HEIDEGGER IN RUINS

OTHER BOOKS BY RICHARD WOLIN

Walter Benjamin: An Aesthetic of Redemption

The Politics of Being: The Political Thought of Martin Heidegger

The Heidegger Controversy: A Critical Reader (editor)

The Terms of Cultural Criticism: The Frankfurt School, Existentialism, Poststructuralism

Karl Löwith, *Martin Heidegger and European Nihilism* (editor)

Labyrinths: Explorations in the Critical History of Ideas

Heidegger's Children: Hannah Arendt, Karl Löwith, Hans Jonas, and Herbert Marcuse

The Seduction of Unreason: The Intellectual Romance with Fascism from Nietzsche to Postmodernism

The Frankfurt School Revisited and Other Essays on Politics and Society

Herbert Marcuse, *Heideggerian Marxism* (coeditor)

The Wind from the East: French Intellectuals, the Cultural Revolution, and the Legacy of the 1960s

RICHARD WOLIN

Heidegger in Ruins

BETWEEN PHILOSOPHY AND IDEOLOGY

Yale

UNIVERSITY PRESS

NEW HAVEN & LONDON

Published with assistance from the foundation established in memory of Henry Weldon Barnes of the Class of 1882, Yale College.

Yale University Press books may be purchased in quantity for educational, business, or promotional use. For information, please e-mail sales.press@yale.edu (U.S. office) or sales@yaleup.co.uk (U.K. office).

Set in Times Roman and Scala Sans type by IDS Infotech Ltd., Chandigarh, India
Printed in the United States of America.

Library of Congress Control Number: 2022931859
ISBN 978-0-300-23318-6 (hardcover : alk. paper)

A catalogue record for this book is available from the British Library.

This paper meets the requirements of ANSI/NISO Z39.48-1992 (Permanence of Paper).

10 9 8 7 6 5 4 3 2 1

For Caroline, *ma femme lumineuse*

Error of philosophers: *The philosopher believes that the value of his philosophy lies in the whole, in the building. But posterity discovers it in the bricks that he used and which others will often make use of again for better building; in the fact, that is to say, that the building can be destroyed and nevertheless possess value as material.*

—Nietzsche, *Human, All Too Human* (1878)

CONTENTS

A NOTE ON SOURCES

IN ADDITION TO HEIDEGGER'S BEING a prolific philosopher—as his hundred-plus volume *Gesamtausgabe* readily attests—he was also a prolific letter writer. Over the course of his long, productive life (1910–1976), he corresponded with some two hundred interlocutors. Over ten thousand of Heidegger's letters remain extant.

After some initial hesitancy, Heidegger ultimately signed off on the publication of his correspondence. He viewed the *Briefausgaben* as an integral part of his *Gesamtwerk*, or oeuvre. In keeping with Heidegger's directives, in 2010 there began, under the auspices of the Freiburg-based Karl Alber Verlag, an ambitious project to publish a thirty-five-volume edition of Heidegger's correspondence.[1]

In this book, I have, at various points, relied on the informative accounts concerning Heidegger's philosophical path that he himself provided in these various epistolary exchanges. Conversely, for the most part, orthodox Heideggerians have steered clear of the letters, which they view as a form of non- or extraphilosophical discourse (although one would think that, in light of their allegiance to Heidegger's program of "Overcoming Metaphysics," the disruptive effects of epistolary testimony might offer a welcome to source of "otherness"). In this note, I wish to explain my decision to rely on the letters as a valuable and legitimate source for understanding the twists and turns of Heidegger's *Denkweg*.

Heidegger's correspondence is intellectually significant for several reasons. For one, it is widely acknowledged that, as Heidegger was a philosopher of *Existenz*, many of his fundamental philosophical impulses derived from his own life experiences: his "conversion" to Protestantism circa 1917, the *Kriegerlebnis* (war experience) of World War I—the defining event of Heidegger's "Generation"— the collapse of the Weimar Republic, and the rise of National Socialism.

Heidegger's letters offer invaluable testimony concerning the ways that these transformative existential episodes impacted his *Denken*. As Heidegger avowed in a letter to Karl Löwith of 19 August 1921: "I work in a concrete factical manner, from out of my 'I am'—from out of my spiritual, factical heritage/milieu/life context, from out of that which becomes accessible to me as living experience."[2] To discount the letters would be to neglect the existential basis or ground of Heidegger's thought.

Moreover, Heidegger's correspondence includes exchanges with some of the outstanding figures in twentieth-century philosophy and letters: among them, Heinrich Rickert, Karl Jaspers, Rudolph Bultmann, Hannah Arendt, Hans-Georg Gadamer, Ernst Jünger, and René Char. In these cases, Heidegger's letters are, quite obviously, of intrinsic philosophical and/or cultural significance.

Equally revealing are Heidegger's epistolary exchanges with close friends and family members such as Elisabeth Blochmann, Elfride Heidegger (the philosopher's wife), and his brother, Fritz. This is true insofar as, in the course of these colloquies, Heidegger often paused to shed invaluable light on the nature and substance of his philosophical trajectory.

Lastly, such conceptual clarification is especially welcome in the case of a philosopher like Heidegger who, in keeping with his emphatic disavowal of "publicness," inclined toward hermeticism. As Heidegger avowed in *Contributions to Philosophy* (1936–38), "Only the great and secretive individuals ensure the stillness necessary for the advent of the god."[3] And in *Anmerkungen I–V*, he affirmed, "Whoever knows me only on the basis of my published work does not really know me at all."[4]

Given Heidegger's predilection for philosophical esoterics, the elucidations that the letters provide remain valuable and indispensable.

HEIDEGGER IN RUINS

Heidegger in Black

The Ontological Privilege of "German Dasein"

THE *BLACK NOTEBOOKS*' PUBLICATION, BEGINNING IN 2014, has generated a new wave of Heidegger scholarship. To date, eight installments, comprising volumes 94–101 of the mammoth, 102-volume Heidegger *Gesamtausgabe*, have appeared. (For purposes of comparison, the comprehensive Hegel edition published by Felix Meiner Verlag, which was completed in 2018, contains "only" 47 volumes.) In light of the fact that the *Notebooks* have added nearly three thousand pages of source material to Heidegger's voluminous corpus, it is understandable that scholars have felt compelled to reassess Heidegger's legacy in the wake of their publication. In *Poesie der Vernichtung: Literatur und Dichtung in Martin Heideggers "Schwarzen Heften,"* Judith Werner has justifiably characterized the *Black Notebooks*' publication as an "earthquake" that provoked "a far-reaching caesura in Heidegger scholarship."[1]

As a philosophical notebook or diary that Heidegger meticulously maintained over the course of four decades, from 1931 to 1969, the *Black Notebooks* are unique. They provide unprecedented insight into the gestation of Heidegger's thought: a metacommentary that sheds significant light on Heidegger's philosophical development and self-understanding, especially with respect to his "Turn" from "existential ontology" to the "history of Being." They are also unique insofar as they vividly document Heidegger's philosophical engagement with the *Zeitgeist*: the interplay between fundamental ontology and *Zeitgeschichte*, or the historical present, is on display on nearly every page. In an afterword to volume 1, the *Black*

Notebooks' editor, Peter Trawny, has felicitously characterized Heidegger's approach in the *Notebooks* as the "attempt to arrive at ontological insights in the areas of 'science,' 'religion,' 'politics,' and 'culture' on the basis of 'signs' or 'characteristics' of daily life under National Socialism."[2]

One of the central reasons that the *Black Notebooks*' publication has spurred a reevaluation of Heidegger's legacy concerns the numerous, compromising "ideological" avowals that they contain. Had the assertions in question been extraneous asides, in all probability, Heidegger's philosophy itself would have remained unimpugned. Disturbingly, Heidegger articulated many of these dubious "metapolitical" judgments in the idiolect of his own characteristic "essential thinking."

As such, the *Black Notebooks* confirm that the *cordon sanitaire* that Heidegger's supporters have sought to maintain between "philosophy" and "worldview" in his oeuvre—ever a dubious interpretive stratagem—is hermeneutically flawed. This is especially true for *Notebooks* II–XV, which span the years 1931–41 and document Heidegger's response to the advent and consolidation of Nazi rule. *Notebook* III ("Überlegungen und Winke III"), which Heidegger began in fall 1932, is especially revealing, insofar as it coincided with Heidegger's twelve-month tenure as Freiburg University *Führer-Rektor*.

As Trawny's observations suggest, the *Black Notebooks* have heightened our awareness concerning the entwinement of philosophy and ideology in Heidegger's work. Heidegger consistently described himself as a philosopher of "temporality" and "historicity," a characterization that resonated in the title of his chef d'oeuvre, *Being and Time* (1927). The *Black Notebooks* attest prodigiously to the *timeliness* of Heidegger's work, to the crucial dynamic between metaphysics and *Zeitgeschichte*. As such, they are *saturated with historicity*, in ways that the existing secondary literature has yet to fully explore.

The *Black Notebooks*' status with respect to the other main divisions of the *Gesamtausgabe*—lectures, seminars, and treatises—is anomalous. For the most part, the entries consist of abbreviated reflections on themes or topoi that spurred Heidegger's philosophical curiosity yet whose treatment did not fit in harmoniously with his more conventional scholarly commitments: monographs, essays, and lecture courses. Because of their "discursive" nature, it would be inaccurate to describe the entries as "aphorisms" or "maxims." As a rule, their intention is not to "jolt" or "provoke" the reader but instead to tentatively elaborate or stake out "positions" and "views." Heidegger himself described the entries as "Versuche": "experiments" or "attempts."

Although the aperçus that compose the *Black Notebooks* may seem disjointed and telegraphic in comparison with Heidegger's more sustained philosophical undertakings, they are not unpolished. In fact, Heidegger often returned to earlier entries in order to emend and improve them, which also provides an important clue concerning the high regard in which he held them. In a text of 1937–38, "The Wish and the Will (On Preserving What Is Attempted)," in which Heidegger listed his philosophical accomplishments to date, he included the *Black Notebooks* on the list. One would be hard-pressed to disagree with Peter Trawny and Andrew Mitchell's conclusion that "Heidegger considered [the Black Notebooks] groupable with the selected best of his philosophical authorship."[3]

Another indication of the *Notebooks*' importance for Heidegger was that he earmarked them to appear as the final nine volumes of his mammoth "Collected Works" edition and, hence, as the crowning achievement of his philosophical life's work. This meant postponing their publication until several decades after his death. One of the motivations underlying this decision, it seems, was that Heidegger felt that his contemporaries were too benighted to grasp the clairvoyance of his "metapolitical" insights. Heidegger was convinced that only a future generation—one that was less small-minded and more attuned to the "emanations of Being"—could do them justice.

Like Nietzsche, a self-described "posthumous man," who, in *The Will to Power*, claimed that he would narrate the "history of the next two centuries," Heidegger, in the *Black Notebooks*, also staked a claim to prophecy. In *Notebook* XII, circa 1939, he forecast that not until the year 2327 would his name finally emerge from *Vergessenheit*, or oblivion. Serendipitously, 2327 also happened to be the four-hundred-year anniversary of the publication of *Being and Time*.[4]

At another point, Heidegger arbitrarily attributed a numinous power to names beginning with the letter *H*. He invoked, as evidence, Heraclitus, Hölderlin, and Hegel. But Hitler would also seem to belong to the list, as would, of course, Heidegger himself.[5]

Whereas, in May 1945, many Germans greeted the Allied victory as a "liberation" from the tyranny of Nazi rule, Heidegger, conversely, insisted that it was merely another episode in the long history of *Seinsvergessenheit*, or the forgetting of Being. Heidegger held that Nazi Germany's excesses paled in comparison with the criminality of the Allied occupation, which, having unleashed its "machinery of death" (*Tötungsmaschinerie*), could only culminate in the "total annihilation" (*vollständige Vernichtung*) of Germany and the Germans.[6] Heidegger prophesied that a final judgment concerning the predominance of "Americanism" would take place in the year 2300.[7]

In material terms, the *Black Notebooks* highlight the depth and extent of Heidegger's Germanophilia: his conviction that *Deutschtum* possessed a salvific historical mission, a "calling" that *elevated it metaphysically above other peoples*. Heidegger maintained that the Germans, as a *Volk*, displayed an *ontological singularity*: a "Seinsart" that justified his commitment to the ideology of "German exceptionalism." On this point, Heidegger could not have been clearer or more insistent, hence his declaration in *Überlegungen* II that "*only someone who is German [der Deutsche] is capable of poetically articulating Being in an originary way*"—an avowal that confirms that Heidegger articulated his commitment to the idea of German superiority in *ontological terms*.[8]

The *Black Notebooks* reaffirm that Heidegger's understanding of *Seinsgeschichte* (the history of Being) was inherently tied to his "metaphysical" wager on the redemptive capacities of *Deutschtum*. Time and again, they demonstrate that Heidegger's ontological "Turn" during the 1930s was integrally bound with an intensification of his commitment to the regenerative attributes of "German Dasein" and "German destiny." Heidegger's ontological-historical wager on Germany emerged, unambiguously, in his paeans to the attributes of "Western-Germanic historical Dasein": a crypto-theological construct in which "German destiny" held the key to actualizing "another Beginning," conceived as a renewal of the "Greek Beginning."[9]

The *Black Notebooks* demonstrate that Heidegger construed *Germanentum* as *authentic historicity incarnate*. It was an ontological status that Germany's geopolitical rivals—England and France, to say nothing of the *Untermenschen* who inhabited of the Slavic lands to the East—could never possibly match. Whereas Heidegger maintained that the Germans had an ontological-historical "calling" (*Auftrag*) to fulfill, he viewed Germany's existentially flawed adversaries as carriers of "nihilism": hence, as peoples who threatened to *undermine* Germany's eschatological "destiny" and "mission."

Accordingly, Heidegger divided the world into *historical* and *unhistorical* peoples. Whereas Heidegger exalted the Germans as the "most metaphysical of peoples," he disqualified Germany's geopolitical "enemies" (*Feinde*) as *devoid of historicity*.[10] Thereby, Heidegger summarily consigned them to the purgatory of *Seinsvergessenheit*, or the "oblivion of Being."

The "cosmopolitan spirit" was entirely alien to Heidegger's *Denkhabitus*. How could it be otherwise given his outsized commitment to the ideology of German singularity? Heidegger discounted "universal history" as a metaphysical abstraction bequeathed by Enlightenment cosmopolitanism. Conversely, he maintained that the essential "carriers" of history were *Völker*, or individual "peoples." This conviction confirms Heidegger's status as a *völkisch* thinker.

Heidegger's fidelity to the ethos of German exceptionalism predisposed him to accept Carl Schmitt's infamous *Freund/Feind* (friend/enemy) opposition. In *The Concept of the Political* (1927), Schmitt exalted "war" as the ultima ratio of "Great Politics." As Schmitt remarked, "War, the readiness for death of fighting men, the physical annihilation of other men who stand on the side of the enemy, possesses an *existential . . . meaning*."[11]

Following the Nazi seizure of power, Schmitt's friend/enemy antithesis assumed more tangible and immediate contours in Heidegger's eyes. Hence, in Heidegger's 1934 seminar on Hegel's *Philosophy of Right*, he engaged intensively with Schmitt's *The Concept of the Political*. In agreement with Schmitt's view that "it is the assimilated Jew who is the *true enemy* [*wahre Feind*]," Heidegger identified German Jews as the "inner enemy" par excellence: a corrosive presence that threatened to undermine the unity of the *Volksgemeinschaft*.[12] Accordingly, in "On the Essence of Truth" (1933–34), Heidegger expressed his deep-seated fear that the "[inner] enemy may graft himself onto the innermost root of a *Volk*'s existence in order to oppose its innermost essence." "All the keener, harsher, and more difficult is the struggle," he continued, "*to ferret out the enemy: to force him to reveal himself, . . . to remain ready to attack, . . . and to initiate the attack on a long-term basis, with the goal of total extermination [völligen Vernichtung]*."[13] As Heidegger observed in 1942, around the time that the Nazis formulated the *Endlösung* to the Jewish Question, "In the era of the Christian West—i.e., the era of metaphysics— *world Jewry is the principle of destruction*."[14]

In light of the fact that both Heidegger and Schmitt hailed from solidly Catholic milieus—provincial Baden, in Heidegger's case; the Rhineland, in Schmitt's—the developmental parallels with respect to their anti-Jewish views are more compelling than may at first appear. It has been well documented that, during the early decades of the twentieth century, as racial anti-Semitism spiked, traditional religious anti-Judaism increasingly accommodated the worldview of its profane doppelgänger. Hence, medieval fears about sectarian Jewish practices—well poisoning, blood libel, and ritual murder—that threatened to undermine the integrity of Christian communities metamorphosed into modern fears about Jews as "carriers of modernity," with all of its attendant disorders, dislocations, and disruptions. For both Heidegger and Schmitt, the traditional, religiously based mistrust of Judaism metastasized into a this-worldly, profane paranoia concerning the disintegrative influence of the "Jewish enemy": a paranoia whose best-known incarnation was *The Protocols of the Elders of Zion*. (In response to Karl Jaspers's skepticism about the existence of a "Jewish world conspiracy," Heidegger demurred, insisting, "There really is a dangerous international alliance of Jews.")[15]

In *Political Theology* (1922), Schmitt argued that all modern political precepts are merely secularized variants of what were originally theological concepts. The same may be said for the momentous transition from traditional anti-Judaism to modern anti-Semitism. Here, too, there is a dialectic of "secularization" at work. The idea that the salvation of the modern world is contingent on the elimination of Jewish influence—an idea that was central to the ideology of "redemptive anti-Semitism"—is a manifestation of "political theology" in a modern setting.

As Raphael Gross has shown in *Carl Schmitt and the Jews*, Schmitt's polemical indictments of "parliamentarism," "normativism," "universalism," and "cosmopolitanism" expressed Schmitt's deep-seated fears of postemancipation Jewish domination. Schmitt's anxieties culminated in his overwrought condemnation of Jewish *Bodenlosigkeit* (rootlessness) in his "Großraum" writings of the early 1940s. As Schmitt declaimed, "The real misunderstanding of the Jewish *Volk* with respect to everything that concerns soil [*Boden*], land, and territory is grounded in its style of political existence. A nation's relation to its soil [*Boden*], determined by its own work of colonization and culture, and by the concrete forms of power that arise from this arrangement, is incomprehensible to the spirit of the Jew."[16]

Heidegger's doctrine of *Seinsgeschichte* assimilated the political theology of "redemptive antisemitism." As the *Black Notebooks* attest, he held that the reemergence of Being in its glory and plentitude would not take place until "world Jewry's" disintegrative influence was eliminated.

The affinities between Heidegger's fundamental ontology and Schmitt's political existentialism also shed light on Heidegger's reformulation of first philosophy as an *ontology of violence*. Heidegger often stressed that the trajectory of *Seinsgeschichte* was riven with *violence* and *conflict*. He found a valuable philosophical anticipation of this view in Heraclitus's Fragment 53, "War is the father of all things": a maxim that Heidegger revered as a normative-ontological touchstone.

"Violence" was the midwife of Heideggerian *Seinsgeschichte*. In the *Black Notebooks*, Heidegger declared, "*The path leading from Being to Thinking hews closely to the edge of annihilation* [*Vernichtung*]."[17] And in *Contributions to Philosophy* (1936–38), he declaimed, "Wherever beings are to be changed by beings—not out of Beyng—*violence is necessary*. Every act is one of violence, such that, here, the violence is mastered by means of power."[18]

Heidegger's reformulation of metaphysics in a bellicist—and *bellicose*— register emerged in the martial idiom that pervaded the *Black Notebooks*. Heidegger claimed that the *Notebooks'* goal was to stake out "advance and rear-guard positions" in order to facilitate, through "conquest" (*Eroberung*), the ends of "original questioning."[19] Expressing his contempt for the reigning philosophical orthodoxies, he disdainfully added, "Two years of military service is better preparation for the sciences than four semesters of 'study.' "[20]

The *Black Notebooks* confirm that Heidegger's vision of the destiny of the West was inextricably wedded to a discourse of German chauvinism. Germany's task, as a nation of *Dichter und Denker*, was to reestablish the ontological-historical link between the "Greek Beginning" and "another Beginning." As such, Heidegger's history of Being was simultaneously a *narrative of redemption*: a saga in which "German Dasein" played a paramount role. According to Heidegger, German destiny was the metaphysical key to overcoming European nihilism: hence to redeeming the West from a condition of twofold "abandonment" (*Verlassenheit*): "abandonment by the gods" (*Gottesverlassenheit*) and "abandonment by Being" (*Seinsverlassenheit*).

In this connection, an obvious question that arises is, What role was left for philosophy to play in Heidegger's narrative? In Trawny's afterword to the *Black Notebooks*, volume 1, he provides an extremely troubling—yet wholly plausible—response. "It is undeniable," observes Trawny, "that Heidegger was convinced that, with the [National Socialist] Revolution, *philosophy had reached its end; it must be replaced by the 'metapolitics of the historical Volk.' "*[21]

Thereby, Trawny justly called attention to the pivotal role that Heidegger's commitment to German exceptionalism played in his later philosophy. By wholeheartedly embracing the "metapolitics of the historical *Volk*," Heidegger perceived a path forward: a path that led beyond the "decline of the West" and toward the redemptory promise of "another Beginning." By wagering on the "metapolitics of the historical *Volk*," Heidegger conceived a meaningful alternative to the impotence and inefficacity of contemporary philosophy—his own existential ontology included.

Needless to say, by invoking the "metapolitics of historical *Volk*," Heidegger did not mean *any Volk whatsoever*. He meant the *German Volk*, which, as the *Black Notebooks* repeatedly reaffirm, Heidegger regarded as *the only genuinely historical Volk*.

The "End of Heideggerianism"?

Among the Heideggerian faithful, the *Black Notebooks*' publication has prompted a considerable degree of soul-searching and rethinking. Numerous Heidegger loyalists felt they had been deceived by Heidegger's literary executors, who had systematically purged the philosopher's work of pro-Nazi and anti-Semitic avowals, a practice that, once these omissions came to light, resulted in a series of embarrassing public controversies that have called into question the *Gesamtausgabe*'s viability.[22]

To cite one example of such "soul-searching" and "rethinking": in 2015, both the president and the vice president of the International Heidegger Society abruptly resigned from their positions. The philosopher Günter Figal explained in announcing his resignation as Heidegger Society president that Heidegger's numerous professions of anti-Semitism, as documented in the *Black Notebooks*, prevented him from representing Heidegger's philosophy in good conscience. "To think in this way," averred Figal, "is incompatible with the vocation of philosophy."[23]

The *Black Notebooks*' publication motivated Figal to reevaluate the way that Heidegger, following the German defeat in 1945, had deployed his "technology-critique" in order to relativize and downplay the historical specificity of Nazi criminality. As Figal observed, "Following the end of World War II, Heidegger refused to acknowledge Germany's responsibility for war crimes. Instead of recognizing the Shoah's singularity, with the war's termination, Heidegger situated the existence of the extermination camps in an eschatological frame of reference that reduced all historical events to undifferentiated consequences of 'modern technics.' "[24]

Figal's prognosis concerning the future of Heidegger studies in the wake of the *Black Notebooks*' appearance was correspondingly bleak. "The philosophi-

cal future," claimed Figal, "portends the end of Heideggerianism." Shortly
thereafter, the president of Freiburg University, where Heidegger had taught for
four decades, announced the university's plans to decommission the *Lehrstuhl*,
or academic chair, that had been named in Heidegger's honor.[25]

Figal's misgivings with respect to Heidegger's betrayal of the "vocation
of philosophy" amounted to a de facto admission that Heidegger's critics had
been correct all along: that the filiations between Heidegger's *Denken* and the
"German ideology" of the 1920s and 1930s were *intrinsic* rather than ephemeral and contingent. Otto Pöggeler—arguably, Heidegger's foremost German
interpreter—had already raised this specter during the 1990s, when he inquired,
"Was it not through a definite orientation of his thought that Heidegger fell—
and not merely accidentally—into the proximity of National Socialism, *without
ever truly emerging from that proximity?*"[26]

Nevertheless, not all of Heidegger's disciples have responded to the *Black Notebooks'* publication with the combination of forthrightness and indignation displayed
by Figal. Instead, there have been numerous attempts to rationalize and discount
Heidegger's more objectionable transgressions in the interest of restoring Heidegger
studies, with the greatest possible speed, to the status quo ante.

The Italian philosopher and former Heidegger student Giorgio Agamben established a precedent for many of the apologetic discussions of the *Black Notebooks* in a 2015 interview with the French weekly *L'Obs*. What took readers
aback were not merely Agamben's efforts to trivialize Heidegger's various pro-
Nazi claims and assertions but his sympathy for the discourse of European anti-
Semitism, whose decline Agamben seemed openly to mourn. As Agamben
asserted, "The polemic surrounding [the *Black Notebooks*] . . . rests on an
equivocation concerning the usage and meaning of the word 'anti-Semitism.'
For well-known historical reasons, this word designates something that has to
do with the persecution and extermination of Jews. . . . But if every assertion
that is critical or negatively disposed toward Judaism—even that which is contained in private diary entries—is condemned as anti-Semitic, the net effect is
to place Judaism outside of language."[27]

By misrepresenting "anti-Semitism"—a paradigmatic example of "race
thinking" and its attendant persecutions—as statements that are "critical or
negatively disposed toward Judaism," Agamben deliberately masked the gravity of the issues at stake. Agamben's subterfuge notwithstanding, none of
Heidegger's critics has disputed the permissibility or legitimacy of criticizing

Judaism. Nor have they sought, as Agamben suggested, to "place Judaism out-side of language." Instead, they have criticized Heidegger's reliance on "race discourse," a habitude and practice that belies the claim that his thinking was constitutionally immune from the temptations of the *Rassengedanke*.[28]

One refrain that has repeatedly punctuated the recent wave of Heidegger apologetics is the claim that, today, *we need Heidegger more than ever*. Often, such assertions invoke the value of Heidegger's *Technik-Kritik* as a challenge to the shortcomings of Western "nihilism," while charitably overlooking the pronounced neo-Spenglerian, antidemocratic, *zivilisationskritisch* overtones of Heidegger's perspective. Paradoxically, by elevating the reign of technology to the status of a *primum movens* or Absolute, Heidegger's framework discounted the capacities of democratically minded citizens to contest technology's im-placable "sway." Already in *Being and Time* (paragraph 127), Heidegger had devalued "publicness" (*Öffentlichkeit*) as a manifestation of inauthenticity *sim-pliciter*. "As expressions of 'das Man,' " remarked Heidegger, "averageness and leveling characterize the ontological modes of 'publicness.' "[29]

Frequently, the claim that "we need Heidegger more than ever" has been cou-pled with the delusional assertion that the most effective antidote to Heidegger's philosophical shortcomings is *even more Heidegger*—at which point, the dis-course of Heidegger-adulation accedes to the pinnacle of self-caricature. Thus, as the editors of *Heidegger's "Black Notebooks": Responses to Anti-Semitism* confi-dently assert, should we wish to interrogate the "anti-Semitism . . . in Heidegger's thinking . . . *the best defense against such a construction is Heideggerian thought itself*"! They proceed to justify this self-serving conclusion as follows: "Heidegger's anti-Semitism is . . . tied to a position operating within an *oppositional logic*. . . . [Hence, it] is tied to a *metaphysical position*. To overcome this anti-Semitism, then, will require *overcoming metaphysics. But this is precisely what Heidegger has taught us!*" In other words, if we seek to probe the nature of Heidegger's anti-Semitism, there is no need whatsoever to consult sources external to Heidegger's magisterial and sovereign corpus. All of the answers we could ever hope to find are contained therein.[30]

Similarly, according to French philosopher Jean-Luc Nancy, the central ques-tion raised by the *Black Notebooks'* publication has nothing to do with Heidegger's philosophical failings or misjudgments. Instead, the main issue at stake concerns the persistence of "Heideggerophobia": a prejudice that, as Nancy asserts, in a profession of obsequious fealty, "*prevents us from understanding the world as it is*." Thereby, Nancy has rewritten the historical record in order to make Heidegger into the "victim": someone who has been unfairly targeted by—as Nancy puts it—the "guardians of political correctness" (*les bien pensants du correct politique*).[31] According to Nancy, scholars who critically challenge Heidegger's views are little more than latter-day inquisitors, *emissaries of intolerance*. Hence, he dismisses their arguments a priori as expressions of bad faith.

Although Nancy readily acknowledges that, in the *Black Notebooks*, Heidegger castigated Judaism as the "principle of destruction," like Agamben, he trivializes Heidegger's anti-Semitism on the (specious) grounds that "philosophy is not immune from the earthquakes" of the times.[32] Nancy's reliance on the metaphorics of "natural catastrophe" seems calculated to render questions of individual or group culpability null and void. (In similar fashion, in postwar Germany, the Nazi debacle was often explained away as a *Betriebsunfall*, an "industrial accident.") In *The Banality of Heidegger* (2015)—Nancy's contribution to the *Black Notebooks* debate—his central argument that Heidegger's anti-Semitism was "banal," hence, unworthy of serious scrutiny, is little more than a rhetorical smokescreen contrived to obviate further questioning.[33]

Nancy's argumentation, which reverses the relationship between "victims" and "perpetrators" to Heidegger's advantage, is a textbook example of "Holocaust inversion." Nancy places Heidegger's critics—the purported "Heideggerophobes"—in the dock; conversely, he lets the Master off the hook by suggesting that further investigation of his "case" is unwarranted.

In *Heidegger, the Jews, and the Shoah*, Donatella di Cesare, pursuing a similar strategy, apotheosized Heidegger—his vicious anti-Semitism notwithstanding—qua "philosopher of the Shoah." "Heidegger," exulted di Cesare, "must be credited with having developed those concepts that, today, *make reflection on the Shoah possible*: from 'Enframing' [*Gestell*] to 'Technique' [*Technik*], from the 'banality of evil' to the 'fabrication of corpses.' "[34] Thereby, di Cesare has transformed a thinker who, in many respects, pioneered the art of Holocaust denial—for example, Heidegger's claim, in *Anmerkungen I–V* (GA 97), that the Holocaust was a paradigmatic example of "Jewish self-annihilation"—into a progenitor of Holocaust studies. As Pierre Bourdieu aptly remarked, "When I hear people say that Heidegger alone makes it possible for us to think the Holocaust—but perhaps I am insufficiently 'postmodern'—I think I must be dreaming!"[35]

In Heidegger's defense, it should be acknowledged that, on various occasions, he expressed his misgivings concerning select aspects of Nazi rule. A good example was his critique of "vulgar National Socialism" in *Überlegungen* III (GA 94), an ideological approach that Heidegger brusquely dismissed as suitable for "journalistic scribblers" and "cultural entrepreneurs."[36]

However, upon closer scrutiny, it is apparent that Heidegger's criticisms of "really existing" National Socialism consistently refrained from challenging the movement as a whole. Instead, Heidegger proposed replacing "vulgar National Socialism" with what he termed "spiritual National Socialism": an understanding of the movement's philosophical "essence" that was more in line with his own ontological-historical approach.[37]

In order to distance himself from "vulgar anti-Semitism," Heidegger adopted the persona or mien of a "spiritual anti-Semite" (*ein geistiger Antisemit*): a standpoint that Heidegger felt was required in order to combat Germany's escalating Jewish "infestation" (*Verseuchung*).[38] On the basis of this remark, it is clear that Heidegger was in no way averse to relying on the (biopolitical) lexicon of "virology" when necessary.

Heidegger reprised the opposition between "vulgar" and "spiritual" National Socialism in *An Introduction to Metaphysics* (1935), when he contrasted the movement's "inner truth and greatness" to the inferior perspectives that, "nowadays, are peddled about as the philosophy of National Socialism."[39] Once again, Heidegger refrained from renouncing National Socialism, *tout court*. Instead, by distinguishing between "authentic" National Socialism and Nazism's epigones or vulgarizers, his aim all along was to *save* National Socialism rather than to *disown* it.

The conclusion one should draw from these ongoing, contentious debates over Heidegger's legacy is not, as some commentators have argued, that one should *abandon* Heidegger's philosophy as irreparably contaminated and, hence, *irredeemable*. Instead, Heidegger's thought must be patiently and systematically reevaluated in view of the revelations that the *Black Notebooks* and other recently published sources have brought to light. *Heidegger in Ruins* is intended as a modest contribution to a more demanding and long-term process of rethinking and reconsideration.

"Heidegger in Ruins"

Since the early 1950s, the reception of Heidegger's work has repeatedly been marred by a series of textual controversies that have highlighted significant discrepancies between the published editions of Heidegger's writings and the original manuscript versions. In chapter 1, "The Heidegger Hoax," I review these troubling developments on the basis of recent discoveries that have shed important light on the dubious editorial practices that have governed the publication of Heidegger's texts.

The first case in which such divergences emerged concerned Heidegger's controversial homage in *An Introduction to Metaphysics* (1953)—a lecture course that was originally presented in 1935—to the "inner truth and greatness of National Socialism." The controversy has become somewhat legendary, in no small measure insofar as it was catalyzed by a review essay written by a little-known twenty-four-year-old philosophy student, Jürgen Habermas—at the time hard at work on a Schelling dissertation.

Heidegger's willingness to allow the disputed passage to stand uncommented, a mere eight years after Nazi Germany's "collapse," provoked a storm of criticism. The textual debate focused on a parenthetical remark that Heidegger had inserted in order to clarify what he meant by National Socialism's "inner truth and greatness": "the confrontation between planetary technology and modern man."[40] Heidegger insisted that the disputed passage had been contained in the original manuscript of the lecture course and that he had retained it in the published version as a matter of "honesty": in keeping with his editorial practice of reproducing earlier texts verbatim, thereby yielding a faithful record of his thoughts and views at the time. Yet subsequent testimony by one of Heidegger's research assistants, Rainer Marten, confirmed that Heidegger had added the parenthetical explanation *après coup*, as he was reviewing the page proofs, in order to forestall anticipated criticism.

In retrospect, the 1953 dispute established a significant precedent. Only recently have we learned the extent to which the published versions of Heidegger's texts from the Nazi era have repeatedly been subject to far-reaching editorial manipulation. In numerous cases, Heidegger's professions of loyalty to the regime as well as his anti-Semitic utterances have been systematically excised in order to rewrite the historical record, thereby standing Heidegger's oft-stated claim that his texts were being reproduced in their original manuscript versions on its head.

At the time, the personal and professional stakes involved were considerable. Following Heidegger's classification by the French occupation authorities in 1945 as a "typical Nazi" (*un Nazi typique*), his reputation lay in shambles. In addition, he was saddled with an onerous teaching ban that lasted five years.

The fact that similar episodes involving textual "cleansing" have repeatedly surfaced raises an important issue: When we read Heidegger's work today, what are we actually reading? Given the numerous instances of editorial distortion that have come to light, how representative are these texts of what Heidegger actually thought and wrote at the time? The problem is especially acute in the case of extant Heidegger translations, since the likelihood of a foreign-language publisher devoting the time, energy, and expense to printing corrected editions is negligible. Although the *Gesamtausgabe* has remedied numerous falsifications and omissions, in recent years, additional cases of textual doctoring have repeatedly emerged.

In chapter 2, "Heidegger in Ruins," I survey the ways that our knowledge of Heidegger's philosophical self-understanding has been transformed as a result of the publication of new materials: the *Black Notebooks* as well as Heidegger's correspondence with his brother and confessor, Fritz. Their epistolary exchange sheds invaluable light on Heidegger's political formation during the early 1930s, as the prospect of National Socialist rule became increasingly imminent. The correspondence refutes the myth of Heidegger as an apolitical *Luftmensch*: a figure who unwittingly stumbled into the orbit of National Socialism, before rapidly rectifying his "error," twelve months later, by resigning as Freiburg University rector.

The correspondence with Fritz details Heidegger's efforts to keep pace with and assess the tumultuous shifts of German politics, as the Weimar Republic descended into a series of terminal crises that culminated in the Nazi seizure of power. We learn, for example, that Heidegger subscribed to the conservative revolutionary monthly *Die Tat* (The Deed), edited by Hans Zehrer. He was also enamored of *Deutschland in Ketten* (Germany in Chains; 1931), a revanchist, virulently anti-Western diatribe that was written by Werner Beumelburg, one of the leading exponents of German "military nationalism" (*soldatischer Nationalismus*). "Anyone who really wants to know about the fate of Germany over the last 12 years," Heidegger counseled, "should read this book."[41]

We also learn how, in response to the accelerating political disequilibrium, Heidegger increasingly succumbed to Hitler's charisma. Heidegger set great store by the fact that both he and Hitler were born in the same year (1889)—a fact that, in Heidegger's eyes, confirmed that their "destinies" were entwined. In the *Black Notebooks*, Heidegger went so far as to credit Hitler with having prepared the way for new and productive approaches to "philosophical questioning." It is a "stroke of good fortune," he enthused, that "the Führer has awakened a new reality that has redirected our thinking along the right path and infused it with new energy."[42]

In chapter 3, "Heidegger and Race," I seek to clarify a fundamental misunderstanding concerning the philosophical grounds of Heidegger's support for National Socialism. Much of the previous literature has assumed that Heidegger's National Socialist commitments were insincere, since, as a champion of *Existenzphilosophie*, Heidegger opposed Nazism on epistemological grounds. Heidegger's defenders have presumed that, since the Nazi worldview was predicated on "biological racism"—a doctrine whose origins may be traced to nineteenth-century scientism—and since Heidegger was an inveterate critic of modern science and its attendant ills, an unbridgeable gulf separated his thought from the predominant Nazi credo. Ergo, Heidegger's "enlistment" for National Socialism must have been sharply at odds with his understanding of the aims and objectives of fundamental ontology.

However, careful scrutiny of the basic tenets of Nazi race doctrine indicates that it had very little in common with "scientism." Instead, Nazi race thinking was an inherently *ideological construct* that emerged in polemical opposition to nineteenth-century positivism. As such, it was saturated with *mystical* and *spiritualist* elements. The end result was a confused, yet highly potent, amalgam of German Romanticism, fin-de-siècle esotericism (Ariosophy), Aryan supremacism, and old-fashioned *Machtpolitik*. Each of these paradigms was significantly at odds with the empiricist orientation of the natural and social sciences.

The idea of Nazi "race science" was, fundamentally, a *contradictio in adjecto*. Instead, National Socialist race doctrine was a paradigmatic instance of *modern political myth*. As myth, it was untethered by the customary empirical and disciplinary constraints of the "logic of scientific discovery."

Moreover, Heidegger's views on race thinking were far from unilaterally negative, as his champions have alleged. In the *Black Notebooks II–VI*, for example, he avowed that "*race* [*is*] *a necessary and mediate condition of historical Dasein*."[43] Attentive scrutiny to Heidegger's texts suggests there are very few qualitative or essential differences between his defense of "spiritual racism" and the understanding of race thinking propagated by the likes of as Hans Günther and Ludwig Ferdinand Clauß. In the view of the philosopher and Heidegger student Karl Löwith, Heidegger "was not merely a distinguished representative of the 'German Revolution'; he was so in a manner *much more radical* than Ernst

Krieck or Alfred Rosenberg."[44] As Löwith's remarks suggest, doing justice to Heidegger's "case" means acknowledging the radical philosophical impulses that subtended his existential "enlistment" for National Socialism.

Following the Nazi seizure of power, Heidegger became preoccupied with the philosophical significance of "work" or "Arbeit." In texts such as "Labor Service and the University," "The Call to Labor Service," and "The German Student as Worker," Heidegger sought to provide *Arbeit* with a philosophical grounding consistent with the existential ontology he had developed in *Being and Time*. It goes without saying that Heidegger's valorization of *Arbeit* reflected the enormous influence that Ernst Jünger's *Der Arbeiter* (1932) had on his political formation during these years.

In light of these precedents, it is all the more surprising that, in the extensive secondary literature on Heidegger, his abiding concern with the ontological meaning of *Arbeit* has been largely ignored.[45] In chapter 4, "*Arbeit macht frei*: Heidegger and the German Ideology of Work," I reexamine Heidegger's treatment of the philosophical significance of *Arbeit*, an endeavor that he viewed as a meaningful extension of his own fundamental ontology.

For example, in his May 1933 rectoral address, "The Self-Assertion of the German University," Heidegger exalted "labor service" (*Arbeitsdienst*), along with "military service" (*Wehrdienst*) and "service-in-knowledge" (*Wissensdienst*), as one of the three essential pillars of "National Socialist Education." Heidegger praised *Arbeitsdienst* as "the force that binds students to the *Volksgemeinschaft*," fearing that, in lieu of the existential constraints that *Arbeitsdienst* provided, the integration of German youth within the "national community"—which was indispensable for national unity—would miscarry.[46]

In *Logic as the Question Concerning the Essence of Language* (1933–34), Heidegger subjected *Arbeit* to intense philosophical scrutiny. Attention to this text suggests that Heidegger viewed *Arbeit* as a self-subsistent "existential": as an essential component of Dasein's "Being-in-the-world," one that, as Heidegger suggested, was on a par with well-known "existentials" such as "Care," "Being-with-others," and "Decisiveness."[47]

Heidegger viewed the National Socialist approach to *Arbeit* as a manifestation *of authenticity* (*Eigentlichkeit*). His meditations and reflections on the philosophical meaning of *Arbeit* complement *Being and Time*'s groundbreaking treatment of "tools" and "equipment" as modalities of *Zuhandenheit*, or being "ready-to-hand."

In chapter 5, "Earth and Soil: Heidegger and the National Socialist Politics of Space," I reexamine the systematic role that the notion of existential "rootedness" played in Heidegger's philosophy. Heidegger's deep-seated conviction that "there can be no essential work of spirit without *primordial rootedness-in-soil* [*ursprünglichen Bodenständigkeit*]"—a profession that he repeated on several occasions—links his thought with the doctrines of the German "geopolitical school": a guild that included influential scholar-ideologues such as Friedrich Ratzel, Karl Haushofer, and Carl Schmitt.[48] In the *Black Notebooks*, the ideology of "rootedness" (*Wurzelung*) figured prominently in Heidegger's critique of "world Jewry": "a human type," according to Heidegger, "whose world-historical goal is the *uprooting of all beings from Being* [*die Entwurzelung alles Seienden aus dem Sein*]."[49]

The foregoing quotation makes clear that, in Heidegger's view, "world Jewry's" primary defect was not merely *racial*; it was, more seriously, *ontological*. Hence, in Heidegger eyes, "world Jewry's" corrosive influence jeopardized the ontological-historical project of "another Beginning."

Heidegger consistently praised *Bodenständigkeit*, or "rootedness-in-soil," as a hallmark of authenticity. He maintained that ontologically "rootless" truth-claims—truths that were *bodenlos*—were truths of a lesser order. In essence, they were *pseudo-truths*.

As an indispensable touchstone of value and meaning, *Bodenständigkeit* constituted the basis or "ground" of Heidegger's "existential" critique of Descartes and the "philosophy of the subject." Accordingly, in *Being and Time*, paragraph 77, Heidegger argued that modern philosophy's shortcomings stemmed from its dearth of ontological "rootedness." In support of this claim, he cited Graf Yorck von Wartenburg's declaration, " 'Modern man'—that is, man since the Renaissance—is fit to be interred."[50] Here, one might well inquire, What does it mean to "inter" one's philosophical adversaries?

Heidegger viewed *Bodenständigkeit* as an essential constituent of *Geschichtlichkeit*, or "authentic historicity." In this guise, it played a key role in Heidegger's support for the ideology of German exceptionalism. In Heidegger's eyes, Germany's ontological superiority was predicated on the German *Volk*'s singular capacity for "rootedness-in-soil."

Heidegger revisited the topos of ontological rootedness in *Nature, History, and State* (1933–34). There, he explored its significance for National Socialist "foreign policy" or *Außenpolitik*: above all, with respect to the Third Reich's quest for *Lebensraum*, its "push to the East." In *Nature, History, and State*, Heidegger emerged as an enthusiastic champion of *Raumpolitik*, the National Socialist "politics of space." Relying on Social Darwinist arguments, the geo- political school exalted so-called large-space nations (*Grossraum Völker*) as ra- cially superior "carriers of culture" (*Kulturträger*). On these grounds, they sanctioned the "prerogative" or "right" of large-space nations to subsume small-space nations (*Kleinraum Völker*).

Heidegger's support for the discourse of *Bodenständigkeit* underwent a proc- ess of what one might call—following the lead of the distinguished historian Hans Mommsen—"cumulative radicalization": it advanced from a rhetorical condemnation of "rootless peoples" to the embrace of the Third Reich's racist and genocidal *Bevölkerungspolitik* (population policies).

In recent years, Heidegger's philosophy has featured prominently in the dis- course of European and American New Right circles. Increasingly, a renascent and self-confident New Right (Nouvelle Droite, Neue Rechte) has relied on Heideggerian precepts to justify its program of authoritarian ethnopopulism. In chapter 6, "From Beyond the Grave: Heidegger and the New Right," I review the impact that Heidegger's philosophy has had among the leading representa- tives of the transnational "New Right."

As one might anticipate, Heidegger's influence has been especially keen among proponents of the German and Austrian Neue Rechte. In the German- speaking lands of Mitteleuropa, Neue Rechte publicists have been instrumental in reshaping the worldview of the far-right parties such as the Alternative for Germany (AFD) and the Austrian Freedom Party (FPÖ), both of whose politi- cal fortunes have surged since the Middle East refugee crisis of 2015. By mo- bilizing Heideggerian terminology for contemporary political purposes, their goal has been to discursively camouflage the racist and neofascist aspirations that underlies the Neue Rechte political agenda.

In France, the birth of the Nouvelle Droite coincided with the founding in 1968 of GRECE, a right-wing think tank, whose acronym stands for "Groupe- ment de recherche et d'étude sur la civilisation européene." From its inception, GRECE sought to resurrect the discourse of interwar race thinking: albeit, re- formulated in an idiolect that concertedly sought to mask these unsavory polit- ical origins. Nouvelle Droite strategists were convinced that the most effective method of achieving this aim would be to reanimate the paradigm of "spiritual racism" propagated by conservative revolutionaries such as Arthur Moeller van den Bruck, Oswald Spengler, Ernst Jünger, Julius Evola, and, of course, Heidegger: all of whom rejected narrowly biological justifications of race thinking in favor of spiritual or aristocratic approaches.

Historically, the Nouvelle Droite has shunned electoral politics in favor of "metapolitics": winning the "battle of ideas" as a necessary prelude to assuming political power. Thereby, its proponents sought to lay the groundwork for an era of neofascist "ideational hegemony." In keeping with this objective, the Nouvelle Droite has characterized its approach as a "Gramscism of the Right." In retrospect, Heidegger's celebration of the "metapolitics of the historical *Volk*," in *Überlegungen* III, seems to have anticipated the Nouvelle Droite's strategy with uncanny prescience.[51]

From the very beginning, the Nouvelle Droite made extensive use of Heidegger's philosophy in order to advance its xenophobic, ethnopopulist agenda. In journals such as *Nouvelle École*, *Éléments*, and *Krisis*, the "Grècistes" have repeatedly invoked Heidegger's neo-Spenglerian "critique of modernity" in order to disqualify democratic legitimacy and *Rechtsstaatlichkeit*. Thereby, they seek to replace the normative provisions of "equality before the law" and jus soli (right of birth) with the "right of blood," or jus sanguinis. In a textbook example of ideological "inversion," they have maligned human rights as "totalitarian," owing to their putative insensitivity to ethnocultural "difference." In doing so, however, they seek to disguise their underlying, neoracist agenda: the establishment of a racially homogeneous, white "ethno-state" stretching "from Dublin to Vladivostok."[52]

In a postscript, "Heidegger and *Heimat*," I revisit the way that, during the 1950s, Heidegger reinvented himself as a champion of *Heimat-Literatur*: above all, in his commentaries on the poetry of fellow Schwarzwälder Johann Peter Hebel (1760–1828). During the Cold War, the flame of German nationalism was often preserved, in sublimated form, through the cultivation of a heightened provincial consciousness. Heidegger's numerous Hebel exegeses, which exalted the notion of "Mundart" or "dialect" (Hebel wrote poetry in the Alemannic dialect), conformed to this pattern.

In Heidegger's Hebel commentaries, his repeated appeals to the virtues of "Mundart" and "Heimat" may be construed as a calculated protest against the ongoing division and occupation of Germany during the 1950s: by U.S. troops in the West and by the Soviets in the East. In many respects, Heidegger's turn to Hebel during the 1950s as the poet of the Alemannic *Landschaft* and *Boden* paralleled his celebration of Hölderlin during the 1930s as the "Dichter der Deutschen" (poet of the Germans).

German national consciousness was also kept alive, in less sublimated form, by the revanchist-minded Bund der Heimatsvertriebenen, or League of Displaced Persons. During the 1950s, the Bund—many of whose members were ex-Nazis—metamorphosed into a powerful political lobby. They propagated the image of Germans as "victims" and appealed for the return of Germany's "lost provinces," omitting the fact that these territorial forfeitures were the direct result of the genocidal *Vernichtungskrieg* that the Third Reich had launched in the East against "Jewish Bolshevism."[53]

Heidegger, whose venia legendi had been revoked by the Allies in 1945, also thought of himself as a "displaced person." Hence, he strongly identified with the League's view of the Germans as "victims" and with their irredentist territorial claims. In keeping with these sentiments, in "Gelassenheit"—one of Heidegger's most important philosophical texts of the 1950s—Heidegger, in solidarity with the League, openly appealed for the return of Germany's lost provinces, which he proceeded to mention by name: East Prussia, Silesia, and Bohemia.[54] Readers who had hoped for an acknowledgment on Heidegger's part of the mass criminality that Nazi Germany had visited on its Slavic neighbors would, once again, be seriously disappointed.

Whither Heidegger Studies?

The challenges of rethinking Heidegger's legacy have immediate, practical consequences for the future of Heidegger pedagogy and Heidegger scholarship. From an instructional standpoint, following the *Black Notebooks'* publication, it is no longer acceptable to proceed as if nothing has changed: as though one could, in good conscience, reinstate the cordon sanitaire between "philosophy" and "worldview" in Heidegger's work, a firewall that his more inflexible champions have consistently sought to maintain.

Heidegger instruction and Heidegger scholarship, instead of averting their gaze, must directly confront the moral and interpretive challenges that have been raised by the Master's commitment to the "inner truth and greatness of National Socialism." Correspondingly, the customary insular and narrowly textual approaches to Heidegger's work must yield to new interpretive paradigms: models that are willing to integrate and reflect seriously on the circumstantial and contextual aspects of Heidegger's thought. To reassess Heidegger's legacy in these terms is entirely consistent with Heidegger's own self-understanding as a philosopher of *temporality* and *historicity*: albeit, in a qualitatively different—that is, *critical*—register.

The *Black Notebooks* confirm that Heidegger's enthusiasm for the Third Reich was more than a short-lived and ephemeral dalliance. Recent documentation has significantly enhanced our understanding of Heidegger's aspirations to assume a position of philosophical leadership or *Führung*. Heidegger was convinced that he alone could provide the metaphysical substance and direction that was required for the "movement" to fulfill its appointed ontological-historical "destiny." The *Black Notebooks* reveal that, as late as 1939, Heidegger persisted in the view that his support for National Socialism was "*more necessary than ever*": not for pragmatic or circumstantial reasons but, as Heidegger put it, on "*philosophical grounds*": that is, for reasons that were based on the salvific "mission" that Heideggerian *Seinsgeschichte* had imputed to the German *Volk* as the "most metaphysical *Volk*."[55]

In formulating the arguments and criticisms that follow, I have been acutely conscious of the mistrust and ill-will they are likely to arouse among Heidegger's more dogmatic supporters. Be that as it may, there is one potential objection that I would like, if possible, to counter in advance: the allegation that my reconstruction of Heidegger's *Denkweg* contains *nothing new*, that "we have seen it all before." Judging by past experience, such accusations tend to be little more than a pretext for refusing to engage with perspectives and positions that challenge the pieties and idées fixes of Heideggerian orthodoxy.

This orthodoxy extolls Heidegger's legacy for having transcended the shortcomings and debilities of "Western metaphysics"—in truth, a caricatural and simplified image thereof. For the most part, however, Heidegger's more rigid partisans fail to acknowledge that, in his efforts to overcome the depredations of metaphysics, Heidegger frequently *regressed behind the* normative attainments of philosophical inquiry. As the philosopher Emil Angehrn has observed in "Ursprungsdenken und Modernitätskritik,"

> Given the premises of Heidegger's philosophy, it is an open question how far he
> is genuinely capable of critical thinking. . . . As Ernst Tugendhat has emphatically
> suggested, the epistemological premises of Heidegger's thought . . . make it impossible to raise questions of the truth and falseness [of propositions]. On these
> grounds, he has linked Heidegger's political errors directly to his philosophical

deficits. . . . In the case of an "originary" thinker like Heidegger, it is not really his "susceptibility" to ideological currents that is at issue. At stake is whether his thinking . . . *inherently produces ideological results.*[56]

Profound skepticism concerning Heidegger's purported "overcoming of metaphysics" is warranted by the manifest contempt in which he held inherited standards of validity, argumentation, evidence, and communication. As Heidegger avowed in *Logic: The Question of Truth* (1925), "At bottom, this magic word 'validity' is a *tangle of confusion, perplexity, and dogmatism.*"[57] The philosophical component of *Heidegger in Ruins* maintains that, in his efforts to transcend the "confusions" and "perplexities" of our inherited understanding of "validity," Heidegger consigned philosophy to a new series of "confusions, perplexities, and dogmatisms."[58]

A Caveat and Disclaimer

I conclude this introduction with an important caveat concerning the aims of the present study: a disclaimer meant to obviate potential misunderstandings.

In the pages that follow, I do *not* argue that Heidegger was a "Nazi philosopher" and that, on these grounds, his work should be condemned and dismissed. On the contrary: Heidegger's reformulation of transcendental phenomenology opened up significant new pathways and possibilities. By decentering the "transcendental subject," Heidegger revolutionized the meaning of intentionality. As such, *Being and Time*, as has been widely acknowledged, initiated a crucial paradigm shift away from the narrow concerns of "epistemology" and "cognition" and toward the phenomenology of "everydayness" and "Being-in the-world."

Heidegger reconceived "transcendental phenomenology" as "existential phenomenology." In the wake of his reformulation of the phenomenological project, "moods," "curiosity," "ambiguity," "idle talk," "solicitude," "falling," and "inauthenticity" became legitimate and propitious philosophical topoi. Heidegger's reformulation of transcendental phenomenology inspired Emmanuel Levinas to justly praise *Being and Time* as a *"sovereign exercise of phenomenology."* With Heidegger's *Daseinsanalyse*, observed Levinas, "one does not reach 'nothingness' through a series of *theoretical steps, but in anxiety* [*Angst*]." Thereafter, "existence itself . . . was animated by . . . the primordial, ontological meaning of *nothingness.*"[59]

Levinas's account helps us to understand why the "war youth generation" (*Kriegsjugendgeneration*), disillusioned with the philosophical commonplaces of the prewar era and confronting a crisis of "meaninglessness," viewed Heidegger's *Existenzphilosophie* as akin to a revelation. A philosophical idiolect that interpreted "Angst," the "Abgrund" (abyss), and "das Nichts" (nothingness) as occasions for the summons to "authenticity" (*Eigentlichkeit*)—an authenticity that is, in each case, "mine" (*jemeinig*)—satisfied what Theodor Adorno, in *Negative Dialectics*, described as a deep-seated generational "ontological need."[60]

Günther Anders's appraisal of Heidegger's legacy echoed Levinas's verdict concerning the transformative nature of Heidegger's existential demarche. Anders paid tribute to Heidegger's singularity, as exemplified by his *"being drawn to philosophizing not by academic problems, but by the most elementary philosophical terrors."* According to Anders, what was unprecedented about Heidegger's approach was its ability to "discern the structure of intentionality in the whole of *pre-theoretical life*: in the making of things, interacting with them, using them. . . . By expanding Husserlian intentionality . . . he was describing the way *one is in the world*: not exclusively as a *task of consciousness*, but in all those acts of everyday life that [*are*] *usually unsuited for philosophical study.*"[61]

Nevertheless, Heidegger's understanding of "authentic Dasein"—his "Lutheran -existential" reconceptualization of Aristotelian *phronēsis*—culminated in the forlornness of "Being-toward-death." To quote Anders, Heideggerian *Eigentlichkeit* terminated in a "new pseudo-radicalism, . . . even a sort of escapism: . . . in the sham-freedom of '*Sterbenkönnen*' als '*eigenster Möglichkeit*' "—the "capacity for death" as one's "innermost possibility." "What a miserable and desperate form of freedom," concluded Anders: "to live-toward-death instead of liking to live or living for a cause."[62] Heidegger's elevation of "Being-toward-death" as the ne plus ultra of "authentic existence" reminds us—should such a reminder be necessary—of the enormous impact that the discourse of central European *Zivilisationskritik* had on his conception of "Being-in-the-world."

Thus, in lieu of a simplistic *dismissal* of Heidegger's philosophy, my intentions—in keeping with the appreciative readings of Levinas and Anders—are decidedly more nuanced. At the same time, in the pages that follow, I have consciously shunned the reverential, text-immanent approach to understanding Heidegger's work that has often prevailed among his more reverential disciples: a framework that treats his texts as compendia of numinous, self-evident

Higher Truths. By systematically expunging questions that bear on the genealogy or *Herkunft* of Heidegger's thought—by spurning questions of context—
his champions have repeatedly blinded themselves to its potential shortcomings
and limitations. I have sought to historicize Heidegger's work, not to impugn
its originality but to broaden our understanding its scope and aims. In doing so,
I have sought to honor hermeneutical directives that Heidegger himself provided.

A cursory perusal of *Being and Time* confirms that Heidegger was, in the first
instance, a philosopher of *Zeitlichkeit* and *Geschichtlichkeit*: of *temporality* and
historicity. These features explain his aversion to Western metaphysics, conceived as a repository of timeless and eternal truths. Working through the correspondence between Wilhelm Dilthey and Graf Yorck von Wartenburg in
1923–25, Heidegger attained a new awareness concerning historicity's centrality for fundamental ontology. Heidegger realized that, as historical beings, we
are not merely *in history*; we ourselves *are history*.

However, in the numerous commentaries on the theme of "Heidegger and
practical philosophy," rarely has the crucial nexus between "historicity" and
"authenticity" been adequately treated. This oversight is hardly fortuitous,
since, in *Being and Time*, it is Heidegger's articulation of "historicity" that reveals his profound indebtedness to the *Zeitgeist* of the interwar period—hence
the indelible ideological biases of his framework.

Pathbreaking studies by Christian von Krockow, Johannes Fritsche, Charles
Bambach, Daniel Morat, and Florian Grosser have convincingly shown that
Heidegger's existential ontology is *shot through with the idiolect of the conservative revolution*.[63] (Regrettably, only Fritsche's and Bambach's contributions are available in English.) The insights and criticisms of von Krockow et
al. are amply corroborated by Heidegger's persistent recourse, in *Being and
Time*, to the conservative revolutionary semantics of "Entscheidung," "Volk,"
"Gemeinschaft," "Heldentum," "Schicksal," and "Kampf." In a pathbreaking
essay on "Heidegger, Nietzsche, and National Socialism," Otto Pöggeler has
underlined the markedly ideological valances of Heideggerian "Geschichtlichkeit." As Pöggeler concludes, *"Historicity* connected the individual and his
or her 'fate' to history and to an encompassing *Gemeinschaft*: *to the destiny of
a 'Generation' and a 'Volk.' "*[64] Pöggeler's pithy summation offers an invaluable hermeneutic clue concerning the philosophical "grounds" of Heidegger's
existential "decision" for National Socialism in 1933.

Heidegger's appropriation of this right-radical, conservative revolutionary idiom was of paramount importance, since, as I will argue, it provided him with a criteriological basis to distinguish between *authentic* and *inauthentic* historicity. Thus, viewed from a "metapolitical" standpoint, the existential analytic of *Being and Time* appealed for the "destruction" of the heritage of "1789" and its replacement by a *Revolution von Rechts* (revolution from the right).[65] Apart from this background, Heidegger's embrace of the "metapolitics of the historical *Volk*" in the *Black Notebooks* and related texts remains, sensu stricto, *unintelligible*.

1

The Heidegger Hoax

Heidegger is like a fox who sweeps away the traces behind him with his tail.
—Otto Pöggeler, *Heidegger in seiner Zeit* (1999)

A Politically Sanitized Corpus

A CURSORY EXAMINATION OF THE PUBLICATION history of Heidegger's texts explains why, in the secondary literature, the scope and degree of his National Socialist allegiances have been consistently downplayed and misconstrued. Among Heidegger scholars, this extremely compromised and checkered textual history is something of an open secret. Yet, in light of the elevated stakes with respect to Heidegger's reputation, rarely have these "open secrets" been publicly discussed.

For decades, Heidegger's philosophical legacy has been systematically manipulated by a coterie of well-disposed literary executors. Among this group, immediate family members have played—and continue to play—a disproportionate role. Hence, following Heidegger's death in 1976, the supervision and publication of his manuscripts was not primarily entrusted to trained scholars but, instead, to interested parties possessing limited professional competence. This disturbing situation motivated one knowledgeable commentator to charge that, because of this blatant disregard for conventional scholarly criteria, Heidegger's collected works edition was, in effect, being run as a "family business."[1]

Much of the editorial deception resulted from Heidegger's belated directive that his manuscripts be published as they were found at the time of his death: in a so-called *Ausgabe letzter Hand*. This decision foreclosed the possibility of producing a critical edition of Heidegger's work: one that, in accordance with prevailing scholarly standards, would have documented the textual history of Heidegger's manuscripts. The willful violation of those standards has opened the door to a series of highly compromising editorial falsifications and distortions. Compounding the original error, prospective readers were misleadingly informed that Heidegger's manuscripts were being published *tel quel*: that, aside from minor stylistic and grammatical changes, no substantive alterations or emendations had been made.[2]

One of the main objectives of this influential clique of Heidegger loyalists was to spare the Freiburg philosopher additional disrepute and opprobrium related to his National Socialist involvements. Ultimately, the "machinations" resulted in the publication of *politically sanitized versions of Heidegger's texts*: editions in which evidence of Heidegger's pro-Nazi and anti-Semitic convictions was consistently masked and expunged. Hence, beginning with the publication of Heidegger's lecture courses during the postwar years, numerous passages that attested to the magnitude and depth of his ideological zealotry during the Nazi years were systematically elided.

One such example concerned Heidegger's encomium in *Schelling's Treatise On the Essence of Human Freedom* (1936) to Hitler and Mussolini for having "introduced a *countermovement to nihilism*": a remark that was contained in the manuscript version of Heidegger's lecture course but that was suppressed in the published edition. Heidegger's paean to Hitler and Mussolini exalted the fascist leaders as exemplars of "active nihilism," a well-known Nietzschean coinage. In *The Will to Power*, Nietzsche characterized "active nihilism" as "*a violent and destructive force*." In contrast to the "passive nihilism" of a bourgeois *Zivilisation*, Nietzsche viewed "active nihilism" as a salutary, life-affirming standpoint: a force that articulated "the conditions under which [a living creature] *prospers, grows, and gains power*."[3]

Nietzsche's exaltation of "active" or "radical" nihilism exemplified the entwinement of "destruction" and "rebirth," "violence" and "renewal," that distinguished Heideggerian *Seinsgeschichte*. Heidegger's praise for Hitler and Mussolini for having "introduced a countermovement to nihilism" attests to the fact that, in 1936, he continued to view fascism as a source of European spiritual renewal. He qualified these expectations by adding, "the *authentic metaphysical realm of Nietzsche* has not yet been realized."[4]

Heidegger's remarks concerning "the authentic metaphysical realm of Nietzsche," which were omitted in the initial publication of his Schelling lectures, are significant, insofar as they indicate the sweeping transfiguration of the European cultural and political landscape that Heidegger expected fascism to provide. They also attest to his endorsement of the conservative revolutionary view that held the egalitarian ideals of Western humanism responsible for the advent and growth of European nihilism. Heidegger, conversely, wagered on political formations that were predicated on *violence, hierarchy, and race* as the optimal hope for European "spiritual" renewal.

Heidegger's effusive praise of Hitler and Mussolini for having "introduced a countermovement to nihilism"—deliberately omitted from the published version of his Schelling lectures—raises a pivotal question about the reception history of his work: To what extent might scholarly opinion have been modified or transformed had access been permitted to the unexpurgated version of Heidegger's texts?

"The Inner Truth and Greatness National Socialism"

Another illustration of the way that Heidegger's publications were politically doctored concerns *An Introduction to Metaphysics* (1935/1953), the first of his lecture courses from the Nazi era to be published after the war.[5] In contrast with other instances of textual suppression, this case is better known, since Jürgen Habermas took it upon himself to raise public awareness concerning the persistence of profascist themes in Heidegger's postwar texts. Reflecting on the dispute some twenty years later, Habermas commented, "In 1953, Heidegger published his lectures from 1935 on the *Introduction to Metaphysics*. I was, as a student, at the time so impressed with *Being and Time* that reading these lectures, *fascist right down to their stylistic details*, actually shocked me."[6]

The leitmotif of Habermas's review essay concerned the imperative to "work through" the social pathologies of the German past as means of ensuring that the past would not repeat itself. In keeping with this theme, he viewed the publication of Heidegger's lectures as a valuable opportunity to "probe the rootedness of fascist motives in the core of the German tradition and to uncover the dispositions that, in a period of 'decline' [*Untergang*], could lead to fascism."

For Habermas, Heidegger's forthright "ontological" justification of Nazi Germany as "the most metaphysical of nations" raised the prospect that "that fascism has more to do with German traditions than one would ordinarily like to admit."[7] Importantly, the profascist elements of Heidegger's lecture course belied the conventional assumption—as formulated, for example, by Hannah Arendt in the *Origins of Totalitarianism*—that National Socialism, as a phenomenon of the "gutter," had nothing to do with the life of the mind or higher spiritual pursuits.[8]

Habermas took particular exception to Heidegger's encomium to the "inner truth and greatness of National Socialism," which, eight years after the German "collapse" of 1945, he had retained in the text, uncommented—thereby implying that it was a standpoint he continued to support.

Philosophically, Habermas objected to Heidegger's "ontological fatalism": his attempt to vindicate National Socialism as an *Ereignis* (Event) that had been mysteriously "decreed" by "Being," independent of human volition. He regarded Heidegger's "ontological-historical" account of Nazism as a case of historical-conceptual subterfuge: a framework that, instead of shedding light on Nazism's political excesses, *merely explained away* those excesses. Heidegger's reliance on the "history of Being" as explanatory trope proved doubly problematic, since it rendered questions of moral and historical responsibility superfluous.

Habermas distilled the gist of his critique in the following passage: "Can the planned murder of millions of human beings, which we all know about today, be made understandable in terms of the history of Being as a fateful 'going astray'? Is this murder not the actual crime of those who, with full accountability, committed it? Have we not had eight years since then to take the risk of confronting what was and what we were? Is it not the foremost duty of thoughtful people to clarify the accountable deeds of the past and keep the knowledge of them awake?"[9]

At the time, Habermas was unaware that Heidegger's parenthetical remarks concerning the "confrontation between planetary technology and modern man"—comments Heidegger appended in order to clarify what he meant by National Socialism's "inner truth and greatness"—had been added after the fact. In other words, although Heidegger had tried to pass off the published text as a faithful reproduction of the manuscript version, it had been editorially "retouched." As Otto Pöggeler disclosed some twenty years later in *Heidegger's Path of Thought* (1983), while preparing the text for publication, Heidegger had substituted "this movement" (*diese Bewegung*) for "National Socialism" in the hope of preempting further controversy. According to Pöggeler, "In 1953, Heidegger had obviously wanted to avoid the term 'National Socialism,' whose historically unambiguous nature was clear after 1935."[10]

In Pöggeler's discussion of the episode, he faulted the editors of the *Gesamtausgabe* edition of *An Introduction to Metaphysics* for allowing Heidegger's unacknowledged editorial tampering to stand, thereby perpetuating the masquerade that had begun with the publication of the Max Niemeyer edition in 1953.[11] Pöggeler's critique was directed at the editor of the *Gesamtausgabe* volume, Petra Jaeger, who had merely compounded the original subterfuge by insisting on "an author's indisputable right in the case of a lecture manuscript to make improvements and clarifications."[12] Admittedly, few persons would dispute that "right." By the same token, few scholars would countenance an author's "right" to misrepresent "improvements and clarifications" inserted eighteen years after the fact as being contained in the original manuscript, especially insofar as the alterations in questions served to mask or distort the author's disturbing political loyalties.

Pöggeler called attention to an additional falsification that marred the *Gesamtausgabe* version of *An Introduction to Metaphysics*: the inclusion of a letter that Heidegger had written in 1968 to an Israeli scholar in which Heidegger misrepresented his controversial endorsement of National Socialism's "inner truth and greatness" as a concession to Nazi security personnel, who, he alleged, were monitoring his lectures. Heidegger reiterated this claim in the *Der Spiegel* interview "Only a God Can Save Us," asserting, "My lectures were constantly under surveillance."[13] Obviously, if the *Sicherheitsdienst*, or state intelligence services, were scrutinizing Heidegger courses, the regime must have regarded him as a potentially dangerous adversary. Heidegger concluded his letter to the Israeli professor by claiming that "those who knew how to listen" could readily discern that his words were those of a political critic and dissident.[14]

In *Heidegger's Path of Thought*, Pöggeler—a Heidegger intimate, whose loyalties to his mentor are above suspicion—pointedly disputed Heidegger's claim that his avowal concerning the "inner truth and greatness" of National Socialism had been insincere: lip service that was intended to placate the (nonexistent) Nazi security apparatus. According to Pöggeler, "*The disputed statement of 1935 appears to be no crumb for informers, but rather the expression of Heidegger's innermost conviction.*"[15] Already in 1945, shortly after the German "collapse," Karl Jaspers had summarily and definitively set the record straight in the appraisal of Heidegger's "case" that he submitted to the university de-Nazification commission: "Heidegger, Alfred Baeumler, and Carl Schmitt were . . . the professors who attempted to reach a position of intellectual leadership under National Socialism."[16]

At this point, another contradiction emerged to undermine Heidegger's ex post facto apologetics. Heidegger's claim, in his letter to the Israeli scholar, that his 1935 lecture course *An Introduction to Metaphysics* had been surveilled by representatives of the Nazi state security apparatus contradicted his earlier testimony, in "The Rectorship: Facts and Thoughts" (1945), in which he contended that *police surveillance of his lectures only began in 1937.*[17]

In the passage that exalted National Socialism's "inner truth and greatness," Heidegger criticized the failings of NSDAP ideologues who "fish in the troubled waters of 'values' and 'totalities.' " In the "The Rectorship: Facts and Thoughts" (1945) and the *Der Spiegel* interview, Heidegger misrepresented this criticism as a *renunciation of National Socialism tout court.* However, as Lutz Hachmeister has shown in *Heidegger's Testament* (2014), Heidegger's critique was less a rejection of National Socialism than an indictment of his philosophical rivals—Ernst Krieck and Alfred Baeumler—with whom he was engaged in a struggle for ideological "leadership" of the movement: political competitors who, in Heidegger's view, lacked the ontological-historical insight required to fathom National Socialism's ultimate significance in the history of Being. As such, Heidegger's remarks contested neither the historical legitimacy of National Socialism nor Hitler's appointed role as secular "redeemer."[18]

At the time of the 1953 debate, Heidegger belatedly entered the fray. However, his intervention, instead of shedding light on the controversy, perpetuated the falsehood that his parenthetical remarks concerning the "confrontation between planetary technology and modern man" had been contained in the original manuscript. As Habermas explained in a later essay, "Work and Weltanschauung: The Heidegger Controversy from a German Perspective" (1988), thereby, Heidegger had "falsely projected a later self-understanding [of technology] back to 1935 . . . even though that self-understanding rested on a clause that Heidegger had added to the manuscript in 1953."[19]

Hence, in addition to falsifying the text, Heidegger misrepresented the philosophical basis of his support for National Socialism in 1935. Whereas during the early 1930s, Heidegger, influenced by his reading of Ernst Jünger's work, had supported National Socialism as a "heroic" response to the challenges of "planetary technology," in 1953, he misleadingly claimed that he had rejected National Socialism as merely another manifestation of technological "decline." Heidegger's misrepresentation—in the form of a September 1953 letter to *Die Zeit*—was significant, insofar as it foreshadowed subsequent attempts on his part to "backdate" the critique of technology that he developed during the late 1940s in order to deceive the public into thinking that, already during the 1930s, he had spurned National Socialism on the basis of this critique.[20]

In retrospect, the textual debate over the furtive editorial reprocessing of Heidegger's remark concerning "inner truth and greatness of National Socialism," as well as his parenthetical qualification of the claim in terms of "the confrontation between planetary technology and modern man," might seem to be a relatively trivial matter. However, to minimize its significance would be a serious mistake, insofar as the episode anticipated numerous future efforts on the part of Heidegger, his editors, and literary executors to disguise the nature of his commitment to National Socialism by manipulating the textual and historical record. Subsequently, a protracted and systematic pattern emerged: one of intentionally falsifying the content of Heidegger's writings in order to suppress the philosophical grounds of his commitment to Nazism as an exemplar of "authentic historicity."

These misleading editorial practices have assumed additional weight in view of the recent controversy over the *Black Notebooks*. In these debates, Heidegger's defenders have repeatedly claimed that his early lexicon of "Entscheidung," "Heldentum," "Schicksal," "Volk," "Generation," and "Gemeinschaft" was *purely formal*. Consequently, this discourse did not predispose his "existential decision" for Nazism in 1933. If this were true, however, then what compelled Heidegger and his literary executors, at a later point, to falsify the dossier? And why did he employ—as the *Black Notebooks* attest—precisely this lexicon in order to justify National Socialism, as he put it in *Überlegungen* XII, on "philosophical grounds" (*aus denkerischen Gründen*)?[21]

The 1953 dispute over the publication of *An Introduction to Metaphysics* was a sorry affair—as well as a dress rehearsal for things to come. It substantiates Pöggeler's allegation that "Heidegger is like a fox who sweeps away the traces behind him with his tail."[22] It also confirms Hannah Arendt's unflattering charge that "Heidegger lies notoriously always and everywhere, and whenever he can."[23]

In 1987, Rainer Marten—a former Heidegger student who had helped prepare the manuscript of *An Introduction to Metaphysics* for publication—

confirmed that the parenthetical phrase concerning the "confrontation between planetary technology and modern man" failed to appear in the original lecture manuscript. Marten testified that Heidegger had added the remarks in 1953, while the manuscript was in page proofs. Thereafter, Heidegger continued to mislead the public by adamantly insisting—in the *Der Spiegel* interview, for example—that the phrase in apposition had appeared in the original manuscript, though it had not been read aloud when the lecture was delivered.[24]

In an effort to resolve the escalating textual dispute, scholars sought to consult the original manuscript. To their dismay, they discovered that the page that contained the disputed passage had inexplicably gone missing—presumably, in a maladroit effort to avoid further embarrassment. However, if this were the case, these efforts backfired spectacularly.

In the article that Marten published in the *Badische Zeitung* in order to clarify these matters, he reflected on the ideological transformation that Heidegger's philosophy had undergone following the Nazi seizure of power. He returned to one of the central themes of Habermas's 1953 review essay: "the rootedness of fascist motives in the core of the German tradition."

According to Marten, one of the defining features of Heidegger's "Turn" from "existential ontology" to the "history of Being" had been to equate "authentic historical existence" with "*das Völkische*." This equivalence was aggravated and reinforced by Heidegger's obsessional preoccupation with "Deutschtum" and its various cognates and corollaries. The most frequent variants of this term that Marten detected in Heidegger's *Werk*, circa 1933–35, were " 'deutsche Wissenschaft,' 'deutsches Recht,' 'deutsche Wirklichkeit,' 'deutsches Dasein,' and 'deutsches Gewissen.' "[25]

Marten realized that Heidegger's *Deutschtümelei*—his maniacal obsession with "things German"—was not merely an occasional or episodic feature of his *Denken*. Instead, it betrayed a fundamental transformation of Heidegger's understanding of the *Seinsfrage*. The end result was that, from then on, *Germanic Dasein* assumed a talismanic primacy in Heidegger's fundamental ontology. It became the measure and criterion of "historicity" or *authentic historical existence*. Concomitantly, the ontological centrality that Heidegger assigned to *Deutschtum* impelled him to consign non-German peoples to the nether regions of "inauthenticity."

Fittingly, Marten titled his essay "A Racist Concept of Humanity." As he explained, "Heidegger's traditional Alemannic belief in the superiority of German

Geist predisposed him to accept a racist concept of humanity. This tendency emerged in 1933, with his Freiburg University *Rektoratsrede*, in which ethnicity [*Volkstum*] and language became the criteria that determined which nations were endowed with a historical 'mission' and which ones were not. In Heidegger's philosophical 'axis' of (ancient) Greeks and Germans, the *völkisch*-based racism was unmistakable, insofar as *one Volk* possessed greater existential legitimacy than all of the others."[26]

Heidegger and Nietzsche: Democracy as "Nihilism"

If we turn our attention to the publication of Heidegger's extensive Nietzsche lectures—which were published in 1961, in an influential, two-volume edition by Neske Verlag—we find that entire pages were excised or rewritten. Nevertheless, the far-reaching nature of these emendations and omissions was never publicly acknowledged. To this day, Anglo-American readers who consult the standard English-language translation, which was published by Harper & Row in four volumes between 1981 and 1984, would remain ignorant of the fact that the lectures had been substantially doctored.

In making these alterations, one of Heidegger's central aims was to mask the nature and extent of his antidemocratic convictions: an ideological disposition that conditioned his hostility toward the Weimar Republic and predisposed him, in 1933, to support the Nazi seizure of power. Another motivation on Heidegger's part was to forestall, in light of the 1953 debacle, yet another public controversy over his commitment to National Socialism.

Heidegger's scorn for democracy was deep-seated and pervasive. According to H. W. Petzet, Heidegger embraced Jacob Burckhardt's view that democracy had been responsible for the downfall of the ancient polis. After the war, Heidegger lamented the "democratized disintegration" (*demokrasierter Verfall*) of contemporary institutions, a critique that was widespread among archconservative champions of "philosophical anthropology," such as Arnold Gehlen and Hans Freyer.[27] (During the 1930s, Freyer and Heidegger were members of the *Ausschuss für Rechtsphilosophie,* a subcommittee of the Academy of German Law that was chaired by the future Nuremburg war criminal Hans Frank.)

In *What Is Called Thinking?* (1954), Heidegger praised Nietzsche's denigration of democracy as "a form of decline [*Verfallsform*] of the state": as a slack form of political rule that, according to Nietzsche, lacked *"will, instinct, and authority* [which are] *anti-liberal to the point of malice.*"[28] Even after the Second World War's whorl of carnage and destruction, Heidegger insisted there were no "essential" differences between "communism, fascism, or world democracy." In his view, all three forms of political rule merely expressed the "universal domination of the will to power."[29]

Heidegger's antipathy to democracy was philosophically overdetermined. As I have already pointed out, in *An Introduction to Metaphysics*, he asserted, "*Truth is not for every man, but only for the strong.*"[30] Heidegger's standpoint discounted the possibility that truth might emerge from the *sensus communis*: an open exchange of opinions and views in the public sphere. This conclusion followed logically from his understanding of language as an "emanation of Being," as opposed to a human institution or construction. Moreover, if one scrutinizes Heidegger's critique of "average, everyday Being-in-the-world" and "das Man" in *Being and Time*, one readily discerns the familiar refrains of the "reactionary modernist," antidemocratic critique of mass society.

In a section that he omitted from the first edition of the Nietzsche lectures, Heidegger lamented that "Europe always seeks to cling to 'democracy,' failing to recognize that *the latter will be its historical death.*" He continued by lauding Nietzsche's realization—a view to which Heidegger himself subscribed—that "*Democracy is nothing but an expression of nihilism*": "*The devaluation of the highest values, to the point where they have become no more than simple 'values'*: in other words, they have ceased to be constructive forces. Hence, 'the ascendancy of the rabble,' '*the social mishmash*,' 'equal men.' . . . The phrase 'God is dead' is . . . the formulation for the fundamental experience of an *Ereignis* of Western history. I took up this phrase in full awareness in my 1933 Rector's Address."[31]

That Heidegger made a point of emphasizing the thematic continuity between his Nietzsche lectures and the pro-Nazi sentiments that were expressed in his 1933 *Rektoratsrede* suggests that, in the intervening years, his "worldview" remained essentially unchanged.

World Jewry's Predilection for "Planetary Criminality"

Many of the expunged passages have been restored in Heidegger's 102-volume *Gesamtausgabe*. Nevertheless, it has recently come to light that it, too, is beset with errors, omissions, and distortions. In 2014, *Black Notebooks* editor Peter Trawny revealed that, during the late 1990s, while preparing Heidegger's

1939 lectures *Die Geschichte des Seyns* (The History of Being) for publication, he had been pressured by Heidegger's literary executors, Friedrich von Herrmann and Hermann Heidegger (the philosopher's son), to excise Heidegger's shockingly anti-Semitic assertion that "it would be worthwhile inquiring into world Jewry's [*Judentums*] predisposition toward planetary criminality."[32]

One would urgently like to know on what editorial grounds Trawny consented to this elision as well as why he waited *sixteen years* before finally revealing the truth?

Heidegger's allegation concerning "world Jewry's" inclination toward "planetary criminality," far from being a trifle, constitutes an avowal of "exterminationist anti-Semitism." It posits that all Jews are "guilty" by virtue of having been born as Jews. It inculpates Jews not because of their actions or deeds but purely and simply because of their "racial character" as Jews.[33] As such, it belies the misleading claim, frequently advanced by Heidegger's diehard defenders, that Heidegger rejected race thinking as a matter of principle.

Heidegger expressed these remarks in his lecture course—hence publicly—shortly after Hitler's notorious 30 January 1939 Reichstag speech, in which he declared, "If the international Jewish financiers in and outside Europe should succeed in plunging the nations once more into a world war, then the result will not be the Bolshevization of the earth, and thus the victory of Jewry, but *the annihilation of the Jewish race in Europe!*"[34] When viewed in this light, Heidegger's comments seem to represent a profession of solidarity with Hitler's views.

"National Socialism" versus "Natural Science"

In 2015, the German news weekly *Die Zeit* revealed a striking transcription error afflicting Heidegger's 1934–35 lecture course *Hölderlin's Hymns "Germanien" and "Der Rhein."* Heidegger's lectures on Hölderlin are suffused with paeans to the virtues of "Führertum" and "Kampf." Heidegger lauded Hölderlin as *"the poet of the Germans"* (*Dichter der Deutschen*) and as the foremost "power in the history of our *Volk*" (*die Macht in der Geschichte unseres Volkes*).[35] Although Heidegger began these lectures six months after his resignation as Freiburg University rector, his effusive praise for the *Volksbegriff* indicates that his ideological ardor remained keen.

However, in an attempt to downplay Heidegger's commitment to Nazism, the abbreviation "N. soz.," which Heidegger had unambiguously employed as shorthand for "Nationalsozialismus," was misleadingly transcribed as "Natur-wissenschaft" (natural science). The marked ideological tenor of the lecture course made the mistaken rendering even more preposterous.[36]

As a result, suspicions arose that the textual manipulation of the Hölderlin lecture course was part of a more general plan to camouflage Heidegger's Nazi past. Writing in *Die Zeit*, Adam Soboczysnki reasonably inquired whether the growing list of editorial omissions and falsifications was merely the "tip of the iceberg," hence part of a systematic effort on the part of Heidegger's literary executors to whitewash his Nazi sympathies. Soboczysnki summarized these suspicions in his article as follows: "There is a widespread suspicion that has arisen concerning the Heidegger edition, one that, to judge by international research, has become the basis for numerous essays and book publications: has there been an attempt to present a version of Heidegger's philosophy that has been purged of references to National Socialist doctrine? Are the errors that have surfaced with respect to the 'last hand edition' begun in 1975 merely the tip of the iceberg?"[37]

"Rewording the Past"

However, not only did Heidegger and his editors consistently *suppress* pro-Nazi avowals and claims. As it turns out, following the war, Heidegger fabricated and rewrote entire passages, inserting them in earlier texts in order to promote the myth that, during the 1930s, he had acted "heroically," as an intellectual and political dissident. To enhance the masquerade, Heidegger passed over these later alterations in stony silence. Instead, he misleadingly sought to pass off the rewritten texts as faithful versions of earlier manuscripts.

The most egregious case of such editorial deceit concerns Heidegger's 1938 lecture "The Age of the World Picture," which was first published in *Holzwege* in 1950. In the secondary literature on Heidegger, "The Age of the World Picture" has been regarded as an important milestone in his maturation as a critic of modern technology. In addition, following its publication in *Holzwege*, the essay became a central pillar of the legend of Heidegger as a spiritual *Wider-standskämpfer* (resistance fighter), corroborating Heidegger's claim, in "The Rectorship: Facts and Thoughts" (1945), that, during the 1930s, his lecture courses had become sites of philosophical "resistance."[38]

In "The Age of the World Picture," the evidence attesting to Heidegger's status as a *résistant* was based on the last of the essay's nine *Zusätze*, or "appendices." In appendix 9, Heidegger elaborated his by-now-familiar critique of the philosophical "subject." Heidegger employed this critique to browbeat the failings of "Western metaphysics." However, what is novel about this iteration of Heidegger's critique is that he applied it obliquely to the legacy of National Socialism. According to Heidegger, "The human being as the rational being of the Enlightenment period is no less a subject than the human being who grasps himself as a nation, wills himself as a *Volk*, breeds himself as a race and, finally empowers himself as Lord of the earth. . . . In the planetary imperialism of the technically organized human beings, the subjectivism of human beings reaches its highest point, from which it will descend to the flatness of organized uniformity and establish itself there. This uniformity becomes the instrument for total, namely technological, dominion over the earth."[39]

In and of itself—that is, even were one, for the sake of argument, to suspend judgment about the editorial deception that resulted in its inclusion—the reasoning that informs this passage is deeply problematic. To suggest that the understanding of subjectivity that informs "the rational [human] being of the Enlightenment" and the Nazi conception of "the human being . . . as a *Volk* [who] breeds himself as a race" are, in essence, *one and the same* is to posit an unacceptable moral and political equivalence. Here, it is important to point out—especially in light of the profound influence that Heidegger's *Vernunftkritik* (critique of reason) has had among representatives of the academic and cultural Left—that they are not at all the same. The Enlightenment standpoint—with its respect for *droits de l'homme*, limited government, constitutionalism, and popular sovereignty—represents an indispensable antidote and counterweight to the "totalitarian temptation" of which Heidegger was so enamored.[40]

Heidegger's myopic equation of "the rational [human] being of the Enlightenment" with the excesses of Nazi race thinking foreshadowed his equally disturbing assertion, in the "Bremen Lectures" on the evils of modern technology (1949), that "mechanized agriculture [is] in essence, the same as the fabrication of corpses in gas chambers and extermination camps"—a claim that belies the canard concerning Heidegger's "silence" with respect to the Holocaust.[41] In the present context, it is worth noting that, in yet another instance of editorial sleight-of-hand, the preceding passage from Heidegger's Bremen Lectures was omitted from the original publication of the "The Question Concerning Technology," in *Vorträge und Aufsätze* (1954).[42]

In "Work and Weltanschauung: The Heidegger Controversy from a German Perspective," Habermas called attention to Heidegger's dishonesty after the war. Instead of acknowledging the extermination of the European Jews, Heidegger, in the "Letter on Humanism" (1947), trained his sights on the transgressions of Western "humanism," thereby insinuating that "reason," "subjectivity," and "metaphysics" were ultimately responsible for the *Endlösung*. According to Habermas, Heidegger's efforts to shift the blame for the European catastrophe from the deformations of German historical development to "Western" ideals represented a continuation of the German Right's ideological assault on the "ideas of 1789":

> Heidegger dealt with the theme of humanism at a time when the images of the horror that the arriving Allies encountered in Auschwitz and elsewhere had made their way into the smallest German village. If his talk of an "essential Event" [*wesentliches Ereignis*] had any meaning at all, the singular event of the annihilation of the Jews would have drawn his attention. . . . Instead, he directed himself against the "humanistic interpretations of man as *animal rationale*, as 'person' " . . . because "the highest determinations of the essence of man in humanism do not realize the proper dignity of man."[43]

Heidegger's persistent efforts to establish a misleading moral equivalence between the Enlightenment and National Socialism were part of a deliberate campaign on his part to *minimize* Nazi criminality by portraying modern "technology" (*Technik*), along with its "Western" cultural origins, as the more fundamental and essential culprit. His revisionist view of the "German catastrophe" insinuated that National Socialism's depredations were primarily—even exclusively—the result of Western cultural and intellectual influences: "humanism," "Cartesian subjectivity" and "Technics."

An important clue concerning the ideological valences of Heidegger's Descartes critique emerged in a passage from "The Fundamental Question of Philosophy" (1933–34), in which Heidegger disparaged the teaching of Descartes at German universities as a form of "spiritual depravity [*geistigen Verlotterung*]."[44] Conversely, his Spenglerian "technology narrative" left the developmental deformities of the German *Sonderweg*—with its inflated veneration of the *Volksbegriff*—entirely out of account. It misleadingly suggested that—as Heidegger continued to believe—"Germanic Dasein" remained the key to Europe's cultural and spiritual renewal. In his view, everything depended on

Germany's ability, as the "most metaphysical of nations," to rebuff deleterious "Western" influences. As Adorno once observed, "Germans are human beings who can't tell a lie without believing it themselves."[45]

For decades, Heidegger scholars have cited his critical observations about "Volk" and "race" in "The Age of the World Picture" as concrete proof that, during the 1930s, Heidegger staunchly opposed National Socialist *Rassenpolitik*. Moreover, the remarks contained in appendix 9 seemed to corroborate Heidegger's claim that, to the detriment of his own safety, he practiced "spiritual" resistance to Nazism: a situation that resulted in his lectures being monitored by the Gestapo. (Recently, however, this pretense on Heidegger's part has been discredited by Lutz Hachmeister.)[46]

However, a comparison of the original 1938 manuscript of "The Age of the World Picture" with the version that was published twelve years later in *Holzwege* reveals that appendix 9 was actually a later addition. Heidegger had written this paragraph after the war, as part of a campaign to rehabilitate his reputation.

Yet, when *Holzwege* was published in 1950, Heidegger deceptively sought to pass it off as part of the original lecture course, thereby providing a pseudoevidentiary basis for the myth that he had actively opposed the regime. In order to consummate the deceit, in the 1950 edition of *Holzwege*, Heidegger appended a prefatory note to "The Age of the World Picture," claiming that "*the Appendices were written at the same time but not delivered.*"[47]

In "Rewording the Past: The Postwar Publication of a 1938 Lecture by Martin Heidegger," Sidonie Kellerer adjudged Heidegger's assertion a "decisive falsification." As Kellerer explains, "[There is] a striking discrepancy between the original manuscript of 1938 and the published version of 1950: the last and longest of all the nine 'appendices' (*Zusätze*) included in *Holzwege* after the main text is absent in the original manuscript. Its insertion into *Holzwege* is crucial—it is in fact *a decisive falsification*—because only here, and nowhere else in the text, is there an explicit political distancing from Nazism. In all earlier writings, Heidegger applied the label 'subject,' his characterization of those who lost their deeper roots of existence, to the adherents of the Enlightenment."[48]

One factor that, undoubtedly, influenced Heidegger's decision to falsify the composition date of appendix 9 was the prospect that the teaching ban that had been imposed on Heidegger for his role in burnishing the credentials of the Nazi dictatorship could be reevaluated.[49]

Heidegger's deliberate falsehood concerning the composition date of appendix 9 has been parroted on numerous occasions by sympathetic scholars who have sought to defend him. It resurfaced in the English translation of "The Age of the World Picture" (in *The Question Concerning Technology and Other Essays*; 1977). In 2002, Cambridge University Press published an English-language edition of *Holzwege, Off the Beaten Path*. An editorial remark reprised Heidegger's misleading assertion that "the Appendices were written at the same time but not delivered."[50]

To this day, the brazen misstatement contained in "The Age of the World Picture," appendix 9, has never been rectified or corrected: neither in the *Gesamtausgabe* nor in the existing English translations. Instead, it remains one among many "dirty secrets" that have characterized the publication history of Heidegger's work.

An Escalating Editorial Debacle

At this point, the edition politics surrounding the Heidegger *Ausgabe* has metamorphosed into an embarrassing public controversy: a scandal that has called into question the integrity of the *Gesamtausgabe* itself. In 2015, in order to rescue the edition's credibility, the publisher Vittorio Klostermann felt compelled to issue a desperate appeal to the *Gesamtausgabe* editors, asking them to step forward with any knowledge they might have concerning other instances in which compromising passages had been intentionally omitted from the published versions of Heidegger's work.

Klostermann noted in his missive that, following the *Black Notebooks'* publication, the press had received "numerous inquiries as to why Martin Heidegger's anti-Jewish enmity [*Judenfeindschaft*] hadn't surfaced in *Gesamtausgabe* volumes that had been previously published." Fearing that a point of no return had been reached, Klostermann underlined the gravity of the metastasizing editorial debacle: "Recent discoveries have raised the concern that a search for further inaccuracies in the *Gesamtausgabe* will arise. Every additional discrepancy that third parties are able to point out risks placing the press and the editors on the defensive, and could potentially damage the reputation of the *Gesamtausgabe* as a whole." There followed Klostermann's appeal to editors who were responsible for volumes from the Nazi era to come forward with any information they might have concerning "questionable deviations from the authorized copies of Heidegger's manuscripts, be it a question of omissions or transcription errors."[51]

Klostermann's plea was widely viewed as a belated attempt at damage control: as an acknowledgment not only that such instances of editorial malfeasance had been widespread but also that they had been sanctioned at the highest editorial levels—by Heidegger's literary executors and by the editors who were responsible for individual *Gesamtausgabe* volumes.

However, despite the admirable intentions underlying Klostermann's appeal, his strategy contained an obvious flaw: if the editors themselves were responsible for the "questionable deviations, omissions [and] transcription errors," how likely was it that they would step forward of their own volition to confess, thereby, effectively incriminating themselves?

What was becoming increasingly clear was that the original edition policy that had conceived and sanctioned the *Gesamtausgabe* as, in essence, a Heidegger "family business" had backfired. The problems began when Heidegger's son Hermann, who lacked the requisite scholarly qualifications, was named as one of the estate's principal literary executors. Moreover, it is well known that the editors of the individual *Gesamtausgabe* volumes were selected primarily on the basis of their "loyalty" to Heidegger's legacy rather than for reasons of professional competence and that Heidegger family members were granted final say in approving or rejecting prospective editors.[52]

As Klostermann's missive tacitly acknowledged, one of the central problems with the edition concerned the "authorized copies of Heidegger's manuscripts." For decades, family members had assumed primary responsibility for producing "fair copies" of Heidegger's handwritten texts. This meant that, if in the view of family members, a specific passage was deemed potentially embarrassing, it was simply elided. The suppression of Heidegger's dictum concerning "world Jewry's predisposition toward planetary criminality" in *The History of Being* at the behest of Hermann Heidegger represents one egregious instance of a "questionable deviation" from Heidegger's original manuscripts to which Klostermann alluded.

In a 2015 interview, the University of Siegen philosopher Marion Heinz, who had edited *Gesamtausgabe* 44, openly lamented the ineptitude that has characterized the publication history of Heidegger's texts, including the *Gesamtausgabe*. In her view, the dearth of professional oversight has resulted in wholesale editorial chaos. It has produced a situation in which "no one knows which passages have been omitted, or whether, in the case of transcriptions or copies [of original manuscripts], insertions have been made." As Heinz concluded, "In sum, we have no reliable basis at our disposal to research and evaluate Heidegger's philosophy."[53]

In January 2014, yet another instance of editorial malfeasance surfaced, when it came to light that a volume of the *Black Notebooks* that had long been presumed "missing"—*Anmerkungen* I, which Heidegger began in 1942—had inexplicably reappeared. It seems that, all along, the manuscript had been in the possession of an extended "family member": Silvio Vietta, a professor of German at the University of Hildesheim. When pressed to explain the circumstances surrounding the notebook's enigmatic peregrinations, Vietta revealed that, decades earlier, Heidegger had given the manuscript to Vietta's mother, Dorothea, as a "gift" when the two were having an affair.[54]

The missing volume returned by Vietta is merely one among many editorial irregularities besetting the *Black Notebooks*. The public has yet to receive a satisfactory explanation concerning the absence of the initial volume, *Winke* x *Überlegungen* (I), which Heidegger began in 1930. (In an editorial note appended to *Anmerkungen I–V*, Trawny simply states that "[the volume's] whereabouts are unknown.")[55] In *Heideggers "Grosse Politik"* (Heidegger's "Great Politics"; 2018), Reinhard Mehring offers a pithy summary of the most salient problems afflicting the *Gesamtausgabe*. Mehring's conclusions amplify Marion Heinz's skeptical verdict:

> Increasingly, questions that have been raised about the edition's academic substance, editorial quality, and political biases have caused the *Gesamtausgabe* to fall into disrepute. . . . As far as the individual volumes are concerned, we still lack an honest discussion of the editorial principles and terms of "authorization." . . . None of the individual volumes from Division III—the so called "*Seinsgeschichtliche Abhandlungen*" [ontological-historical treatises] . . . has had much of an impact on contemporary philosophical discussion. The philosophical content of Heidegger's "anderes Denken" has largely been ignored by the academic mainstream, and the "esoteric" divisions of the *Gesamtausgabe* [Abteilungen III and IV] have provoked an uptick of political scandal, . . . thereby, sullying Heidegger's reputation as a philosophical "classic."[56]

Mehring's contention that "we still lack an honest discussion of the editorial principles and terms of authorization" with respect to the *Gesamtausgabe* alludes to the fact that there is no extant documentation of the agreement that was putatively struck between Heidegger and Klostermann Verlag in Heidegger's hand. Instead, the negotiations on Heidegger's behalf were transacted by his assistant and—following the philosopher's death—literary executor, Friedrich-Wilhelm von Herrmann. Consequently, the only written authorization we have attesting to the editorial guidelines—the consent to an edition "aus letzter Hand" and so forth—are based on von Herrmann's claims.

In April 1970, Heidegger suffered a stroke that left him considerably weakened. In 1973—a mere three years before his death—he belatedly consented to the idea of a *Werkausgabe*.[57] Thereafter, von Herrmann seized the initiative with respect to the *Gesamtausgabe* planning—a circumstance confirmed by the fact that all communications with Klostermann concerning the edition were negotiated by von Herrmann in Heidegger's name.

When pressed to explain these unusual circumstances—that is, Heidegger's absence from the discussions that culminated in the publishing arrangement with Klostermann—von Herrmann referred cryptically to a "waxen, black notebook" in which Heidegger allegedly consigned his "Weisungen" or "editorial directives." The only flaw in von Herrmann's explanation was that the "directives" in question had been *dictated* by Heidegger to von Herrmann himself. Hence, scholars had no means at their disposal to independently verify von Herrmann's claim that the instructions in question stemmed directly from Heidegger.[58]

In practice, the idea of an "Ausgabe aus letzter Hand" has served as little more than a convenient fiction, one that has been repeatedly dishonored or suspended in order to accommodate the *Gesamtausgabe* editors' shifting whims. The potential for editorial licentiousness became clear, in 1986, when von Herrmann issued a statement to clarify the organization of *Gesamtausgabe*, Division II, "Lecture Courses: 1919–1944."[59] Von Herrmann's declaration included a stunning profession of editorial "sovereignty": an assertion of his unfettered "right" as literary executor to impose "enhancements" (*Erweiterungen*), "abridgments" (*Kürzungen*), and "transpositions" (*Umstellungen*) on Heidegger's manuscripts. In the eyes of many observers, such editorial arbitrariness was tantamount to dispensing with "guidelines" *tout court*.[60]

A comparable series of editorial miscues and distortions has marred the *Black Notebooks'* publication. In directives dating from the late 1930s, Heidegger referred to the *Notebooks* as *Überlegungen* (Reflections) and

Aufzeichnungen (Notes). Explicit reference to "Black Notebooks" is nowhere to be found. There is no evidence to suggest that the "Black Notebooks" appellation was approved by Heidegger. Instead, the epithet seems to have been a marketing ploy that was jointly conceived by the philosopher's publisher and his literary executors.

The inconsistencies that have plagued earlier *Gesamtausgabe* volumes are also in evidence in the *Black Notebooks*. Periodically, one encounters comments that Heidegger inserted that refer the reader to related discussions elsewhere in the text. These remarks indicate that Heidegger revised and reedited the *Black Notebooks* with an eye toward their future publication.

Regrettably, none of these emendations or "signposts" is dated. Nor is there any reliable information concerning the extent of Heidegger's revisions. Were specific passages excised? Were other passages added? How long after the *Notebooks*' original composition were these textual redactions made? Until there has been a systematic comparison between the original manuscript versions of the *Black Notebooks* and the published editions, we have no way of knowing. If past experience is a reliable benchmark, there is little cause for optimism. It is little wonder that, in a widely cited article, Theodore Kisiel denigrated the *Gesamtausgabe* as an "international scandal of scholarship," owing to the editors' arrogant disregard of customary editorial standards and practices.[61]

The numerous textual omissions have severely prejudiced the international reception of Heidegger's work. In the case of a philosopher of Heidegger's stature, influence, and renown, such brazen attempts to manipulate the scholarly record seem especially unconscionable. Not only have the repercussions been far-reaching. Much of the damage that has been done appears to be irreparable.

The editorial manipulation of Heidegger's texts was meant to deflect critical attention from the fraught nexus between *Seinsgeschichte* and *Seinspolitik*. As a result, for decades, the public has been presented with a misleading, politically "sanitized" image of Heidegger's thought: a bowdlerized version in which Heidegger's profascist political allegiances have been extensively airbrushed.[62]

As far as the numerous translations and foreign-language editions of Heidegger's works are concerned, from a publishing standpoint, it is essentially too late—too cumbersome and too expensive—to implement the requisite corrections and emendations. As a result, for the foreseeable future, generations of students encountering Heidegger's work for the first time will be exposed to editorially doctored, politically cleansed versions of Heidegger's thought.

These significantly flawed texts have, meretriciously, become the de facto standard editions.

Moreover, in the voluminous secondary literature on Heidegger, this web of editorial deception is rarely mentioned. Were it acknowledged, it would risk exposing a deliberate policy of textual manipulation that, by masking the philosopher's ideological loyalties, has sought to marginalize fundamental questions bearing on the intellectual and moral integrity of his work.

Rehabilitation through Translation

The international reception of Heidegger's work has also benefited immensely from the efforts of sympathetic translators. As a rule, these translators have been Heidegger loyalists: scholars who have a vested interest in presenting as favorable an image of Heidegger's thought as is philologically tenable. Given Heidegger's enduring commitment to the discourse of German exceptionalism, the intellectual stakes involved in translating his work are enormous. Since, in the case of translations, questions of interpretation inevitably arise, it has been relatively easy to camouflage Heidegger's ideologically freighted language.

The English translation of Heidegger's 1933–34 seminar *Nature, History, and State*, which was published in 2013, is a good example of these misleading translation practices. In the introduction, the editors provide readers with interpretive guidelines concerning the translation of politically charged terms such as "Volk" and "Führer." Although both terms are used in colloquial German, following Hitler's seizure of power in January 1933, they had indisputably become keywords in the lexicon of *Nazi-Deutsch*.[63] Moreover, since Heidegger employed them in conjunction with his efforts to provide National Socialism with the requisite ontological grounding, his usage coalesced with their predominant ideological employment.

In *Nature, History, and State*, Heidegger employed "Volk" in order to justify Nazi geopolitical thinking: specifically, the "Drang nach Osten" or "push to the East." The *Drang nach Osten* was implicitly genocidal, since it required subjecting Slavic peoples to the imperatives of Nazi racial domination. Himmler once described the Third Reich's plans for the conquest of Poland as follows: "We are not bringing these people civilization. I can only repeat to you word for word what the Führer wishes. It will be enough if: (1) the children learn to read the traffic signs so that they do not run under vehicles; (2) if they learn their 2 × 2 so they can count up to 25; and (3) if they can write their names; no more is necessary."[64]

Nevertheless, in an explanatory note to *Nature, History, and State*, the editors, abstracting from the historical context in which alone Heidegger's employment of such terms makes sense, explain that they decided to translate "Volk" as "people." Not only does the semantic deception mask the depth of Heidegger's commitment to an especially brutal iteration of Nazi ideology; it comes close to transforming Heidegger into a putative champion of Jeffersonian democracy. Heidegger's supporters can find solace in the editors' comment that the German "term *Volk* is related to [the English word] 'folk,' " as well as in their misleading assurance that *Volk* was "often, *but not always*, understood in racial terms."[65]

These elucidations, instead of clarifying Heidegger's ideological intentions in utilizing such terms, intentionally sow confusion. Although "Volk" and "folk" are etymologically related, this explains nothing about Heidegger's employment of "Volk" under Nazism, at a point in time when he was actively vying for a position of philosophical *Führertum*. An honest treatment of the linguistic issues at stake would confirm that Heidegger's use of the term did not differ substantially from the way that other Nazi ideologues employed it.

The editors' related claim that that *Volk* was "often, *but not always*, understood in racial terms" is little more than a blatant falsehood. Under the Third Reich, "Volk" was indeed a racial concept. Moreover, it was inextricably tied to the reigning *Herrschaftsideologie*: a discourse of German mastery and German superiority. As a member of the Nazi Party and as a thinker who supported the Third Reich in numerous official capacities—for example, his role in rewriting the Baden educational charter in line with the *Führerprinzip*—Heidegger's use of "Volk" unambiguously coincided with its employment by other Nazi potentates. The evidence at our disposal overwhelmingly suggests that Heidegger supported the Third Reich's racial agenda. When Heidegger used the word *Volk* in his seminars, lecture courses, and public addresses, he was fully aware of the term's racial implications.

Much of the same holds true for Heidegger's use of "Führer," whose ideological valences the translators of *Nature, History, and State* seek to mask by mistranslating it as "leader." They attempt to camouflage this deception by informing readers that "Führer is the ordinary German term for leader," neglecting to mention that an even more "ordinary" German term for leader is "Leiter."[66]

The "Führerprinzip" was central for National Socialism's political self-understanding as a charismatic dictatorship. As applied to Hitler, the term "Führer" assumed an emotional, quasi-religious significance. It conveyed Hitler's unique position within the NSDAP (National Socialist German Worker's Party) and the *Volksgemeinschaft* as a leader whose legitimacy derived from his status as the personification of the *Volkswillen*.

Heidegger's employment of "Führer" indisputably imbibed these semantic valences. In Heidegger's "political ontology," *Führertum* and *Führersein* attested to superhuman ontological powers and capacities. These powers and capacities, which were redolent of Nietzsche's *Übermensch*, elevated the bearer beyond the realm of "average everydayness" inhabited by "das Man" and toward the holy sanctum of "Being" (*Seyn*) itself. In Heidegger's view, authentic *Führertum* transcended the sociological criteria of Weberian "charisma." Instead, in the form of *Führersein*, it was tantamount to a profane apotheosis, a transfiguration that elevated the bearer to quasi-divine status.[67]

By rendering *Führer* as "leader," the translators of *Nature, History, and State* abstract from the conceptual history of *Führer* as a Nazi neologism. Hitler was canonized as the *Führer* of the Nazi Party during the early 1920s. Although the term had been previously used, the inclusion of the definite article, as in the expression *der Führer*, dates from 1925 and was unique to Nazism.[68] In 1934, a leading dictionary of contemporary usage explicitly linked the term *Führer* to the person of Hitler: yet another example of the way that *Nazi-Deutsch* had commandeered colloquial German.[69]

The *Führerprinzip* was the Third Reich's central organizational principle. According to the *Organizational Handbook of the Nazi Party*, "The Führerprinzip determines the pyramidal construction of the organization in its details and as a whole. At the head stands the Führer. At the Reich, party, and state levels, he designates the leaders of the various spheres of competence. Thereby, the assignment of tasks at the party level becomes clear. They become *Führerorden* [Führer-Orders]."[70]

Heidegger's employment of "Führer" in *Nature, History, and State* demonstrated that he had fully internalized the predominant Nazi usage, as is evidenced by his fulsome summons that "the Might of the Führer become fused with Being and the soul of the *Volk*."[71]

Nor was Heidegger's commitment to the *Führerprinzip* merely rhetorical. To judge by Heidegger's seminar on Hegel's *Philosophy of Right* (1934–35), which he held in conjunction with his participation in Hans Frank's Academy of German Law, Heidegger strove to enshrine the *Führerprinzip* as the legal-constitutional cornerstone of the National Socialist *Führerstaat*.[72]

Another example of linguistic deception via the ruse of translation pertains to Heidegger's assimilation of conservative revolutionary discourse. By relying on this idiom, Heidegger underlined his solidarity with the "Front Generation" or "community of the trenches." Like other radical nationalists, Heidegger viewed the *Kriegerlebnis* as a "spiritual event": a reawakening of the *Volksgeist* from the torpor and disarray of nineteenth-century "materialism." As Heidegger declaimed in 1934, "At the Front there transpired *an entirely new experience*: an entirely new idea of *Gemeinschaft* emerged. . . . The awakening of the *Frontgeist* during the war, and its reaffirmation after the war, is nothing less than *the creative transformation of this Event into a formative power of future Dasein*."[73]

Thus, it is hardly a coincidence that, in Division II of *Being and Time*, the concept of "Generation" figured prominently as an expression of authentic "Being-with-others." "In communication and struggle [*Kampf*], the power of destiny [*Macht des Geschickes*] becomes free. *Dasein's fateful destiny in and with its 'Generation' constitutes the authentic occurrence of Dasein*," proclaimed Heidegger.[74] In light of this assertion—and others like it—it is difficult to deny that Heidegger's understanding of "authenticity" (*Eigentlichkeit*) was integrally tied to the "warrior ethos" of the *Kriegerlebnis* and the *Frontgeneration*.

Similarly, Heidegger's appeal to "heroism" (*Heldentum*) as an exemplar of authentic Being-in-the-world betrayed his indebtedness to the discourse of German "military nationalism" (*soldatischer Nationalismus*). "Dasein wählt sich seinen Helden"—"Dasein chooses its hero"—declared Heidegger.[75] "Heldentum," "Sein-zum-Tode," "Kampf," "Volk," and "Gemeinschaft": in *Being and Time*, these terms play a key role in Heidegger's construction of "authentic historicity." As Daniel Morat has aptly concluded in *Von der Tat zur Gelassenheit*, "With his recourse to these concepts . . . Heidegger offered *a brilliant summary of the politics of the revolutionary Right*."[76] As Morat continues, "The 'heroic existentialism' of [*Being and Time*] and its call for individuals to embrace 'authenticity' and reject the 'dictatorship' of the 'they' constitute a kind of 'inner activism' that anticipated key elements of a *political existentialism*. Heidegger was able to build on these elements when he assumed the rectorship of Freiburg University in May 1933. Thereafter, he set about reworking them in line with his understanding of intellectual leadership within the Nazi State."[77]

In *German Science and National Socialism*, Arno Münster reached a conclusion strikingly similar to Morat's: "The practical application of [Heidegger's] conservative revolutionary project to the historical circumstances of the times . . . was only possible insofar as Heidegger's existential ontology . . . had already prepared the terrain conceptually by relying on categories such as 'decisiveness' [*Entschlossenheit*], the 'destining of Being' [*Seinsgeschick*], fatherland, 'anticipation-toward-death' [*Vorlaufen-zum-Tode*], and so forth. Consequently, *there was a distinct, immanent categorial predisposition . . . in Heidegger's thought that facilitated its accommodation with National Socialism.*"[78]

In *Being and Time*, the pervasiveness of such bellicose, conservative revolutionary semantics casts doubt on of the plausibility of the liberal democratic, "Heidegger and pragmatism" demarche.[79] (Unsurprisingly, in *Being-in-the-World: A Commentary on Heidegger's "Being and Time"*—one of the most influential exposés of Heidegger's thought in English—Hubert Dreyfus refused to treat Division II entirely, on the grounds that it "*contains the 'existentialist' side of Heidegger's thought, which focuses on anxiety, death, guilt, and resoluteness.*")[80] After all, pragmatists are unlikely to appeal to the "warrior ethos" of *Entscheidung, Heldentum, Kampf, Sein-zum-Tode*, and *Schicksal* that, in *Being and Time*, pervaded Heidegger's *Daseinsanalyse*. By exalting the lexicon of "military nationalism," Heidegger—who avoided serving at the front owing to an alleged heart ailment—remained true to the foundational experiences of his "Generation."

As Karl-Heinz Bohrer noted in *Ästhetik des Schreckens*, already during the 1920s, Heidegger's *Existenzphilosophie* had assimilated the "aesthetics of terror" propagated by like-minded fascist sympathizers: Oswald Spengler, Ernst Jünger, and Carl Schmitt. Heidegger's existential ontology was suffused with a "combative" (*kämpferisch*) idiom that was entwined with fantasies of *Untergang* or catastrophe: a Nietzschean-apocalyptical idiolect in which the imagery of "impending rupture, destruction, decline, and ruin" predominated.[81]

Nevertheless, in the standard translations of *Being and Time*, Heidegger's appropriation of this conservative revolutionary idiolect has been entirely airbrushed. By rendering the ideological valences of Heidegger's terminology unrecognizable to an Anglo-American public, the translations of his work have facilitated a politically anodyne reception of his thought. (Already during the 1970s, Pierre Bourdieu, in *Heidegger's Political Ontology*, convincingly exposed the conservative revolutionary biases of Heidegger's *Denken*.)[82] Only by suppressing this dimension of Heidegger's "existential semantics" might one smoothly assimilate his work to the lineage of American pragmatism, as represented by Charles S. Peirce, William James, John Dewey, George Herbert Mead, and Richard Rorty.

Similar criticisms apply to the standard English-language translations of *Bodenständigkeit*—"rootedness-in-soil"—and its etymological corollaries: *Boden, bodenständig,* and *bodenlos.* The 2011 edition of the *Brockhaus Wahrig Deutches Wörterbuch* instructively defines *bodenständig* as "not introduced from outside, bound to *Heimat,* bound to place, rooted [*nicht von außen eingeführt, Heimat gebundenen, ortsgebunden, verwurzelt*]." It defines *Bodenständigkeit* as "being bound to the *Heimat* [*Gebundenheit an die Heimat*]." Both of these definitions clarify the ethnocentric and parochial sense in which Heidegger employed these terms, already during the 1920s.

One of the reasons that Heidegger valorized Greek philosophy pertained to its *Bodenständigkeit,* in sharp contrast to the free-floating—hence ontologically superficial—"lack of rootedness," or *Bodenlosigkeit,* of Western liberalism. To exalt a school of thought as *bodenständig,* as did Heidegger on numerous occasions, meant praising its "ethnic substance," which was rooted in the *Boden,* or "native soil," of the *Volk.*

In *The Basic Concepts of Aristotelian Philosophy* (1924), Heidegger identified *Bodenständigkeit* as one of Greek philosophy's outstanding attributes. The conceptual integrity of Aristotle's thought, claimed Heidegger, derived from "the way in which its various conceptual moments are *bodenständig.*" "We must investigate the *Bodenständigkeit* of this [Aristotelian] conceptual skein," asserted Heidegger. "We need to examine how the Greek manner of thinking [*die griechische Begrifflichkeit*] appears in its *Bodenständigkeit.* Only if we proceed in this way can we be certain of discovering the true nature of Aristotle's philosophical approach."[83]

Heidegger embraced *Bodenständigkeit,* or "rootedness-in-soil," as an emblem of philosophical authenticity. He held that *bodenständige,* or "rooted," philosophies were *existentially superior* to their *bodenlose* competitors. Heidegger viewed *Bodenständigkeit* as an ontological manifestation of *authentic Being-in-the-world.* Worldviews that were *bodenständig* transcended "subjective" judgment or opinion. They expressed "primordial" (*anfängliche*) truths that were *rooted in Being itself.* Correspondingly, Heidegger viewed peoples who were existentially "unrooted," or *bodenlos,* as *inauthentic.* He regarded such insights as an unarguable, *factical-ontological truths.*

Consequently, in Heidegger's *Denken*, *Bodenständigkeit* possessed a "crypto-normative" status. It exalted "rooted" *Völker*, such as the Germans, at the expense of "unrooted" *Völker*, such as "world Jewry." On these grounds, Heidegger condemned Jews as *untrustworthy cultural interlopers*: as a spiritual-biological threat to integrity of the *Volksgemeinschaft*.[84] In the *Black Notebooks* (*Anmerkungen I–V*), Heidegger denigrated "world Jewry" as the "principle of destruction," *simpliciter*—a remark that speaks volumes about the ontological prejudice intrinsic to Heideggerian *Seinsgeschichte*.[85]

The idiom of *Bodenständigkeit* intersected semantically with the ideology of *Blut und Boden* as espoused by Walther Darré, the Nazi agricultural tsar and the author of *New Aristocracy of Blood and Soil* (*Neuadel aus Blut und Boden*; 1930). (Darré was a protégé of the leading Nazi race theorist Hans "Rasse" Günther. Because of the commonalities between Darré's *Blut und Boden* perspective and Heinrich Himmler's worldview, he has often been regarded as the "real ideologue behind Himmler.")[86]

The discourse of *Blut und Boden* that Heidegger embraced has had a disturbing afterlife. In the guise of "ethnopopulism," it has reemerged as one of the ideological linchpins of the European and American New Right: as a key argument against the perils of *métissage*, or "racial mixing." In August 2017, at the infamous "Unite the Right" rally in Charlottesville, Virginia, white supremacists expressly reprised the terminology of *Blut und Boden* with their chants of "blood and soil" during an ominous torchlight parade reminiscent of the Sturmabteilung (SA) processions that accompanied the Nazi *Machtergreifung*.[87]

English speakers unfamiliar with the German original would remain clueless with respect to the *völkisch*, racially exclusionary valences of Heidegger's existential lexicon. Instead, as a rule, they have been offered a narrow range of anodyne semantic equivalents: translation choices that mask the ideological resonances of Heidegger's protofascist idiolect. Thus, by rendering *Bodenständigkeit* as "indigenous character," the translator of *Basic Concepts of Aristotelian Philosophy* effectively expunged the term's *völkisch*-ideological connotations.[88]

In and of itself, to speak of the "indigenous" qualities of a discourse is unobjectionable. Among anthropologists, such usage is common practice. Conversely, to praise the virtues of *Bodenständigkeit* in interwar Germany, at a time when a revanchist, national revolutionary consciousness was menacingly on the rise, meant something else entirely. It conveyed support for an *existential geopolitics* that consciously exalted the protofascist values of *Volk*, *Boden*, and *Erde*.

Heidegger's philosophy was rife with politically freighted *Kampfbegriffe*. It was suffused with the idiom of—to borrow Kurt Sontheimer's expression— "antidemocratic thinking."[89] Whereas in the German original, the conservative revolutionary semantics of Heidegger's discourse are unmistakable, readers who encounter his thought in politically sanitized English translations have consistently been deceived concerning fundamental ontology's inherent ideological predispositions.

Scholars have frequently analyzed the "reenchantment" and "remythologization" of language that was characteristic of *Nazi-Deutsch*.[90] In *The Myth of the State*, Ernst Cassirer observed that Germany's "rearmament" had begun prior to 1933. The first step had been the rhetorical and semantic transformation that culminated in the embrace of Nazism as a form of *political myth*: "If nowadays I happen to read a German book published in these last ten years . . . I find to my amazement that I no longer understand the German language. New words have been coined, and even the old ones . . . have undergone a deep change of meaning. . . . Words that were formerly used in a descriptive, logical or semantic sense are now used as *magic words* that are destined to produce certain effects and stir up certain emotions."[91]

To illustrate his point, Cassirer cited a compendium of *Nazi-Deutsch* that had recently been published by a group of German scholars-in-exile. Despite their noble intentions, the project foundered: the idiom in question was so culturally and linguistically "rooted" that, in effect, it defied translation. According to Cassirer, what distinguished these terms was less their "objective meaning than the emotional atmosphere that surrounded . . . them." "The men who coined these terms," Cassirer continued, "were masters of the art of political propaganda. They attained their ends—the stirring up of violent political passions— via the simplest means. The word, or even the change of a syllable in the word, was often good enough to serve this purpose. If we hear these new words, we feel in them the whole gamut of human emotions: hatred, anger, fury, haughtiness, contempt, arrogance, and disdain."[92]

Cassirer's analysis reminds us why, in Heidegger's case, the issue of translation/mistranslation is so imperative. After all, how might non-German speakers discern the ideological resonances of Heidegger's *Existenzphilosophie*—its indebtedness to a protofascist, national revolutionary idiom—if keywords are consistently and deliberately misrendered?

Vernunftkritik: The "Unreasonableness" of Reason

The intellectual ramifications of the debates over Heidegger's philosophical legacy transcend the often-parochial domain of Heidegger studies. Heidegger's influence on postwar intellectual life has been incalculable. Heidegger's radical critique of humanism became the epistemological cornerstone of poststructuralism. Taking Heidegger's declaration that "reason, glorified for centuries, is the most stiff-necked adversary of thought" as a point of departure, proponents of French theory concluded that the pursuit of knowledge, instead of setting us free, has only further inscribed us in the entrapments of "logocentrism" and the "disciplinary society." In 1977, Michel Foucault pithily summarized these developments when he declared, "La torture, c'est la raison": "Reason is torture."[93] Thereby, the discourse of *Zivilisation-kritik*, which played a pivotal role in discrediting democracy in the eyes of the German *Bildungsbürgertum* (educated middle classes), secured a new lease on life in the postwar period. It became the hallmark of an academically fashionable "left Heideggerianism": an "antiphilosophy" that derived its inspiration from Heidegger's view that questions of "validity" (*Geltung, Gültigkeit*) are inherently detrimental, since they are destined to degenerate—as Heidegger put it—into a "tangle of confusion, perplexity, and dogmatism."[94] Ultimately, as with Nietzsche's doctrine of the "will to power," the systematic denigration of discursive reason and "force of the better argument" inexorably leads to the veneration of the discourse of "force."[95]

Heidegger's "antihumanism," as mediated through the prism of French theory, paved the way for the impasse of our contemporary "post-truth" universe. The self-undermining nature of radical *Vernunftkritik* (critique of reason) was presciently diagnosed by Hegel. In the *Phenomenology of Spirit*, Hegel expressed his fear that a systematic "distrust of science [*Wissenschaft*]" would culminate in "fear of truth."[96] As Herbert Schnädelbach has aptly observed, "*Vernunftkritik* has become the philosophical commonplace of our century: a platitude that distinguishes itself from other platitudes by virtue of its ceaseless claims to originality. . . . *Vernunftkritik* becomes 'radical' once it is no longer the weaknesses, the self-understanding, or the excesses of reason that are at issue, as was true for the tradition of philosophical enlightenment initiated by the sophists. Instead, it is reason *simpliciter* that now stands under attack."[97]

As Schnädelbach's remarks suggest, *criticism of reason* is the lifeblood of philosophy. Conversely, *Vernunftkritik*—a German specialty that was initiated by Schelling and the Romantics and that culminated in Heidegger's "anderes Denken"—is another matter entirely. It supplanted the immanent critique of reason via recourse to totalizing claims and demonization. Nietzsche's philosophical vitalism, epitomized by the proposition that we must learn to "philosophize with our instincts," proved to be an indispensable waystation along this path—hence Nietzsche's attendant claim that his books were "assassination attempts" (*Attentate*) rather than "literature" and his predilection for "philosophizing with a hammer" in lieu of reasoned argument.[98]

Heidegger's canonization—as evidenced by the oft-heard refrain, "Today, we need Heidegger more than ever!"—along with *Vernunftkritik*'s elevation as a new theoretical orthodoxy, have diminished the means we have at our disposal to defend democracy and "public reason" against a formidable array of authoritarian encroachments. As I demonstrate in chapter 6, Heidegger's arguments have consistently played into the hands of "spiritual reactionaries" who, in recent years, have led the charge against rule of law and human rights and, thereby, have helped to incite a global upsurge of illiberal ethnopopulism.

To judge by the *Gesamtausgabe*'s most recent installments, not only have the aforementioned dubious editorial practices continued, but they have escalated exponentially. To take only one example, in 2016 and 2020, a comprehensive, two-volume edition of Heidegger's collected *Vorträge* (lectures)—corresponding to *Gesamtausgabe* volumes 80.1 and 80.2—appeared. Inexplicably, however, the chronological sequence is marred by a conspicuous two-year gap. Volume 1 spans the years 1915–32; volume 2 covers the time frame lasting from 1934–67. Hence, the period of Heidegger's rectorate, which lasted from May 1933 to April 1934, has been brazenly and deliberately elided. True to the pattern I have described, materials that might shed valuable light on Heidegger's National Socialist commitments have been meretriciously excised—a fact that has been duly noted in the recent scholarly literature. As one commentator recently quipped, in view of the escalating history of distortions and manipulations of Heidegger's philosophical texts, it would be more accurate to speak of an "Ausgabe letzter Hände" (last *hands* edition), rather than an "Ausgabe letzter Hand" (last *hand* edition).[99]

Moreover, recent reports confirm that, following the death of Hermann Heidegger in 2019, the legacy of the *Gesamtausgabe* as a Heidegger "family business" will endure. Thus, in keeping with family tradition, the new executor of

Heidegger's literary estate will be the philosopher's granddaughter Almuth Hei-degger. Announcing her plans for the *Gesamtausgabe* in *Die Zeit*, Heidegger's new *Nachlassverwalter* revealed her intention to publish "supplementary vol-umes" (*Ergänzungsbände*)—precisely how many remained unspecified—to the current 102-volume edition. (At one point, Almuth Heidegger raised eyebrows by speaking of an independent *Ergänzungsausgabe*, or "supplemental edition.") According to Heidegger's new literary executor, the additional volumes would consist of materials from the philosopher's estate that were currently barred from public viewing until 2046, when the existing copyright was due to elapse. She added, suggestively, that an initial glance at the texts in question revealed the existence of "politically tricky passages [*politisch heikle Stellen*]," declining to specify what "politically tricky" meant or entailed—an avowal that led to speculation that the so-called *Ergänzungsausgabe* was meant to serve as a "depot" or "bad bank" for a subset of politically toxic materials.[100]

2

Heidegger in Ruins

My father was critical of world Jewry [Weltjudentum] *without being an anti-Semite. However, after Auschwitz, it has become impossible to make this distinction. Nevertheless, anyone who was alive during the 1930s readily understands its meaning.*
—Hermann Heidegger, defending his father against accusations of anti-Semitism, *Sezession* 60 (2014)

"The Metaphysics of German Dasein"

BLACK NOTEBOOKS II–VI DOCUMENT THE "TURN" in Heidegger's thought from "existential ontology" to the "history of Being." They also attest to the heightened "metapolitical" focus of Heidegger's *Denken*: his pivot away from the "sterile" concerns of first philosophy and toward—as Heidegger phrased it—the *"metaphysics of German Dasein."*[1]

In *Überlegungen* II, Heidegger characterized this "metapolitical" shift as follows: "The metaphysics of Dasein must, in accordance with its inner structure, deepen itself and be extended to the *metapolitics of the historical Volk*."[2] With this formulation, Heidegger highlighted the eschatological role that he ascribed to "German Dasein" in the narrative of the history of Being. The *Black Notebooks* attest to Heidegger's mounting conviction that philosophy must yield to the ontological-historical imperatives of "German Dasein" as the "historical *Volk*," par excellence.

The *Black Notebooks* confirm that Heidegger attributed a *redemptory mission* to "German Dasein": a salvific role that belies all modish discussions concerning his aversion to the blandishments of "onto-theology" (a perspective that has become canonical among deconstructionist readings of Heidegger). The *Black Notebooks* show that Heidegger esteemed "German Dasein" as the fundament or ground of "another Beginning" (*anderer Anfang*). The German *Volk*'s exceptional status bespoke a metaphysical capacity or potential that Heidegger denied to other *Völker*, or peoples. Instead, relying on a Nietzschean idiolect, Heidegger implicated non-Germanic peoples in the dissolution and ruination of "European nihilism."

Heidegger's commitment to the ideology of German "exceptionalism" is one of the *Black Notebooks'* fundamental leitmotifs. His support for this perspective emerged, unmistakably, in his assertion that "*only someone who is German [der Deutsche] is capable of poetically articulating Being in an originary way.*"[3] On the basis of this remark and others like it, it becomes clear that Heidegger's partisanship for National Socialism was ontologically overdetermined. It was predicated on his view *that Being discloses itself historically only to certain metaphysically privileged peoples*: peoples whom Heidegger regarded as an ontological-historical "elect."

Heidegger's insistence on the German *Volk*'s metaphysical "election" was by no means a "one-off." Nor was it an ad hoc, "occasional" political remark. It was an assertion that Heidegger imbued with essential, ontological-historical significance. As such, it went to the very heart of his understanding of the history of Being.

Scrutiny of the *Black Notebooks*, as well as Heidegger's so-called ontological-historical treatises of the 1930s, confirms that he regarded the capacity for ontological insight as *racially coded*. Heidegger maintained that specific *Völker*, or peoples, such as the Germans, stood out by virtue of their unique, existential-cognitive aptitude to discern the "sendings of Being" (*Schickungen des Seins*). Conversely, other *Völker*—the Jews and like-minded peoples who adhered to the "rootless" (*bodenlos*) worldview of Western "liberalism"—remained bereft of this capacity. Heidegger viewed such peoples as existentially and ontologically deficient. Accordingly, in the *Black Notebooks*, Heidegger, speaking of "world Jewry" (*das Judentum*), proclaimed, "The more primordial and original [*ursprünglicher und anfänglicher*] future decisions and questions become, the more inaccessible they remain for this 'race.' "[4]

Heidegger maintained that the most essential "primordial and original decisions and questions" were prescribed by *Seinsgeschick*, or the "destinings of

Being." Since such "decisions and questions" concerned fundamental ontological matters, they remained indiscernible to "world Jewry," insofar as, as
Heidegger repeatedly claimed, Jews as a "race" were ontologically flawed.

In the just-quoted passage, Heidegger's insistence on placing the word "race"
in quotation marks was ideologically fraught. It reflected his view that, measured by racial criteria, "world Jewry" as a "race" was essentially fraudulent. It
qualified not as a "race" but as an "antirace"—in Nazi parlance, a *Gegen-Rasse*
or "counterrace"—insofar as it lacked one of the indispensable criteria of authenticity: *Bodenständigkeit*, or "rootedness-in-soil."

Although we have been repeatedly told by Heidegger's champions that
Heidegger systematically shunned race thinking, his insistence on portraying
"world Jewry" as an "antirace" reprised one of the fundamental tenets of
Nazi race doctrine. Proponents of race thinking held that "world Jewry," as a
"counterrace," embodied an *existential threat* to superior, "Nordic" races like
the Germans. They repeatedly invoked this claim as a justification for combating Jewish influence via recourse to the most violent and radical measures: for
example, "total extermination."

Heidegger's conviction that a people's cognitive capacities were inherently
linked to questions of "rootedness-in-soil" emerged clearly in *Nature, History,
and State* (1933–34), a text in which Heidegger reflected on the relationship
between *Raum* and *Erfahrung*, "space" and "experience." "On the basis of a
Volk's specific knowledge of the nature of its space [*Raum*], we first experience
the way that nature is revealed in it," observes Heidegger. "The nature of our
German space [*Raum*] is revealed in a distinctly different manner to a Slavic
Volk than it is to us. *In the case of Semitic nomads, it will perhaps never be revealed at all.*"[5]

Heidegger held that the Jews' status as a "rootless" and "nomadic" people ac-
counted for their endemic experiential and cognitive incapacities, as exempli-
fied by their inability to grasp the existential distinctiveness of "German space."
Reformulated in terms of the history of Being, this incapacity meant that the
Jews were permanently consigned to a type of ontological perdition. "World
Jewry's" condition of ontological deprivation came to light in Heidegger's as-
sertion that "primordial and original decisions and questions" concerning the
Seinsfrage were fated to remain "inaccessible to this 'race.' "

Heidegger's commitment to the ontological singularity of *Deutschtum*—his
understanding of "German Dasein" as an *Ereignis*, or "Event," in the history of

Being—predisposed his commitment to National Socialism as a reenactment of the "Greek Beginning": a "repetition" that took place on a higher ontological plane. Heidegger's *Deutschtümelei*—his attachment and devotion to things German—bespoke a "metaphysical" conviction. As such, it proved impervious to countervailing arguments and empirical refutation. Thus, at the apogee of World War II, as the battle of Stalingrad raged and there could no longer be any doubt concerning the atrocities and depredations that defined the essence of Nazi rule, Heidegger persisted in his view that the West's "redemption," should it ever come to pass, could only emerge from "German Dasein": a judgment that was consistent with his earlier veneration of Germany as the "most metaphysical of nations."[6] As he declared in 1943, *"Only the Germans—and they alone—can redeem [retten] the West and its history. . . . The planet is in flames. The essence of man is out of joint. Only from the Germans, provided that they discover and preserve their Germanness, can world-historical consciousness arrive."*[7]

The *Black Notebooks* confirm that Heidegger supported National Socialism not *despite* its "barbarian" methods—the *Totens-* and *Vernichtungslager* (death and extermination camps), the SS (Schutzstaffel) *Totenskopf* brigade, the *Vernichtungskrieg* (war of annihilation) in the East; concepts that stemmed from Nazi *Herrenrasse* ideology—*but because of them.*

Following Nietzsche's recommendation that, if something is falling, the merciful thing to do is to give it a final push, in the *Black Notebooks*, Heidegger praised "National Socialism [as] *a barbaric principle*," adding, with breathtaking frankness, "Therein lies its essence and its capacity for greatness." "The danger," Heidegger cautioned, "is not [National Socialism] itself, but instead, *that it will be rendered innocuous via sermons about the True, the Good, and the Beautiful.*"[8] "Everything must be exposed to complete and total devastation [*völlige Verwüstung*]," Heidegger continued. "In this way alone might one shatter the 2,000-year reign of [Western] metaphysics."[9]

In the *Black Notebooks*, Heidegger displayed a remarkable fondness for the lexicon of "military nationalism" (*soldatischer Natonalismus*). Adverting to the rhetoric of the *Frontgeneration*, Heidegger characterized the philosophical perspective purveyed by the *Notebooks* as "stealthy advance and rearguard positions [*unscheinbare Vorposten- und Nachhutstellungen*]."[10] Invoking the National Socialist idiolect of "racial hygiene," Heidegger asserted, "The breeding [*Züchten*] of ever-higher thought-forms [*Denkarten*] is of greater importance than the mere communication of knowledge [*Kenntnismitteilung*]."[11] In his capacity as Freiburg University rector, one of Heidegger's first steps was to introduce *Wehrdienst* (military service) as a required component of the curriculum.[12]

Heidegger's defense of Nazism as a "barbaric principle" exemplified his conviction that the only way to surmount "nihilism" was via recourse to *nihilistic methods*: by relying on a strategy of "*complete and total devastation*." Heidegger held that only a maximum of brutality would eliminate, once and for all, the detritus and decay of a Western civilization on the brink of collapse. One of the hallmarks of Heideggerian *Seinsgeschichte* was the attempt to supersede Nietzsche's *Wille zur Macht* (will to power) via a *Wille zur Zerstörung* (will to destruction).

In crafting these arguments, Heidegger relied on an understanding of history that may be felicitously described as an inverted Hegelianism, insofar as it consciously stood the Enlightenment notion of historical progress on its head. According to this revisionist view, the emancipatory strivings of bourgeois society led not to "progress in the consciousness of freedom," as Hegel had prophesied.[13] They culminated instead in a paroxysm of retrograde democratic "leveling": in a "negative apocalypse" or "twilight of the idols" that Nietzsche had discerned in his works of the late 1880s.

The German Right's rebirth during the 1920s as an amalgam of national revolutionary and protofascist movements is a story that cannot be told apart from Nietzsche's titanic influence.[14] Following World War I, Nietzsche's negative transmogrification of "progress" was reborn as the ideological cornerstone of the conservative revolutionary worldview: a standpoint cultivated by Oswald Spengler, Ernst Jünger, and Carl Schmitt. Heidegger venerated these thinkers as fraternal spirits. On the basis of his "confrontation" with their work, Heidegger fully internalized the post–World War I ethos of *Wille* and *Macht*, whose trademark was an "unyielding commitment to *masculinity, heroism, hardness, danger, courage, and daring*."[15]

Heretofore, Heidegger's *Denkweg* has been interpreted as the product of a conversation among like-minded "Great Thinkers."[16] However, the standard view changes dramatically once one takes into account the impact that the conservative revolutionary intellectuals had on his philosophical formation.

A closer examination of Heidegger's existential idiolect suggests that his attraction to the lexicon of "complete and total devastation" was a habitude that predated his conversion to Nazism. For example, in *Being and Time*, Heidegger urged not a "course correction" of Western metaphysics but a "destruction of the history of ontology."[17] Similarly, in *Kant and the Problem of Metaphysics* (1929), Heidegger demanded "the destruction [*Zerstörung*] of the founding principles of Western metaphysics: 'spirit,' 'logos,' and 'reason.' "[18] Finally, lecturing on "the essence of human freedom" in 1930, Heidegger tellingly re-defined "philosophical debate [qua] *interpretation as destruction*."[19]

Throughout the various phases of Heidegger's thought, it displayed a predi-lection for the amalgam of "barbarism and civilization" that distinguished fas-cist discourse.[20] A proverb dear to "spiritual fascists"—it is cited by Nietzsche and Spengler—held that "God vomits out the lukewarm." If bourgeois civiliza-tion is neither hot nor cold, if it is simultaneously "what it is and what it is not," then salvation from liberal indeterminacy can only be obtained by embracing "destruction." From this perspective, death and devastation are infinitely pref-erable to the "entropy of feeling."[21]

The *Frontgeist* and Discourse of "Military Nationalism"

With the publication of Heidegger's correspondence with his brother Fritz, in 2016, his enthusiasm for a wide array of protofascist, radical conservative topoi has become a matter of public record. In a letter of October 1932, for ex-ample, Heidegger disclosed that he subscribed to *Die Tat* (The Deed), which, during the twilight of the Weimar Republic, had metamorphosed into the flag-ship organ of the Young Conservative movement.[22] In 1929, *Die Tat*, under the editorial stewardship of Hans Zehrer (1899–1966), underwent a significant radicalization—a pronounced shift to the right. During the ensuing four years, its circulation escalated to an astonishing thirty thousand per issue. Initially, the *Tatkreisler* had scorned the NSDAP as insufficiently elitist: too plebeian and excessively committed to the strategies of "mass politics." Be that as it may, in 1933, Zehrer et al. celebrated the Nazi seizure of power for having finished off the liberal "System": hence, for having effectuated a much-needed "Revolution von Rechts." As Zehrer exulted in April 1933, " 'Liberal man' has ceased to ex-ist; he no longer has a future. . . . With the [National Socialist] Revolution . . . the deep will of the *Volk* has been brought to fulfillment."[23]

Another right-wing scribe whom Heidegger admired was Werner Beumel-burg (1899–1963), a representative of the *Frontgeneration* who specialized in a genre of combat literature known as "military nationalism" (*soldatischer Na-*

tionalismus).[24] Military nationalism glorified the ethos of male camaraderie that, according to legend, characterized the *Fronterlebnis*—a *mentalité* that contrasted sharply with the boredom and convention of civilian life. Narratives of military nationalism exalted the *Kriegerfahrung* as a "primal scene" of German heroism: a proving ground for the virtues of manliness and virility, hence as a wellspring of *Männerphantasien*.[25]

Following the armistice, fidelity to the "Ideas of 1914" became a litmus test of German patriotism. Pacifists, internationalists, and those who criticized the war in any way were dismissed as traitors. As Beumelburg's biographer Florian Brückner aptly notes, "During the Weimar Republic, the spread of such authoritarian, proto-fascist conceptions of domination and social hierarchy . . . contributed to the destruction of parliamentary democracy in Germany."[26]

Not only did the exponents of military nationalism seek to mask the war's horrors and traumas. They posited that the *Kriegerlebnis* had been a crucible of Germany's spiritual and political rebirth. As one writer put it, *"We needed to lose the war in order to gain our Nation."*[27] Among radical nationalists, the "front experience" became the cornerstone of an aggressive, revanchist worldview, a standpoint that fused a "hunger for experience" with an irrational glorification of *Herrschaft* and *Dienst*, "authority" and "service." Thereby, the *Fronterlebnis* developed into the prototype of a renascent German state: a highly regimented, combat-ready *Volksgemeinschaft*.

In a major address on "the German university" (1934), Heidegger celebrated the *Kriegerlebnis* and the *Frontgeist*—the war experience and the spirit of the front—as crucial waystations on Germany's path toward National Socialism, hence as transformative and regenerative "Events" in history of the German *Volk*:

> The genuine preparation for the National Socialist Revolution began in earnest . . . during and by means of the World War. At the Front, there occurred an entirely new experience: an entirely new idea of *Gemeinschaft* took shape. This new spirit from the Front bore within itself *a strong will*: a will that, after the war, became effective as the defining power of the *Dasein* of the *Volk*. . . . For *every Volk*, the World War is the great test that determines whether or not it is capable of inwardly transforming this Event *spiritually* and *historically*. . . .
>
> The awakening of the *Frontgeist* during the war and its reaffirmation after the war is nothing other than the creative transformation of this Event into a formative power of future *Dasein*. . . . The *Frontgeist* is the knowing will to a new

> *Gemeinschaft*. . . . This *Gemeinschaft* is characterized by *camaraderie*: a mutual belonging in which every person in every situation unconditionally vouches for everyone else.[28]

During the Weimar years, Beumelburg became one of Germany's best-selling writers. The sales of his novels and popular histories often rivaled those of better-known authors like Jünger.

The Beumelburg text that Heidegger, in his correspondence with Fritz, singled out for special praise was *Deutschland in Ketten: Von Versailles bis zum Youngplan* (Germany in Chains: From Versailles to the Young Plan; 1931). As Heidegger avowed in a 1932 letter, "One needs only to view this 'history' of Germany clear-sightedly in order to understand what is at stake today."[29]

Deutschland in Ketten was a long-winded, histrionic diatribe that lamented Germany's mistreatment at the hands of the Triple Entente, from the Versailles Treaty (1919) to the Young Plan for the restructuring of Germany's war debt (1929–30). Beumelburg maintained that the Western powers' postwar diplomacy was essentially a continuation of war by other means. By imposing a republican political system on a defenseless Germany, France and England sought to annihilate Germany's cultural distinctiveness, as defined by Prussian militarism and the "National Idea."

Beumelburg denounced internationalism and pacifism, claiming that, by disqualifying the *Volksbegriff*, they lacked an awareness of the "highest deed." He lionized *Frontsoldaten* camaraderie while downplaying the war's sanguinary and destructive aspects. Beumelburg excoriated the treason of the "November criminals"—Social Democrats, Jews, and internationalists—whose actions putatively benefited Western interests rather than Germany's.

Among the long list of postwar humiliations that Germany was forced to endure, Beumelburg reserved a place of honor for the French military occupation of the Ruhr district (1923): an episode that Beumelburg denounced as Germany's "Black Humiliation," since French leaders had the gall to include Senegalese and Moroccan legions among the occupying troops. As Beumelburg inveighed, "And then the Blacks arrived some 30,000 strong: Moroccans, Senegalese, and Indochinese [*sic*]. The white robes of the *Spahis* [lightly armed Algerian troops] fluttered across the Rhine bridges. The Negroes' flat noses unnerved even the local cattle. Henceforth, it was open season on German women and girls, as the quivering population broke down. The world reacted:

newspaper stories were published, non-partisan professors arrived to document the crimes, committees formed to denounce Germany's 'Black Humiliation.' But the Western governments remained completely silent, and France felt not in the least compelled to withdraw a single Negro soldier from the Rhineland."[30]

Among the national revolutionary literati whom Heidegger esteemed was the novelist Hans Grimm, author of the runaway best-seller *Volk ohne Raum* (1926). (By the end of the 1930s, Grimm's "settler colonialism" bildungsroman had sold five hundred thousand copies.) As Heidegger observed to Fritz in a March 1932 letter, "Are you familiar with Hans Grimm's *Volk ohne Raum*? Whoever is still in the dark learns from this book the meaning of *Heimat* as well as the fate of our *Volk*."[31]

Volk ohne Raum furnished an urgent, prolix (over twelve hundred pages) endorsement of the imperatives of German geopolitical expansion. In "Overpopulation and the Colonial Problem" (1922), Grimm explicated the premise of *Volk ohne Raum* as follows: "In Germany today, every third man is one too many! . . . Thus, for the German the problem of *the third man*—and that means for the German moral problem, and it means for the German social problem—there is only one solution: *the procurement of space [Raum]*."[32]

Teeming with bluster, *Volk ohne Raum* was a blunt political allegory. The novel's protagonist, Cornelius Friebott, was a German everyman. The dislocations of *Zivilisation* had cruelly expulsed Friebott from the agrarian tranquility of his native Saxony and exposed him to the hardships and injustices of modern industrialism. Ultimately, the claustrophobia of Friebott's German *Heimat* compelled him to seek his fortunes in colonial southern Africa. *Volk ohne Raum* became the paradigmatic novel of German "settler colonialism" (*Siedlungskolonialismus*).

Volk ohne Raum was at its core a novel of Germany's betrayal by a long list of enemies, near and far. The domestic enemies consisted predominantly of socialists, communists, internationalists, and, of course, Jews. Jewish characters were portrayed in the novel as leftists, powerful financiers, and cutthroat diamond merchants. Jews were mentioned in *Volk ohne Raum* on thirty-two occasions. In twenty-two of those instances, the characterizations were unflattering or negative.[33]

Grimm's title provided Nazi foreign-policy elites with a valuable rallying cry. Unsurprisingly, *Volk ohne Raum* rapidly acquired a place of honor in National Socialist leadership circles.

Redemption through "Active Nihilism"

A passage from *Beyond Good and Evil* (1886) sheds valuable light on the rationale underlying Heidegger's embrace of the Nietzschean "will to destruction" paradigm. In it, Nietzsche clarified how one might reinterpret the *Götzendämmerung* (twilight of the idols) unleashed by modern democracy as a blessing in disguise. According to Nietzsche, the dialectic of Western civilization, when correctly understood, harbored the capacity to metamorphose into its opposite:

> The same new conditions under which . . . a levelling and mediocratization of man will take place—a useful, industrious, serviceable, and gregarious herd animal—are in the highest degree suitable to give rise to exceptional men of the most dangerous and attractive qualities. Although . . . the democratization of Europe will tend to the production of a "type" prepared for slavery in the most subtle sense, in individual and exceptional cases, *the strong man will necessarily become stronger and richer than ever before.* . . . Consequently, the democratization of Europe is at the same time an involuntary arrangement for the cultivation of tyrants—taking the word in every sense, including the most spiritual.[34]

Nietzsche's observations concerning the felicitous potential for "reversal" contained in the "dialectic of enlightenment" sheds important light on Heidegger's endorsement of a negative eschatology or *politique du pire*: the "accelerationist" view that embracing catastrophe is a precondition for cultural renewal or the realization of "another Beginning." As Klaus Vondung has shown in *The Apocalypse in Germany*, the imagery of negative apocalypse was a defining feature of the conservative revolutionary worldview. Its proponents exalted the idiolect of catastrophe as an effective mechanism of counteracting the bourgeois narrative of "progress."[35] In *Ecce Homo*, Nietzsche anticipated a future dominated by "upheavals, convulsions of earthquakes, a moving of mountains and valleys, the like of which has never been dreamed of. . . . All power structures of the old society will have been exploded. . . . There will be wars the like of which have never yet been seen on earth."[36] In keeping with the ethos of "active nihilism," Nietzsche regarded these cataclysms and disasters as necessary purgatives: *cleansing mechanisms* required to clear a path for the advent of the *Übermensch*.

Heidegger enthusiastically endorsed Nietzsche's visions of catastrophe. Among Nietzsche's conservative revolutionary heirs—exponents of *Kulturpessimismus* such as Oswald Spengler and Arthur Moeller van den Bruck—his narrative of European "decline" became an essential pillar of what Fritz Stern denominated the "politics of cultural despair."[37] The imagery of negative apocalypse reinforced Heidegger's "inverted Hegelianism": his view of modernity as heightened catastrophe as opposed to Hegel's "progress in the consciousness of freedom."

Heidegger's hyperbolic *Zeitdiagnose* accentuated the eschatological tendencies of his doctrine of *Seinsgeschichte*. His understanding of the "destiny of the West" as a history of "decline"—a "Fall" from pristine "Origins," or the Greek *Anfang*—was ontologically tied to a metapolitical vision of the German *Volk* as "redeemer." Consequently, Heidegger characterized *Seinsgeschichte* as a process of *"decline, darkening, and devastation*: a movement away from the ontological rootedness of the pre-Socratic *archē*." The "Fall" from "Origins," which resulted in the perdition of *Seinsverlassenheit* (abandonment by Being), could only be rectified by the redemptive powers of the German *Volk*: by appealing to "verborgene Deutschheit," or "hidden Germanness."[38] Heidegger maintained that "only the Germans, the *Volk* of thinkers and poets, had the power to retrieve the force of the first Greek beginning and prepare the path for the arrival of another Beginning."[39]

A similar Nietzschean leitmotif, emphasizing the benefits of cataclysm and upheaval, underlay Heidegger's enthusiasm in the *Black Notebooks* for the Spenglerian trope of *Untergang* (downfall).[40] "*Untergang*," declared Heidegger, "is not something that should be *feared*." Instead, insofar as it anticipated "the transition to another Beginning," it should be *welcomed* as "the essential precondition for historical greatness." "Man's truth for Being [*Seyn*]," declaimed Heidegger, "first manifests itself in *Untergang*."[41]

Thus, in fidelity to Nietzsche, Heidegger endorsed the idea of a "purification of Being" (*Reinigung des Sein*s), notwithstanding the fact that, as Heidegger acknowledged, this eventuality was destined to culminate in "*the self-obliteration of the earth and the disappearance of contemporary humanity*," hence in the wholesale annihilation of life as we know it. Heidegger was quick to add that this anticipated catastrophe should neither be "feared" nor construed as a "misfortune" (*kein Unglück [ist]*). Instead, he insisted that humanity should *welcome* this act of "self-obliteration," since it portended the "purification of Being from the thoroughgoing distortions resulting from the predominance of 'beings.' "[42] As *Black Notebooks* editor Peter Trawny has noted, Heidegger's glorification of the "purification of Being" paralleled National Socialism's obsession with racial purity, thereby revealing the extent to which his *Denken* had become entangled in the "cleansing fantasies" of Nazi race doctrine.[43]

Heidegger fused Nietzsche's vision of imminent apocalypse with the dystopian perspective of contemporary *Zivilisationskritiker* such as Spengler and Jünger. In the *Black Notebooks*, Heidegger reaffirmed Spengler's "diagnosis of the times," declaring at one point, "We cannot find the most trifling reason or occasion to oppose Spengler's findings."[44] Heidegger's admiration for Jünger's allegory of political totalitarianism, *Der Arbeiter* (1932), has been copiously documented. As Heidegger acknowledged in 1945, by the early 1930s, Jünger's glorification of a "totally mobilized" *Arbeiter-Soldatengesellschaft* had become the template or prism through which he interpreted contemporary politics.[45]

In the discourse of central European *Kulturkritik*, the specter of "decline" has consistently played a pivotal ideological role. However, as a diagnostic tool or concept, it had little empirical or objective value. As Michel Winock has shown in "The Eternal Refrain of 'Decadence,' " the principal elements of the worldview in question are existential revulsion of the historical present, nostalgia for a Golden Age, anti-individualism, a longing for authority and a new elite, and fear of genetic degeneration.[46]

Heidegger's appropriation of the conservative revolutionary standpoint not only influenced his "political formation," narrowly construed but also significantly impacted the existential ontology of *Being and Time*. The "conservative revolutionary critique of modern technology, rootless capitalism, and political liberalism" *suffused* Heidegger's critique of "average, everyday Being-in-the-world" in Division I.[47] As Jürgen Habermas concluded in a retrospective evaluation of Heidegger's work that was published on the occasion of Heidegger's seventieth birthday, "Under the label of the everyday mode of being of *das Man*, one finds the current concepts of cultural criticism from Oswald Spengler down to Alfred Weber, reconceived as ontology."[48] Heidegger's dark portrayal of the "fallen" (*verfallen*) nature of "society" (*Gesellschaft*) consistently reprised the central elements of "reactionary modernist" *Zivilisationskritik* that was so widespread among radical conservative intellectuals.[49]

Heidegger was, first and foremost, a philosopher of "temporality" and "historicity." He was equally a philosopher of "Being-in-the-world." He held traditional philosophy's preoccupation with eternal verities in low esteem.

A cursory glance at the existential analytic of *Being and Time*—especially, those sections devoted to a critique of "everyday Being-in-the-world"—indicates that Heidegger regarded his philosophy as a response to the "crisis of modernity": a predicament that Heidegger understood, following Nietzsche, as the triumph of "European nihilism." Hence, it should not come as a surprise that, as a philosopher of *Zeitlichkeit* (temporality), Heidegger was convinced that his thinking had something essential to contribute to resolving the modern crisis.

Heidegger held—no doubt, immodestly—that in order to surmount the "decline of the West," it would be necessary to radically reformulate the *Seinsfrage*. In Heidegger's mind, what set his *Denken* apart from competing philosophies was that it had adequately reformulated this problem. He viewed rival approaches, uncharitably, as little more than symptoms or emanations of "decline." Instead of helping to combat the crisis, they merely aggravated and perpetuated it.

The Quest for a "Teutonic Messiah": Germany's Response to the "Decline of the West"

The publication of Heidegger's correspondence with his brother, Fritz, in 2016, has broadened our understanding of Heidegger's engagement with the *Zeitgeist*. Their epistolary exchange refutes the myth of Heidegger as an otherworldly spirit: a maladroit *Luftmensch* unaccustomed to dealing with the imperfections of the sensible world. Hannah Arendt established the template for this view of Heidegger's "error" in her essay "Heidegger at Eighty" (1969). Rising to Heidegger's defense, she insisted that, in 1933, when the "hour of decision" struck, Heidegger stumbled around in confusion for a few months before quickly regaining his balance.[50]

However, the correspondence with Fritz (1895–1980)—which Heidegger's literary executors sought to withhold from public view for as long as possible; only a chance miscue at the German Literary Archive at Marbach finally forced their hand—tells a very different story.[51] Although Heidegger did not officially join the NSDAP until May 1933, Heidegger's letters reveal that his "spiritual enlistment" for National Socialism began much earlier. The letters also expose Heidegger's conviction that a cabal of powerful Jews was manipulating German politics from behind the scenes: a situation that was ultimately rectified by the Nazi seizure of power.

Accordingly, Heidegger regarded the government of Catholic Center Party Chancellor Franz von Papen, which lasted from June to December 1932, as a tool of Jewish bankers and financiers, thereby reprising a central tenet of anti-Semitic doctrine. As he wrote to Fritz in October 1932, "It was already clear at the beginning of August that the Jews were [once again] on the upswing, having gradually overcome the state of panic to which they had succumbed. That the Jews were successful in orchestrating the von Papen ministry shows how difficult it will be to counteract 'big capital' [*Grosskapital*] and everything related to it [*dergleichen Gross-*] in the future."[52]

The correspondence with Fritz also reveals the extent to which Heidegger was mesmerized by Hitler's charisma. According to the University of Siegen philosopher Marion Heinz, Heidegger esteemed Hitler as a Teutonic Messiah, "as the person who was uniquely capable of redeeming the West."[53]

Thus, in a letter of December 1931, Heidegger urged Fritz to "engage with the Hitler-book"—that is, *Mein Kampf*—which he had sent to Fritz as a Christmas gift. Ultimately, the letter devolved into a fulsome paean to the Führer's unmatched leadership capabilities:

> No one who is insightful will dispute the fact that, whereas often the rest of us remain lost in the dark, this is a man who is possessed of a sure and remarkable political instinct. In the years to come, many other forces will fuse with the National Socialist movement. It is no longer a question of petty party politics. *Instead, what is at stake is the redemption or destruction* [*Rettung oder Untergang*] *of Europe and Western Culture.* Whoever fails to grasp this fact today will succumb to the gathering chaos. Reflection on such matters does not stand in opposition to the peace of the Christmas season. Instead, it leads us directly to *the essence and mission of the Germans*—that is, to the "origin" of this wonderful celebration.[54]

In retrospect, Heidegger's attempt to reconcile the political promise of National Socialism with "the peace of the Christmas season" seems especially macabre. It presaged the distinctive amalgam of "barbarism and civilization" that, in so many respects, defined the essence of Nazi rule.[55]

For the most part, Fritz's contributions to the epistolary exchange were irregular and deferential. He seemed content to act as the sounding board for his older brother's ideas. At one point, however, when the topic of Hitler's charisma resurfaced, he conveyed the following impressions: "I'm not sure whether or not it's an illusion; but, Hitler's bearing and countenance, as conveyed by contemporary photographs, remind me of you. This comparison alone leads me to conclude that Hitler must be an extraordinary fellow [*Kerl*]."[56]

In the months following the Nazi *Machtergreifung*, Germany's path toward totalitarian dictatorship was firmly established. After declaring martial law, Hitler suppressed the left-wing trade unions, incarcerated hundreds of political opponents, and erected the first concentration camps. On 23 March, the Reichstag—which had already been purged of communist deputies—passed the Enabling Act, which, with the blessing of the conservative establishment, allowed Hitler to rule by decree. A few months later, dispensing with all legal formalities and constitutional restraint, Hitler permanently dissolved the Reichstag and banned political parties.

During the initial months of Nazi rule, the regime's treatment of its political opponents was particularly heartless and cruel. As Ian Kershaw notes in his Hitler biography, "The rounding up of communist deputies and functionaries . . . during night raids [was] carried out with massive brutality. Communists were the main targets. But Social Democrats, trade unionists, and left-wing intellectuals . . . were also among those dragged into improvised prisons . . . and savagely beaten, tortured, and in some cases murdered."[57]

The correspondence with Fritz demonstrates that Heidegger was capable of seeing beyond the brutality. He greeted the Nazi seizure of power with unbridled enthusiasm. As Heidegger rhapsodized in a letter of 13 April 1933, "With every passing day, Hitler's greatness as a statesman is becoming increasingly apparent. The world of our *Volk* and our *Reich* is undergoing a transformation. Everyone who has eyes to see, ears to hear, and a heart to act has been gripped with excitement and transposed into an authentic and deep state of enthusiasm. We are encountering once again a *powerful Actuality* [*eine grosse Wirklichkeit*]. However, there is a pressing need *to realize this actuality concretely in the spiritual world of the Reich and in the secret mission of German essence* [*in den geheimen Auftrag deutschen Wesens*]."[58]

In the letter, Heidegger lamented the Third Reich's recently decreed anti-Jewish proscriptions: not because these measures had cruelly put Nazi race thinking into actual practice but because they had resulted in the loss of three research assistants, thereby adding to his already considerable workload.

Heidegger informed Fritz that he would need to postpone an upcoming visit due to a prior political commitment: the inaugural meeting of the Nazi philosopher and pedagogue Ernst Krieck's *Kulturpolitische Arbeitsgemeinschaft deutscher Hochschullehrer* (Cultural-Political Working Group of German University Professors). The portentous appellation of Krieck's "working group" masked its insidious intent. It had been established in March, in the spirit of *Gleichschaltung*, to provide a Nazi alternative to the existing "liberal" Association of German University Professors, which was perceived as an atavism from the Weimar era. In April, Krieck would be named as Germany's first Nazi university rector.

"Deutschtümelei"

The two missives to Fritz, from December 1931 and April 1933, attest to Heidegger's obsessional "Germanocentrism": his conviction that the West's redemption, should it come to pass, could only result from an act of German "self-assertion." Heidegger rejected the Enlightenment conception of "universal history." Instead, following in the footsteps of Johann Gottfried Herder and German historicism, he held that the individual *Volksgeister*, viewed along ethnic and racial lines, were the primary carriers of "historicity." Consequently, for Heidegger, *ethnos*, rather than *demos*, became the driving force of *Seinsgeschichte*.

Heidegger's attendant conviction—reiterated in countless treatises, essays, and lecture courses—that the German *Volk* had been endowed by Providence with a unique, world-historical eschatological "mission" was also a linchpin of National Socialist ideology. This belief played an essential role in Heideggerian *Seinsgeschichte*. Heidegger made retrieval of the "Anfang" contingent on the German *Volk*'s awareness concerning its salvific, world-historical task. Otherwise, the long night of *Seinsvergessenheit* would continue to hold sway, or "perdure."

Thereby, Heideggerian *Geschichtlichkeit* furnished an ontological-historical warrant for Germany's providential self-understanding qua *Herrenrasse*. In the *Black Notebooks*, Heidegger could not have been any clearer or more unequivocal on this point. As he affirmed, *"The anticipatory and essential moment of decision [Entscheidung] concerning the essence of history is reserved to the Germans."*[59]

The *Volksbegriff* anchored a worldview that was pan-German, anti-Semitic, and millenarian. As such, it expressed a hypertrophic, delusional consciousness of German superiority. By the late 1920s, at the very latest, it had become the exclusive prerogative of the radical Right.

Proponents of the *Volksbegriff* contrived "political visions that were as divorced from reality as their creators were from their society."[60] Hence, throughout the concept's various and sundry semantic shifts, it remained, at base, a pseudoscientific, ideological construct: an ad hoc mélange of often irreconcilable physiological and spiritual elements. This diverse ideational admixture is important to keep in mind, since it reminds us that Nazi "race thinking" was never an exclusively "biological" question.

In light of such evidence, Heidegger's avowal, in the 13 April 1933 letter to Fritz, that National Socialist revolution augured a qualitative transformation of the "spiritual world of the Reich," hence, a realization of the "secret mission of German essence," assumes new import and significance. It confirms that "Heidegger developed a form of *spiritual nationalism* that . . . elevated the *Volk* to a *metaphysical entity*."[61] Heidegger's reflections on the "spiritual world of the Reich" and the "secret mission of German essence" were entirely consistent with the "spiritual" and "mystical" understanding of German "destiny" that was advanced by the movement's ideological Führer such as Hitler, Himmler, and Rosenberg. As George Mosse remarks in *The Crisis of the German Ideology*,

> While it is true that the anti-Semitism of the Nazis had a practical intent—the elimination of the Jews as an economic and political force—it also rested its case on purely *spiritual, ideological, and cultural grounds*. The anti-Jewish dynamic . . . made great headway through various spiritualist beliefs, theosophical religions which had a *völkisch* tradition. . . . Heinrich Himmler believed in *karma* and was convinced that he was the reincarnation of Henry the Fowler. . . . Hitler . . . [believed] that contact with the life force, springing from nature, is the only valid introduction to the cosmos. . . . No wonder that he told [Hermann] Rauschning that knowledge must once again take on the characteristics of a "secret science." . . . The theosophical impetus . . . [culminated] in the adoption of *a purely Germanic faith*.[62]

Those who have claimed that Heidegger's *Denken* was constitutionally opposed to Nazi race doctrine insofar as it steadfastly opposed "biologism" are tilting at windmills. As Susanne Lettow observes in "Heideggers Politik des Rassenbegriffs," "Heidegger's statements distancing himself from the [biological conception of race] do not represent a 'critical distancing from National Socialism.' Instead, *they are interventions on the terrain of National Socialist race discourse itself.* They are directed against a specific variant of the *Rassenbegriff*, namely, a biological-genealogical conception that focuses on heredity and the physical constitution of human and national types."[63]

Nazi race thinking shunned the evidentiary straitjacket of "bourgeois" natural science. Instead, it was, first and foremost, the archetypal expression of modern "political myth." As political myths, the *Rassengedanke* and the

Volksbegriff fused to the point where, ultimately, they became indistinguishable. As Kurt Sontheimer remarks in *Antidemocratic Thought in the Weimar Republic*, in the long run, " '*Volk*-ideology' and 'race-theory' *merged.* The myth of
the *Volk* transformed itself into the myths of *blood* and *race.* Even those who
disdained the biological naturalism of the *Volksbegriff* upheld the power and
sanctity [*Macht und Heiligkeit*] of *blood* and the value of *race.* A *Volk* remains
great and powerful if it maintained the purity of its blood and subsisted as a
community-of-blood [*Blutgemeinschaft*]."[64]

The 1928 edition of the *Große Brockhaus Lexikon* sheds useful light on the
ideological transformation that the *Volksbegriff* underwent during the interwar
years. It defined "Volk" appositely as the "Germanization [*Verdeutschung*] of
the word 'national,' *in accordance with a racially defined, profoundly anti-
Semitic nationalism.*"[65]

Heidegger's profligate employment of the *Volksbegriff* was entirely consonant with the substance and gist of the *Große Brockhaus* definition. On these
grounds, it is safe to conclude that Heideggerian *Seinsgeschichte*, which was
predicated on the ideology of German "exceptionalism," coalesced with the essential tenets of Nazi race doctrine.[66] Heidegger never abandoned his conviction that, as he put it during the mid-1930s, the German *Volk* possessed
privileged access to "*the primordial realm of the powers of Being.*"[67]

On these grounds, Heidegger's doctrine of the history of Being accorded
Deutschtum a redemptory role that was denied to lesser *Völker*—peoples who
were ontologically benighted or less advanced. Heidegger explored the nature
of Germany's "ontological singularity" in detail in a 1935 lecture course: "Situated in the middle, our *Volk* . . . is the most endangered. Despite this, it is *the
most metaphysical of Völker.* . . . As a historical *Volk*, our *Volk* must move itself,
and thereby the history of the West . . . into *the primordial realm of the powers
of Being.* If the great *Entscheidung* [decision] regarding Europe is not to bring
annihilation, that *Entscheidung* must be made in terms of *new spiritual energies unfolding historically from out of the middle.*"[68]

Heidegger's allusion to "new spiritual energies unfolding historically from
out of the middle" was intended as an encomium to National Socialism's status
as an *ontological-historical watershed:* a turning point in the history of Being.
In the *Rektoratsrede*, Heidegger's endorsement of the "Glory and Greatness of
the National Awakening" was predicated on his understanding of National Socialism as an ontological caesura: an *Ereignis* that presaged the overcoming of

Western "decline" (*Untergang*). Heidegger's attribution of an eschatological role to the Germans—whom he lionized as "the most metaphysical of Völker"—exposes the indelible flaw of his putative "overcoming of metaphysics" (*Überwindung der Metaphysik*): his demarche was inherently beholden to the ideology of German exceptionalism; that ideology, in turn, was predicated on an unshakable belief in German racial superiority.[69]

"To Lead the Leader"

Heidegger's fascination with Hitler as a neopagan *roi thaumaturge* soon found its way into his philosophy. This claim is amply supported by Heidegger's enthusiasm for the *Führerprinzip*, allusions to which suffused his lecture courses and seminars. In his lectures on Hölderlin, Heidegger exalted "Führersein" as the noblest of "fates." "The true and only Führer," declaimed Heidegger, "anticipates in his Being the realm of the Demigods."[70] In the *Black Notebooks*, Heidegger credited Hitler and the German Revolution with having catalyzed a much-needed regeneration of his *Denken*. "It is a great stroke of fortune," enthused Heidegger, that "the Führer has awakened a new reality: a reality that has *galvanized* my *Denken* and redirected it along the right path. A glorious and electrifying popular [*volklicher*] Will has disrupted the contemporary world-darkening. . . . An upsurge of Belief courses throughout our nation."[71]

Delusional though it may seem, Heidegger regarded himself as National Socialism's *philosophical* Führer: as the thinker who, by virtue of his privileged insight into the history of Being, could impart to Nazism the philosophical direction it needed in order to realize its ultimate metaphysical potential. Thereby, Heidegger sought—to cite Otto Pöggeler's apt characterization—"to lead the leader": to play philosopher king to the twentieth-century German *tyrannis*, Adolf Hitler.[72]

For these reasons, Heidegger felt compelled to recalibrate his doctrine of *Seinsgeschichte* in order to take into account the historic "total transformation German Dasein" heralded by the Nazi *Machtergreifung*.[73] Henceforth, the new imperative governing Heidegger's thought mandated reconciling fundamental ontology with—as Heidegger put it in his April 1933 letter to Fritz—the "*secret mission of German essence*."[74]

Heidegger conceived this "secret mission" as the reenactment, on a higher ontological plane, of the "Greek Beginning." Hence, in the *Rektoratsrede*, brimming with optimism concerning the "Glory and Greatness" of Germany's political future, Heidegger declared, "The Beginning *exists* still. It does not lie behind us, as something long past, *but stands before us*."[75] The "National Awakening" of 1933 reinforced Heidegger's view that the Germans possessed a unique, salvific historical mission: they alone, as a *Volk*, were capable of redeeming the ontological promise of the Greek Beginning. Thus, Heidegger venerated the National Socialist seizure of power as a watershed event, or *Ereignis*, in the destiny of "Western-Germanic historical Dasein."[76]

As we have seen, in *An Introduction to Metaphysics*, Heidegger asserted that the Germans, owing to their *Mittellage*—their geopolitical positioning between East and West—as well as their "existential" affinities with the ancient Greeks, possessed privileged access to "the primordial powers of Being."[77] In this way, Heideggerian *Seinsgeschichte* doubled as a justification or writ for Nazi Germany's imperial mission or "push to the East."

An important part of that mission meant keeping the "red hordes" of Bolshevism at bay. As Heidegger wrote to Herbert Marcuse in 1948, "I expected from National Socialism the spiritual renewal of life in its entirety . . . and a deliverance of Western Dasein from the dangers of Communism."[78] Heidegger clarified the geopolitical implications of the *Seinsfrage*, as informed by Carl Schmitt's *Freund-Feind* distinction, in a 1934–35 lecture course: "The name Heraclitus is not the title of a Greek form of philosophy that has expired long ago. Nor is it a formula for a hackneyed form of cosmopolitan humanity. Instead, it is the name of *an originary power of Western-Germanic historical Dasein in its confrontation with the Asiatic*."[79]

Heideggerian *Seinsgeschichte* was predicated on a twofold logic of racial-ideological exclusion: (1) a rejection of "the West" qua the apogee of technological nihilism and (2) a denial of "the Asiatic" qua *furor orientalis*: the imminent threat—following Nietzsche's lead in *The Birth of Tragedy*—of a rootless and shapeless barbarism. In the context at hand, it is worth recalling that, among advocates of the *Volksbegriff*, Jews were consistently vilified as an "Asiatic" people.[80]

"Redeeming the Fatherland": The *Rassengedanke* as "Myth"

In a March 1932 letter to Fritz, Heidegger reaffirmed his conviction that, given the current political landscape, National Socialism represented Germany's "*only hope of salvation*." He warned that an excessive preoccupation with pragmatic and tactical considerations would merely confuse and distort the larger picture. In Heidegger's view, what was needed, above all, in order to realize this "hope" was a superhuman "act of Will": "It is not a question of whether a *Volksbewegung* [i.e., National Socialism] seeking to awaken the nation has 'standing' among a few anxiety-ridden members of the educated classes. Nor is it a question of those who, by chance, happen to 'represent' the movement, or of those who support it. Instead, it is a question of whether every one of us is willing to support [the movement] by virtue of *an act of Will* [*Willensentscheidung*], insofar as it represents *the fatherland's only hope of salvation* [*die einzige Rettung des Vaterlandes*]."[81]

Heidegger's claim that the "redemption of the fatherland" depended on a forceful and decisive *Willensentscheidung*—an "act of Will"—betrayed his "decisionism": the conviction that he shared with conservative revolutionary thinkers such as Schmitt and Jünger that the ends of action were of secondary importance in relation to the sheer quantum or force of will underlying the act itself. "Decisionism" elevated the "state of exception"—the Schmittian "Ausnahmezustand"—above the prosaic, rule-governed consistency of the bourgeois *Rechtsstaat*.

In retrospect, it is clear that Heidegger's "eschatological" understanding of Germany's historical "mission" got everything backward. The wager he placed on *Deutschtum* as "the most metaphysical *Volk*" culminated not, as he had foreseen, in Europe's *redemption* but, instead, in its wholesale *ruination*: an unprecedented whorl of misery, destruction, and carnage. As Hannah Arendt aptly remarked, "In less than six years, Nazi Germany destroyed the moral fabric of the Western world by committing crimes that no one previously considered to be possible." In *The Origins of Totalitarianism*, Arendt characterized the Nazi *Vernichtungslager* as "absolute evil," insofar as what transpired there *"could no longer be deduced from humanly comprehensible motives."* Thereby, Arendt recognized Auschwitz's status a *Zivilisationsbruch*: a qualitative and irreparable "rupture" in the fabric of civilization.[82]

Heidegger, conversely, pioneered the art of Holocaust denial.[83] To have acknowledged German responsibility for the *Zivilisationsbruch* would have conflicted with his commitment to the ideology of German "exceptionalism," which, as we have seen, was the linchpin of Heidegger's doctrine of *Seinsgeschichte*. Consequently, in *Anmerkungen I–V*, Heidegger characterized the Holocaust as "essentially"—that is, when viewed from the standpoint of the history

of Being—an act of "Jewish self-annihilation." Ultimately, the Jews bore responsibility for their own industrialized mass murder, since, as the leading
"carriers" of modern technology, they had, in the death camps, fittingly died by
their own hand. According to Heidegger, "When the essentially 'Jewish' [*das
wesenhaft 'Jüdische'*] in the metaphysical sense struggles against what is Jewish, the *zenith of self-annihilation has been achieved.* This means that the 'Jewish' has, everywhere, appropriated for itself the mechanisms of domination, so
that even the struggle against what is 'Jewish' devolves into obedience to what
is Jewish."[84] In other words, the National Socialist machinery of annihilation,
by turning the apparatus of modern "technics" against the Jews themselves, had
essentially resorted to Jewish methods. Thus, in Heidegger's eyes, the *Endlösung* was merely another example of what Wilhelm Marr characterized as
Der Sieg des Judenthums über das Germanenthum (The Triumph of Judaism
over Germany; 1879).

By characterizing the Holocaust as an act of "Jewish self-annihilation,"
Heidegger elevated the technique of "Holocaust inversion" to new heights.[85]
Holocaust inversion is a classic example of what the Frankfurt School identi-
fied as "secondary anti-Semitism." As Monika Schwarz-Friesel explains in
"Language as 'Crime Scene' in Germany: Anti-Semitism in the Public Sphere
of Communication," secondary anti-Semitism arises when "historical facts
concerning the extermination of the Jews are distorted or misrepresented, and
German responsibility for the Holocaust is relativized or denied. . . . The strat-
egy of reversing perpetrators and victims is characteristic of post-1945 anti-
Semitism: German shame and guilt are rejected or trivialized and responsibility
[*Täterschaft*] is shifted to the Jews."[86]

By insinuating that European Jews, as "shifty" disseminators of *Machenschaft*, had been responsible for their own extermination, Heidegger's anti-
Judaism achieved two ends at once: it denied to the Jews their status as
"victims," and it absolved the perpetrators—Heidegger's *Volksgenossen*, or fellow Germans—of responsibility for their crimes. From the standpoint of *Vergangenheitsbewältigung* (coming to terms with the past), Heidegger's ruse
diverted critical scrutiny from the pathologies of German historical development and redirected it toward the hypostatizations and pseudoexplanations of
Seinsgeschichte: "technology," "Western metaphysics," "subjectivity," the
"Will-to-Will," "Enframing," and so forth. By shifting the plane to "metaphysics," he diverted attention from Nazism's historical situatedness.

In *Die Geschichte des Seyns* (The History of Being; 1939), Heidegger declared, "It would be worthwhile inquiring into world Jewry's [*Judentums*] predisposition toward planetary criminality."[87] Heidegger's assertion inculpated "world Jewry" as the leading exponent of "Machenschaft": the reduction of the totality of Being to "standing reserve" (*Bestand*). To declare an entire people guilty of "planetary criminality" constitutes, in no uncertain terms, an appeal for collective retribution or punishment. It is also, unequivocally, a *racial indictment*: a blanket condemnation of the Jews as a "race" or "Volk."

In the *Black Notebooks* (*Überlegungen* XII), Heidegger, in remarks that reprised the calumny of a "world Jewish conspiracy," explicated the nature and substance of the Jews' "planetary criminality" by invoking their role as the progenitors of *Machenschaft*: "Contemporary Jewry's temporary increase in power has its basis in the fact that Western metaphysics—above all, in its modern incarnation—offers fertile ground for the dissemination of an empty rationality and calculability, which, in this way, gains a foothold in 'spirit,' *without ever being able to grasp from within the hidden realms of Decision* [*Entscheidung*]."[88]

By declaring that "Jews"—wherever they might be found and in whatever guise they assumed—were constitutionally incapable of fathoming the "hidden realms of Decision," Heidegger reaffirmed their endemic racial inferiority and ontological difference. The Jews' ineradicable, existential shortcomings and debilities stood in stark contrast to the salvific mission that Heidegger consistently attributed to *Deutschtum*. Heidegger's condemnation of the Jews' *Seinsverlassenheit*—their "abandonment by Being"—was merely the corollary or flip side to his abiding conviction that "only the Germans are capable of redeeming the West in its history."[89]

Heidegger's related assertion in the *Black Notebooks* that "world Jewry, . . . wherever it may be found, is '*ungraspable*' [*unfassbar*]" similarly attested to his belief in a Jewish world conspiracy. As a people or race composed of devious cultural interlopers and "Drahtzieher" (string-pullers), Heidegger defined world Jewry as a force that was omnipresent as well as impossible to "pin down."[90] In declarations such as these, Heidegger's anti-Semitism did not differ qualitatively from that of leading Nazi ideologues such as Himmler, Rosenberg, and Hitler.

Danielle Cohen-Levinas has reflected on the systematic role that anti-Semitism played in Heidegger's fundamental ontology as follows: "In

Heidegger's eyes, the Jews represented a formidable threat to the German *Volk*'s realization of its destiny. The German *Volk* found itself stifled in its mission, which was to prepare the terrain for a return of the gods. For Heidegger, to link the Germans to this 'other Beginning' signified a way of preventing the triumph of *Machenschaft*. The hermeneutical violence enacted by Heidegger's philosophy—which culminated in the argument that *the Jews programmed their own destruction*—runs deep. Heidegger reprised the arguments of anti-Semites who affirmed that the Jew is *an essentially destructive being*."[91]

As Christian Tilitzki explains in *Deutsche Universitätsphilosophie in der Weimarer Republik und im Dritten Reich*, "During the 1920s, the assumption that each *Volk* possessed an 'unalterable racial character'—that every *Volk* disposed over an irreducible store of naturally determined behavioral norms and fundamental values—had acquired the status of an indisputable fact."[92] Heidegger's conviction that a *Volk*'s *racial characteristics*, or "Seinsart," explained its innermost epistemological abilities and capacities fits the pattern described by Tilitzki to a tee. A paradigmatic illustration of Tilitzki's point was Heidegger's telling avowal that "only someone who is German [der Deutsche] is capable of poetically articulating Being in an originary way."[93]

Heidegger's paranoia with respect to contemporary Jewry's "planetary" implementation of *Machenschaft* qua "empty rationality and calculability" was much more than a restatement of an amorphous and widespread anti-Semitic "cultural prejudice." In the German *Kulturbereich*, by the late 1930s, anti-Jewish "cultural prejudice" had yielded to the paradigm of "exterminationist anti-Semitism." To wit, on 30 January 1939, Hitler delivered an infamous speech commemorating the sixth anniversary of the Nazi *Machtergreifung* in which he prophesied the "Final Solution" to the "Jewish Question." "I have often been a prophet in my life, and I was mostly laughed at," remarked the Führer. "I want to be a prophet again today: if international Finance Jewry in Europe and beyond should succeed once more in plunging the peoples into a world war, then the result will not be the Bolshevization of the earth and thus the victory of Jewry, but *the annihilation of the Jewish race in Europe*."[94]

Heidegger's "strategy of avoidance" vis-à-vis the depredations and misdeeds of the Nazi past—as illustrated by his treatment of the Holocaust as an act of Jewish "self-annihilation"—exemplified the "pseudo-concreteness" of his fundamental ontology.[95] While claiming to have *transcended* the mystifications and pseudoexplanations of "metaphysics" and "first philosophy," in point of fact,

Heidegger remained inextricably in their thrall. As Theodor Adorno observed in *Against Epistemology*, "However close to experience Heidegger's pronouncements may seem, they simply do not connect with the reality of society. . . . Heidegger's tendency [is] to camouflage irresolvable contradictions, like those between timeless ontology and history, by ontologizing history itself as 'historicity' and turning the contradiction as such into a 'structure of Being.' "[96]

By hewing closely to the ethereal plane of *Seinsgeschichte*, Heidegger avoided having to confront the missteps of German history. His narrative of the history of Being functioned as a *Verdrängungsapparat*: a mechanism of "repression." As Habermas pointed out during the late 1980s, "With the help of an operation that we might call 'abstraction through essentialization,' *Seinsgeschichte* remained disconnected from political and historical events." Heidegger's inveterate refusal to forthrightly confront the *Schuldfrage*—the "question of German guilt"—epitomized his "disconnect[ion] from political and historical events." This "strategy of avoidance" attested to Heidegger's abiding philosophical *mauvaise foi*.[97]

As a citizen, Heidegger failed his fellow Germans not once but *twice*: first, by opting for Nazism in 1933; second, following the war, by employing his "*Technik*-critique" as a metaphysical cudgel with which to disparage the values of democratic self-determination, ignoring the quintessential fact that "under the rubrics of 'self-consciousness,' 'self-determination,' and 'self-realization,' there emerged a normative content of modernity that must not be reduced to blind subjectivity or self-preservation."[98]

Emmanuel Levinas insightfully highlighted the hypocrisy of the later Heidegger's self-understanding as a critic of modern technology: "Although Heidegger inveighed against the reduction of the intellect to *technics*, this did not prevent him from supporting a brutal regime [*un régime de puissance*] more inhuman than the machine age he criticized."[99]

Ultimately, Heidegger was endemically blind to the virtues of what Claude Lefort has termed the "democratic invention": the joys of public liberty, of associative solidarity, of people "acting in concert" for the sake of realizing shared values.[100] No one exposed this deficit in Heidegger's *Denken* more forcefully than Hannah Arendt. As she wrote in *On Revolution*, "The ultimate end of revolution was . . . the constitution of a public space where freedom could appear, the *constitutio libertatis*, . . . the [creation] of elementary republics . . . where everyone could be free." The experience of dictatorship sensitized Arendt to the virtues of participatory politics. Whereas political isolation is proto-totalitarian, the establishment of "public spaces where freedom could appear" meant that "no one may be called free without his experiencing *public freedom*, and that no one could be called either happy or free without participating, and having a share, in public power."[101]

Heidegger also failed profoundly as a thinker. According to Habermas, this failure resulted from his dogmatic elevation of the *Seinsgedanke* to the status of a *fundamentum inconcussum*, an irrefragable Absolute. As Habermas explains, "By rejecting the proto-humanism of the Socratic School—i.e., the so-called Greek Enlightenment—in favor of pre-Socratic philosophy, Heidegger regressed behind cognitive-moral threshold of the 'Axial Age' (800–300 BCE): the break-through of transcendence and the dawn of self-conscious humanity. Thereby, Heidegger committed treason against the caesura that is marked by the prophetic-awakening Word from Mount Sinai, and by the Enlightenment of a Socrates."[102]

The *Black Notebooks* confirm that Heidegger's "*Technik*-critique"—a stand-point that has garnered Heidegger's later thought so much acclaim—was insep-arable from his anti-Semitism. As he avowed circa 1938, "One of the stealthiest forms of Gigantism [*das Riesige*], and perhaps the most ancient, is the fast-paced *cleverness of calculation, huckstering, and intermingling* [*die Zähe Geschicklichkeit des Rechnens und Schiebens und Durcheinandermis-chens*] whereby [world] Jewry's *worldlessness* is established."[103] In light of such claims—and many others like them—it has become increasingly difficult to deny that Heidegger's castigation of modern "technics," in "The Question Concerning Technology" and related texts, doubled as a critique of Jewish "ma-terialism": of the baneful influence that the Jews' dissemination of "empty ra-tionality and calculability" had inflicted on the realm of "Geist," or "spirit."

In the foregoing passage, Heidegger's denunciation of Jewish "worldlessness" —as an outgrowth of Jewish "cleverness, calculation, and huckstering"—served to highlight Judaism's "corrosive" role in what Heidegger characterized as the "uprooting" (*Entwurzelung*) of "Being by beings." Such accusations were, of course, a standard component of the Nazi *Weltanschauung*. That Heidegger en-dorsed these claims during the late 1930s, as the Third Reich reached its political zenith, demonstrates that he made no attempt whatsoever to distance himself from the reigning mind-set of "eliminationist anti-Semitism."

Heidegger repeatedly rebuked "world Jewry" as the executors and benefi-ciaries of "planetary *Machenschaft*." He condemned Jewish "rootlessness" for having unleashed a dynamic of "total deracialization" (*totale Entrassung*): a process that, Heidegger claimed, culminated in the "self-alienation of peoples" (*Selbstverfremdung der Volker*).[104] In *Überlegung* XIV, Heidegger reprised his critique of Jewish "rootlessness," asserting, "The question of world Jewry's role is *not a racial question but a metaphysical one*: a question about what sort of human being can take up *the uprooting of all beings from Being as a 'world-historical' task* [*die Entwurzelung alles Seienden aus dem Sein als 'weltge-schichtliche' Aufgabe*]."[105] With these remarks, Heidegger added specificity and substance to his accusation concerning world Jewry's penchant for "planetary criminality." As Thomas Assheuer, in a judicious assessment of the *Black Notebooks*, concluded appositely, "The hermeneutic trick of acknowledging Heidegger's anti-Semitism only in order to permanently cordon it off from his philosophy proper is no longer convincing. The anti-Jewish enmity of the *Black Notebooks* is no afterthought. Instead, it forms the basis of Heidegger's philosophical diagnostics."[106]

Assheuer's remarks confirm that Heidegger's judgmental myopia was not merely an accidental miscue, a philosophically inconsequential *lapsus*. Instead, it was an ontological misjudgment that went to the very heart of his understanding of the history of Being. Heidegger's abiding commitment to the ideology of German exceptionalism incited heightened paranoia concerning the threat that "world Jewry" posed to the Third Reich's plans for racial self-assertion and continental hegemony.

The *Black Notebooks* confirm that, whatever misgivings Heidegger may have had concerning specific National Socialist policies or practices, until the very end, he upheld his commitment to the movement's "inner truth and greatness." Hence, in 1939, Heidegger reaffirmed his support for what he described as National Socialism's "genuine power and inner necessity"—not as a matter of convenience but *on philosophical grounds*."[107]

An Apologist's Jubilee

To judge by the proliferation of apologetic literature on the *Black Notebooks*, it is clear that many of Heidegger's disciples have gone to great lengths to circumvent Assheuer's verdict concerning anti-Semitism's centrality for Heidegger's *Denken*. It is in this spirit of avoidance that one Heidegger loyalist has claimed that "not one iota of [Heidegger's] history of Being would have to be changed if one removed all references to Jewish matters."[108] Taken at face value, this statement seems to be a classic example of Freudian "wish-fulfillment." (In the *Black Notebooks*, Heidegger treats Freud in passing but only to disqualify him as a "Jew" who, like all Jews, sought to trace everything back to the "instincts.")[109] If only "all references to Jewish matters" in Heidegger's work were excised, then we could blissfully return to the status quo ante, reading and interpreting his philosophy with a clear conscience. (In the just-quoted remarks, the author carefully avoids using the word "anti-Semitism," substituting instead the more anodyne expression "Jewish matters," thereby evading the issue of Heidegger's indebtedness to "race thinking.")

The author's thought experiment is also noteworthy insofar as the scholar in question displays no interest whatsoever in fathoming how such incriminating anti-Semitic claims infiltrated Heidegger's discourse to begin with. He seems similarly unconcerned with the ways that these anti-Semitic dicta intersect with other components of Heidegger's "essential thinking." Yet a closer examination of these themes suggests telling, long-term continuities with respect to Heidegger's anti-Semitic disposition: from the *Zivilisationskritik* of *Being and Time* to the "Germanocentrism" of *Seinsgeschichte*, in which "world Jewry" emerged as a significant obstacle to the goals of German "self-assertion."

Heidegger's assimilation of the *Rassengedanke* (race thinking) was not merely a later adventitious political accretion. It was profoundly "rooted" in tendencies that were extant in his early philosophy. It was implicit in the ontological distinction that he formulated in his 1924 Kassel lectures on "the concept of time" between *bodenlose* and *bodenständige Völker*: "rooted" and "rootless" peoples. Already in *Being and Time*, Heidegger exalted *Bodenständigkeit*—"rootedness-in-soil"—as a criterion of authenticity (*Eigentlichkeit*). As Heidegger asserted during the mid-1920s, "I am convinced that there is no essential work of the spirit that does not have its root in primordial 'Bodenständigkeit.' "[110] An abiding feature of Heidegger's Germanocentrism was his conviction that the Germans, as a *Volk*, possessed a superior capacity for *existential rootedness*: a perspective that meshed seamlessly with the ideology of German singularity.[111]

Heidegger's supporters have deflected accusations of anti-Semitism by pointing out that anti-Semitic utterances are entirely absent from his pre-1933 philosophical texts. However, this assertion is misleading on several counts. As a state employee, or *Beamter*, Heidegger was obliged to observe stringent protocols concerning the admixture of political views in his classroom instruction as well as his scholarly work. Those who violated these strictures risked serious sanctions or reprisals. A good case in point is that of the Nazi philosopher Ernst Krieck. In 1930, Krieck was dismissed from his position at the Academy for Pedagogy in Frankfurt because of his pro-Hitler politicking.[112]

Heidegger was careful to avoid such transgressions in his professional duties. Nor could he afford any such missteps, insofar as, prior to the appearance of *Being and Time* in 1927, he had published very little. Not until 1923 was he finally granted an associate professorship at the University of Marbach.

Conversely, abundant testimony confirms Heidegger's expression of anti-Semitic opinions and views *en privée*. As Toni Cassirer remarks in her account of the storied Davos encounter between Heidegger and her husband, Ernst, "[Heidegger's] tendency toward anti-Semitism was not unknown to us." She and Ernst approached the debate with trepidation, fearing that Heidegger intended to drag the work of Hermann Cohen—the Jewish founder of neo-Kantianism—"into the dust and, if possible, to destroy Ernst."[113]

In Heidegger's defense, his supporters have also insisted that his understanding of "race" had little in common with the customary, narrowly biological approaches to race thinking. They have repeatedly invoked this distinction to support their claim that Heidegger's thought was light-years removed from the essential precepts of Nazi race doctrine. Hence, when all is said and done, Heidegger's Nazism must have been insincere: a faux Nazism and a disingenuous racism.

However, rudimentary familiarity with National Socialist race thinking indicates that the movement's leading ideologues accepted scientific-biological racism only in a highly qualified sense. Hence, their understanding of race was consistently suffused with mythical and spiritual elements. The view of Germans as a *Herrenrasse*, or "master race," was one such mythologem. In fact, among the "master thinkers" of Nazi race doctrine, there was broad agreement about the need to *transcend* the limitations of nineteenth-century "materialism" and "scientism."

Conversely, the idea of reanimating prehistoric *myths* metamorphosed into an ideological obsession. The preoccupation with myth echoed in the title of Rosenberg's programmatic exposition of the National Socialist *Weltanschauung*, *The Myth of the Twentieth Century* (1930). "The longing to give the Nordic race soul [*Rassenseele*] its form as a German church under the sign of the

Volksmythos," claimed Rosenberg, "that, for me, is the greatest task of our century."[114] The "myth" of Rosenberg's title was, of course, *the myth of race*.

In the present context, Rosenberg's portentous subtitle, *An Evaluation of the Psychic and Spiritual Ideological Struggles of Our Age*, is also highly significant, since it highlighted the chasm that separated Nazi race thinking from run-of-the-mill "biologism." Rosenberg insisted that "psychic and spiritual struggles" merited independent consideration; hence, it would be a grave disservice to explain their inner workings as a causal efflux of, as he put it, "cell biology." In fact, none of the leading *Rassentheoretiker*—Ludwig Ferdinand Clauß, Walther Darré, or Hans Günther—conceived "race" in exclusively biological terms. All maintained that "race" entailed an ineffaceable "spiritual" or "mystical" dimension, as suggested by Rosenberg's subtitle.

As a "discourse" or "episteme," the ideology of anti-Semitism proved to be semantically diffuse and remarkably polyvalent. Thus, in portraying the "deformations" of political modernity, pejorative allusions to "capitalism," "commerce," "banking," "finance," "rootlessness," and "cosmopolitanism" consistently functioned as "stand-ins"—Lacanian "points de capiton" (quilting points)—for Jews and their disintegrative cultural influence. As Shulamit Volkov has argued in her pathbreaking study "Anti-Semitism as a Cultural Code," by the early twentieth century, anti-Semitism had become an omnipresent and indispensable component of central European, antimodernist *Kulturkritik*: "The 'German Ideology' that [emerged] in the 1890s [was] a radical anti-modern mentality, rejecting liberalism, capitalism, socialism, in a nostalgic passion for a long-lost world. It implied a series of political views including an opposition to democracy and a call for the reestablishment of a 'national community.' . . . It was associated with extreme nationalism, a colonial and imperial drive, an enthusiasm for war and an advocacy of a pre-industrial moral code. . . . In one way or another, *it was always combined with anti-Semitism*."[115]

Yet another confirmation of anti-Semitism's ideological lability is the fact that it was regularly applied not only to "capitalists," "financiers," and "entrepreneurs" but also to representatives of the *political Left*: Marxists, Social Democrats, "Jewish Bolshevists," and so forth. Nor, of course, were "liberals" exempt from this familiar litany of denunciations and inculpations. Hence, as an ideological template, anti-Semitism ranged across the entire ideological political spectrum, encompassing capitalists, socialists, and liberals. Anti-Semites viewed these political currents as the expressions of a wider conspiracy to "Judaize the world."[116]

The *Zivilisationskritik* paradigm exemplified by Heidegger's critique of everyday Being-in-the-world was inseparable from a strand of anti-Semitic prejudice that disparaged Jews as the leading "carriers" of cultural modernity and capitalism, in particular. Following World War I, the idiolect of *Zivilisationskritik* metamorphosed into a lingua franca among a wide array of "reactionary modernists": Werner Sombart, Arthur Moeller van den Bruck, and Oswald Spengler—"spiritual reactionaries" from whom Heidegger borrowed much and whom he regarded as kindred intellectual spirits.[117]

Heidegger's preoccupation with disproportionate Jewish cultural influence suffused the *Black Notebooks*. As he commented at one point, "To appropriate 'culture' as a means of power, and therewith to promote oneself and claim that one is superior, is essentially a Jewish tactic."[118]

As a discursive template, *Zivilisationskritik* held that *Gemeinschaft* was the natural and authentic mode of human belonging. *Gesellschaft*, conversely, was artificial and inauthentic. Jewish "intellection" was, purportedly, a cultural attribute that thrived under *Gesellschaft*, which, increasingly, became a stand-in for the dislocations of "capitalist modernity." "Modernity," with Jews in the lead, corroded the traditional mores of *Volk* and *Gemeinschaft*: a process that culminated in the "soul-destroying" standardization and massification of life that was the hallmark of "Gesellschaft," which reactionary modernists denigrated as the "graveyard of *Kultur*." Consequently, *Zivilisationskritiker* viewed "modernity" and "Gesellschaft" as "a *downward plunge* in which the real principle of history—namely, *Gemeinschaft* or community—has been pushed aside by the former. At some point in this downward plunge—with the beginning of World War I, for instance—'fate' raised its head and demanded that people demolish *Gesellschaft* in order to realize the proper *Gemeinschaft*."[119]

Sombart's monograph *Jews and Modern Economic Life* (1912) was a watershed in the cultural discourse identifying Jews as conspiratorial "string-pullers" behind the rise of modern capitalism. Sombart denounced Judaism as a belief system peculiar to a rootless and nomadic, "desert people." In Sombart's view, the Jews' nomadic origins accounted for their innate affinities with the "extraterritoriality" of international finance. Sombart alleged that the Jewish covenant with God predisposed Jews toward abstraction, a contractual *mentalité*, and the numerical calculation of sin: qualities that afforded them innumerable cultural advantages with respect to entrepreneurship.[120]

Nearly all of the aforementioned anti-Semitic tropes and prejudices pervaded Heidegger's *Denken* from early on: from his lamentations about the "Jewification of our culture and our universities [*die Verjudung unsrer Kultur u. Universitäten*]" in 1916 to his insistence on "rootedness," or *Bodenständigkeit*, as a sine qua non of philosophical *Eigentlichkeit* (authenticity) during the 1920s to his complaint about the "*Verjudung* of German spiritual life" in 1929 to his indictment of "Jewish nomads" in *On the Essence of Truth* (1933–34).

Paradoxically, one of the reasons for anti-Semitism's success as a "cultural code" was that, as a species of political myth, it bore little relationship to reality. Instead, as a "worldview," its value was primarily *functional*: its effectiveness derived from its ability to reinforce the ideological belief system of its adherents—hence the kernel of truth to the adage, "Anti-Semitism tells us more about anti-Semites than it does about actual Jews." As Jean-Paul Sartre remarked in *Anti-Semite and Jew*, "If the Jew did not exist, the anti-Semite would have to invent him." As David Nirenberg, echoing Sartre, observed appositely in *Anti-Judaism: The Western Tradition*, "[Anti-Semitism] has generated the 'Jewishness' it criticizes in the world."[121]

A parable that circulated widely during the 1920s, based on a hypothetical encounter between a hardened anti-Semite and a more sober representative of the German *Bildungsbürgertum*, helps to illustrate this point. Confronted with an anti-Semite's embrace of the "stab-in-the-back myth," alleging that the Jews had been responsible for Germany's defeat in World War I, his more skeptical countryman countered, "Yes! The Jews and the bicyclists!" Noticeably perplexed, the anti-Semite inquired haltingly, "Why the bicyclists?" To which his interlocutor rejoined, "Why the Jews?"[122]

"Overcoming Metaphysics"

For quite some time, a Heideggerian orthodoxy has prevailed: a received wisdom that, faithful to the Master's self-interpretation, has exalted Heidegger as the thinker who, his failings and limitations notwithstanding, single-handedly "emancipated" philosophy from the stranglehold of "Western metaphysics." One might characterize this demarche as the "Heidegger-as-redeemer" paradigm. It insinuates that Heidegger's thought possesses a unique soteriological value, insofar as it points the way toward a nebulous and ill-defined "other Beginning." Hence, despite Heidegger's regrettable political *lapsus*, he merits our gratitude, insofar as his *Denken* points beyond our current ontological-historical impasse: a "blockage" that Heidegger portrayed as a condition of *Gottesverlassenheit*, or "abandonment by the gods." Heidegger held that the present age was marked by a twofold "abandonment": the "no longer" of the gods that have fled and the "not yet" of the gods to come.

At present, such rationalizations of Heidegger's philosophical and political lapses have congealed into a litany of commonplaces and idées fixes. They have been popularized by a guild of Heidegger loyalists who, it seems, have exchanged their intellectual autonomy for fealty to the Master's portentous prescriptions concerning the inscrutable "sendings of Being" (*Schickungen des Seins*). Heidegger's champions have invested so much "cultural capital" in his legacy that, were they to back down now, the entire gambit would collapse into "Nothingness," or *das Nichts*.

One impassioned advocate of the "Heidegger-as-redeemer" paradigm has lionized his efforts to transcend the "metaphysics of subjectivity" and its attendant dysfunctions (a very long list, as it turns out). The advantage of Heidegger's approach, we are told, is that it offers an invaluable critique of the "violence of representation and manipulation, of possession and use-relations": of an imperious "will-to-knowledge" that is responsible for the dysfunctions of Western modernity. Heidegger's alternative, conversely,

> imagines a "releasement" inherent in a poetic response to the World and to Earth—a letting-be of things as a letting-go of representational consciousness, of the exclusivity of rational, conceptual truth claims. . . . Attendance to things in their own elusive self-unfolding becomes possible outside the reduction to metaphysical-technological measures. *Gelassenheit* [letting-be] involves the resignation of subjectivity . . . as the desire to master and define, and requires . . . a more phenomenologically genuine kind of thinking. One can then ask about technology's essence, how to live with technology and at the same time preserve a critical distance from it. . . . Heidegger's thought poses questions . . . that are of urgency for our own attempts to think philosophically. . . . Are there not truths and meanings, possibilities and experiences, textures and processes of factical life that are ignored, or even destroyed, by the monopoly that technological rationality holds onto claims and exerts over reality and over us? . . . Do we not have a relationship to language that is other than merely instrumental? . . . Does not poetic language, long neglected by philosophical thinking, hold a source for that thinking, a source for a *possible liberation*?[123]

Such effusive praise for Heidegger's thought as a panacea for the afflictions of Western modernity conceals a host of problematic assumptions and unexamined presuppositions. For one, it has uncritically internalized Heidegger's prejudices concerning the history of philosophy as a "history of error": as an unending tale of "representational violence," "manipulation," and "(dis)possession"—in sum, a narrative of Spenglerian *Untergang* that attests to the perils of "obliviousness to Being" (*Seinsvergessenheit*). Equating the history of metaphysics with "errancy" (*Irrnis*), Heidegger concluded during the early 1930s that "*it* [*was*] *time to put an end to philosophizing*" (*sic*), insofar as it had failed to measure up to the "metapolitical" challenges of the times. In his view, the time had come to *jettison* first philosophy in favor of the "metapolitics of the historical *Volk*."[124]

In opposition to the history of philosophy as a continuum of metaphysical violence, Heidegger lauded *Seinsgeschichte* as a form of secular eschatology, assuring his devotées that the "other Beginning" contained the seeds of redemption. However, since the "saving power" (*das Rettende*) that Heidegger invoked derived from a sphere that was beyond "reason" and "representation"—as Heidegger once remarked, "Making itself intelligible is suicide for philosophy"[125] —interpreters were often obliged to accept his assurances at face value. By arrogantly disqualifying competing academic disciplines, Heidegger sought to immunize himself against discordant facts and potential criticism—hence his haughty avowal in *Anmerkungen I–V* (GA 97) that "the historian is the personified negation of history."[126]

Heidegger's assertion, in *An Introduction to Metaphysics*, that "mysteriousness [*Geheimnischarakter*] constitutes the authenticity and greatness of historical knowledge" suggests that he regarded occult knowing as a catalyst and prerequisite for the transition to the "other Beginning." "*Truth*," declared Heidegger, "*is not for everyone, but only for the strong*."[127] In the *Black Notebooks*, Heidegger's appeal to the Messianic promise of "hidden Germanness" (*verborgene Deutschheit*) confirms that, in his mind, the "other Beginning" was inextricably entwined with the ideology of German exceptionalism.[128]

In *Heidegger's Ways*, Hans-Georg Gadamer rightly called into question the obscurantist turn that Heidegger's later ontological-historical thinking had taken. Gadamer feared that *Seinsgeschick*, or the "destining of Being," had succumbed to the temptations of a neopagan "mythology or poeticizing gnosis." Thereby, it had devolved into what Gadamer disparagingly characterized as a "Seinsmystik," or "Being-mysticism."[129] In "The Great Influence," Habermas, invoking the later Heidegger's notion of the "Fourfold"—gods and mortals, heaven and earth—raised a set of parallel objections: "Along with the 'subjec-tivistic' ossification of more recent thought, [Heidegger] also abandoned its normativity. The evocation of Myth is legitimated as a form of spiritual exer-cise. . . . As an antidote to crisis and a notion to counter metaphysics, Heidegger invoked not *Kritik* but *Mythos*."[130]

Numerous commentators have expressed similar reservations with respect to the later Heidegger's avowed preference for "poeticizing gnosis" vis-à-vis Hegel's "labor of the concept" (*Anstrengung des Begriffs*). In contrast with Heidegger, Hegel insisted that "concepts alone can produce the universality of knowing, which is not the common indeterminateness and paltriness of plain common sense, but rather that of culturally mature and accomplished cogni-tion."[131] Hegel's defense of the "concept," in contrast with Heidegger's "devo-tional submissiveness to Being," signified a declaration of intellectual freedom.[132] In *Negative Dialectics*, Adorno, in solidarity with Hegel, added, "it is never enough just to make a critical case; the task of philosophy—what dis-tinguishes philosophy from mere cultural chatter—is to analyze rigorously what has been criticized; to set the object of criticism in motion in order to com-prehend it in its necessity."[133]

Following Kant, Hegel recognized the "autonomy of reason" as *Geist*'s rai-son d'être. Spirit's freedom resided in its unremitting, principled resistance to the regressive temptations of "origins" and "primordiality." Conversely, the re-gressive blandishments of *Ursprünge* and *Anfänge* were expressly revived in Heidegger's glorification of "originary thinking" (*anfängliches Denken*). Heidegger's passive fealty to the "sendings of Being" was tantamount to an act of *spiritual self-renunciation* and hence a philosophical standpoint incompati-ble with the requirements of *Mündigkeit*, which, in "What Is Enlightenment?," Kant sagaciously defined as "humanity's emergence from a state of self-incurred tutelage."[134]

Heidegger's critics have rightly feared that his preoccupation with "Geheim-nischarakter" of knowledge caused him to abandon philosophy's commitment to rigor, coherence, and argument: criteria that the later Heidegger expressly derided.[135] In *Self-Consciousness and Self-Determination*, Ernst Tugendhat rec-ognized that "Heidegger's need to disengage himself from the [philosophical] tradition was so strong that instead of casting these familiar phenomena [cate-gories pertaining to volition and action] in a new light, he chose to elucidate the subject matter by means of a series of terms that were idiosyncratically adopted and inadequately explained. This procedure of explication through sheer accumulation of words occurs often in *Being and Time*. It is connected to what I have called the evocative method."[136]

Following Tugendhat, Winfried Franzen has called into question the "binding" character of Heidegger's originary thinking, "especially, insofar as his philosophy claims to yield immediate access to the truth of Being, while, nevertheless, renouncing minimal standards of communicability and objectivity." Ultimately, concludes Franzen, Heidegger's "purportedly more rigorous 'essential thinking' [*wesentliches Denken*], which is predicated on a strict *obedience to Being* [*Gehorsam zu Sein*], merely betrays arbitrariness and willfulness."[137]

In *Heidegger: A Thinker in an Age of Affliction*, Karl Löwith summarized many of the central philosophical objections to Heidegger's thought, observing, "Heidegger's claim concerning the necessity of his *Denken* will only convince those who already believe that his *Denken* has itself been 'sent' by Being: a 'destining of Being' [*Seinsgeschick*] that expresses 'decrees concerning the truth of Being.' Such matters resist rational adjudication."[138] Although Heidegger's shortcomings may seem most obvious in his unguarded attempt to think "the inner truth and greatness of National Socialism," they emerge even more undeniably in his efforts to " 'dissolve the idea of logic in the turbulence of a more originary questioning': in his reading of the entire history of Western metaphysics as 'nihilism' and in his consistent endeavor to restore to thinking . . . 'leadership in the whole of human existence.' "[139]

The Rejection of "Validity"

In *Logic as a Question of Truth*, Heidegger dismissed the idea of "validity" on the grounds that it was fated to devolve into a "tangle of confusion, perplexity, and dogmatism."[140] To be sure, in the past, philosophers have contentiously debated the meaning of "validity," disagreeing about which criteria are best suited to define it. Nevertheless, they have, quite sensibly, refrained from *banishing* the idea of "validity" *simpliciter*, realizing that to do so would propel philosophical reflection into a senseless freefall from which it would probably never recover. It was left to Heidegger to endorse this dubious philosophical caesura or breach with tradition. Unfortunately, it seems that many Heidegger loyalists have followed his lead by imitating this destructive *salto mortale*.

In a similar vein, in *Hölderlin's Hymns "Germanien" and "Der Rhein,"* Heidegger derided the epistemological value of "explanation" and "understanding" (*Erklären* and *Verstehen*), asserting, "Once something is *explained* [*erklärt*], then there is nothing more to *understand* [*verstehen*]." "This means," he continued, "that, strictly speaking, 'Understanding' [*Verstehen*] has no prerogative and no entitlement."[141] In the *Black Notebooks*, Heidegger fulminated against what he called "the dictatorship of the comprehensible."[142] Too often, Heidegger's more unctuous partisans have misconstrued such professions as signs of profundity.

Heidegger's reflexive demonization of "reason" and "logos," instead of "overcoming metaphysics," caused him to regress behind it, thereby losing sight of indispensable benchmarks of knowledge and truth. As Heidegger avowed in "Nietzsche's Word: 'God Is Dead' " (1945), "Thinking begins only when we have come to know that Reason, glorified for centuries, *is the most stiff-necked adversary of thought* [*Denken*]."[143]

To abstractly dismiss Plato's *Ideenlehre* for equating "Ideas" with "correctness" (*orthotos*)—as did Heidegger's in "Plato's Doctrine of Truth"—is both destructive and philologically untenable. In the aftermath of Kant's critique, metaphysics—Plato's included—has been "disenchanted." Hence, it no longer poses the same risks of dogmatism that it did in an earlier point in time. Instead, today, we court a greater risk by slavishly following Heidegger's admonition that metaphysics should be summarily "abolished" or "overcome."

Kant's conception of "Ideas of Reason" sought to preserve the "truth content" of metaphysics, in order to safeguard a niche for it amid the rampant skepticism of a "postmetaphysical" age. "Morality" was one such "Idea of Reason." Despite the fact that, as an Idea of Reason, morality possessed no basis in experience, we are required to think it, counterfactually, in order to conceive of persons as "noumenal" beings—hence as inhabitants of a putative "kingdom of ends." As Kant observed in the *Critique of Pure Reason*, "That no human being will ever act adequately to what the pure idea of virtue contains does not prove in the least that there is something chimerical in this thought. For it is only by means of this idea that any judgment of moral worth or unworth is possible; and so it necessarily lies at the ground of every approach to moral perfection, even though the obstacles in human nature . . . may hold us at a distance from it."[144] Thereby, Kant recognized, paradoxically, that just when we thought that we could dispense with metaphysics entirely, we needed it the most.

True to the critical legacy of German Idealism, the Frankfurt School also sought to preserve the "autonomy of reason." It recognized that, in light of the pacification of class struggle and the ascendancy of the "totally administered world," reason and metaphysics remained indispensable sources of negation and critique:

> Under the name of Reason, philosophy conceived the idea of an authentic Being in which all significant antitheses—subject and object, essence and appearance, thought and being—were reconciled. Connected with this idea was the conviction that our existence is not immediately and already rational but must rather be brought to Reason. Reason represented the highest potentiality of man and of existence. . . . Thereby, Reason was established as a *critical tribunal*. . . . Man, the individual was to examine and judge everything given by means of the power of his knowledge. Thus, the concept of Reason contains the concept of freedom as well. For such examination and judgment would be meaningless if man were not free to act in accordance with his insight and to bring what confronts him into accordance with Reason.[145]

The Politics of "Post-Truth"

Heidegger's *Denken*, by virtue of its summons to "overcome metaphysics," inaugurated the "post-truth" era. The problem derived from Heidegger's harsh indictment of "propositional truth" in favor of the more "archaic," ontological notion of truth as "unconcealment": an orientation that culminated in Heidegger's dubious insistence on the equiprimordiality of "truth" and "error." As Heidegger asserted in "The Origin of the Work of Art," "The clearing [*Lichtung*] is provided by a constant *concealment* in the double form of *refusing and dissembling. . . . Truth is in its nature untruth*." However, by conflating "truth" and "error," Heidegger risked rendering them indistinguishable. Thus, on the one hand, Heidegger denigrated the vacuity of propositional truth: truth as "idea," "representation," or "correctness." On the other hand, in keeping with his quest for a more "primordial" conception of truth—a quest that was reflected in his attraction to the *Naturphilosophie* of the pre-Socratics—in his so-called ontological-historical treatises, he praised "Irrnis," or "erring," as covalent with truth itself.[146]

Today, the shortcomings of Heidegger's risky philosophical chess move have become increasingly apparent, as the post-truth perspective has devolved into the de facto credo of would-be despots and tyrants across the globe.[147] Among champions of the European New Right, Heidegger's political cachet has skyrocketed. As the leader of the Austrian Identitarian Movement, Martin Sellner, avowed in "My Path to Heidegger" (2015), "There is no such thing as a 'free-floating subject' that lies encrusted beneath the layers of Tradition. Instead, the quest for Dasein's Essence and Being shows that it is always rooted in a *concrete, ethno-cultural soil* [*ethnokulturellen Boden verwurzelt*]. . . . Heidegger realized that an understanding of Being [*Seinsverständnis*] always derives from a *Volk*. . . . It grows out of the soil [*Boden*]."[148] Sellner, who, in 2015, was legally banned from entering Great Britain owing to his racist views, heralded the *Black Notebooks*' publication as a valuable confirmation of the Identitarian worldview, which seeks to redefine citizenship in accordance with the precepts of "ethnicity": in essence, a euphemism for "race."[149]

Nor have the antidemocratic valances of Heidegger's endorsement of ethnocultural "rootedness" passed unnoticed among white nationalists who ply their trade on the American side of the Atlantic. As Thomas J. Main remarks in *The Rise of the Alt-Right*, numerous "Alt-Right sites, especially *Radix Journal* and *Counter-Currents* Publishing, devote considerable attention to political . . . thinkers such as Carl Schmitt, Martin Heidegger, and a range of European New Rightists."[150]

In a 2013 interview, the *Counter-Currents* founder and *Occidental Quarterly* editor Greg Johnson disclosed that his "anti-Jewish *Weltanschauung* crystallized after encountering the controversy surrounding Heidegger's National Socialism": a debate, Johnson added, that "called forth a lot of rhetorical thuggery . . . on the part of Jewish commentators." (Are we to presume that such "rhetorical thuggery" is nonexistent among Alt-Right circles? Johnson's hypocrisy is truly delectable.) Falsifying the historical record, Johnson praised Heidegger as a "dissident National Socialist" who, in the *Black Notebooks*, presented "the outlines of a post-totalitarian, postmodernist New Right." In Johnson's eyes, the *Black Notebooks* were a political epiphany. They demonstrated that Heidegger had developed an "intellectually coherent foundation for National Socialism," an approach that explained the movement's "inner truth and greatness" with respect to "the confrontation of historical man with global technological civilization."[151] As Graham Macklin confirms in *Key Thinkers of the Radical Right*, "Heidegger had an enduring influence upon the New Right and on Johnson personally."[152]

Although exponents of the "Heidegger-as-savior" standpoint are willing to acknowledge the Master's limitations with respect to this or that point, such reservations rarely dampen their enthusiasm for Heidegger's "originary think-ing" as a whole. Nor, as a rule, are these limitations explored in earnest. Instead, for the most part, Heidegger's disciples have accepted at face value his mislead-ing characterization of "metaphysics" as the archenemy of *Denken*. Hence, they regard his brand of "antiphilosophy" as a locus of redemption. Since Heidegger's devotées view his thought as a ne plus ultra, in a gesture of intellectual submis-sion, they assume the role of authorized exegetes. In this way, the entrapments of "onto-theology"—which, Heidegger acolytes contend, it is our ethical duty to transcend—return through the back door in the form of Heidegger veneration.

Heidegger loyalists rarely perceive the link between his endorsement of *Vernunftkritik*—his denegation of "reason" and "metaphysics"—and his embrace of fascism. Nor do they bother to correlate Heidegger's quest for the "other of Reason" with his demonstrable enthusiasm for "Mythos," "Blut," and "Herr-schaft." They fail to heed Hannah Arendt's well-placed caveat that Heidegger's attraction to "concepts of this kind can only lead us *out of philosophy into some kind of nature-oriented superstition.*"[153] Heidegger's supporters rarely subject his *Logosvergessenheit*—his "forgetting of reason"—to sustained critical scrutiny. Hence, they dismiss the link between his rejection of the "ideas of 1789" and his disconcerting embrace of the ideology of German "particularism."

Seinsgeschichte: Between *Herrschaft* and Heteronomy

In retrospect, Heidegger's attempt to attribute the European catastrophe of 1939–45 to "Western metaphysics," the Cartesian "subjectum," and "Technik" stands out as, perhaps, his greatest act of deception. The upshot of Heidegger's "anticivilizational" animus—a standpoint that was profoundly indebted to the worldview of central European *Kulturpessimismus*—was to disqualify the democratic norms that, in point of fact, are the sine qua non for *contesting* and *restraining* modernity's scientific-technological excesses: norms capable of subjecting scientific expertise and political technocracy to the mollifying balm of public reason and democratic will-formation. Even were we to assume, for the sake of argument, that Heidegger's Spenglerian *Zeitdiagnose* concerning the negative apocalypse of modern "technics" were correct, the antidemocratic thrust of his standpoint ultimately disqualifies it.

Throughout the various iterations of Heidegger's fundamental ontology, it re-mained committed to the precepts of *Herrschaft* and heteronomy. As such, one of its hallmarks was demanding strict obedience to fate. Heideggerian *Seinsgeschick* was a recipe for human passivity, a blind capitulation to destiny. As Heidegger avowed in the "Letter on Humanism" (1947), "Man does not decide whether and how beings appear, whether and how god and the gods or history and nature come forward into the clearing of Being, come to presence and depart. *The advent of beings lies in the destiny of Being.*"[154] Nearly twenty years later, in the *Der Spiegel* interview (1966) "Only a God Can Save Us," Heidegger reaffirmed his retrograde belief in humanity's powerlessness and impotence. "The sole possibility that is left for us," he counseled, "is to prepare a sort of readiness . . . for the appearance of the god or for the absence of the god in the time of decline [*Untergang*]; for in the god's absence, we perish [*untergehen*]."[155]

Heidegger's trademark explanation-from-*Seinsgeschichte* excelled in obfuscation and denial. Its forte was its capacity to *explain away*: to muddle and confuse historical circumstances, rather than illuminating them.

As a thinker, Heidegger failed by elevating the *Seinsgedanke* to the status of a *fundamentum inconcussum*: an unchallengeable, philosophical Absolute and, hence, a precept that remained impervious to humanity's capacities for contestation and critique. As one disillusioned Heideggerian observed resignedly upon reading the *Black Notebooks*, "If the History of Being is itself a sending by and of Being, a sending in which Being withdraws and conceals itself, what decision of mortals can make a difference?"[156]

In "Why Still Philosophy?," Adorno directly confronted this failing in Heidegger's "primordial thinking" (*anfängliches Denken*): his "ontological fatalism" and glorification of heteronomy. In Adorno's eyes, this debility shed light on the philosophical motivations underlying Heidegger's "enlistment" for National Socialism. "For Heidegger," observed Adorno, "thinking would be the passive harkening to Being without any right to critique, constrained to capitulate before everything that can appeal to the shimmering might of Being. Heidegger's falling in with Hitler's *Führerstaat* was no act of opportunism. Instead, it was a consequence of a philosophy that equated *Being* and *Führertum*."[157]

National Socialism and the Transition to "Another Beginning"

Heidegger never relinquished the view that, as he put it in the *Der Spiegel* interview, "*National Socialism moved in the right direction.*"[158] A review of Heidegger's postwar thought confirms that he never renounced National

Socialism, per se. He merely rejected the ideologically deficient versions of
Nazism promoted by his political rivals. As Lutz Hachmeister observes in *Heidegger's Testament*, "Heidegger's so-called 'polemics' against National Socialism were much ado about nothing. His criticisms were directed against
political-ideological competitors such as Ernst Krieck and Alfred Baeumler.
*They never called into to question National Socialism's intrinsic historical le-
gitimacy nor Hitler's*."[159]

A revealing avowal in *Überlegungen VII–XI*, circa 1939, provides telling evidence in support of Hachmeister's assertion that whatever misgivings
Heidegger may have had with respect to specific National Socialist policies
never caused him to doubt the movement's ultimate "metaphysical" significance. Heidegger explained that, despite his earlier ambivalences about National Socialism, he was fully convinced, "on philosophical grounds," of the
movement's ontological-historical import:

> Thinking purely "metaphysically" (that is, in terms of the history of Being), in the
> years 1930–1934 I took National Socialism for the possibility of a transition to an-
> other Beginning. . . . With this, I misunderstood and underestimated this "move-
> ment" in its *authentic forces* and *inner necessities* as well as in the kind of
> *Greatness* . . . that is proper to it. . . . On the basis of full insight into the earlier de-
> ception about the essence and historical essential force of National Socialism,
> there results the *necessity of its affirmation, and indeed on philosophical grounds*
> [*aus denkerischen Gründen*]. . . . This "movement" remains independent of its
> contemporary shape . . . and of the duration of its specific visible forms.[160]

Although the preceding passage remains undated, it was clearly written at some
point in 1939. In all probability, the political enthusiasm it evinced reflected the
outbreak of World War II on 1 September: an *Ereignis* that reanimated
Heidegger's fantasies of *Vernichtung* and *Zerstörung* as measures required to
vanquish nihilism, in keeping with his oft-stated conviction that nihilism could
only be surmounted via methods that were themselves nihilistic. This accounts
for Heidegger's—morally irresponsible—endorsement, circa 1941, of "*Extermination* [*Vernichten*] as that which assures us against the prospect of defeat."[161]

Nevertheless, in the secondary literature, an exculpatory consensus has
emerged crediting Heidegger with having definitively broken with the regime at
the time of the Battle of Stalingrad (1942–43): in other words, once it had become
clear that Nazism had been soundly defeated. However, these *verstehende* inter-

pretations of Heidegger's conduct overlook the fact that, by then, to all intents and purposes, there was very little of the "Third Reich" as a "utopian political project" left to support. Palingenetic hopes that Nazism might lead to the birth of a "New Man"—or, to employ Heidegger's idiolect, "another Beginning"—were permanently dashed with the onset of war in 1939. It is well known, moreover, that, during the last two years of the war, Nazi loyalists began bolting in droves.[162]

Heidegger's "enlistment" for Nazism had always been primarily *ideational* and *philosophical*. It derived from his belief in the transformative-eschatological capacities of National Socialism qua "movement" rather than a commitment to the NSDAP qua "party" or "regime."[163] In sum, Heidegger's belated disillusionment with "really existing" National Socialism would seem to count for very little, since it left the ideational basis of his engagement untouched.

Ultimately, there was never any *prise de conscience* on Heidegger's part concerning the inherent criminality of the regime he supported. The Freudian trope of "working through the past" never held any significance for him. Instead, in keeping with the Nietzschean ethos of "active nihilism," Heidegger proved to be quite adept at rationalizing Nazi brutality as *ontologically necessary*: as required by the imperatives of *Seinsgeschichte*.

In *Self-Consciousness and Self-Determination*, Ernst Tugendhat observed that the shortcomings of Heidegger's "de-rationalized concept of truth" can be deduced from his justification of the Nazi seizure of power as an "*Ereignis . . . in which the Volk recovers the truth of its Will as Dasein.*" For Heidegger, Tugendhat continued, "Truth is the disclosure of what makes a *Volk certain, clear, and strong in its acting and knowing.*" Ultimately, "Heidegger's Nazism was no accidental affair. . . . [Instead,] a direct path led from his philosophy—from its de-rationalized concept of truth and the concept of self-determination defined by this—to Nazism."[164]

At the same time, Tugendhat appended an important caveat to this critique. The fact that Heidegger *retained* the concept of "truth"—albeit in an unsatisfactory form—indicates that even his "de-rationalized conception of truth" continued to stand in an unmistakable "relation to reason." Consequently, "we would be relinquishing philosophical insight if we did not try to learn what we can from Heidegger. . . . The point is to recognize precisely the position that led to irrationalism, and not to throw the baby out with the bath water."[165]

3

Heidegger and Race

"Race": the defining feature of the National Socialist Weltanschauung.
*Race posits an ideology of Aryan superiority, the subhumanity of world
Jewry, and advocates the practice of racial hygiene in order to realize the
goal of "Nordic breeding."*
—*Vokabular des Nationalsozialismus* (2007)

Race doctrine [der Rassengedanke] *has two main principles and two
main goals: (1) the elimination of Jewish and so-called "colored" blood
with respect to our* Volk; *and (2) the unequivocal affirmation of* Germanic
blood *as the origin, basis, and future of everything that we call
"German." The contours and content of* German statecraft
[Staatsführung] *are based on these two principles.*
—Walther Darré, "Wir und die Leibesübungen" (1935)

"Spiritual National Socialism"

IN APPROACHING THE TOPIC OF "HEIDEGGER and race," one finds oneself in a
quandary reminiscent of Edgar Allan Poe's "The Purloined Letter": what exists
in plain sight or seems fairly obvious is incessantly denied or deliberately en-
shrouded in a miasma of deliberate obscurity. After all, in Heidegger's impassioned endorsements of National Socialism, as well as his actions as Freiburg
University *Führer-Rektor*, he consistently comported himself as *a committed
political radical: a Nazi true believer*. According to Heidegger's student
and biographer Ernst Nolte, "Heidegger wanted to be a *revolutionary of the*

'*Volksgemeinschaft,*' in which the various estates and professions coexisted in joyful harmony, and where 'leading' and 'following' [*'Führen' und 'Folgen'*] were clearly distinguished."[1] The ideological inflection of Heidegger's discourse, as documented in numerous seminar protocols, lecture transcripts, and philosophical treatises, underlines the unwavering nature of his philosophical and political engagement. In nearly every respect, Heidegger was *plus royaliste que le roi*. "Le roi," in this case, was none other than Hitler.

Nevertheless, despite the ever-expanding dossier, Heidegger's supporters have persisted with their brusque denials. As one Heidegger loyalist recently put it, "Heidegger's anti-Semitism, however crude it may appear, . . . seems fundamentally to have been based on a form of *cultural anti-Semitism* of a sort that was widespread in Germany and Europe before the Second World War and did not disappear afterward (not even from German academic circles)."[2] In other words, efforts to further explore the gravity of Heidegger's anti-Semitism are superfluous, since, when all is said and done, it merely expressed a widespread cultural prejudice. Not only does the author fail to distinguish between "cultural anti-Semitism" and the stipulations of Nazi race doctrine that Heidegger dutifully implemented as Freiburg University rector, but his remarks are a classic expression of "moral conventionalism": since anti-Semitism was a perspective that was shared by so many Germans before and after the war, it would be unfair to single out Heidegger for criticism.

Heidegger's zealous enlistment for Germany's "National Awakening" would have been inconceivable apart from his support for the fundamental claims of the *Rassengedanke*, the central pillar of Nazi ideology. Nazi ideologues never concealed their adherence to this hate-filled *Weltanschauung*, nor did they seek to mask its murderous implications for groups that they regarded as racially inferior. As Hitler declared proleptically in *Mein Kampf*, "If twelve or fifteen thousand of the Jews who were corrupting the nation had been subjected to poison gas at the beginning of . . . World War I, . . . then the millions of sacrifices made at the front would not have been in vain."[3]

"Race thinking"—and anti-Semitism, as its necessary corollary—was the alpha and omega of National Socialism's political self-understanding. Nazi potentates such as Alfred Rosenberg, Hans Frank, and Walther Darré invoked it repeatedly in their verbal diatribes and political treatises. Had Heidegger regarded National Socialist race doctrine as intellectually and morally unacceptable, it is doubtful that he would have signed on with the "movement," as he did with great fanfare, on 1 May 1933.[4]

Heidegger retroactively denied having supported the *Rassenbegriff*. In the apologia that Heidegger composed for the Freiburg University de-Nazification commission in 1945, he alleged that he had staunchly opposed the dogmas of National Socialist "biologism."[5] Nevertheless, Heidegger's disclaimer was question-begging and beside the point. Under National Socialism, there flourished a wide variety of competing approaches to race thinking. As Thomas Rohkrämer has pointed out in "Heidegger, Kulturkritik, und völkische Ideologie," "Even among leading National Socialists, very different [ideological] conceptions predominated, from the *Germanen*-mania of Alfred Rosenberg to Goebbels' cult of modern 'steely romanticism,' to Heinrich Himmler's mystical gibberish and the sober fanaticism of his right-hand man, Reinhard Heydrich, to the party-loyalist Martin Bormann, for whom National Socialism was defined by Hitler's Will."[6]

Although Heidegger opposed "scientific" race thinking, he did so merely in the name of a competing ideological strand of Nazi race doctrine, a current that he believed more closely approximated National Socialism's "inner truth and greatness." Hence, in any future discussion of Heidegger's attitudes toward race, it is important to keep in mind that his disavowal of Nazi "biologism" was never intended as a rejection of National Socialism per se. Instead, such denials always entailed an underlying solidarity with the Nazi project.

Heidegger referred to the ideological current of Nazism that he favored as "spiritual National Socialism." In an outburst of political euphoria, Heidegger exalted National Socialism as the embodiment of *"new spiritual energies unfolding historically from out of the middle."*[7] On another occasion, he praised the "National Socialist Revolution as . . . the work of men who seek to realize *a new spiritual order* [*eine neue geistige Ordnung*] and who are motivated by a deep sense of responsibility vis-à-vis the fate of their *Volk*."[8] And in the *Black Notebooks*, Heidegger characterized himself as a proponent of *"spiritual National Socialism* [*geistiger Nationalsozialismus*]," a perspective that he contrasted with "vulgar National Socialism."[9]

Moreover, during the early 1920s, Heidegger had expressly described himself as a "spiritual anti-Semite" (*ein geistiger Antisemit*), a comportment he viewed as an effective means of combating Germany's escalating Jewish "infestation" (*Verseuchung*).[10] To describe the presence of Jews on German soil as an "infestation" is, in point of fact, to unambiguously partake of the language of biological racism. This avowal on Heidegger's part—along with many simi-

lar statements and assertions—casts a long shadow over his subsequent professions of innocence.

By endorsing "spiritual National Socialism," Heidegger remained no less
committed to the fundamental tenets of race thinking than did the movement's
other devotees. The only difference was that Heidegger's "enlistment" for Nazism proceeded under the guise of *a different epistemology*—an epistemology
based on the *Seinsgedanke*. Moreover, as a rule, among the National Socialist
faithful, debates over Nazi ideology proved to be "family disagreements."
They left untouched the disputants' fundamental commitment to the National
Socialist *Weltanschauung*.

Heidegger's affirmation of "spiritual National Socialism" sheds important
light on his controversial encomium to the "inner truth and greatness of
National Socialism" in *An Introduction to Metaphysics* (1935).[11] Allowing this
phrase to stand in the postwar publication of the lecture course was Heidegger's
way of indicating that, in his own mind, he *felt that he had nothing to apologize
for*. Its inclusion attests to the hypocrisy of his postwar political tergiversations.

Following in the Master's footsteps, Heidegger loyalists have seriously misconstrued the persistence and intensity of his political engagement. To claim
that, in the aftermath of Heidegger's rectorate, he "distanced himself" from
National Socialism constitutes, at best, a partial truth.[12] Heidegger's purported
"retreat" from politics merely reflected the fact that he found himself on the losing end of a struggle for ideological supremacy. Once the outcome of these ideological battles had been settled—once it became clear to Heidegger that his
understanding of National Socialism's "inner truth and greatness" had failed to
win out—Heidegger retreated to the sphere of "metapolitics." As he avowed in
the *Black Notebooks*, "We must abolish [philosophy] in order to prepare the
way for the entirely 'Other': *Metapolitics*."[13] The *Black Notebooks* present a
detailed record of the "metapolitical" struggles that Heidegger continued to
wage on behalf of Nazism.

To be sure, at various points, Heidegger formulated criticisms of specific
Nazi policies, such as the "vulgar," biological understanding of the Nazi
Rassengedanke. However, in this respect, his comportment differed little from
that of other NSDAP loyalists, many of whom also harbored a long list of com-
plaints and grievances. Historians have long identified internecine strife as a
defining feature of Nazi rule.[14] Heidegger's misgivings and reservations about
specific Nazi practices or policies notwithstanding, he repeatedly insisted, as he

put it in 1936, that *"National Socialism is the right way for Germany; one must merely 'hold out' long enough."*[15] When all is said and done, his fundamental commitment to National Socialism's intrinsic, world-historical significance remained unabated.

Race Thinking and Racial Hygiene

Heidegger's acceptance of Nazi race doctrine was not purely attitudinal or theoretical. As Freiburg University rector, Heidegger was charged with implementing the discriminatory provisions of Nazi race law. Despite his subsequent prevarications and disclaimers, he did so conscientiously and enthusiastically.

A good case in point concerns Heidegger's enforcement of the anti-Semitic provisions of provincial race law. After staging a "coup" on 6 April 1933, the Nazi leadership in Baden promulgated a decree banning Jews from university instruction. Their zealotry gave rise to an unforeseen conflict with Berlin, since at the Reich level, the ban on Jewish instructors allowed for certain exemptions, such as World War I veterans.

The competing edicts provoked a jurisdictional crisis over which law should be granted priority. The confusion was especially acute in Freiburg, where the recently elected non-Nazi rector, Wilhelm von Moellendorff, had been deposed following a vicious campaign of denunciation by the Nazi press. On 21 April, Heidegger was named as von Moellendorff's successor.

Heidegger rashly entered the fray, weighing in decisively in support of the more rigid, provincial version of the anti-Jewish ban. In one of his first actions as rector, Heidegger wrote to the Baden minister of culture, Dr. Otto Wacker, declaring that he favored a "clear and unqualified implementation of the [provincial] decree." Its strict enforcement, Heidegger added dishonestly, would be the best way for the university to support "endangered colleagues."[16]

In Heidegger's capacity as *Führer-Rektor*, he displayed few moral qualms about restructuring the university in accordance with the *Rassenprinzip*. His ideological zeal was well-nigh unbridled. Heidegger's outsized political ambitions surfaced in the role he played in reformulating the provincial educational charter, in August 1933, in accordance with the *Führerprinzip*. As a result of his efforts, a long-standing tradition of university self-governance was annulled. This ministerial fait accompli provoked consternation among Heidegger's colleagues, many of whom were traditional conservatives who abhorred political

extremism as destructive of the university's pedagogical mission. The economist Walter Eucken wrote to Heidelberg rector Willy Andreas to complain
about Heidegger's high-handedness: "The fruits of Heidegger's diligence have
become clear. The new university governance regulations in Baden constitute a
radical break with tradition. They are tantamount to a *destruction of the old university*. . . . The situation has really become unimaginably serious."[17]

Nor were Heidegger's political ambitions confined to the regional or provincial level. Instead, he was fully committed to extending his understanding of
National Socialism's "inner truth and greatness" to the national level. From the
outset of his tenure as rector, Heidegger engaged in an intensive and concerted
lobbying effort with the Nazi leadership in Berlin for the sake of realizing his
vision of "The University in the New Reich."

In this respect, Heidegger's most egregious transgression was, undoubtedly, the
telegram that he sent on 20 May 1933 directly to Hitler, urging the postponement
of an upcoming conference of German university rectors until the requisite *Gleichschaltung* measures had been implemented: in other words, until the group had
been purged of members who were not committed National Socialists.[18]

The institutional support that Heidegger, as *Führer-Rektor*, provided for Nazi
race doctrine was consistent with his long-term objective of transforming Freiburg
into *a model National Socialist university*: a paragon of what he termed, in a 30 November 1933 address, "National Socialist Education."[19] Heidegger's endorsement
of Nazi race policy was consistent with his goal of acceding to a position of *geistige
Führung*, or "spiritual leadership." In keeping with this objective, Heidegger reconceived the university's pedagogical mission. Henceforth, it would become a crucible for training "spiritual leaders" (*geistige Führer*).

Ample evidence confirms that Heidegger regarded the precepts of Nazi race
doctrine as compatible with the essential tenets of his own *Existenzphilosophie*.
For example, Heidegger's June 1933 address "The University in the New Reich" attested to his rhetorical infatuation with the Social Darwinist idiom of
Kampf und Überleben—"struggle" and "survival"—an indispensable hallmark
of the *Rassengedanke*. "Whoever does not survive the struggle [*Kampf*]," declaimed Heidegger, "will fall by the wayside. The struggle [*Kampf*]," he continued, "will be based on the forces of the New Reich that are being realized
by *Volkskanzler* Hitler. *A hard race*, with no thought for itself, must fight the
battle . . . to determine the *new configuration of instructors and leaders* [*Führer*]
at the university."[20]

During Heidegger's rectorate, the director of the Race Bureau of the Freiburg branch of the SS, Dr. Helmut Haubold, was invited to lecture at the university on "Rassenhygiene" (eugenics).[21] Within months, attendance at Haubold's lectures became mandatory for all students. In fall 1933, at the urging of Nazi students, Heidegger installed Dr. Heinz Riedel, a "race specialist" from the local psychiatric clinic, to lecture on "problems of the *Rassenfrage*."[22]

Heidegger's vigorous support for Nazi race policy also became clear in other areas of university life. As rector, Heidegger oversaw hiring guidelines mandating that teaching vacancies would only be filled by instructors who were loyal to National Socialism.

Another illustration of Heidegger's endorsement of race thinking emerged in the course of his efforts to purchase the literary estate of one of Germany's leading race theorists, Ludwig Schemann (1852–1938). A native Freiburger, Schemann was a leading authority on Arthur de Gobineau, whose *Essai sur l'inegalité des races humaines* (1853–55) was the *Ur*-text of European race thinking. Schemann was president and founder of the German Gobineau Society as well as the executor of Gobineau's papers and personal library. Following the Nazi seizure of power, Schemann's standing rose considerably, since party ideologues viewed his work as a valuable source of doctrinal legitimacy.

In a June 1933 letter to Minister Wacker, Heidegger proposed the idea of purchasing Schemann's papers. "It would be highly desirable," urged Heidegger, "if the entirety of Schemann's literary state could be kept in Freiburg. Hopefully, a decision on this matter by the Baden government will soon be forthcoming."[23] To bolster his case, Heidegger appended a missive he had solicited from the university librarian, Joseph Rest. Invoking the Schemann-Gobineau filiation as leverage, Rest vaunted Freiburg's status as a mecca of European race science: "Currently, much of race science is based on Gobineau's work, which, consequently, . . . represents an important area of academic study. Since research on Gobineau is associated with Freiburg, and since the most important German race scientists were trained here, Gobineau's library should unquestionably remain in Freiburg."[24]

In conjunction with these efforts, Heidegger enlisted the support of the notorious physical anthropologist and race scientist Eugen Fischer. In Fischer's capacity as director of the Kaiser Wilhelm Institute of Human Heredity and Eugenics in Berlin, he attained notoriety as the Third Reich's leading expert on eugenics and racial hygiene.

During the waning years of the *Kaiserreich* (1871–1918), Fischer had made a name for himself by publishing a controversial monograph on the so-called Rehoboth Bastards, who were the progeny of Boer colonizers and indigenous women of the Nama tribe. In 1892, the Rehobothers came under German administration in German Southwest Africa (contemporary Namibia). By inserting the word "bastards" in the title, Fischer had significantly prejudiced the reception of his monograph, which was regarded as a "pioneering" study in the up-and-coming field of "race mixing."

Fischer concluded his study with a heartless policy recommendation: the Germans should protect these "*Mischlinge* [individuals of mixed race] as long as it served their interests"; thereafter, "*destruction* [*Untergang*]."[25] During the 1930s, Fischer's insistence that "those who are genetically diseased and, therefore, racially unassimilable to the *Volk*, must be eradicated [*ausgemerzt*]" furnished the template for Nazi eugenic policy: for example, the infamous "T-4" euthanasia program.[26]

Fischer took Heidegger's prodding to heart, and in his missive to Minister Wacker, he stressed Schemann's indispensability with respect to "the spiritual lead-up to National Socialism, as well as his unique significance for its racial and genetic-biological legacy."[27]

During the next few months, Fischer's and Heidegger's paths intersected repeatedly. In May 1933, the Nazis named Fischer to the prestigious post of rector of the University of Berlin. A few months later, Fischer seems to have played a key role in the behind-the-scenes machinations that led to Heidegger being offered a *Lehrstuhl*, or chair, at the University of Berlin.[28]

On 11 November 1933, Heidegger's and Fischer's paths crossed again, when both appeared as featured speakers at a University of Leipzig rally in support of a Nazi plebiscite that called for Germany's withdrawal from the League of Nations. The Leipzig event was tantamount to a declaration of intellectual surrender to totalitarianism. The rhetoric that the speakers employed exemplified Nazi ideological doublespeak: it invoked a pseudodemocratic idiom that exalted every nation's right to "spiritual self-development and cultural freedom." The final statement implored "educated persons around the world to [support] the struggle of the German *Volk*, united behind Adolf Hitler, for freedom, honor, law, and peace."[29]

At the Leipzig rally, National Socialism's ruthless, pseudo-Nietzschean "transvaluation of values" was unabashedly on display. The speakers redefined "freedom" as enslavement to dictatorship; they reconceived "bondage" as a form of "emancipation."

Heidegger participated enthusiastically in this charade, claiming that, by announcing the plebiscite, "the Führer demanded nothing from the *Volk*. Instead, he *granted* it the possibility of the *highest free decision* [*höchsten freien Entscheidung*]: whether the entire *Volk* wills its own Dasein or not." He lauded the Nazi dictatorship for having "liberated" Germans from the "deification of [an approach to] thinking that is *powerless and insufficiently rooted-in-soil* [*eines boden-und machtlosen Denkens*]."[30] Commenting on Heidegger's address, the University of Freiburg historian Gerd Tellenbach observed, "It was an impassioned National Socialist who spoke: bereft of wisdom and a sense of political responsibility, devoid of concern for adequate differentiation."[31]

The political semantics of Heidegger's speech merit further scrutiny, since they explain why he regarded National Socialism as an *Ereignis*, an "Event" of metaphysical significance in the history of Being. Heidegger exalted National Socialism for having created a "space" in which "the lucid severity of . . . simple questioning concerning the essence of Being" could flourish. In Heidegger's view, the liquidation of "thinking that was *powerless and insufficiently rooted-in-soil*" was an unmixed blessing, since it had cleared the way for "völkische Wissenschaft": an approach to "knowledge" in which *völkisch* concerns acceded to their rightful position of primacy.[32]

Let there be no mistake: the opposition between "völkische Wissenschaft" and "boden-und machtlosen Denken"—"thinking that is powerless and insufficiently rooted-in-soil"—that Heidegger proposed was, fundamentally and unavoidably, a *racial contrast*. It was a schema that endorsed a set of discriminatory, racial-ideological stereotypes. In Heidegger's *Denken*, the contrast between "rooted" and "rootless" thinking expressed a fundamental *ontological antagonism,* an opposition that was *grounded in the nature of Being*. Heidegger invoked this contrast repeatedly in his denigration of Jewish intellectual habitudes.

When, in Heidegger's Leipzig address, he praised National Socialism as an "Event" that facilitated the reinstatement of "simple questioning concerning the essence of Being," he chose his words with the utmost philosophical precision. He regarded the National Socialist *Volksgemeinschaft*—which was itself an irreducibly racial construct—not merely as a political watershed. It was also a watershed in the history of Being.

Accordingly, in the *Black Notebooks*, Heidegger credited National Socialism with having catalyzed the renewal of his *Denken*, for having, as Heidegger put it, "*rejuvenated our thinking and redirected it along the proper path* [*eine neue Wirklichkeit erweckt hat, die unserem Denken die rechte Bahn und Stoßkraft gibt*]." "Otherwise," he continued, "in spite of everything, it [our thinking] would have remained lost within itself, and only with great difficulty would it have succeeded in influencing reality."[33]

In sum, Heidegger exalted National Socialism not merely as a *political break-through* but also as a *metaphysical caesura*: an ontological *novum* that struggled heroically against the corrosive influence of *"boden- und machtlosen"* Jewish intellectual habitudes. Heidegger regarded such "unrooted" intellectual paradigms as detrimental to *Seinsgeschichte* as an *Ereignis*, on which the "destiny of the West" depended. As he avowed in the *Black Notebooks*, "The question of world Jewry's role is . . . a *metaphysical question* about the type of human being that, itself unrooted [*ungebunden*], can adopt the uprooting of all beings from Being as its 'world-historical' task [*die Entwurzelung alles Seienden aus dem Sein als 'weltgeschichtliche' Aufgabe*]."[34] The National Socialist worldview was itself predicated on a "metaphysical-racial anti-Semitism [insofar as] it demanded the exclusion of Jews from the *Volksgemeinschaft*." Conceived of as a life-or-death struggle, this logic of exclusion took the form of an "either-or": "world Jewry's" influence on the life of the German *Volk* must be eliminated, or else the *Volk* will perish.[35]

In Heidegger's eyes, "world Jewry's" misdeeds did not hinge on specific wrongs perpetrated by individual Jews or Jewish groups. Instead, as the just-quoted remarks confirm, the problem lay with the degenerative tendencies of "world Jewry" *as a race*. Consequently, for Heidegger, the redemption of "world history" from "world Jewry's" disintegrative influences was not primarily *a political question*. Instead, it was a matter of fundamental ontology qua profane eschatology. As Heidegger affirmed in "The Anaximander Fragment" (1946), "As 'destining' [*geschickliches*], Being itself is inherently *eschatological*."[36]

Bodenständigkeit versus *Verjudung*

The opposition between "rooted" and "rootless" thinking had also been foremost in Heidegger's mind in the letter that he wrote, in October 1929, to the assistant director of the *Notgemeinschaft der deutschen Wissenschaft* concerning a fellowship application by Eduard Baumgarten. Heidegger maintained, hyperbolically, that the stakes of Baumgarten's application concerned a momentous "choice": "whether to provide our *German* spiritual life once again with genuine, 'rooted' [*bodenständig*] manpower and educators, or to deliver it over definitively . . . to increasing *Verjudung* [*Jewification*]."[37]

In the discourse of anti-Semitism, the term *Verjudung* occupied a prominent and ignominious niche. Richard Wagner employed it in "The Jews in Music" (1850), in which he bemoaned the "*Verjudung* of modern art."[38] In *The Triumph of Judaism over Germany* (1879), Wilhelm Marr characterized Germany's battle against *Verjudung* as an "existential struggle," a "Kampf um's Dasein"— a description that Heidegger, the *Existenzphilosoph*, certainly would have endorsed.[39] In *Mein Kampf*, Hitler—not to be outdone—complained about the rampant "*Verjudung* of the [German] soul and the mammonization of our drive to reproduce." If left unchecked, he continued, these developments "would prove ruinous for the entirety of our genetic progeny."[40]

In the 1929 letter, Heidegger's anxiety about the threat posed by the "Verjudung des deutschen Geistes" was by no means an isolated instance, a "one-off." Instead, it expressed a persistent leitmotif of his *Denken*. In 1916, Heidegger had employed remarkably similar language in a missive to his future wife, Elfride Petri. In the letter, Heidegger expressly lamented the "*Jewification of our culture and our universities* [*die Verjudung unsrer Kultur u. Universitäten*]."[41] These two observations, though separated by thirteen years, confirm Heidegger's understanding of "Jewification" and "rootlessness"—*Verjudung* and *Bodenlosigkeit*— as necessary corollaries.

Heidegger held that Jewish "rootlessness," when viewed from the standpoint of *Seinsgeschichte*, culminated implacably in *nihilism*: in a perilous loss of "essence." By framing the crisis of German spiritual life in this *völkisch*, anti-Semitic idiolect, Heidegger affirmed the necessity and legitimacy of race thinking.

Another example of Heidegger's commitment to race thinking concerns his dogged pursuit of a faculty appointment in *Rassenhygiene*, or "eugenics." It is worth noting that Heidegger's insistence on hiring in this area explicitly contravened a policy directive issued by Wilhelm Frick, the Nazi minister of the interior, that discouraged such appointments because of a paucity of qualified scholars.

So eager was Heidegger to make an appointment in *Rassenhygiene* that, on 4 April 1934, he wrote to the minister of culture to request the dismissal of the current lecturer in the field, in the hope of securing a permanent position. At one point, fearing that his intensive lobbying efforts might come to naught, Heidegger vented his frustration in a letter. "For months," Heidegger grumbled, "I have sought to come up with a suitable person to fill this position, so that I could apply to the Interior Minister [Frick] for funding for a *Lehrstuhl* in *Rassenkunde und Erbbiologie* [Race Studies and Biology]."[42]

Heidegger's letter to Dr. Wacker, coupled with his persistence in seeking an appointment in *Rassenhygiene*, belie his post hoc claim that, as a matter of principle, he opposed National Socialist "biologism."[43] Instead, when it came to satisfying the demands of Nazi "politicized science," Heidegger's convictions seemed to be infinitely malleable. As long as Heidegger felt that he could tweak the demands of race thinking to accord with his own understanding of "spiritual National Socialism," his reservations and qualms were few.

A final example of Heidegger's efforts to integrate the *Rassengedanke* within the university curriculum concerns his support for an appointment in the field of *Ur- und Frühgeschichte* (Pre- and Early History). Wolfgang Soergel—the dean of mathematics and natural science and a Heidegger appointee—had urged hiring in this area, stressing its centrality with respect to the mission and goals of the "*völkisch* State."[44]

Heidegger endorsed Soergel's proposal unreservedly. In his letter to Minister Wacker, Heidegger stressed, "whomever we hire in this field must be able to *think and educate students historically and politically*." Thereby, Heidegger affirmed that, in the search for a suitable candidate, ideological considerations were paramount. Invoking the strictures of *Geschichtlichkeit*, or "authentic historicity," Heidegger cautioned that, were "historical and political" considerations neglected, the appointment would, in all likelihood, devolve into "*a simple concern with antiquities for the sake of filling up museums*."[45]

The problem was that, under the Third Reich, *Ur- und Frühgeschichte* was closely allied with the disciplines of *Volks-* and *Rassenkunde*, or Nazi "ethnography." Hence, the field was pervaded by racial and ideological themes. As Volker Losemann notes in *Nationalsozialismus und Antike*, to all intents and purposes, the fields of *Ur- und Frühgeschichte* had devolved into handmaidens of Nazi Germany's plans for eastward geopolitical expansion.[46]

In support of these goals, the study of *Urgeschichte* sought to reinforce a predatory and combative image of German identity. Inspired by Tacitus's *Germania*, it exalted the indomitable, warlike vigor of *Ur*-Germanic tribalism.

The myth of the *furor Teutonicus* held that the cultivation of primitive, martial virtues—"loyalty, conviviality, passion, and communalism"—had enabled the ancient German warrior bands to hand the Roman legions, led by the ill-fated Varus, their most costly and humiliating defeat to date in the legendary *Hermannsschlacht* (9 AD).[47] That Tacitus's reconstruction of the events had been predicated on legend and hearsay, rather than firsthand testimony, mattered little.

In Heidegger's reflections on the *Seinsfrage*, he demonstrated that he, too, had been seduced by the blandishments of primeval Teutonic glory. Lecturing on the "essence of truth" in 1933–34, he urged that *Wissenschaft* be reconceived to accord with the values of "archaic Germanic tribalism [*Urgermanischen Stammwesen*]": a disposition that, Heidegger claimed, must be restored to "Herrschaft," or "predominance."[48]

In a revealing letter of September 1930, Heidegger expressly disavowed the path of philosophical "moderation" and the "golden mean," urging instead reanimating the "*actuality of the Volk and of the tribes* [*die Wirklichkeit des Volkes und der Stämme*], in order to *restore their inherent, originary power.*"[49] That Heidegger's interlocutor, Elisabeth Blochmann, was Jewish renders these assertions doubly off-putting.

Heidegger's correspondence with Blochmann is riven with misgivings about contemporary German philosophy as, essentially, a *dead end*. Profoundly disillusioned with the prosaic results of professional philosophy, Heidegger concluded that the key to reenlivening the *Seinsfrage* was to realign it with the "originary powers [of] primal history." In a December 1932 letter to Werner Jaeger, Heidegger characterized this epistemological paradigm shift as a search for sources of "*subterranean philosophy* [*unterirdischen Philosophieren*] . . . *which have not yet been surmised.*"[50] Unquestionably, one of the primary motivations underlying Heidegger's pro-Nazi delirium stemmed from his understanding of the Third Reich—as he put it in the just-quoted letter to Blochmann—as a renewal of the "*inherent, originary power of the Volk and of the tribes.*"

Increasingly, Heidegger came to regard "archaic Germanic tribalism" as a valuable and originary wellspring of "subterranean" knowledge. The semantics of "unterirdischen Philosophieren" highlighted the *chthonic* and *rooted* dimension of this new approach, whose prospects and advantages—in comparison with the desiccated character of modern life and thought—were abundant.

The "Political Plato": Racial-Authoritarian Paideia

Heidegger's fascination with the potentials of "subterranean philosophy" emerged during his correspondence with the renowned German classicist Werner Jaeger. According to Frank Edler, the rapprochement between Heidegger and Jaeger concerned "the importance of the ancient Greeks for the German Revolution." Edler's remarks suggest that Jaeger's "Third Humanism," which was predicated on a political-authoritarian reinterpretation of the Greek polis, influenced Heidegger's conception of "another Beginning" (*anderer Anfang*). As Edler remarks, "Both Jaeger and Heidegger read the approaching [National Socialist] Revolution as a much wider phenomenon than the grabbing of power by a political party. They both saw the Revolution as a *turning point* which could provide *the seedbed for a different future*. Heidegger saw it as a turning toward the possibility of a new relationship to Being. Jaeger saw it as the possibility for establishing a 'Third Humanism.' "[51] Thus, in their perceptions of ancient Greece, Heidegger and Jaeger shared a disturbing "metapolitical" orientation: "disturbing" insofar as it coalesced with a racial-ideological view of the Greeks as an "Indo-Germanic" *Volk* or "proto-Aryans."

In an informative article on the politicization of German classics, the University of London scholar Katie Fleming, following Edler's lead, also examined the metapolitical bond that united Heidegger and Jaeger. According to Fleming, the two men "shared a belief in the messianic powers not only of Greece, but also of Germany as a mediator of the ancient culture." As Fleming concludes, "Seen through the lens of [National Socialist] debates on education and humanism, their writing on Paideia appears *irrecoverably tainted*."[52]

The idea of a racial association between Greeks and Germans dates from the nineteenth century. During the interwar period, however, this filiation developed into one of the cornerstones of Nazi ideology. Hitler, for example, exalted the "racial bond" (*Rasse-Einheit*) that united Greeks and Germans, two peoples who were engaged in a common "existential struggle." As he remarked in *Mein Kampf*, "The struggle that rages today is for very great aims. A millennial culture that encompasses Hellenism and Germanism is fighting for its existence."[53]

As Jonathan Chapoutot has shown in *Greeks, Romans and Germans*, among Nazi ideologues, the understanding of Greek antiquity exhibited a "remarkable consistency": "In the canon of Nazi ideology—from *Mein Kampf* to the construction of the great edifices of Nuremberg and throughout all the school textbooks and scholarly treatises published during the [Third Reich]—there was a coherent discourse on antiquity, which depicted the era as the first . . . and the only great epoch of Nordic Indo-Germanic history. Greco-Roman antiquity was reread and rewritten through a variety of media to forge a worldview that offered the reader, listener, spectator, student, and subject of the new Reich a vigorous and robust narrative of their past."[54]

During the 1920s, Jaeger's "Third Humanism" oversaw a racial-authoritarian reconfiguration of German classics. As William M. Calder comments in "Werner Jaeger and Richard Harder: An *Erklärung*," for Jaeger, "Greek acceptance of slavery alone was decisive. Indeed, Jaeger's Greek politics easily boil down to Homeric wisdom and Platonic authoritarianism. . . . It was the *Dienstbarkeit* of Jaeger's politics, . . . the preference for accommodation over reform[,] that made them unacceptable."[55]

Jaeger's approach, colloquially known as the "Political Plato," consciously abandoned the narrow philological concerns of an earlier generation of classics scholars, as represented, for example, by Jaeger's mentor, Ulrich von Wilamowitz-Moellendorf.[56] Instead, this Jaeger-led current sought to *actualize* Plato's corpus—hence the parallel with Heidegger's trademark "symptomatic" readings of ancient texts—by foregrounding the merits of "educational dictatorship" (*Erziehungsdiktatur*), "spiritual selection" (*geistige Auslese*), and the *Führerprinzip*. Along with many radical conservatives, Jaeger held that the only way to staunch modern democracy's degenerative tendencies was to entrust the reins of power to a knowledgeable elite: a guild of latter-day guardians and philosopher kings. Understandably, the model text in this regard was Plato's *Republic* or *Politeia*, tendentially translated into German as *Der Staat*.

Jaeger's celebration of "racial-authoritarian Paideia" highlighted the draconian, *Spartan* features of Plato's proposals for political reform in the *Republic*. Following Plato's lead, Jaeger exalted the merits of "guardianship," "breeding," and the "noble lie" propagated by the philosopher king for the good of the hoi polloi. As Jaeger asserted in "Die griechische Staatsethik im Zeitalter des Plato" (The Greek Attitude toward the State during the Age of Plato), "The State is prior to man, man is only man by virtue of belonging to the State."[57]

Following the Nazi seizure of power, Jaeger, like Heidegger, sought to intercede as a latter-day philosopher king, especially, with respect to the field of National Socialist pedagogy, or "tutelary Paideia." In order to ascend the National Socialist educational hierarchy, Jaeger allied himself with the Nazi philosopher and onetime Heidegger ally Ernst Krieck. In "Die Erziehung des politischen Menschen und die Antike" (The Education of Political Man and the Ancient World), which was published in Krieck's *Volk im Werden*, Jaeger exalted Plato as the "State-founder and Lawgiver" (*Staatsgründer und Gesetzgeber*) par excellence. "The special task with which history has confronted the present-day German *Volk*," remarked Jaeger, "*concerns the formation of the political human being. . . .* At present, when a new political type of human being is forming and shaping itself, we will have need of antiquity as a formative force."[58]

Heidegger's affinities with the "Political Plato" vogue were readily discernible in his May 1933 *Rektoratsrede* "The Self-Assertion of the German University." It was there that Heidegger first articulated his ontological understanding of National Socialism as a reenactment of the "Greek beginning": hence as a world-historical turning point in the history of Being. As Heidegger affirmed, "The beginning of our spiritual-historical existence . . . is the beginning [*Aufbruch*] of Greek philosophy. That is when, from the culture of one *Volk* and by the power of that *Volk*'s language, Western man rises up for the first time against the totality of what is and questions it and comprehends it as the *Being* that it is. For the Greeks, science was not merely a 'cultural artifact' [*Kulturgut*]. It was the innermost, formative capacity of the of ethno-political [*volklichstaatlichen*] Dasein in its totality."[59] Two months earlier, in a letter to his Freiburg University colleague, the art historian and Nazi Party member Kurt Bauch, Heidegger characterized the guidelines for university reform that he had formulated as a member of Ernst Krieck's *Kulturpolitsche Arbeitsgruppe deutscher Hochschullehrer* as a "Platonic Program."[60]

Jaeger, for his part, was deeply impressed by Heidegger's portrayal of the Greek "Anfang" in the *Rektoratsrede* as a "spiritual-historical" touchstone with respect to political present. Jaeger sought to republish "The Self-Assertion of the German University" in the "Third Humanism's" flagship journal, *Die Antike: Zeitschrift für Kunst und Kultur des klassischen Altertums*, which Jaeger had founded in 1925. However, for unknown reasons, his efforts were unsuccessful.[61]

Another attestation of the Jaeger camp's enthusiasm for Heidegger's demarche in the *Rektoratsrede* emerged in the florid review by the political Platonist and Jaeger ally Richard Harder, which appeared in *Gnomon*: the prestigious classics journal that Jaeger founded in 1925 to spread the Third Humanist gospel. (After Jaeger emigrated to the United States in 1936, Harder

succeeded Jaeger as *Gnomon*'s editor in chief.) Praising Heidegger as the "leading philosopher of our time," Harder asserted that, in the *Rektoratsrede*, "by
virtue of the comparison with Greek thought, German thinking acquires enhanced power and esteem. Once again, the radical new Beginning [an allusion
to the Nazi seizure of power] benefits by contact with founders of Western heritage."[62] Heidegger's receptiveness to the "Political Plato" paradigm stood in
stark contrast to his subsequent denigration of Plato, in "Plato's Doctrine of
Truth" (1940), as the founder of "Western metaphysics"—hence as the initiator
of *Seinsvergessenheit*.[63]

During the early 1930s, as confidence in the Weimar Republic's staying
power waned, Heidegger explored the virtues of political Platonism in his
lecture course *On the Essence of Truth: Plato's Cave Allegory* (1931–32). Heidegger's reflections on Platonism's potential as a ground for political authority
reveal much about his political self-understanding at this point.

Heidegger was especially impressed by the typology of the "guardians" that
Plato had outlined in the *Republic*, book 2. On the basis of this discussion,
Heidegger endorsed guardianship as a model of political *Herrschaft* and sought
to reconcile this idea with his own understanding of the entwinement of politics
and philosophy.

Hence, in *On the Essence of Truth*, Heidegger, aping Plato, insisted that "philosophers must become guardians [*Wächter*]" and that "the authentic guardians
of the unity of human being-with-one-another in the polis must be philosophers
[*philosophierende Menschen*]."[64] Heidegger interpreted the Weimar Republic's
political unraveling as a repetition of Plato's "luxurious polis" or "city of pigs"
in the *Republic*, book 2. In the *Republic*, Plato had constructed the "city of
pigs" as a parable of *negative fraternity*. Its inhabitants' aspirations failed to
rise above the crass pursuit of, as Plato phrased it, "perfumed oils, incense,
prostitutes, and pastries" (373a). Thus, the "city of pigs" was a veritable *anti-
polis*, in which comity and civic harmony are destroyed by appetite, lascivious-
ness, and unbridled egotism (372b).

Although the guardians were an invaluable source of order and authority in
Plato's Kalliopolis, or "best city," at one point, Plato-Socrates, owing to their
servility, mockingly likened them to a pack of "well-bred dogs": creatures who
are "swift to overtake the enemy when they see him and strong too, if, when
they see him, they have to fight with him" (375e). In Plato's portrayal, the
guardians might be accurately described as "proto-Schmittians," insofar as

their outstanding attribute was their capacity to distinguish "friend" from "enemy." As Plato, in keeping with the humorous "well-bred dog" analogy, explained, "a dog, whenever he sees a stranger, is angry; conversely, when he sees an acquaintance, he welcomes him, although the one has never done him any harm, nor the other any good."[65] Plato regarded the guardians' innate ability to distinguish *Freund* from *Feind* as indispensable, since it prevented these vicious "attack dogs" from redirecting their ferocity toward the Kalliopolis itself.

Plato concluded his account of the guardians by appending a sardonic twist. Mocking the pretensions of his philosophical rivals, the Sophists, Socrates declaims, "Your 'dog' is a true philosopher!" To assuage the confusion of his youthful interlocutors, Glaucon and Adeimantus, Socrates explains that the guardian, as a "well-bred dog," qualifies as a "philosopher" since he relies on the criterion of "knowledge" in order to distinguish "friend" from "enemy." Any animal that "determines what he likes and dislikes by the test of *knowledge*," continued Socrates, must be regarded as "a lover of learning"—hence as a "philosopher" (376b,c).

In *On the Essence of Truth*, Heidegger's discussion of the guardians' role seemed strangely tone deaf to the satirical ambivalences of Plato's account. Although, as we have seen, Plato's depiction of the guardians as "well-bred dogs"—hence, as *philosophical imposters*—was suffused with ridicule, Heidegger, for his part, seemed to approach their role in the Kalliopolis with the utmost seriousness.

Plato viewed the guardians as a Praetorian Guard *avant la lettre*. Hence, the education that he prescribed for them was *narrowly Spartan*: it was confined to the subaltern domains of physical culture, music, and art. In keeping with these limitations, Plato ruled out exposing the guardians to the *higher epistemological forms* of "dialectic" and "pure reasoning" (*noein*), a level of instruction that he reserved for "authentic rulers," that is, the "philosopher kings." Thus, in contrast with Heidegger's reading, Plato, in keeping with the "well-trained dogs" analogy, insisted that the guardians were not persons "who have an aptitude for philosophizing."[66]

Heidegger, conversely, depicted the guardians as a more elevated and intellectually exalted breed. Hence, he praised them as "philosophierende Menschen," "men who philosophize." As Heidegger affirmed, "The order of domination [*Herrschaft*] in the state must be *suffused with men who philosophize*: men who, from the deepest . . . knowing, establish the standards and rules, and who disclose the paths of decision [*Bahnen der Entscheidung*]. As men who philosophize, they must be capable . . . of *knowing what man is and how things stand with respect to his Being and capacity-for-Being* [*Sein-können*]"—attributes that Plato had reserved for the "philosopher kings."[67]

In sum, Heidegger transposed the attributes and traits of philosopher kingship to a caste—the guardians—that, in the *Republic*, Plato had denigrated ironically as "well-bred dogs."

Another example of Heidegger's indebtedness to Jaeger's "Third Humanism" concerned his endorsement, in the *Rektoratsrede*, of three forms of "service [*Dienste*]": *Arbeitsdienst* (labor service), *Wehrdienst* (military service), and *Wissensdienst* (knowledge service). Heidegger's schema reprised the threefold hierarchy outlined in Plato's *Republic*: (1) philosopher kings, (2) guardians, and (3) workers. Although Heidegger would become an unremitting critic of Plato's *Ideenlehre*—in "Plato's Doctrine of Truth" (1930/1942), he characterized Plato's theory of Ideas as the downfall of Western philosophy—during the early 1930s, he was profoundly enamored of the draconian-authoritarian features of Plato's Spartan-influenced political doctrine.

"Spiritual Leadership"

Heidegger's indebtedness to the "Political Plato" model also emerged in his exaltation of "geistige Führung," or "spiritual leadership." It was an orientation that manifested itself in Heidegger's own aspirations to philosopher kingship: "to lead the leader" (*den Führer zu führen*), following the precedent of Plato's ill-fated entanglement with the tyrant Dionysius at Syracuse.[68]

Heidegger's attraction to the paradigm of "geistige Führung" reflected his growing attraction to the mystique of the Stefan George-*Kreis*. Among George-*Kreis* disciples, "spiritual leadership" had gradually metamorphosed into a quasi-official credo and raison d'être. The publication of Max Kommerell's study *The Poet as Führer in the Age of German Classicism* (1928) signified a crucial way station in these developments.[69]

The appearance of Kommerell's book represented a spiritual turning point for Heidegger. It opened his eyes with respect to the transformative, demiurgic potentials that were lodged in the model of "geistige Führung." The influence of the "spiritual leadership" paradigm was evident in the new, political-poetological typology that Heidegger developed during the mid-1930s. This typology or scheme impelled

Heidegger to exalt the demiurgic capacities of "poets, thinkers, and statesmen" as founders of the "historical Dasein of a *Volk*." As Heidegger affirmed in *Hölderlin's Hymns "Germanien" and "Der Rhein,"* "The primordial, historical epoch of *Völker* is the epoch *of Poets, Thinkers, and Statesmen* [*Dichter, Denker, und Staatsschöpfer*]. It is they who authentically ground and establish the historical Dasein of a *Volk*."[70]

One of the reasons that Kommerell's *The Poet as Führer in the Age of German Classicism* became so important for Heidegger concerned Kommerell's interpretation of Hölderlin as an unrivaled prophet of German nationalism: as "the most *German* poet of *German* fate" (*deutschesten Dichter deutschesten Schicksals*) and as the "clarion of heroic reality" (*Künder der heldischen Wirklichkeit*).[71]

During the 1930s and 1940s, Heidegger and Kommerell developed an intense spiritual camaraderie that was reflected in their correspondence.[72] A cursory glance at Heidegger's lectures on Hölderlin's hymns "Germanien" and "Der Rhein" (1934–35) attests to the transformative impact that Kommerell's view of Hölderlin as a "spiritual leader" had on Heidegger. It permanently altered his understanding of the import and potential of *geistige Führung*.[73] Thereby, Kommerell's approach complemented and reinforced the spiritual elitism of Jaeger's Third Humanism.

The ideal of "spiritual leadership" had been assiduously cultivated by members of the Stefan George-*Kreis* during the lead-up to the Great War. Attuned to the growing mood of civilizational crisis, and in an effort to cultivate a following among *Jugendbewegung* circles, circa 1910, George and his disciples began to distance themselves from their earlier "aestheticism." Increasingly, they defined themselves as the emissaries of a supersensible "spiritual state" whose mission it was to transpose the poet's "Reich," or "realm," from the plane of "aesthetic form" to "sensible reality." Kurt Hildebrandt, the George-*Kreis*'s resident Plato expert, described the cenacle's new self-understanding as follows: "Instead of a circle of readers, now a circle of disciples would find its fulfillment in forming a *spiritual state*, which will gradually penetrate the outlying regions in ever farther reaches."[74]

Hildebrandt played a key role in popularizing the George-*Kreis* gospel of "spiritual leadership" among members of the German classics guild. As Hildebrandt commented in his protofascist monograph *Plato: The Struggle of Spirit for Power* (*Platon: Der Kampf des Geistes um die Macht*; 1933), "With respect to what, today, goes under the name of the Total State, there is no more perfect model than Plato's *Republic*."[75]

Another prophet of the "spiritual leadership" model was the George-*Kreis* hagiographer Friedrich Wolters. "It belongs to the nature of *spiritual* power," avowed Wolters, "that it seeks to fashion the physical realm after its own image, to subject it to a design of its own making." According to Wolters, the desired transformation of reality would be accomplished by a "geistige Tat": a "spiritual deed" that emanated from the "Herrscher," or "sovereign."[76]

Needless to say, George-*Kreis* acolytes regarded George—whom they were obligated to address as "der Meister"—as the ultimate spiritual "sovereign," or "Herrscher." Correspondingly, they viewed George's *Dichtung* as the consummate "spiritual deed." George, for his part, regarded himself as the "Herrscher" (ruler) of a "spiritual empire"—a "geistiges Reich"—and "as a politician of the spirit."[77] George invariably referred to the Circle's publications as "spirit books" (*Geistbücher*), proclaiming that "*spirit books are political books.*"[78]

One representative of the German classics guild who attentively registered Hildebrandt's and Wolter's efforts to define the parameters of "geistige Führung" was Werner Jaeger.

Since the time of the Great War, the George-*Kreis*'s understanding of "geistige Führung" had been infused with a commitment to the values of German nationalism. George-*Kreis* loyalists lauded Hölderlin as a poet of the *Vaterland* and as the "Dichter der Deutschen." In support of this interpretation, they invoked Hölderlin's passing allusion to his self-professed "vaterländische Umkehr," or "turn to the fatherland."[79]

The catalyst for the reading of Hölderlin as a prophet of German destiny was Norbert von Hellingrath. In 1915, von Hellingrath, in a lecture, characterized the Germans as "the *Volk* of Hölderlin." He exalted Hölderlin as "*the most German of Germans*," a "seer" who had forecast the advent of "secret Germany"— a George-*Kreis* signature that Heidegger incorporated within the eschatological framework of *Seinsgeschichte*. In von Hellingrath's view, Hölderlin's mystical insight into the "German essence" made him the prophet of a "secret *Reich*."[80]

The topos of "secret Germany" was integral to the George-*Kreis*'s self-understanding as a coterie of "geistige Führer," or "spiritual leaders." George's final poetry collection, *Das neue Reich*, was published in 1928, five years prior to the advent of the Third Reich. Five years earlier, in 1923, the conservative revolutionary publicist Arthur Moeller van den Bruck published *Das dritte Reich*, in which he forecast Germany's rebirth as a bellicose *Volksgemeinschaft* and central European hegemon. In retrospect, it would be foolish to gainsay the prophetic quality of these anticipations of a "secret Reich," a "neues Reich," and a "drittes Reich"—all of which emerged in polemical opposition to the Weimar Republic, whose legitimacy the German Right had contested from its inception.

During the 1930s, Heidegger enthusiastically endorsed von Hellingrath's and Kommerell's readings of Hölderlin qua prophet of German renewal. On the basis of this poetic-eschatological template, Heidegger interpreted the Third Reich's advent as an *Ereignis* that signaled the fulfillment of German destiny. In *Hölderlin's Hymns "Germanien" and "Der Rhein,"* Heidegger, aping George-*Kreis* rhetoric, recurred to the trope of "secret Germany." "The great 'secret' that carries the entire historical Dasein of the *Volk* within itself," affirmed Heidegger, "is announced by the poet." Thereby, he embraced the George-*Kreis*'s reading of Hölderlin qua soothsayer of Germany's resurrection.[81]

Heidegger revisited the leitmotif of "secret Germany" as he reflected on the upsurge of German national sentiment during the Wars of Liberation. Along with many Germans nationalists, Heidegger regarded this era as a critical turning point in the consciousness of German unity. Heidegger perceived important parallels between this period and the resurgence of national "resolve" under National Socialism. Both epochs of German renewal had succeeded periods of national humiliation, thereby attesting to "secret Germany's" resilience. In Heidegger's eyes, these developments confirmed Hölderlin's singularity as a prophet of German rebirth:

> At the turn of the eighteenth and nineteenth centuries, the Germans were anything but free. The unity of the old Reich had dissolved into a disorganized and rootless *Kleinstaaterei*. In 1806–7, Prussia, which was the only fully autonomous German state, was defeated by Napoleon and his allies. Nevertheless, despite this political impotence, despite this political fragmentation, despite this impoverishment of the *Volk*, there survived—*and there survives today*—a *secret Germany*. Under conditions of inner affliction and of external bondage, there arose a new sense of freedom. This confirms that the meaning of freedom was reconceived and implanted in the knowing and will of the Germans.[82]

Führersein: "Self-Sacrifice" and "Proximity to Death"

Under the Third Reich, a cottage industry arose honoring Hölderlin as the "poète maudit" of German national self-assertion. The groundwork for this interpretive approach had been laid by the pioneering readings of von Hellingrath and Kommerell. In the essay "Kriegskamerad Hölderlin," Norbert Rath distilled the gist of the National Socialist reading of Hölderlin as follows: "Hölderlin's texts were refunctioned as advertisements for submission to fate and self-sacrifice—gobbledygook in support of the '*Deutschland-Mythos.*' . . . Hölderlin's poetry was wrenched from its original context and elevated to the dizzying heights of mythical soothsaying. Recast as a *priest, a seer, a prophet, a lawgiver, and a warrior*, 'Hölderlin-as-Führer' was 'conscripted' for war on behalf of another Führer, fulfilling his 'ideological duty' by glorifying sacrifice and downfall [*Opfer und Untergang*]. . . . Thereby, his poetry shriveled to material for the embellishment of 'total war.' "[83]

Heidegger's understanding of Hölderlin qua prophet of *völkisch* regeneration owed much to Kommerell's views, in *The Poet as Führer*, on the imperatives of "spiritual leadership." Accordingly, in *Hölderlin's Hymns "Germanien" and "Der Rhein,"* Heidegger feted Hölderlin as the "poet of German destiny" (*Dichter des deutschen Schicksals*): a seer and clairvoyant who spoke the "primordial language of a *Volk*" (*Ursprache eines Volkes*).[84]

Following Kommerell's lead, Heidegger insisted that the *Volk*'s apotheosis was forged in the crucible of "war" and "struggle." Their respective Hölderlin interpretations highlighted the role that *Heldentum* (heroism) played in catalyzing Germany's "national awakening." As Kommerell observed in *The Poet as Führer*, "The apotheosis of the entire *Volk* in war is the secret wellspring of Germany's future. . . . Only then does the *Volk* attain the standing attributed to it by Hölderlin: *to wander among the gods, and thereby engender heroes.*"[85]

In *Hölderlin's Hymns "Germanien" and "Der Rhein,"* Heidegger followed suit. Exalting "death-in-war" as the founding event of the *Volksgemeinschaft*, Heidegger perpetuated the intoxications of the "war experience" (*Kriegserlebnis*) as forged by the First World War's "community of the trenches" (*Gemeinschaft der Schützengraben*). By claiming that "death" and a "readiness for sacrifice" place the individual in the "metaphysical proximity to the Unconditioned" (*metaphysische Nähe zum Unbedingten*), Heidegger embraced the "metaphysics-of-death" that was integral to the fascist *Weltanschauung*:

> The *most original community* [*ursprünglichste Gemeinschaft*] originates . . . in situations in which proximity to death [*die Nähe des Todes*] places each of us in the same proximity to nothingness. . . . Death and a readiness for sacrifice [*der Tod und die Bereitschaft zu seinem Opfer*] first create the space for community [*Raum der Gemeinschaft*] out of which comradeship develops. . . . Comradeship also develops from *Angst* when it is conceived in terms of . . . the highest metaphysical

proximity to the Unconditioned . . . when death [is understood] as a free sacrifice that challenges the core of individual's Dasein.[86]

Following Kommerell's example, Heidegger lauded Hölderlin as an avatar of "geistiger Führertum." In his discussion of "the being of demigods and the poet's calling" (*Das Seyn der Halbgötter und die Berufung des Dichters*), Heidegger elevated the *Dichter-Führer* to the realm of the "Halbgötter," or "demigods." In this capacity, he assigned them the sacred mission of mediating between "gods and men." "The true and only Führer," claimed Heidegger, "by virtue of his Being [*Seyn*], points the way to the realm of the demigods. *Führersein* [Being-a-Führer], is a form of finite Being, a 'fate.' "[87] As Heidegger uttered these words in winter 1935, Germany was entering its third year of dictatorial rule. The political message conveyed by Heidegger's unsubtle paeans to the virtues of *Führertum* and *Führung* was not hard to discern. Heidegger's words were hardly those of a spiritual *Widerstandskämpfer*.

Heidegger dedicated "Hölderlin and the Essence of Poetry"—his first major publication on Hölderlin—to the memory of von Hellingrath, who perished in 1916 in the battle of Verdun. The essay appeared in 1936, in honor of the twentieth anniversary of von Hellingrath's death. In the epigraph that preceded the essay, Heidegger urged German youth to honor the memory of this "fallen hero." As Claudia Albert has shown in her essay on "Kulturarbeit" under National Socialism, by 1936, dedications to von Hellingrath, such as the one that preceded "Hölderlin and the Essence of Poetry," had become obligatory emblems of solidarity with the Nazi cause.[88] Heidegger's patriotic epigraph was suppressed in all postwar editions of "Hölderlin and the Essence of Poetry," including its republication in the *Gesamtausgabe*, notwithstanding Heidegger's misleading statement that "the commentaries on several of Hölderlin's poems that were previously published individually have been regathered *unaltered* [*unverändert*]."[89]

Heidegger published "Hölderlin and the Essence of Poetry" in *Das innere Reich*, a title that expressly invoked the glories of "spiritual *Führung*." *Das innere Reich* was a "Nazi-Zeitschrift" whose "spiritual mission" was to provide cultural legitimation for the Third Reich and its policies.[90] In the inaugural issue, the editorial committee defined the journal's mission in terms of the complementary aims of "das innere Reich" and the "das dritte Reich." The editors explained that both of these tropes derived their strength from the "primeval *Reich* of the German soul [*Urreiche des deutschen Seele*]":

A miracle has taken place! The Germans have become a single and united *Volk*. . . . Providence has inscribed this miracle in the heart and the force of every German man who stood shoulder to shoulder among millions in times when the inner meaning of sacrifice, obedience, and duty [*Opfer, Obrigkeit, und Pflicht*] . . . remained unclear. . . . Today, however, we recognize that, under the *Führung* of Adolf Hitler, the *Volk* . . . must restore, whatever the cost, what it means to live in a genuine *Vaterland* . . . and thereby, simultaneously, to do justice to the primordial Reich of the German soul [*Urreiche des deutschen Seele*].[91]

From *Das Neue Reich* to the Third Reich

Reviewing *The Poet as Führer in the Age of German Classicism* in 1930, Walter Benjamin, although not entirely unsympathetic to Kommerell's demarche, observed laconically that, in Kommerell's monograph, "the monk's cowl hangs next to a steel helmet [*Stahlhelm*]."[92]

Benjamin's insight proved to be inordinately prescient. As the Nazis consolidated their grip on power, the ideological nexus between George-*Kreis* loyalists and the Third Reich intensified. As Edith Landmann—one of the few women participants in what was otherwise decidedly a *Männerbund*—noted in retrospect, many of George's disciples had long harbored political views that accorded with those of the Nazis.[93] Among many of George's followers, it seemed obvious that the Third Reich, as a self-described *Führerstaat*, embodied the synthesis of *Geist und Macht* toward which they had long aspired.

Was the George-*Kreis*'s chauvinistic understanding of German "destiny" and German "essence" predicated on race thinking? In light of the Circle's ever-changing cast of participants, and in view of the Master's numerous Jewish followers, simple answers to this question are best avoided.

Nevertheless, in an important essay on the George-*Kreis* and National Socialism, the historian Peter Hoffmann claimed that the Circle's notion of "spiritual leadership," as developed by Kommerell and others, "rivaled and paralleled that of the National Socialists." Hoffmann pointed out that it was George himself who, following World War I, took the lead in popularizing the notion of *geistiger Führertum*, whose long-term consequences proved so destructive. As one commentator has remarked, "George's call for a Messianic leader or Führer who would redeem Germany was increasingly honored by the thousands of young men who translated his words into support for Hitler."[94] Hoffmann reminded readers that, "between 1916 and 1934, no fewer than 18 books written by members and associates of the George Circle . . . carried a swastika on their covers and title pages."[95]

Hence, it should not come as a surprise that the George-*Kreis*'s attraction to the blandishments of "spiritual leadership" was accompanied by a growing commitment to the lexicon of race thinking as an integral component of its plans for a "secret Germany." As the editors of a recent anthology on the politics of the George-*Kreis* have confirmed, "The most ominous transformation of the concept of Germanness in the Circle . . . was its increasing preoccupation with the issue of race."[96]

Among George-*Kreis* associates, the Master's growing openness to racial thinking was something of an open secret. On one occasion, George remarked that the "white race" (*die weiße Art*) had to be saved from the "yellow apes" of Asia as well as from miscegenation with African peoples. George blamed French "decline" on the proliferation of interracial marriage, which, adverting to racial terminology, he characterized as "Blutschmach" (blood-shame). When Kurt Hildebrandt published a study of racial degeneration, *Norm und Entartung des Menschen* (1920), George rose to Hildebrandt's defense in the face of objections that were raised by Edgar Salin, one of the Circle's Jewish members.[97]

Following the Nazi seizure of power, Frank Mehnert, who had been George's protégé and companion during the Master's final years, demanded from Nazi leaders a greater role for "secret Germany." Lecturing at the University of Tübingen, another George disciple, Woldemar Uxkull-Gyllenband, informed his audience that the *Führerprinzip* and a "heroic worldview" had always been the core precepts of George's "vision," thereby suggesting that the Third Reich was the realization of the Master's prophecies concerning the advent of a "Neues Reich."[98]

Notwithstanding the Circle's numerous Jewish adherents, anti-Semitism—especially among the George intimates Wolters and Kommerell—had long been rife. Hildebrandt confirmed this fact, matter-of-factly, in 1935, observing, "Already during the [First] World War, George was convinced, both politically and intellectually, that the role of the Jews was *corrosive*."[99]

By foregrounding the fascist themes of "war, visionary leadership, and artistic and military heroism," George's final poetry collection, *Das neue Reich*, underwent what might be characterized as a "military-nationalist" turn. As such, it was a textbook example of what Walter Benjamin termed the "aesthetics of violence." Inspired by von Hellingrath's reading of Hölderlin, *Das neue Reich* prophesied a new era of *völkisch* and national renewal. George's glorification of a "secret-Germany-in-arms" foreshadowed Heidegger's kindred, ontological-historical preoccupation with German rebirth through the powers of "geistige Führung."[100]

The esteem in which Heidegger held George's *Dichtung*—and *Das neue Reich*, in particular—is clear from Heidegger's 1939 lecture course *On Herder's Treatise "On the Origins of Language,"* in which he praised *Das neue Reich* for having anticipated the "Übergang" (transition) from the "first Beginning" to "another Beginning."[101]

George died in December 1933. During the ten months preceding his death, he successfully fended off the efforts of Nazi cultural potentates to enlist his support for the "New Reich." Ultimately, however, George found it impossible to resist taking credit for Nazism's political "success." In May 1933, upon declining the presidency of the Prussian Academy of Poetry, George, in a letter to the Nazi minister of education, Bernhard Rust, proudly staked his claim as National Socialism's "spiritual" progenitor. "I don't deny," George avowed, "having fathered the new national movement, nor shall I choose to withhold my spiritual support."[102]

In 1930, upon reading volume 1 of *Mein Kampf*, Kommerell dismissed it as "narrowminded and uncouth." Upon further reflection, however, he qualified this negative judgment, observing that the book's "instincts are often sound and correct": "It is an achievement that merits respect. And in our age of indecision, to clench one's fist in this way is always a plus. Hopefully, I will soon get hold of volume two."[103] Kommerell's ambivalences vis-à-vis National Socialist rule remained unresolved until 1939, when he elected to join the NSDAP.

Following the Nazi seizure of power, Benjamin, in response to the growing intimacy between George-*Kreis* acolytes and Hitler dictatorship, appositely remarked, "If ever God has punished the prophet by fulfilling his prophecy, then that is the case with George."[104]

Ultimately, the differences between Heidegger's "spiritual National Socialism" and the Nazi ideological mainstream were trivial and insignificant. This is true insofar as Heidegger consistently strove to fuse "spirit" with the central precepts of the *Rassengedanke*: "Volk," "Blut," "Gemeinschaft," and so forth. The Nazi leadership, for its part, was entirely at ease with Heidegger's efforts to reconcile "spirit" with "race." As a *Weltanschauung* averse to rigid orthodoxy, National Socialist "doctrine" had always been a multifarious hodgepodge, persistently subject to compromise and emendation. Hence, on 30 January 1933, when the "hour of decision" (Spengler) struck, Nietzscheans, Neo-Hegelians, Social Darwinists, Nordicists, race mystics, and biological determinists began avidly competing for intellectual leadership.

When the dust cleared, nearly all of those who had striven for position of ideological *Führung* were left by the wayside, since, in the Führer's eyes, conflicts over doctrinal purity mattered little. As Hannah Arendt observed in the *Origins of Totalitarianism*, "Total domination does not allow for free initiative in any field of life, for any activity that is not entirely predictable."[105] As a rule, intraparty ideological squabbles were settled on the basis of *Machtpolitik*. Innovative theoretical contributions were largely beside the point.

Jaeger and Heidegger: "The Poet as Legislator"

Werner Jaeger outlined his conception of the "poet-as-legislator" (*der Dichter als Gesetzgeber*) in a 1932 essay on the Spartan poet Tyrtaeus. Faithful to Kommerell's notion of "the poet as Führer," Jaeger extolled Tyrtaeus's "war poetry" as the "foundational charter of the Spartan *Machtstaat*."[106] In December 1932, Jaeger sent a copy of his Tyrtaeus essay to Heidegger. In Heidegger's response, he praised Jaeger's recovery of "subterranean philosophy." According to Heidegger, by abandoning the strictures of arid and lifeless "philology," Jaeger had succeeded in grasping "the reality and strength . . . of Greek Dasein."[107]

Jaeger's Plato interpretation set the stage for Heidegger's apotheosis of the "Greek beginning." It reinforced Heidegger's conviction that philosophers could—and should—"rule" (*herrschen*). Similarly, Kommerell's treatment of Hölderlin lent support to Heidegger's view that the poet's true vocation was to become a "spiritual legislator."

The essay by Jaeger that Heidegger singled out for praise in their correspondence, "Tyrtaeus and True *Aretē*," exemplified the *völkisch*-ideological reading of Sparta that was popular among the Nazis. It reflected an interpretive trend widespread among *Althistoriker* (ancient historians) alleging that ancient Spartans and contemporary Germans shared a common racial heritage. According to this view, both Spartans and Germans were descended from the ancient Dorians, who, in turn, were arbitrarily classified as a "Proto-Germanic" *Volk*.

In "The Classics and the Second World War," Volker Losemann detailed the various ways that the racial-authoritarian image of Sparta as a precursor of the

Nazi *Machtstaat* informed Jaeger's work. According to Losemann, "Jaeger's way of characterizing the Greek tribes, which ultimately resembled a racial typology, was not far removed from the basic precepts of Nazi ideology. In *Paideia* [1934], the section entitled 'Spartan State Education' is a eulogy to 'the ethical greatness of the [Aryan] Dorians.' . . . Jaeger praised the Dorian 'Master Race' and the fifth-century B.C.E. poet Pindar as personifications of the 'ideal of the blonde, high-racial type of man': . . . of the 'aristocratic teaching about blood' and the Ideal of the Hellenic racial aristocracy."[108]

A parallel set of ideological themes suffused "Tyrtaeus and True *Aretē*," which was published in 1932, two years prior to *Paideia*, vol. 1. In the essay, Jaeger expressly lionized Tyrtaeus's war poetry as the "foundation charter of the Spartan *Machtstaat*." With one eye fixated on the historical present, Jaeger attributed Sparta's greatness to its indomitable spirit of "racial and communal solidarity." In Sparta, Jaeger continued, "citizen rights" were based on one's "status as a soldier." Tyrtaeus, to his credit, "was the first writer to describe this ideal of the citizen-soldier that, at a later point, came to fruition in the Spartan educational system." According to Jaeger, Tyrtaeus's outstanding contribution to the evolution of Greek Paideia was having "recasted the Homeric ideal of heroic *aretē* as the heroism of *patriotism* [*Vaterlandsliebe*]." Thus, in his dual capacity as *Dichter-Staatsgründer*, Tyrtaeus's goal was "to create an entire Volk and an entire State of heroes [*ein Volk, ein ganzer Staat von Helden*]." "Death is beautiful," Jaeger gushed, "if it is a hero's death; and to die for one's country is a hero's death."[109]

Following Jaeger's lead in "Tyrtaeus and True *Aretē*" and echoing Kommerell's emphasis, in *The Poet as Führer in the Age of German Classicism*, on "the apotheosis of the *Volk* in war," Heidegger, too, exalted "death-in-war" as a paragon of "Eigentlichkeit" (authenticity): as the ultimate expression of "patriotism," or *Vaterlandsliebe*.

One reason that Jaeger's Tyrtaeus essay resonated powerfully with Heidegger was that, in *Being and Time*, alluding to World War I's "community of the trenches," Heidegger had lauded "Being-toward-death" (*Sein-zum-Tode*) as the high point of "authenticity." Moreover, in his discussion of "The Basic Constitution of Historicity" in Division II, Heidegger highlighted the link between "Being-toward-death" and "Heroism," a nexus that crystallized in "authentic Dasein's" capacity for "choosing-a-Hero" (*einen Helden zu wählen*). As Heidegger declaimed, "The possibility that Dasein may choose its Hero is

grounded existentially in anticipatory decisiveness [*Entschlossenheit*]. In decisiveness, one first makes a choice that makes one free for the struggle of loyally
following in the footsteps [*die kämpfende Nachfolge und Treue*] of that which
can be repeated."[110] Thereby, Heidegger anticipated Jaeger's thesis in the Tyrtaeus essay concerning the paramount role that sacrificial death had played in
ancient Sparta.

The discussion of "Being-toward-death" was Heidegger's way of keeping
alive the "warrior ethos" of World War I. The "metaphysics of death" conditioned the worldview of the numerous paramilitary veterans' organizations that
had proliferated after the war: the *Freikorps*, the *Stahlhelm*, and, in Italy, Mussolini's *Fasci di Combattimento*. As the 1920s wore on, these groups provided
the "human matériel" that was essential for the rise of European fascism.

In the eyes of Herbert Marcuse, the fascist resonances of Heideggerian
Being-toward-death were unmistakable. In Marcuse's view, the "existential"
coined by Heidegger in *Being and Time* reprised "fascism's and Nazism's emphasis on sacrifice as an end-in-itself." As the Frankfurt School philosopher and
former Heidegger student continued, "There is a famous phrase by Ernst Jünger,
the Nazi writer, who speaks of the necessity of sacrifice 'on the edge of the
abyss,' or 'on the edge of nothingness' [*am Rande des Nichts oder am Rande des
Abgrunds*]. In other words, a sacrifice that is good because it is a sacrifice, and
because it is freely chosen . . . by the individual. Heidegger's notion [of Being-
toward-death] recalls the battle cry of the fascist Futurists: *Viva le muerte!*"[111]

In *Being and Time*, one variant of "Being-toward-death"—"Vorlaufen-zum-
Tode," or "anticipation-toward-death"—rendered the martial semantics of
Heidegger's existential ontology even more explicit. "Vorlaufen-zum-Tode"
conjured trench-warfare imagery of "going over the top": making a conscious
"decision" (*Entscheidung*) to "sally forth" (*Vorlaufen*) in order to meet one's
"fate" *heroically*. In *Historical Destiny and National Socialism in Heidegger's
"Being and Time,"* Johannes Fritsche proposed parallels between Heideggerian
"Vorlaufen-zum-Tode" and the myth of the "heroes of Langemarck," who,
according to legend, marched to their death en masse while singing the
"Deutschland-Lied."[112]

In *The Jargon of Authenticity*, Adorno, echoing Marcuse's comments concerning the parallels between fundamental ontology and the fascist "cult of
death," remarked, "Death, as the existential horizon of Dasein, . . . becomes the
Absolute in the form of an Icon. Here, there is a regression to the *cult of death*.

The 'jargon' has from the beginning gotten along well with military matters."
Adorno recalled a "female Heidegger devotée" who, during the 1920s, praised
Heidegger for having reconnected German youth with the experience of death.
"Now, as earlier," observed Adorno, "[Max] Horkheimer's response remains
valid: . . . [General] Ludendorff accomplished the same goal much more effec-
tively."[113]

Heidegger reinforced the semantic link between the existential analytic and
the *Kriegerlebnis* of the "Front Generation" by foregrounding "Generation" as
a constituent feature of authentic "historicity." The Great War had been the
defining experience of Heidegger's own "Generation." In *Being and Time*,
Heidegger sought to resuscitate the "warrior ethos" of the *Frontsoldaten* by affirming that only in "*Kampf* does the power of *destiny* become free. Dasein's
fateful *destiny* in and with its 'Generation' consummates the full authentic his-
toricizing of Dasein."[114]

In the wake of World War I, the idea of what it meant to be German changed.
It no longer signified an elective decision or a voluntary commitment. Instead,
as Heidegger's inordinate emphasis on "fate" and "destiny" suggested, among
proponents of the *Volksbegriff*, to be "German" meant belonging to a *Schicksalgemeinschaft*, a "community of fate."

By glorifying the ideas of *Generation*, *Gemeinschaft*, and *Schicksal* (destiny)
in *Being and Time*, Heidegger perpetuated the bellicose mind-set of the
Schützengraben Gemeinschaft—the "community of the trenches"—that had
been forged amid the First World War's "storms of steel."[115] His adumbration of
Geschichtlichkeit anticipated the "*Gemeinschaft* mania" that, a few years later,
would become one of the defining features of Nazi rule.

Gemeinschaftsempfang was the term that the Nazis used to describe the requirement that Germans listen to radio addresses that were held by the Führer
and other NSDAP leaders. *Gemeinschaftslager*—also known as *Lehrerlager*—
referred to the ideological training camps that teachers were required to attend.
As a rule, such *Lager* included a mandatory *Wehrsport*, or "military exercise,"
component.[116] The goal of *Gemeinschaft* training was to weld the various strata
of German society into a racially homogeneous *Volksgemeinschaft*, in accordance with the Nazi slogan, "Ein Volk, Ein Reich, Ein Führer."

In Heidegger's capacity as *Führer-Rektor*, he was obsessed with defining the
nature of the "true *Volksgemeinschaft*." Rejecting the traditional ideal of "Wissenschaft" (scholarship), Heidegger reconceived the university under National

Socialism as an "erzieherische Lebensgemeinschaft": an "educational community of life." By honoring the "spirit of true camaraderie and authentic socialism," Heidegger sought to restore the "honor" that Germany's "previous political officeholders had taken from the *Volk*."[117]

As rector, Heidegger proved to be an enthusiastic advocate of *Gemeinschaftslager*. In October 1933, he personally organized a *Wissenschaftslager* retreat in Todtnauberg, thereby fulfilling a promise he had made in his *Rektoratsrede* concerning *Wissensdienst*, or "knowledge service." In a memorandum that he circulated among the participants, Heidegger declared that the *Lager*'s objective was to forge *"an authentic German community [echte deutsche Gemeinschaft]."* "Authentic *Lagerarbeit*," remarked Heidegger, "is conducive to reflecting on the methods of struggle [*Erkämpfung*] for the sake of advancing higher education of the German spirit [*des deutschen Geistes*]. . . . The *Lager*'s success will depend on a new sense of courage, on clarity and attentiveness with respect to the future, . . . and on the decisiveness of the will to *loyalty, sacrifice, and service [zu Treue, zu Opfer und Dienst]*. From these sources, there will emerge a new train of followers [*Gefolgschaft*] that supports and consolidates *an authentic German community [echte deutsche Gemeinschaft]*."[118]

The Ontological Mission of Poets and State-Founders

Heidegger regarded Jaeger's Tyrtaeus essay as invaluable for another important reason: it was one of the few works of scholarship that appreciated the *state-founding capacities of Dichtung*, poetry's constitutive role in establishing the nature and parameters of *aretē* ("virtue" or "excellence'). "Tyrtaeus and True *Aretē*" had an enduring impact on Heidegger's thought, insofar as it transformed his understanding of the interrelationship between *Dichtung, Denken,* and *Staatsführung*: poetry, philosophy, and statecraft.

Echoing Jaeger's portrayal of Tyrtaeus as a "poetic Lycurgus"—as the spiritual progenitor of the Spartan "Machtstaat"—Heidegger attributed an analogous "state-founding" capacity to Hölderlin. In "Tyrtaeus and True *Aretē*," Jaeger had lionized Tyrtaeus as a poetic prophet who transformed *aretē* from the celebration of *individual heroism* during Homeric times into a glorification of sacrificial death for the greater good of the polis. According to Jaeger, with Tyrtaeus's poetry, "the Homeric ideal of heroic *aretē* was transformed into the heroism of love of country [*Vaterlandsliebe*]. The poet suffuses the citizenry with this spirit. Thereby, he creates a *Volk*, an entire state of heroes."[119] Heidegger's apotheosis of Hölderlin qua "poet of the Germans" (*Dichter der Deutschen*) and as the "founder of German Being" (*Stifter des deutschen Seyns*)[120] reprised, nearly word for word, Jaeger's characterization of Tyrtaeus as the "voice of the fatherland" (*Stimme des Vaterlandes*) and the "voice of his country."[121]

Inspired by Jaeger's Tyrtaeus's interpretation, Heidegger honed his conception of the ontological vocation of poets and statesmen, whom he exalted as "die eigentlich Schaffenden," or "authentic creators." For Heidegger, these "authentic creators" embodied an ontological elite: *Führerschichten*, or "leadership cadres," that established the Dasein of a *Volk*: "The historical Dasein of *Völker*—their emergence, flowering, and decline—originates from poetry. Out of the latter, there originates authentic knowledge in the sense of philosophy, and hence, the realization of a *Volk* as a *Volk* through the State—*politics*. This primordial, historical epoch of peoples is the epoch of poets, thinkers, and state-founders [*Staatsschöpfer*]: the epoch of those who authentically ground and establish the historical Dasein of a *Volk*. They are the *authentic creators*. . . . [Through their actions], the *Volk* is brought to itself qua *Volk*."[122]

Heidegger explored the relationship between artists as "authentic creators" and "state-founding" in "The Origin of the Work of Art" (1935–36), an essay that stands in close thematic and temporal proximity to his Hölderlin lectures of 1934–35. However, in the secondary literature on Heidegger's "Kunstwerk" essay, interpreters have, as a rule, charitably overlooked the racial-authoritarian implications of Heidegger's understanding of *Staatsgründung* and *Führertum*, as though his reliance on such concepts were unrelated to his support for the Third Reich.[123]

In "The Origin of the Work of Art," Heidegger addressed the interrelationship between the *Seinsfrage* and *Geschichtlichkeit*. Such concerns went to the heart of Heidegger's fundamental ontology, since they treated the all-important link between "Being" and "Time." In his reflections on these topoi, Heidegger explained how "Being" becomes "Historical." As such, they reflected his reformulation of existential ontology qua *Seinsgeschichte*. In this schema, *Deutschtum* occupied a central role, since Heidegger regarded the Germans as the "historical *Volk*" par excellence—hence the privileged role that *Germanentum* played in Heidegger's doctrine of "another Beginning."

In the "Kunstwerk" essay, Heidegger reformulated "Being-in-the-world" as the "self-revealing openness and . . . essential decisions with respect to the *des-*

tiny of a historical Volk [*wesentlichen Entscheidungen im Geschicke eines geschichtlichen Volkes*]." "The self-affirmation of 'essence,'" Heidegger insisted, "means surrendering oneself to the *hidden primordiality of the heritage of one's own Being* [*die verborgene Ursprünglichkeit der Herkunft des eigenen Seins*]."[124]

These formulations are of fundamental importance: they illustrate the way that Heideggerian *Geschichtlichkeit* was inexorably tied to the particularity of the *Volksbegriff* and, more specifically, to the singularity of *German Existenz*. Heidegger never relinquished the view that "historicity" was beholden to the "mission" of "*German* Dasein" and "*German* destiny." His reference to "hidden primordiality" (*die verborgene Ursprünglichkeit*) alluded to the pivotal role that "subterranean philosophy" and the retrieval of "the archaic" (*das Ursprüngliche*) played in catalyzing the "other Beginning."

In the passage just quoted, Heidegger's reference to the "heritage of one's own Being" (*der Herkunft des eigenen Seins*) was a euphemism: a stand-in for the ontological singularity of German Dasein. Thereby, it reaffirmed the centrality of the ideology of German exceptionalism for Heidegger's doctrine of *Seinsgeschichte*.

Time and again, Heidegger linked the *Seinsfrage* to the particularity of *völkisch* belonging: to the "heritage of one's own Being" as a placeholder for *German Being*. This correlation was neither contingent nor accidental. Instead, it expressed an ontological imperative that went to the heart of Heideggerian *Seinsgeschichte*.

Heidegger was convinced that "world history" could only be meaningfully comprehended in *völkisch* terms. Hence, along with like-minded advocates of the *Volksbegriff*, he regarded "universal history" as a *sham*: little more than a nightmare of *Seinsvergessenheit*. "Authentic" Dasein was necessarily *völkisch*, which is merely another way of saying that, in order for Dasein to be authentic, it must be conceived in racial terms.

"Active Nihilism": *Macht* versus *Moral*

Both Heidegger and Jaeger insisted that the "state-founding" mission of poetry was dependent on race. As we have seen, Jaeger regarded the Spartans as racial progeny of the "Indo-Germanic" Dorians. During the Third Reich's early years, among classicists it became obligatory to contrast the Dorians, as a race of fearless Aryan conquerors, with the racially inferior Ionians. It was in this spirit that, in 1934, the poet and Nazi sympathizer Gottfried Benn (1886–1956) jumped on the Dorian bandwagon, publishing an essay titled "The World of the Dorians: An Investigation of the Relationship between Art and Power."[125]

Heidegger's recourse to the *Volksbegriff* was both *racial* and *racist*. Under the Third Reich, to think in *völkisch* terms necessarily meant thinking *in racial terms*. Committing oneself to the *Volksbegriff* meant endorsing the "salvific" mission of *Deutschtum*. Hence, it also meant embracing the idea of German racial superiority. Thereby, proponents of the *Volksbegriff*, such as Heidegger, underwrote Germany's "right" to "dominate" (*herrschen*) "inferior" peoples or *Völker*.

This conclusion followed implacably from National Socialism's reformulation of "natural law" (*Naturrecht*) in accordance with the Social Darwinist notion of the "survival of the fittest." Nazi legal theorists systematically divested the natural law tradition of its universalistic components. They restyled "natural right" qua "German right" (*deutsches Recht*): as "law" that was conducive to the benefit of the *Volk*. Reformulated in Heidegger's characteristically Germanocentric idiolect, this meant according ontological primacy—as Heidegger put it in "The Origin of the Work of Art"—to "the heritage of one's own Being." Thus, Heidegger, too, embraced the Social Darwinist conviction that *Macht* is the sole guarantor of *Recht*, that "might makes right."

A good example of Heidegger's elevation of *Macht* over *Moral* emerged in his lecture course on Nietzsche and "European nihilism" (1940). Like Nietzsche, Heidegger regarded himself as an "active nihilist." Instead of resting content with "half measures" and "compromises," he held that one must *consummate nihilism* prior to overcoming it, in accordance with the maxim, "the worse the better."

In Heidegger's Nietzsche lectures, he paused to reflect on the moral significance of Great Britain's destruction of the French fleet at Oran, Algeria. Faithful to Nietzsche's doctrine of the "will to power," Heidegger denounced "universal morality" as an illusion that possessed only "propaganda value." Instead, he embraced the Social Darwinist standpoint, according to which "every power . . . has its own law, and only through impotence does it become illegal," thereby glorifying moral cynicism. As Heidegger observed, "When [in July 1940] the British bombed and sank French Navy vessels docked at Oran, it was thoroughly 'justified' from their point of view. Here, 'justified' is *that which serves to augment power*. . . . Every power, metaphysically considered, has its own law

[*Recht*], and only through impotence does it become illegal [*Unrecht*]. It is a metaphysical tactic on the part of all powers never to regard the adversary or his actions in relation to their point of view, but instead, according to a universal human morality, which, however, possesses only mere propaganda value."[126]

Heidegger's discussion exemplified the "might makes right" perspective. Although Heidegger's defenders have consistently praised his philosophical legacy for its pathbreaking "critique of metaphysics," in the preceding passage, the morally disastrous consequences of "postmetaphysical thinking" are apparent, especially once one insists, following Nietzsche, that universal morality is little more than—as Heidegger put it—a "metaphysical tactic," an expression of the "will to power."

Rectorate and *Rassengedanke*

As rector, Heidegger did nothing to restrain—and much to encourage—the persecutions of National Socialist youth. Under his stewardship, the civic and moral fabric of university life rashly deteriorated. Heidegger consistently acted in accordance with National Socialist standards of "justice," which redefined "right" as conduct that furthered the aims of the *Volksgemeinschaft*—another illustration of the way that, under the Third Reich, "justice" was redefined in terms of "race."

Among convinced Nazis, it went without saying that the privileges that pertained to the Germans qua *Herrenrasse* were inapplicable to racial inferiors—so-called *Minderwertigen* (persons of lesser value) or *Untermenschen* (subhumans). Had Heidegger been genuinely opposed to "Nazi justice," presumably, he never would have joined Hans Frank's Academy of German Law—an organization that was dedicated to destroying *Rechtsstaatlichkeit* (rule of law) and replacing it with "German law."[127]

The numerous persecutions that transpired under Heidegger's rectorate were justified on the basis of Nazi race doctrine. Among Jews and opponents of National Socialism, the consequences were often devastating. The civic chaos that resulted was depicted in a June 1933 article in the *Karlsruher Zeitung*: "Upon learning that the Jewish student association, Neo-Freibürgia—whose quarters on Baseler Strasse had already been occupied by the SA—wanted to reconvene elsewhere, all hell broke loose among the [pro-Nazi] Freiburg Student Association. Hundreds of students gathered in front of the Jewish student residence hall, demanding its closure and the arrest of its inhabitants. Six Jewish students were taken into 'protective custody' by the SS. The house was immediately placed under additional surveillance by the SA and bedecked with a Swastika flag. Shortly thereafter, in order to avoid further disturbances, the house was permanently closed by the police."[128]

It is doubtful whether any of these actions would have been tolerated had Heidegger's attitude toward the *Rassengedanke* been ambivalent or lukewarm. When Heidegger joined the NSDAP in May 1933, he did so after having read *Mein Kampf*. Recently, it has emerged that he was also an avid reader of the *Völkischer Beobachter*.[129] In sum, Heidegger was fully cognizant of National Socialism's ideological program and political goals, which were unambiguously predicated on the *Rassenprinzip*. As the German legal historian Bernd Rüthers has written, "There was nothing the least ambiguous about National Socialism's political aims. They were readily discernible to anyone who could read."[130]

The race thinking that animated the Nazi *Weltanschauung* was on display at every party rally. It pervaded nearly every speech that Hitler delivered. Point 4 of the 1920 NSDAP Program proclaimed, "None but those of German blood, whatever their creed, may be members of the *Volk*: No Jew, therefore, may be a member of the *Volk*."[131] As the Heidegger biographer Hugo Ott has remarked, "Anyone capable of exalting Hitler's rule as licensed by the 'writ of Being' necessarily partook of his lethal anti-Semitism."[132]

Nazi anti-Semitism was denuded of any and every semblance of moderation. Instead, it assumed the characteristics and traits of a political religion: of an all-encompassing, salvific worldview. Consequently, racial anti-Semitism was suffused with an eschatological dimension that contrasted sharply with more moderate and traditional religious criticisms of Judaism, in which "conversion" offered an option of last resort.

In light of the various interpretive mystifications that have arisen with respect to Heidegger's commitment to Nazism, it is worth stressing that Heidegger never raised any principled objections to Nazi race doctrine. Instead, he consistently sought to reconcile race thinking with the tenets of his own fundamental ontology. To do so required no great intellectual adjustment on Heidegger's part, since, from the very beginning, his *Denken* was profoundly indebted to the dogmas of German particularism—a standpoint that was indebted to the tenets of race thinking.

Well attuned to the *Zeitgeist*, Heideggerian *Seinsgeschichte* consciously fused fundamental ontology with a *völkisch* understanding of history. *Geschicht-lichkeit*, in its Heideggerian iteration, furnished an ontological-historical warrant for *Deutschtum*'s providential self-understanding qua *Herrenrasse*. Heidegger never sought to mask his conviction that "*only someone who is German [der Deutsche] is capable of poetically articulating Being in an originary way.*"[133]

Heidegger's declaration surpassed the chauvinism of "normal nationalism." Its perlocutionary effect condemned non-German *Völker* qua facilitators and abettors of "European nihilism." Heidegger viewed "world Jewry" as the leading carrier of social decay or "Machenschaft." Hence, his eschatological prognostications concerning the history of Being could only come to pass once "world Jewry" was soundly eliminated.

Not only did Heidegger invoke the *Volksbegriff* in order to legitimate Germany's salvific historical "mission," or *Sendung*. His employment of "Volk" was entirely consistent with the racial semantics of pan-German nationalism. In this employment, "Volk," as a cultural and racial unit, was apotheosized as an *absolute value*.

As I indicated previously, following World War I, the *Volksbegriff* was racially recoded: it was reconceived in accordance with "a racially defined, profoundly anti-Semitic nationalism."[134] In *Logic as a Question Concerning the Essence of Language* (1934), Heidegger acknowledged that *Volk* and *Rasse* had, to all intents and purposes, become lexical equivalents. "We often use the word 'Volk' in the sense of 'race,' " he avowed.[135]

"The Mystical Origins of National Socialism": The Epistemology of the *Rassenbegriff*

Heidegger's defenders have consistently alleged that his understanding of "race" was radically opposed to Nazi "biologism." On these grounds, they have perpetuated the fiction that, under the Third Reich, Heidegger practiced "spiritual resistance" to National Socialism. It was a myth that Heidegger himself contrived in his 1945 apologia "The Rectorate, 1933–34: Facts and Thoughts," in a desperate attempt to avoid the *Lehrverbot* (ban on teaching) that he ultimately received.[136]

However, in the words of one prominent historian, "Heidegger's reconstruction of the past has been characterized by an ongoing, conscious strategy of reality-fabrication via the techniques of embellishment and distortion": "As far as [Heidegger's] purported acts of 'spiritual resistance' are concerned, *there is no factual evidence to support these claims*, either in the form of archival documents or eyewitness accounts. The only exception concerns his attacks against 'false,' competing views of National Socialism advanced by more powerful rivals. . . . In refutation of these claims, one finds [Heidegger's] numerous letters of denunciation and his zealous, pro-Nazi *Lager* discourses, all of which are very well-documented."[137]

Apologetic attempts to vindicate Heidegger on the grounds that he opposed National Socialist race doctrine founder, since they rest on a fundamental misunderstanding concerning the epistemology of race thinking. Nazi race discourse was consistently suffused with mystical and spiritual elements. As such, it was awash in pseudoscience. Hence, in all its variants, race thinking promoted an antiscientific "sacralization" of *Blut*, *Volk*, and *Boden*. The idea of *Deutschtum* qua *Herrenrasse*, or "master race," was one such "element." Moreover, among the "master thinkers" of Nazi race doctrine, there was broad agreement about the need to *transcend* the limitations of nineteenth-century "materialism" and "scientism."

A good example of the spiritual-mystagogical side of Nazi race thinking was the SS *Ahnenerbe*, or "Racial Ancestry," initiative. This undertaking devoted significant monetary, material, and scholarly resources to unearthing archaeological traces of a mythological Aryan *Ur-Rasse*—the "Hyperboreans"—that had putatively perished in a prehistoric natural catastrophe. This fanciful quest led Nazi archaeologists to the upper reaches of the Himalayas and—nearly—to the heights of the Peruvian Andes.[138] By the late 1930s, the *Ahnenerbe* had significantly expanded its institutional heft to include two-dozen research institutes, spanning the fields of linguistics, prehistory, and *Volkskunde*.

Himmler had hoped that, by reconnecting Germans with their primeval roots, he would succeed in remaking them as *warriors*. By reestablishing the links between the *Volk* and ancient paganism, he had hoped that the Germans would be better able to shed Christianity's "effeminizing" cultural influence. Thereby, the *Volksgemeinschaft* would be able to redouble its resolve in view of the impending *Weltanschauungskrieg* with Stalin's "Asiatic hordes."

Himmler was also an adherent of so-called Cosmic Ice Theory (*Welteislehre*), which explained sublunary occurrences as the result of intergalactic antagonisms between "sun planets" and "ice planets." Himmler held that Cosmic Ice Theory—also known as "Glacial Cosmology"—could explain global catastrophes, such as the mysterious disappearance of Atlantis, the conjectural *Ur-Heimat* of the aforementioned Nordic *Herrenrasse*.[139]

Implausible though it may seem, Nazi ideologues frequently extolled the National Socialist *Weltanschauung* as an "Idealism." Thereby, they sought to contrast the movement's orientation toward "higher pursuits" with the base "materialism" of the regime's political opponents: Marxists, liberals, and Jews. The SS's commitment to the values of "honor" and "loyalty"—as exemplified by the motto, "Mein Ehre heißt Treue" (My honor is called loyalty)—is a textbook example of Nazi "Idealism."

By infusing race thinking with a "mystical" dimension, the Nazi leadership sought to spiritualize race thinking, thereby sharply distinguishing it from the determinism of nineteenth-century "scientism." In *The Myth of the Twentieth Century*, Rosenberg's commitment to the worldview of "spiritual racism" was evident on nearly every page.

A good place to start is the book's subtitle: *An Evaluation of the Spiritual and Psychic Struggles of Our Age* (*Eine Wertung der seelisch-geistigen Gestaltenkämpfe unserer Zeit*). Nazi ideology regarded "blood" and "race" as functional equivalents. Consequently, in *The Myth of the Twentieth Century*, Rosenberg's validation of "race mysticism" was simultaneously a validation of "blood mysticism."

In part, Rosenberg's affirmation of "blood mysticism" was intended as a polemical rejoinder to the scientific aspirations of historical materialism. Similarly, his understanding of history as a "struggle for spiritual values"—*ein Kampf um geistige Werte*—was formulated in opposition to the Marxist notion of history as the outcome of "class struggle." Rosenberg's numerous elegies to the mystical powers of "race" and "blood" were meant to highlight National Socialism's "spiritual" qualities, in contrast to the crude determinism of modern natural science—an approach that Rosenberg rejected, since it sought, as he put it, to "reduce blood to a chemical formula."[140]

Rosenberg's understanding of National Socialism as a form of "blood mysticism" also coalesced with his view of "race" as an expression of "soul." As Rosenberg explained, "Soul means race seen from within. Conversely, race is the external side of the soul. . . . The struggle of the blood and the intuitive awareness of life-mystique are simply two aspects of the same thing. Race is the image of the soul. . . . Racial history is simultaneously natural history and soul mystique."[141]

Historically speaking, the idea of "race-soul" as a mystical source of German unity had a dynamic career. Although Germany, qua *pays légal*, might seem hopelessly riven by regional, confessional, and linguistic divisions—conflicts that dated back to the Thirty Years' War (1618–48)—to compensate, proponents of the *Volksbegriff* sought to reimagine Germany as a racial utopia whose unity was predicated on the mystical, hence supernatural and indomitable, forces of *Blut* and *Boden*.

Ultimately, there was nothing the least bit "scientific" about such grandiose racial visions. At base, they were an extravagant ideological confabulation: a delusional projection of German supremacy that culminated, inexorably, in catastrophe.

To be sure, in view of the phenomenological rigor of Heidegger's fundamental ontology, it was light-years removed from the intellectual charlatanism of Rosenberg and his ilk. At the same time, at a later point, his discursive assimilation of racialist ideologemes such as "Blut," "Volk," "Boden," and "Erde" fluidly intersected with the "spiritualist" currents of Nazi race thinking.[142]

Recent scholarship on the cultural origins of Nazi race doctrine has confirmed its fundamentally ideological—hence "antiscientific"—character. As Waldemar Gurian confirms in *Um des Reiches Zukunft* (1932), "That National Socialist race doctrine . . . had nothing to do with natural scientific theories of race is clear from the fact that leading [German] nationalists explicitly and demonstratively distanced themselves from such theories. Instead, the belief in 'race' was an attempt to return to a condition of simple and immediate unity in the face of the complexities and confusions of the present. *'Race' was not a natural scientific fact, but instead an ideational construct that both reflected the current situation and projected a series of ideal demands.*"[143] Hence, in the genesis of Nazi race thinking, reputable scientific research on genetics played a subordinate role. It was merely used as a springboard for a series of underlying cultural and political prejudices.

Moreover, when it came to the planning and implementation of National Socialist race policy in the eastern territories, scientists played a subaltern role in comparison with "race mystics" such as Hans Günther, Walter Gross, Alfred Rosenberg, and Himmler. It was their grandiose, dystopian racial visions that served as the template for the Third Reich's brutal politics of conquest and colonization.[144]

Similar conclusions hold with respect to another key component of the *Rassengedanke*, "redemptive anti-Semitism." The rationale that the Nazi lead-

ership provided for the "Final Solution" was not based on demonstrable empirical findings derived from the natural sciences. Nor did Hitler, Himmler, et al.
seek to justify the exterminations in narrowly scientific terms. Instead, as one
historian of Nazi race discourse has pointed out, "The very idea of the Jews as
a separate race with particular, dangerous traits . . . grew from a mystical notion
of 'thinking with the blood' . . . far more than it did from eugenic or anthropological research into Jews' physical or psychological characteristics."[145]

The "mystical" or "spiritual" dimension of Nazi race thinking reflected the
movement's ideological origins in Ariosophy: a theosophical justification of
Aryan racial supremacy that, during the early twentieth century, flourished
among anti-Semites in German-speaking lands.[146] As one scholar has pointed
out, Ariosophy was a "case study in Nazi religiosity." Ariosophists "combined
völkisch nationalism and Aryan racial theories with occultism. They articulated
a defensive ideology of German identity and illiberalism, since they were concerned with counteracting the political emergence of subject nationalities in
Austria-Hungary. Since their ideas in respect of putative ancient Aryan homelands ('Hyperborea' and 'Atlantis'), Germanic religion, and runic wisdom later
filtered through to Heinrich Himmler and his SS research departments, Ariosophy offers a model case study in Nazi 'religiosity.' "[147]

Following World War I, the disparate precepts of race mysticism coalesced
into a Aryanized "political theology." As a "total" political worldview, Nazism
sought to counter the existential uncertainties of "modernity"—doubts and
fears that, on historical grounds, were especially acute in Mitteleuropa—by
popularizing a panoply of regressive, political myths, many of which were
predicated on delusional visions of German superiority.

As a form of secular religion, one of Nazi ideology's key functions was to
provide the *Volk* with a profane theodicy: ideational solace for *Gesellschaft*'s
rash erosion of "meaning." National Socialist race thinking, in a manner that
reflected its roots in Social Darwinism, was more closely related to superstition
and myth than it was to empirical science. Hence, it was imbued with numerous
cultural, mythological, and mystical elements—a fact that explains what one
scholar has aptly termed the "occult roots of Nazism."[148]

Not only were such mystical and occult components integral to Nazi
ideology. In many ways, they were the key to its success as a species of political religion. As George Mosse noted in "The Mystical Origins of National Socialism,"

At the very center of this development were ideas that were not so much of a *na-tional* as of a *romantic* and *mystical* nature—part of the "revolt against positivism" that swept Europe at the end of the nineteenth century. In Germany, this revolt took a special turn, perhaps because romanticism struck deeper roots there than elsewhere. This German reaction to positivism became intimately bound up with a belief in nature as *a cosmic life force*: a dark force whose mysteries could be un-derstood, *not through science, but through the occult*. An ideology based upon such premises was fused with the glories of the Aryan past and, in turn, that past received a thoroughly romantic and mystical interpretation.[149]

In the German-speaking lands of Mitteleuropa, mystical approaches to race fused with the ideology of Aryan chauvinism: a worldview that was predicated on a series of archaizing and regressive myths. Ultimately, with the Nazi sei-zure of power, the champions of race-and-blood mysticism migrated from the margins of society to the political center, with results that were catastrophic for Germany and Europe alike. As Mosse explains, "In Germany, the recovery of the unconscious, in reaction against the dominant positivist ideologies, laid the groundwork for the German form of twentieth-century totalitarianism. This re-action combined the deep stream of German romanticism with the mysteries of the occult as well as the 'Idealism' of deeds. What sort of 'deeds' these turned out to be is written in blood on the pages of history."[150]

Under National Socialism, the *Rassengedanke* was never formalized qua "doctrine." Instead, as with other aspects of Nazi ideology, "race" was beset by competing currents and tendencies. In *Behemoth: The Structure and Practice of National Socialism*, Franz Neumann stressed the eclectic and contradictory na-ture of Nazi race thinking.[151] "National Socialist ideology was constantly shift-ing," observed Neumann. "It had certain *magical beliefs*—leadership adoration, the supremacy of the Master Race—but its ideology was never laid down in a series of categorical and dogmatic pronouncements."[152]

Neumann's description of the Nazi worldview as an ideology in perpetual flux applies even more emphatically in the case of the *Rassengedanke*. Al-though Hans Günther—the so-called Race Pope and an exponent of the "Nor-dic Idea" (*der nordische Gedanke*)—was one of the leading Nazi race thinkers, his approach to race thinking was widely recognized as amateurish and subjec-tive.[153] Günther's racial typologies inclined toward the methods of "aesthetic caricature." In many respects, they represented a throwback to the imprecisions of physical anthropology. Be that as it may, Günther's racial impressionism was shared by countless Nazi geneticists and biologists, which indicated the extent to which Nazi "science" had succumbed to ideological demands and constraints.

A remark from the *Black Notebooks* suggests that the racial connotations of the "Nordic Idea" were not entirely foreign to Heidegger's thinking. In an entry from 1938–39, he excoriated Catholicism owing to its "Roman" and "Spanish" origins. What Heidegger deemed especially objectionable about this Latinate spiritual lineage was that it was "in every respect *un-Nordic* and wholly *un-German* [*ganz und gar un-nordisch and vollends undeutsch*]," thereby implying that "Nordic" and "German" were functional equivalents.[154]

In keeping with the antiscientific biases I have outlined, the goal of reanimating primeval myths soon gained the upper hand. The superiority of "myth" over "reason" informed the title of Rosenberg's opus, *The Myth of the Twentieth Century*. (Over the lifespan of the Third Reich, Rosenberg's book sold over one million copies.) The "myth" of Rosenberg's title was, of course, the myth of *race*. Needless to say, if race is the stuff of *myth*, it has very little, if anything, to do with natural science.

Among Nazi race theorists, efforts to reconcile *Rasse* and *Geist* in the name of "race mysticism" were widespread. In an article on "*Volksgeist* and law," the Nazi legal theorist Karl Larenz extolled the dialectical confluence of "blood" and "spirit" as a cornerstone of National Socialist legal doctrine. According to Larenz, "Blood must become Spirit, and Spirit must become Blood. . . . Because Spirit can decline, Blood must come to Spirit's rescue. In the end, Spirit will triumph when it is renewed by Blood."[155]

Among Nazi jurists, attempts to "spiritualize" the *Rassengedanke*—and thereby to free it from the trammels of bourgeois "materialism"—became increasingly popular. In *Die Rassengesetzliche Rechtslehre* (Racial Legislation as Legal Doctrine), Helmut Nicolai—one of Heidegger's colleagues on the Committee for the Philosophy of Law—explored the entwinement of *Rasse* and *Geist*. Defining Germany as a "Rassengemeinschaft" (racial community), Nicolai insisted that it was imperative for Nazi legal scholarship to acknowledge the *Volksgemeinschaft*'s qualities and capacities qua "Rassen-Seele."[156]

Heidegger's characterization of the Germans as the "most metaphysical of peoples"—as the *Volk* that stands in the closest "proximity" (*Nähe*) to Being—confirms his affinities with the "spiritualist" current of National Socialist race doctrine. His ascription of a redemptive mission to *Germanentum* resembled the Ariosophists' profane eschatology, which had similarly sacralized *Deutschtum*.

As we have seen, Heidegger's doctrine of *Seinsgeschichte* frequently recurred to the leitmotif of the German *Volk* as "redeemer." In the *Black Notebooks*, his appeal to the Messianic promise of "die verborgene Deutschheit," or "hidden Germanness," paralleled Ariosophy's salvific, pan-German longings. His assertion in *An Introduction to Metaphysics* that "mysteriousness [*das Geheimnischarakter*] constitutes the authenticity and greatness of historical knowledge" suggests that he regarded occult knowledge as an indispensable catalyst for the transition to "another Beginning."[157]

The real-world consequences of the *Rassengedanke* could be—and often were—quite lethal. From a scientific standpoint, however, its merits were negligible. Ultimately, Heidegger acolytes who praise the Master for having rejected Nazi "biologism" are, in essence, tilting at windmills. They are scratching where it doesn't itch.[158]

"Spiritual Racism"

Heidegger's understanding of race was *existential* and *völkisch*. He sought to integrate features of earlier approaches to race thinking—for example, the "cultural" understanding of race—with popular and widespread biological conceptions. At the same time, he added another dimension to race doctrine, a component that reflected the fin-de-siècle "revolt against scientism" discussed by Mosse and that was profoundly indebted to the legacy of German Romanticism.[159] He sought to endow race with an enduring and profound *spiritual orientation*.

Heidegger's defense of "spiritual racism" surfaced in the *Rektoratsrede*, in which he emphasized the entwinement of *Geist*, *Erde*, and *Blut*: "spirit," "earth," and "blood." "The spiritual world of a *Volk*," claimed Heidegger, "is not its cultural superstructure. Instead, it is the power that comes from preserving . . . *forces that are rooted in the soil and blood of a Volk* [*erd-und bluthäftigen Kräfte*]."[160] In *Logic as a Question Concerning the Essence of Language*, Heidegger lauded "blood"—"Blut und das Geblut"—as the ground of the *Volk*'s "spirituality": "The spirituality of our Dasein [*die Geistigkeit unseres Daseins*]," claimed Heidegger, emerges from the "voice of blood."[161] Here, "blood" was merely a substitute for "race." For Heidegger, the paradigm of "spiritual racism" served as an important prophylaxis against the temptations of interpreting race in accordance with the regressive epistemology of the "bourgeois" natural sciences.

In approaching the problem of race, Heidegger insisted on the complementarity of its "spiritual" and "material" sides. Hence, he developed an understanding of race that equitably combined the elements of *Geist*, *Erde*, and *Blut*. By stressing the "embodied" character of *Geist*—or, as Heidegger put it, *Geist*'s fusion with "forces that are rooted in the soil and blood of a *Volk*"—Heidegger sought to *deepen* the inherited understanding of *Geist materially* and *existentially*. Thereby, he also sought to demonstrate the superiority of the *German* understanding of *Geist*, or "spirit," vis-à-vis the predominant Western conceptions.

According to Heidegger, an important index of German *Geist*'s supremacy was its rejection of "spirit" qua "cultural superstructure." The German approach accomplished this feat by deriving spirit from *Erde* and *Blut*. Heidegger consistently dismissed interpretations of "mind" or "spirit" that lacked these qualities as *bodenlos*. From the standpoint of fundamental ontology, they were inferior, insofar as they trafficked in unrooted "abstractions."

Although it may seem paradoxical, countless fascist intellectuals exalted fascism as a spiritual phenomenon or movement—above all, since fascism presented itself as an alternative to nineteenth-century positivism and materialism. Consequently, they welcomed fascism as a form of spiritual deliverance from the failings of reason and democracy, two evils that had been bequeathed by the Enlightenment.

Spiritual fascists held this Enlightenment legacy accountable for Europe's rash descent into nihilism. Conversely, they regarded fascism as a *life-affirming force*, often based on a selective reading of Nietzsche's work. Proponents of spiritual fascism were convinced that fascism, by combating materialism and scientism, presaged a return to the values of *virility*, *vitality*, *energy*, and *strength*. They emphatically rejected parliamentary "decadence" and sought to replace "discussion" and "rule of law" with "the deed" (*die Tat*). The champions of spiritual fascism viewed the Bolsheviks' storming of the Winter Palace and Mussolini's March on Rome as the templates for a return to Nietzschean "Great Politics."

As Zeev Sternhell observed in his study of fascist ideology *Neither Right, nor Left*, "pure fascists . . . such as Drieu la Rochelle and Robert Brasillach . . . [and fascist sympathizers] like [Thierry] Maulnier, [Bertrand de] Jouvenel, and

[Marcel] Deát . . . were agreed on this point: *fascism was a revolt against materialism, a revolt of the spirit, the will, and instinct.*"[162] The trope of spiritual fascism allows one to make sense of de Jouvenel's counterintuitive (and egregiously myopic) characterization of Germany's blitzkrieg victory over France, in June 1940, as a "triumph of the spirit."[163] Thereby, de Jouvenel sought to contrast Nazi Germany's "spiritual superiority" with the French Republic's widely bemoaned moral decay. It also helps to explain why, at the time, antidemocratic French intellectuals—the so-called Jeune Droite, for example—viewed themselves as the Gallic counterpart to Germany's conservative revolutionaries. Lastly, the allure of "spiritual fascism" also helps to explain a widespread rationale for "collaboration" during Vichy, since Maréchal Pétain's *État français* portrayed itself as a regime of "national regeneration."[164]

Nevertheless, among spiritual fascists, race thinking and anti-Semitism remained ideological constants. Writing in *La Flèche*, the spiritual fascist and *collaborateur* Gaston Bergéry justified anti-Semitism as an ideological imperative via recourse to a parable. A friend who had recently visited a government office groused that "he had been sent from Rosenthal to Rosenfels and from Rosenfels to Blumenthal." Reflecting on his friend's encounters, Bergéry concluded, "A Jewish Frenchman is a Frenchman like any other; but if one goes to see ten Frenchmen and they turn out to be ten Jews, they are no longer Frenchmen like any other."[165]

"*Volk* as Spirit"

In *Being and Time*, Heidegger had sought to ground spirit "existentially," in order to free it from the epistemological missteps of Idealism. During the 1930s, he explored the ideological semantics of "spiritual National Socialism" in a variety of contexts. Given "spirit's" prominence in the history of German philosophy, the stakes involved in reassessing its legacy were considerable. Above all, Heidegger sought to highlight spirit's relevance with respect to *Geschichtlichkeit*, or authentic historicity.

In *Logic as a Question Concerning the Essence of Language*, Heidegger addressed these themes explicitly in a discussion of "*Volk* as Spirit" (*Volk als Geist*). "In every case in which questions concerning self-organization, alignment, and decision [*Entscheidung*] arise," asserted Heidegger, "the *Volk* remains an inherently *historical, knowing, willing, and spiritual* entity."[166] In part, Heidegger's understanding of "*Volk* as Spirit" was intended as a rejoinder to ideological rivals who sought to construe race biologically.[167] At the same time, what stood out in Heidegger's treatment of this topos were his efforts to amalgamate *Geist* and *Volk*: to reconcile "spirit" with the demands of race thinking—hence the praise that Heidegger bestowed on the "*völkisch* movement's" (*völkische Bewegung*) efforts to rekindle the "purity of the *Volk*'s tribal origins [*das Volk zur Reinheit seiner Stammesart zurückbringen*]."[168]

Heidegger complemented his treatment of "*Volk* as Spirit" with a related inquiry concerning "*Volk* as Soul" (*Volk als Seele*). Here, Heidegger was primarily interested in the idea of *Volk* as "expression": the way that the *Volk*'s inner capacities objectivated or manifested themselves externally. What seized Heidegger's attention were the correspondences between "*Volk* as Soul," on the one hand, and "Volkskunde" and "Siedlungen" (dwellings), on the other.

Under the Third Reich, "Volkskunde," or "folklore" merged with "Rassenkunde," or Nazi "ethnology." National Socialist ethnographers were busily preoccupied with finding traces of earlier German settlements (*Siedlungen*), primarily, in "the East," in order to provide a cultural warrant for the Third Reich's colonization plans.

Heidegger exalted the objectivations of "Volkskunde" and "Siedlungen" as manifestations of "*Volk* as Soul." He described them as "metaphorical imprints of the *Volk*'s basic-attitudinal Dasein":

> The emotional life a *Volk* reveals itself in *Volkslieder* [folk songs], *Volksfeste* [folk festivals], and customs. These elements are the metaphorical imprint of the *Volk*'s basic-attitudinal Dasein. In such instances, the *Volk* is no longer arbitrarily understood as merely a "population" or as "inhabitants," but instead as a determinate human group that is lodged in established dwellings [*Siedlungen*]. . . . In these settlements, the *Volk* first comes into its own through its customs and leaves its imprint on the land. . . . However, in a sequence of temporal events—birth, marriage, death, and seasonal change—the landscape also imprints itself on the everyday life of "collective Dasein" [*gemeinschaftlichen Daseins*].[169]

Although the examples that Heidegger provided may seem perfectly innocent, from an ideological standpoint, there is much more at stake than meets the eye. Heidegger's ruminations on "Volkskunde," "Volkslieder," "Volksfeste," and "Siedlungen" as the outward manifestations of "*Volk* as Soul" were formulated in 1934. As such, they attested to the ideological intoxications of the

Volksbegriff. Heidegger's commentary on the ethnographic richness of "folk songs," "folk festivals," and "settlements" were not meant as *generic* discussions of these topoi. Instead, they were intended as contributions to the reigning mood of *Deutschtümelei.* They were *racial discussions* that were meant to highlight the specificity and superiority of German "rootedness."

Volk and *Rasse*

Heidegger readily acknowledged the existential value of race. He regarded race as a valuable and legitimate corollary to *Being and Time*'s stress on the *embodied* character of human existence. As Heidegger avowed in *Logic as a Question Concerning the Essence of Language,* "What we call 'race' is related to the bodily."[170]

In *Being and Time,* Heidegger depicted the formal constituents of *Existenz,* the essential structures of Dasein's Being-in-the-world. Among these basic structures, Heidegger included "average everyday Being-in-the-world," "Discourse," "Care," "Angst," "Being-with-others," and "Being-toward-death." In *Logic as a Question Concerning the Essence of Language,* Heidegger sought to validate "race" as an "Existential": as a filter or prism that, along with the aforenamed "structures," conditioned Dasein's encounters with "the Being of beings."

Heidegger claimed that the existential value of race was best understood by way of analogy with the "Stimmung," or "mood. In *Being and Time,* "mood" suggested an emotive, noncognitive basis for Dasein's Being-in-the-world. As Heidegger asserted, "Mood makes manifest 'how one is,' and how one is faring." "In this 'how one is,' " he continued, "having a mood brings Being to its 'there.' "[171]

Heidegger's efforts to amalgamate "race" and "mood" was neither cursory nor pro forma; nor was it a rote gesture of ideological *obéissance.* Instead, it was Heidegger's way of differentiating his own "spiritual" understanding of race from the materialist or biological approaches. By foregrounding this comparison, Heidegger sought to certify the existential legitimacy of race, in opposition to the misguided and destructive attempts to foist on race a scientific epistemological pedigree.

In *Logic as a Question Concerning the Essence of Language,* Heidegger clarified his views on the existential significance of race, arguing that race, like "mood," was a formal precondition for Dasein's "Being-in-the-world": "Blood and race determine man essentially . . . only when they are co-determined by moods [*Stimmungen*]. The voice of blood [*Stimme des Blutes*] derives from the foundational mood [*Grundstimmung*] of man. As such, it is not autonomous. Instead, it belongs to the unity of mood. The same might be said of the spirituality [*Geistigkeit*] of our Dasein, which occurs as 'work' [*Arbeit*]."[172]

By emphasizing the racial character of "Being-in-the-world," Heidegger— faithful to the fundamental ontology of *Being and Time*—sought to make an "existential" point. We experience the world not merely as *res cogitans*—as disembodied, "cognitive subjects"—but also as *racial beings*. Race, as filtered by "mood," is an integral component of *Mitsein*, of our Being-with-others. For Heidegger, race signified a fundamental and inalienable expression of human embodiment. In this respect, it constituted a sine qua non of Being-in-the-world. Race helped to define what Heidegger called the "who" of Dasein. Insofar as Dasein's *Existenz* was *geschichtlich*, or historical, its acts of ontological self-assertion were necessarily and unavoidably filtered through the prism of race.

All of which is to say that Heidegger viewed race as a sine qua non for *Geschichtlichkeit*. Accordingly, in the *Black Notebooks*, he embraced race as a "necessary and mediate condition of historical Dasein."[173] Heidegger regarded race as an essential aspect of "historical Dasein's" capacity to *actualize* its past in accordance with a prefated "mission" (*Sendung*) and "task" (*Auftrag*). He insisted that Dasein retrieved its past not as an "atomized subject" or "punctual self" but, instead, as part of a determinate historical *Gemeinschaft*: as a member of a *particular Volk*. For all of these reasons, Heidegger held that *Existenz* was fundamentally and inevitably *racial*.

As Heidegger became increasingly convinced of metaphysics' inefficacity— its inability to impact "historicity"—he turned toward race as an existential-historical guarantor of *Gemeinschaft*, *Eigentlichkeit*, and *Wahrheit*: "community," "authenticity," and "truth."

Heidegger's "Kehre"—his "Turn" away from *Dasein* and toward *Sein*— simultaneously reflected his wager on "race." The centrality of race emerged in Heidegger's shift toward what he denominated the "metaphysics of German Dasein."[174] Heidegger's *völkisch* transmutation of fundamental ontology meant that, henceforth, race began to play an increasingly prominent role in his understanding of *Seinsgeschichte*. One might accurately characterize this development as Heidegger's "racial *Kehre*."

Heidegger's turn toward the "metaphysics of German Dasein" signified a radical disillusionment with the powers of first philosophy. Increasingly, he became convinced that an excessive focus on metaphysical questioning impaired the efficacy of *Volk* and race. In Heidegger's view, *Volk* and race possessed a transformative ontological-historical potential that far outstripped philosophy's comparatively meager, cerebral capacities. Consequently, in the *Black Notebooks*, he emphatically declared, "Today, we must finally put an end to philosophizing, since *Volk* and race are no longer adequate to it. Its [philosophy's] power shrivels and is degraded to the point of impotence."[175]

"The Metapolitics of the Historical *Volk*"

Heidegger's racial recasting of the *Seinsfrage* meant replacing the *Daseinsanalyse* of *Being and Time* with the "metapolitics of the historical Volk." In one of the *Black Notebooks'* most revealing avowals, he asserted, "The metaphysics of Dasein must, in accordance with its inner structure, deepen itself and be extended to the metapolitics of the historical Volk."[176] Heidegger's appeal confirmed his "Turn" toward the racial-ontological mission of *Deutschtum*. In keeping with his preternatural and abiding Germanocentrism, Heidegger regarded *Deutschtum* as the "historical *Volk*" par excellence.

For Heidegger, "metapolitics" occupied an intermediate sphere between "fundamental ontology" and the "ontic." It also bore significant affinities with Nietzsche's conception of "Great Politics." In contrast to the timorousness and compromises of bourgeois "parliamentarism," "metapolitics" affirmed politics qua *Tat* and *Kampf*, "deed" and "struggle."

To deny that Heidegger's endorsement of the "metapolitics of the historical *Volk*" was, essentially, a racial judgment would be to falsify the historical record. Racial evaluations suffused Heidegger's understanding of *Seinsgeschichte*. Heidegger's doctrine of "another Beginning" was predicated on the redemptory role of *Deutschtum*, a standpoint that itself reflected his commitment to "spiritual National Socialism." In this respect, it too involved a racial judgment. Heidegger could hardly have been clearer on this point. As he affirmed in the *Black Notebooks*, "The anticipatory and essential moment of decision concerning the essence of History is reserved to the Germans."[177]

Heidegger augmented these remarks about race with insights concerning the power and capacities of "blood." In *Sein und Wahrheit* (1934), he haled "*Blut und Boden* as necessary and powerful," yet ultimately insufficient, "conditions for the Dasein of the *Volk*."[178] By appending this qualification, Heidegger sought to leave the door ajar for the contributions of "spiritual racism."

Like other proponents of the *Rassengedanke*, Heidegger maintained that *Blut und Boden* displayed "spiritual" qualities and attributes, characteristics that transcended their chemical and physical makeup. As rector, Heidegger justified the dismissal of a Jewish colleague on racial grounds. However, in his view, the reasons for dismissal were not simply biological or genetic. They also touched on questions of "worldview." As such, they entailed a "spiritual" dimension.

Heidegger's objections concerned his colleague's proximity to "neo-Kantianism" and "liberalism," perspectives that Heidegger regarded as spiritually deficient, since they were inadequately grounded in "*Boden und Blut.*" Heidegger explained that the basic problem with these excessively *Westernized* philosophical perspectives was that "the essence of man is dissolved into a free-floating consciousness [*freischwebendes Bewusstein*] . . . and a universally logical 'world reason' [*Weltvernunft*]. Thereby . . . attention is diverted from man *in his historical rootedness*, his folkish [*volkhaften*] tradition, and his origins in *soil* and *blood* [aus *Boden und Blut*]. . . . [Hence,] man becomes a servant of an indifferent universal world culture."[179]

In an August 1933 address, Heidegger, employing similar arguments, exalted "blood" and "soil" as guarantors of "authenticity" and "greatness." "Every *Volk* possesses the guarantee of its own authenticity and greatness," claimed Heidegger, "*in its blood, its soil, and its corporeal growth* [*in seinem Blut, seinem Boden und seinem leiblichen Wachstum*]." "Should these qualities dissipate or grow weak," he continued, "every political effort on the part of the State—all economic and technical know-how, all spiritual capacities [*geistige Wirken*]—will, in the long run, prove useless and pointless."[180]

Although Heidegger's treatment of "race" fluctuated, when it came to the *Volksbegriff*, all hesitancies on his part quickly dissipated.

Over the course of World War I, the *Volksbegriff* metamorphosed into toxic ideological amalgam: a composite of late Romantic emotionalism, decisionistic *Machtpolitik*, secular eschatology, *Lebensphilosophie*, and Social Darwinism. Taken as a whole, these elements fused to shape and inform the *Rassengedanke*.

In "The Self-Assertion of the German University," Heidegger referenced "das Volk" no fewer than thirty-eight times. "The will to the essence of the German university," asserted Heidegger, "is the will to [realize] the historical-spiritual mission of the German *Volk* as a *Volk* that knows itself in its State." "The spiritual world of a *Volk* is a power that derives from . . . *forces that are rooted in the soil and blood of a Volk*": forces that possess the "power to arouse . . . and to shake up the *Volk*'s existence."[181]

In referencing *das Volk*, Heidegger did not mean any *Volk* whatsoever. He meant the German *Volk*, or *Deutschtum*, to which he consistently attributed an eschatological, salvific role. Heidegger held that the West's redemption from the nightmare of European nihilism hinged on the "metaphysics of German Dasein."[182] In his view, the German *Volk* possessed metaphysical traits and capacities that other *Völker* egregiously lacked. Time and again, Heidegger insisted that the "saving power"—*das Rettende*—should it materialize, could only come from the Germans.

Heidegger's frequent employment of *Volk*, in philosophical treatises as well as in political texts, offers a number of important clues concerning his attitudes toward race thinking. By the late 1920s and early 1930s, when Heidegger began utilizing the *Volksbegriff* extensively, it had merged indistinguishably with the idea of race. Research on the "language of totalitarianism" has shown that, between 1871 and 1900, the meanings of "national" and "völkisch" diverged. According to *Meyers Enzyklopädisches Lexikon*, "völkisch" increasingly became synonymous with "*an ethnically exclusive, antisemitic nationalism*." The *Brockhaus Wörterbuch* reaffirmed this finding, remarking that, during this time frame, " 'völkisch' assumed the contours of *an emphatically antisemitic nationalism that was grounded in the Rassengedanke*."[183] Finally, the conceptual historian Reinhart Koselleck, in his contribution to the article "Volk, Nation, Nationalismus, Masse" in *Geschichtliche Grundbegriffe*, confirmed the semantic entwinement of these two terms. Koselleck explained that, by the early 1930s, "Volk's ideological, illocutionary, and perlocutionary functions had been subsumed by the concept of 'race.' "[184]

Hence, with the twilight of the Weimar Republic, *Volk* had all but forfeited its earlier, democratic-constitutional valences. Instead, it connoted the impassioned allegiance to an irrational, race-based *Weltanschauung*. In its racial iteration, *Volk* vigorously opposed the Rousseauian ideal of democratic sovereignty, as embodied by the *volonté générale*. Instead, it posited that the goal of meaningful politics was to "express" the inner life of the *Volk*, thereby giving concrete form to an organic, prepolitical *Volksubstanz*.

Since the specific content of this *Volksubstanz* remained nebulous and ill defined, it required the political "will" of a Führer to give it shape and direction.
In addition to positioning *Führer-Schichten*, or leadership cadres, another paramount responsibility of the "State" was to protect the *Volk* from the contamination of alien racial influences.

Volk and Historicity

Heidegger's account of *Geschichtlichkeit* in *Being and Time*, Division II,
offers a propitious starting point for understanding his approach to the *Volksbegriff*. Heidegger regarded *Geschichtlichkeit* and *Volk* as "existential"
corollaries. He understood both notions as expressions of *Eigentlichkeit*, or authentic Being-in-the-world.

In line with a problematic cultural lineage stemming from J. G. Herder,
Heideggerian *Geschichtlichkeit* pointedly rejected cosmopolitanism in favor of
the *Volksbegriff*.[185] In keeping with this tradition, Heidegger held that the primary historical "actors"—the "carriers" of *Geschichtlichkeit*—were *Völker*, or
"peoples," rather than "humanity" (*die Menschheit*), a concept that proponents
of *völkisch* thought belittled as an insubstantial abstraction. During the 1930s,
Heidegger expressly warned against "hackneyed," "cosmopolitan" interpretations of pre-Socratic philosophy, readings he contrasted unfavorably with the
imperatives of "Greco-Germanic mission."[186]

In his exposition of *Geschichtlichkeit*, Heidegger, in a passage that invoked,
seriatim, the concepts of *Gemeinschaft*, *Geschick*, and *Generation* (community,
fate, and generation), lauded *Volk*'s centrality. As Heidegger asserted, "If fateful
Dasein . . . exists essentially in Being-with-others, its co-historizing is determinative for it as *destiny [Geschick]*. This is how we designate the *historizing of
the community [Gemeinschaft]*, of a *Volk*, . . . Dasein's *fateful destiny in and
with its Generation*."[187]

The terms that Heidegger employed in the foregoing passage were talismans
of the conservative revolutionary worldview. Viewed as an ensemble, they
were emblematic of an antidemocratic, protofascist idiom, whose perlocutionary effect accustomed the *Bildungsbürgertum*, or educated middle classes, to
accept the political excesses of Nazism.[188] As Kurt Sontheimer has remarked in
"Antidemocratic Thought in the Weimar Republic," these ideas formed the cornerstone of a metapolitical orientation that provided "spiritual preparation" for

National Socialism.[189] The "Generation" that Heidegger had in mind was, of course, the *Frontgeneration*, whose members proudly regarded themselves as a *Schicksalgemeinschaft*, a "community of fate."

In a study of Heidegger and Jünger, Daniel Morat, commenting on Heidegger's endorsement of "*völkisch* historicity" in *Being and Time*, reached a similar conclusion: "With the sequence involving *Geschick*, *Gemeinschaft*, and *Volk*, Heidegger delineated a mode of authentic Being-with-others that clearly qualifies as the conservative-*völkisch* counterweight to democratic publicness. . . . These passages from *Being and Time* clearly anticipate Heidegger's National Socialist engagement. They demonstrate the indebtedness of his existential ontology to the 'decisionistic' thinking of the conservative revolution."[190]

Race and *Erkenntnis* (Knowledge)

Heidegger's commitment to "spiritual racism" was also reflected in his view that a people's capacity for *Erkenntnis*, or knowledge, was determined by race. As we have seen, Heidegger maintained that, when it came to the *Seinsfrage*, the Germans possessed an incontestable metaphysical advantage. According to Heidegger, the ability to productively reflect on the essential nature of Being was existentially tied to "the deepest necessity of German Dasein."[191]

Heidegger's belief in an ontologically conditioned racial hierarchy derived from his embrace of the *Volksbegriff*. This demarche led him to the "racialist" conclusion that the capacity for truth was not equally distributed among the world's *Völker*, or peoples. *Deutschtum's* exceptional and unique capacity for truth was counterbalanced by the defective understanding of truth displayed by inferior, "unhistorical" races or peoples: Jews, Slavs, and "Negroes." In Heidegger's view, their ontological deficiencies reduced them to avatars of *Seinsvergessenheit*.

Heidegger perceived the history of Being as, inherently and unavoidably, a racial struggle, or *Kampf*. At its center lay an ontological confrontation in which the "destiny of the West" hung in the balance. In order for Germany's salvific role to be fulfilled, it was necessary to do battle with the ideological and geopolitical adversaries that threatened to impede or obstruct the path to "another Beginning."

The "ontological differences" among peoples that Heidegger discerned—their hierarchical standing in the "epochal" trajectory of *Seinsgeschichte*—were predicated on racial distinctions: on the confluence of *Volk*, *Boden*, and

Geschichte that Heidegger regarded as the keys to deciphering the fluctuations and rhythms of *Geschichtlichkeit*.

Heidegger's understanding of truth's "ontological rootedness" conditioned his view of *Deutschtum*'s historically privileged relationship to truth, hence his asseveration in the *Black Notebooks* that "*the German alone . . . will conquer the essence of theoria.*"[192] Heidegger was convinced that the "question of truth" and the question of German "destiny" (*Schicksal*) were inherently intertwined. On these grounds, he accorded *Deutschtum* an exceptional status in the metanarrative of *Seinsgeschichte*. Consequently, in Heidegger's view, resolving the *Wahrheitsfrage* depended on reinstating what Heidegger described as the "primordial laws of our Germanic tribal heritage [*Urgesetze unseres germanischen Menschenstammes*]."[193]

Heidegger's endorsement of "German exceptionalism"—the view that the German *Volk* harbored an ontological capacity for truth that other *Völker* lacked—provided an epistemological warrant for his commitment to German racial superiority. As such, *race thinking infected the core of Heidegger's fundamental ontology*. Such judgments suffused his philosophical texts, especially, in cases where questions of *Geschichtlichkeit* were at issue.

The tenets of race thinking were also apparent in Heidegger's excoriation of inferior races, or *Völker*: Slavs, Africans, and, especially, Jews, whom Heidegger held responsible for the total degradation of Being. Viewed in historical context, Heidegger's condemnations of "world Jewry" were tantamount to rhetorical summonses to genocide. Lecturing on "Nietzsche's metaphysics" in 1941–42, as the Third Reich began finalizing its plans for the "Endlösung," Heidegger praised "Extermination"—"das Vernichten"—as "that which assures [Germany] against the prospect of defeat."[194]

In *Logic as a Question Concerning the Essence of Language*, Heidegger grappled with the seemingly contradictory proposition that "although Negroes [Neger] are men, they have no history." Via recourse to italics, Heidegger explained that, in order to vindicate this assertion, it was necessary to distinguish between "Geschichte" and "*Geschichte*," "history" and "*history*." As Heidegger tantalizingly suggested, "history and *history* are not always the same."[195]

In Heidegger's view, the distinction at issue depended on the ability to differentiate between mundane, empirical history and *Geschichtlichkeit*: *historicity qua authenticity*. For Heidegger, *Geschichtlichkeit* meant "being-historical" in the sense of advancing *Seinsgeschichte*, or the "history of Being."

Heidegger feared that, in lieu of the distinction between "average everyday" history and *historicity* proper, one risked countenancing a congeries of meaningless, inauthentic histories. The examples of ontologically "meaningless" history that Heidegger provided were "the history of animals, of plants, . . . [and] the history of the entire earth." The "history of Negroes," Heidegger continued, was on a par with the aforementioned instances of "natural history." The linchpin of Heidegger's argument was his claim that not everything that "passes away" deserves to be treated as "historical" in the strong sense of *Geschichtlichkeit*: "Might *nature* be said to have history? In that case, however, *Negroes would also have history.* . . . As something that passes away, nature enters into the past. Yet, not everything that passes away becomes 'historical.' When an airplane propeller turns, then nothing *essential* 'occurs' [*geschieht*]. Conversely, if the airplane in question brings the *Führer to Mussolini, then history takes place. The flight becomes history. And the airplane itself enters into history.* It might even be displayed in a museum! The historical character of the airplane does not depend on the turning of the propeller, but instead on what grows out of this meeting."[196]

In the just-quoted passage, the repercussions of Heidegger's abandonment of universal history in favor of the racialist *Volksbegriff* emerge. Moreover, since Heidegger's *völkisch* understanding of history was profoundly infused with Social Darwinism, it did not shy away from celebrating the "existential" right of so-called large-space nations, such as Nazi Germany, to subsume "small-space" nations within its geographical orbit. Consequently, agreeing with the architects of Nazi geopolitics, Heidegger held that, in an era of unrestrained *Machtpolitik*, "small-space" nations had forfeited their *Existenzrecht*.[197]

Heidegger's condemnations of "ontologically defective" *Völker* frequently devolved into a litany of dehumanizing, anti-Semitic stereotypes. In the *Black Notebooks*, he alleged that Germany's geopolitical adversaries—England, the United States, and Bolshevism—were pawns of "world Jewry": "a type of humanity that, lacking permanent ties [*schlechthin ungebunden*], assumed the world-historical 'task' of *uprooting* [*Entwurzelung*] *the totality of beings from Being*." In Heidegger's view, world Jewry, by reducing "history" to "Machenschaft" and by virtue of its "planetary" spread, managed to "entrap all comers equally in its net."[198]

According to the strictures of fundamental ontology, to denounce a "people" or "race" for "uprooting the totality of beings from Being" was the most serious indictment imaginable. It meant accusing them of having sinned against the

Seinsgedanke. Hence, no form of retribution would be too severe. In "On the Essence of Truth," the remedy that Heidegger urged was "völlige Vernichtung": "total annihilation."[199]

Volksgemeinschaft and German Singularity

"Volksgemeinschaft"—another Nazi idiom that Heidegger employed profusely—was also inseparable from the *Rassengedanke*. By the mid-1920s, it, too, had been fully racialized. *Volksgemeinschaft* excluded from the national community "racially alien" groups whose ethnic difference was adjudged potentially injurious to the *Volk*'s well-being. As Hitler ominously avowed in 1934, "Only by realizing an authentic *Volksgemeinschaft*, one that annuls antagonistic interest groups and classes, might one permanently eliminate deformations of the human spirit."[200]

Heidegger's use of *Volksgemeinschaft* was wholly consistent with the term's ideological employment under Nazism. For example, in the *Rektoratsrede*, Heidegger lauded *Arbeitsdienst* (labor service) as "the bond that unites the *Volksgemeinschaft*. It entails the obligation to share fully . . . in the toil, the striving, and the abilities of all estates and members of the *Volk*." In "Arbeitslager und die Universität" (Labor Camps and the University), Heidegger exalted *Arbeitslager* as a "new institution for the direct revelation of the *Volksgemeinschaft*." And in a June 1933 address on "the university in the New Reich," Heidegger urged that "the university be integrated again within the *Volksgemeinschaft* and be joined together with the State."[201]

As the Second World War neared its apocalyptic crescendo, Heidegger persisted in his belief that the West's "redemption" was, necessarily, an exclusively German affair. Heidegger's conviction, far from being a contingent or occasional insight, was an ontological judgment: it was predicated on his view that the Germans alone were privy to the hidden "truth of Being" (*Wahrheit des Seyns*). As Heidegger observed, "Whatever may lie in store 'externally' with respect to the destiny of the West, the authentic test for the Germans still lies ahead: . . . whether they, as Germans, *in accordance with the truth of Being* [*Wahrheit des Seyns*] *and in readiness for death*, can remain strong enough in the face of the small-mindedness [*Kleingeisterei*] of the modern world to redeem the [Greek] 'Origin' [*das Anfängliche*]." "*Only the Germans*," added Heidegger, "*are capable of redeeming the West in its history*."[202]

Hence, as late as 1943, Heidegger remained oblivious to the catastrophic consequences that the ideology of "German exceptionalism" had wrought. Instead, he continued to insist that only the Germans—in contrast with other peoples or races, whom he accused of "Kleingeisterei"—stand in a privileged relationship to the "truth of Being." Heidegger's ontological chauvinism served as the philosophical basis of his political chauvinism. Heidegger's ontological racism functioned as the epistemological "ground" and "condition of possibility" of his political worldview.

The privileged role that Heidegger attributed to *Deutschtum* in the developmental trajectory of *Seinsgeschichte* also sheds valuable light on his understanding of "spiritual racism." Heidegger's support for this credo helps to explain his frenetic efforts to accede to a position of "geistige Führung," or "spiritual leadership."

Heidegger's ideological zeal was reflected in the various measures he undertook during his *Rektorat* to transform the German university system into a training ground for *Führer-Schichten*, or "leadership cadres."[203] It was with this end in mind that, in the *Black Notebooks*, Heidegger redefined "education" as the "binding application of state-power [*Staatsmacht*] toward the ends of the [German] *Volk*'s will to self-assertion"—a formulation that surrendered "education" and "truth" to the ends of the National Socialist state.[204]

Fifteen years earlier, as World War I neared its sanguinary climax, Heidegger prophesied that Germany's "salvation" (*Rettung*) would only come to pass if "truly spiritual men seized the reins: . . . a decisive leadership stratum [*eine entschlossene Führung*] capable of training the *Volk* to recognize . . . the authentic value-ideals . . . of Dasein."[205] Similarly, at the dawn of the Third Reich, he asserted that it was necessary to "destroy" the German university in its liberal-Humboldtian guise so that a "new spiritual-political leadership [*Führung*]" could take control. "We need a new constitution for the university," claimed Heidegger, "one that will secure a new spiritual-political leadership [*geistige-politische Führung*]. To what end? Not for the sake of 'reconstructing' what is already at hand, but instead, *in order to destroy the university [zur Zerstörung der Universität*]. This 'negative goal' will only prove to be effective if a new race [*eines neuen Geschlechtes*] seizes the reins of education."[206]

Heidegger viewed the German university system as the "breeding ground" or "crucible" for the creation of this "new race." Accordingly, in the *Rektorat-srede*, he proposed that, under National Socialism, the university's goal must be the "Auslese der Besten": "selection of the best."[207] In the idiolect of National Socialism, *Auslese* was associated with the imperatives of "positive" and "negative" breeding. Both approaches were esteemed as methods of strengthening the "racial community," or *Volksgemeinschaft*. "Auslese" required "(1) the enhancement of the German *Volk*'s racial character by targeting, increasing, and strengthening biologically superior elements; (2) the identification and cultivation of biologically superior and gifted individuals for the sake of ensuring future leadership cadres [*Führernachwuchses*]."[208]

Auslese was predicated on the Social Darwinist view that laws of "natural selection" were the key to racial survival. As Hitler observed, "The universe in its entirety appears to be driven by a single idea or precept: never-ending selection [*Auslese*]. Ultimately, those who are stronger secure the right to live and those who are weaker die off. . . . It is the law of 'selection' [*Auslese*] that, in accordance with the natural struggle for existence [*Kampf ums Dasein*], grants victory to the healthy, to the strong, and to superior natures over the sickly, the weak, and the inferior natures."[209]

In the *Rektoratsrede*, Heidegger's appeal to *Auslese* emphasized its value with respect to "selecting" *Führerschichten*, or spiritual "leadership cadres": an orientation that reflected Heidegger's campaign to abolish the "liberal" conception of knowledge as a disembodied "cultural superstructure" (*der Überbau einer Kultur*). In Heidegger's view, one exemplary method of achieving this end was to subordinate knowledge (*Wissenschaft*) to the goals of the *Volksgemeinschaft*.[210]

Heidegger, Evola, and "Spiritual Fascism"

Heidegger's understanding of "*Volk* as *Geist*" resembled the "spiritual racism" of the Italian fascist Julius Evola (1898–1974), whose views on race consistently outflanked Mussolini to the right.[211] It has recently come to light that, in 1935, Heidegger read Evola's chef d'oeuvre, *Revolt against the Modern World* (1934), in German translation. A careful reading of *Überlegungen II–VI* indicates that Evola's "spiritual fascism" influenced Heidegger's iteration of conservative revolutionary *Zivilisationskritik*.[212]

During the 1930s, Evola refused to join the Fascist Party, which he regarded as excessively prone to compromise—hence as ideologically and politically flaccid. In *Pagan Imperialism* (1928), Evola excoriated Italian fascism's rapprochement with Catholicism, incensing the fascist authorities, who promptly removed him from the editorial board of Giuseppe Bottai's *Critica Fascista*.[213]

In Nazi Germany, Evola's books were widely translated and well received. In a review of *Revolt against the Modern World*, Gottfried Benn heralded Evola's efforts to propagate the ethos of "spiritual fascism" as a significant ideological breakthrough. As Benn enthused, "Whoever reads this book will see Europe differently!"[214]

In recent years, Evola's "Traditionalism" has made a noteworthy comeback among exponents of the European and U.S. extreme Right. For example, in a controversial Vatican speech (2014), Donald Trump's future campaign manager Steve Bannon lauded Evola's political views for their usefulness in the "global war against Islam." Bannon went on to praise Russian president Vladimir Putin as the only world leader who appreciated the value of "Julius Evola and different writers . . . who are the supporters of . . . the 'Traditionalist' movement"—notwithstanding the fact that, as Bannon grudgingly acknowledged, Evola's Traditionalism "eventually metastasized into Italian Fascism."[215]

Bannon's encomium to Putin reflected the fact that, at the time, one of the Russian president's leading political advisers was Alexander Dugin, an Evola devotee—during the early 1980s, Dugin translated *Pagan Imperialism* into Russian—as well as Russia's leading Heideggerian. In summer 2014, Putin embraced Dugin's "neo-Eurasianism" as a geopolitical warrant for Moscow's annexation of Crimea and invasion of eastern Ukraine.[216]

The fascist organization that Evola most admired was Heinrich Himmler's SS: a point that Evola drove home in his 1938 article "Le SS: Guardia e ordine della rev-olutizione crociuncinata" (The SS: Guard and Order of the Swastika Revolution).[217] Evola especially revered the *Ordensburgen*: training centers for a new racial elite that were modeled, in part, after the medieval Knights of the Teutonic Order. Although Evola's proximity to the Italian fascist regime grew over time, he "felt more at home among the German reactionaries. He saw Adolf Hitler, Nazism, and the SS as more nearly embodying his ideas than any of their counterparts in Italy. In particular, Evola had an 'almost total adherence' to the principles of the SS and an 'almost servile admiration' for Himmler, whom he knew personally."[218]

Proficient in German, Evola undertook several lengthy stays during the late 1930s in Nazi Germany, where he rubbed elbows with Nazi elites and attempted to ingratiate himself among the SS leadership. In June 1938, Evola presented a lecture cycle at the German-Italian Society in Berlin. In "The Weapons of Secret War," Evola outlined the global threat posed by the putative Jewish world conspiracy. His anti-Semitism made *The Protocols of the Elders of Zion*—in 1938, Evola penned a long preface to the Italian translation of the *Protocols*—look like the work of a neophyte. In another address, "The Aryan Doctrine of Holy War," Evola sought to convince Nazi leaders that the Italians, as the spiritual heirs of *Imperium Romanum*, deserved to be viewed as a "Nordic" race on a par with other full-blooded Aryans.[219]

Evola's early brush-up with the fascist regime notwithstanding, during the 1930s, he continued to publish in a wide array of fascist literary organs. Following the "Pact of Steel" with Nazi Germany, Mussolini, who was impressed by Evola's *Sintesi di doctrina della Razza* (A Summary of Racial Doctrine), sought out Evola's expertise with the aim of strengthening Italy's race laws, since Evola was widely regarded as one of fascist Italy's foremost authorities on race matters.[220] As Aaron Gillette observes in *Racist Theories in Fascist Italy*,

> Evola adopted racism because it allowed him to better express on the physical level several of his fundamental transcendental concepts: tradition, communal identity, inequality, and the predominance of spiritual values. He had no trouble accepting the . . . deprecation of blacks and Jews as . . . racial vermin. The Jewish stereotype was particularly convenient as a symbol of modernism. Race also served as a vehicle for the transmission of ancient Aryan values. As Evola explained it: "Racism conceives and valorizes the individual as a function of a given community either in space—as a race of living individuals—or in time, as a unity of race, of tradition, of blood."[221]

Following the war, Evola assumed the role of political mentor to a new generation of fascist activists, who broke with Italy's official neofascist party, the Movimento Sociale Italiano (MSI), owing to its entanglement in the web of bourgeois democracy. As the MSI's founder, Giorgio Almirante, once commented on Evola's mesmerizing influence on Italian youth, "He was our Marcuse, only better!"[222] It was Evola who, in widely read books such as *Men among the Ruins* (1951) and *Ride the Tiger* (1961), anticipated the neofascist strategy of political destabilization via gratuitous acts of violence that, in 1980, culminated in the horrific Bologna train-station bombing, in which eighty-five people were killed and over two hundred wounded.

Evola and Heidegger shared a Gnostic understanding of Western modernity as a "site of catastrophe."[223] Heidegger's sympathies for Gnosticism were evident in his neo-Augustinian view of "everyday Being-in-the-world" qua "Falling" (*Verfallen*): a condition in which *Angst, Schuld* (guilt), and "inauthenticity" predominated. In *Being and Time*, Heidegger denigrated "everyday Being-in-the-world" as pervaded by "temptation, tranquillizing, alienation, and self-entangling." Heidegger claimed that Dasein's existence was characterized by a "downward plunge" into the "groundlessness and nullity of inauthentic everydayness."[224]

In *Revolt against the Modern World*, Evola adopted the controversial "Indo-European" doctrine of "Tripartism." Writing in a full-blown Orientalist mode, Evola portrayed modernity as the "Kali Yuga": Sanskrit for the "Age of Darkness." In the Mahabharata's account of the four ages of Hindu spirituality, the Kali Yuga is the most forsaken and iniquitous. The modern world, qua Kali Yuga, was dominated by the debased spirituality of international Jewry, whose preeminence Evola regarded as inimical to the higher spirituality of "Tradition." In "The Weapons of Holy War," Evola defined "Tradition" as "being bound to the 'metaphysical-formative.'" "Tradition," Evola continued, "is the secret of all that possesses 'form' in the higher sense; hence, all that signifies *race* and *culture* in the higher sense."[225]

Evola maintained that the "conspiracy" or "plot" that had been set in motion by world Jewry portended an epidemic of "reverse assimilation"—a challenge that Evola illustrated by way of the following parable. An Aryan approached a rabbi in the interest of racial comity. The rabbi, however, would accept this conciliatory gesture only under one condition. "We Jews are circumcised," said the rabbi. "Hence, for the sake of comity, you Aryans must also be circumcised."[226]

At the core of *Revolt against the Modern World* stood a theory of Aryan supremacy. Drawing on René Guénon's *Crisis of the Modern World* (1927), which Evola translated into Italian in 1938, Evola glorified a mythical pre-Christian, Indo-European polity that was allegedly dominated by an elite coterie of warrior-priests: the "shock troops" of pagan spirituality.[227] This aristocratic warrior caste was composed of "sun people" whose Nordic *Ur-Heimat* had been destroyed by a natural catastrophe. The remaining members of this fictive, Indo-European *Herrenrasse* purportedly scattered across the Earth, seeking high ground in order to escape the deluge, or *Sintflut*.

"Traditionalists" seek to restore this lost race of proto-Aryan "sun people" to their rightful position of spiritual-political predominance—notwithstanding the fact that no archaeological evidence attesting to their existence has ever been discovered.[228]

In an article titled "Ur-Fascism," Umberto Eco helpfully clarified the ideological nexus between historical fascism and Evola's Traditionalism. According to Eco, Evola's "cult of Tradition" represented *Ur-fascism incarnate*: "One has only to look at the syllabus of every fascist movement to find the major 'Traditionalist' thinkers. The Nazi gnosis was nourished by traditionalist, syncretistic, and occult elements. The most influential theoretical source of the theories of the Italian *Nuova Destra*, Julius Evola, merged the Holy Grail with *The Protocols of the Elders of Zion*, alchemy with the Holy Roman and Germanic Empires."[229]

Three aspects of Evola's doctrine impacted Heidegger's worldview: (1) Evola's critique of science, (2) his antihumanism, (3) and his Nietzschean rejection of Christianity as an orientation suitable for slaves. Both Heidegger and Evola agreed that "world Jewry" was the prime mover behind the construction of Western modernity as a technological Moloch: a civilization in which a crude, all-encompassing "materialism" had anathematized all higher aspirations and goals.

Both Heidegger and Evola rejected attempts to validate race thinking via appeals to natural science. Both insisted that "spiritual fascism"—or, to employ Heidegger's expression, "*Volk* as Spirit"—represented a valuable corrective to this widespread misapprehension. In a recent article, one scholar has helpfully summarized these intellectual affinities as follows: "For Heidegger, as for Evola, the world was facing an apocalyptical decision. In Evola's case, it was the struggle between the traditional and the modern world that was at issue. In Heidegger's case, it was the struggle between the 'preeminence of *Machenschaft* and the authority of Being.' For Evola, the modern world had to perish in order for rebirth to occur; for Heidegger, history culminated in the 'self-annihilation of man.' However, far from being a misfortune, according to Heidegger, this situation paved the way for a 'purification of Being from the deep-seated disfigurations of beings [*das Seiende*].' "[230]

Following Steve Bannon's banishment from the White House in August 2017—in the heat of the 2016 election campaign, Bannon famously quipped that he wanted to make Breitbart News a "platform for the alt-right"—Trump's former chief political strategist had ample time to reflect on other European thinkers whose ideas might be serviceable for the ends of the transatlantic New Right. In a 2018 interview with the German news magazine *Der Spiegel*, he revealed that Heidegger's name had risen to the top of his list. In the words of the *Der Spiegel* journalist Christoph Scheuermann, "We sit down at the dining room table and [Bannon] picks up a book, a biography of the philosopher Martin Heidegger. '*That's my guy!*', Bannon says. Heidegger, he says, had some good ideas on the subject of Being, which fascinates him. . . . [Bannon] jumps from the depths of politics to the heights of philosophy, from the swamp to Heidegger in five seconds. What sets us apart from animals or rocks, Bannon asks? What does it mean to be human? How far should digital progress go?"[231]

Seinsgeschichte as *Heilsgeschichte*

Heideggerian *Seinsgeschichte* embodied a profane, quasi-mystical version of Christian *Heilsgeschichte*, one in which *Deutschtum*, instead of Christ, had been elevated to the role of *Erlöser*, or "redeemer."

The *Volk*-centered dynamic of redemption and catastrophe that conditioned Heidegger's history of Being was deeply rooted in German history. Its origins are traceable to the confluence of the Thirty Years' War and the rise of Pietism: developments that culminated in the political theology of Anabaptist Messianism. A similar eschatological dynamic fed the Ariosophists' pan-German delirium in the years preceding World War I.[232]

Another groundswell of pan-German, apocalyptic fervor arose during the Wars of Liberation, as poets and thinkers, in a secular recasting of *Heilsgeschichte*, sought to interpret the outpouring of nationalist sentiment as the manifestation of a preexisting divine plan.

Heidegger's ontological-historical treatment of *Kairos*, *Volk*, and *Führertum* closely tracked the discussion of similar themes in Johann Gottlieb Fichte's *Addresses to the German Nation* (1808). Fichte regarded the Germans as an "Ur-Volk": a "primordial people," whose uniqueness derived from its having "retained . . . the primordial language of its ancestral stock." On the basis of this view, Fichte developed his conception of Germany's distinctive, salvific-historical mission. "Should the German not assume world government through philosophy, the Turks, the Negroes, the North American tribes, will finally take it over and put an end to the present civilization," he warned.[233] "If you go under," Fichte warned, addressing his fellow Germans, "all humanity goes under with you, without hope for any future restoration." In *Addresses to the German Nation*, Fichte concluded by exalting the German *Volk* as "die

Auserwählte": the "elect" or the "chosen."[234] Other *Völker*, conversely, were consigned to perdition.

Fichte maintained that the Germans' linguistic and spiritual authenticity provided them with privileged insight into "the eternal archetype [*Urbild*] of all spiritual life." Hence, in his view, the Germans were the only Europeans who possessed an authentic culture. According to Fichte, the only other language that merited comparison with German was Greek. Anticipating Heidegger's conception of Germany's metaphysical singularity, Fichte concluded, "True philosophy is . . . uniquely German: that is, *primordial*."[235]

Thereafter, *völkisch* nationalism emerged as the linchpin of a new, salvific-Germanocentric national mythology: a mythology replete with its own symbols, dogmas, and myths. In the *Nationalization of the Masses*, George Mosse described the ethos of *völkisch*-salvific nationalism as follows: "The myths that formed the basis of the new national consciousness . . . stood outside of the contemporary flow of history. They were meant to make the world whole again and to restore a sense of community to the fragmented nation."[236]

In an essay that was written shortly after the Congress of Vienna (1815), Friedrich Schlegel, reflecting on the contemporary political situation, drew attention to the malignant spirit of *völkisch* nationalism that pervaded the German Confederation. "What bodes ill for the future," foresaw Schlegel, "is that, throughout Germany . . . many groups that pay lip service to the fanaticism of 'national character' [*Volkstum*] carry destructive discord and conquest in their hearts."[237]

In *The Apocalypse in Germany*, Klaus Vondung has shed light on the Manichean oscillation between destruction and redemption that, in times of crisis, increasingly defined Germany's self-understanding. As Vondung observed, "The phoenix of German spirit rises out of the ashes of its incinerated enemies. Only *ex negativo*, out of the struggle against a '*nonspirit*,' can German spirit exist. *Only in destruction does it gain any meaning*." Especially in times of war and catastrophe, "when the feelings of threat, disorientation, helplessness, and despair become so strong that absolutely no more meaning can be found, then . . . an apocalyptic reaction is likely to follow. The whole world is perceived as meaningless and is consigned to destruction. Meaning is expected from *a* New World. . . . Redemption alone makes the incomprehensible comprehensible. It transforms chaos into order, . . . gives suffering a purpose and eliminates the feeling of insecurity and powerlessness."[238]

Heideggerian *Geschichtlichkeit* consciously reprised this idiolect of secular-ized *Heilsgeschichte*, a discourse that exalted Germany's *Sendungsbewusstein*: its "special mission" as the West's divinely appointed savior. Inspired by Fich-te's and Hölderlin's prophecies, he extolled the Third Reich as a premonition of ontological-historical redemption.

Similarly, Heidegger demonized Germany's opponents as "unholy" champi-ons of "nihilism" and *Seinsvergessenheit*. He portrayed the struggle to elimi-nate nihilism as a quasi-theological battle to unmask and destroy "evil." It was in this vein that, in *An Introduction to Metaphysics*, Heidegger vilified "Amer-ica and Russia" as nations for which the "quantitative temper . . . aggressively destroys all rank and all that is world-spiritual [*welthaft-Geistige*]. . . . This is the onslaught of what we call *the demonic*, in the sense of *destructive evil*."[239]

In the just-quoted remarks, Heidegger's insensitivity to the nuance and com-plexity of historical circumstance becomes painfully apparent. As a rule, his po-litical judgments are indistinguishable from crude prejudice. They derive from a penchant for a priori reasoning that surpasses, by far, the alleged missteps of "Western metaphysics."

In order to combat the "demonic and destructive evil" that had triumphed in the United States and Russia, Heidegger cast his lot with the "inner truth and greatness of National Socialism." His support for National Socialism was not merely a personal-biographical *lapsus*. Instead, as Herbert Marcuse recog-nized, it was tantamount to *a betrayal of philosophy*: "A philosopher can be de-ceived regarding political matters. . . . But he cannot be deceived about a regime that killed millions of Jews, merely because they were Jews, that made terror into an everyday phenomenon, and that turned everything that pertains to the ideas of Spirit, Freedom, and Truth, into its bloody opposite."[240]

One consequence of Heidegger's approbation of Nazi race thinking was his endorsement of the regime's genocidal practices and policies. Heidegger de-fended the view that, in order to make the world safe for Being, one needed to make it *Judenrein*, "free of Jews." This conclusion followed from his convic-tion that "every philosophy is in-human—an all-consuming fire."[241] Heidegger's assertion proved eerily prophetic. Within a few years, European Jewry would perish, as Heidegger had forecast, in an "inhuman, all-consuming fire." Having dismissed the idea of "validity" as little more than a "tangle of confusion, per-plexity, and dogmatism," having endorsed the view that " 'understanding' has no [philosophical] prerogative and no entitlement," Heidegger's *Denken* entered into a destructive, downward ontological-historical spiral from which it never fully reemerged.

The *Judenfrage* as *Seinsfrage*

Heidegger's critique of Jewish *Machenschaft* relied on a quasi-theological oscillation between perdition and redemption. In Heidegger's view, the struggle against "world Jewry" constituted an *ontological struggle* in which, as he put it, nothing less than the "uprooting of beings in their entirety" (*die Entwurzelung alles Seienden*) was at stake. In Heidegger's mind, the *Judenfrage* and the *Seinsfrage* were, of necessity, ontologically intertwined.[242]

Toward the end of the 1930s, Heidegger commented that the historical present bore witness to "the end of the Great Beginning of Western humanity in which man was summoned to the guardianship of Being [*Seyn*]." What emerged instead was a new "age of darkness" or "Kali Yuga": "a technological monstrosity [*machenschaftlichen Unwesen*] in which . . . a sense of what is truly historical is lost and what is rootless takes on the most variegated and contradictory forms, unable to recognize itself as the monstrosity it is, in the extreme enmity and penchant for destruction. Victorious in this struggle—insofar as it merely struggles with no end in view, and therefore counts only as distorted image of struggle [*Kampf*]—is the greater rootlessness that is deprived of all ties [and that makes] everything useful (that is, *Jewry*)."[243]

Heidegger's reflections on *Seinsgeschick* are suffused by the eschatological dynamic described by Vondung. To offset the groundswell of "rootlessness," Heidegger endorsed the idea of a "purification of Being" (*Reinigung des Seins*): notwithstanding the fact that, by his own avowal, this "Reinigung" was fated to culminate in "the self-obliteration of the earth and the disappearance of contemporary humanity"—that is, in the wholesale annihilation of life as we know it. Heidegger was quick to add that the anticipated catastrophe should neither be feared nor construed as a "misfortune" (*kein Unglück* [ist]). Instead, he insisted that humanity should *welcome* this act of "self-obliteration," since it portended the "purification of Being from the thoroughgoing distortions resulting from the predominance 'beings.'"[244] Heidegger's glorification of the "purification of Being" paralleled National Socialism's obsession with *racial purification*, thus revealing the extent to which his *Denken* had become entangled in the "cleansing fantasies" of Nazi race doctrine.[245]

In the *Black Notebooks*, a similar dynamic arose in conjunction with Heidegger's appropriation of the Spenglerian theme of "Untergang," which he refunctioned for the ends of *Seinsgeschichte*. "*Untergang*," exulted Heidegger, "is not something that should be feared!" Instead, Heidegger continued, insofar as it anticipated "the transition to another Beginning," it should be *welcomed* as "the essential precondition for historical Greatness." "Man's truth for Being [*Seyn*]," added Heidegger, "first manifests itself in *Untergang*."[246]

Heidegger's persistent efforts to endow Nazi criminality with a patina of ontological dignity are, to say the least, deeply troubling. They cast doubt on the cogency and viability of his doctrine of *Seinsgeschichte* as a whole. After all, how might one reconcile Heidegger's insistence on the interrelatedness of the *Seinsgedanke* and the *Wahrheitsfrage* with the notion that "Man's truth for Being first manifests itself in *Untergang*"? Such assertions, instead of clarifying historical circumstances, threaten to shunt insight and lucidity into an unfathomable abyss from which they are unlikely ever to resurface.

National Socialist ideology held that "world Jewry" was engaged in a global conspiracy to undermine the racial integrity of other *Völker*—especially, the Germans. Consequently, champions of the *Volksbegriff* regarded the Jews as a *Gegen-Rasse*, or "antirace"—hence the necessity of eliminating their influence from German life. In "The Jews in Music" (1850), Wagner excoriated Judaism as "the evil conscience of modern civilization."[247] Thereafter, the campaign to remove Jews from German life advanced by degrees. It began with the assertion, "you may not live among us as Jews." It was succeeded by the command, "you may not live among us." It culminated in the "annihilationist" edict, "you may not live."[248]

Heidegger's justification of the "Final Solution" was "racial-ontological." As he observed in the *Black Notebooks*, "The Jews, on the basis of their manifestly cunning talents [*rechnerischen Begabung*], have 'lived' on the basis of the principle of race [*Rassenprinzip*] longer than any other people. Yet, they defend themselves to the hilt against the application of that principle."[249]

It is worth noting that, in the preceding quotation, Heidegger elected to place the word "live" in quotation marks. This diacritical qualification was no *lapsus* on Heidegger's part. Instead, by proceeding in this manner, he sought to highlight the "existential" truth that the Jews, as a people or race, did not really "live." It was an ontological deficiency that reflected their incapacity to "have a world."

Heidegger regarded the ability to "have a world" as one of the ontological preconditions for "being human," in the sense of Dasein or *Existenz*. Conversely, he regarded Jews as an essentially *worldless Volk*, insofar as they lacked the ability to "have a world." In Heidegger's eyes, a "rootless" *Volk* was, by definition, a "worldless" *Volk*.

These conclusions followed inexorably from Heidegger's disparagement of Jews as "nomads": a condition of permanent dissociation and flux—a state of existential perdition—that resulted from the Jews' preternatural *Bodenlosigkeit*, or "rootlessness." In Heidegger's view, so integral was the nexus between *Volk* and *Boden*, "people" and "soil," that peoples who *lacked* this connection suffered from a type of *existential-cognitive impairment*—hence Heidegger's claim that the "realm of essential decision" was forbidden to Jews. As Heidegger explained in *Nature, History, and State*, "*Volk* and *Raum* are mutually interrelated. On the basis of a *Volk*'s specific knowledge about the nature of its 'space,' we experience the way that nature manifests itself to it. German space [*deutscher Raum*] reveals itself in a different way to a Slavic *Volk* than it does to us Germans. *In the case of Semitic nomads, it is likely that German space will never reveal itself at all.*"[250]

Since the Jews were incapable of *Existenz* in the Heideggerian sense, they were also incapable of *Geschichtlichkeit*. Hence, ontologically speaking, they were incapable of *authenticity*. Proceeding from these premises, Heidegger—in basic agreement with leading proponents of the *Rassengedanke*—regarded "world Jewry" as a *Gegen-Rasse*, or "anti-*Volk*." According to Heidegger, the Jews' "worldlessness"—a consequence of Jewish "rootlessness"—meant that Jewish *Existenz* had more in common with the Being of "stones" and "plants" than it did with Dasein, or human Being.

Heidegger's "ontological" disqualification of the Jews was directed against Jews as a "race" or "Volk." As such, it was, at base, a *racial disqualification*.

4

Arbeit macht frei: Heidegger and the German Ideology of Work

Under the Third Reich, the true meaning of the pseudo-revolutionary concept of Arbeit *was best demonstrated by Heidegger. Taking his cue from Ernst Jünger, Heidegger exalted work "existentially." He demanded that his students surrender their academic insularity for the more demanding and risky life of* Arbeitsdienst *or "labor service." Emblematic of these developments was the unspeakable motto that greeted prisoners as they entered the* Arbeits- *and* Todeslager *at Auschwitz: "Arbeit macht frei."*
—Frank Trommler, "The Nationalization of *Arbeit*"

With Heidegger, everything became "Gestalt": either the Führergestalt *or the* Gestalt *of Stefan George or the Gestalt of der* Arbeiter, *or the* Gestalt *of the* Gemeinschaft. *Ernst Jünger's* [Der Arbeiter: Gestalt und Herrschaft] *exerted a tremendous influence on Heidegger. Heidegger was convinced that it was* concrete Gestalten, *rather than abstract values and norms, that were obligatory. . . . The Gestalt required to shape the* Volk *was the "Werk."*
—Max Müller, in *Martin Heidegger: Ein Philosoph und die Politik*

Arbeit and "Authenticity"

DURING THE 1930S, ONE OF THE most noteworthy features of Heidegger's *Denken*—albeit one that, in the secondary literature, has remained largely unremarked—concerns his preoccupation with the philosophical meaning of

Arbeit. Following the Nazi seizure of power, Heidegger highlighted *Arbeit*'s sa-
lience repeatedly and in a wide variety of contexts: in lectures courses, seminars, treatises, and various political settings. The titles of these texts confirm
Arbeit's centrality for Heidegger's political self-understanding: "*Arbeitsdienst*
and the University," "The German Student as *Arbeiter*," and "The Call to *Arbeitsdienst*."[1] Moreover, in Heidegger's *Rektoratsrede*, "The Self-Assertion of the
German University," he denominated *Arbeitsdienst* (labor service)—along with
Wehrdienst (military service) and *Wissensdienst* (service-in-knowledge)—as
one of three essential *Dienste*, or forms of "service," vital for the consolidation
of a unified *Volksgemeinschaft*. The distinctive, "existential" idiolect that
Heidegger employed to discuss these themes attested to the philosophical seriousness with which he approached them.

Heidegger's lecture course *Logic as a Question Concerning the Essence of Language* (1933–34) provides additional evidence concerning *Arbeit*'s existential-
philosophical centrality. Careful textual scrutiny suggests that Heidegger regarded
Arbeit as a topos that was on a par with the other "existentials" or "formal indica-
tions" of *Being and Time*. Heidegger understood *Arbeit* as *a fundamental modality
of Dasein's Being-in-the-world*, one that was covalent with other "existentials"
such as "everydayness," "care," "Being-with-others," and "historicity."

Equally important, Heidegger viewed *Arbeit* as a manifestation of "authenticity." On these grounds, he assigned it a distinctive metaphysical capacity or
function as a form of *Existenz*, or Being-in-the-world, that facilitated the disclosure or unveiling of beings. In all of these respects, *Arbeit* played a crucial role
in Heidegger's narrative of *Seinsgeschichte*. As Heidegger declaimed in *Logic
as a Question Concerning the Essence of Language*, *Arbeit* "transports Dasein
into the openness of what is": "*Arbeit = the Present* [*die Gegenwart*]. The
present is not the 'Now' [*das Jetzige*]; rather, it is the Present insofar as it transposes our Being into the work-related emancipation of beings [*werkgerechte
Befreiung des Seienden*]. As someone who works [*Arbeitender*], man is transported into the openness of what is. This Being-transported toward things belongs to the essence of our Being."[2]

The emphasis that Heidegger placed on the philosophical value of *Arbeit* broad-
ens our understanding of "Heidegger and practical philosophy."[3] From a philosophical standpoint, Heidegger's treatment of *Arbeit* complements the discussions
of "tools" (*Werkzeuge*), "equipment" (*Zeug*), and "readiness-to-hand" (*Zuhandenheit*) that are contained in the existential analytic of *Being and Time*. "The work

[*Werk*] to be produced," specifies Heidegger, "as the 'towards which' of such things as the hammer, the plane, and the needle . . . has the kind of Being that belongs to *equipment*. . . . The work that is to be found when one is 'at work' on something [*das in Arbeit befindliche*] has a usability which belongs to it essentially and that allows us to encounter the 'towards which' for which it is usable."[4]

Heidegger's treatment of *Arbeit* also stands as a positive counterweight vis-à-vis his subsequent indictment of "technics" as "enframing" (*Gestell*) and "standing reserve" (*Bestellen*): a development that he regarded as the "consummation" (*Vollendung*) of European nihilism. Heidegger's *Arbeit* enthusiasm explains why he construed National Socialism's "inner truth and greatness" in terms of its potential for resolving the disequilibrium "between planetary technology and modern man."[5] In sum, Heidegger held that National Socialist *Arbeit* possessed the capacity to transcend and overcome (*Verwindung*) the nihilism of Western "technics."

Heidegger took his cue from Ernst Jünger's writings and elevated *Arbeit*, in ontological-historical terms, as a manifestation of *völkisch* authenticity. Heidegger also assigned *Arbeit* an epistemological role in the dialectic of "concealment" (*Verborgenheit*) and "unconcealment" (*Unverborgenheit*): that is, as a mode of "unveiling" that facilitated the disclosure of the "Being of beings." Heidegger's ideological proximity to Jünger goes far toward explaining his abiding preoccupation with concepts such as *Arbeitslager*, *Arbeitsdienst*, and *Arbeitsfreude*: notions that became indispensable to Heidegger's post–*Being and Time* recalibration of "historicity."[6]

Hence, if one is serious about fathoming the meaning and implications of Heidegger's understanding of Being-in-the-world, assessing the ontological significance of *Arbeit* is paramount.

A Brave New World of "Total Mobilization"

On several occasions, Heidegger avowed that, during the 1930s, his understanding of contemporary politics had been decisively shaped by Ernst Jünger's vision of a protofascist, ultramilitarized *Arbeitergesellschaft*—a perspective that Jünger had honed in his 1932 monograph *Der Arbeiter: Herrschaft und Gestalt* (The Worker: Domination and Form).

In Heidegger's 1937 lecture course *Nietzsche's Metaphysical Centrality for Western Thought*, he extolled Jünger and Oswald Spengler as the only "authentic heirs to Nietzsche."[7] In light of Heidegger's unabashed reverence for Nietzsche's work during this period, this avowal carries considerable weight. Following a theoretical template that Nietzsche had formulated in *The Will to Power*, Heidegger held that Jünger and Spengler had consummately unmasked the West's headlong descent into "nihilism." Moreover, both authors, to their credit, had identified the implacable rise of modern technology as a leading precipitant of Western "decline" (*Untergang*). In the *Black Notebooks*, Heidegger sought to subsume the various manifestations of nihilism under the rubric of *Machenschaft*.

In *Zu Ernst Jünger*—the *Gesamtausgabe* volume that collates the notes and reflections that Heidegger recorded in preparation for the three seminars that he conducted during the 1930s on Jünger's work—Heidegger returned to the Jünger-Nietzsche filiation, in order to clarify the "metaphysical" significance of their pathbreaking exposés of European nihilism. Heidegger claimed, "Ernst Jünger was the only figure to produce an interpretation of World War I that grasped the war's military essence [*seinem kriegerischen Wesen*]. His interpretation is based on his excruciating [*härtesten*] experiences as a platoon leader in the battles of matériel. Jünger's account is *unequalled* in the way that it grasps the metaphysical precept that defines this age . . .: *Nietzsche's 'will to power.'* Jünger replaces . . . Nietzsche's principle with a term that is more adequate to our century, one that stems from the tradition of German metaphysics after Leibniz: '*Arbeit.*'" Heidegger concluded these reflections by reaffirming that the terms *Arbeit* and *Arbeiter*, properly understood, are metaphysical concepts.[8]

Eight years later, in "The Rectorship: Facts and Thoughts" (1945), Heidegger explained that he esteemed Jünger's work owing to its astute *Zeitdiagnose* of the modern age as an *Arbeitszeitalter*, an "age of work":

> In 1930, Ernst Jünger's essay on "Total Mobilization" appeared. There, he outlined the basic features of his 1932 book, *Der Arbeiter*. At the time, I discussed the book in a small group and sought to show how it expressed *an essential understanding of Nietzsche's metaphysics*, insofar as the horizon of this metaphysics [was] correctly perceived and anticipated the history and present-day status of the West. On the basis of the conceptual foundations that these texts provided, we sought to fathom the nature of What Was to Come [*das Kommende*]; in other words, we sought to confront and to debate it.[9]

In *Der Arbeiter*, Jünger apotheosized modern society's metamorphosis qua technocratic behemoth: as a battle-ready, totalitarian monolith that was dominated by a caste of interchangeable and robotic "soldier-workers" and "worker-soldiers."

The political-military template for Jünger's Orwellian vision was the advent of "total mobilization" during the Great War. World War I's titanic "battles of matériel" had demanded the total integration of all sectors of society for the sake of the war effort. Women and retirees were also "conscripted" to serve as *Arbeiter* on what became known as the "home front." Toiling long hours in outsized armaments factories and in other war-related industries, they constituted a new *Arbeiterheer*: an "army of labor." The Great War confirmed the effacement of the customary distinction between military and civilian life. Under National Socialism, the trend toward the militarization of everyday life accelerated, thereby reaffirming Jünger's dystopian prognosis. Workers were commonly referred to as *Soldaten der Arbeit*, or "soldiers of labor."

With these developments in mind, Jünger forecast the advent of an all-encompassing *Arbeitzeitalter*: an "Age of Work" that, henceforth, would define and determine all forms of human activity. As Jünger observed,

[Total mobilization] conveys the extensively ramified and densely veined power supply of modern life towards the great current of martial energy. . . . Total mobilization is far less consummated than it consummates itself. In war and peace, it expresses the secret and inexorable claim to which our life in the age of masses and of machines subjects us. The end result is that each individual life unambiguously resembles *the life of a worker*. Hence, following the wars of knights, of kings, and of citizens, we now have *wars of workers*. The first great twentieth-century conflict [i.e., World War I] has offered us a presentiment of their rational structure and of their mercilessness.[10]

In Jünger's view, the ascendancy of "mechanized warfare" meant that the contributions to the war effort made on the home front by the "army of labor" were no less important than those of the *Frontsoldaten*. The sheer scale of "mechanization"—in the munitions factories behind the lines and at the front itself—provided support for Jünger's assertion that, to all intents and purposes, the duties of workers and soldiers had become interchangeable. Both groups had effectively become appendages of a titanic, superhuman "war machine."

These developments culminated in the advent of a totalitarian *Arbeitergesellschaft*, at whose apex there stood a Leviathan-like "total state." As Jünger remarked, "The image of war as armed combat merges into the more extended image of a gigantic *Arbeitsprozess*. In addition to the armies that meet on the battlefields, there originate the modern armies of commerce and transport, foodstuffs, and the manufacture of armaments: *the Army of Work* [*Arbeiter-heer*]. . . . In this unlimited marshaling of energies, one that transforms the warring industrial nations into *volcanic forges*, we find the most striking sign of the dawn of the *Age of Work* [*Arbeitszeitalter*]." As Jünger jubilantly concluded, "In their world-historical import and significance, these developments by far transcend the French Revolution. Thereby, they put paid to the loathsome 'ideas of 1789.' "[11]

Jünger greeted these trends enthusiastically, since, in his view, they portended the end of the diffident and risk-averse "bourgeois individual." Confronted with the totalitarian demands of the *Arbeitszeitalter*, the bourgeois subject's timorous longings for tranquility and security would, deservedly, be crushed to a pulp. Jünger savored the irony that Enlightenment reason, instead of yielding "perpetual peace," had metamorphosed into "total wars" of unprecedented scope and proportion.

In "The Turn toward the Total State" (1931), Carl Schmitt acknowledged the uncanny prescience as well as empirical cogency of Jünger's perceptive *Zeit-diagnose*. As Schmitt observed, "All sectors are included in this new state. [It] encompasses not only the military . . . but everything else: industry and the economic preparation for war, intellectual and moral development, as well as the education of the citizens. Ernst Jünger has arrived at a pregnant formula to describe this astonishing process: *total mobilization*. [Jünger's] formulation . . . is fitting . . . insofar as it . . . conveys the idea of a great and profound transformation."[12]

However, as Walter Benjamin pointed out in "Theories of German Fascism"—his insightful review of *Krieg und Krieger* (1930), the Jünger-edited volume in which "Total Mobilization" first appeared—Jünger's "heroic realism" intentionally shunned all discussion of the devasting effects of modern industrialized warfare. It systematically glossed over and abstracted from its disfiguring, terrifying features. Instead, readers were left with a celebratory account of war as a vehicle for self-realization and aesthetic transfiguration. "It is more than a curiosity," observed Benjamin; "it is a *symptom*, that *Krieg und Krieger*, a text from 1930, ignores all of these developments": flamethrowers, machine guns capable of firing up to six hundred rounds per minute, aerial bombardment, dreadnoughts, gas warfare, and "mega-howitzers," such as the

420-millimeter "Big Bertha." So extensive was the range of new-generation artillery that the crews had to take the Earth's rotation into account before firing. Instead, in Jünger's texts, we are offered the "apotheosis of war": a gratuitous, cult-like veneration of carnage-for its own sake. As Benjamin concluded, "The most rabidly decadent origins of this new theory of war . . . is nothing other than an uninhibited translation of the principles of *l'art pour l'art* to war itself."[13]

Prussian Socialism

Jünger's image of a technofascist *Arbeitergesellschaft* was profoundly indebted to Oswald Spengler's monograph *Prussianism and Socialism* (1919), which Spengler had written as a political pendant to *The Decline of the West*. Germany's defeat in the Great War had been preceded by the November Revolution: a working-class uprising in protest of the Ludendorff dictatorship's inflexible prosecution of an unwinnable war. Thereafter, the German Right became obsessed with redirecting working-class loyalties away from "Marxist internationalism" and toward the patriotic ends of German nationalism.

Spengler's pamphlet epitomized this widely held conviction. There was no need, he argued, for German workers to seek out *international* solutions for their grievances, especially since the left-wing organizations claiming to represent them—which Spengler portrayed as money-grubbing and Jew-ridden— rarely had the workers' best interests at heart. He prophesied that, in the future, international socialism would cede to an authentically German, "national socialism."

The "national socialism" that Spengler envisioned incarnated the traditional "Prussian" virtues of *Pflicht*, *Gehorsamkeit*, and *Zucht*: "duty," "obedience," and "discipline." Spengler claimed that traditional Prussian values were best exemplified by three institutions: "the Prussian Army, the Prussian bureaucracy, and Bebel's workers [*Arbeiterschaft*]." Auguste Bebel, of course, was one of the founders of German social democracy. By including the *Arbeiterschaft* in this series, Spengler sought to rally the working class to the cause of German nationalism. Echoing Nietzsche's appeal for a "Superman," Spengler summarized his position as follows: "We need . . . a caste of *socialist Master-types* [*Herrennaturen*]. . . . Socialism means *power* [*Macht*], . . . and the recipe for attaining power is clear: combining the most valuable segment of German workers with traditional Prussian *étatisme* [*altpreussisches Staatsgefühl*]."[14]

Spengler derided theoreticians of "international socialism" as irresponsible *littérateurs*: men whose political ideas were predicated on unrealistic "programs" and "dogmas." The values of *Preussentum*, conversely, "were based on blood."[15]

Spengler's template for "Prussian Socialism" exuded nostalgia for the glories of the recently defeated *Kaiserreich*. In many respects, in *Der Arbeiter*, Jünger parroted the credo of "barracks socialism" that Spengler had celebrated twelve years earlier in *Preussentum und Sozialismus*. As one commentator has remarked, "Often, Jünger seems to have copied directly from Spengler. One finds exactly the same exaltation of *travailler pour le roi de Prusse*, *Arbeit* as an 'end-in-itself,' for the 'greater good of Prussia,' in Spengler. . . . Jünger's praise of *Arbeits-Pflicht* [work-as-duty] as the highest form of activity, and of the highly disciplined functioning of the 'Army of Work' [*Arbeiter-Armee*], had already been conceived by Spengler."[16]

At the same time, Jünger *actualized* Spengler's analysis, providing it with an "archeofuturist" twist by basing his *Gestalt* of the *Arbeiter* on the experiences of "total war."[17] In *Der Arbeiter*, Jünger praised German workers (*das Arbeitertum*) as "*Preussentum's only possible heir*," claiming that, since they had "experienced firsthand the destruction of all previous social bonds," they were exceptionally well positioned to rise to the challenges of "total mobilization." On these grounds, Jünger glorified "the worker" as the anthropological material of "a new aristocracy." "The worker" embodied the fulfillment of Nietzsche's prophecy concerning the advent of the "Superman" as a force capable of reversing the "dwarfing" of man under the constraints of "total mechanization."[18] As one insightful Jünger exegete has remarked, "*Der Arbeiter* praised a form of domination [*Herrschaft*] that was anonymous and unintelligible. Jünger's *Arbeiter* is the representative of a new *Herrenrasse*. Consequently, Nietzsche's idea of the *Übermensch* plays a key role. As the product of a specifically *German* form of 'training' [*Züchten*], the *Arbeiter* is racially and functionally superior to all other peoples, a *Gestalt* that shapes the human 'material' for German world-mastery [*Weltherrschaft*]."[19]

In sum, in *Der Arbeiter*, Jünger's *Gestalt* of the worker heralded the ascendancy of the "new man" qua "fascist man." In contrast with Spengler, his understanding of fascism as a combat-ready, mechanized colossus was decidedly future-oriented. Hence, in the pantheon of fascist literati, Jünger carved out a revered niche as a type of *Frontgeneration* Jules Verne.

"German Socialism"

Following the precedents established by Spengler and Jünger, Heidegger weighed in on the merits of "German socialism" in "The German Student as Worker" (*Der deutsche Student als Arbeiter*; 1933), an article that attested to *Der Arbeiter*'s influence on Heidegger's understanding of contemporary politics. (In a letter to the art historian Kurt Bauch, Heidegger acclaimed Jünger as "the only genuine literary figure that Germany possesses.")[20] Following Jünger's lead, Heidegger understood Nazism, first and foremost, as an *Arbeitswelt* and an *Arbeitergesellschaft*. He regarded the universalization of the *Arbeiter-Gestalt* as an unmitigated "metaphysical" blessing: already, the National Socialist *Arbeitersstaat* had made great strides in surmounting the lacerations and divisions of political liberalism, thereby paving the way for a renascent "national community" that was united in *Kampf*. As Heidegger remarked, "On what basis does the *Volk* attain its true composition and unity? Only insofar as the actions and reactions of every individual, group, and social stratum is conceived as *Arbeit*. Thanks to the new spirit of *Gemeinschaft*, *Arbeit*, for the first time, attains its authentic meaning. 'Der Arbeiter' is not, as Marxism would have it, a simple object of exploitation . . . whose salvation lies in class struggle. *Arbeit* is neither a commodity, nor does it merely serve to produce goods for others."[21]

Heidegger extolled "German socialism" as "a struggle [*Kampf*] that is concerned with the *Volk*'s essential organizational forms." "German socialism," he continued, "demands *hierarchy*, unconditional *service*, and the irreproachable honor of *Arbeit*. For us, this is the meaning of Freedom."[22]

By endorsing the "Prussian" virtues of "hierarchy," "service," and "work" (*Rangordnung*, *Dienst*, and *Arbeit*), Heidegger aligned himself clearly with the protofascist, national revolutionary *Weltanschauung* of Spengler and Jünger. His contention that "hierarchy" and "service" embody "the meaning of Freedom" is a classic case of Nazi ideological doublespeak: a rhetorical tactic that, on the one hand, trivialized the democratic understanding of freedom as "licentiousness" and, on the other hand, exalted servitude and obedience as "emancipatory."

Heidegger's encomium to *Arbeit* and "German socialism" betrayed his ideological affinities with "National Bolshevism," a worldview that Jünger propagated during the years that preceded *Der Arbeiter*'s publication. (From 1927 to 1933, Jünger and Germany's leading National Bolshevik, Ernst Niekisch, coedited the journal *Widerstand*.)[23] In this respect, it is significant that, in "The Rectorship: Facts and Thoughts," Heidegger claimed that his disillusionment with National Socialism dated from the Röhm purge of 30 June 1934. At the time, the SA has been clamoring for a "second revolution" that would make good on the Party's "socialist" commitments, in keeping with its claims to be an "Arbeiterpartei" (*workers'* party).[24]

Stressing the political significance of Germany's *Mittellage*, the National Bolsheviks favored a geopolitical alliance with the Soviet Union. They believed that the Versailles *Diktat* had saddled Germany with a set of anomalous, "Western" political institutions that undermined Germany's tradition of political authoritarianism. The National Bolsheviks emulated Lenin's ruthless embrace of dictatorial methods: his refusal to shy away from political violence, if called for, as well as his militarization of the economy during the period of "war communism" (1918–21). Jünger, for his part, found Lenin's definition of socialism as "the Soviets plus electrification" especially attractive: a no-nonsense approach to organizational questions that presaged his own doctrine of "total mobilization." The National Bolsheviks also esteemed the idea of a "command economy," which suited their Prussian veneration of *étatisme*. When Stalin launched the Soviet Union's first five-year plan in 1928, Bolshevism's cachet rose considerably, as did the idea of "state planning," more generally, following the Great Crash of 1929.

In 1924, Stalin had abandoned communist "internationalism" in favor of "Socialism in One Country." The National Bolsheviks viewed this heresy as a course correction on Stalin's part, as a de facto endorsement of "national communism." At the time, many observers began to wonder whether there was any meaningful difference between Stalin's brand of authoritarian national communism and the political Right's veneration of "national socialism." A popular witticism that described a Nazi as a "beefsteak"—"brown on the outside and red on the inside"—captured the presumptive ideological affinities of the two political extremes.[25]

The left-wing of the Nazi Party—its Berlin-based, northern faction, which was led by the brothers Gregor and Otto Strasser—also displayed a marked admiration for the Bolshevik dictatorship. The Strasser wing took seriously National Socialism's claims to being an anticapitalist *Arbeiterpartei*—a party that took to heart the well-being of the German working class—in contrast to the Munich branch headed by Hitler.

"Barbarians of the Twentieth Century"

During the 1880s, Nietzsche observed, "A dominant race can grow up only out of terrible and violent beginnings. . . . *Where are the barbarians of the twentieth century?*"[26] In *Der Arbeiter*, Jünger, writing in an apocalyptical register, sought to provide a response to Nietzsche's prophetic summons.

Following Nietzsche, Heidegger and Jünger hoped that the "barbarians" of the twentieth-century *Arbeiterwelt* would deliver a merciful *coup mortel* to a Western civilization in a state of terminal "decline" (*Untergang*). They viewed the sack of Rome by the Visigoths, in 410 CE, as a relevant historical precedent.

In keeping with Heidegger's veneration of "active nihilism," he subscribed to Nietzsche's maxim, "If something is falling, it must be given a final push!" As he remarked in *On Ernst Jünger*, "Nietzsche's nihilism is not the nihilism of the 'weak' that so readily slides into pessimistic indifference; instead, it is '*active nihilism.*' " Accordingly, Heidegger embraced Nietzsche's glorification of "the basic instinct of strong natures," adding, "one must not hesitate to produce *human victims*: [one must] court every danger, take upon oneself everything that is bad, including the very worst."[27]

Heidegger held that, for the new to be born, the old must be swept away without a trace—a conviction that, combined with his visceral antipathy to political liberalism, helps to explain his abiding attraction to the Nazi idiolect of *Sturm und Kampf*. As he remarked in 1936, "National Socialism's beauty [is] as a *barbaric principle*. It must take care lest it become bourgeois."[28] Recalling the 1929 Davos debate, Hans Jonas commented that, in the eyes of many attendees, the encounter pitted "Heidegger-the-barbarian" vis-à-vis Ernst Cassirer's "homo humanus."[29]

In an August 1935 letter to Kurt Bauch, Heidegger extolled Jünger's political clairvoyance. Alluding to Jünger's vision of an ultramilitarized, technocratic *Arbeitergesellschaft*, Heidegger asserted, "It seems to me that Jünger's vision has been confirmed." National Socialism, Heidegger continued, must be " '*spiritual*,' but also *severe* and *militarily firm*, in an entirely different sense than what, today, passes itself off as *Weltanschauung*."[30]

Reactionary modernists like Heidegger and Jünger were convinced that "Germany could be both technologically advanced and true to the soul. . . . [Their] accomplishment within the conservative revolution was to demonstrate that this national cultural protest could serve to celebrate, rather than to denounce, the mechanization of war and labor."³¹ In their eyes, one of the advantages of the fascist "industrial-warrior" state glorified by Jünger was that it portended the end of a moribund bourgeois *Zivilisation*. Among *fascisant* literati, few social types were as loathsome as "Der Bourgeois," which was also the title of a polemical, anti-Jewish tract penned by Werner Sombart on the eve of World War I.

Conservative revolutionary intellectuals regarded the Jews' as the "string-pullers" or "orchestrators" of modern capitalism. In *The Jews and Modern Capitalism*, Sombart characterized Jews as "rootless, restless, and coldly rational. They pushed the material calculus of profit and loss to its logical consequence, without regard for human interest. They invented virtually every modern commercial institution, from instruments of exchange, to fixed prices, to competitive advertising, to securities of uniform denomination, and security speculation."³²

For the febrile anti-Semitic imagination, the association of Jews with capitalism would harden into an unassailable idée fixe. In this way, the allegation that capitalism was a fundamentally Jewish contrivance—the result of a Jewish "plot"—became a central axiom of central European *Zivilisationskritik*.³³ According to this template, Jews were "merchants and traders, whereas the Aryans were producers and initiators. Jews were actors, imitators, and 'virtuosos'; Aryans were artists, creators, and 'amateurs.' . . . Jews were 'progressive,' whereas the Aryans were 'conservative.' Jews were 'shifty,' whereas the Aryans were 'principled.' "³⁴ Ultimately, such overheated polemics against "das Jüdische" reached a point where they did not need to be linked explicitly to Jewish themes. "The Jewish" became a metaphor for all that was fleeting and ephemeral, hence for uncontrollable social change. It became synonymous with "social mobility, the non-immediately-graspable, 'secretive practices,' and abstraction."³⁵

Spengler's *Decline of the West* embodied the *fons et origo* of the *Zivilisationskritik* paradigm. His writing overflowed with familiar anti-Semitic stereotypes. Spengler grudgingly conceded that, prior to the Jews' expulsion from Spain in 1492, they had registered numerous cultural achievements. However, once the Jews had forfeited their rootedness-in-soil, they became a dangerous and corrosive cultural presence.

Hence, in *Decline of the West*, Spengler denigrated "western European Jews" as "a coolie-mass characterized by a civilized, cold, superior intelligence and an unfailing eye for business." He asserted that the central tension animating

Western civilization was the conflict between "the Race-Ideal of the Gothic springtime . . . and that of the Sephardic Jew, which was formed in the ghettos of the West." "*It is want of race*," declaimed Spengler, "and nothing else, that makes intellectuals—philosophers, doctrinaires, Utopists—incapable of understanding the depths of this metaphysical hatred between these two groups. . . . *Jewry has been . . . destructive where it has intervened.*"[36]

Heidegger trafficked in many of the same anti-Semitic tropes and stereotypes as Spengler. Thus, following World War I, he attributed economic shortages and the growth of a black market to the Jews' predatory economic practices: "Here, there is a lot of talk about how many cattle now get bought up from the villages by Jews. . . . Everything is swamped with Jews and black marketeers," lamented Heidegger. Upon reading a study of Hölderlin by a German-Jewish scholar, Heidegger described the book as "so grotesque one can only laugh. One wonders whether from this contamination we will ever return to the primordial freshness and rootedness of life." "It is enough," Heidegger continued, "to make one become *a spiritual anti-Semite*." Apparently, Heidegger regarded "spiritual anti-Semitism" as the necessary antidote or a countermeasure to the Jewish cultural "contamination" that he detected in the aforementioned Hölderlin study. These remarks foreshadow Heidegger's acerbic denunciation, during the late 1920s, of the "Jewification [*Verjudung*] of German spiritual life."[37]

The epithet "Weltjudentum," to which Heidegger recurred without compunction in the *Black Notebooks*, is a keyword in the lexicon of modern anti-Semitism. It immediately calls to mind the idea of a "Jewish world conspiracy": a notion to which Heidegger subscribed by virtue of his characterization of "world Jewry" as the leading progenitor of "planetary" *Machenschaft*.[38] In light of these avowals of anti-Jewish paranoia, it is little wonder that Heidegger insisted in a conversation with Karl Jaspers that "there really is a world conspiracy of Jews."[39]

"Bard of Carnage"

During the 1920s, Jünger (1895–1998) gained notoriety as Germany's foremost literary representative of the *Frontgeneration*. In his war diaries, *In Stahlgewittern* (Storms of Steel) and *Kampf als inneres Erlebnis* (Struggle as Inner Experience), he glorified the brutality of the *Fronterlebnis*, transfiguring it into material for aesthetic contemplation.

In *Der Kampf als inneres Erlebnis*, Jünger described combat in mystical-or-gasmic terms—as an experience comparable to a religious epiphany:

> At last: ecstasy! As is true for a saint, a great poet, and great love, ecstasy also per-tains to instances of outstanding courage. Here, enthusiasm so suffuses manliness to a point where the hot, coursing blood threatens to burst through veins and over-whelm the heart. It is an intoxication beyond all intoxication, an unbinding beyond all constraint. It becomes a mad dash beyond restraint and limitation, comparable only to the forces of nature. Under such conditions, man becomes a gathering storm, a frothing sea, and rolling thunder. Then, suddenly, he is pulverized into thin air, traveling headlong to the gates of death like a speeding bullet. And as the purple ripples begin to pummel him, he is wholly unaware of the transition that lies in store for him. It is as though he were gliding on a wave.[40]

Jünger described his experiences as a platoon leader as an event akin to a reli-gious conversion, a profane illumination: "For many of us, the war experience produced a *total transformation of our essence*—one that can only be compared with the religious phenomenon of 'mercy,' through which a man is unexpect-edly and totally transformed."[41]

Although in the secondary literature, much has been made of Jünger's talents as an aesthete and *littérateur*, this emphasis downplays his tireless efforts to promote a bellicist, masculinist ethos of combat. Jünger's efforts to immortal-ize the *Fronterlebnis* were a classic case of Freudian *Nachträglichkeit* (posteri-ority). By retrospectively lionizing the *Kriegerlebnis*, Jünger sought to exalt and to redeem battles that the *Reichswehr* had, in reality, already *lost*. Thus, as a writer, one of Jünger's central aspirations was to bestow, *après coup*, an aura of meaning and purpose on an otherwise ignominious military defeat.

Just as Homer commemorated poetically the great deeds of the Trojan War combatants, Jünger sought to immortalize the experiences of the "community of the trenches" (*Schützengraben-Gemeinschaft*). However, in contrast with Homer, Jünger's narratives of atrocity and carnage took place in an era of in-dustrialized mass warfare, in which acts of individual heroism were dwarfed and overshadowed by a new generation of weaponry.

In *Zu Ernst Jünger*, Heidegger expressed his esteem for Jünger's influential combat narratives. In Heidegger's eyes, Jünger's singularity as a chronicler of destruction was that he fully appreciated the Great War's *metaphysical sig-nificance*: its status as a caesura or breach in Western Dasein. Hence, Jünger's perspective heralded a new epoch in which the political concepts of the bourgeois world ceased to apply. In sum, Heidegger venerated Jünger's war diaries as harbingers of a "total mobilization" that was still to come. As Heidegger remarked, "In a manner that is unequaled, [Jünger] experienced the World War metaphysically: as an event relevant to beings in their totality [*Seienden im Ganzen*]. His thinking after the war went beyond traditional understandings of 'destiny' and 'mankind.' . . . This allowed him to do justice to the World War's essence as qualitatively 'other.' . . . Ultimately, Jünger recognized Nietzsche's doctrine of the *Will to Power* as *the* metaphysical basis of the way that the World War . . . became historical."[42]

Jünger recognized that the "planetary" triumph of industrial methods meant that *Arbeit* had assumed a *totalizing* character. At the same time, it was clear that the individual *Arbeiter* had been reduced to an expendable appendage or supernumerary of a titanic mechanism. As Jünger observed, "[Today,] many things appear as 'work' in ways that, previously, would have been inconceivable—football matches, for example. Henceforth, a *total work-character* [*totaler Arbeitscharakter*] will implacably permeate all spheres of life."[43] Whereas the Left bemoaned these developments as examples of the "alienation" and "reification" that were endemic to capitalism, Jünger, in a Nietzschean spirit of *amor fati*, effusively welcomed them. According to Jünger, by surrendering to more potent cosmological forces, the individual attained a higher ontological dignity.

From "Total War" to "Total Mobilization"

In Jünger's eyes, the advent of "total war" was a key development in the transition from the nineteenth-century's minimalist, "nightwatchman state" to the totalitarian *Arbeitersstaat*. Not only did "total war" render the traditional distinction between combatants and civilians obsolete; it also blurred the difference between war and peace, since henceforth, peacetime demanded preparation for the next war. According to Jünger, another one of "total war's" advantages was that it replaced the bourgeois longing for security and material comfort with a steely "warrior ethos." Standing Clausewitz on his head, Jünger claimed that "total mobilization" meant that, from now on, politics would become the continuation of war by other means. The logic of "total war" guaranteed that *Kriegsführung* (warfare) would become modern society's central raison d'être.

In the future, states that shunned the totalitarian imperatives of the military-industrial *Soldaten-Arbeitersstaat* would be doomed to extinction.

For Jünger, the *Arbeitszeitalter*, or "Age of Work," embodied a "total institution." Its all-enveloping nature meant that, henceforth "there was nothing that could not be conceived as *Arbeit*. *Arbeit* determines the rhythm of the hand, of thought, of the heart, of life by day and by night, of science, love, the arts, faith, religious practice, and war. *Arbeit* determines the circulation of energy and of the atom; it impels the stars and the solar system."[44]

In a parallel development, the advent of industrial behemoths such as Krupp and I. G. Farben seemed to refute the Enlightenment's optimistic prognoses. They demonstrated that science and technology, instead of facilitating emancipation, led only to greater bondage. Thereby, humanity became increasingly dependent on a leviathan-like network of autonomous and uncontrollable technological processes. By turning society into what Jünger described as an "ungeheure Schmiedewerkstätte"—a gigantic industrial forge—the *Arbeiterszeitalter* sounded the death knell of the bourgeois *principium individuationis*.

Jünger embraced these developments enthusiastically, insofar as they portended deliverance from the superficial blandishments of bourgeois *Existenz*. One commentator has felicitously summarized Jünger's worldview as follows: "Jünger reconceived the impersonalization and standardization inherent in modern technology along the lines of a totalitarian political doctrine. . . . Decisive for Jünger was that the process of standardization did not come about consciously and intentionally; instead, it had been effectuated by the increasing automatization of technological and organizational subsystems."[45]

Anticipating the later Heidegger's ontological fatalism—as Heidegger declared in the "Letter on Humanism," "The History of Being bears and determines every situation and *'condition humaine'* "—in *Der Arbeiter*, Jünger characterized *Arbeit* as a "superordinate Principle of Being [*übergeordnetes Seinsprinzip*]" and as a "unitary and unalterable Being [*einheitliche und unveränderliche Sein*]."[46]

Amor fati—surrendering to "fate"—was a favored Nietzschean trope. As Nietzsche observed in *Ecce Homo*, "My formula for greatness in a human being is *amor fati*: that one wants nothing to be different, not forward, not backward, not in all eternity. Not merely bear what is necessary, still less conceal it—all idealism is mendaciousness in the face of what is necessary—*but love it*."[47] Among conservative revolutionary thinkers, the idea that surrendering to destiny was the true meaning of freedom became a widely held shibboleth. The systematic role that Heidegger's fundamental ontology attributed to "fate" (*Geschick*) and "destiny" (*Schicksal*) faithfully reflected the reactionary modernist understanding of temporality.

Technics as "Steely Romanticism"

Jünger's and Heidegger's reflections on the *Arbeitergesellschaft*'s underlying "metaphysical" meaning touched on a leitmotif that was of central importance for the self-understanding of the national revolutionary Right. One of the crucial lessons that the German Right had extracted from the First World War's colossal "battles of matériel" was that, in an age of "total mobilization," the aesthetics of German Romanticism had been rendered permanently anachronistic. Hence, going forward, it was imperative that the Right constructively engage the forces of "mechanization," since their influence had, in no small measure, determined the Great War's outcome. There seemed to be little doubt that, henceforth, they would decide the outcome of future wars.

Given modern industrialism's status as a negative totem, or *Schreckbild*, in the discourse of German *Kulturkritik*, this desideratum presented itself as a challenge. However, in the long run, among revolutionary nationalists, the reconciliation of *Geist* and *Technik* proved inordinately successful. Thomas Mann called attention to the fraught amalgam of "spirit" and "technics" in his essay on "Germany and the Germans," describing it as a *"highly technological romanticism."* As Mann remarked, "The really characteristic and dangerous aspect of National Socialism was its mixture of robust modernity and an affirmative stance toward progress, combined with dreams of the past: in other words, a highly technological romanticism."[48] Although, at various points, the Nazis had flirted with visions of a *völkisch*-agrarian utopia,[49] circa 1936, as rearmament began in earnest, their embrace of "technological romanticism" definitively gained the upper hand.

This ideological reconciliation of *Geist* with *Technics* was epitomized by Goebbels's infamous "German Technology" speech, which he delivered in 1939 at the German auto show in Berlin. As Goebbels asserted,

> We live in an era of technology. The racing tempo of our century affects all areas of our life. There is scarcely anything that happens that can escape its powerful in-

fluence. Therefore, the danger unquestionably arises that modern technology will make men soulless. National Socialism never rejected or struggled against technology. Instead, one of its main tasks was to consciously *affirm it, to fill it inwardly with soul*, . . . and to place it in the service of our *Volk* . . .

National Socialist public statements used to refer to the "steely romanticism" of our century. Today this phrase has attained its full meaning. We live in an age that is both romantic and steel-like, that has not lost its depth of feeling. On the contrary, *it has discovered a new romanticism in the results of modern inventions and technology*. While bourgeois reaction was alien to and filled with incomprehension, if not outright hostility, toward technology, and while modern skeptics believed it was profoundly responsible for the collapse of European culture, *National Socialism understood how to take the soulless framework of technology and fill it with the rhythm and hot impulses of our time*.[50]

From an ideological standpoint, Goebbels's characterization of National Socialism's efforts to *"fill [technology] inwardly with soul"* was extremely revealing. On the one hand, it sought to combat the sterile and counterproductive, neo-Romantic *demonization* of technology, an orientation that was at odds with the Third Reich's rearmament plans. At the same time, Goebbels's remarks reprised a long-standing Nazi claim that *its* approach to technology was *revolutionary*, insofar as it had transcended the *soulless* and *utilitarian* understanding of "technics" that predominated in the West, where, unlike Germany, "international Jewry" remained in control. One of National Socialism's main selling points was that, by infusing modern industrialism with race qua "primal life instinct," it would counteract the "titanic power of money." Thereby, it would ensure—as one Nazi ideologue put it—the triumph of "spirit over matter." In this way, "technical *Geist* and the Nazi racial myth would form a common front against Jewish materialism."[51] Here, we find another compelling illustration of the way that National Socialism understood race in *spiritual terms*.

Goebbels's glorification of "steely romanticism" sheds important light on Heidegger's view of technology, as shaped by Jünger's and Spengler's views. It also helps us to understand his controversial avowal in *An Introduction to Metaphysics* that National Socialism's "inner truth and greatness" emerged in its efforts to resolve the antagonism "between planetary technology and modern man."[52]

Heidegger was convinced that National Socialism's vision of a racially unified *Volksgemeinschaft* represented an ontologically adequate response to the dysfunctions and dislocations of Western modernity. These manifestations of Spenglerian "decline" culminated in the triumph of *Machenschaft*: the instrumentalization of the totality of Being by "technics." In Heidegger's eyes, National Socialism embodied the remedy or solution to the domination of "technics" qua *Unwesen*, or "monstrosity."

Heidegger regarded "world Jewry" as the hidden force or power that was busily orchestrating *Machenschaft* behind the scenes. In the *Black Notebooks*, he explained the link between (Jewish) *Machenschaft* and "Western metaphysics" as follows: "Contemporary Jewry's temporary increase in power has its basis in the fact that Western metaphysics—above all, in its modern incarnation—offers fertile ground for the dissemination of an empty rationality and calculability, which in this way gains a foothold in 'spirit,' without ever being able to grasp from within the hidden realms of decision."[53]

Heidegger's "metaphysical" indictment of "world Jewry" as the progenitors of planetary *Machenschaft* culminated in his justification of the *Endlösung* as a form of *défense légitime*. "Total extermination" (*völlige Vernichtung*) was the only way to safeguard Being from the disintegrative effects of Jewish "Entrassung": "world Jewry's" destruction of "racial substance" on a planetary scale.[54]

Heidegger was seduced by National Socialism's veneer of "steely romanticism," a quality that had been forged amid the *Stahlgewittern* (storms of steel) experienced by the Front Generation and immortalized in Jünger's work. Heidegger glorified Nazism's unequaled success in reconciling *Geist* with *Technics*—a capacity that contrasted sharply with the failings and shortcomings of the Western democracies.

In sum, Heidegger regarded National Socialism as authentic *Geschichtlichkeit* incarnate. On these grounds, not only was he was willing to overlook its inherent penchant for mass criminality. He justified its criminality "metaphysically" as indispensable to the advancement of *Seinsgeschichte*.

"The German Student as *Arbeiter*"

Heidegger presented "The German Student as Worker" as a radio address in November 1933, hoping that his proposals would become key points of reference in the contentious debate over National Socialism's plans for university reform. Heidegger delivered the address in Munich. It was simultaneously broadcast on six regional stations: Frankfurt, Freiburg, Kassel, Trier, Cologne, and Stuttgart—a circumstantial aspect that attests to its importance.

When Heidegger wrote the "The German Student as Worker," he was actively vying for a position of philosophical leadership. Hence, apart from Heidegger's May 1933 *Rektoratsrede*, "The German Student as Worker" offers the most comprehensive account of his understanding of National Socialism's "metaphysical" potential: its status as an *Ereignis* in the continuum of "Western-Germanic historical Dasein."[55] As of this writing, this pivotal document remains untranslated in English.

The main theme of Heidegger's address concerned *Arbeit*'s centrality with respect to National Socialism's world-historical "Auftrag," or "mission." Heidegger maintained that National Socialism's understanding of *Arbeit* represented an ontological watershed, or *novum*, insofar as, for the first time, *Arbeit* had emerged as the ground of *Geschichtlichkeit*, or authentic historicity. Consequently, with the Nazi seizure of power, "The essence of work [*Arbeit*] determined the Dasein of man." "[German] Dasein," Heidegger exulted, "is beginning to transpose itself to a different ontological 'type' [*Seinsart*], whose nature I defined years ago as 'care' [*Sorge*], although professional philosophers unanimously rejected this designation. More recently, *Ernst Jünger*, basing himself on a creative understanding of Nietzsche and on the experience of the First World War's 'battles of matériel,' has interpreted the ontological reality of man that is characteristic of the new age on the basis of *the Gestalt of the Worker*."[56]

Heidegger's assertion in "The German Student as Worker" that Jünger's portrayal of the "Gestalt of the Worker" was predicated on a "creative understanding of Nietzsche" merits additional scrutiny.

Both Heidegger and Jünger regarded Nietzsche's diagnosis of "European nihilism"—the bankruptcy of the West's highest ideals—as unarguable. It signified the coup de grâce with respect to the bourgeois illusion of "progress." Thereby, it settled in advance all questions pertaining to the philosophy of history. Spengler's *Decline of the West*—which, among the conservative revolutionary thinkers, had acquired a type of totemic status—represented a pseudoerudite extrapolation of Nietzsche's thesis.[57] Both Heidegger and Jünger were mesmerized by Nietzsche's prophecies concerning the "fateful" character of the "machine age" as well as by his correlative appeal for a *Herrenrasse*: a race of *Übermenschen*, capable of rising to the challenges of modern technology.

It was Nietzsche who, more than any other thinker, had set the precedent for Jünger's conception of *Der Arbeiter: Gestalt und Herrschaft*. In *The Will to Power*, Nietzsche prophesied that, in the future, the vocation of "workers" and "soldiers" would coincide. "*Workers should learn to feel the same way as soldiers*," declaimed Nietzsche. Alluding to the "Spartan" *ethos* that shaped Plato's portrayal of the guardians in the *Republic*, Nietzsche proffered a protofascist version of "careers open to talent": "An honorarium, an income, but no being paid! . . . Instead, placing the individual, each according to his kind, in such a way that he can achieve the highest which lies in his sphere." "In the future," Nietzsche concluded, "workers should live like citizens [*Bürger*] live today: but *in a more exalted way*, distinguishing themselves by their freedom from need, *like a higher caste: thus poorer and simpler*, while possessing *power*."[58] Thereby, Nietzsche outlined his own "Gestalt" of *Der Arbeiter*.

In a passage from *The Will to Power* that both Heidegger and Jünger regarded as uniquely prophetic, Nietzsche forecast the "Superman's" emergence as a necessary "countermovement" to the diminution of "mankind" in the "machine age": the individual's reduction to the status of a "cog" in the service of "total administration." According to Nietzsche,

> Once the imminent and inevitable total economic administration of the earth [*Wirtschafts-Gesamtverwaltung der Erde*] comes to pass, mankind will find its highest meaning as a cog in total administration's service: as a tremendous clockwork of ever smaller, ever more finely 'adapted' *cogs*. . . . Against this dwarfing and adaptation of men to an increasingly specialized utility, *a reverse movement is required*. . . . I designate this *countermovement* as the secretion of *a luxurious surplus of mankind*, which shall bring about *a stronger species, a higher type*, the conditions of whose genesis and survival are different from those of the average man. . . . My metaphor for this type is the "Superman."[59]

Heidegger viewed Nietzsche's prognostications concerning the "Superman" as a "countermovement" to the "dwarfing" of man in advanced industrial society as especially auspicious. Seduced by Nietzsche's *Zukunftsphilologie* (philology-of-the-future)—Nietzsche once claimed, "Only fifty years from now will perhaps a few . . . have eyes to see what has been done through me"[60]—yet equally attentive to Jünger's dystopian visions in *Der Arbeiter*, Heidegger perceived National Socialism as the ontological-historical embodiment of Nietzsche's and Jünger's prophecies. "Both Jünger and Heidegger believed that the technological era could reach fulfillment only under the leadership of an Elite. . . . Both of them awaited the Nietzschean Superman who would complete the nihilistic process."⁶¹ According to Daniel Morat, Heidegger envisioned National Socialism's "metaphysical" task as one of "breaking technology's preeminence, and thereby restoring an equitable relationship between nature and man."⁶²

Hence, in the schema of Heideggerian *Seinsgeschichte*, National Socialism embodied a metaphysical breakthrough: the dawn of "another Beginning" that would *reverse* the course of Western "nihilism," whose dislocations were evident in the "confrontation between planetary technology and modern man."⁶³ The eschatological allure of Nietzsche's prophecy concerning workers-of-the-future as "a *higher caste, . . . poorer and simpler*, while possessing *power*" conditioned Heidegger's enthusiasm for the *Arbeitszeitalter* heralded by National Socialism. Lecturing on Nietzsche's doctrine of "Eternal Recurrence" in 1937, Heidegger reiterated his view that "*Der Arbeiter* represents a sobering appellation for the *Gestalt* of man that Nietzsche refers to as the 'Superman.' "⁶⁴ Heidegger's avowal sheds light on his subsequent claim that, during the 1930s, he understood politics through the lens of "Nietzsche's metaphysics": a vantage point that had "correctly perceived and anticipated the history . . . of the West."⁶⁵

In *Besinnung*—written in 1938 but published in 1997—Heidegger restated his understanding of the "metaphysical" lineage leading from Nietzsche to Jünger:

> Spengler's historical metaphysics of "Caesarism" and Jünger's metaphysics of the "Worker" are the only worthwhile elucidations of the completion of modernity [*Vollendung der Neuzeit*] in the sense of Nietzsche's understanding of Western metaphysics. Spengler regards man as a "beast of prey"; the process ends with the domination of a "Caesar," whom the masses—organized and ordered by the economy, technics, and world war—are obligated to serve. Jünger, for his part, understands the *Gestalt* of "the Worker" as a *planetary development* . . . in which modern man is reduced to a component of an "organic construction" of Being as a whole.⁶⁶

Contrary to a widespread misconception, Heidegger did not simply *dismiss* the powerful *Zeitdiagnosen* that had been proffered by Nietzsche, Spengler, and Jünger. This point is worth stressing, since it has been alleged that, by the late 1930s, Heidegger *rejected* Jünger's dystopian-Nietzschean vision of "Der

Arbeiter" as merely another failed instance of the "metaphysics of subjectivity" and the "Will to Will." Purportedly, by criticizing Jünger's prophecies, Heidegger also permanently disavowed National Socialism. However, a closer examination of Heidegger's interpretation demonstrates that he *endorsed* Spengler's and Jünger's views as exemplars of (Nietzschean) "active nihilism."

Consequently, in *On Ernst Jünger* (1939), Heidegger praised Jünger effusively as a figure who "surpasses all contemporary 'Dichter' (i.e., writers) and 'Denker' (i.e., professional philosophers) by his matchless intuitive perception [*Sehen*] of the 'Real' [*des Wirklichen*]: an intuitive perception that transcends mere 'gawking' and that, therefore, is existentially accomplished and understood." In a similar vein, Heidegger praised "Nietzsche's nihilism [as] not the 'nihilism of the weak,' or the self-oblivion of the pessimist's 'nothing matters,' but rather, '*active nihilism*.' "[67]

In sum, following a path that had been delineated by Nietzsche and Jünger, Heidegger rejected bourgeois-democratic approaches as inadequate "half measures": as remedies or solutions that would merely prolong the agony of *Untergang* and *Seinsvergessenheit*. This realization shaped Heidegger's conclusion that only "absolute" or "total nihilism" would prove adequate to the ontological-historical challenges at hand. "Nietzsche," affirmed Heidegger, "demands that the advent of nihilism be perceived as the introduction of *an absolute return and a new beginning*, unhindered by half measures, rather than as the means of spreading the belief in the 'decline of the West.' "[68]

Thus, Heidegger, inspired by his reading of Nietzsche and Jünger, wagered on "active nihilism" to prepare the terrain for the transition to "another Beginning." In *European Nihilism*, Heidegger reconceived "active nihilism" as "ecstatic nihilism." "Extreme nihilism," observed Heidegger, "develops into an *active nihilism*; the latter does not allow what exists to simply fall little by little into ruins by limiting itself to the role of spectator. Instead, *it actively intervenes to overthrow it*. By revolutionizing inherited values, a space is created for a New Order of values. *Extreme, active, space-producing nihilism* is *ecstatic nihilism*."[69]

In *Heidegger and the Ideology of War*, Domenico Losurdo felicitously summarizes Heidegger's understanding of "active" or "ecstatic" nihilism as follows:

> [Heidegger] transfigured philosophically the unscrupulous brutality with which the Third Reich actualized the National Socialist "New Order" as *absolute, active nihilism*. . . . Heidegger followed the events of the war, attempting to interpret the

Third Reich's dazzling victories philosophically . . . [as] the victory of . . . *active nihilism* over *incomplete nihilism*. . . . The victor was a new humanity . . . that transcended modern man: . . . the "Superman" who is commensurate to the absolute "machine economy." . . . [The Superman and the absolute "machine economy"] depend on one another in order to establish "absolute dominion over the earth."[70]

The *Arbeitergesellschaft* as "Ereignis"

Heidegger's lecture course on "European nihilism," which was held during the summer semester of 1940, coincided with the *Wehrmacht*'s stunning blitz-krieg victory over France. At one point, Heidegger paused to reflect on the "metaphysical" significance of the French defeat: its meaning as an *Ereignis*, or "Event," in the history of Being. Heidegger contended that, when perceived in this light, Germany's victory revealed the bankruptcy of Cartesian metaphysics. Heidegger alleged that the French defeat expressed a "secret law of history": a law that exposes "a *Volk* [the French] as *no longer adequate to the metaphysics that has emerged out of its own history*." Conversely, viewed from a German perspective, the Nazi victory confirmed Nietzsche's "metaphysical" insight that "*a new humanity is needed that is thoroughly equal to the fundamental essence of modern technology and its metaphysical truth; that is*, [*a humanity*] *that lets itself be totally dominated by the essence of technology*, in order to guide and utilize the individual technical procedures and possibilities."[71]

Thus, Heidegger affirmed that the "metaphysical lesson" of the German victory was quintessentially Nietzschean: it validated Nietzsche's prophecy that "only the Superman is adequate to the unlimited 'machine economy,' and vice versa: the former is in need of the latter to establish *unconditional domination over the Earth*." "Technics" and the "master race" were necessary corollaries. The *Wehrmacht*'s triumph reaffirmed Nietzsche's insight in the *Will to Power* concerning the "Superman" as "a stronger species [and] higher type": an indispensable "countermovement" to the "total economic administration of the Earth," a bureaucratic Moloch that Heidegger, agreeing with Nietzsche and Jünger, rejected, insofar as it resulted in the "dwarfing and adaptation of men to an increasingly specialized utility."[72]

For Heidegger, the imperatives of *Seinsgeschichte* justified *Deutschtum*'s "right," qua *Übermenschen* and *Herrenrasse*, to establish its "unconditional" planetary domination. Heidegger regarded French "metaphysics" as little more than an expression of Western "decline." Conversely, he lauded German metaphysics—which, in Heideggerian parlance, bespoke "nearness [*Nähe*] to Being"—as embodied by the *Wehrmacht*, as the reenactment of the "Greek beginning." Thus, as late as 1940, Heidegger reaffirmed National Socialism's ontological uniqueness in terms of its making the world safe for the *Seinsfrage*.[73]

Heidegger's damning verdict with respect to France's "strange defeat"[74] confirmed his view of the National Socialist *Arbeitergesellschaft* as an *Ereignis*: a "metaphysical" breakthrough that facilitated humanity's "proximity" to "another Beginning." Nazism's unprecedented reconciliation of *Arbeit* and *Technik* signified a qualitative advance beyond the degraded and exploitative *Western* understanding of "work." Viewed in Nietzschean terms, National Socialist *Arbeit* was an expression of authenticity. It presaged the "self-overcoming" (*Selbstüberwindung*) of the "average man"—the "Last Man"—as prophesied by Nietzsche, and the ascendancy of the "Superman" or "Master Race."

Jünger and National Socialism

During the 1920s, Nietzsche's appeal for a *Herrenrasse* as a countermovement to the entrapments of the "machine age" galvanized conservative revolutionary thought in profound and surprising ways. According to one observer, "Weimar's right-wing intellectuals presented war, militarism, and nationalism as the breeding ground for a new, post-decadent, anti-bourgeois man. Nietzsche provided these thinkers with an anti-bourgeois language as well as the pathos of a heroic struggle against convention."[75] In this respect, Heidegger's enthusiasm for Nietzsche as a sworn enemy of the bourgeois "shopkeeper" mentality and Western "decline" reflected a widespread cultural trend.

Writing in *Die Standarte: Wochenschrift des neuen Nationalismus* in 1925, Jünger, too, extolled Nietzsche's uncanny clairvoyance: his realization that *Technik* and *Geist*, far from being antitheses, were ultimately *complementary*. As Jünger effused, "[Nietzsche] taught us that life is not only a struggle for daily existence, but also a *struggle for higher and deeper goals. Our task is to apply this doctrine to the machine*."[76] In retrospect, Jünger's remarks anticipated the central argument of *Der Arbeiter*: only "total mobilization," as the embodiment of "active nihilism," facilitated the "self-overcoming" of technics.

It permitted technics to shed the trappings of "bourgeois domination" (*Herrschaft*). Via recourse to the mechanisms of "total mobilization," technics was reborn as the cornerstone of a monolithic fascist dystopia.

In 1936, Heidegger restated his understanding of fascism's world-historical significance by invoking Nietzsche's doctrine of "European nihilism" as the relevant touchstone and precedent. Fascism, claimed Heidegger, embodied a "countermovement to nihilism." "It is well known," he continued, "that the two men who, in different ways, . . . have introduced a countermovement to nihilism, Mussolini and Hitler, were influenced in essential ways by Nietzsche, without, however, having realized the authentic metaphysical realm of Nietzsche's thought."[77] Hence, in Heidegger's view, much work remained to be done.

In *Storms of Steel* (1920) and *Der Arbeiter* (1932), Jünger established a reputation as the Front Generation's premier aesthetician of *Kampf* and *Schlacht*, "struggle" and "slaughter." His war diaries, *In Storms of Steel* and *Struggle as Inner Experience*, were among the most widely read books of the 1920s. By glorifying the *Kriegerlebnis*, Jünger's narratives celebrated the spirit of "soldatischer Nationalismus" (military nationalism), thereby providing aesthetic consolation to compensate for Germany's battlefield losses. Thus, among radical nationalists, Jünger's works rapidly acquired the status of canonical texts. In the words of one scholar, "[Jünger] inflated war memories into mythic proportions to justify the enormous loss of life on the battlefields and to create a nationalist and collectively utopian narrative as an alternative to the unpopular Republic. . . . In [Jünger's] view, war brings men back into a natural, unchanging order, subject to elementary forces that reveal the primordial violent rhythms of life beneath the thin veneer of civilization. . . . Critics such as Klaus Theweleit have accused Jünger of thereby legitimizing the embrace of death and destruction by means of a Fascist literary imagination."[78] More than any other German writer, it was Jünger who, in works such as "Total Mobilization" and *Der Arbeiter*, cleared the way for Goebbels's elegy to "steely romanticism" in "German Technics."

During the 1920s, one of Jünger's greatest admirers was the Nazi Party leader Adolf Hitler. In 1926, Hitler contacted Jünger to arrange a meeting. The Führer briefly corresponded with Jünger and sent him an autographed copy of *Mein Kampf*. Jünger, for his part, praised Hitler as a "new type of leader" and as "Germany's greatest speaker." He dedicated a copy of *Feuer und Blut* (Fire and Blood; 1925) enthusiastically to "The National Leader, Adolf Hitler!"[79]

Given Jünger's profile as a war hero and best-selling author, he was one of the Weimar Republic's most prominent public figures. Hence, among the *Bildungsbürgertum*, Jünger's antidemocratic animus and glorification of "military nationalism" carried enormous weight.

Following World War II, a series of contentious debates ensued over Jünger's relationship to Nazism. Jünger's defenders pointed out that he never formally joined the NSDAP and that his relations with the Third Reich were often tempestuous. Jünger's 1939 novel *On the Marble Cliffs* has frequently been interpreted as an antitotalitarian allegory. Jünger's biographer Hans-Peter Schwarz, who had also served as Jünger's personal secretary, went so far as to portray Jünger as an "anarchist"—albeit a "conservative anarchist."[80] Schwarz's apologetic account insinuated that Jünger's earlier appeals for an ultramilitarized, proto-Orwellian *Arbeitergesellschaft* were an anomaly. Jünger, in his own defense, claimed that his writings were tantamount to a "seismograph" and that it would be the height of prejudice to blame the seismographer for the earthquake.[81]

Ultimately, these efforts to sanitize Jünger's ideological past proved enormously successful. By the time Jünger died in 1998, at the advanced age of 102, he had been showered with numerous accolades and tributes. In 1982, despite a public outcry and accompanying street protests, Jünger was awarded the Goethe Prize by the city of Frankfurt. In 1993, French President François Mitterrand and German Chancellor Helmut Kohl paid homage to Jünger at visit at his home in Wilflingen, Swabia.

Yet, on closer inspection, the "official" version of Jünger's political past has proven to be untenable: woefully selective and misleading. Hence, it reinforced a politically anodyne account of Jünger's robust career as a writer, activist, and political publicist.

During the postwar period, Jünger's reputation profited enormously from a series of beneficent and selective editorial decisions. The Stuttgart-based firm Klett-Cotta published two editions of Jünger's collected works.[82] In both instances, Jünger's editors agreed to omit his political journalism from the 1920s, thereby suppressing the approximately 130 articles that Jünger had published in a wide array of prominent conservative revolutionary organs. In addition to his editorial involvement with *Die Standarte* and Ernst Niekisch's *Widerstand*, Jünger also coedited and contributed to *Arminius: Kampfschrift für deutsche Nationalisten* and *Die Kommenden: Überbundische Wochenschrift der deut-*

schen Jugend. Both publications sought to mobilize the "spirit" of Front Generation militarism against Germany's fledgling democracy. As organs of
"military nationalism," they consistently advocated replacing the Weimar *Rechtsstaat* with dictatorship, a form of political rule that they regarded as consonant with Germany's authoritarian traditions.

The full of extent of Jünger's career as a political publicist during the 1920s
remained relatively unknown until several years after his death.[83] Consequently,
in the contentious debates over Jünger's literary and political legacy, they rarely
figured in the discussions. When queried about these articles and essays during
the postwar period, Jünger disingenuously responded that he simply did not remember them.[84]

Jünger's activities as a political journalist belie the image, carefully honed by
his supporters, of Jünger as an independent-minded nonconformist and an aesthete: someone who consistently maintained a safe distance above the fray of
contemporary politics. Instead, they reveal Jünger as a committed, right-wing
political militant who consistently engaged in ideological warfare in order to
undermine the hated republic. Moreover, as a political activist, Jünger had ties
to National Socialism that were considerably more substantial than had been
widely assumed. In fact, his very first political essay, "Revolution and Idea,"
which was published in September 1923, appeared in the National Socialist
daily, the *Völkischer Beobachter*. The article attests to Jünger's willingness to
employ political violence in order to overthrow Germany's legally constituted
government. "The *real revolution* has not yet occurred," declared Jünger. "Its
forward march cannot be halted. . . . Its idea is *das Völkische*, sharpened to as
yet unknown hardness; its banner is the swastika, its expression is the concentration of the will in a single point: *dictatorship*."[85] As editor of *Arminius*,
Jünger had few qualms about opening up the journal's pages to the likes of Joseph Goebbels and Alfred Rosenberg.

To judge by Jünger's activities as a political publicist, he was also not a
stranger to the lures of political anti-Semitism. In a 1927 article, he described
Jews as "scum." And in a 1930 essay, he insisted that Germans and Jews were
as different as "oil and water." Jünger reaffirmed his aversion the "trick" of
Jewish assimilation. The only "solution" for Jews in Germany, he concluded,
ominously, was "either for them to be a Jew in Germany, *or not to be*."[86] In "Total Mobilization," Jünger could not resist taking a swipe at Foreign Minister
Walter Rathenau, who was felled by a coterie of far-right assassins in 1922,

claiming that, as a Jew, Rathenau remained an eternal stranger to the "inner requirements" of "total mobilization."[87]

As Nicolaus Wachsmann has observed in "Marching under the Swastika," even when Jünger appeared to distance himself from National Socialism, it was less because he disagreed with the movement's practices and objectives than because, like Hans Zehrer and the *Tatkreisler*, he believed that the Nazis, by virtue of their willingness to play the parliamentary game, had sold out. As Wachsmann concludes,

> To celebrate the "western-humanist tradition" of a writer who, for years, consistently undermined democracy and who declared that "the day the parliamentary state crumbles in our clutches, and on which we proclaim the national dictatorship, will be our greatest day of celebration," displays a profound ignorance of Jünger's political position during the 1920s. . . . By systematically denying any legitimacy to Weimar, Jünger contributed to the climate of crisis which favored the rise of the Nazis. Jünger helped the Nazis to gain support in a more direct way of giving Nazism intellectual credibility and making it acceptable to nationalist readers as a force for change. He hailed the NSDAP as a radical movement of nationalism in the mid-1920s, when most other opponents of Weimar held it in very low esteem.[88]

It is little wonder that, in 1945, Thomas Mann dismissed Jünger as "a prophet and ice-cold dandy of barbarism."[89]

Arbeit as an "Existential"

In "The German Student as Worker," Heidegger's claim that *Arbeit* bore comparison with *Sorge*, or "Care"—one of the fundamental "existentials" of *Being and Time*—confirms that he viewed *Arbeit* with the utmost philosophical seriousness.

In *Being and Time*, Heidegger exalted *Sorge* as "the most primordial phenomenon of truth."[90] Heidegger viewed *Sorge* as a fundamental structure of human intentionality. It indicated how Dasein related to its "world" *existentially*: that is, in a manner that distinguished Dasein ontologically from other "beings": animals, plants, and stones.[91] As a form of intentionality, *Sorge* facilitated the "open region" or "clearing" (*Lichtung*) that was existential ontology's sine qua non. Ultimately, truth qua predication or correspondence could only emerge against the backdrop of this more primordial, existential precondition. As Charles Guignon has remarked in *Heidegger's Theory of Knowledge*, "What is *primary* is a historically unfolding 'clearing' or 'opening' which cannot be coherently set over against a reality distinct from the clearing. . . . [Heidegger] wants us to see that truth . . . is possible only against the background of 'truth' in the sense of an 'opening' or 'clearing.' . . . Elementary predication is possible only in a world in which things have already been taken out of their hiddenness through Dasein's disclosing of the intelligible world."[92]

By proposing that *Arbeit*, as an "existential," was covalent with *Sorge*, Heidegger confirmed that he regarded *Arbeit* as an indispensable form of "world disclosure." Like *Sorge*, *Arbeit* opened up a primordial "space" or "clearing" that facilitated Dasein's encounters with the "worldhood of the world." Moreover, just as there were "authentic" and "inauthentic" forms of *Existenz*, there were also authentic and inauthentic forms of *Arbeit*.

The analogy between *Sorge* and *Arbeit* underlines the ontological continuity that Heidegger perceived between the existential analytic of *Being and Time* and the *Seinsarten*, or ontological modalities, of National Socialism. By asserting that, under National Socialism, Germans' "*Dasein is beginning to transpose itself to a different ontological plane*," Heidegger highlighted the unprecedented nature of the historical transformation at issue. "Arbeit," claimed Heidegger, "transposes the *Volk* effectively into reality *as an essential power of Being*." He continued, "The structure that, in and through *Arbeit*, transforms *völkisch Dasein* is the *State*. The National Socialist State is an *Arbeitsstaat*."[93] Heidegger maintained that, under Nazism, *Arbeit*, *Volk*, and *Staat* coalesced to form an essential ontological-historical triad.

As the preceding remarks confirm, Heidegger's understanding of "the German student as *Arbeiter*" portended the destruction of the German university's traditional, Humboldtian-humanitarian mission, insofar as it required the university's *Gleichschaltung* within the National Socialist state.

Heidegger endorsed the transformation of "the German student as *Arbeiter*" as an effective means of surmounting the separation between intellectual and manual labor or, as Heidegger put it, "of establishing a living bridge between the worker of the 'hand' and the worker of the 'brain.'"[94] Overcoming the divide between intellectual and manual labor had been a long-standing Nazi political goal, since minimizing class tensions advanced the cause of national unity.

Heidegger wholeheartedly supported this aim. He believed that, by redefining German students as "workers," one could eliminate sterile intellectualism: scholarly pursuits that were insufficiently "rooted" in the life of the *Volk*. Accordingly, Heidegger's program for university reform meant redefining knowledge in light of the goals of *völkisch* "self-assertion" (*Selbstbehauptung*). As he remarked in "The German Student as *Arbeiter*," "The student's awareness of his role in the implementation of *völkisch* claims to knowledge is what *makes him a worker*. Heretofore, students were 'workers' only insofar as they studied. Conversely, today's student 'studies' *because he is a worker.* 'Studying' means: *unfolding of the will-to-knowledge for the sake of affirming and advancing the knowledge that makes our Volk historical [geschichtlich].*"[95]

In Heidegger's view, grounding "spirit" in the life of the *Volk* signified a qualitative improvement over the aimless, "free-floating" approaches to knowledge that predominated under liberalism. Heidegger regarded National Socialism as a watershed in German spiritual life, insofar as it freed the university from the anarchy and licentiousness of "so-called academic freedom"—a mentality that, as Heidegger put it, underwrote "complacency and indifference: arbitrariness of intention as well as the steadfast avoidance of commitment."[96] As Heidegger explained, "Freedom is not '*freedom from*' Obligation, Order and Law. Freedom is '*freedom for*': for a decisive commitment to our collective spiritual deployment on behalf of German destiny [*Entschlossenheit zu gemeinsamem geistigen Einsatz für das deutsche Schicksa*l]."[97]

For Heidegger, Nazism represented a *breakthrough*, insofar as it permitted the "German *Volk* to reconnect with its historical-spiritual mission [*Auftrag*]." "Academic youth," to their credit, had risen to the challenge, so that, in the years to come, they could assume a position of "spiritual-political leadership [*Führerschaft*]." Reimagining German students as "workers" would play a key role in solidifying their commitment to the *Volksgemeinschaft*.[98]

The Existential Analytic as a "Black Forest Idyll"

Heidegger's *Arbeitsanalyse* constituted an extension and refinement of the "pragmatic" orientation of *Being and Time*. In the existential analytic, Heidegger accorded primacy to *pragmata* and *Zuhandenheit*: Dasein's symbiotic rapport with objects of everyday use, such as "tools" (*Zeuge*). This focus reflected Heidegger's basic insight that "theoretical reason" and "think-ing substance," instead of being "primary," were derivative of "Being-in-the-world."

Consequently, Heidegger's concern with the philosophical meaning of *Ar-beit* signified a continuation of his commitment to "practical philosophy." It re-flected Heidegger's efforts to surmount the legacy of epistemological "dualism": the bifurcated subject bequeathed by Descartes and his heirs. As Heidegger ex-plained, "When Dasein grasps objects, it does not somehow first get out of an *inner sphere* in which it has been proximally encapsulated. Instead, its primary kind of being is such that it is always outside alongside the beings that it en-counters and that belong to a world." "A *commercium* of the subject with a world," he continued, "does not get created for the first time by knowing, nor does it arise from some way in which the world acts upon a *Subject. Knowing is a mode of Dasein founded upon Being-in-the-world.*"[99]

Heidegger's phenomenological treatment of Dasein's dealings with "tools" and "equipment" is widely regarded as a major philosophical breakthrough. These discussions, which reflect Heidegger's efforts to transcend the limita-tions of monadic, self-enclosed subjectivity, must be numbered among the book's most consequential advances. As Heidegger explains,

> We shall call those entities that we encounter in concern [*Fürsorge*] "equipment" [*Zeug*]. . . . To the Being of equipment there always belongs a *totality of equip-ment*. . . . Equipment is essentially "something in order to." . . . A totality of equip-ment is constituted by various ways of the "in order to": serviceability, conduciveness, usability, and manipulability. . . . Equipment . . . always is in terms of its belonging to other equipment: ink stand, pen, ink, paper, blotting pad, table, well, furniture, windows, doors, room. . . . The kind of being which equipment possesses . . . we call "readiness to hand" [*Zuhandenheit*].[100]

Heidegger maintained that the objects-for-use that we encounter as "equip-ment" are not discrete or autonomous entities. Instead, our interactions with ob-jects that are "ready-to-hand" depend on a preexisting network of relations (*Bewandtniszusammenhang*) in terms of which our actions (*Handlungen*) make sense or become meaningful. "Objects never reveal themselves individually and such as they are," insists Heidegger, "but only . . . as part of a 'totality of equipment.'" "If we look at things merely 'theoretically,'" he continued, "we get along without understanding readiness-to-hand." Conversely, in our everyday interaction with tools, there arises a type of practical knowledge "from which things acquire their thing-like character."[101]

Heidegger's understanding of equipment's "existential" meaning stemmed from his intensive engagement with Aristotle's *Nicomachean Ethics* during his Marburg years (1923–28). The confrontation with Aristotle impelled Heidegger to reformulate his earlier "hermeneutics of facticity" through the prism of *phronēsis*, or "practical wisdom": a concept that stood in contrast with the "pure knowing" associated with *theoria*, or "contemplation."[102]

The Greeks distinguished *phronēsis* from the purely instrumental manufacture or production of objects, which they denominated *poēsis*. What is relevant for our purposes is that, in Heidegger's later work, *Arbeit* signified a composite of *phronēsis* and *poēsis*. It embodied a form of "practical reason" (*praxis*) that surpassed the purely instrumental manipulation of objects.

Heidegger devalued the instrumentalism of *Arbeit* qua *poēsis*, or "labor," insofar as it was devoid of "mission" (*Sendung*) and "mandate" (*Auftrag*) and hence unrelated to the concerns of *phronēsis*, or "practical wisdom." In this respect, *poēsis* prefigured "technics," which derived from the Greek *technē* and which became a central target of critique in Heidegger later work.

Conversely, what distinguished Heidegger's understanding of *Arbeit* was that it *transcended* the purely "instrumental" sphere of production/*poēsis*. Thereby, it qualified as a higher existential modality: as a form of *action* or *praxis*. In Heidegger's view, this dimension of *Arbeit* enabled it to surmount considerations of mere utility and hence, ultimately, to qualify as an expression of "authenticity."

As an "existential," *Arbeit* represented an essential form of Dasein's interaction with the object-world of *Seiende*: entities or beings. It signified a modification of the "equipmental totality" that, in *Being and Time*, Heidegger had described as an integral dimension of Dasein's dealings with the thing-world of the "ready-to-hand." In phenomenological terms, such entities constituted an essential component of Dasein's "horizon of experience."

As such, *Arbeit* exemplified Dasein's capacity to "have a world": a capacity that attested to Dasein's ontological uniqueness and that distinguished Dasein's *Seinsart* (mode of Being) from that of ontologically inferior beings: animals, plants, and inorganic nature. Heidegger also regarded *Arbeit* as a manifestation of authentic temporality.

According to Heidegger, lesser "beings"—animals, plants, and stones—in contrast with Dasein, were incapable of *Existenz*. Unlike Dasein, they were *unec-*

static, insofar as their *Seinsart* hindered them from *projecting themselves* (*sich entwerfen*) *toward the future*. As Heidegger explained, "Stones, animals, and plants are themselves not temporal, as we are. They assume no mandate [*Auftrag*], they possess no mission [*Sendung*], *they do not work* [*sie arbeiten nicht*]—not because they are carefree, but because *they are incapable of work*. The horse may be said to work only insofar as it is incorporated into a human work-event. The machine does not work either. That it 'works' [*arbeitet*] is a misinterpretation of the nineteenth century, when man was also degraded to a machine. Thereby, his attitude toward history and time became similarly degraded."[103]

In the *Black Notebooks*, Heidegger invoked these basic ontological distinctions as a metaphysical warrant for anti-Semitism. He claimed that "world Jewry's" lack of "roots"—its *Bodenlosigkeit*—confirmed its incapacity to "have a world."[104] On these grounds, he adjudged Jews as, racially, *less than human*.

Heidegger held that, insofar as Jews were *ontologically impoverished*— "weltarm" or "poor-in-world"—they had more in common with "animals" and "stones" than they did with Dasein. Translated into the idiom of *Nazi-Deutsch*, this meant that Jews were an "antirace," or *Gegen-Rasse*. Conversely, *Germanentum*'s existential superiority—its status qua *Herrenrasse*—derived from its privileged ontological rapport with the "Greek beginning."

Following the war, Heidegger revisited the question of the Jews' existential inferiority in his Bremen lectures on "technology" (1949), "Insight into That Which Is." There, he argued that the Jews who perished in the *Vernichtungslager* manifested a demonstrative incapacity for "Being-toward-death," since they had endured an irresolute, "industrialized" mass death. Hence, according to the strictures of existential ontology, their deaths were "inauthentic." Heidegger explained his reasoning in following passage, which belies the commonplace concerning his "silence" about the Holocaust: "Hundreds of thousands die en masse. Do they die? They perish. [*Sie kommen um.*] They are cut down. They become items of material available for the manufacture of corpses. [*Bestandstücke eines Bestandes der Fabrikation von Leichen.*] Do they die? Hardly noticed, they are liquidated in extermination camps [*Vernichtungslager*]. And even apart from that, in China millions now perish of hunger."[105]

A striking feature of the preceding passage is that Heidegger pointedly refrained from mentioning the victims of the *Vernichtungslager* by name. By perpetuating their anonymity, Heidegger underwrote a further injustice, while simultaneously aping the impersonal nature of the extermination process itself.

There are additional distortions. The number of victims was not in the "hundreds of thousands," as Heidegger falsely asserted. Instead, as is well known, the number of "liquidated" Jews was close to six million. Moreover, by 1949, these figures were well known.

Heidegger also erred in speaking of the "millions who now perish of hunger in China." By making this claim, Heidegger sought to fabricate a misleading equivalence between the crimes of Nazism and communist crimes. But, in this case too, the figure he invoked—"millions"—was wildly inaccurate.[106] Moreover, the hunger that followed the communist victory in 1949, far from being a deliberate policy, was the product of Japan's ruthless, fifteen-year occupation of China and the ensuing civil war.

In addition to refusing to name the victims who "died en masse," Heidegger also declined to identify the perpetrators. In lieu of *actual* perpetrators and *actual* victims, he presented an anodyne and impersonal account of Nazi criminality: a pseudoexplanation in which the prime mover or culprit was the anonymous power of "technics." Reading Heidegger's account, one would never suspect that the ideological template that inspired these mass atrocities— Nazism—was one that Heidegger himself enthusiastically embraced and whose implementation he oversaw in his capacity as Freiburg University rector. Thereby, true to form, Heidegger allowed the mystifications of *Seinsgeschichte* to substitute for meaningful historical understanding.

Heidegger's understanding of "tools" and "equipment" in *Being and Time* was distinctly "antiquarian" and "pre-industrial." By idealizing the work-world of premodern craftsmanship, his account resembled a premodern "Black Forest idyll."[107] His discussion of Dasein's interaction with tools was decidedly out of step with the nature and demands of advanced industrial society. Adorno was not far off the mark when he observed in "Why Still Philosophy?" that, with Heidegger, "Nietzsche's 'backworldsmen' [*Hinterweltler*] have literally become backwoodsmen."[108]

Although some analysts have praised Heidegger's *Daseinanalyse* for its forthright treatment of the problem of "alienation"—above all, his critique of "average everydayness" ("curiosity," "idle talk," "das Man," and so forth)—left-wing critics have objected that, by viewing alienation ontologically and ahistorically, Heidegger disguised the class basis of social suffering. Thus, by treating alienation as endemic to Being-in-the-world, Heidegger portrayed it as an eternal and unalterable aspect of the human condition, rather than as a corrigible, class-determined phenomenon.

Adorno criticized Heidegger's thinly disguised paeans to craftsmanship and guild production as inherently ideological: as examples of the "jargon of authenticity." Thus, instead of unmasking social contradictions, Heidegger's approach meretriciously concealed them. "In the midst of our all-embracing functionalism," claimed Adorno, "every ontological light on the remnants of so-called *Zuhandenheit* 'gilds' the context." "The jargon," Adorno continued, "pursues artisanship under the shadow of industry, as carefully chosen as it is cheap; it gathers reproductions of kitschy life-reforming impulses that real life has buried. . . . Language rolls up its sleeves and lets it be understood that right action . . . is worth more than reflection. Thereby, a contemplative attitude, without any perception of the *praxis* which brings about change, sympathizes all the more strikingly with the here and now, the servicing of obligations presented within the given."[109]

"German Work" as "Joy-in-Work"

Heidegger's critique of the nineteenth century's understanding of *Arbeit* as utilitarian and exploitative prepared the terrain for his own reflections on *Arbeit* qua "authenticity." In line with the precedents that had been furnished by Spengler, Sombart, and Jünger—all of whom he read attentively—Heidegger associated "authentic work" and "joy-in-work" with *German work*.[110] From a phenomenological perspective, Heidegger's understanding of *Arbeit* in terms of "readiness-to-hand" and "craftsmanship" implied a higher degree of intentionality in comparison with the *degraded understanding of work* characteristic of modern industrial society—an approach that effectively reduced the worker to an "object": to a work-existence in which *Vorhandenheit* (being present-at-hand) substituted for *Zuhandenheit* (being ready-to-hand).

However, the rigid dichotomy between handicraft and technology on which Heidegger relied, though seductive, was both historically inaccurate and misleading. As numerous critics have pointed out, Heidegger romanticized to a fault conditions of life in rural Germany, although they were frequently rife with hardship and want. Rural circumstances can prove as oppressive and unforgiving—if not more so—than the social situation of modern industrialism. Moreover, over the course of the nineteenth century, the *Arbeiterbewegung* (workers' movement) was, on the whole, remarkably successful in ameliorating conditions of "alienated labor" that prevailed under the modern factory system. Heidegger's account failed to take any of these developments into consideration.[111] Conversely, the "equipment" at the farmer's disposal often remained quite primitive, and the prospects for a successful harvest were constantly exposed to the vagaries of climate. The potential advantages of labor-saving technology, which, under conditions of rural life, were often considerable, remained entirely outside Heidegger's diagnostic purview. Here, too, his approach succumbed to a self-defeating "pseudo-concreteness": it remained steadfastly aloof with respect to the relevant historical and empirical analyses of *Arbeit*, resting content with abstract flights of speculation.

Arbeitslager

Careful examination of Heidegger's *Arbeitsbegriff* shows that he equated nonalienated labor—*Arbeit* as an expression of "spirit"—with National Socialism's racial-totalitarian approach to this topos. Heidegger viewed National Socialist *Arbeit* as the fulfillment of "existential" qualities and characteristics that, six years earlier, he had outlined in the *Daseinsanalyse* of *Being and Time*.

Heidegger's reasoning proceeded as follows. Heidegger's aversion to "self-positing subjectivity"—which he regarded as an atavism of Cartesianism—impelled him to subordinate "intentionality" to the "destiny" and "mission" (*Schicksal und Sendung*) of the National Socialist *Volksgemeinschaft*. Heidegger held that *Arbeit-als-Eigentlichkeit*—work as authenticity—could only emerge once work was yoked to a higher, *völkisch* sense of purpose: linked to a "fate" that transcended the vulgar, *Western* understanding of *Arbeit* as narrowly instrumental and profit-oriented. Heidegger insisted that meaningful work—work as "well-ordered action"—occurred only when it was performed "in service to the *Volk*." As Heidegger averred, " 'Arbeit' is the title of every well-ordered action that is born by the responsibility of the individual, the group, and the State and which is thus in service to the Volk. . . . *Arbeiter* and *Arbeit*, as National Socialism understands these words, do not divide into classes, but bind and unite *Volksgenossen* and the social and occupational groups into one great will of the State."[112]

In keeping with this *völkisch* understanding of work, during Heidegger's rectorship, he repeatedly emphasized the ideological value of *Arbeitslager*, or "labor camps." Under the auspices of the *Reichsarbeitsdienst* program, *Arbeitslager* had become an official organ of the National Socialist state. Heidegger lauded *Arbeitslager*, insofar as they "[situated] the educational powers of the *Volk* in a *new, rooted unity*, on the basis of which the *Volk*, in its state, is obligated to act in accordance with its *destiny [zum Handeln für sein Schicksal verpflichtet]*."[113]

Among German workers, it soon became clear that the *völkisch*, "fate-laden" understanding of *Arbeit* that Heidegger praised was little more than a swindle that provided ideological cover for the rigid subordination of German workers to National Socialism's draconian policies. As Joan Campbell observes in *Joy in Work, German Work*,

> Heidegger became an enthusiastic Party member in May 1933. [He] used his posi-
> tion publicly to praise the new regime, and actively supported student participa-
> tion in Labor Service on the grounds that it constituted an educational device to
> imbue the new academic generation with a proper attitude to work and commu-
> nity, while creating a much-needed bond between workers of the "brain" and the
> "fist." . . . By vigorously promoting a German work ethic indistinguishable from
> that to be found in *Mein Kampf* or the propaganda of [state-sponsored] "Labor
> Service" [*Arbeitsdienst*], and by failing at any point explicitly to repudiate Na-
> tional Socialism, Heidegger helped to rally ideological legitimacy to the regime.[114]

Heidegger's subordination of *Arbeit* to ends that were defined by *Volk* and *Staat* coalesced with his more general attempt to redefine "freedom" as subor-dinating oneself to a higher "destiny" (*Schicksal*) and "mission" (*Sendung*). In the *Beiträge zur Philosophie*, Heidegger described bourgeois freedom as "tyrannical," insofar as it "demanded that everyone be left to his or her own opinion."[115] Heidegger's philosophical chess move was consistent with his re-formulation of *Geschichtlichkeit* as *Seinsgeschick* (the "destining of Being"). Proceeding from these premises, Heidegger regarded National Socialism—notwithstanding its brutal and repressive features—as a superior embodiment of freedom. Correspondingly, he insisted on the need to reconceive the defi-cient, Western doctrine of "negative freedom" as "freedom-for the spiritual mission of the German *Volk*": "Freedom is not freedom-*from* commitment, law, and obligation. Freedom is *freedom-for* decisive collective-spiritual 'de-ployment' for the sake of Germany's fate [*gemeinsamen geistigen Einsatz für das deutsche Schicksal*]. . . . Matriculation means committing oneself to the community of educators and combatants [*Kampf-und Erziehungsgemeinschaft*] for whom the spiritual mission of the German *Volk* is the be-all and end-all."[116]

In *Der Arbeiter*, Jünger glossed the relationship between freedom and necessity in a manner that paralleled Heidegger's inversion of the "misguided" Western understanding of their rapport. Both Jünger and Heidegger agreed that the superiority of the "German idea of freedom" consisted in sacrificing the individual to "fate." According to Jünger, the *Arbeitswelt*'s superiority was that, as an "organic construction," it negated "freedom" in the name of "obedience" (*Gehörsamkeit*): "To belong to an 'organic construction' [i.e., the *Arbeitswelt*] is neither an individual act of will nor an expression of bourgeois freedom. It is a factual assignment that is determined by the specific type of labor at issue. . . . Henceforth, freedom ceases to be the be-all and end-all of the individual's existence. . . . Instead, we have arrived at a point where freedom and obedience have become identical."[117]

"Holy Work" and the Nationalization of Work

Heidegger's attempt to appropriate *Arbeit* for the ends of National Socialism coalesced with the German Right's concerted efforts to lure the working class over to the cause of the *Volksgemeinschaft*. Alarmed by the November Revolution (1918–19)—which had accelerated Germany's military collapse and precipitated a divisive civil war—right-wing nationalists strove to develop a more proactive and integrationist approach to *Arbeit*. The refounding of the German Workers Party (Deutsche Arbeiterpartei) under Hitler's leadership, in 1919—at which point it was renamed the National Socialist German Workers Party—was part and parcel of these efforts to "nationalize" German workers.

In the plan to permanently sever the proletariat's loyalties to international socialism, Nietzsche's philosophy played a significant role. One of the leading proponents of the movement to rechannel working-class allegiances toward the ends of German nationalism was Paul Horneffer: a professor of religion at the University of Giessen and a convinced Nietzschean. It was Horneffer who, in 1900, delivered the commemorative address at Nietzsche's funeral. Subsequently, he became the executor of Nietzsche's literary estate.

Horneffer was convinced that Nietzsche's doctrines were ideally suited for advancing the ends of German nationalism. He regarded Nietzsche's trenchant critique of democratic "leveling" as valuable ideational fodder for Germany's ideological confrontation with the West. Horneffer maintained that Nietzsche's "aristocratic radicalism," as well as his understanding of life qua "will to power," meshed seamlessly with the values of Prussian militarism. Moreover, Nietzsche's worldview, which underwrote the "right" of the strong to express their strength unconditionally, contrasted sharply with the timorousness of left-wing pacifism. Lastly, since Nietzsche's "joyful wisdom" was inherently "life-affirming," it offered a welcome contrast to the "negativism" of orthodox Marxism, which thrived on fomenting class antagonisms.

In 1925, a coterie of Ruhr industrialists established "Dinta," the German Institute for Technical and Industrial Training (Deutsche Institut für Technische Arbeitsschulung), as the institutional cornerstone and bridgehead of their project to win over the working class to the cause of German nationalism. One of Dinta's main goals was to jump-start productivity by creating a more benevolent, labor-friendly work environment. Dinta sought to improve employer-employee relations by soliciting worker feedback on matters related to workplace safety and company benefits. It sought to enhance communication between labor and management by arranging regular meetings at which "bosses" could directly respond to worker concerns. These improvements and adjustments were implemented in the name of the "humanization of the workplace."

The Dinta initiatives were realized during the high tide of "Taylorism," which aimed at the administrative rationalization of the workplace. Hence, integral to the Dinta approach was the incorporation of the latest psychological assessment techniques to evaluate workers for job placement and supplementary occupational training.

In retrospect, the Dinta episode stands out as an object lesson in ideological cynicism. Under its auspices, German employers paid lip service to the "human factor's" importance by liberally referencing the rhetoric of psychological well-being. Ultimately, however, the technocrats and "organization men" who were running the show were "more interested in raising productivity and averting social discord than in minimizing the psychological trauma experienced by the individual worker and rationalizing production."[118]

Horneffer's most significant contribution to Dinta was his adaptation of Nietzsche's idea of "the joyful science" (*Die fröhliche Wissenschaft*; 1882) for the ends of workplace indoctrination. Horneffer's discursive fine-tuning of Nietzsche's philosophy culminated in the notion of *Arbeitsfreude*—"Joy in Work"—which became one of the ideological hallmarks of Dinta's project of working-class pacification.

Horneffer held that instilling Nietzschean values among German workers was a surefire method of alleviating "alienated labor." To that end, in 1919, Horneffer and his brother, August, coauthored a pamphlet titled *Heilige Arbeit* (Holy Work), whose objective was to foster an "ethical" understanding of work: reconceptualizing work as both a national duty and a means of Nietzschean "self-overcoming."

In 1922, Horneffer pursued the theme of "holy work" in a programmatic essay on "the religion of work." Invoking *Thus Spoke Zarathustra* (1882) in support of his positions and claims, Horneffer extolled *Germanentum* as the "genius-race of work" (*Genie-Volk der Arbeit*). He argued that, by embracing work as a "religion of human creativity," Germans would ensure their redemption as a *Volk*.[119]

Conversely, according to Horneffer, Social Democracy, by indoctrinating workers with the hyperrationalist credo of "scientific socialism," weakened their natural and instinctual patriotism, just as Marxism, by inciting class antagonism, acted as a vehicle of anticapitalist *ressentiment*. Ultimately, left-wing ideologies only aggravated the workers' feelings of "alienation" and discontent.

Horneffer praised "Nietzsche's individualistic *Lebensphilosophie*" as a panacea "for the fundamental sickness of the entire epoch," which he attributed to the generalized rejection of *Führertum*. Horneffer contended that only by restoring the *Führerprinzip* to its rightful position of primacy might Germany surmount its current economic woes, since only "genuine leaders" were capable of restoring German productivity to its prewar levels.[120]

In 1928, Horneffer published a sequel to "The Religion of Work" titled *Der Weg zur Arbeitsfreude* (The Way to Joy in Work).[121] Quoting extensively from Nietzsche's *Joyful Science* as well as from Schiller's "An die Freude" (Ode to Joy), Horneffer argued that Germany urgently needed a "spiritual social policy" to complement the material advances in social welfare that had been achieved under Bismarck.

Horneffer claimed that it was the responsibility of German elites—artists, politicians, and educators—to promote *Arbeitsfreude* in order to guarantee the realization of a well-adjusted and harmonious *Volksgemeinschaft*. Among Horneffer's pantheon of "leaders" (*Führer*), engineers took pride of place. As Horneffer explained, given their "knowledge of the joy to be derived from creation and their appreciation of the beauty of technology, [engineers] could do the most to enhance the German worker's innate capacity to feel 'something in the presence of the mighty enterprise of which he forms a part' and to experience pride in mastering his work."[122]

As a matter of principle, Horneffer's "Joy in Work" approach refused to address matters that pertained to the workers' concrete, material needs—concerns that he dismissed as crass and undignified. Consequently, in keeping with Horneffer's insistence on the need for a "spiritual social policy," none of Dinta's policy proposals focused on higher wages or enhanced social benefits. Instead, Dinta's approach concentrated exclusively on psychological measures that aimed at "curing alienation" and, thereby, defusing working-class rebelliousness. Horneffer's efforts were part of a more general strategy on the part of the German Right—an orientation that was already in evidence during the First World War—to deploy Nietzsche's philosophy in order to advance the worldview of authoritarian German nationalism.

The Ecstasies of *Arbeitsfreude*

Like Horneffer, Heidegger was a radical nationalist and avowed Nietzschean whose understanding of the European crisis was indelibly conditioned by Nietzsche's views. Following the Nazi *Machtergreifung*, Heidegger, under the tutelage of another prominent Nietzsche enthusiast, Ernst Jünger, regarded the "nationalization" of *Arbeit* as one of the keys to National Socialism's "total transformation of German Dasein."[123] In light of this background, it is not difficult to discern the similarities between Heidegger's paeans to the nobility of "German work" and the standpoint of authoritarian nationalists, such as the Horneffer brothers and the captains of industry who headed Dinta.

In Heidegger's seminar "On the Essence of Truth" (1933–34), he further explored the ontological meaning of work: the constitutive role that *Arbeit* played in Dasein's practical dealings with "Being of beings." Heidegger viewed *Arbeit* as a manifestation of "Dasein's becoming essential . . . in its practical encounters with the essence of things." He associated *Arbeit* with "the essence of [the German] State as a form that permanently structures and compels self-responsibly acting Dasein [*selbstverantwortlich handelndes Dasein*]." Well attuned to the *Zeitgeist*, Heidegger defined the "essence of work" (*Wesen der Arbeit*) as an activity that is concerned with "the empowerment of our Dasein [*Ermächtigung unseres Daseins*]." Thus, as a modality of Being-in-the-world, *Arbeit* licensed a certain primordial violence: a violence that was directed toward "beings" or "things." According to Heidegger, "[*Arbeit*] suffuses Dasein's attainment of world-mastery [*Weltbemächtigung*] on the most trivial as well as on the most exalted level."[124] It would be fair to say that Heidegger's characterization of the "essence of work" in "On the Essence of Truth" was a crucial way station in the militarization of existential ontology.

In *Logic as a Question Concerning the Essence of Language*, Heidegger broadened his conception of *Arbeit* as a form of "world-mastery" by appending an affirmative account of *Arbeitsfreude* or "Joy in Work": a focus that suggested additional parallels between Heidegger's treatment of *Arbeit* and the authoritarian nationalist approach that was promoted by Horneffer and the German notables associated with Dinta. In an idiolect reminiscent of the existential analytic of *Being and Time*, Heidegger exalted *Arbeitsfreude* as one of Dasein's *Grundstimmungen*, or "foundational moods," as well as a "condition of possibility for authentic work."[125] His valorization of "Joy in Work" in the *Logic* lectures is intellectually and politically significant, since, with the consolidation of Nazi rule, lip service to the ecstasies of *Arbeitsfreude* became one of the regime's defining ideological features.

Arbeitslager as Sites of Racial Discipline

With the Great Crash of 1929, the German industrialists' strategy for labor underwent a qualitative change. The immediate challenge concerned Germany's skyrocketing unemployment rate: as of 1932, approximately twelve million workers—some 30 percent the workforce—were out of work. Faced with the material distress of a rapidly expanding pool of unemployed workers, Dinta was forced to reassess its industrial training strategies. In many instances, Dinta was obligated to retrain these workers—many of whom were unskilled—in the hope that they would eventually reenter the labor force.

In response to this predicament, there emerged a new focus on the benefits of *Arbeitsdienst*, or "labor service." During the twilight of the Weimar Republic, Freiwilliger Arbeitsdienst established a network of voluntary public-works programs for the unemployed. Following the Nazi seizure of power, these programs gradually became compulsory.

Initially, *Arbeitsdienst* became mandatory for university students. Often, they were put to work in the countryside to ensure that they remained *bodenständig*, or "rooted": untempted by cerebral flights of fancy. As of 1935, Freiwilliger Arbeitsdienst, or "Voluntary Labor Service," was transformed into Arbeitsdienstpflicht, or "Mandatory Labor Service." Soon, *Arbeitsdienst* became obligatory for German men under the age of twenty-one.

From a National Socialist perspective, compulsory labor service possessed several distinct advantages. For one, it was a valuable source of under- or unpaid labor. The average wage was a risible two Reichsmark per hour. It also acted as a solvent with respect to class differences, acculturating German youth to the values of the *Volksgemeinschaft*.

In keeping with the Third Reich's expansionist aims, under the direction of Konstantin Hierl, the *Reichsarbeitsdienst* (RAD) bureau introduced a military training component. As Hierl observed, "The newly forged type of the *Arbeitsmann* results from a fusion of three basic elements: soldiers, the peasantry, and workers." As a "means of correct training" (Foucault), *Arbeitsdienst* aimed to inculcate the values of "discipline" (*Zucht*), "loyalty" (*Treue*), and a heightened appreciation of the demands of "Blut und Boden."[126]

Following the Nazi seizure of power, Dinta operatives became assiduous proponents of compulsory labor service. They viewed obligatory *Arbeitsdienst* as a valuable method of inculcating discipline and positive work habits among those sectors of the German working class that remained beyond the reach of the organization's own educational training programs.[127]

National Socialist ideology was saturated with *Arbeitsrhetorik*, a lexicon of "work," "labor," and "service." In essence, the Third Reich substituted a *labor ideology* for a meaningful and consequential *labor policy*. Nazi officials appealed "to the pride, patriotism, [and] idealism" of German workers. The focal point of Nazi labor ideology was the intrinsically uplifting character of work, rather than the well-being of the individual worker. One of the more popular slogans was, "work ennobles" (*Arbeit adelt*). The infamous maxim inscribed on the gate at Auschwitz, "Arbeit macht frei," was merely a grotesque variation on this theme.[128]

In a 1934 interview, Hitler addressed *Arbeit*'s significance for the National Socialist worldview. He explained that, from the very beginning, one of Nazism's central goals was to destroy socialism. Once Marxism was eliminated, the path would be clear to rechannel working-class support toward the ends of German nationalism. "I chose the word 'worker' [for the NSDAP, or National Socialist German *Workers* Party]," remarked Hitler, "because I wanted *to* reconquer it for the forces of the Nation. . . . The comrade with the red cloth cap must become a member [*Volksgenosse*] of the *Volksgemeinschaft*." The ulti-mate goal, he continued, was to "transform the sociological concept of 'worker' into an emblem of the 'nobility of work' [*Edel der Arbeit*]. This emblem alone represents an effective oath of allegiance to the Nation on the part of soldier and farmer, merchant and scholar, worker and capitalist."[129]

In a major speech delivered at the First Congress of the Deutsche Arbeits-front (DAF), the Führer added the following clarification: "The movement rep-resented by me and my co-combatants intends, with all due speed, to exalt the word 'Arbeit' as an emblem of the German Nation. . . . If popular and direct participation of the German *Volk* in the actions of the German State is at all pos-sible, it will only occur through *Arbeit*. In this sense, the German Reich is the *Reich of German Socialism*, a state of *Arbeit* and *Arbeiter*."[130]

Hitler was adept at deploying his humble origins for political gain. He was proud to be known as a *Volkskanzler*—the People's Chancellor—and as a "leader from the rank and file" (*Führer von unten*). During the mid-1930s, in a speech to construction workers, he described himself as "one who went forth from among you": a person of modest means who prided himself on being "a man without estate, stocks, or bank account." Addressing the Reichstag in 1938, the Führer boasted, "During the past five years, I too have been a worker!"[131]

Although the Nazi worldview was suffused with the rhetoric of *Arbeit*, the *Arbeitdiskurs* itself was permeated by military metaphors. It was simultane-ously a *Soldaten-Diskurs*, in which the idiom of *Sturm und Kampf*, "attack" and "struggle," predominated. (During the 1920s, Heidegger characterized his phil-osophical friendship with Karl Jaspers as a *Kampfgemeinschaft*: a "community of struggle.")[132] It was as though National Socialism's *Arbeitsideologie* had transformed German society into a replica of Jünger's dystopian, ultramobi-lized *Arbeitergesellschaft*.

Hence, the National Socialist *Arbeitersstaat* was effectively a *Soldatenstaat*. Under Nazism, the *Volksgemeinschaft* was regarded as an extension of the First World War's *Grabenschutzgemeinschaft* (community of the trenches). To all in-tents and purposes, the Third Reich offered everyone the opportunity to become a soldier! As Hitler observed during the early 1930s, "The political leader is al-ways a soldier!"[133]

The National Socialist Ministry of Labor was known as the Deutsche Arbe-itsfront. In German, the military connotations of *Front* were numerous and wide-ranging. Among them were *Frontgeneration*, *Fronterlebnis*, and *Front-*

soldaten. Deutsche Arbeitsfront was an appellation that called to mind the "fighting spirit" of the *Frontgeneration*: an uncanny confirmation of Jünger's thesis in *Der Arbeiter* that, with the advent of "total mobilization," "soldiers" and "workers" would become interchangeable.

It was in this spirit that Deutsche Arbeitsfront officials described the challenges of combating unemployment as "winning the battle of labor" (*Arbeitsschlacht*). *Einsatz*, a military expression for the deployment of combat troops, became the term of art for the implementation of "work details" in conjunction with *Reichsarbeitsdienst*. Workers were commonly referred to as "soldiers of labor" (*Soldaten der Arbeit*), a description that accurately reflected their condition of servitude and regimentation under Nazism. Members of the SA, or Sturmabteilung (Attack Division), were commonly referred to as "political soldiers."

Nazi leaders sought to model the *Volksgemeinschaft* after the First World War's "community of the trenches." Robert Ley, the head of the *Reichsarbeitsfront*, reaffirmed that "German socialism" took its bearings from the camaraderie among the *Frontsoldaten*. As one highly placed *Reichsarbeitsfront* official put it, "The German has always found military leadership to be the optimal form of social organization. . . . Under our political leadership we stand . . . in a marching column whose visible expression is the uniform."[134]

In Konstantin Hierl's inaugural address as *Reichsarbeitsdienstführer*, he emphasized the importance of the "militarization of work" for Nazi social policy. Reflecting on Germany's unacceptably high unemployment rate, Hierl remarked,

> Deeds alone [*nur die Tat*] can extricate us from our current state of affliction. In keeping with the moral precepts of Aryan man, poverty can only be alleviated through *Arbeit*. . . . The goal of compulsory labor service [*Arbeitsdienstpflicht*] is to produce for the benefit of the State an army of labor [*Arbeitsheer*] for deployment as a political force in the economic struggle for survival [*Kampf um unser Leben*], so that we can regain our national economic independence. . . . Like the term "soldier," the term "worker" must become emblematic of the supreme duty [*Pflicht*] of each and every German.[135]

In another address, Hierl lauded the National Socialist *Arbeitslager*, which he described as indispensable "bulwarks against the Jewish-materialistic conception of work, which perceives work solely in terms of monetary gain and which understands work exclusively as a commodity."[136]

Anti-intellectualism among the Nazi leadership was something of an open secret. Hence, within months of the seizure of power, Hitler et al. made *Arbeitsdienst* obligatory for university admission. From a National Socialist standpoint, this measure possessed several advantages. It would discourage elitism by introducing university students to the hardships of rural life. It would also furnish the Third Reich with additional manpower, at minimal cost, for its outsized public-works programs. Last but not least, it would inculcate National Socialist values among privileged German youth.

Hierl's description of *Arbeitslager* as "bulwarks against the Jewish-materialistic conception of work" epitomizes the racially coded nature of the Nazi *Arbeitsbegriff*. National Socialism consistently attributed a *positive* valuation to "Aryan work," which, purportedly, valued work as an "ethical" task. Jewish attitudes toward work, conversely, were deemed "unethical," since Jews allegedly viewed work in a narrowly egoistic, self-interested manner. A cursory glance at Hitler's *Arbeitsdiskurs* shows that it was rife with platitudes that played on the opposition between "German work" and "Jewish work." "Aryanism," claimed the Führer, "means an ethical approach to work. Socialism demands the primacy of common use [*Gemeinnutz*] rather than selfish use [*Eigennutz*]. . . . Judaism signifies Mammonism and materialism. In other words, it is diametrically opposed to German socialism."[137]

In Hitler's 13 August 1920 speech in Munich—which is commonly regarded as the *Ur*-text of National Socialist racial doctrine—he defined anti-Semitism by invoking the antithesis between "Aryan work" and "Jewish work." As the Führer explained, because the Nordic races inhabit cold climates, they understand work as an imperative for survival—hence as a "duty," or *Pflicht*. Conversely, the Jews, who take their ethical bearings from the Old Testament, *shun productive work*, which they perceive as punishment for Original Sin. Thus, whereas the Aryan *Arbeitsethos* led to the "purity of racial breeding" and "the strength to establish States," the Jewish strategy of work avoidance, "led to inbreeding and to a lack of the strength to build States." "Jewish internationalism" posed a special risk, insofar as it threatened to "denationalize the races." Anticipating the Final Solution, Hitler concluded by claiming that the only plausible remedy for this imbalance was "the removal of the Jews from the midst of our people."[138]

In assessing the National Socialist *Arbeitslager*, it is important to take into account the *longue durée*. Under the Third Reich, the *Arbeitslager* would soon become an integral component of a sinister and extensive *Lager* system or network. Hence, the *Arbeitslager* administered by Hierl and his staff established a fateful precedent. As Peter Dudek has shown in *Erziehung durch Arbeit* (Education through Work), although the *Arbeitslager* had modest beginnings, they rapidly metamorphosed into a much greater evil:

> With the introduction of National Labor Service [*Reichsarbeitsdienst*], National Socialism created a comprehensive system of forced labor for German youth. Ultimately, it would systematically transform the "camp" function into an integral component of its education and annihilation system. The *Lager* played an essential role in establishing a "community of coercion" . . . above all, with respect to the expulsion and removal of political opponents and racially persecuted groups. Groups that, in keeping with the tenets of Nazi ideology, were deemed *incapable, unwilling*, or *unworthy* of "integration" [*als nicht gemeinschaftsfähig, -willig und -würdig*] were ultimately plunged into the maw of a comprehensive network of "camps" that included *reeducation camps, pedagogical work camps*, and *extermination camps*: an escalation that exemplified National Socialism's "cumulative radicalization." . . . Thereby, the regime created a new social constellation that implacably linked the idea of "camps" to terror, compulsion, and annihilation.[139]

Heidegger endorsed *Arbeitslager* as an indispensable component of Nazi social policy and as an important catalyst for achieving a racially homogeneous *Volksgemeinschaft*. As Heidegger observed in *"Arbeitsdienst* and the University,"

> With the *Arbeitslager*, a new institution for the direct revelation of the *Volksgemeinschaft* is being realized. In the future, young Germans will be governed by the knowledge of *Arbeit*, in which the *Volk* concentrates its strength in order to experience the severity of its existence, to preserve the momentum of its Will, and to learn anew the value of its manifold abilities. The *Arbeitslager* also functions as a camp for training leaders [*Führer*] in all social groups and professions. What counts in the *Lager*, above all, is exemplary acting and working together. . . . The *Arbeitslager* awakens and educates to the knowledge of the laboring community of all social groups [*die arbeitende Gemeinschaft aller Stände*].[140]

Kraft durch Freude: The Institutionalization of *Arbeitsfreude*

Following the Nazi *Machtergreifung*, eliminating the trade unions became one of National Socialism's highest priorities. Their continued independence meant the ever-present risk of strikes, protests, and other forms of resistance, especially in the case of the Social Democratic unions, which boasted four and a half million members. Hence, trade-union autonomy represented one of the primary obstacles to the realization of a totalitarian state. As one scholar has observed appositely, "The step from bureaucratic authoritarian dictatorship to total rule required the smashing or absorption of all voluntary organizations. . . . Authoritarian regimentation and total mobilization . . . accorded with a theory in which all social organizations were assigned the function of transmitting the will of the party and its leaders to the masses. The elimination of the tradition-rich and . . . powerful socio-political organizations of the working class was an important step toward readying the economic and social sector for rearmament."[141]

Following the Enabling Act of 23 March 1933, which allowed Hitler to rule by fiat, the Third Reich enacted a series of repressive decrees that were aimed at emasculating the trade unions. Foremost among these measures was a 4 April 1933 law that underwrote the on-the-spot dismissal of Communist workers and Social Democratic Party (SPD) shop stewards. A few weeks later, the Nazis achieved an important coup against a dispirited political Left by restyling May Day as the "National Day of Labor," declaring that, henceforth, it would be a paid national holiday. On 2 May—that is, the very next day—the SS and the SA forcibly occupied trade-union offices throughout Germany. By divesting the labor movement of its legal prerogatives and autonomy, these actions brought one of the last bastions of civic resistance to its knees.

The Deutsche Arbeitsfront, under the direction of Robert Ley, was the Nazi bureau that was constructed on the ruins of the German trade-union movement. Under the Third Reich, it was responsible for ensuring the cooperation and docility of the German working class. As Karl Dietrich Bracher remarks in *The German Dictatorship*, "The DAF was a compulsory organization subservient to the party. In line with *Volksgemeinschaft* ideology, it stripped the concept of the 'worker' of its class-sociological meaning. Employees and employers were locked into one gigantic organization, which ultimately embraced more than 25 million members. . . . A Law for the Regulation of National Labor (January 20, 1934) and the official designation of the DAF as an 'auxiliary of the NSDAP' . . . made the DAF the sole organization of the 'soldiers of labor,' 'depending solely on the will of the leadership of the NSDAP.' "[142]

The DAF was also the organization charged with promoting the idea of *Arbeitsfreude*—a forseeable development, in light of the fact that, during the

1920s, Ley had been an avid supporter of Dinta's plans to alleviate working-class dissatisfaction by "spiritualizing" and "humanizing" industrial relations.

To facilitate this goal—and as an ultimate expression of National Socialism's ideological cynicism vis-à-vis the German working class—in 1933, the DAF established an office for the "Beauty of Labor" (*Schönheit der Arbeit*): "In Beauty of Labor, the utopian promise of an industrial society where work was beautiful and the class struggle abolished was given political and administrative form. Its goal was the domestication of labor. . . . The aestheticization of machine technology, Taylor's work processes, and efficiency provided the new requirements of the machine with a cultural *raison d'être*. . . . As industrial psychology, Beauty of Labor extended the domination of material nature to the nature of the worker, whose consciousness was reduced to an environmental factor, to be transformed in the interest of productivity and habituation."[143]

Beauty of Labor was a subsidiary of the DAF's *Kraft durch Freude* (Strength through Joy) leisure and vacation division. David Schoenbaum has described *Kraft durch Freude* as "the Third Reich's best publicized and best received contribution to industrial relations": "Conceived in a moment of embarrassment as a scheme to win friends and . . . find use for the confiscated assets of the trade unions, *Kraft durch Freude* overcame both worker resistance and the gloomy prophecies of [Robert] Ley's [National Socialist] Party colleagues. Its expansive programs soon included subsidized theater performances and concerts, exhibitions, sport and hiking groups, dances, dancing, films, and adult education courses. Its most famous feature was a grandiose system of subsidized tourism whose practical economic by-products included visible benefits to thousands of rural hotel keepers and the State railroad." As the beneficiary of vast subsidies, *Kraft durch Freude* soon came to resemble a state-run megacorporation. By 1935, thanks to the construction of two ocean liners, it had transformed itself into a shipping company. By 1937, with the development of the Volkswagen, which was originally known as the "KdF Wagen," it simultaneously became a major automobile manufacturer. These *Kraft durch Freude* activities contributed to the economic might of the regime. During the lead-up to war, they were militarily refunctioned. The ocean liners became troop ships. And the Volkswagen was redeveloped as an all-purpose military vehicle.[144]

Like the *Reichsarbeitsdienst* program, *Kraft durch Freude* was regarded as a means of leveling class distinctions, thereby enhancing national unity.

Nevertheless, these plans, however laudable in theory, were never realized in practice. Since the Volkswagen was only affordable for Germans with middle-class incomes, it effectively became a bourgeois status symbol. A similar fate befell *Kraft durch Freude*'s mass tourism program, despite the inclusion of employers and members of the middle class among the tourist groups and the construction of single-class cruise ships.

Beauty of Labor was overseen by the future Nazi minister of armaments Albert Speer. Its goal was to employ the blandishments of "schöner Schein," or "beautiful appearance," to cement the ideological loyalty of German workers—despite the fact that, under Nazism, their wages never rose above Depression-era levels.

Beauty of Labor's official motto was, "German everyday life shall be beautiful." The bureau earmarked vast sums of money to ensure that German factories were outfitted with an aesthetically pleasing veneer. Resources were devoted to the construction of gleaming kitchens, sparkling restrooms, and state-of-the-art recreational facilities. Within the first two years, over one hundred million Reichsmark were expended on renovating the German workplace: the facades of over twelve thousand plants were cosmetically improved, factories were repainted, floors were washed, and new washing and sanitation facilities were installed.[145]

In addition to these material improvements, the Beauty of Labor office initiated a campaign against excessive plant noise. Under the auspices of the slogan, "Good light—Good work!" it sought to remedy the problem of poor factory lighting. The "Clean People and Clean Factories!" campaign took steps to improve workplace hygiene and factory ventilation systems. What had begun in 1933 as a modest undertaking with limited resources had, by 1938, expanded into an immense bureaucratic apparatus that housed five fully staffed subdivisions.

In 1936, in order to highlight the bureau's achievements, DAF chief Robert Ley published a book titled *Germany Is Becoming More Beautiful!* (*Deutschland ist schöner geworden!*). The Führer praised Beauty of Labor as a shining example of "Socialism of the Deed" (*Sozialismus der Tat*). "In the future," Hitler exulted, "there will be only one nobility, *the nobility of labor! [Adel der Arbeit]*."[146]

Ultimately, what the DAF offered German workers as a substitute for union representation—appeals to a "spiritual" work ethos, the cosmetic enhancement of factories, and the growth of mass tourism under the auspices of "Strength through Joy"—failed to mask the working class's increasingly draconian conditions of servitude. German workers' brief respite from Depression-era hardship ended abruptly, in 1936, with the regimentation of the four-year plan, which was implemented with a view toward "total war."

Arbeitswelt and *Schollenromantik* (Romanticism of the Soil)

One of the fundamental pillars of Nazi ideology sought to combine a nostalgia-oriented *Schollenromantik*—a "romanticism of the soil"—with an enthusiasm for modern industrialism that was essential to the movement's expansionist geopolitical aspirations.

Heidegger's attraction to National Socialism oscillated between these two poles. The tension between them—agrarian traditionalism, on the one hand, and the celebration of Germany's matchless technological prowess, on the other—seems less extreme once one takes into account the seductive nature of National Socialist *Arbeitsideologie*. The Nazi "ideology of labor" promoted an aesthetic definition of labor that masked the dislocations and hardships of industrialization. Ultimately, "the peasant with his plow and the *Arbeiter* at the blast furnace could appear as complementary aspects of a seamlessly integrated *Arbeitergesellschaft*: a unified '*Volksgemeinschaft*-at-work.' "[147]

Nevertheless, in 1936, with the implementation of the four-year plan, the Nazis sided squarely with the technocratic orientation of Germany's leading industrialists, on whose proficiency the Third Reich depended for the steady supply of armaments that, a few years later, would help to determine the outcome of the "battles of matériel."

Heidegger's advocacy of *Arbeit-als-Beruf*—labor as a "calling"—provided the Third Reich with a valuable source of intellectual and political legitimacy. His defense of *Arbeit-als-Metaphysik* dovetailed with National Socialism's *Arbeitsideologie*: a "swindle" that Max Horkheimer and Theodor Adorno deftly exposed in *Dialectic of Enlightenment*: "That the hygienic factory and everything pertaining to it, Volkswagen and the *Sportspalast*, are liquidating metaphysics does not matter in itself; but that these things are themselves *becoming metaphysics*—an ideological veil within the social whole behind which real doom is gathering—matters considerably."[148]

Heideggerian "metapolitics" sought to reconcile these two seemingly antithetical dimensions of the National Socialist *Arbeitsethos*: the technocratic-industrial dimension that Ernst Jünger had celebrated in *Der Arbeiter*; and the *Schollenromantik* aspect that, during the 1920s, conditioned Heidegger's embrace of *Bodenständigkeit* as a normative topos.

Heidegger consistently shunned the role of "professional philosopher." Instead, he regarded himself as an *Arbeiter*, a self-understanding that was closely tied to the *Heimat* ideology of his native Alemannia. Thus, in "Why We Remain in the Provinces" (1934), Heidegger praised the Alemannian landscape as his *Arbeitswelt* (work world). "My philosophical work," he avowed, "is intimately rooted in and related to the work of the peasants." "The inner relationship of my own *Arbeit* to the Schwarzwald and its *Volk*," Heidegger continued, "comes from a centuries-long and irreplaceable *Alemannian-Swabian Bodenständigkeit* [rootedness]." Both of these observations are entirely consistent with *Schollenromatik* ideology.[149]

A year earlier, in the *Rektoratsrede*, Heidegger advanced similar arguments—albeit in a more ideologically charged register—concerning the spiritual and cultural merits of "rootedness." "The spiritual world of a *Volk*," he asserted, "is not its cultural superstructure. Instead, it is the power that comes from preserving . . . the forces that are rooted in the soil and blood of a *Volk* [*erd- und bluthäftigen Kräfte*]."[150] By invoking "*the forces that are rooted in the soil and blood of a Volk*" as a normative topos, Heidegger recurred to a classic trope of *Blut und Boden* ideology. This demarche consciously subverted—and inverted—Idealism's claims concerning the primacy of "Spirit." Instead, Heidegger reconceived "Spirit" as something "rooted in the soil and blood of a *Volk*": that is, as essentially *chthonic* and hence as more "primordial" (*ursprünglich*).

In "Why We Remain in the Provinces," Heidegger explained how the topography of his native Schwarzwald had impacted his personal *Arbeitsethos*. He defined *Arbeit* as a modality of "unconcealment": an activity that opened up a *Lichtung*, or "clearing," in which the "Being of beings" became manifest. In the passages that follow, Heidegger rhapsodized about the entwinement of *Landschaft* and *Arbeit*:

> On the steep slope of a wide mountain valley in the Schwarzwald, at an elevation of 1,150 meters, there stands a small ski hut. . . . Scattered at wide intervals throughout the narrow base of the valley . . . lie the farmhouses with their large overhanging roofs. . . . *This is my work world* [*Arbeitswelt*]. . . . The gravity of the

mountains and the severity [*Härte*] of their primeval rock, . . . the rush of the mountain brook in the long autumn night, the stern simplicity of the flatlands covered with snow—all of this . . . penetrates daily existence up there . . . only when one's own Dasein stands in one's *work* [*nur, wenn das eigene Dasein in seiner* Arbeit *steht*]. . . . The *Arbeit* alone *opens up* space, viz., the reality that is these mountains. *The Arbeit's trajectory remains embedded in what happens in the region.*

A deep winter's night when a wild, pounding snowstorm rages around the cabin . . . *is the perfect time for philosophy.* Only then can working through each thought become tough and focused [*hart und scharf*]. The struggle to mold something into language is akin to the resistance of the towering firs against the storm.

My philosophical work . . . is intimately rooted in and related to the work of the peasants. . . . The inner relationship of my own *Arbeit* to the Schwarzwald and its people comes from a centuries-long and irreplaceable *rootedness in the Alemannian-Swabian soil* [*Bodenständigkeit*]. . . . My entire work is sustained and guided by the world of these mountains and their people.[151]

The lyricism of Heidegger's portrayal of "Alemannian-Swabian *Bodenständigkeit*" is impressive. Nevertheless, his depiction also signified a ringing endorsement of *Schollenromantik* provincialism.

Heidegger's defense of Alemannian-Swabian regionalism reflected his ideological aversion to life in the Jew-infested modern metropolis. "The world of the city runs the risk of falling into a destructive error," Heidegger warned.[152] He disparaged the urbanites who inhabit the modern metropolis as "rootless individuals [*entwurzelte Menschen*]."[153] In *The Fundamental Concepts of Metaphysics* (1929–30), he denigrated "contemporary city man" as "the ape of civilization" for whom "homesickness" had lost all meaning.[154]

The Heidegger intimate H. W. Petzet claimed that Heidegger felt ill at ease in large cities, owing to "the mundane spirit of Jewish circles that is at home in the metropolitan centers of the West."[155] And in a letter of recommendation that Heidegger wrote in 1929, he insisted, "at stake is nothing less than the urgent awareness that we stand before a choice: once again to provide our German spiritual life with genuinely rooted forces and educators [*echte bodenständige Kräfte und Erzieher*], or to deliver it over definitively . . . to *increasing Jewification* [*Verjudung*]."[156] Heidegger's use of "Verjudung"—a patently racist term that was predominantly employed by anti-Semites—demonstrated a fear of racial contamination or defilement.

"A New Aristocracy of *Blut und Boden*"

Heidegger's embrace of *Schollenromantik* tracked the *Blut und Boden* ideology that was propagated by the Nazi minister of agriculture Walther Darré. In *Der Feldweg*, Heidegger praised German farmers, or *Bauern*, as "bondsmen to heritage [*Herkunft*] rather than slaves to *Machenschaft*." In *Das Bauerntum als Lebensquell der Nordischen Rasse* (*The Peasantry as a Vital Source of the Nordic Race;* 1929), Darré advanced a remarkably similar claim: "To be a farmer [*Bauer*] means *being free*, neither bondsman nor servant."[157]

Among *völkisch* intellectual circles, Darré's writings were responsible for popularizing *Schollenromantik* ideology. In 1932, Himmler acknowledged Darré's talents as a proponent of Nordic superiority by appointing him as director of the SS Race and Settlement Main Office.[158] Darré maintained that the twin evils of urbanization and modern industrialism were responsible for Germany's cultural and demographic decline. The remedy that he recommended was a return to the soil, or *Boden*. Darré held that only a new nobility could restore Germany to "racial health." He advocated the idea of a Nordic elite, whose claim to superiority was based on "purity of blood" as opposed to the rootless and corrupt accoutrements of wealth.

For Darré, the embodiment of this new aristocracy, or *Adeltum*, was the German "farmer" (*Bauer*), a caste that he revered as the savior of the German race. Darré asserted that the overcrowding of German cities—which advocates of Nazi race doctrine held responsible for a wide array of social ills, including genetic degeneracy and population depletion—could only be remedied by a concerted policy of eastward colonization and the acquisition of *Lebensraum*. Thereby, the *Volksgemeinschaft*, led by a vanguard of hardy peasant-farmers, could escape the suffocating constraints of the metropole and return to "health." To be sure, this scenario remained unconcerned with the fate of the expendable, "racially inferior" Slavs currently occupying these lands.

During the 1920s, Darré, along with Himmler and Alfred Rosenberg, had been a member of the Artamanen Order, which envisioned the creation a racial elite by subjecting Aryan youth to the rigors of agricultural labor.[159] Darré's distinctive contribution to the Nazi worldview is conveyed by the titles of the two books he published in the years preceding the Nazi seizure of power: *The Peasantry as a Vital Source of the Nordic Race* and *A New Aristocracy of Blood and Soil* (*Neuadel aus Blut und Boden*; 1930). In these works, Darré described the link between *Blut und Boden* ideology and Nazi *Lebensraum* doctrine:

> The German people cannot avoid coming to terms with the Eastern Problem. . . . We look on with dumb resignation as formerly pure German cities—Reval, Riga, and Warsaw—are lost to our *Volk*. . . . Why shouldn't other German colonial settlements of past centuries—Breslau, Stettin, even Leipzig or Dresden—be next in line? . . . The German *Volk* cannot avoid a life or death struggle with the advancing East. Our people must prepare for the *struggle*. . . . There is only one solution for us: Absolute Victory! The concept of *Blut und Boden* gives us the right to take back as much Eastern land as is necessary to achieve harmony between the body of our people and geopolitical space.[160]

According to Darré, *Blut und Boden* ideology was predicated on the distinction between "settler peoples" and "nomads." Settler peoples, by virtue of "the work of their hands, [developed] the riches of the soil as a permanent abode." Conversely, the shifty and untrustworthy "nomad" represented the antithesis of Nordic-aristocratic rootedness.[161] Nomads were archetypal *parasites*: their rootlessness, or *Bodenlosigkeit*, was matched by an innate, reprehensible aversion to work.

Like all parasites, nomads knew only one way to prosper: by feeding off and exploiting their hosts. As Darré explained, "The life of the nomads is always a life of *pure parasitism*. . . . From this parasitic attitude, the world knows that the people of these nomadic tribes work nowhere and at no time."[162] Since the nomad was constitutionally unable to "construct," he could only "exploit." To compensate for this deficiency, nomads ravaged and plundered their hosts, engaging in depredations such as "ambushes, destruction, death, and robbery."[163]

In the discourse of Nazi race doctrine, "nomads" was a commonplace stand-in for "Jews." This negative cultural stereotype was predicated on the Ahasverus myth of the wandering Jew. Such characterizations forcefully conveyed the Jewish nomad's corrosive impact on the existential and racial well-being of his hosts. In *Mein Kampf*, Hitler included a lengthy diatribe against "Jewish nomads," to which he added an important qualification: even were these "Jewish nomads" to reform themselves and become sedentary, their efforts could never be more than a ruse contrived to deceive the indigenous races whose hospitality they exploited. Ultimately, it would be impossible for such reforms to mitigate the Jews' deleterious cultural influence.[164]

In order to stave off the risks of racial degeneration, Darré recommended the adoption of two measures: (1) breeding and (2) the forcible exclusion from the gene pool of those who were weak and impure, since Darré was convinced that "there is no difference between breeding men and breeding animals; [consequently,] it is practical to apply the lessons learned from animal breeding to human propagation."[165]

Darré's elaborated his theory of Jewish nomadism in the essay "Swine as the Criterion for Nordic Peoples and Semites." His point of departure was the contrast between the traditional Jewish dietary proscription against eating pork as opposed to the healthy German peasant's ravenous appetite for the same. Since Darré associated swine with the "rooted" agricultural habitudes of the German peasantry, he viewed the Jewish aversion to pork consumption as further evidence of the unbridgeable racial divide separating Germans and Jews: the Aryan farmer-settler versus the rootless and parasitical Semitic nomad.[166]

The Metaphysics of Ontological "Rootedness"

Heidegger shared Darré's concerns regarding the disintegrative cultural influence of nomadic peoples and their destructive impact on the life of "rooted" peoples who inhabited settled "national communities." Heidegger's views were conditioned by his trademark metaphysics of ontological rootedness: the sacralization of "the forces of blood and earth" that he embraced as a counterweight to the advanced cultural decomposition of Western modernity.

Heidegger shared this orientation with like-minded champions of "Integral Nationalism": "spiritual reactionaries" who invoked the prerogatives of jus sanguinis, or the "right of blood," in opposition to the "ideas of 1789." "The rootlessness [*Bodenlosigkeit*] of contemporary life is the basis [*Wurzel*] of an escalating disintegration [*Verfall*]," claimed Heidegger. "All attempts at renewal and innovation will remain hopeless," he continued, "unless we succeed in returning to the nurturing powers of our native soil [*heimatlichen Boden*]."[167] Heidegger's vindication of "native soil," or *heimatlichen Boden*, presupposed the "existential" affinities between *Volk*, *Blut*, *Raum*, and *Erde*. These correlations were of central importance for Heidegger's ontologically grounded "metapolitics." He regarded competing approaches that neglected these "factical" elements as ontologically deficient. They failed to measure up to the depth and profundity of the *Seinsgedanke*.

"A *Heimat*," claimed Heidegger, "is something I have on the basis of my birth. . . . A *Heimat* expresses itself in *rootedness-in-soil* and *being bound to the earth [Bodenständigkeit und Erdgebundenheit]*."[168] Heidegger's conviction that *Deutschtum*, in contrast with other races or peoples, possessed a unique, re-demptory ontological mission infused his worldview with a prejudice-laden ideological virulence.

Heidegger's expatiated on the perils and depredations of "nomadism" in *Na-ture, History, and State* (1934). As the following passage demonstrates, his per-spective coalesced with the racist orientation of Nazi geopolitics (*Raumpolitik*):

> Every *Volk* has a space that belongs to it. People who live by the sea, in the moun-tains, and on the plains are different. History teaches us that nomads have been made nomadic by the desolation of wastelands and steppes. However, often, *no-mads have also left wastelands behind them* even when they found fruitful and cultivated land. Conversely, peoples who are rooted-in-soil have known how to make a home for themselves even in the wilderness.
>
> From the specific knowledge of a *Volk* about the nature of its space [*Raum*], we first experience how nature reveals itself to this *Volk*. In the case of a Slavic *Volk*, the nature of our *German space* would definitely be revealed differently from the way it is revealed to us. Conversely, to Semitic nomads, *it will perhaps never be revealed at all.*[169]

Nazism invoked an analogous conception of racial geopolitics to justify its claims to European hegemony. This orientation justified the prerogatives of *Germanentum* qua *Herrenrasse*, in contrast with the racial inferiors or *Unter-menschen* that it targeted for colonization, slave labor, or extermination. Ac-cording to the left-wing writer Kurt Tucholsky, Nazi *Schollenromantik*, "started off green, but soon became bloody-red."[170]

Lager-Mania

During the 1930s, Heidegger championed the *Lager* idea. Under the Third Reich, the *Lager*, or "camps," became the central disciplinary institution for en-suring mass loyalty to the regime. As such, they played a pivotal role in turning "Germans into Nazis."[171] The *Lager* were a decisive instrument for realizing what the historian Peter Dudek has described as the National Socialist "com-munity of forced obedience [*Zwangsgemeinschaft*]."[172]

Heidegger's enthusiasm for the *Lager* idea was intimately related to his conception of the ontological mission of *Arbeit*. Under National Socialism, the *Lager* idea assumed a wide variety of forms. There were "camps" for university professors (*Dozentenlager*), for secondary-school instructors (*Lehrerlager*), for jurists (*Juristenlager*), and for doctors (*Ärztelager*), as well as the more sinister and familiar concentration camps (*Konzentrationslager*) and extermination camps (*Vernichtungslager*). Nevertheless, *Arbeitslager*, or "work camps," embodied the germ or model for all subsequent camps.[173] As the *Reichsarbeitsdienstführer* Konstantin Hierl observed, the goal of *Reichsarbeitsdienst* was "educating German youth, in the spirit of National Socialism, for the sake of the *Volksgemeinschaft* and in order to inculcate a genuine idea of labor [*zur wahren Arbeitsauffassung*]."[174]

The *Lager* aimed at fortifying total ideological adherence to the Third Reich and its institutions. As such, they proved to be a crucial mechanism for consolidating totalitarian rule. The *Lager* exemplified the sociologist Erving Goffman's notion of "total institution."[175] They removed determinate social groups from the comforts and familiarity of everyday life in order to subject them to more concentrated and refined methods of social conditioning. They were closed to the outside world, and the officials who oversaw them made it impossible for attendees to leave. The *Lager* aimed at inculcating unconditional obedience and respect for authority. Their organizational basis was the *Führerprinzip*.

In whatever guise the *Lager* assumed, they aimed at becoming a *Volksgemeinschaft* in miniature. They strove to reproduce the "spirit of camaraderie" that prevailed among the *Frontsoldaten*. Following the World War I, this spirit had been kept alive by (illegal) paramilitary organizations such as the *Freikorps* and veterans groups such as the *Stahlhelm*. Jünger joined the *Freikorps* in 1924.

Another important model for the *Lager* was Ernst Röhm's SA, or Sturmabteilung. By 1932, membership in Röhm's "Brown Shirts" had risen to four hundred thousand. A year later, owing to heightened unemployment levels, SA membership spiked, reaching nearly two million. In keeping with the SA template, the *Lager* were conceived predominantly as a *Männerbund*: an association that stressed the virtues of male bonding.[176]

The *Lager* exemplified the militarization of everyday life under Nazism. Accordingly, *Wehrsport*, or military exercises, became a prominent feature of *Lager* life. *Wehrsport* were complemented by additional paramilitary activities and practices. *Geländesport*, or track-and-field competitions, were especially encouraged, in keeping with the Third Reich's emphasis on health and fitness as desirable national attributes. Another popular *Lager* activity was *Flaggenparaden*: marching in formation under outsized Nazi banners, which was also a favored SA pastime.

Following the Nazi seizure of power, the *Lager* idea rapidly gained currency. "It became fashionable to refer to any type of meeting or mass gathering as a 'Lager.' *Lager* connoted a 'way of life' [*Lebensform*] as opposed to merely another form of social organization. . . . To refer to something as a 'Lager' became a sign of approbation."[177] One Nazi official described the popularity of the *Lager* form as follows: "There are *Lager* in tents and *Lager* in houses, *Lager* that are composed of thirty people, of several hundred, even thousands of participants; there are *Lager* in which manual labor [*körperliche Arbeit*] predominates, and others in which the primary focus is intellectual training. There are *Lager* that barely last a week, as well as long-term *Lager*, in which one receives certification after six weeks or six months; there are *Lager* that have a permanent staff, and others that take shape with a bare minimum of formal organization."[178]

Under National Socialism, the *Lager* functioned as positive and negative vehicles of socialization. Prominent among its negative forms were *Arbeitslager*, also known as *Arbeitserziehungslager*: "labor camps" whose mission was to discipline shirkers, wayward youth, and political dissidents by subjecting them to arduous—and often quite pointless—physical tasks. Nazi *Arbeitsideologie* placed a high premium on "work" as a central method of contributing to the well-being of the "national community." "Persons who avoided making a productive contribution were excluded from the *Volksgemeinschaft*. Those who shunned work were confined to 'workhouses' and 'welfare camps,' so that they could be forcibly educated through work. Those who were deemed 'unreformable' were often relocated to *Konzentrationslager*."[179]

The first *Konzentrationslager* (KZ) at Dachau, Pappenwege, Kemna, Sonderburg, and Flössenburg (1933) were also known as *Arbeitslager*. As Georges-Arthur Goldschmidt observes in "Labor and National Socialism," "From the very beginning, it was impossible to separate National Socialism's *univers concentrationnaire* from the sphere of 'labor.' The essence of the concentration camp system was collective labor carried out in an absurd and physically onerous manner."[180]

The KZ were originally constructed as detention centers or holding cells for the regime's political opponents: communists, socialists, liberals, and Jews. Initially, their numbers were relatively small. Conversely, following the outbreak of war and Third Reich's initial military conquests, their numbers—as well as the number of internees—escalated exponentially.[181]

During the 1940s, the *Lager* form metastasized into the infamous *Vernichtungslager*, or extermination camps, all six of which were situated in Poland. The most notorious, of course, was Auschwitz, where inmates and deportees were greeted by the infamous slogan, "Arbeit macht frei."

Auschwitz functioned as both an *Arbeitslager* and a *Vernichtungslager*—a "workcamp" and an "extermination camp." At Birkenau, or Auschwitz II, approximately one million European Jews met their deaths by gassing. In the words of Dolf Sternberger, "As harmless as the word *Lager* might have been in the past and as harmless as it may once again become, today, we can no longer think of it without thinking of Auschwitz."[182]

Lager as the Privileged Site for the "Total Transformation of German Dasein"

From the very beginning of National Socialist rule, Heidegger actively sought a position of leadership in the politics of German university reform. In that capacity, he became a vociferous advocate of the *Führerprinzip* and of the *Lager-Begriff*. "We need a new constitution for the university," declared Heidegger, "one that will secure a new spiritual-political leadership [*Führung*]. To what end? Not for the sake of 'reconstructing' what is already at hand, but instead, *in order to destroy the university* [*zur Zerstörung der Universität*]. This 'negative goal' will only prove to be effective if a new race [*eines neuen Geschlechtes*] seizes the reins of education."[183]

As *Führer-Rektor*, Heidegger sought to ensure the *Herrschaft*, or rule, of "a new spiritual-political leadership" stratum by implementing the *Lager* idea in a variety of forms and settings. In addition to his efforts to integrate *Wehrdienst* and *Arbeitsdienst* as mandatory components of the curriculum, Heidegger dutifully organized *Wissenschaftslager* (knowledge camps) and *Ferienlager* (ideological summer camps). Heidegger perceived German universities as privileged sites of political activism. As Otto Pöggeler has observed, "Heidegger was convinced that the National Socialist Revolution had begun with the universities and that its success or failure would depend on them."[184] The precedents of the *Turngesellschaften* (gymnastics societies) and the *Jugendbewegung* attested to German youth's pivotal role in advancing the cause of *völkisch* nationalism. By May 1933, when Heidegger joined the NSDAP, the Nationalsozialistischer Deutscher Studentenbund was the only student organization left standing.

During the initial months of Heidegger's rectorship, he regularly traveled to Berlin in order to lobby for reforms that would effectively transform the German university system into the institutional vanguard of Nazism. In June 1933, at a conference organized in Berlin by the Main Office for the Political Education of German Students, he delivered a keynote address titled "The University in the New Reich." In his speech, Heidegger rejoiced that, henceforth, German students would be "bound together by an approach to science [*Wissenschaft*] that derives from our [German] spirit: an approach to science that reawakens the existential realities of nature and history from the somnambulism of an unreal and barren 'Ideologism' to which science succumbed as a result of Christianity's influence on German spiritual life—which, with the advent of National Socialism, has recently freed itself from its imprisonment in the positivist fetishization of factuality."[185]

As rector, Heidegger supported numerous measures to hasten the militarization of German university life. In one of his first official acts, he requested that Freiburg municipal authorities provide the university with a police detail, so that, in the course of its "military exercises [*Wehrdienst*], . . . the student body could benefit from strict and professional supervision."[186] The 17 May letter was merely one of several steps that Heidegger took to integrate *Wehrsport*, in addition to *Arbeitsdienst* and *Wissensdienst*, within the curriculum. These measures were consistent with Heidegger's plans to ensure that German universities played a key role in National Socialism's "total transformation of German Dasein."[187]

Heidegger's plans for *Wissensdienst* and *Arbeitsdienst* were formulated with the *Lager* idea foremost in mind. *Wissensdienst*, too, would be organized through "camps": self-contained structures that, for the sake of efficiency and group cohesion, were sealed off from the outside world. Under the Third Reich, *Arbeitsdienst* was transformed into a major instrument of socialization. This was especially true with respect to the millions of German workers who were unemployed. The Nazis valued *Arbeitsdienst* for fostering a rigorous ethic of "work discipline" and as "the ultimate manifestation of 'German Socialism' and *Kameradschaft*."[188] In light of the *Reicharbeitsdienst*'s paramilitary features, it is significant that the director, Hierl, was a retired army officer.

Heidegger esteemed the *Lager* as effective organs of political indoctrination. In the *Rektoratsrede*, he had praised *Wissensdienst*, or "knowledge service," although, at the time, the precise institutional form that this "service" would assume remained indeterminate.

Heidegger clarified his intentions by organizing *Wissenschaftslager* and *Ferienlager*. Both were, in essence, "indoctrination camps." By relying on time-honored disciplinary techniques—marching, military exercises, propaganda lectures, and a spirit of *Kameradschaft*—the *Lager* sought to mold students, younger faculty, and workers into "human material" suitable for the *Volkgemeinschaft in statu nascendi*. As one Nazi official put it, the *Lager* form's distinct advantage was that it permitted the "deep capture of the whole person."[189]

Heidegger's proposals for *Wissenschaftslager* were consistent with the Nazi doctrine of *politische Wissenschaft* (politicized science). In "The University in the New Reich," Heidegger excoriated the old university system, in which "research was directionless, and disorientation was camouflaged by the idea of international scientific progress. The aimlessness of instruction concealed itself behind pointless examination requirements." Today, Heidegger implored, "a fierce battle must be waged in the National Socialist spirit. That spirit must not be stifled by humanizing, Christian ideas that suppress its imperatives."[190]

Heidegger refined his conception of "political education" (*politische Erziehung*) in a seminar that he held in 1934 on the political thought of Hegel and Carl Schmitt. He insisted, "*All education is 'political.'* In other words: education co-founds, develops, and maintains the *Dasein of the State*. The *Volk* is educated and shaped in conformity with the State. In this way alone does it *become* a *Volk* properly so-called."[191]

Heidegger's views on National Socialist *Wissensschulung*—"education" or "schooling"—harmonized with the Nazi idea of "politicized science." As the preceding quotations from "The University in the New Reich" and the Hegel-Schmitt seminar attest, *Wissensschulung*'s operative principle required subordinating education to the ends of the *Volksgemeinschaft*. Heidegger viewed *Wissenschaftslager* as the perfect vehicle for negating the antiquated, liberal-Humboldtian university by integrating the pedagogical aims of "politicized science."

In sum, Heidegger viewed the university as a training site for the formation of National Socialist political elites. Heidegger clarified this desideratum in "The University in the New Reich," in which he proposed that the university be reconstituted as an "educational site for training leaders [*Erziehungstätte der Führenden*]." "The university," Heidegger added, "must be integrated within the *Volksgemeinschaft* and allied with the State. The university must once again become a pedagogical force that educates the nation's political elite [*Führerschicht im Staat*] to knowledge [*zum Wissen*]." This goal demanded "courage, since the struggle for the educational site of new leaders [*Erziehungstätte der Führenden*] will be a long one. It is a struggle that is based on the powers . . . that *Volkskanzler* Hitler is making into a reality."[192]

The goal of establishing *Wissenschaftslager* at the national or Reich level was formalized at a conference on the goals of National Socialist higher education that was organized by the Main Office for the Political Education of German Students in July 1933. Not only did Heidegger attend this meeting. Correspondence between Nazi officials and Heidegger's assistant, Rudolf Stadelmann, indicates that Heidegger's *Rektoratsrede*, "The Self-Assertion of the German University," had provided the ideological template for the conference.[193]

The National Socialist hierarchy endorsed Heidegger's view that it was necessary to replace "so-called academic freedom" (*sogenannte akademische Freiheit*) with a new, "rooted" approach to pedagogy: an orientation that accorded primacy to the political goals of the state. In his *Rektoratsrede*, Heidegger belittled the pursuit of knowledge as an end in itself. Instead, as we have seen, in keeping with the aims of "politicized science," he redefined higher education in terms of various forms of "service" (*Dienste*): "Military Service" (*Wehrdienst*), "Labor Service" (*Arbeitsdienst*), and "Service in Knowledge" (*Wissensdienst*). By highlighting the importance of "service," Heidegger sought to replace "academic freedom" with the authoritarian precepts of "obligation" and "duty" (*Gehorsamkeit* and *Pflicht*).

The *Wissenschaftslager* reflected the militarization of everyday life under Nazism. In the *Rektoratsrede*, Heidegger's celebration of *Wehrdienst*, or "military service," coalesced with this agenda. Nazi authorities regarded the *Wissenschaftslager* as "positive" complements to the book-burning rallies that had convulsed German universities in May 1933. In the months to come, spurred by the rallying cry "Awakening of the German Spirit!" (*Aufbruch des deutschen*

Geistes), *Wissenschaftslager* increasingly gained a foothold in German university life.

The *Wissenschaftslager*'s goal was to construct a new "university community": a *Hochschulgemeinschaft* "based on a new conception of science" that reflected a new "intimacy between the professorate and the student body." The new *Hochschulgemeinschaft* explicitly sought to "foster an alliance between the university and the vocational life of the *Volk*: an alliance that would result from a university-based collaboration [*gemeinsamer Arbeit*] between the student body and vocationally active workers [*berufstätiger Arbeiterschaft*]."[194]

The *Wissenschaftslager* were modeled on the *Arbeitsdienst* program. They brought professors, students, and workers together for a series of communal National Socialist consciousness-raising sessions. Their goal was to ameliorate class and professional differences, thereby facilitating the realization of a harmonious *Volksgemeinschaft*. Heidegger regarded the persistence of class and status differences as a fraught legacy of the Weimar "System." Under the Third Reich, it would be imperative to extirpate "difference" as a potential source of cultural and political divisiveness. In *On the Essence of Truth*, Heidegger, never one to mince words or soft-peddle hard truths, underlined the need to root out and "annihilate" (*vernichten*) the "domestic enemy," or *innere Feind*.[195]

Heidegger formally delineated his views on the *Wissenschaftslager* in "National Socialist Education" (*Nationalsozialistische Wissenschulung*), a lecture that he delivered to six hundred *Notstandsarbeiter* (unemployed workers) who were participating in a municipally sponsored *Arbeitsdienst* program. Heidegger's address was held in a university lecture hall. Student attendance was made obligatory.

Heidegger described the central aim of National Socialist pedagogy as preparing German youth "to become strong for *a fully valid Dasein* as *Volksgenossen* [comrades] in the German *Volksgmeinschaft*."[196] This formulation is philosophically significant since it confirms Heidegger's understanding of the *Wissenschaftslager* as crucibles of political authenticity.[197]

The thematic overlap between Heidegger's January 1934 *Wissenschulung* address and "Why We Remain in the Provinces" is also philosophically and politically telling. In both texts, Heidegger extolled the *Arbeit* of "farmers," "woodcutters," and "miners," which he contrasted favorably with abstract and barren "scientific knowledge" (*Wissen*). Heidegger regarded *Handarbeit*, or manual labor, as *existentially superior*, since it was *bodenständig*, or "rooted-in-soil."

In Heidegger's reflections on "National Socialist education," he sought to level the distinction between "tilling the soil and felling a tree," on the one hand, and the scientific study of nature and history, on the other. Seeking to curry favor with his working-class audience, Heidegger contended,

> What we thought up to now when we used the words "Wissen" and "Wissenschaft" has assumed another meaning. . . . *Wissenschaft* is not the possession of a privileged class of citizens to be used as a weapon in the exploitation of working people [*werktätigen Volkes*]. Instead, *Wissenschaft* is merely *the more rigorous* and hence *more responsible* form of that knowledge which the entire German *Volk* requires for its historical existence as a State. . . . Essentially, the knowledge of *Wissenschaft* does not differ significantly from the knowledge of the farmer, the woodcutter, the miner, or the artisan. . . . Knowledge [*Wissen*] means . . . to be up to the task that is assigned to us, whether this task be to till the soil or to fell a tree or to dig a ditch, to inquire into the laws of Nature or to illuminate the fate-like force of History.[198]

Heidegger's observations reflected his understanding of fundamental ontology qua "practical philosophy" circa the mid-1930s. His contention that philosophy, like farming, woodcutting, and mining, should be "rooted" conditioned his aversion to *thēoria*, Platonism, Idealism, and the "philosophy of the subject." It alienated him from the Western philosophical tradition and propelled him into the arms of one of the most murderous and destructive regimes known to human history. Having accepted, as did so many members of his generation, Nietzsche's verdict on the nullity of all inherited Western values, Heidegger felt justified in reconciling *Existenzphilosophie* and the National Socialist discourse of *Sturm* and *Kampf*.

Heidegger's propagation of the *Lager* concept also emerged in the case of the *Ferienlager*—so named because they took place during the break between summer and winter semesters—that he organized during his rectorship. The *Ferienlager* targeted younger faculty members, *Dozenten*, and assistant professors. Like the *Arbeits-* and the *Wissenschaftslager*, the *Ferienlager* were intended—in the spirit of *Gleichschaltung*—as vehicles of political "socialization," to ensure that junior faculty members possessed an adequate grasp of the national revolution's values and goals.

In a memorandum that Heidegger circulated to the organizers of the weeklong camp, he outlined the objectives that he hoped to achieve. "Authentic camp

participation [*eigentliche Lagerarbeit*]," observed Heidegger, "must be conducive to reflecting on the paths and methods of struggle [*Erkämpfung*] with respect
to the future of the higher education of the German spirit [*deutschen Geistes*]."
Among the political gains that Heidegger expected from the *Ferienlager* was
"hands-on familiarization with the goals of the National Socialist transformation
of the university system." Heidegger concluded his missive with a paean to the
virtues of the *Lager* concept. "*Lagerarbeit*," Heidegger insisted,

> must not be the window-dressing for an [ideologically] vapid program. It must de-
> velop from genuine leadership [*Führung*] and followership [*Gefolgschaft*], and on
> this basis, produce its own Order. A select few lectures presented before the entire
> camp community [*Lagergemeinschaft*] should catalyze the "basic mood" [*Grund-
> stimmung*] and the "basic attitude" [*Grundhaltung*]. Decisive interventions [by the
> leadership] during the group sessions must shape and define the discussions.
>
> The *Lager*'s success will depend on the *courage* that is displayed, on a *clarity*
> and *alertness* that are oriented toward the future [*das Künftige*], on the decisive-
> ness of the Will to loyalty, sacrifice, and service [*zur Treue, zu Opfer und Dienst*].
> These are the virtues of true followership: virtues that support and affirm true Ger-
> man community [*echte deutsche Gemeinschaft*].[199]

Heidegger's remedy for the "anarchic freedom" characteristic of bourgeois liberalism was a theory of political obedience (*Gehörsamkeit*) that redefined "freedom" as subordination to *Herrschaft*, or higher authority.

On 3 September 1933, Heidegger was a featured speaker at the twenty-second
annual congress of the Baden Master Carpenters Association. His speech addressed the importance of rectifying the imbalance between higher education
and the trades (*Handwerk*), a division that, from the standpoint of national
unity, boded ill. Heidegger's discourse offers further evidence concerning his
understanding of National Socialist *Arbeitsideologie*, which appealed to labor's
centrality with respect to the productive capacities of the *Volksgemeinschaft*.
(During the early years of the Nazi dictatorship, "deine Hand dem Handwerk"—
"lend a hand to craftsmanship"—was a popular Nazi slogan.)[200]

Heidegger remarked in his address that one of National Socialism's fundamental aims was transcending the opposition between intellectual and manual
labor. *Volkskanzler* Hitler's efforts to reawaken among the *Volk* a genuine sense
of *Gemeinschaft* had placed this goal well within reach.

Heidegger acknowledged that the national revolution had presented traditional estates, social strata, and occupational groups with a new set of challenges and responsibilities. Hence, in the future, it would be necessary to
establish a new set of ideologically suitable institutions to target "youth," "trade
associations," and "labor camps" (*Arbeitslager*). These vehicles of National
Socialist acculturation would act as organs of socialization, thereby supersed-
ing the traditional institutions that, as vestiges of the ancien régime, could not
be trusted to fulfill Germany's national "mission."

Heidegger emphasized the value of "workshops" (*Werkstätte*), while
urging that, henceforth, they should be reconstituted as sites of practical
education, in which the *Meister* (Masters) became "Führer." Reprising a
theme found in many of his political texts, Heidegger insisted that every type
of "*German* work" (*deutsche Arbeit*) exemplified the fusion of "intellectual labor and manual labor." Hence, it was imperative that the university and the
trade associations (*Handwerkbände*), such as the Baden Master Carpenters
Association, cooperate in order to confer on the state the honor and esteem it
was due.[201]

National Socialist *Arbeitsideologie* stressed the importance of surmounting the
separation between manual and intellectual labor, the division between "*Arbeiter der Faust und dem Arbeiter der Stirn*." Heidegger's frequent allusions to
this objectionable dichotomy—in "Nationalsozialistische Wissensschulung,"
he spoke of the need to "erect a living bridge between manual and intellectual
labor" (*zwischen dem Arbeiter der "Faust" und dem Arbeiter der "Stirn" eine
lebendige Brücke zu schlagen*)—are a further indication of his proximity to National Socialist *Arbeitsideologie*.[202]

Heidegger also addressed this problem in "The Call to Labor Service" (*Der
Ruf zur Arbeitsdienst*), in which he praised *Arbeitsdienst* as an effective mechanism of surmounting this worrisome threat to national unity.

In order to make this argument plausible, Heidegger felt that it was necessary
to reassess the meaning of *Geist*, or "spirit." He insisted that it was essential to
uncouple "spirit" from the ethereal realm of "intellectual pursuits." Heidegger's
remedy for the idealistic "deformations" of classical German philosophy was to
reconceive "spirit" in relationship to *Arbeit*. Henceforth, "spirit" must limit itself to articulating "the afflictions that are part of the *Volk*'s historical Dasein."
Heidegger argued in favor of a *völkisch* reorientation of "spirit," since the *Volk*

"is more directly . . . exposed to the severity and danger [*Härte und Gefahr*] of human Dasein."[203]

Reviewing the afflictions of "spirit," Heidegger recurred to the benefits of *Arbeitsdienst* as a remedy or panacea. Among its virtues, *Arbeitsdienst* "offered the basic experience of severity [*Härte*], proximity to the soil and to the implements of labor," observed Heidegger.

> Such *Dienst* provides the basic experience of a daily existence in an *Arbeitsgemein-schaft* [laboring community]. . . . *A complete transformation of German existence is taking place.* Within the German university, a new fundamental attitude toward scholarly work [*wissenschaftliche Arbeit*] is developing. As this happens, notions of the "Spirit" [*Geist*] and "intellectual work" [*geistige Arbeit*] *will completely disappear.* . . . So-called intellectual work [*geistige Arbeit*] is not "spiritual" [*geistig*] because it relates to "higher spiritual things." It is spiritual because *work* reaches back more deeply into the afflictions that are part of the *Volk*'s historical Dasein and since it is more directly . . . exposed to the severity and danger of human Dasein.[204]

These remarks expose the ideological subtext underlying Heidegger's rejection of the German Idealist trope of the "sovereignty of spirit." They also help to explain his disaffection with contemporary German university life, as well as the intellectual basis of his commitment to the Nazi program of restructuring higher education in accordance with the values of the "racial community." Heidegger's innate political radicalism, which was abetted by his abhorrence of bourgeois cultural complacency, convinced him that "half measures" (*Halbheiten*) would not suffice.[205] Consequently, he embraced political "violence" (*Gewalt*) as the form of "praxis" best suited to advancing the goals of *Germanentum*'s rebirth.

Fundamental Ontology and "Joy in Work"

As we have seen, Heidegger's interest in *Arbeit* was not exclusively political. It was, first and foremost, *ontological*, in keeping with his understanding of National Socialism's privileged role in narrative arc of *Seinsgeschichte*. Heidegger interpreted *Arbeit* as a manifestation of *Eigentlichkeit* and *Geschichtlichkeit*, "authenticity" and "historicity." Hence, in *Logic as a Question Concerning the Essence of Language*, Heidegger highlighted the pivotal role that "authentic work" played in the transition from the "Ich-Zeit" (egotism) of Western liberalism to the "Wir-Zeit" (communitarianism) of the National Socialist *Volkgemeinschaft*.

In a passage laced with superlatives and italics, Heidegger emphasized that "the *Arbeit* of historical man is not a matter of minor concern. *Arbeit* refers to a mission [*Sendung*] that is both *determinate* and *temporal*. It unifies our acting and existing in each historically determinate moment, thereby making that moment *effective*. *Arbeit bespeaks the manner in which historical man comes to presence. Historical coming-to-presence = Arbeit. Arbeit is Orientation and Mission, Future and Past.*"[206]

Heidegger viewed "German *Arbeit*" as "ecstatic," in the sense of the "ecstases" of existential temporality. He contrasted the existential value of *German Arbeit* with the "alienated" understanding of work that prevailed in the West, where, unlike Nazi Germany, *Arbeit* and *Arbeiterschaft*—"work" and "workers"—were instrumentally degraded qua "objects" that are "present-at-hand." The ontological superiority of German work came to fruition in *Arbeitsfreudigkeit* or "Joy in Work": a capacity that Germany's geopolitical opponents distinctly lacked.

Heidegger developed his views on the ontological benefits of *Arbeitsfreudigkeit* in response to the unemployment crisis of the early 1930s. As a matter of principle, Heidegger refused to view unemployment (*Arbeitslosigkeit*) as a strictly *economic* problem. Instead, he interpreted it, in the first instance, as an *existential* deficiency or lack. In Heidegger eyes, unemployment was a symptom of *ontological privation*, insofar as it negatively impacted the worker's capacity for *authenticity*. As Heidegger asserted in "National Socialist *Wissenschulung*," "In the first instance, job creation [*Arbeitsschaffung*] must ensure that our unemployed and non-gainfully-employed *Volksgenossen* become *existentially capable* [*daseinsfähig*] *in and for the State* and, thereby, for the *Volk* as a whole."[207]

Heidegger maintained that the loss of the "existential capacity" (*Daseinsfähigkeit*) to work was significant for two reasons: (1) from a political standpoint, it deprived the *Volksgemeinschaft* of necessary labor power, or *Arbeitskraft*; (2) on the individual level, it undermined Dasein's capacity for self-actualization, since *Arbeit* bespoke an essential component of authenticity.

In sum, Heidegger held that *Arbeitslosigkeit*, or unemployment, constituted a significant obstacle to Dasein's potential for "Being-a-Self." In *Logic as a Question Concerning the Essence of Language*, he heightened the "existential" stakes, claiming that "unemployment leads to *psychic dissolution*, since to be without work prevents us from becoming *enraptured with 'things.'*"[208]

Not only did Heidegger regard *Arbeit* as an essential modality of "unveiling" or "world-disclosure." He conceived *Arbeitsfreudigkeit* as a "Grundstimmung," or "basic mood," that enabled Dasein to merge with the "rapture of things" (*Entrücktheit in die Dinge*). As a form of ontological "rapture," or *Entrücktheit*, *Arbeitsfreudigkeit* transported Dasein into greater proximity to Being qua *Ereignis*: "The question of Joy in Work [*Arbeitsfreudigkeit*] is important. . . . 'Joy,' as a foundational mood, is the condition of possibility for authentic work [*echte Arbeit*], which first renders man *Daseinsfähig*. In work, as presence, the making-present of beings takes place. Work is presence [*Gegenwart*] in the primordial sense. . . . *Through work we expose ourselves to the historicity of beings*. . . . Out of the great moods of *struggle* [*Kampf*], *astonishment* [*Staunen*], and *reverence* [*Ehrfurcht*], we regulate [*verwalten*] Being and assume a place within its Greatness."[209]

Heidegger's "ontological" elevation of *Arbeit* and *Arbeitsfreudigkeit* coalesced with the central themes of National Socialism's "Beauty of Labor" and "Strength through Joy" discourse. It reflected a significant tendency of his *Denkweg*: to transfigure the prosaic, everyday realities of Nazism by *discursively embellishing them*: by attributing to them a higher, existential significance and meaning.

In stark contrast to the mood of *Kulturpessimismus* that suffused *Being and Time*, Heidegger's championing of *Arbeitsfreudigkeit* during the 1930s cannot help but come as a surprise. An additional surprise emerged with his attempt, also in the *Logic* lectures, to include a perfunctory discussion of "Love" (*Liebe*).

"Love," proposed Heidegger, is also a manifestation of *Sorge*, or "Care." "Love" is an outgrowth or manifestation of what Heidegger referred to as Dasein's "exposure to beings": "I have called and still call exposure to beings, as consignment to Being [*das Sein*], 'Care' [*Sorge*]—however, Love [*die Liebe*] also belongs to human life."[210] Heidegger's allusion to "love" is surprising, since, at the time, he sought to reconfigure the idiolect of existential ontology in accordance with the National Socialist lexicon of "hardship" and "severity" (*Härte und Schwere*).[211]

However, a closer examination reveals that there was a specific political motivation that impelled Heidegger to explore the existential semantics of *Arbeitsfreude* and *Liebe*. Under the Third Reich, Heidegger's efforts to assume a position of intellectual leadership had been hampered by criticisms that his "philosophical pessimism" was incompatible with upbeat and joyous qualities of the Nazi spirit. Heidegger's portrayal of human existence in *Being and Time* as "Sorge," or "Care," had been exposed to especially withering criticism. In his *Logic* lectures, at one point, Heidegger expressly bemoaned the unfairness of these objections and the misunderstandings of his work they had engendered.

An especially mean-spirited rebuke came from one of Heidegger's chief ideological rivals, the University of Marburg psychologist Erich Jaensch. In 1934, Heidegger and Jaensch were competing with each other for the directorship of the Prussian Academy of University Lecturers: a Nazified, or *gleichgeschaltet*, version of the academy that had existed under the Weimar Republic. Jaensch's intemperate denunciation of Heidegger—which, ultimately, found its way to Alfred Rosenberg's desk—reads as follows: "The products of Heidegger's thinking . . . are not just the usual kind of hairsplitting sophistry . . . but a special sort of sophistry, so extreme as to border on the pathological; one constantly wonders how much of this is just eccentric . . . and how much already qualifies as the untethered musings of a schizophrenic mind. Since this type of thinking is naturally exploited and propagated by clever scribblers and profit-minded publishers . . . we shall end up with our universities in the grip of an epidemic of intellectual sickness: a type of *mass psychosis*."[212]

Jaensch's anti-Heidegger vituperations will not concern us, per se. Of greater interest is their tenor and direction. They focused primarily on two considerations: the alleged prominence of Jews in Heidegger's milieu prior to 1933 and the lachrymose orientation of Heidegger's "existential anthropology" in *Being and Time*. Heidegger's detractors maintained that his existential ontology, in which concepts such as *Angst*, *Schuldig-Sein* (Being-Guilty), *Verfallen* (Falling), and *Sein-zum-Tode* (Being-toward-death) predominated, was incompatible with the mentality of petty-bourgeois cheerfulness that the Nazis sought to inculcate—an orientation whose paradigmatic instances were the "Strength through Joy" and "Beauty of Labor" programs.

Arbeit and Technics

Notwithstanding phenomenology's avowed orientation toward "concreteness" and "the things themselves," Heidegger's treatment of *Arbeit* often failed to rise above the level of platitudes and generalities. Ultimately, it proved unable to transcend what the philosopher and former Heidegger student Günther

Anders characterized as the "pseudo-concreteness of Heidegger's existential-ism."[213] In order to mask the contentlessness of his assertions and positions, Heidegger often sought refuge in portentous abstractions and hollow circumlo-cutions. It was a shortcoming that also informed Heidegger's later, ontologi-cally inflected indictment of modern technology (*Technik*) qua "enframing."

As we have seen, Heidegger's preoccupation with the ontological nature of *Arbeit*—*Arbeit* reconceived according to the stipulations of "Eigentlichkeit," or "authenticity"—was one way that Heidegger responded to the challenges of modern "technics." Basing himself on Jünger's vision of a highly regimented *Arbeiter- und Soldatenstaat*, Heidegger hailed National Socialism for the steps that had been taken toward constructively resolving the "confrontation between technology and modern man." In the West, "alienated labor" predominated. With "deutsche Arbeit," conversely, there arose a "steely romanticism," as prophesied by the texts of Nietzsche, Spengler, Horneffer, and Jünger.

The lack of a genuinely historical orientation consistently handicapped Heidegger's perception of modern technology, rendering his views static. For want of a developmental perspective, his standpoint was unable to register the historically changing nature of modern technology. Instead, he subsumed all varieties and manifestations of *Technik* under the simplifying rubrics of "en-framing" (*Gestell*) and "standing reserve" (*Bestand*). As Graham Harman has remarked, "For Heidegger, technology is a gloomy drama in which every in-vention merely strips the mystery from the world and turns all things into a ma-nipulable stockpile of present-at-hand slag. A mass-produced umbrella is no different from a cinder block or an aircraft carrier. . . . The problem with his analyses is not their pessimism, but their monotony."[214]

As Harman's comments imply, Heidegger's understanding of "technics" lacked differentiation. Throughout its various phases, Heidegger's *Technik* cri-tique remained uniform. Ultimately, nearly all manifestations of modern social life were reduced to and dismissed as "enframing" or "metaphysics." But such interpretive rigidity is conducive to misapprehension and distortion. Heidegger made no attempt to distinguish between the productive and destructive uses of *Technik*. Nor did he make an effort to conceptualize the transition from "Ford-ism" to "postindustrialism," even though this transformation took place during his lifetime. Since Heidegger systematically scorned the social sciences, his analyses lacked an empirical dimension that might have enriched his philo-sophical framework with significant detail and rigor.

The mystifications of Heidegger's philosophical idiom were a primary target of Adorno's critique in *The Jargon of Authenticity*. Adorno found fault with Heidegger's lexical tumescence, which, in his view, harmonized with fascism's ideological masking of social tensions and contradictions. According to Adorno,

> The jargon . . . sees to it that what it wants is on the whole felt and accepted through its mere delivery, without regard to the content of the words used. . . . This formal element favors demagogic ends. Whoever is versed in the jargon does not have to say what he thinks, does not even have to think it properly. The jargon takes over this task and devalues thought. . . . The words of the jargon sound as if they said something *higher* than what they mean. . . . As frozen emanations, the terms of the jargon of authenticity are products of the disintegration of the aura. . . . Those who have run out of Holy Spirit speak with mechanical tongues.[215]

It is not known whether Adorno was aware of Heidegger's reflections on the existential singularity of German *Arbeit*. In *The Jargon of Authenticity*, nowhere does he cite these texts. Instead, his criticisms focused primarily on the pomposity and pretension of Heidegger's existential argot: on the role it played in cementing ideological allegiance to the Nazi project. By virtue of the seemingly limitless capacity of Heidegger's ontological idiom to elevate National Socialist ideologemes to the level of "authenticity"—National Socialism's *Arbeitsideologie* being merely a case in point—its philosophical limitations come clearly into focus.

5

Earth and Soil: Heidegger and the National Socialist Politics of Space

By Bodenständigkeit, Heidegger . . . meant to convey a profoundly
metaphysical relation to Earth as a place of dwelling, to the landscape as
one's indigenous home, and to language as the expression of one's
rootedness: . . . as the name for an understanding of history as destiny to
which we primordially belong and through which we are appropriated by
the gift-giving power of Being . . . [as] Ereignis. Only when we are
fundamentally attuned to the Earth, . . . only when we are rooted in it and
let this rootedness take hold of us, can we find our proper dwelling place
with the Fourfold. . . . Heidegger considered Bodenständigkeit as a
relationship to the Earth that acknowledged its hidden, concealed,
nocturnal, and chthonic dimensions.
—Charles Bambach, *Heidegger Roots*

The higher compulsion of the Earth does not first emerge with the
everyday and the deed, but already in the creative questioning and the
world-forming power of a Volk.

[Der höhere Zwang der Erde ist nicht erst beim Alltag und der
Tat, sondern schon in der schöpferischen Fragekraft und der
weltbildenden Macht eines Volkes.]
—Heidegger, *Überlegungen und Winke* III, GA 94

Earth and Soil: Heidegger and the National Socialist Politics of Space

COMMENTATORS ON HEIDEGGER'S THOUGHT HAVE OFTEN acknowledged the central role that the ideas of "Earth" and "Space"—in German, *Erde* and *Raum*—play in his work. In *Being and Time*, for example, one of the defining features of Heidegger's attempt to renew the meaning of first philosophy was his distinctly *spatial* reinterpretation of cognition (*Erkenntnistheorie*) as "Being-in-the-world." The paradigm of *Existenz* consciously abandoned the presuppositions of transcendental subjectivity in favor of the embodiment and situatedness of the knowing subject. The "Da" (there) of "Dasein" already depended on a spatial metaphor.

Heidegger's *Daseinsanalyse* was predicated on a hermeneutical, nonobjective understanding of "world" and "worldhood." He expressly understood "world" and "worldhood" in terms of their "spatial" and "environmental" features. "We shall seek the *worldhood* of the *environment* [*Umwelt*]," explained Heidegger; "the expression 'environment' implies . . . spatiality."[1] Beings that are "ready to hand," such as "tools" or "equipment," are also "spatial," Heidegger continued, insofar as they belong to a "region" (*Gegend*). Heidegger's hermeneutical approach to "spatiality" entailed an "existential" critique of the "mathematicized" space of physics and the natural sciences. As Heidegger observed in paragraph 23 of *Being and Time* ("The Spatiality of Being-in-the-World"), in the case of physicalist approaches to space, "environmental regions get neutralized to pure dimensions. . . . The whole circumspectively-oriented totality of places belonging to equipment ready-to-hand gets reduced to a multiplicity of positions for random Things. The spatiality of what is ready-to-hand within-the-world loses its involvement-character, . . . [and] the environment becomes the world of Nature. The 'world,' as a totality of equipment ready-to-hand, becomes 'spatialized' to a context of extended Things which are just present-at-hand and no more."[2]

Interpreters have also commended the prominence of "Earth" and "Space" in Heidegger's later thought as a dimension that furthered his rejection of the Cartesian "punctual self" and that, hence, opened vistas to a set of more concrete, topographical and ontological truths. On these grounds, they have proposed that Heidegger be regarded as a "topological thinker."[3] In *Aus der Erfahrung des Denkens* (1954), Heidegger himself recurred to this expression, describing the "Topology of Being" as the "place" (*Ortschaft*) where the essence of Being becomes manifest.[4] And in *Pathmarks*, in opposition to the reigning "topography of nihilism," Heidegger proposed a "topology" capable of "gathering Being and Nothingness in their essence."[5]

Heidegger's attentiveness to considerations of "topography" and "space" nourished his pathbreaking critique of modern technology, whose ravages have been so destructive of tradition and place. As a result, since the rise of the modern environmental movement, Heidegger has increasingly gained followers on the political left who believe that Karl Marx's critique of modernity was insufficiently radical.[6]

Recently, commentators have suggested that Heidegger's attunement to the "politics of space" provides the basis for an "antiauthoritarian" understanding of Heidegger's work: an understanding that belies his "transitory" allegiance to National Socialism. These interpreters have proposed that Heidegger's understanding of "place" represents a template of emancipation, insofar as it facilitates "the opening up of the world and of things in their essential questionability." Heidegger's "topology" is not "a 'violent' mode of revealing," we are told, but one that "allows things to come forth in their difference and unity." As such, it signifies a "turning away from all modes of 'decision' or 'authoritarianism.'" Heidegger's "topological" approach provides the basis for a critique of the "technological ... 'tyranny' that is ... destructive of the human community [and] of the things of 'nature.'" Thus, approaching Heidegger as a "spatial thinker" allows us to recover the "democratic" dimension of Heidegger's work, since his attention to "things in their essential questionability" entails "a mode of politics that, [like democracy], is tied to contestation [and] negotiation."[7]

Heidegger's 1925 assertion, "Unless we succeed in returning to the essential and sustaining powers that derive from our native soil [*aus heimatlichem Boden*], all attempts at renewal and improvement will remain hopeless," suggests that "rootedness" and "native soil" and the related concepts of "earth" and "blood" were recurrent and enduring leitmotifs of his *Denken*.[8] An attentive reconsideration of the developmental trajectory of Heidegger's topography of "space" and "soil," *Raum* and *Boden*, belies the suggestion that his approach to *Raumpolitik* culminated in a dialectic of emancipation.

Instead, Heidegger's allegiance to the paradigm of "reactionary modernism," before and after 1933, suggests a very different conclusion concerning the metapolitical valences of his *Denken*. As Hans Jonas has confirmed in "Heideggers Entschlossenheit und Entschluss," "A certain 'blood-and-soil' point of view was

always present. Heidegger emphasized his Black Forest roots a great deal. . . .
This attitude reflected his ideological commitments: one had to be close to na-
ture, and so on. And certain remarks—ones he sometimes made about the
French, for example—manifested a . . . primitive nationalism."⁹

Indicative of this orientation was Heidegger's characterization of his philosophical "mission" in *An Introduction to Metaphysics* (1935) as focused on "restoring historical Dasein's rootedness-in-soil." "Through our questioning,"
claimed Heidegger, "we are entering a *landscape* [*Landschaft*]; to be in this
landscape is the fundamental prerequisite for restoring rootedness to historical
Dasein [*dem geschichtlichen Dasein seine Bodenständigkeit zurückzugewin-
nen*]."¹⁰ Since, at this point in time, the preoccupation with *Bodenständigkeit*
was also a linchpin of the National Socialist worldview, Heidegger's avowal
can only be construed as a profession of ideological solidarity.

One year earlier, in *Logic as the Question Concerning the Essence of Language* (1934), Heidegger expressly associated " "history-making" with the
"production of space and soil." He insisted that "national histories" are existentially entwined with the forces of *Raum*, *Erde*, and *Boden*.¹¹ Thereby, Heidegger
underlined the confluence between his own distinctive hermeneutic-ontological
approach to the "politics of space" and the Nazi *Lebensraum-Gedanke*, as canonized by seminal precursors such as Friedrich Ratzel (1844–1904) and Karl
Haushofer (1869–1946).

As we have seen, Heidegger's endorsement of the "production of space and
soil" by a *Volk* harmonized with the "peasant" or "agrarian" strain of National
Socialism that was codified by the Nazi minister of agriculture Walther Darré
in his *Blut und Boden* manifesto *New Aristocracy of Blood and Soil* (1930).¹² In
The Language of the Third Reich, Victor Klemperer characterized this current
of Nazi ideology as follows: "The glorification of the *Bauer* [farmer or peas-
ant], wedded to the earth, steeped in tradition and hostile to all things new, remained constant to the end. The declaration of faith expressed in the formula
BLUBO—*Blut und Boden*—. . . derived directly from his way of life."¹³

The German *Volk*'s orientation toward *Blut und Boden* was regarded as an
expression of authenticity. In the *Black Notebooks*, Heidegger extolled *Boden*,
or "native soil," claiming, "In *Bodenständigkeit* alone does one find the rootedness [*Verwurzelung*] that grants growth into the universal."¹⁴

In the *Der Spiegel* interview, which was conducted some twenty years after
National Socialism's collapse (1966), Heidegger recurred to the thematics of

"Heimat" and "rootedness," reaffirming, unapologetically, "Everything essential and everything great originates from the fact that man had a home and was rooted in tradition [*dass der Mensch ein Heimat hatte und in einer Überlieferung verwurzelt war*]." In the same passage, he dismissed "modern literature," tellingly, as "predominantly destructive" owing to its lack of "rootedness."[15]

Heidegger's disparagement of aesthetic modernism was of a piece with the "reactionary modernist" rejection of "degenerate art," whose decadent qualities reflected the "rootlessness" of modern "society." From here, it was but short step to Heidegger's repeated denunciations of "world Jewry" as a perennial cultural interloper and corrupter of ethnically homogeneous "communities." Time and again, Heidegger excoriated European Jewry as the leading "carriers" of *Machenschaft*: a code word for the corrosive tendencies of (modern) "Zivilisation." Heidegger's hostility toward Jews was consistent with Shulamit Volkov's construal of anti-Semitism as a "cultural code": a network of demeaning stereotypes that, by the time of the Nazi *Machtergreifung*, had coalesced into an objectively lethal discursive paradigm.[16]

Far from being contingent or adventitious, Heidegger's aversion to Jewish influence was an *existential judgment*: a conviction that was largely predicated on his *ontology of rootedness*. Heidegger regarded Jewish "rootlessness" as an emblem of Jewish perdition: an ontological stain that permanently consigned the Jewish people to "inauthenticity," insofar as Heidegger embraced "rootedness" as a sine qua non for "authenticity." Heidegger's enduring preoccupation with *Boden* and *Raum* underlines the extent to which his thought was suffused with ideological elements that he imbibed from the conservative revolutionary *Zeitgeist*.

During the 1930s, Heidegger's recourse to a semantics of "Earth" and "Soil"— *Erde* and *Boden*—reflected his ontological-historical "Turn" from the existential ontology of *Being and Time* to the "metaphysics of German Dasein."[17] This reorientation of Heidegger's *Denkweg* was accompanied by a heightened infusion of *mythical*, *chthonic*, and *obscurantist* themes in his work. "The higher compulsion of the Earth does not first emerge with the everyday and the deed," declared Heidegger, "but already in the creative questioning and the world-forming power of a *Volk*."[18]

Heidegger's dissatisfaction with traditional *Erkenntnistheorie* impelled him to defend the epistemological superiority of myth vis-à-vis "cognition" or rational knowledge. "*Mythos*," Heidegger enthused, "*names Being in its primor-*

dial looking-into and shining-forth." Heidegger exalted "*Mythos* [as] the only appropriate mode of the relation to appearing Being."[19]

Heidegger's advocacy of the epistemological benefits of "myth" reflected his blossoming intellectual friendship with Alfred Baeumler, whose three-hundred-page introduction to Johann Jakob Bachofen's *Der Mythos von Orient und Occident: Eine Metaphysik der Alten Welt* (1926) Heidegger revered.[20] It also coincided with a more general and worrisome shift in German spiritual life during the 1920s, whose signature was a heightened antipathy to "reason" and a correlative infatuation with "prehistory" and the "archaic."

In "Greek Mythology and the Intellectual History of Modernity," Walter Burkert pithily summarized the generational fascination with "myth" and the "archaic" that characterized the worldview of reactionary modernist *Kulturkritik*. According to Burkert, this trend was "influenced by Expressionism, by phenomenology, by the Youth Movement, and by the Stefan George-*Kreis*. It was far removed from the Christian tradition, opposed to 'Der Bourgeois' and to Reason. It was elitist and latently 'fascistic.' The shock of the Great War was a decisive formative element, but not its sole cause: the rational world of the nineteenth century seemed to have *shattered* and primordial depths [*Urgründe*] emerged and came to the surface."[21]

Geopolitics as Political Eschatology

The most comprehensive discussion of Heidegger's "politics of space" is Charles Bambach's *Heidegger's Roots: Nietzsche, National Socialism, and the Greeks*. In his study, Bambach meticulously reconstructs the toxic categorial admixture that subtended Heidegger's endorsement of the Third Reich's exterminatory "push to the East": a vision of "continental mastery" that was predicated on Germany's entitlement, qua *Herrenrasse*, to dominate its racial inferiors: Slavs, Jews, Sinti, and Roma.

Bambach convincingly demonstrates that Heidegger's embrace of "rootedness" was not merely a contingent or occasional political disposition. Instead, from the very beginning, Heidegger's thought was predicated on a commitment to "ontological rootedness" as a paramount factical-existential value. In Heidegger's first lecture course, *On the Definition of Philosophy* (1919), he characterized philosophy as an "Urwissenschaft": a "science of origins" that was engaged in a phenomenological quest to "disclose" (*entdecken*) *a primordial substratum of Being*—an archaic stratum that "Platonism" and "Western meta-physics" had "concealed."[22] Two years later, in *Phenomenological Interpretations of Aristotle* (1921–22), Heidegger restated the epistemic centrality of this longing for the "primordial," observing that we must "hold onto the beginning [*den Anfang*], while understanding it *radically*; remaining within the *Anfang*, we must grasp and retain it."[23]

For Heidegger, "originary thinking" (*anfängliches Denken*) meant "boden-ständiges Denken": a thinking that was rooted-in-soil. Conversely, Heidegger consistently condemned intellectual paradigms that shunned "rootedness" as nihilistic and degenerative, insofar as they abetted the technological mastery of Being and beings. The tendential racism that was "always already" latent in Heidegger's predilection for thought-forms that were "rooted" and "originary" emerged with his declaration in *Überlegungen XII–XV*, "The more primordial and original [*ursprünglicher und anfänglicher*] that future decisions and questions become, *the more inaccessible will they remain for this 'race'* "—that is, *for the Jews.*[24]

As Bambach has shown in *Heidegger's Roots*, this fundamental ontological prejudice on Heidegger's part engendered numerous ontic missteps. It conditioned his receptiveness to National Socialism as a political form that, in the *Rektoratsrede*, Heidegger praised for having vanquished the "moribund pseudocivilization [of the West]" in the name of a "more primordial and replete concept of knowledge [grounded] in the historical-spiritual world of the *Volk*."[25] As Bambach remarks, "Heidegger was convinced that 'originary philosophy' could only be done in dialogue with politics . . . as the historical-ontological site within which Dasein struggled to find its own sense of *being rooted*: in a *community*, a *Volk*, a *tradition*, and a *history*. On this reading, politics is a *politics of the Earth*, a *geopolitics*, whose ultimate meaning is *ontological* in the sense that it becomes *the site for the unfolding of basic human possibilities*. . . . The Earth becomes what the ancient Greeks called 'chton,' the place where humans go and form a homeland."[26]

Heidegger's defense of ontological rootedness betrayed a long-standing German Romantic prejudice concerning the unique spiritual confluence between the *Volk*, on the one hand, and *Heimat, Boden, Landschaft* (landscape), and "Mother Earth," on the other. This paradigm represented a distinctly German response to the upsets and dislocations of "modernity": especially, the risks of destabilization and loss of identity associated with the transition from *Gemein-*

schaft to *Gesellschaft*. The discourse of "rootedness" in "landscape" and "native soil" situated the individual in a greater cosmic whole: a force that guaranteed unity and provided an "existential" prophylaxis against atomization. It signified a rejection of *Gesellschaft* and the "division of labor" and a return to "primordiality." Since nature was endowed with spiritual properties, the "return" was viewed as "regenerative": as a quasi-theological *restitutio in integrum*. As the philosopher and former Heidegger student Wilhelm Kamlah observed in 1943, "Race and *Volkstum* [folklore], Blood and Mother Earth, are *cosmic powers* that determine *Thereness* [*Dawesen*] in a manner different than historical tradition."[27]

Heidegger's efforts to amalgamate *Geopolitik* and *Heilsgeschichte*—the "politics of space" and a "politics of redemption"—dominated his middle period. In "The Origin of the Work of Art" (1935–36), Heidegger expressly linked the interplay between "Earth" and "World" to a neopagan eschatology in which the German *Volk*—which Heidegger exalted as "the most metaphysical of peoples"—emerged as the catalyst and pivot.[28] "*World*," claimed Heidegger, "is the self-revealing openness . . . concerning the simple and essential decisions [*Entscheidungen*] in the fate of a historical *Volk* [*im Geschick eines geschichtlichen Volkes*]."[29] "The great turning points among peoples [*Völker*]," he remarked, "emerge . . . when a *Volk* penetrates to the Earth in order to take possession of its *Heimat* [*in seine Erde hinabreicht und Heimat besitzt*]."[30]

The oscillation between "Earth" and "World" governed the dynamic of "concealment" (*Verborgenheit*) and "unconcealment" (*Unverborgenheit*) that, according to Heidegger, defined the ontological precondition for the emergence of truth qua "alētheia." However, in keeping with Heidegger's commitment to the ideology of German "exceptionalism," he construed *Deutschtum*—the uniquely "historical" *Volk*, whose singularity emerged in its status as a nation of "Dichter und Denker"—as the ontological-historical axis on which the consummation of *Seinsgeschichte* depended. "Unconcealment," observed Heidegger, "does not subsist off somewhere in itself or even as some property of things. *Being happens as the history of human beings, as the history of a Volk.*"[31] "The governing expanse [*Weite*] of this open relational context [the polis] is the world of the historical *Volk*. Only on the basis of this site does the *Volk* return to itself, thereby fulfilling its mission."[32]

In Heidegger's eyes, the German Revolution's salvific, ontological-historical thrust portended restoring the *Volk* to its chthonic "origins," thereby offsetting the degenerative influences of "Enlightenment" and "progress." Heidegger railed against the "urbanization of German man [*Verstädterung des deutschen Menschens*]." Conversely, he praised National Socialism for promising to return the Germans to "soil and the country through resettlement [*dem Boden und der Land in der Siedlung*]."[33] During the 1930s, Heidegger reconceived *Geschichtlichkeit* as *Seinsgeschichte*: a development that he claimed was driven by a cryptic dialectic of "rootedness" (*Verwurzelung*) and "redemption" (*Rettung*).[34] In "The Origin of the Work of Art," Heidegger defined tragedy as the "speech of the *Volk* [*Sagen des Volkes*]," as the site of the "battle [*Kampf*] of the new gods against the old." In this capacity, it determined the "decision" (*Entscheidung*) concerning "what is holy and unholy."[35]

Heidegger's metaphysics of *Erde* and *Boden* endowed "German Dasein" with a higher mission and purpose. As Dieter Thomä comments appositely in *Die Zeit des Selbst und die Zeit danach*, "Heidegger's recourse to 'Earth' as 'Event' [*Geschehen*] served as a mechanism of strengthening the primordial 'action' [*ursprüngliches Handeln*] of the *Volk*. 'Earth' became the 'higher imperative' to which the *Volk* needed to subordinate itself in order to escape 'idle talk' [*Gerede*]. . . . The *Volk* developed itself not as a determinate, isolated human 'type,' but instead in relationship to the 'Earth.' On this basis, the German *Volk* assumed its 'fate.' "[36]

Thomä's remarks lend support to Hannah Arendt's contention in "What Is Existential Philosophy?" that Heidegger's exaltation of "mythologized and muddled concepts such as '*Volk*' and 'Earth' " reflected his efforts "to supply the isolated selves [of *Being and Time*] with a shared, common ground." Arendt correctly foresaw that "concepts of that kind can only lead us out of philosophy into some kind of nature-oriented superstition."[37]

The discourse of "rootedness-in-soil" was pronouncedly "anti-Enlightenment" and "anti-Western." Over time, it hardened into a worldview that was intolerant vis-à-vis "otherness": especially in the case of ethnic groups such as Poles and Jews, who, purportedly, incarnated threats to *völkisch* unity. On these grounds, such groups were denigrated as (racial) "enemies" of the *Volk*. "Foreign presence [*Fremdes Wesen*]," bemoaned Heidegger, "distorts and disrupts our specific type of Being." "Why is it," he continued, "that the Germans are so susceptible to being seduced by *that which is foreign* [*zu fremdem Wesen*]?"[38]

In *The Crisis of German Ideology*, George Mosse explained that the ideology of "cosmic rootedness" entailed a set of enduring metaphysical attributes:

The term "rooted" was constantly invoked by *völkisch* thinkers. . . . [It] conveyed the sense of man's correspondence with the landscape through his soul and thus with the *Volk*, which embodied the life-spirit of the cosmos. It provided the essential link in the *völkisch* chain of being. Moreover, rural rootedness served as a contrast to urban dislocation, or . . . "uprootedness." It also furnished a convenient criterion for excluding foreigners from the *Volk*. . . . Having no roots stigmatized a person as being deprived of the life-force and lacking a properly functioning soul. Rootlessness condemned the whole man, whereas rootedness signified membership in the *Volk* which rendered man human.[39]

Over the course of the nineteenth century, the idiolect of "rootedness" played a key role in defining the ideology of German "exceptionalism." The *Sonderweg* paradigm demanded the rejection of the "civic" understanding of citizenship associated with the French Revolution (jus soli). Instead, it favored an "ethnic" definition of citizenship (jus sanguinis) that was closely allied with the discourse of *Heimat*, *Boden*, and *Volk*.

Like so many aspects of German ideology, following World War I, the discourse of *Bodenständigkeit* underwent a radicalization that reflected an escalating rhetoric of German superiority. Correspondingly, the inferiority of non-Germanic peoples was portrayed in harsh and defamatory, racial terms.

To be sure, there was nothing prefated or inevitable about the catastrophic dénouement of the discourse of German "rootedness." Nevertheless, historically speaking, it culminated in Goebbels's notorious dictum, formulated in the aftermath of the Nazi *Machtergreifung*, "The year 1789 has hereby been effaced from history."[40]

Although Heidegger's habitual recourse to the terminology of "Heimat" and "rootedness" was not inherently reducible to his support for Nazism, his reliance on this idiom, already during the 1920s, was inherently ideological. It betrayed Heidegger's indebtedness to the discourse of the "German exceptionalism." According to Bambach, the imperatives of *Bodenständigkeit* conditioned Heidegger's

reading of German history in terms of a *völkisch* bond to the homeland and to the native Earth: a *völkisch* myth of destiny that offered a way of preserving and transforming the German *Volk* against forces of industrialization, urbanization, and the threat of foreign influence. . . . Only if a *Volk* is rooted in its own Earth can it summon the historical energy necessary for embracing and transforming its own destiny. . . . In Heideggerian terms, this *völkisch* commitment to rootedness was transformed . . . into a myth of autochthony that claimed a privileged, originary

relation between the ancient Greeks and the German *Volk*. Based on this autochthonous bond of "originary" *Völker* . . . Heidegger framed his own account of the
history of Being.[41]

The tenets of Heideggerian *Seinsgeschichte* maintained that the "authenticity"
of the Greeks and the Germans and the key to their secret bond derived from
their exceptional capacity for ontological "rootedness." He esteemed both
peoples (*Völker*) as *Kulturträger*: "carriers of culture." In Heidegger's view,
their ontological superiority underwrote their "right" to dominate lesser peoples.

As Bambach's remarks suggest, in Heidegger's thought, *Raumpolitik* and
Seinspolitik—the "Politics of Space" and the "Politics of Being"—went hand
in hand. The "Politics of Space" provided Heidegger with a post-Nietzschean,
"extramoral" standpoint that grounded his endorsement of the *Volksgemeinschaft* as a "rooted" alternative to the nihilistic "sham culture" (*Scheinkultur*) of
the modern West.[42]

Phenomenology as "*Völkisch* Science"

The seeds of Heidegger's exaltation of *Raum* and *Boden* were firmly planted
during the 1920s. In his Kassel lectures, *The History of the Concept of Time*
(1925), in which Heidegger outlined the research program of existential phenomenology, he stressed *Bodenständigkeit*'s indispensability as a methodological desideratum. According to Heidegger, the essence of "things" (*Sachen*)
could only be "disclosed" once the *Seinsfrage* had been properly posed; *Bodenständigkeit* played an indispensable role, insofar as it *mediated* between *Seindes*
and *Sein*, "beings" and "Being." In sum, Heidegger regarded "rootedness-in-
soil" as an ontological precondition for experiencing Being.

Thereby, Heidegger revised Husserl's transcendental phenomenology in a
telling and unsettling manner. During phenomenology's formative years, Husserl had proclaimed "To the things themselves!" (Zu den Sachen selbst!) as the
school's guiding methodological precept. Husserl's adage conveyed transcendental phenomenology's aversion to the speculative assumptions of German
Idealism, whose unwarranted presuppositions blocked the attainment of "ei-
detic" knowledge, or the intuition of "essence."

In *The History of the Concept of Time*, Heidegger lauded Husserl's adage,
while insisting that it needed to be radically reformulated. Heidegger feared

that, were phenomenology to accede to "the things themselves" in a manner that conformed with Husserl's directives, it would remain mired in superficiality. Hence, in opposition to Husserl, Heidegger reenvisioned phenomenology's mission as one of restoring things to their *Bodenständigkeit*. Only by returning to *Bodenständigkeit*, claimed Heidegger, could philosophy reinstate the lost dimension of "Ursprünglichkeit," or "primordiality." On these "grounds," Heidegger reformulated the telos of phenomenology as "*bodenständig ausweisend forschen*": "investigations that disclose the *bodenständig* character of things." Phenomenological research, Heidegger insisted, must "affirm and secure this 'ground' [*diesen Boden*]."[43] "The more originally [*ursprünglicher*] and the less prejudicially the elaboration of what is put into 'preview' is brought about," Heidegger added, "then all the more surely will concrete research into Being attain its ground [*Boden*] and remain rooted-in-soil [*bodenständig*]."[44]

Heidegger's conflation of "Boden" and "bodenständig" was of paramount epistemological significance. In his eyes, their etymological confluence suggested a metaphysical correlation: that the key to determining the "ground" or "cause" (*Boden*) of a phenomenon was necessarily tied to unearthing its "rootedness" (*Bodenständigkeit*).

The ideological dimension of Heidegger's approach emerged when he trained his sights on Descartes's "ego cogito sum": a precept that Heidegger rejected because of its alleged "Geschichtsfeindlichkeit," its "aversion to history." Accordingly, Heidegger accused Descartes's cogito of having provided philosophy with a "false origin": a "ground that is no ground" (*ein Boden, der kein Boden ist*). This fateful misstep, he added, resulted from Descartes's attempt to base philosophical inquiry on the "bodenlos" (rootless) "I think."[45]

Heidegger held that modern philosophy's *Bodenlosigkeit* reflected a more far-reaching and acute condition of cultural "decline": a crisis of European nihilism, which Heidegger viewed ideologically as an expression of "degeneration," or "Entartung." These concerns informed his critique of "discourse" (*Rede*) and "propositional truth" in *Being and Time*. As Heidegger admonished, "It is possible for every phenomenological concept and proposition that is derived from genuine origins to *degenerate* [*Entartung*] when communicated as a statement. It gets circulated in a vacuous fashion, loses its rootedness-in-soil [*Bodenständigkeit*] and becomes a free-floating thesis."[46] "The lack-of-rootedness [*Bodenlosigkeit*] of contemporary life," he remarked, "is the basis of its growing *decline* [*Verfall*]. Unless we succeed in returning to the essential and sustaining powers that derive from our native soil [*aus heimatlichem Boden*], all attempts at renewal and improvement will remain hopeless."[47]

Heidegger believed that the remedy for this predicament was to redirect fundamental ontology toward its "primordial" (*ursprünglich* and *anfänglich*) bases in *Boden* and *Erde*. In this way, alone, might it recover the *depth dimension* it had forfeited by following the "bodenlose" paths of "consciousness" and "subjectivity." Heidegger's remedy for the problem of "dissociated subjectivity" entailed "replacing the self-reflection of consciousness and the rational norms that derive therefrom with the blind power [*Macht*] of rooted tradition," hence with a philosophical approach that openly courted the risk of cognitive and ethical regression.[48]

Heidegger's yearning for "primordiality" was accompanied by a nostalgia for a mythical *Urzeit*. As Stefan Günzel has shown in *Geophilosophie*, this yearning was already discernible in Heidegger's treatment of "Tradition" (*Überlieferung*), "Repetition" (*Wiederholung*), and authentic "historicity" (*Geschichtlichkeit*) in *Being and Time*, Division II. In a revealing avowal, Heidegger described fundamental ontology's mission as a quest for "those primordial experiences [ursprüngliche Erfahrungen] in which we achieve our first ways of determining the nature of Being."[49] Both of these assertions suggest that Heidegger—in a manner that was consistent with the "reactionary modernist" fascination with "prehistory" as a guarantor of experiential integrity—equated "authentic experience" with "primordial experience."

Ontological Rootedness and Authenticity

A recurrent leitmotif of Heidegger's early lecture courses was the idea that the superiority of ancient Greek thought derived from its *Bodenständigkeit*, in stark contrast with the "lack-of-rootedness" (*Bodenlosigkeit*) that characterized the thought paradigms of Western modernity.

Thus, in *The Basic Concepts of Aristotelian Philosophy* (1924), Heidegger claimed that the conceptual integrity of Aristotle's thought stemmed from "the way in which the various conceptual moments are *bodenständig*." On these grounds, he urged his contemporaries to "seek out the *Bodenständigkeit* of this [Aristotelian] conceptual skein." "We need to examine," Heidegger continued, "how the Greek manner of thinking [*die griechische Begrifflichkeit*] emerges in its *Bodenständigkeit*. Only if we proceed in this way can we be certain of discovering the true nature of Aristotle's philosophical approach."[50] These assertions demonstrate that, during the mid-1920s, Heidegger regarded *Bodenständigkeit* and *Eigentlichkeit* as necessary corollaries. Increasingly, he perceived "rootedness-in-soil" as a precondition and guarantor of "authenticity."

There is a direct line of continuity between Heidegger's reflections on the *Bodenständigkeit* of Greek thought in *The Basic Concepts of Aristotelian Philosophy* and his manifestly ideological treatment of these themes, nine years later, in the *Rektoratsrede*. "For the Greeks," Heidegger insisted, "science [*Wissenschaft*] was not a 'cultural treasure' [*Kulturgut*], but the innermost determining center of their *völkisch*-political Dasein [*völkisch-staatlichen Daseins*]. Science is not simply the means of making the unconscious conscious, but the power that keeps all of existence in focus and embraces it."[51]

In *Being and Time*, Heidegger explored the idea of *Bodenständigkeit* as a guarantor of *Eigentlichkeit* in his discussion of the recently published Graf Yorck–Wilhelm Dilthey correspondence. Heidegger credited Yorck's "dynamic" understanding of *Geschichtlichkeit* with having transformed his own view of "historicity." Consequently, Heidegger praised Yorck for having developed the ontological distinction between the *ontic* and the *historical*: history as something "present-at-hand" (*vorhanden*) as opposed to history qua *Existenz*. Thereby, Yorck anticipated Heidegger's own conception of *Geschichtlichkeit* or "authentic historicity."

Yorck's conception of *Geschichtlichkeit* as a "reanimation" of the past clarified Heidegger's understanding of the link between *Bodenständigeit* and German "destiny." Thus, "By reconfiguring German identity in terms of *Bodenständigkeit* . . . Yorck . . . pointed to an essential dimension of Germanic *Dasein*: *its rootedness in an Earth* whose authentic meaning was *historical* rather than geological or topographical. . . . Yorck's understanding of the *native earth* and the *local landscape* as *determining forces in the shape of German historical destiny* provided Heidegger with a model for a way of thinking through a connection between *Bodenständigkeit* and history."[52]

In *Being and Time*, Division I, Heidegger had analyzed Dasein from the standpoint of *Zeitlichkeit*, or "temporality." In Division II, conversely, he treated Dasein "essentially" or "authentically": as belonging to a "Volksgemeinschaft," or "historical community." Hence, in Heidegger's sketch of authentic *Geschichtlichkeit* in *Being and Time*, Division II—especially, paragraphs 74–77—the *völkisch* stamp of Heidegger's existential ontology acceded to prominence.

Yorck's treatment of *Bodenständigkeit* was disturbingly anti-Semitic. In "Katharsis," Yorck denigrated Jews as "a tribe that lacks the feeling for a psychic and physical ground or soil": a widespread, anti-Jewish canard that repeatedly reemerged in Heidegger's work.[53]

Following Yorck's lead, Heidegger claimed that, in order to be genuinely "geschichtlich," or "historical," a *Volk* must *actualize* its heritage. However, in order to do so—and, hence, to qualify as "authentic"—it must be *bodenständig*: *existentially rooted*. Consequently, Heidegger perceived *Bodenständigkeit* as *an ontological capacity that allows one to distinguish "historical" from "nonhistorical" peoples*. "Historical" peoples are capable of *actualizing* their heritage, whereas "nonhistorical" peoples notably *lack* this capacity: yet another example of the way that *Seinsgeschichte* and *Seinspolitik* were entwined in Heidegger's work.

Heidegger viewed nonhistorical peoples as a living anachronism, insofar as they ceased to be meaningful historical actors. In Heidegger's view, they failed to contribute positively to the narrative arc of *Seinsgeschichte*. More seriously, this meant that, from an ontological-historical standpoint, they had forfeited their "right to exist."

Here, an illustration drawn from Heidegger's work may prove helpful. Lecturing in 1940 on "Nietzsche and European nihilism," Heidegger claimed that France's humiliating blitzkrieg defeat at the hands of the *Wehrmacht* was not merely a *military* or *political* victory on Germany's part. Instead, he viewed it as an *Ereignis*: an "Event" that was replete with *metaphysical significance*. According to Heidegger, the French defeat expressed "a mysterious law of history which states that one day a people [i.e., the French] no longer measures up to the metaphysics that arose from its own history."[54] In sum, France's downfall attested to the obsolescence of Descartes's "metaphysics of subjectivity" and of the triumph of the *Seinsgedanke*. As Robert Minder summarized Heidegger's interpretation in *Dichter in der Gesellschaft*, "[Heidegger] triumphantly perceived the French collapse [of 1940] as a confirmation of his view that it was not the *French generals* who had lost the war, *but Descartes!*" Consequently, he "disqualified French philosophy since Descartes as a lifeless *Vernunftdenken*. German philosophy since Leibniz, conversely, yielded organic and vital knowledge."[55]

In the case of the European Jewry, the metaphysical stakes of Heidegger's negative ontology of "bodenlose Völker" (rootless peoples) were raised considerably. As Louis Valencia-Garcia affirms in *Far-Right Revisionism and the End of History*, "*Bodenständigkeit* was a belief propagated by . . . Martin Heidegger, as well as Nazi eugenicist Hans Günther, who believed that what distinguished Germans from Jews was the German *connectedness-to-the-soil*, as opposed to the supposed 'uprootedness' of the Jews. . . . In essence, without 'Being,' those who are 'unbound' from the soil are denied their humanity."[56]

According to Heidegger, world Jewry's "lack of roots," or *Bodenlosigkeit*, rendered the Jews not merely "ahistorical" but also an *ontologically disintegrative force*. World Jewry's ontological-historical role as "carriers" of "machination"—a force that was inherently destructive of "rootedness" and "tradition"—meant that, in Heidegger's eyes, Jews were emissaries of the Anti-Christ. As Heidegger remarked in the *Black Notebooks*, "The Anti-Christ must, like any 'anti-matter,' originate from the same essential ground as that against which it is 'anti'—namely, like 'the Christ.' . . . In the era of the Christian occident or metaphysics [world Jewry] has been the *principle of destruction*."[57]

In Schmittian parlance, the Jews were not merely the "enemy" (*hostis*); they were a "scourge" (*inimicus*): *the enemy of humankind*. Hence, from the standpoint of *Seinsgeschichte*, their extermination was an ontological-historical imperative: a view that helps to explain Heidegger's refusal, following the war, to condemn their annihilation. (Moreover, to combat the "Anti-Christ" is, presumably, to do God's work.) When Heidegger deigned to address the Nazi "Endlösung," he trivialized it as merely another instantiation of the evils of modern technology, hence comparable to the dislocations of "motorized agriculture and the blockading of nations."[58] Here we have another example of Heidegger's penchant for pseudoexplanations: insights that, instead of shedding light, rationalize or "explain away." By attributing responsibility for the Holocaust to "Western metaphysics," Heidegger conveniently abstracted from the developmental pathologies of the German *Sonderweg*.

In paragraph 77 of *Being and Time*, Heidegger endorsed Graf Yorck's contention that the central debility afflicting modern philosophy was its inability to conceive of thought "as a manifestation of life." Yorck maintained that, as a result of this failing, philosophy had degenerated into the " 'expectoration' [*sic*] of uprooted thinking [*bodenloses Denken*]." "The uprootedness of thinking [*Bodenlosigkeit des Denkens*] and the belief in such thinking," Yorck contended, "was [itself] a historical product." Yorck's accusation of *Bodenlosigkeit* functioned as a *Kampfbegriff*: a conceptual "weapon" that trained its sights on the deficiencies of modern subjectivity. In *Being and Time*, Heidegger approvingly cited Yorck's

remark that " 'modern man'—man as he has existed since the Renaissance—
would be better off dead and buried [ist fertig zum Begrabenwerden].' "⁵⁹

In *The Role of Consciousness and History*, Yorck commented that Jewish
monotheism's superficiality was a consequence of the Jews' "extraterritoriality": *their lack of historical rootedness.* As Yorck explained, "It has often been
remarked that the extraterritorial character of Jewish exile is responsible for the
Jewish conception of God. Hence, since Jewish life is characterized by *absence
of soil [Bodenlosigkeit]*, absence of land, and absence of power, resulting in the
Jews' abstract conception of God, the Jews are, to all intents and purposes, *a
people without history.*"⁶⁰ Since Yorck, under the influence of Social Darwinism, regarded history as "*a struggle between historical and ahistorical peoples
[Völker]*," he held that the future of civilization depended on the Jews' demise
(*Untergang*).⁶¹

In *Citizenship and Nationhood in France and Germany*, Rogers Brubaker remarks that, in Germany, the "ideas of 1789" provoked a "'holy war' of ethno-
national resistance": a struggle that entailed the elevation of "feeling over
desiccated rationality; of unconscious, organic growth over conscious, artificial
construction; of the vitality and integrity of traditional, rooted folk cultures as
over against the soullessness and artificiality of cosmopolitan culture."⁶² The
discourse of *Raum* and *Boden* that Heidegger, in fealty to Graf Yorck von Wartenburg's understanding of "historicity," embraced was entirely consonant with
such views. It urged eliminating "free-floating" approaches to knowledge that
had prevailed under political liberalism—a worldview that, by perpetuating the
confusion and disorientation of *Bodenlosigkeit*, prevented the attainment of
"essence."

Two years later, in *The Fundamental Concepts of Metaphysics* (1929–30),
Heidegger lamented the "groundlessness of philosophy" (*Bodenlosigkeit der
Philosophie*) and the correlative triumph of "free-floating speculation."
Heidegger viewed both of these phenomena as expressions of ontological "decline." They culminated in an *Existenz* in which "no one stands with anyone
else and no community [*Gemeinschaft*] stands with any other in the rooted
[*wurzelhaften*] *unity of essential action.*"⁶³

In 1930, expatiating on "the essence of truth" at the Baden *Heimattag*—an
annual patriotic gathering that was held at the provincial seat in Karlsruhe—
Heidegger proclaimed that truth is beholden to the "roots of the *Heimat*."
Truth's mission and purpose, claimed Heidegger, come to fruition in "strength-

ening the Heimat." The following day, a local newspaper summarized the philosophical gist of Heidegger's address as follows: "Heidegger sought to establish
the foundations for the essence of truth with concepts such as 'sincerity' and
'rootedness-in-soil' [*Bodenständigkeit*]. . . . 'Truth' and 'reality' [*Wahrheit und
Wirklichkeit*] unite on the soil of the *Heimat* [*auf dem Boden der Heimat*]. . . .
Thereby, one surmounts the abyss of human existence. 'Angst' in the face of the
'Nothing' reflects modern man's lack of 'rootedness.' "[64]

Heidegger's evolution as a "geophilosopher" tracked the radicalization of
the German ideology between the Great War and the Nazi seizure of power.
This trajectory culminated in his celebration in the *Rektoratsrede* of the "powers of earth and blood" (*erd- und bluthaftigen Kräfte*) that had emerged in the
course of the "German Revolution." Heidegger welcomed the Nazi seizure of
power as a form of ontological "deliverance": as an existential "Event" that
presaged a "decision" for "primordiality" and "origin," a *Heimkehr* that augured
the reintegration of *Bodenständigkeit*, *Volk*, and *Erde*. The "Beginning [*Anfang*] is not behind us," Heidegger exulted; "it lies before us!"[65] In keeping with
the widespread reactionary modernist quest for "origins"—an understanding of
historicity meant to contest the Enlightenment narrative of (linear) progress—
Heidegger was convinced that the "way forward," of necessity, passed through
"prehistory" as a locus of "Ursprünglichkeit." Consequently, in *Being and
Time*, Heidegger defined authentic historicity as the capacity to retrieve historical events in the "primordiality of their Being [*Ursprünglichkeit seines Seins*]."[66]

The day after the *Rektoratsrede*, Heidegger presented his controversial
Schlageter-*Rede*, in which he glorified acts of sabotage by the Freiburg native
and Nazi martyr Albert Leo Schlageter. In the course of his remarks, Heidegger
glossed the attributes of *Boden* and *Erde* as they manifested themselves in the
local Schwarzwald landscape: Schlageter's *Heimat* as well as Heidegger's.

Heidegger's discourse was couched in the "heimisch," or "nativist," idiom of
the *Jugendbewegung*, which, during the pre–World War I period, had been a
crucible of *Schollenromantik* ideology: the "romanticism of native soil." In his
address, Heidegger, true to the semantics of "rootedness," highlighted the correspondences between *Boden* (native soil) and *Heldentum*, thereby suggesting
that Schlageter's "heroism" had been forged by the rugged provincial topography: "Students of Freiburg! German students! When on your hikes and outings
you set foot in the mountains, forests, and valleys of this Black Forest, which is
the *Heimat* of this hero [Schlageter], experience this and know: the mountains

among which the young farmer's son grew up are of primitive stone, of granite. They have long been at work hardening the Will."[67]

In *Logic as the Question Concerning the Essence of Language* (1934), Heidegger revisited the thematics of *Erde* and *Boden* as the "ground" of authentic "historicity." The academic context required Heidegger to formulate his views with greater rhetorical circumspection and philosophical precision than the Schlageter-*Rede*.

In the quotation that follows, Heidegger reflected on the relationship between "geopolitics" and "historicity," emphasizing that "national histories" remain unintelligible apart from the elemental forces of *Raum*, *Erde*, and *Boden*: "We say that a stretch of land is rich in history. In this way, Earth and Soil [*Erdboden*] also become part of history. Not, however, as geology would have it, as a chronological sequence. Instead, *national histories* [*die Geschichte der Völker*] *are lodged in the soil* [*geht in den Boden ein*], *and peoples* [*Völker*] *'make history' insofar as they produce space and soil* [*den Raum und Boden schaffen*]."[68]

Implicit in Heidegger's assertion that "national histories are lodged in the soil" is the related claim that a *Volk*'s "Raumbezogenheit"—its "relationship to space"—is an existential determinant of racial and national "difference." Heidegger explored this theme in earnest in *Nature, History, and State* (1933–34), observing, "Every *Volk* has a space that belongs to it. People who live by the sea, in the mountains, and on the plains are *different*." "Space [*Raum*]," Heidegger stipulated, "*belongs to the concrete Being of a Volk*." On these grounds, Heidegger insisted that the idea of a "Volk ohne Raum"—a "people without space"—was an ontological impossibility, since *Volk* and *Raum* are mutually determinative.[69]

Heidegger's observations about the interrelatedness of *Volk* and *Raum*, as well as his related assertion that "*peoples 'make history' insofar as they produce space and soil*," dovetailed with the expansionist designs of the *völkisch* geopolitical school. As Wilhelm Volz, director of the Leipzig-based *Stiftung für deutsche Volks-und Kulturbodensforschung*, declared in "Lebensraum und Lebensrecht des deutschen Volkes" (1925), "Every space has its *Volk*. . . . Space is co-determining for history. . . . The *Volk* makes the space its own but space also creates its *Volk*."[70]

On first blush, Heidegger's claims concerning the ontological correspondences between *Volk* and *Raum*—as represented by his assertion that "every *Volk* has a space that belongs to it. . . . People who live by the sea, in the mountains, and on the plains are *different*"—might appear to be little more than a descriptive affirmation of environmentally conditioned cultural differences. However, a closer examination reveals that Heideggerian *Raumpolitik* was predicated on an inflexible, metaphysical conception of "ontological difference." This explains Heidegger's conviction that differences between *Völker* reflected different "ontological capacities," or "Seinsweisen." As Heidegger affirmed, "Relationship to space [*Raumbezogenheit*], that is, the mastery of space and being marked by space, belongs to the essence and ontological distinctiveness [*Seinsart*] of a *Volk*."[71]

Heidegger's views reflected the escalating ideological symbiosis between *Lebensphilosophie* and the *Volksbegriff*. According to this perspective, "the very capacity to think and see nature as a 'whole'—the art of so-called *Ganzheitsbetrachtung*—was a trait peculiar to the 'Indo-Germanic' mind, while the Jewish mind was fundamentally analytic, dissolutive, and materialistic."[72] As Anne Harrington remarks appositely in *Reenchanted Science*, insofar as "the German and the Jewish races had radically different ways of experiencing and interacting with the natural world—ways apparently rooted in their *different biologies*—then one possible conclusion was that . . . truth, by definition, always carried the stamp of a particular *Volk and Blut* and served that *Volk*'s 'political reality' and 'fateful struggle.' "[73]

Heidegger fully subscribed to this view. He held that *geopolitical differences* entailed *racial differences*: they accounted for a *Volk*'s "ontological specificity," or "Seinsart." In Heidegger's eyes, Germany's *ontological superiority*—its loftier "Seinsweise"—justified the Third Reich's geopolitical and territorial entitlements. Conversely, Heidegger denigrated "unrooted" peoples. He adjudged them ontologically deficient, insofar as they lacked a symbiotic relationship with their environment. As paragons of such ontological deprivation, Heidegger singled out "Jewish nomads," who, "having been made nomadic by the desolation of wastelands and steppes," lacked a fixed relationship to "space" and "soil."[74]

Heidegger held that a *Volk*'s "Raumbezogenheit," or "relationship to space," combined with its ability to "produce space and soil," determined its capacity for *Geschichtlichkeit* and *Eigentlichkeit*: "historicity" and "authenticity." In his view, the ultimate determinant—the aspect that distinguished *historical* from *unhistorical* peoples—concerned a *Volk*'s ability to "master space": Heidegger's euphemism for the ontological and Social Darwinist imperatives of geopolitical "self-assertion." Whereas authentically historical peoples *succeeded* in this task, unhistorical peoples *perished*. Accordingly, during the 1930s, Heidegger increasingly justified his commitment to the "metaphysics of German Dasein" via references to political geography and the "politics of space."[75]

The Entitlements of *Lebensraum*: The "Law of Expanding Spaces"

Following the Great War, the "politics of space" devolved into a febrile discourse of revanchist nationalism. Geopoliticians dismissed international law as a baseless, insubstantial "abstraction," hence a doctrine that violated the state's "natural right" to increase its power via the quest for *Lebensraum*. As Karl Haushofer (1869–1946), the doyen of the German geopolitical school, put it, "Among life forms struggling for *Existenz* on the face of the Earth, the lofty vocabulary of international law has no relevance or meaning." Instead, it was necessary to supplant this outmoded idiom—an atavism of Enlightenment "natural right" discourse—with the nebulous concept of "biologically correct borders."[76]

Proponents of geopolitics rejected the claims of international law as inherently ideological: a stalking horse for Western aggression and territorial expansion, hence little more than an ideational smokescreen for Western "interests." Conversely, they argued that the "politics of space" offered an "objective," nonideological alternative to the West's moral-legal hypocrisy, especially with respect to "indemonstrable" claims of modern natural law.

To remedy these subterfuges and injustices, German *Raumpolitiker* proposed that, henceforth, the criterion of legitimacy in international politics should be the "law of expanding spaces." As formulated by Haushofer, the "law of expanding spaces" sanctioned the entitlement of so-called "large-space nations" to dominate "small-space nations."

The "politics of space" advanced by the German geopolitical school transposed Social Darwinist arguments to the plane of interstate relations. At base, its champions merely reprised the idea of the "right of the strongest." The geopoliticians dismissed approaches to international law predicated on norms of equity and fairness as little more than humanitarian hypocrisy. They claimed that the only realistic, nonideological solution to politics among nations would be to replace existing international law with the unvarnished brutality of *Machtpolitik*.

The "law of the growth of spaces" and the "right" of "large-space peoples" to rule "small-space peoples" harked back to Friedrich Ratzel's *Lebensraum* doctrine. According to Ratzel (1844–1904), the cornerstone of geopolitics was "the law of movement from narrow to broad spaces."[77] Nations that failed to expand their boundaries "degenerated." Hence, geopolitical expansion was deemed a matter of life or death. Nations that shunned the "law of expanding spaces" jeopardized their own survival.

The proponents of National Socialist *Raumpolitik* regarded the continuous expansion and growth of states as an existential imperative. In the dog-eat-dog world of Great Power *Machtpolitik*, a *Volk* that ignored this imperative was destined to *perish* (*unterzugehen*). Territorial aggrandizement was viewed as a sine qua non for the survival of "large-space nations," which were simultaneously extolled as the "carriers" of culture or civilization.

The geopolitical school claimed that *Raumpolitik* presaged a new era of legal "objectivity." However, in keeping with the tradition of German Romanticism, its proponents elevated *Boden* and *Erde* to the rank of supernatural powers: entities that were *alive* or *ensouled*. As Adolf Grabowsky observed in *Staat und Raum* (1933), "If we can no longer attribute all progress to the intervention of great personalities, as a more naïve time did, and can, therefore, no longer unreservedly profess a heroic worldview, we can still *render the Earth itself a hero* . . . as the mighty foundation that man battles to subdue and upon which he remains, in the last analysis, ever dependent."[78]

In essence, the geopolitical standpoint provided a series of threadbare rationalizations for predatory acts of German self-assertion. It sought to replace "normative" approaches to dispute resolution, such as Hans Kelsen's doctrine of "peace through law," with racially driven imperialism. One of the primary reasons for geopolitics' ascendancy derived from its opposition to the emerging consensus in favor of cosmopolitan law as a peaceable alternative to unregulated armed conflict. By reducing international politics to a single, arbitrary and subjective variable—the acquisition of "territory," or *Raum*—geopolitics simplified, at great cost, the complexities of international law.

By equating "history-making" with the "production of space and soil," Heidegger fused fundamental ontology with the worldview of the German geopolitical school, whose leading exponents were Haushofer, Ratzel, and Hans Grimm (1875–1959). Heidegger's geopolitical "Turn" sought to address the dilemma—to invoke Grimm's thesis—of a *Volk ohne Raum*. It was a challenge that Heidegger and the German geopoliticians sought to resolve via the quest for *Lebensraum*, a notion that Heidegger defined euphemistically as the way that a "*Volk* that lacks sufficient *Lebensraum* [achieves] its positive unfolding."[79]

The Dilemmas of a "Volk ohne Raum"

Going back to Kant and Herder, the relationship between geography and philosophy had been a prominent feature of German *Geistesgeschichte*. Since the age of German Romanticism, discussions of *Erde* and *Raum* had been oriented toward "holism," the cosmological interconnectedness of "life" in its totality. According to this perspective, human cultural evolution could not be thought apart from natural history. Instead, the two spheres were regarded as mutually complementary.[80]

During the late nineteenth century, the field of geopolitics was significantly influenced by the *Lebensphilosophie* vogue—an orientation that profoundly impacted the work of Ratzel, the de facto founder of the German "geopolitical school," who coined the term *Lebensraum*. Ratzel's understanding of political geography internalized German Romanticism's holistic understanding of space. Ratzel's approach was significantly influenced by Nietzsche's vitalism and the rising tide of Social Darwinism.

Ratzel viewed the "state" as a "space organism": as an organic "life form" whose roots were planted firmly in the soil, or *Boden*, and whose survival depended on successful adaptation to its geophysical environment. Ratzel maintained that

> it was natural and desirable for a healthy "space organism" to add to its strength
> through territorial expansionism. . . . Hence, the growing state will tend to absorb
> the less successful ones and will also aim to expand into what is strategically and
> economically the most valuable territory. . . . Every state needs to grow in this way
> if it is to flourish or it will decline and eventually disappear, incorporated into the
> territory of another more successful state. . . . The acquisition of *Lebensraum*
> makes the dynamic state more powerful; it will also make its people stronger and
> more enterprising: fit to dominate ever larger territories.[81]

Heidegger's understanding of geopolitics displayed a familiarity with Ratzel's doctrines. For the most part, however, his understanding of geopolitics derived from his esteem for Hans Grimm's novel *Volk ohne Raum* (1926).

Heidegger singled out Grimm's work for praise in a March 1932 letter to his brother, Fritz. "Are you familiar with Hans Grimm's *Volk ohne Raum*?" inquired Heidegger. "Whoever does not already know about the meaning of *Heimat* and the fate [*Schicksal*] of our *Volk* learns about it here."[82]

Grimm's long-winded novel faithfully anticipated Nazi *Grossraum* doctrine: the abandonment of *Weltpolitik* (overseas colonialism), which had prevailed during the *Kaiserreich* (1871–1918), in favor of "continental imperialism"—a standpoint that was predicated on the Social Darwinist entitlement of large-space nations to subsume "small" nations. In *The Ideological Origins of Nazi Imperialism*, Woodruff Smith summarized *Volk ohne Raum*'s central thesis as follows: "If the German people are to survive without losing the fundamental spiritual and material elements of their culture . . . [and] if Germany as a political entity is not to be destroyed by foreign enemies and internal division, *Germans require 'large spaces' for expansion*."[83] Franz Neumann, reflecting on Grimm's towering influence—the Nazis' promotion of Grimm's novel helped propel it to best-seller status—remarked, "With *Volk ohne Raum*, we are given a popular, emotional treatment of geopolitics. The entire 1200 pages constitute one long outcry against British power and the preparation for German imperial expansion."[84]

In the *Black Notebooks*, Heidegger revisited Grimm's theses in *Volk ohne Raum*. He praised Grimm's "dynamic" understanding of "space"—a euphemism for *Lebensraum*—as a genuine ontological breakthrough. Grimm's singular achievement, Heidegger gushed, was having facilitated the "opening and upsurge of Being."[85]

Heidegger maintained that pre-Socratic ontology—especially Heraclitus's understanding of Being as "polemos," or "war"—provided a metaphysical writ for German territorial aggrandizement: the *Drang nach Osten*, or "push to the East." As Otto Pöggeler aptly commented in "Heidegger, Nietzsche, and Politics," "Heidegger linked the beginning of philosophizing to the teaching of Heraclitus on 'war as the father of all things' and the depths of *physis*. . . . It was the study of the pre-Socratics . . ., combined with the study of Nietzsche, that led Heidegger to choose National Socialism."[86] In Heidegger's mind, Heraclitus's conception of Being as *polemos* and Grimm's depiction of the Germans as a *Volk ohne Raum* became inextricably fused.

During the 1930s, Heidegger attempted to combine Heraclitus's notion of Being qua *polemos* with Carl Schmitt's controversial "friend/enemy" distinction.

"The pinnacle of Great Politics," claimed Schmitt in *The Concept of the Political*, "is the moment when the enemy comes into concrete clarity as the enemy."[87] Heidegger, impelled by his reading of Schmitt, reinterpreted *polemos* in light of the "metaphysical" value of "*standing against the enemy, . . . standing firm in confrontation [Stehen gegen den Feind, . . . das Durchstehen in der Auseinandersetzung]*."[88]

However, the aspect of Schmitt's doctrine that made the deepest impression on Heidegger was Schmitt's treatment of the "domestic enemy," or "inneren Feind." In *The Concept of the Political*, Schmitt argued, "The requirements of internal peace compel [the state], in critical situations, to decide upon the domestic enemy. Every state provides some kind of formula for the declaration of an internal enemy."[89] Consequently, Heidegger sought to merge Heraclitus's ontological treatment of "polemos" with Schmitt's justification of the state's entitlement to suppress the "internal enemy."

Heidegger's concerns pertained especially to German Jews. Since 1929, Heidegger had been increasingly disturbed by the "Jewification of the German spirit [*Verjudung des deutschen Geistes*]."[90] Inspired by the views of Schmitt and Heraclitus, Heidegger asserted, "It is a fundamental requirement to *find the enemy, to unmask the enemy* . . ., so that this standing-against-the-enemy may happen and so that Dasein does not lose its 'edge.' " Heidegger contended that, in light of the unique risks that German Jews, as the "domestic enemy," posed to the unity and homogeneity of the *Volksgemeinschaft*, the ultimate goal in combating this threat must be "total annihilation." As Heidegger explained,

> The domestic enemy can attach itself to the innermost roots of the Dasein of a *Volk*; it can set itself against the *Volk*'s own essence and act against it. The *Kampf* is all the more *fierce* and all the more *difficult* . . . since it consists in a *mutual coming to blows*. It is often far more difficult and wearisome to catch sight of the [domestic] enemy as such, to bring the enemy into the open, to harbor no illusions about the enemy, *to keep oneself ready for attack*, to cultivate and intensify a constant readiness, and to prepare the attack, looking far ahead with the goal of *total* annihilation [*völlige Vernichtung*].[91]

Thus, some eight years prior to the Wannsee Conference, at which the "Final Solution" to the Jewish question was set in motion, Heidegger, inspired by this amalgamation of Schmitt and Heraclitus, donned the mantel of a prophet of "völlige Vernichtung," or "total annihilation."

Heidegger's appropriation of Heraclitus's Fragment 53—"war is the father of all things"—for National Socialist purposes was hardly original. In a speech of July 1927, Hitler demonstrated that he, too, appreciated the value of Heraclitus's maxim as a writ for "struggle" and the quest for *Lebensraum*. The Führer's Social Darwinist reading of Heraclitus's adage did not differ qualitatively from Heidegger's interpretation:

> *Struggle* [*Kampf*] *is the father of all things.* This means *the selection of the best results through struggle.* Without struggle the world suffocates through the overgrowth of the mediocre and the inferior.
>
> Imperialism is the *Kampf* for the survival of the *Volk*, . . . and whoever refuses to struggle surrenders his future. He is no longer the *hammer* but instead the *anvil*. *Whoever does not want to be either hammer or anvil . . . will be crushed between hammer and anvil.*[92]

It was Haushofer—a retired army general—who, from his perch at the University of Munich, did the most to endow the nascent field of geopolitics with an aura of academic legitimacy. In 1924, following the Nazis' ill-fated Munich Beer Hall Putsch, Haushofer became a habitué of Landsberg prison, where he found an attentive disciple in Rudolf Hess, the Führer's second in command. In effect, he became Hess's political mentor. In 1934, Haushofer dedicated his influential primer on geopolitics, *Weltpolitik von Heute*, to Hess. During the 1930s, the Nazis, under Haushofer's tutelage, established the Reichstelle für Raumforschung (National Office for Research on Space), whose findings were published in the journal *Raumforschung und Raumordnung*.[93]

The extent to which Haushofer came into direct contact with Hitler at Landsberg prison during the composition of *Mein Kampf* is a matter of dispute. Be that as it may, the fruits of Haushofer's tutelage were readily apparent in the book's penultimate chapter, "Eastern Orientation and Eastern Policy," in which Hitler lauded geopolitics as a template for restructuring the political boundaries of Mitteleuropa. "A nation's sustenance," Hitler declared, "is assured by the amount of its existing soil [*Boden*], . . . which, ultimately, . . . is determined by military-geopolitical [*wehr-geopolitische*] considerations." He conceived his mission as Führer as "leading this *Volk* from its present, restricted *Lebensraum* to new land and soil."[94] Hitler repeatedly stressed the "metapolitical" entwinement of *Boden*, *Volk*, and *Raum*. Viewed as an ensemble, this admixture proved to be a lethal semantic cocktail: a sinister template for Nazi *Bevölkerungspolitik*.

Germany's aspirations to continental predominance were predicated on a nebulous confluence of geopolitical, demographic, and racial-cultural factors. Like Nazi race doctrine, "geopolitics" was fundamentally a pseudoscience: ideological camouflage that served as a pretext for the colonization of the Third Reich's eastern neighbors.

The concepts of "location" (*Ort*) and "space" (*Raum*) constituted the ideational cornerstone of *Raumpolitik* doctrine. "Location" referred to the dangers of the German *Mittellage*: a notion that invoked Social Darwinist arguments to justify Germany's claims to central European hegemony. The ideology of *Raumpolitik* suggested that, the greater Germany's "endangerment," the more it was entitled to pursue an aggressive foreign policy—purportedly, on the grounds of "self-defense."

Haushofer's influence proved decisive in reorienting Germany's quest for *Lebensraum* away from the goals of *Weltpolitik*, or "overseas colonialism," toward the benefits of "continental imperialism." As we read in *Mein Kampf*, "It is not in colonial acquisitions that we must see the solution to the problem of [*Lebensraum*], but exclusively in the acquisition of a territory or settlement, which will enhance the area of the Motherland. . . . Should it fail to extend its soil [*Boden*], a great *Volk* is doomed to destruction. This is especially true when not some little negro nation or other is involved, but the Germanic Mother of Life, which has provided the contemporary world with its cultural model."[95]

In *An Introduction to Metaphysics* (1935), Heidegger restated, nearly verbatim, the ideology of the German *Mittellage*, which, by this point, had become the central justification for Nazi continental expansion and the *Drang nach Osten*. As Heidegger observed, in another example of his confluence of *Seinsgeschichte* and *Seinspolitik*, "Today, [Germany] is caught in a pincer. Situated in the middle, our *Volk* incurs the severest pressure. It is the *Volk* with the most neighbors, and, hence the most endangered *Volk*, and for all that, the most metaphysical 'Volk.' As a historical *Volk*, our *Volk* must move itself, and thereby the history of the West, . . . into *the primordial realm of the powers of Being*. If the great *Entscheidung* [decision] regarding Europe is not to bring *annihilation*, that *Entscheidung* must be made in terms of *new spiritual energies unfolding historically from out of the middle*."[96]

Heidegger's "pincers" metaphor alluded to Germany's long-standing fear of geopolitical "encirclement." On one side stood the Western powers; on the other side, the threat of "Jewish Bolshevism." From a Social Darwinist perspective,

Germany's *Mittellage* entailed a right to "self-defense." As we have seen, it was widely believed that, in the predatory sphere of interstate relations, nations that failed to expand ultimately perished. Heidegger's ruminations on the German *Mittellage* reflected this dilemma. The influence of geopolitics also explains his claim that the only alternative to national "self-assertion" is "annihilation."

In addition, by exalting *Deutschtum* as "the most metaphysical 'Volk,'" Heidegger sought to furnish an ontological justification of the Third Reich's drive for continental hegemony. Heidegger's endorsement of Nazi Germany's "push to the East" emerged directly from his doctrine of the "history of Being." According to this narrative, Russia and the United States were the preeminent representatives of planetary *Machenschaft*. Their influence resulted in "the boundless etcetera of Indifference and Always-the-sameness, . . . the domination of . . . the indifferent Mass, [combined with] an active onslaught that destroys all Rank and every world-creating impulse of Spirit." As Heidegger concluded, "This is the onslaught we call *the demonic* (in the sense of *destructive evil*)."[97] As exemplars of "European nihilism," the United States and Russia posed a significant stumbling block to Germany's prospects of realizing "another Beginning." For these reasons, Heidegger felt compelled to provide an ontological-historical rationale for their elimination.

"State-Founders" as the "Violent Ones"

Heidegger's geopolitical "Kehre" also conditioned his understanding of the transformative role that art and poetry played in the process of "state-founding" (*Staatsschaffen*): that is, their contribution to establishing the ontological parameters of the *Volksgemeinschaft*. Thus, in "Hölderlin and the Essence of Poetry" (1930)—whose composition predated the advent of the Nazi dictatorship by three years—Heidegger designated "Dichtung" as the "Primordial language [*Ursprache*] of a historical *Volk*."[98] "Language," declared Heidegger, "is the *Ur*-poetry [*Urdichtung*] through which a *Volk* poeticizes Being. . . . By virtue of great poetry, a *Volk* enters into *history*."[99]

Heidegger apotheosized "Poets, Thinkers, and Statesmen" as an existentially privileged caste. They embodied an *ontological elite* that Heidegger lionized as the "three creative powers of historical Dasein." Heidegger charged this guild—the "shock troops" of fundamental ontology—with the mission of establishing "fundamental attunement as the truth of a *Volk* [*die Grundstimmung als Wahrheit eines Volkes*]."[100]

In all of these respects, "Poets, Thinkers, and Statesmen" played an indispensable role in furthering the ends of *Seinsgeschick*, or the "destining of Being." As Heidegger explained, "The historical Dasein of *Völker*—their rise, their pinnacle, and their decline—originates from *poetry*; out of poetry there arises a proper knowing in the sense of *philosophy*; and from both of these, the construction of the Dasein of a *Volk* as a *Volk through the State*—i.e., *politics*. The primordial, historical epoch of *Völker* is the epoch *of Poets, Thinkers, and Statesmen* [*Dichter, Denker, und Staatsschöpfer*], those who authentically [*eigentlich*] ground and establish the historical Dasein of a *Volk*."[101]

Thereby, Heidegger reprised a leitmotif that derived from the political philosophy of German Romanticism: the trope of the "Aesthetic State."[102] Heidegger held that Hölderlin's distinct contribution to the ethos of "Staatsschaffen" was exemplified by the poem "Der Tod fürs Vaterland" (1800). By lauding the "*Volk* of this Earth as a historical *Volk*," remarked Heidegger, Hölderlin highlighted the essential nexus between "rootedness-in-Earth" and "historicity."[103] Heidegger claimed that "Earth-related" (*Erdbezogen*) *Völker* were ontologically superior to "unrooted" or "ungrounded" peoples. This superiority conferred on them the prerogatives of "Herrschaft": the right "to rule" or "to dominate."

As I indicated in chapter 3, Heidegger's *völkisch* appropriation of Hölderlin as the "Stimme des Volkes" (voice of the *Volk*) meshed seamlessly with the protofascist interpretations of Hölderlin's work that had been pioneered by George-*Kreis* luminaries such as Norbert von Hellingrath and Max Kommerell. From Kurt Hildebrandt to Alfred Baeumler, one finds the same apotheosis of Hölderlin as the "embodiment of the German *Volksgeist* and the *Führerprinzip*": the "antagonist of an alien, excessively Westernized, rationalistic Idealism" and the "redeemer of a Germanic-Greek *Mythos* that derives from the essential root and ground of humanity.' "[104] As Baeumler observed in "Hellas und Germanien" (1937), "By honoring Hölderlin, we honor . . . the man of our destiny. His path established the fateful path of the German spirit [*Schicksalsweg des deutschen Geistes*]. By way of *Hellas*, it finds its way back to *Germanien*."[105] Faithful to these interpretations, in *Hölderlin's Hymns "Germanien" and "Der Rhein"* (1934), Heidegger lauded Hölderlin as a prophet of "German destiny" and as the "poet of the Germans." In order for the Germans to fulfill their appointed "mission," claimed Heidegger, it was imperative for them to acknowledge Hölderlin as the foremost "power in the history of our *Volk* [*die Macht in der Geschichte unseres Volkes*]."[106]

Heidegger's bellicose Hölderlin interpretation exalted the ethos of the "community of the trenches," or *Grabenschutzgemeinschaft*, that, in *Being and Time*, had served as the "ontic" point of reference for the concept of "Being-toward-death." Similarly, in his lectures on Hölderlin, Heidegger proclaimed, "The basis for *Frontsoldaten* camaraderie . . . is the *proximity of death*, each man's sacrifice in the face of the same Nothingness." "Death and a readiness for sacrifice," Heidegger continued, "produce the *space of community* [*Raum der Gemeinschaft*] from which camaraderie springs." Thereby, *Angst* in the face of death metamorphosed into a touchstone of existential profundity. It facilitated what Heidegger described as a "metaphysical proximity to the unconditioned." "Were it not for death as free sacrifice," Heidegger concluded, "camaraderie would not exist."[107]

Heidegger's "metapolitical" instrumentalization of Hölderlin as a "German Homer" or a "German Tyrtaeus" was accompanied by a litany of geophilosophical aperçus that exalted the imperatives of "historicity," "rootedness," and "dwelling." "As founding [*Stiftung*]," claimed Heidegger, "poetry secures the ground of possibility so that human being can settle upon the Earth . . . [and] become *historical* [*geschichtlich*], which means: to be a *Volk*." "This authentic *Being-settled and rooted-in-soil* [*bodenständig zu sein*], this 'dwelling,'" he continued, "is grounded in and through poetry." Highlighting the "metapolitical" value of these insights, Heidegger claimed that they epitomized "politics in the highest and most genuine sense."[108] As interpreters, we would be remiss if we declined to take Heidegger at his word.

During the 1930s, Heidegger reprised this conception of the "state-founding" capacities of poetry and art in a wide variety of contexts. These efforts were part of a more general effort on his part to develop an aestheticized political ontology. As Heidegger declaimed in *Hölderlin's Hymns "Germanien" and "Der Rhein,"* the *Volk*'s "Being [*Seyn*] is founded poetically. . . . [It is] rooted in the deeds [*Täterschaft*] of the State-Founders of the Earth [*Staatsgründer der Erde*], and in historical space [*Raum*]."[109] Heidegger elevated the poet, by virtue of his capacity as a "Staatsgründer" or "state-founder," to the pantheon of "Halbgötter," or "demigods." Thereby, Heidegger sought to provide an ontological warrant for the *Führerprinzip*. Heidegger clearly regarded himself as a philosophical Führer, a latter-day "philosopher king." As Heidegger observed, "The true and only Führer points the way, by virtue of his Being [*Seyn*], to the realm of the demigods. *Führersein* [Being-a-Führer], as a form of finite Being, is a 'fate.'"[110]

Since the poet's "mission" was to mediate between the spheres of "gods and men," he metamorphosed into a "Dichter-Führer."

Heidegger's attempt to enlist *Dichtung* in the service of "state-founding"—a recurrent leitmotif of his *Denken* during the 1930s—coalesced with National Socialism's self-understanding as a "national aestheticism." Nazi leadership cadres were rife with self-styled "artist-statesmen." Prior to emigrating to Germany, Alfred Rosenberg, who was born in Reval, Estonia, studied architecture in Riga and Moscow. Goebbels, for his part, trained as a Germanist at the University of Heidelberg under the supervision of Max von Waldberg and Georg-*Kreis* loyalist Friedrich Gundolf. He was also the author of a novel, *Michael.* Hitler, who viewed himself as a great architect, had tried his hand at painting during his "wilderness years" in Vienna. He had also sought to enroll—unsuccessfully—in the Vienna Academy of the Arts.

According to Manfred Frank, the Nazi elite's training in the arts was a "legacy of nineteenth-century German Romanticism, which approached social issues through the lens of art-theory and art-as-religion [*Kunst-Theorie und Kunst-Religion*], and which—as the cases of Rainer Maria Rilke and Stefan George demonstrate—viewed *Dichtung* as a substitute for *Myth.*"[111] The "crypto-aesthetic" orientation that was shared by the NSDAP leadership suggests that they regarded the shift to politics later in life as a second career choice.

During the 1920s, the longing for a New Religion and a New Mythology profoundly influenced the discipline of geopolitics: a fact that helps to account for the gnostic features that distinguished the field.[112] In geophilosophers' search for holistic explanations, they sought to discern the subterranean forces that determined life and history behind the scenes. As one prominent *Raumpolitiker* declared during the 1920s, "Our time is an epic of dissolution that recalls the collapse of the ancient world, the Reformation, and the Renaissance. It is the longing for a New Religion that spills over into the social and political doctrines of the day."[113]

For similar reasons, proponents of geopolitics often insisted that their discipline was closer to "art" than to "science." Writing in *Die Tat* in 1925, Erich Günther asserted that geopolitics embodied a "synthesis of art and science." Hermann Lautensach, one of the most influential political geographers of the 1920s, proposed that geopolitics bore greater resemblance to a "Kunstlehre" than to a science.[114]

Heidegger's fascination with the idea of an "Aesthetic State" crested with his treatise on "the origin of the work of art." There, Heidegger invoked the interplay between "Earth" and "World" to illustrate the dynamic of "concealment" (*Verborgenheit*) and "unconcealment" (*Unverborgenheit*) that he viewed as the ontological precondition for the emergence of truth qua "alētheia," or "unveiling." Faithful to the ideology of German exceptionalism, Heidegger construed *Deutschtum*—whose singularity derived, in part, from its status as a nation of "Dichter und Denker"—as *the* uniquely "historical" *Volk*. "Unconcealment," Heidegger insisted, "does not transpire somewhere in and of itself or as a property of things. *Being happens as the history of human beings, as the history of a Volk*."[115]

Heidegger's claim that "unconcealment" and the "happening of Being" are tied to "the history of a Volk" reinforces the view that *Seinsgeschichte* was predicated on the ideology of "racial difference." Heidegger held that ontological capacities reflected differences in the racial constitution—the "ontological nature," or *Seinsart*—of a *Volk*. Moreover, Heidegger repeatedly insisted that the *German Volk* possessed privileged access to the mysterious "sendings of Being" (*Schickungen des Seins*) and that, consequently, the advent of "another Beginning" was inextricably linked to the unique ontological capacities of *Deutschtum*. As Heidegger declared in the *Black Notebooks*, "The anticipatory and essential moment of *Entscheidung* concerning the essence of history is reserved to the Germans."[116] Conversely, the most one could expect from ontologically, hence racially, inferior races or *Völker*—Slavs, Jews, and "Negroes"—was that they obediently heed the commands of their German *Herrscher* (rulers).

The philosophical inspiration underlying Heidegger's reflections on "state-founders" as "violent ones" (*Gewalt-tätige*) was Nietzsche's portrayal of "state-creators" in *The Genealogy of Morals* as "unconscious artists." Nietzsche characterized "state-creators" as individuals who are "*violent by gesture and deed*": men who "create and imprint forms instinctively." "Where they emerge," remarked Nietzsche, "new . . . structures of domination [*Herrschafts-Gebilde*] arise." According to Nietzsche, the "state-creators'" "shaping of a population" necessarily occurred through "acts of violence": acts that Nietzsche described as "a terrible tyranny that continues working until the raw material of people and semi-animals has been . . . kneaded and made compliant." "The word 'State,'" Nietzsche stipulated, means "a pack of blond beasts of *prey: a conqueror* and *master race*, which, organized on a war footing, . . . unscrupulously lays its dreadful paws on a populace."[117]

Heidegger and the "Law of Expanding Spaces"

In keeping with the Social Darwinist conception of "life" as a "Kampf um Existenz" (struggle for existence), Heidegger maintained that *Völker* who shunned the challenges of territorial expansion—"die über Heimatgebundenheit hinaus nicht vorstossen"—risked forfeiting their "Volkheit," or "peoplehood." In sum, they risked forfeiting their *völkisch* "authenticity" or "substance." Heidegger claimed that the risks of such forfeiture were especially grave among "Volksdeutsche," or "ethnic Germans." As Heidegger explained, although "ethnic Germans" possess a "German *Heimat*, they do not enjoy the prerogatives of belonging to the State or Reich." Consequently, they are in constant danger of "forfeiting their ontological authenticity" [*so ihrer eigentlichen Seinsweise entbehren*]," since the latter is contingent on belonging to a State.[118]

Heidegger's arguments furnished an ontological warrant for Nazi *Lebensraum* doctrine, which demanded (1) the political incorporation of *Volksdeutsche* within the expanded German state, or *Grossdeutsches Reich* and (2) the subordination of the Slavs, who were perceived as racially inferior, to German interests. Heidegger's account of Slavic racial inferiority was ontologically conditioned.

Heidegger held that a *Volk*'s spatially conditioned predisposition for "historicity" manifested itself in its potential for "self-assertion." Its capacity for "self-assertion," in turn, determined whether or not a particular *Volk* was *authentically historical*. A tragic fate awaited peoples or *Völker* that *lacked* this capacity, who were unable to "project themselves into space." Such peoples were demonstrably "unhistorical." As such, they were destined *to perish* (*untergehen*).

Nevertheless, in Heidegger's quest to determine the constituents and parameters of *Raumpolitik*, he, like other representatives of the geopolitical school, ran up against a contradiction. On the one hand, in keeping with the tenets of Nazi race doctrine, Heidegger exalted the ontological superiority of peoples who were *bodenständig*, or rooted-in-soil. However, a potential inconsistency arose as Heidegger sought to reconcile the demands of "rootedness" with the "right to conquest": two desiderata that, on first view, seemed irreconcilable. One emphasized the primacy of "place" (*Ort*), in keeping with geopolitics' embrace of racialized, romantic environmentalism. (The German Romantics, for example, regarded "landscape" as an expression of the German "soul," a perspective that was consistent with eighteenth-century natural philosophy.) The other, conversely, stressed the necessity of transcending rootedness in keeping with the ends of colonial self-assertion, thereby satisfying the geopolitical imperative to "master" spaces inhabited by inferior, "unhistorical" peoples.

Heidegger conceived of an imaginative way to resolve this quandary by relying on an approach known as "dynamic geopolitics." The advantage of "dynamic geopolitics" was that it surpassed the environmental determinism that had bedeviled geopolitics' more traditionally minded, Anglo-American exponents. Advocates of dynamic geopolitics insisted that peoples were not simply at the mercy of environmental factors such as climate, topography, and location. Instead, they maintained that *Volk* and *Ort*, "people" and "place," were "codetermining": they stood in a relationship of mutual reciprocity.

In keeping with the dynamic geopolitical model, Heidegger claimed that it was incumbent on "historical" peoples to surmount the geographical limitations of "location" in order—as Heidegger euphemistically put it—to "strike out" and "interact with wider expanses." In this way alone might historical peoples, such as the Germans, actualize their ontological-historical "right" to self-assertion: an entitlement that Heidegger equated with the "right to conquest." As Heidegger explained in *Nature, History, and State*, "It is not proper for a *Volk* that is rooted-in-soil and nurtured-by-soil to perceive its unique ideal in the 'settled' nature that finds its realization in the *peasantry*: in its [the peasantry's] expansion, growth, and, health. Equally necessary is the domination of territory and space [*Beherrschung des Bodens und des Raumes*], the act of striking out and interacting in wider expanses. The concrete manner in which a *Volk* interacts with space and shapes it necessitates both aspects: rootedness-in-soil and interaction [*Bodenständigkeit und Verkehr*]."[119]

In Heideggerian *Raumpolitik*, the role of the state was paramount, since its power and prowess determined the *Volk*'s effectiveness in its efforts to "master" its geopolitical environment. Consequently, Heidegger held that the state's role was crucial for a *Volk*'s self-understanding, insofar as it determined the *Volk*'s "willingness and power to strike out and expand. . . . We can only genuinely speak of the state," Heidegger continued, "when, in addition to *Bodenständigkeit*, the will to extend its reach, to interaction, also becomes a factor."[120]

However, the task of "striking out and interacting in wider expanses" was problematic in the case of peoples for whom "space" and "state" failed to coincide. Therefore, although in such cases the *Volk* in question may possess a *Heimat*, for want of a state, it lacked the capacity to *expand*. Thereby, a *Volk*'s

Dasein and survival were placed at risk, since it lacked the political means of safeguarding and protecting its *Existenz*.

Heidegger explained the existential divide between *Heimat* and state as follows:

> I possess a *Heimat* by virtue of my birth. . . . *Heimat* is expressed by virtue of being rooted-in-soil and rooted-in-the-earth [*Bodenständigkeit und Erdgebundenheit*]. . . . *Heimat* becomes the ontological modality of a *Volk when it strikes out into wider expanses . . . in the form of a state*. . . . Peoples or population groups that *fail* to expand the borders of their *Heimat*-spaces . . . are in constant danger of losing their *Volk* identity and perishing. This is the great problem of the Germans who live beyond the borders of the Reich, who have a German *Heimat*, but who do not belong to the German state or the German Reich, and who are, therefore, deprived of their ontological authenticity. . . . The space of a *Volk* and the soil of a *Volk* extends as far as the members of the *Volk* have found a *Heimat* and have become *bodenständig*. The space of the state and its territory find their borders *by striking out into wider expanses*.[121]

Faithful to the ideology of the *Großdeutsches Reich*, Heideggerian *Raumpolitik* endorsed the goal of unlimited German territorial aggrandizement.

The *Großdeutsches Reich* was a geopolitical fiction: a rationalization of the German drive toward eastward colonial expansion. Proponents of the *Drang nach Osten* (push to the East) justified their expansionist designs by dramatizing the plight of the *Volksdeutsche* or "ethnic Germans"—as Heidegger phrased it, "the great problem of the Germans who live beyond the borders of the Reich"—as a pretext. However, as a rule, advocates of Germany's "push to the East" neglected to mention that many of the *Volksdeutsche* had migrated to the east centuries earlier, no longer spoke German, and had little desire to return to the "Fatherland."

Sidestepping these inconvenient truths, Heidegger highlighted the predicament of the *Volksdeutsche*, whom he described as "Germans who live beyond the borders of the Reich, who have a German Heimat, but who do not belong to the German state or the German Reich."[122] He supplemented these traditional justifications of German expansion by adorning them with a "metaphysical" claim concerning the imperative of restoring the "ontological authenticity" of the "stateless" *Volksdeutsche* by reincorporating them within the Reich.

Heidegger's contention that ethnic Germans who lived beyond the Reich's borders "have a German *Heimat*" was an ideological fiction that had been fabricated by archaeologists, ethnologists, and demographers who sought to prove that Slavic peoples were inherently *kulturlos*—"incapable of culture"—and that, historically, they had been dependent on their German overlords for whatever meager trappings of "civilization" they had acquired.[123] By exaggerating the archaeological significance of ancient German settlements in the East, these nationalistically inclined scholars prepared the way for a German "reconquista."

Heidegger's endorsement of the *Drang nach Osten* harmonized with Hitler's discussion of Nazi foreign-policy goals in *Mein Kampf.* Celebrating Germany's *Sendungsbewusstsein*, or "special mission," Hitler justified the Third Reich's colonial entitlements in terms of *Deutschtum*'s *völkisch* and *racial* superiority. "The basic ideas of the National Socialist movement are *völkisch*," claimed Hitler, "and *völkisch* ideas are National Socialist. If National Socialism wants to *conquer*, it must unconditionally espouse this truth."[124]

Hitler vindicated Nazism's "right to conquer" in terms of the racial inferiority of Germany's Slavic neighbors. As the Führer explained,

> The organization of a Russian state formation was not the result of the political abilities of the Slavs. Instead, it was a wonderful example of the state-forming efficiency of the German element in an inferior race. . . . Inferior nations, led by German organizers and overlords, have, on more than one occasion, evolved into mighty state formations that have endured as long as the racial nucleus of the creative state-race maintained itself. Whereas, for centuries, Russia drew nourishment from the German nucleus of its upper leading strata, today . . . it has been replaced by the Jew, . . . [who] has no talent for organization, but is instead a ferment of decomposition.[125]

Hitler's characterization of "the Jew" as a "ferment of decomposition" confirmed that, among the champions of Nazi race thinking, world Jewry's disintegrative influence was an ever-present obsession. As the alpha and omega of the Nazi worldview, the *Judenfrage* rarely receded from view.

Nazi "Nomadology"

In *Nature, History, and State*, Heidegger broached the "Jewish Question," relying on the precepts of the German geopolitical school. The constraints of an academic setting necessitated recourse to euphemism. Thus, instead of speaking of Jews directly, Heidegger relied on the negative stereotype of "Semitic

nomads." Heidegger's discussion was intended as a parable concerning the deleterious influence of Jewish "nomads" on German *Boden*.

In the discourse of anti-Semitism, the denigration of Jews as "nomads" had
a long and unsavory pedigree. The Austrian Orientalist Adolf Wahrmund's
1883 tract *The Law of Nomadism and Contemporary Jewish Dominance* (*Das
Gesetz des Nomadentums und die heutige Judenherrschaft*) established a fateful precedent. Wahrmund, who was a professor of Arabic, stressed the cultural
affinities between Jews and Arabs as Semitic peoples. On the basis of these affinities, he characterized the Jews as a "desert people," thereby reinforcing the
prejudicial image of Jews as "nomads." Wahrmund argued that the Jews, as
"non-Aryans," represented an alien ethnic presence amid the "Indo-European"
cultural landscape. As racially undesirable trespassers, they could only have an
influence that was corrosive and malign.

Among conservative revolutionaries, Werner Sombart's (1863–1941) treatise *The Jews and Modern Capitalism* (*Die Juden und das Wirtschaftsleben*;
1911) proved especially influential in popularizing the image of Jews as shifty
cultural interlopers. Opposing Max Weber's thesis in *The Protestant Ethic and
the Spirit of Capitalism* (1905) that the Protestant Reformation had unleashed
the "demons" of modern entrepreneurialism, Sombart reasserted the Jews' centrality in the developmental history of capitalism, thereby reconfirming one of
the ideological linchpins of modern anti-Semitism. In order to make his case,
Sombart relied on Wahrmund's portrayal of the Jews as nomads. He argued that
the Jews' rootless, protean nature was especially conducive to their geographical and social mobility under capitalism.

For the most part, Sombart's characterizations rarely rose above the level of
base and indemonstrable stereotypes. "In the desert," claimed Sombart, "where
the shepherd's flock of sheep could grow quickly and be destroyed with equal
rapidity by disease or hunger, the idea of unlimited acquisition and production
took root among the Jews as it never could in a settled agricultural community."[126] In contrast with races that possessed a meaningful attachment to place,
Sombart alleged that the Jews, as perennial meddlers and go-betweens, were
able to flourish in trades such as banking and commerce that required transcending the constraints of national borders.

Sombart alleged that Jewish "rootlessness" was especially well suited to an
economic system in which the free circulation of money and capital was central. Hence, money united "both factors of the Jewish essence: *desert* and *wan-*

dering, Saharism and *nomadism*."[127] Reprising yet another widely held stereotype, Sombart claimed that the Jews' nomadic heritage provided them with a distinct advantage with respect to intellectual vocations such as journalism, law, and scholarship—professions that rewarded cleverness and a capacity for abstract thought, rather than deep conviction.

Hitler included a barbed discussion of Jewish nomadism in *Mein Kampf*. He claimed that, although in many cases, nomads successfully assimilated to their host cultures, with the Jews, things were different. Unlike other peoples, the Jews as a race were fundamentally *inassimilable*. He added that, whereas many nomadic peoples displayed a positive attitude toward work, the Jews, conversely, remained unregenerate "parasites": "freeloaders, who extended their influence more and more like a deadly bacillus." Ultimately, claimed Hitler, "through systematic racial defilement, the Jew consciously poisons the blood of the host nation."[128] Hence, to exterminate the Jew was a matter of life or death.

According to Heidegger, the *Bodenlosigkeit* and peripatetic habitudes of nomadic peoples produced overwhelmingly disintegrative consequences and effects, hence his claim that the character structure of nomads was permanently contaminated by "the desolation [*Trostlosigkeit*] of the desert and steppes." Consequently, "they frequently leave behind deserts in cases where, at an earlier point, they had discovered fruitful and cultivated land." Conversely, "rooted peoples know how to create a *Heimat* out of the wilderness."[129]

Heidegger's conviction that the ontological interrelatedness of *Volk* and *Raum* accounted for variations in the racial aptitude or cognitive capacity among *Völker* also played a key role in his disquisition on Jewish nomads, hence his assertion that, whereas Slavic peoples might find it difficult to fathom the nature of "German space," in the case of "Semitic nomads," comprehending "German space" was an *ontological impossibility*: "On the basis of a *Volk*'s specific knowledge of the nature of its space [*Raum*], we first experience the way that nature is revealed [in] it. The nature of our *German* space [*Raum*] is revealed in a distinctly different manner to a Slavic *Volk* than it is to us. In the case of Semitic nomads, *it will perhaps never be revealed at all*."[130]

Heidegger's critique of the Jews' racial-cognitive failings coalesced with the Nazis' excoriation of the Jews as a "Gegen-Rasse," or "antirace," an allegation that underlined the seriousness of the threat they posed to the cultural-political integrity of all races or peoples. Heidegger's endorsement of "Nazi nomadology" confutes defenders who claim that he consistently rejected Nazi race doctrine.

As Sander Gilman has affirmed in "Cosmopolitan Jews vs. Jewish Nomads," an anti-Semitic commonplace alleged that Jews were incapable of grasping the "notion of a national or particularistic Space"—precisely the point that Heidegger sought to make in *Nature, History, and State*.[131] Hence, owing to the Jews' *Bodenlosigkeit*, in their case, the fruitful reciprocity between *Volk* and *Raum* was entirely absent. Among anti-Semites, the Jews' existential taint meant that they were condemned in perpetuity to inauthenticity and alterity. Consequently, the Jews could never become *echt deutsch*, or authentically German, since to belong to the *Volk* and to share in its "destiny" hinged on the entwinement of *Volk* and *Raum*: a capability that Jews, as eternal aliens, or *Fremdlinge*, endemically lacked.

Heidegger's disparagement of Jewish "nomadism" in *Nature, History, and State* was an inherently racial critique. What mattered was not the "real-world" conduct of actual Jews but, instead, their status in the political imaginary of Nazi race doctrine. In the words of one scholar, proponents of anti-Semitism "did not respond to 'real' developments. . . . The nature of their ideas tended to detach them from real events, instead of compelling them to take new developments into consideration."[132]

Heidegger's critique of Jewish "extraterritoriality," or *Bodenlosigkeit*, was a natural outgrowth of his "existential" affirmation of *Raum* and *Erde*, "space" and "earth." As Heidegger, echoing Sombart's disparagement of Jews as untrustworthy meddlers and go-betweens, observed in the *Black Notebooks*, "Contemporary Jewry's temporary increase in power has its basis in the fact that Western metaphysics—above all, in its modern incarnation—offers fertile ground for the dissemination of an empty rationality and calculability, which in this way gains a foothold in 'spirit,' *without ever being able to grasp from within the hidden realms of decision*."[133]

Heidegger's denigration of Jews as the primary carriers of "an empty rationality and calculability" coalesced with *Lebensphilosophie*'s growing tendency to interpret the modern struggle of "life" versus "mechanism" in terms of "a racial struggle between Germans and Jews: a conceit that had been popularized in the early decades of the [twentieth] century by people like [Houston Stewart] Chamberlain and subsequently adopted by Rosenberg and Hitler." The upshot was that "Jewishness, *as a racial condition*, became a flesh-and-blood metaphor for the only apparently divergent ideas of *chaos* and *mechanism*: a force at once *disorganizing* and *sterilizing*, to be contained and conquered by the racial power of German-Aryan Wholeness."[134]

Heidegger's reflections on the ontological shortcomings of Slavs and Jews underlines the fundamental affinities between fundamental ontology and the *Rassengedanke*. It illustrates the extent to which Heidegger had internalized the *völkisch* understanding of racial hierarchy, the ontological gulf separating *Germanentum* from lesser races. The "law of expanding spaces" required that "existentially" superior peoples, such as the Germans, increase their "mastery" of adjacent spaces at the expense of racial inferiors. From the standpoint of *Seinsgeschichte*, it mattered little if the "small-space" peoples who were "displaced"—Poles, Czechs, and Serbs—were annihilated or destroyed.

The threat posed by "Jewish nomads," conversely, was of an entirely different order. In 1933–34, when Heidegger offered his seminar *Nature, History, and State*, some five hundred thousand Jews still resided within the Reich. The Nazis claimed that these Jewish *Fremdlinge* constituted an internal threat to the integrity of the *Volksgemeinschaft*. Hence, the "Final Solution" to the Jewish Question needed to be comprehensive and all-encompassing. As we have seen, Heidegger demonstrated his receptiveness to the notion of an *Endlösung* to the "Jewish Question" when, in 1933–34, he endorsed the idea of the Jews' "völlige Vernichtung": their "total annihilation."[135]

Jewish "Worldlessness": An Indelible Ontological Stain

Heidegger supplemented his condemnation of "Semitic nomads" as an insidious and destructive "counterrace" with an equally harsh denunciation of Jewish "worldlessness." In Heidegger's existential ontology, Jewish "worldlessness" functioned as a corollary to Jewish "rootlessness": the Jews' incapacity to establish a symbiotic relationship to "environment" and "place," *Raum* and *Ort*.

Heidegger's assessment of Jewish "worldlessness" emerged in conjunction with his critique of "Machenschaft": Heidegger's term for the West's maniacal and single-minded preoccupation with the ends of technological world "mastery." Heidegger contended that such developments threatened to reduce Being in its totality to mere "stuff of domination"—"standing reserve" (*Bestand*)— and that the Jews were the *Gegen-Rasse*, or force orchestrating this process from behind the scenes. As he asserted in the *Black Notebooks*, "One of the stealthiest forms of Gigantism and perhaps the most ancient" is "the fast-paced history of calculation, pushiness, and intermixing whereby [world] Jewry's worldlessness is established."[136]

As we have seen, in *Being and Time*, Heidegger defined the distinctive nature of Dasein, or "human being," in terms of its capacity to "have a world." As Heidegger explained in *The Fundamental Concepts of Metaphysics*, "Man is not simply regarded as part of the world within which he appears and which he makes up in part. Man also stands over against the world. This standing over against is a 'having' of world as that in which man moves, with which he engages, which he both masters and serves, and to which he is exposed. Thus, man is, first, a part of the world; and second, as this part, he is at once master and servant of the world."[137]

In *Being and Time*, Heidegger identified the capacity to "have a world" as a hallmark of authentic Selfhood.[138] He held that beings or peoples that were divested of this capacity suffered from a deep-seated and irremediable ontological deficiency. Ultimately, this debility rendered them *subhuman*. To illustrate his point concerning the existential primacy of "Being-in-the-world" and "having a world," Heidegger asserted that stones and plants, in contrast with Dasein, were "worldless." Their inability to "have a world" and to develop constructive "world relations" underlined their ontological impoverishment: their incapacity for authentic "temporality" (*Zeitlichkeit*), or what Heidegger called "projection" (*Entwurf*). According to Heidegger, this profound existential "lack" distinguished stones, plants, and animals from *human* Being-in-the-world. As Heidegger explained,

> Man has world. But then what about the other beings which, like man, are also part of the world: the animals and plants, the material things like the stone, for example? Are they merely parts of the world, as distinct from man who in addition has the world? Or does the animal too have world, and if so, in what way? In the same way as man, or in some other way? And how would we grasp this otherness? And what about the stone?
>
> However crudely, certain distinctions immediately manifest themselves here. We can formulate these distinctions in the following theses: (1) The stone (material object) is *worldless*; (2) The animal is *poor-in-world*; (3) Man is *world-forming*.[139]

On the basis of these remarks, it is clear that, by characterizing Jews as "worldless," Heidegger, in effect, ascribed to them an ontological deficiency that they shared with lower forms of organic and inorganic life: plants, stones, and animals. The upshot of this rather crude normative scheme, in which the capacity to have a "world" (*Weltlichkeit*) proved decisive, is that Jews as a people were

deemed devoid of a raison d'être. In fact, in the existential hierarchy established by Heidegger, Jews ranked below animals: whereas Heidegger deemed
animals "poor-in-world," Jews, as "worldless," were afflicted by a more profound ontological void.

Hence, by characterizing Jews as "worldless," Heidegger subjected them to
an even greater existential sleight. Because of their "worldlessness," Jews were
incapable of acceding to "authenticity" as well as "historicity." The end result
of Heidegger's phenomenology of Jewish "worldlessness" was his denial that
the Jews as a people have a compelling ontological reason to be.

Bodenständigkeit was also an integral component of *Raumpolitik*, which,
during the 1920s, increasingly gained a foothold among *völkisch* and pan-
German intellectual circles. In *Mein Kampf*, Hitler, too, stressed the necessary
entwinement of *Bodenständigkeit*, *Volk*, and *Raum*:

> The strength of our *Volk* is maintained by preserving the *Boden* of its *Heimat* in
> Europe and not in the colonies. We must never consider the Reich to be truly se-
> cure until it can guarantee every individual descendant of our *Volk* his own piece
> of land for centuries to come. We must never forget that the holiest right on this
> earth is *the right to the soil* [*Boden*] . . . and that the holiest sacrifice is the blood
> [*Blut*] that one sheds for this soil [*Boden*].
>
> Only a sufficiently large space [*grosses Raum*] on this earth guarantees that a
> nation is free to continue to exist. . . . Obtaining new land and soil [*Boden*] must
> be the aim of our foreign policy. . . . A *Volk* that protects its own soil [*Boden*] be-
> comes *heroic*. With parasites, conversely, things are different. It leads to lying hy-
> pocrisy and malicious cruelty.[140]

The semantic stipulations of the *Volksbegriff* decreed that peoples who were
bodenständig were existentially and racially superior to those who were "unrooted" or "uprooted," *boden-* or *wurzelos*. Thereby, *Bodenständigkeit* reinforced a series of ideological prejudices against "the West" as a geopolitical
"site" that had been culturally and politically "deformed" by Latinate influences, the Enlightenment, and the "ideas of 1789." Accordingly, in "The Origin
of the Work of Art" (1935–36), Heidegger lamented that the "Latinization of
Greek concepts" had culminated in the wholesale "uprootedness of Western
thought [*Bodenlosigkeit des abendländischen Denkens*]."[141]

The National Socialist employment of *Bodenständigkeit* was both ideological and polemical. It was instrumental in the construction of *Feindbilder*, or

projections of "enmity." Under Nazism, the racial distinction between "rooted" and "rootless"—*bodenständig* and *bodenlos*—peoples underwrote the subjugation and annihilation of races and groups deemed lacking in "roots": socialists and communists, Jews, Sinti and Roma, and so forth. Advocates of the *Volksbegriff* consistently disparaged *bodenlos* peoples and *mentalités* as remaining in thrall to nebulous and superficial abstractions: cultural self-understandings that, purportedly, were profoundly lacking in "substance" and "depth."

Mythos versus *Nous*

Heidegger maintained that the existential affinities between the Greeks and the Germans were grounded in the material semantics of *Erde* and *Boden*. It was the subterranean, ontological-historical kinship between these two *Völker*, Greeks and Germans, that served as the basis for Heidegger's doctrine of "another Beginning." Heidegger regarded the Greeks and the Germans as the only two authentically *"historical"* peoples, in the sense of Heideggerian *Geschichtlichkeit*. As such, they shared a common ontological-historical *Schicksal*, or "destiny."

According to Heidegger, the ontological kinship between Greeks and Germans meant that they were "stammverwandt": "racially" or "ethnically" related.[142] This judgment followed from his conviction that "blood and race [*das Blut und das Geblüt*] are essential determinants of man." "The voice of blood [*Stimme des Blutes*]," Heidegger asserted, "derives from the fundamental attunement of man [*Grundstimmung des Menschen*]."[143] The racial idiolect that Heidegger utilized in such passages was well "attuned" to the precepts of National Socialist *Rassen-* and *Bevölkerungspolitik*.

The heightened terminological prominence of "Erde" in Heidegger's thought bespoke a deepening of ideological elements in his *Denken*. It reflected Heidegger's engagement with the work of contemporary *Zivilisationskritiker* such as the former George-*Kreis* loyalist Ludwig Klages, Leopold Ziegler, Oswald Spengler, and Max Scheler—all of whose writings reinforced Heidegger's perception of the historical present as a nihilistic age of "decline."

During the 1920s, disputes over the ideological valences of "Erde" among spiritual reactionaries metamorphosed into a veritable *Kulturkampf*. The debate pitted a coalition of protofascist, conservative revolutionary thinkers against champions of *Aufklärung* such as Thomas Mann, Sigmund Freud, and Ernst

Cassirer. Widespread disillusionment with the nineteenth-century idols of "progress" and "science" had precipitated a longing for the "primordial." Increasingly, the stakes of the debate concerned the historical status of "myth." Right-wing *Zivilisationskritiker* exalted a return to "myth" as a panacea for the ills of modernity.[144] A flashpoint in the developing controversy over the cultural status of myth was the Bachofen-Renaissance of the mid-1920s.

In "Der Mythos und das Als Ob" (Myth and the As If; 1927), the neo-Kantian philosopher Hans Vaihinger expressed his misgivings concerning myth's rising cultural currency among right-wing literati and *Kulturkritiker*. "For some 25 years," Vaihinger cautioned, "there has been a noticeable increase in the voices demanding a positive evaluation of myth and mythical thinking, in general. Formerly, myth was regarded as part of the study of ancient history and folklore [*Altertumswissenschaft und Volkskunde*]. Today, conversely, myth has emerged as an increasingly important component of *Kultur*. In myth, one discovers forms of representation that no longer belong exclusively to the past; instead, they have assumed an independent role and an essential function in contemporary spiritual life. Hence, the summonses—often quite violent—for a 'New Myth' of the future."[145]

One tenet that united the "spiritual reactionary" camp was the idea that the "way forward" required a return to "prehistory": the revival of a mythical, primordial past that predated the diremptions and lacerations of Western modernity. Representatives of this view held that, by tapping into the values a mythological *Urzeit*, it would be possible to surmount the disintegrative influences of "Enlightenment," "progress," and the legacy of "1789."[146]

Among reactionary modernists, Nietzsche's exaltation of the cultural superiority of myth in the *Birth of Tragedy* (1872) became an obligatory point of reference: a powerful allegory concerning the failures of Enlightenment rationalism and the growing demand for cultural "wholeness." Nietzsche claimed, "Without Myth, all cultures lose their healthy, creative, natural energy. Only a horizon surrounded by Myths encloses and unifies a cultural movement. Only by Myth can all the energies of fantasy and Apollinian dream be saved from aimless meandering. The images of Myth [are] . . . the daemonic guardians under whose tutelage the young soul grows up and by whose signs the grown man interprets his life and his struggles; even the State knows of no more powerful unwritten laws than the Mythical fundament which guarantees its connection with religion and its emergence from Mythical representations."[147]

In the *Myth of the State* (1945), Ernst Cassirer interpreted the revival of myth as a negative cultural caesura: "Among Enlightenment thinkers, myth was viewed as something *barbaric*: an indistinct mass of confused ideas and superstitions; fundamentally: a monstrosity." Conversely, the contemporary advocates of political myth radically contested the idea of human self-determination. In doing so, they sacrificed the goal of *Mündigkeit* (autonomy) on the altar of an obscurantist "higher necessity." In light of fascism's repressive instrumentalization of political myth, Cassirer termed the reemergence of myth a "pathology of symbolic consciousness."[148]

Representative of the heightened esteem for prehistory and myth was the Romanian historian of religion Mircea Eliade's *The Myth of Eternal Return*. During the 1930s, Eliade was an avid supporter of Corneliu Codreanu's fascist "Legionnaire" movement: a filiation that confirms the important nexus between political myth and fascist ideology. In *The Myth of Eternal Return*, Eliade extolled the "longing for a periodic recourse to a mythical age of primordial origins": an era that, in comparison to the degradations of the historical present, stood out as an "Age of Greatness." According to Eliade, such epochs were distinguished by a "metaphysical 'valorization' of human existence" that had disappeared with the advent of political modernity. The outstanding characteristic of "archaic societies," Eliade alleged, was their uncompromising rebellion against history and temporality: "Although they are conscious of a certain form of 'history,' [archaic societies] make every effort to disregard it. In studying these traditional societies, one characteristic has especially struck us: *their revolt against concrete, historical time*, their nostalgia for a periodical return to the mythical time of the *beginning of things*—to the 'Age of Greatness.' . . . In our opinion, it is justifiable to read in this depreciation of history and in this rejection of profane, continuous time, *a certain metaphysical of 'valorization' of human existence*."[149]

Similarly, in *Cosmogonic Eros* (1923), Klages, a Bachofen enthusiast with whose work Heidegger engaged in *The Fundamental Concepts of Metaphysics* (1929), glorified "primal history" as a site of *Urbilder*: "archaic images" that facilitated a mystical communion between "dead souls"—"spirits" of a bygone *Urzeit*—and inhabitants of the historical present. Klages maintained that only an exceptionally gifted cenacle of "spiritual clairoyants" would be able to reconnect with these enigmatic *Urbilder*. In *Cosmogonic Eros*, Klages—who once claimed that "logic is organized darkness"—remarked,

In the ecstatic surging, life marches toward liberation from intellection [*Geist*]. Perfection consists in the awakening of the soul and . . . seeing the reality of the archetypes [*Urbilder*]. With archetypes, the souls of the past reappear. Yet, in order to appear, they need the connection with the blood of physically living beings. This occurs in the act of "seeing," which is a mystical marriage between the . . . soul of the seer and the generating demon. Upon awakening, the ecstatic knows . . . that the world of facts is merely a fantasy . . . [and] that the world of bodies signifies a world of *symbols*: . . . the monstrous products of "seeing" fertilized by the primeval world.[150]

In the *Heritage of Our Time*, Ernst Bloch disparaged Klages's infatuation with the "reactionary usefulness of 'myth' [lodged] in the collective-archaic unconscious" as a regressive "Tarzan philosophy."[151]

In a manner similar to Klages, Heidegger, too, equated "authentic experience" with "primordial experience." In the years that followed the publication of *Being and Time*, Heidegger's appeals to "Ursprünglichkeit" and "Urgeschichte"—"primordiality" and "primal history"—became increasingly frequent. As Stefan Günzel has shown in *Geophilosophie*, Heidegger's longing for a return to "primal history" reflected his conviction that, in order to recapture "primordial experience," it would be necessary to reconnect with a pristine, mythical *Urzeit*: an age that preceded the decimation of Being by Western metaphysics.[152] As Frank Edler has remarked in an article that reconstructs Heidegger's path to the pre-Socratics, as kindled by his interpretation of Hölderlin, "If the second part of *Being and Time* was supposed to include a dismantling of the Western philosophical tradition in order to uncover a more originary understanding of Being, then the dismantling or deconstruction (*Abbau*) would have to deal with the problems of explicating *mythic Dasein* and *scientific Dasein* as two fundamental possibilities of Being-in-the-world, [thereby] retrieving a more originary understanding of the relationship between mythos and logos, and reconstructing the conditions for the possibility of the transformation of the historical existence of a people."[153]

Rejecting Kant's caveat in the concluding paragraphs of *The Critique of Pure Reason* concerning the perils of philosophical dogmatism ("The critical path alone is open to us"), Heidegger increasingly came to regard "cognition" (*Erkenntnistheorie*) as an obstacle or barrier that interfered with the possibility of reviving "primordial experience."[154] Heidegger contended that the "the model of 'consciousness' . . . *obscured* the fundamental question of Being. It remained dependent upon a philosophical tradition that Heidegger aimed to overcome."[155]

Accordingly, following the completion of *Being and Time*, Heidegger's *Denken* displayed an increasing fascination with the epistemological value of myth.

The new prominence that "prehistory" and "myth" assumed in Heidegger's work emerged in the review essay that he penned, in 1928, of Ernst Cassirer's *Mythical Thought* (1925), the second volume of Cassirer's *Philosophy of Symbolic Forms*.[156] In the review, which Heidegger drafted in preparation for the Davos debate, he voiced his reservations concerning Cassirer's neo-Kantian attempt to devalue myth as an autonomous source of insight and meaning. Hence, in the opening paragraphs, Heidegger reproached Cassirer for his deprecatory treatment of "mythical thinking" vis-à-vis "purely logical thought": as a "manner of seeing" (*Anschauungsform*) that was only appropriate for a bygone, primitive "form of life."[157]

In *Mythical Thought*, Cassirer depicted "mythical consciousness" as saturated with "sensuous" and "imagistic" elements. Heidegger, conversely, in a more positive vein, stressed the parallels between "mythical Dasein" and his own concept of "thrownness" (*Geworfenheit*). "Mythical Dasein," asserted Heidegger, "is primarily determined through 'thrownness.' "[158] "Thrownness," explained Heidegger, attested to the fact that Dasein was "overpowered" and "intoxicated" (*benommen*) by the world. Thus, according to Heidegger, "thrownness" corresponded to the way that "mythical Dasein" was "delivered over" to and "overpowered" by "mana," or the "sacred": a comportment that, as Heidegger enthusiastically put it, expressed an openness to what "*is always in each case . . . remarkably extraordinary* [*das überraschende Ausserordentliche*]."[159] "Thrownness" and "mythical Dasein" resembled each other, Heidegger contended, by virtue of their mutual openness to "primordial Being": a receptivity that rational cognition, owing to its intellectualist biases, had foreclosed.

In essence, Heidegger sought to *invert* the priority of *reason* over *myth* that was implicit in Cassirer's Enlightenment-oriented account. In opposition to Cassirer's efforts to consign myth to the realm of "phantasy," Heidegger revalued "*myth* [as] *an essential phenomenon within a universal interpretation of Being*."[160] In support of his claims concerning the cognitive superiority of myth, Heidegger invoked, as a significant precedent, Schelling's "positive" assessment of myth in *Introduction to the Philosophy of Mythology* (1841–42). Heidegger alleged that Schelling's outstanding achievement in *Philosophy of Mythology* was his understanding of "myth" as an expression of the "destiny of the *Volk*."[161]

The correlation between "myth" and the "destiny of the *Volk*" to which Heidegger adverted in his Cassirer critique presaged the centrality that the conceptual triad of "Schicksal," "Volk," and "Mythos" would attain in Heidegger's later *Denken*. Thus, in *On the Essence of Truth*, Heidegger reconceived philosophy's "task" as the "encouragement, struggle, and veneration of a *Volk* for the sake of the *hardness* and *clarity* of its *destiny* [*das Fordern, Hadern, und Verehren eines Volkes um der Härte und Klarheit seines Schicksals willen*]."[162]

For Heidegger, the epistemological superiority of myth resided in its greater "proximity" (*Nähe*) to "primordiality" and to "origins." Accordingly, in *An Introduction to Metaphysics*, Heidegger exalted "Mythology" as "*knowledge of prehistory [Wissen von Ur-Geschichte]*." "The authenticity and greatness of historical knowledge," Heidegger continued, "rests with understanding the mysterious character of this Beginning [*Geheimnischarakters dieses Anfangs*]."[163] Conversely, Heidegger maintained that Cassirer, by consigning myth to a lower rung on the cognitive-evolutionary ladder, had perpetuated philosophy's status qua "Irrnis": a negative continuum of *Seinsvergessenheit*. Heidegger's defense of the ontological value of myth reflected his conviction that only by returning to "prehistory" would it be possible to offset the West's precipitous, headlong descent toward *Untergang*.

Heidegger's reappraisal of myth as an ontological-historical construct sheds light on his abrupt disavowal of first philosophy circa the early 1930s. As he declaimed in the *Black Notebooks*, "We must bring [philosophy] to an end in order to prepare the way for the totally Other: viz., Metapolitics."[164] Heidegger's denigration of metaphysics, owing to its disintegrative and destructive logocentric biases, presaged his pivot toward the "metapolitics of the historical *Volk*."[165]

At Davos, Cassirer was undoubtedly taken aback by the nihilistic, antiphilosophical turn that Heidegger's *Denkweg* had assumed—a development that reflected his growing attraction to *Vernunftkritik*. At one point during their colloquy, Heidegger asserted that essential philosophical questioning "leads man beyond himself into the totality of beings in order to make manifest to him there . . . the nothingness of his Dasein." "Nothingness," Heidegger continued, "is not the occasion for pessimism and melancholy. Instead, it is the occasion for understanding that . . . philosophy has the task of throwing man back into the hardness of his fate from the shallowness of a man who merely 'uses' the work of spirit."[166]

Heidegger's denigration of the "spiritual shallowness" of those who shirk the "hardness of fate" was pointedly directed at Cassirer and his fellow neo-Kantians: a guild that, by devaluing the cognitive potential of myth, re-mained wedded to the anachronistic, "life-denying" value-ideals of the Enlight-enment and Western humanism.

Only in retrospect, or *après coup*, did Cassirer realize that "Heidegger's in-terpretation of myth in the 1920s not only had significant theoretical implica-tions, but also held a certain responsibility for the actual propagation of the most ominous expression of political myth in the modern period"—that is, Na-zism.[167] Cassirer lamented that, under National Socialism, "Germany had re-nounced all of the ideas that were responsible for the form-giving powers of its *Kultur*. . . . It became a *genuine witches' sabbath*: a recrudescence of the most primitive images and beliefs [*Auffassungen*], a profusion of the most violent passions, and an orgy of hatred and rage."[168]

The instrumentalization of myth for political ends was one of the defining hallmarks of the fascist worldview. In *The Myth of the State*, Cassirer sought to evaluate the crucial role that political myth had played in legitimating fascism as a regime of symbolic power. Cassirer demonstrated that the resurrection of political myth—the "myth of race" in the thought of Comte Arthur de Gob-ineau; the "myth of the hero" in the work of Thomas Carlyle—had abetted Nazism's efforts to consolidate a seamless web of ideological illusion: an im-pregnable semantic veil that preempted dissent and manufactured a semblance of totalitarian unanimity.

Cassirer recognized that fascism's aspirations to ideological hegemony were inextricably tied to the "power of myth and myth of power," both of which proved destructive of autonomy and spontaneity.[169] "Nothing," remarked Cassirer, "is more likely to lull asleep all our active forces, our power of judgment and critical discernment, and to take away our feeling of personality and individual responsi-bility than the steady, uniform, and monotonous performance of the same *rites*. . . . In all primitive societies ruled and governed by rites, individual responsibility is an unknown thing. What we find here is only a collective responsibility. Not the individuals, but the group is the real 'moral subject.' The clan, the family, and the whole tribe are responsible for the actions of all the members."[170]

By reconceiving questions of political legitimacy as matters of "faith" or "belief," fascism's instrumentalization of political myth—the "New Man," "Romanità," the "Führer as political Savior"—helped to immunize it against the demystifying powers of reason and critique. The "epistemology of fascism" explicitly scorned science and empirical truth as atavisms of the much-despised "liberal era." Conversely, it exalted myth as the repository of a superior, "meta-historical" reality. In this way, the manipulation of myth for political ends contributed significantly to fascism's trademark "sacralization of politics."[171]

It was in this vein that, in *Mythos oder Religion* (1935), Paul Simon—a prescient and indefatigable Catholic critic of the Nazi worldview—perceptively traced National Socialism's ideological origins to the mythological longings of "Bachofen, Nietzsche, Houston Stewart Chamberlain, and Stefan George."[172] Simon maintained that, by consciously mobilizing the semantics of political religion, Nazi ideologues aspired to "mold" the Third Reich into "a Holy Myth." "The Confessional Creed of the SS" (SS *Glaubensbekenntnis*)—a crucial statement of the National Socialist worldview—declared that Nazism's ultimate goal was a "return to the past in order to build once and for all a new future": "*We return to our roots*: to the roots of the Germanic man, to the roots that shape our destiny."[173]

In the context at hand, it is worth recalling that the most important contribution to the National Socialist ideological canon apart from *Mein Kampf*, Alfred Rosenberg's *Myth of the Twentieth Century*, repeatedly appealed to the regenerative powers of "myth." The "myth" of Rosenberg's title was, of course, the myth of "race."

The Quest for "Primordiality"

In *The Metaphysical Foundations of Logic* (1928), Heidegger refined the positive evaluation of myth that he had outlined in his Cassirer review. Reflecting on temporality's significance for *Seinsgeschichte*, Heidegger highlighted the epistemological entwinement of "myth" and "primal history": a philosophical chess move that culminated in a qualitative transformation of his understanding of "knowledge." Thereafter, Heidegger viewed "mythical thought"—"das Mythische"—as an epistemic modality that, in contrast to theoretical knowledge, permitted access to the experiential fullness of "primal history." Heidegger claimed that the epistemological superiority of myth was reflected in its capacity to facilitate a metaphysical encounter with primordial Being: an encounter that approximated an "epiphany" as opposed to an act of cognition. Such encounters were barred to "first philosophy" qua *Wissenschaft*, or *theoria*.

Heidegger lauded "primordial history"—"Urgeschichte"—as a prelapsarian ontological fundament: an experiential "ground" that was impervious to the decay and ruination of historical time. Following the publication of *Being and*

Time, "primordial history" became the focal point of Heidegger's recalibration of *Geschichtlichkeit*. As the following passage from *The Metaphysical Foundations of Logic* attests, Heidegger's turn toward "Urgeschichte," as a repository of ontological plentitude, was intimately tied to his exaltation of the "metaphysics of myth": "The entrance into the world by beings is *primordial history* [*Urgeschichte*], purely and simply. From this primordial history, there necessarily develops a region of problems that, today, we are beginning to approach with greater clarity: the region of the Mythic [*das Mythische*]. The *metaphysics of myth* must come to be understood on the basis of this primordial history: with the help of a metaphysical construction of a primordial age [*Urzeit*], which is the age [*Zeit*] with which primordial history [*Urgeschichte*] itself begins."[174]

Heidegger's glorification of the "metaphysics of myth" was profoundly motivated by cultural-political considerations. Heidegger maintained that "prehistory" offered a constructive, "holistic" alternative to the spiritual imperfections of Western modernity. In Heidegger's eyes, myth's experiential superiority derived from the unique access it offered to an Edenic "Ur-Zeit": a "primal past" in which the ontological unity of *Geist*, *Volk*, and *Bodenständigkeit* remained intact. In Heidegger's view, the "perdurance" (*Austrag*) of mythical time contrasted sharply with the disintegrative temporality of the "liberal era," which, following Spengler, Heidegger rejected as a time of *Untergang*.

In *Heidegger in seiner Zeit*, Otto Pöggeler confirmed that Heidegger's turn toward "primordial history" and the "metaphysics of myth" represented a caesura or breach in his understanding of "temporality" and "historicity"—a breach that had begun with his review of Cassirer's study of *Mythical Thought*: "Heidegger's review of Ernst Cassirer's study of myth highlighted the 'overpowering nature' of the Mana-idea that resided in Myth, an idea that divided time and the world into sacred and profane. Hence, in Heidegger's summer 1928 lecture course, he declared that one must comprehend the 'metaphysics of myth' with the help of a 'metaphysical construction of primal history': on the basis of 'primordial fact' [*Urfaktum*] and 'prehistory' [*Urgeschichte*]."[175]

Heidegger perceived "primordial history" as the basis or ground of a mythically oriented "counterhistory." It was a perspective that he tasked with overturning the modern narrative of "progress," which he viewed as "lebensfeindlich," or "hostile to life."[176] The heightened prominence of these tendencies in Heidegger's work signified a deepening of the "reactionary modernist" and "zivilisationskritisch" dimension of his thought.[177]

Commenting on the politicization of *Lebensphilosophie* during the 1920s, Georg Lukács noted the increasingly prominent role played by the "mythical element." As Lukács noted, "The more militantly reactionary these myths became, the more directly they anticipated fascist myth."[178]

In *The Mass Psychology of Fascism* (1933), Wilhelm Reich warned—in terms strikingly redolent of Lukács's reflections—that the reactionary modernist glorification of a mythologized "primal past" openly courted the risk of collective-psychological regression. In Reich's view, such retrograde yearnings for a mythological *Urzeit* paralleled fascism's longing for "a cultural period in which life had not yet broken away from the harmony of nature." According to Reich, fascism's longing for "brute nature" misleadingly glorified an "unconscious lawfulness that is always lacking in the works of free reflection." Prophetically, Reich perceived the central danger of fascism as the collective desire "to escape the difficulties of responsibility and the actualities of everyday life . . . by seeking refuge in ideology, illusion, mysticism, or brutality."[179]

In *Pariser Rechenschaft* (1926), Thomas Mann voiced similar misgivings concerning myth's expanding cultural currency among conservative revolutionary intellectuals. During World War I, Mann had been one of Germany's most prominent *Zivilisationskritiker*, as his proto-Spenglerian lamentations about Western "decline" in *Reflections of a Nonpolitical Man* (1918) demonstrate. However, the brutal assassination of the Weimar Republic's Jewish foreign minister, Walter Rathenau, in 1922, by right-wing thugs, compelled Mann to reassess his earlier "antiliberalism."[180]

Reflecting on the retrograde nature of the escalating appeals to "primordiality" and "myth," Mann concluded that it would be politically irresponsible "to expose the Germans to such 'night terrors' [*Nachtschwärmerei*]: this entire Joseph Görres–complex of *Earth, Volk, Nature, Prehistory*, and *Death*, this *revolutionary obscurantism* . . . that, lately, has gained such currency."[181] Little did Mann realize how prophetic his misgivings would prove to be, only a few years later, with the Nazi *Machtergreifung*.

The "Metaphysics of Myth"

Mann's qualms concerning the potential for cultural regression that was lodged in the widespread appeals to the "night terrors of Earth, Volk, Nature, Prehistory, and Death" had been provoked by his reading of Alfred Baeumler's

Bachofen: Der Mythologe der Romantik (Bachofen: The Mythologist of Romanticism; 1926), a three-hundred-page introduction to a recently published anthology of the—academically discredited—Swiss historian and philologist Johann Jakob Bachofen's (1815–87) writings.

Mann's forebodings correctly sensed that the Bachofen renaissance was symptomatic of a troubling spiritual caesura in the life of the fledgling Weimar Republic: a breach that portended the hardening of an anti-Western, antidemocratic metapolitical orientation among the right-wing intelligentsia. A year earlier, the former George-*Kreis* adherent Ludwig Klages had edited and introduced a new edition of Bachofen's *Essay on the Funerary Symbolism of the Ancients*.[182] So poorly received was Bachofen's *Essay* when it first appeared in 1859 that, shortly thereafter, the University of Basel revoked his qualifications as a *Privatdozent*.

Bachofen had been a promising student of the University of Berlin historian and founder of the historical school of law Friedrich Carl von Savigny (1779–1861). However, in midcareer, he turned his back on "scientific" history in favor of an esoteric, divinatory approach to understanding the past that was inspired by the late Romantic Georg Friedrich Creuzer's conception of the "symbol" as an autonomous fount of insight and meaning: a source whose arcana remained inaccessible to the methods of "scholarly" (*wissenschaftlich*) history writing. Instead, the epiphanies lodged in the symbol could only be extracted via the technique of intuitive-imaginary conjuring. By reversing the Enlightenment narrative of "progress" and, thereby, disrupting the linearity of chronological history, Bachofen's "symbolic" approach aimed not merely to *revisit* the archaic past. It sought to *reactivate* prehistory's semantic potentials in the here and now.

Undeterred by the critical acid bath to which *Funerary Symbolism of the Ancients* had been subjected, two years later, relying on his trademark, intuitive-divinatory method, Bachofen published his magnum opus, *Mother Right: An Investigation Concerning Gynocracy in the Ancient World with Respect to Its Religious and Legal Nature* (1861). In *Mother Right* (*Mutterrecht*), Bachofen glorified a prelapsarian age in which humanity and Mother Earth purportedly dwelled in a state of blissful, mutual symbiosis. According to Bachofen, proximity to humanity's chthonic, primordial origins provided a guarantee of cosmological unity. "Generative Motherhood," proclaimed Bachofen, "is the basis of universal brotherhood among men." "The development of paternity, conversely, caused this condition to disintegrate."[183] Thus, in Bachofen's view, the patriarchal warrior societies that superseded ancient matriarchy signified a palpable fall from grace.

The evidentiary basis for Bachofen's conjectures concerning the existence of an archaic-matriarchal Eden was negligible. Following *Mutterrecht*'s publication, whatever remaining credibility Bachofen possessed as a historian and scholar dissipated. As Robert Norton noted in *Secret Germany*, "Poorly printed, cluttered, badly organized, and seemingly formless, [*Mother Right*] came out in only fifty copies and was greeted with stony silence by the scholarly world. Not a single review of the book was ever published. When Bachofen died in 1887, at the age of 72, his passing was barely registered."[184]

Thomas Mann's Baeumler critique in *Pariser Rechenschaft* presciently identified a dilemma or challenge that, within a few years' time, would preoccupy Heidegger's work: a challenge that derived from his efforts to reorient fundamental ontology toward the "metaphysics of myth."

The Heidegger-Baeumler Alliance

Following the publication of *Being and Time*, Heidegger reconceived *Geschichtlichkeit* so that it might accommodate the "subterranean" experiences of a primordial *Urzeit*. In recent years, a critical consensus has emerged suggesting that Heidegger's reformulation of the *Seinsfrage* was inspired by his encounter with Baeumler's profoundly Nietzschean Bachofen interpretation. In the words of one scholar,

> What originally brought [Heidegger and Baeumler] together was their shared concern for the archaic and chthonic sources of Greek culture and its relevance for contemporary Germany. . . . In his essay dealing with the archaic and mythic sources of Western culture [*Bachofen: The Mythologist of Romanticism*], Baeumler set out the principles of a chthonic philosophy of history, a project that caught Heidegger's attention. Drawing on what Bachofen termed "tellurism"—the archaic principle that sees the essential meaning of human life as rooted in and arising from the Earth or Soil—. . . Baeumler focused on the meaning of the Earth in the formation of ancient culture. . . . Rejecting Winckelmann's fable about the "noble simplicity and calm grandeur" of Hellenic culture, Baeumler put forward a forceful account of the *subterranean, telluric, and chthonic elements* that shaped the archaic world of the Greeks that lay dormant in the modern epoch. Only by

recovering the originary power of these chthonic forces, Baeumler argued, could the Germans defeat the new Olympian forces of Enlightenment, democracy, liberalism, and internationalism that threatened to destroy modern Europe.[185]

The friendship between Heidegger and Baeumler spanned the years 1928–33. Heidegger read Baeumler's compendious Bachofen introduction in 1928, in preparation for his Cassirer review and the Davos disputation. So impressed was Heidegger with Baeumler's efforts to "actualize" Bachofen's understanding of "primordial history" that he immediately wrote to Baeumler, urging him to apply for the philosophy chair in Marburg that Heidegger had recently vacated in order to accept the Husserl-*Lehrstuhl* in Freiburg.

Baeumler confirmed these circumstances in a letter of 17 May 1928 to Walter Eberhardt: "Heidegger wrote to me spontaneously to ask for my curriculum vita; he would like to propose me as his successor [in Marburg]."[186] In a missive of 3 November, Heidegger informed Karl Jaspers that he had, indeed, nominated Baeumler for the recently vacated Marburg position.[187] Although Heidegger's efforts to install Baeumler as his successor at Marburg came to naught, a few months later, Baeumler was offered an assistant professorship at the University of Dresden.

Prior to becoming a Bachofen enthusiast and exegete, Baeumler had carved out a respectable niche as a scholar of German Idealism. In 1923, his *Habilitationsschrift* on Kant's *Critique of Judgment* was published by the highly esteemed Max Niemeyer Verlag in Halle. However, upon completing his Kant study, Baeumler rejected German Idealism due to its faulty equation of "cognition" with "intellection" and "rational synthesis": a failing that accounted for Idealism's inability to accede, claimed Baeumler, to a "logic of Totality."[188]

Thereafter, Baeumler shifted his focus to the late Romanticism of the Heidelberg School: a transformation that Baeumler characterized as a "step from eighteenth-century aesthetics and philosophy to the romanticism of [Joseph] Görres."[189] Baeumler claimed that only a new understanding of history as "myth"—as a counterweight to "scientific" history writing—could reunite humanity with its archaic-cosmological origins, its "ground" in primordial Being. In Baeumler's eyes, by interpreting historical artifacts as "symbols," rather than as a disjunctive compilation of empirical-scientific "findings," Bachofen's intuitive-divinatory method was able to reprise the condition of "primordial oneness" characteristic of the long-lost *Ur-Zeit*.

In 1931, Baeumler published his influential monograph *Nietzsche als Philosoph und Politiker*, which set the tone for the National Socialist canonization of Nietzsche. (Baeumler sent an autographed copy to Hitler, whom he had met a few months earlier at the "Brown House" in Munich.) Baeumler's pivot toward Nietzschean "active nihilism" during the late 1920s—a "turn" that was foreshadowed by his 1928 essay on "Nietzsche and Bachofen"—reflected his new "metapolitical" ambitions. It also paralleled his growing rapprochement with National Socialism.[190]

In "Nietzsche and National Socialism" (1934), Baeumler recounted the intellectual trajectory that had led him from "Bachofen to Nietzsche." Baeumler explained that Nietzsche's celebration of "heroism" and "activism" had furnished the elements of "self-assertion" and "will" that were sorely lacking in Romanticism's understanding of "German *Existenz*." According to Baeumler, in contrast to the Enlightenment,

> Romanticism saw man again in the light of his *natural and historical ties*. Romanticism opened our eyes to the *night, the past, our ancestors*, to *Mythos* and *Volk*. The movement that led from Herder to Görres, to the brothers Grimm, Eichendorff, Arnim, and Savigny is the only spiritual movement that is still fully alive. . . . Nevertheless, today, we have discovered new possibilities for understanding the essence of German *Existenz* through Nietzsche, the philosopher of *heroism* . . . [and] *activism*. . . . "Works" result not from the desire for "display" . . . but from *practice*, from the ever-repeated *deed* [*Tat*]. . . . Thereby, [Nietzsche] reestablished the purity of the sphere of action and the political sphere.[191]

Baeumler's vitalistic naturalism, coupled with his harsh polemics against "modernity" and "subjectivity," paved the way for his celebration of "race values" (*Rassenwerte*) that had been "decreed by fate" (*schicksalhaft Gegebenes*). Following his conversion to "Nietzsche and National Socialism," Baeumler viewed history as a Heraclitean "polemos," or "struggle," that pitted "creative" Indo-Germanic races against "destructive" races, such as "international Jewry."[192] As Christian Tilitzki explains in his reconstruction of Baeumler's intellectual-political odyssey, "From the Conservative Revolution to National Socialism," "Those who, like Baeumler, were strongly fixated on the metaphysical distinctiveness of the *Volkscharakter*, who attributed the defeat of 1918 to national disunity, . . . who perceived untrustworthy, liberally minded Jewish intellectuals and politicians lurking behind the ideas of 'humanity' and 'humaneness,' and who regarded Jewish cosmopolitanism as a fifth column, unavoidably came to believe that national unity depended on an ethnically based integration capacity of citizens."[193]

In light of Heidegger's developing fascination with "das Mythische" as a privileged repository of truth, it is not difficult to discern what it was about Baeumler's Bachofen interpretation that aroused his enthusiasm. In solidarity with Nietzsche's rebuke of "antiquarian history" in *The Use and Abuse of History*— as Nietzsche observed, "When the study of history serves the life of the past in such a way that it undermines ... higher life, when the historical sense no longer conserves life but *mummifies it*, ... man is encased in the stench of must and mold, ... in the dust of bibliographical minutiae"[194]—Heidegger, too, rejected desiccated, narrowly scholarly approaches to understanding the ancient world. He became convinced that recovering the "primordial past" depended on resuscitating subterranean forms of knowledge: cognitive strategies that paralleled Bachofen's esoteric efforts to reanimate the glories of the archaic past. In all of these respects, Heidegger perceived Bachofen's oeuvre, as elucidated by Baeumler, as a valuable precedent.

In an informative essay on the "Heidegger-Baeumler relationship," Frank Edler has plausibly suggested that Heidegger's interest in Baeumler's Bachofen-*Deutung* was motivated by three insights: "(1) [Baeumler's] radical reinterpretation of the origin of Greek tragedy based on a chthonic Dionysus associated with the cult of dead heroes; (2) his attempt to uncover a new sense of history based on the exegesis of mythic symbols; and (3) [Baeumler's] claim that Hölderlin and Nietzsche represented attempts, in the German tradition, to liberate Greek antiquity from the domination of Roman and Christian interpretations."[195]

A cursory glance at Heidegger's *Rektoratsrede* provides support for Edler's claim concerning the pivotal role that Nietzsche played in Heidegger's scheme to resuscitate the Greek "Anfang." Praising Nietzsche as "the last German philosopher," Heidegger reformulated the mission of "science/*Wissenschaft*" as "obedience to the distant decree of the Beginning [Anfang]." In this way alone, Heidegger insisted—in other words, by heeding the strictures of Nietzsche's critique of "antiquarian history"—might "science become the fundamental event of our spiritual Dasein as a *Volk* [*geistig-volklichen Daseins*]."[196]

Additional evidence attesting to the value that Heidegger ascribed to Baeumler's "reactionary modernist" Bachofen interpretation stems from a missive that Heidegger wrote, in May 1932, to his trusted correspondent and paramour,

Elisabeth Blochmann, in which he urged Blochmann to consult a text that Baeumler had recently published on Bachofen's theory of natural law. His reservations concerning Bachofen's "methodology," notwithstanding, Heidegger stressed that, in Bachofen's work, "important matters are perceived": "A very useful Bachofen anthology, *Primordial Religion and the Symbols of Antiquity*, has been published by Reclam in three volumes. As you know, much of this is controversial. The methodology is not convincing, nor is it applicable in all places. Nevertheless, *important matters are perceived*. The short text edited by Alfred Baeumler entitled *J. J. Bachofen: Autobiography and Inaugural Address on Natural Law* is excellent on Bachofen himself."[197]

In the years that followed, Heidegger internalized the methods of "subterranean philosophizing" in order to reanimate the repressed, chthonic dimension of pre-Socratic Dasein: a component of archaic *Existenz* that was rooted in *Erde* and *Boden* and that had been obfuscated by the sterile methods of conventional "scholarship."[198] In Heidegger's eyes, the "destinings" (*Schickungen*) of the "Anfang" or "Urzeit" portended a countermovement to contemporary "nihilism." Heidegger perceived the first stirrings and hints of this world-historical "countermovement" in National Socialism's "construction of a world rooted in the *Volk* [*volklich gegründete Welt*]." He perceived National Socialism as an ontological-historical cryptogram: a metapolitical destiny capable of reinvigorating the repressed, "subterranean" trajectory of "Western-Germanic historical Dasein." The task of "science" was to assist in the retrieval and recovery of "origins," a mission that anticipated the West's rebirth following the long night of *Seinsvergessenheit*.[199] As such, Heidegger's commitment to the epistemological value of "myth"—an orientation that had been catalyzed by Baeumler's Bachofen interpretation—would play a pivotal role in his understanding of National Socialism as an *Ereignis*: an "Event" in the "history of Being."

Heidegger's embrace of the "metaphysics of myth" paralleled his turn toward the "metapolitics of the historical *Volk*." However, in order for this "metapolitical" project to become a reality, "the Germans would need to dispense with the complacency of *Altertumswissenschaft* and its scientific model of truth in favor of a new, Nietzschean style of 'subterranean philosophizing': an approach that would retrieve the originality and chthonic forces of archaic *alētheia*. . . . Henceforth, revolutionary upheaval would not be aimed at the history of philosophy, but at the destiny of the Germans within Europe and the West."[200]

In the illuminating essay "Heidegger's Discovery of Myth," Daniel Meyer has proposed that Heidegger's ontological veneration of "myth" was inherently tied to a discourse of fascist political legitimacy. Meyer convincingly argues that the discourse of Heideggerian *Seinsgeschichte* "embedded the National Socialist *Machtergreifung* in an overarching, historico-philosophical narrative. Thereby, Heidegger's understanding of the Greek '*Anfang*' merged with a philosophical justification of National Socialism's political prospects. On these grounds, Heidegger exalted National Socialism . . . as a recrudescence of Myth."[201]

Heidegger's strategy of "retrieval and recovery" culminated in his Hölderlin lectures of 1934–35, in which he interpreted Hölderlin's *Dichtung* as an onto-logical-historical cipher: as an augur or portent of gnostic knowledge in which the "subterranean" affinities between the "Greek *Anfang*" and the "metaphysics of German Dasein" commingled.[202] Hence, Heidegger's celebration of Hölderlin as the "poet of the Germans" (*Dichter der Deutschen*) and as the "founder of German Being" (*Stifter des deutschen Seyns*).[203]

Heidegger, invoking a leitmotif that he had imbibed from the Stefan George-*Kreis*, lauded Hölderlin as the poet of "secret Germany." A similar figure or trope emerged in the *Black Notebooks*, in the course of Heidegger's appeal to the redemptive powers of "die verborgene Deutschheit," or "hidden German-ness."[204] For Heidegger, the meaning of "secret Germany" became clear in his Hölderlin-inspired, eschatological vision of a "Greco-German affiliation, . . . a mythic crossing of pre-Socratic philosophy and National Socialist politics."[205]

Reassessing the "Metapolitics of Myth"

Heidegger's recourse to the metapolitics of myth suggests the timeliness of reconsidering the philosophical stakes of the Heidegger-Cassirer dispute. Cassirer laid the groundwork for this reconsideration in *The Myth of the State*, in which he sought to fathom the causes underlying modern Germany's regression to a politics of full-blown racial idolatry: a moral-cognitive *lapsus* that, during the 1930s, assumed pan-European proportions.

Cassirer based his insights on a spate of recent anthropological findings and noted that, whereas tribal societies typically relied on pragmatic and utilitarian methods of coping with their environments, at times of acute crisis, they regressed to the practices of magic and myth. In Cassirer's view, a parallel situation had emerged in the case of European fascism, one of whose distinguishing traits was a significant recrudescence of political myth. As Cassirer remarked, "In politics, we are always living on volcanic soil. . . . In critical moments of human social life, the rational forces that resist the rise of the old mythical conceptions are no longer sure of themselves. In such moments, the time for *myth* has come again. . . . In desperate situations, man will have recourse to desperate means—and our present-day political myths embody such desperate means. If reason has failed us, there always remains the *ultima ratio*, the power of the miraculous and the mysterious."[206]

The European crisis had been marked by a widespread and acute loss of self-confidence in modern society's intrinsic problem-solving abilities. As the societal collective's self-confidence waned, traditional sources of political legitimacy—respect for custom, law, and inherited social authority—were radically devalued. As a result, the body politic became increasingly receptive to the twin seductions of charisma and political myth. As Cassirer observed, "The call for [charismatic] leadership only appears when . . . all hopes of fulfilling this desire in an ordinary and normal way have failed. . . . What alone remains is the mystical power and authority of the leader." In this way, "the leader's will is elevated to supreme law."[207]

Unlike traditional myths, modern political myths are "ideologies" that have been consciously constructed and manufactured. Hence, in comparison with earlier myths, modern political myth is decidedly more complex. As Cassirer noted, "The new political myths . . . are *artificial things* fabricated by very skillful and cunning artisans." In the future, he continued, "they can be manufactured . . . according to the same methods as any other modern weapons: as machine guns or airplanes."[208]

The "prefabricated" character of modern political myths highlighted yet another regressive feature that accompanied their emergence: a worrisome debasement of the communicative function of language. According to Cassirer, one of the hallmarks of political myth was that the magical use of language superseded its exoteric, denotative capacities. Modern political myth contributed to the mystification of political authority by semantically obfuscating its contours and content. By obscuring social transparency, political myths thwarted the prospects of democratic will-formation and popular sovereignty, desiderata that are the lifeblood of modern democracy.[209] As Cassirer remarked,

In the history of human speech, the word fulfills two entirely different functions. . . . These functions are the *semantic* and *magical* use of the word. . . . In primitive societies, the magical use predominates. . . . In the [magician's or the sorcerer's] hands, the word becomes a powerful weapon. Nothing can resist its force.

If we study modern political myths and the use that has been made of them, we find . . . not only a transvaluation of our ethical values, but a transformation of human speech. *The magic word takes precedence over the semantic word.* . . . Nothing is more likely to lull asleep all our active forces, our powers of judgment and critical discernment . . . than the steady, uniform, and monotonous performance of the same [linguistic] rites.[210]

Cassirer's insights concerning the regressive tendencies that are endemic to political myth underline the risks that beset Heidegger's enthusiasm for the "metaphysics of myth": that is, the way that Heidegger's glorification of the "subterranean" powers of *Boden*, *Volk*, and *Erde* informed his perception of the links between *Seinsgeschichte* and *Seinspolitik*.

Heideggerian *Seinsgeschichte* sought to reestablish a "metaphysics of myth." By reconceiving language fatalistically as an emanation of Being, Heidegger seriously undermined the capacities of language as "critique." By denigrating the defetishizing powers of language, Heidegger downplayed the pivotal role that "discourse" (*Rede*) plays in demystifying dogmatic claims to social authority. If, as Hans Blumenberg claimed, the "legitimacy of the modern age" is necessarily tied to the project of human self-determination, Heidegger's "ontological fatalism" presents itself as a stumbling block to the goal of emancipation in all of its modalities and manifestations.[211]

Seinsgeschichte glorified "fate" by endowing it with a superior and unwarranted ontological dignity. As a result, Heidegger's "ontological fatalism" systematically devalued inner-worldly learning processes.[212] Thereby, it sought to subordinate practical reason to a network of compulsory, preordained ontological antecedents: imperatives that were inimical to the goals of human freedom. Thereby, Heidegger—a thinker who once avowed, "Let not ideas and doctrines be your guide. Today, the Führer alone is the present and future *German reality* and its law"[213]—denigrated the accumulated store of secular human knowledge as an insignificant "blip" amid the continuum of *Seinsvergessenheit*. As Hannah Arendt cautioned in "What Is Existential Philosophy?" (1945), underlying "Heidegger's ontological approach lay a *functionalism* . . . [in which] man is no more than his modes of Being or functions in the world."[214] In Arendt's view,

Heidegger's degradation of being-human to a series of inert and reified functions was already apparent in his portrayal of "everyday Being-in-the-world" in *Being and Time*. So thoroughly enmeshed was Dasein in mechanisms of social conformity that its existence came to approximate the inanimate being of *things*.

Whereas Kant's moral philosophy foregrounded the nexus between moral autonomy and human freedom, Heidegger, in his haste to disqualify the ideal of self-positing subjectivity, consigned human being to new forms of heteronomy. According to Arendt, the problem with Heidegger's "ontological functionalism" was that it rashly "dispensed with all those human characteristics that Kant . . . had defined as *freedom, human dignity, and reason*." Thereby, Heidegger's philosophy suppressed the capacities of "spontaneity" that, as Arendt put it, allowed men and women "*to reach beyond themselves*": to surpass heteronomous, thing-like Existenz in order to become self-actualizing beings.[215]

When pressed in the "Letter on Humanism" to explicate the difference between Being and beings, Heidegger embraced a standpoint that, with breathtaking frankness, glorified humanity's subordination to nameless and mysterious Higher Powers. "*Man does not decide whether and how beings appear, whether and how God and the gods or History and Nature come forward into the lighting of Being, come to presence and depart*," Heidegger avowed. "*The advent of beings lies in the destiny of Being*."[216]

The ontological determinism of Heideggerian *Seinsgeschichte* proved to be little more than an updated version of Greek *moira*: an exaltation of "fate" that contrasted sharply with the humanistic aspirations of the Greek Enlightenment. Socrates and his philosophical heirs proudly concerned themselves with "human things." By sacrificing "autonomy" on the altar of ontological heteronomy, Heidegger's recourse to pre-Socratic "physis" represented a step backward.

Heidegger's understanding of *Seinsgeschichte* consciously rejected Hegel's view of history as "progress in the consciousness of freedom." Instead, Heidegger's *Denken* sought refuge in a "new mythology": a mythology that was predicated on the tropes of *Seinsverlassenheit* and *Gottesverlassenheit*, both of which were atavisms of central European *Kulturpessimismus*. For Heidegger, the modern world was determined by a twofold "absence": the "no longer" of the gods that had fled and the "not yet" of the gods to come. In the postwar period, Heidegger embellished this condition of heteronomy rhetorically qua *Gelassenheit*, or "releasement," thereby apotheosizing it. As Karl Jaspers concluded appositely, Heidegger's *Denken* remained "unfree, dictatorial, and incapable of communication."[217]

6

From Beyond the Grave: Heidegger and the New Right

It should come as no surprise that Heidegger, a life-long man of the Right, is also an important thinker for the New Right in Europe and North America. Heidegger belonged to the German Conservative Revolutionary intellectual current. He fell in and out with the National Socialist movement. His encounter with National Socialism, and his postwar thinking on modernity, technology, and the possibility of a new dispensation, are of enduring relevance to the New Right project of defining a post-totalitarian alternative to both the Old Right and the existing Jewish/Leftist hegemony.

—Greg Johnson, author of *White Identity Politics* and Alt-Right blogger, in *Counter-Currents* (2014)

Black Mass

ON 21 MAY 2013, FRANCE WAS traumatized by a horrific, headline-grabbing episode: a man in his late seventies committed suicide by shooting himself with a pistol in front of fifteen hundred worshipers attending Tuesday-morning services at the Notre Dame Cathedral in central Paris.

In a missive that was sent to a local newspaper, the man claimed that he had taken his own life in order to protest the "Mariage Pour Tous" (Marriage for All) law sanctioning gay marriage that had passed four days earlier. He also expressed his vigorous support for the ongoing wave of pro-Catholic, right-wing counterdemonstrations—the so-called Manif pour Tous (Demonstration for All)—protesting the law's passage.

In the note, the man who had taken his own life sought to encourage the Manif pour Tous participants to address an even greater political injustice: the "conspiracy" launched by French and European political elites to "replace" indigenous (read: white) Europeans with dark-skinned masses from the developing world, most of whom were practitioners of Islam. In support of his point, the man invoked the far-right author Renaud Camus's Islamophobic diatribe *Le Grand Remplacement*. He admonished France's "classe politique," whom he blamed for the ongoing immigration crisis. "Although I defend the identities of all peoples in their native lands," he observed, "I take umbrage at the crime committed by those *who seek to replace our [European] populations*." "It is important to realize," he continued, "that a France that has fallen into the hands of Islamists is an all too probable occurrence. For the last forty years, with the exception of the National Front, politicians of all political parties, as well as employers and the church, have abetted this catastrophe by favoring North African immigration." He suggested that the time for polished words and phrases had long passed. "We are entering a period," he prophesied, "in which *words* need to be backed by *deeds*." Henceforth, he continued ominously, "new measures [would be required], *both spectacular and symbolic*, in order to bestir the lethargy and to jolt an anesthetized consciousness into awakening *the memories of our origins*."[1] Undoubtedly, he viewed his sensational suicide as one such exemplary "spectacular and symbolic" deed.

The suicide's name was Dominique Venner (1935–2013). The day after Venner ended his own life, the editors of *Histoire Coloniale et Postcoloniale*, in an attempt to contextualize this provocative and disturbing episode, published the following note: "Up to the moment of his spectacular suicide, Dominique Venner promoted the bogey of France succumbing 'to the grip of Islamists.' He invoked this specter in his final blog post, in which he referred to the profoundly racist novel, *The Camp of the Saints*, in which Jean Raspail depicts the capitulation of French elites in the face of a column of impoverished Asiatics."[2]

"Jews Will Not Replace Us!"

In retrospect, Dominique Venner's allusion in his May 2013 suicide note to Renaud Camus's "Great Replacement" mythologem seems eerily prescient. As Jean-Marie Le Pen observed in his integral nationalist manifesto *Les Français d'abord* (1984), "Semantics are not neutral. One utilizes them like weapons in a combat where, at times, words kill more assuredly than bullets."[3]

Since *Le Grand Remplacement*'s initial publication in 2012, Camus's anti-immigrant screed has had a toxic and deadly afterlife. In March 2019, Brenton Tarrant, the Christchurch, New Zealand, mosque murderer, claimed that his anti-Muslim killing spree—which took the lives of fifty-one innocents—had been inspired by Camus's "Great Replacement" theorem. Prior to the mass killing, Tarrant posted online an eighty-page xenophobic tirade titled "The Great Replacement." For the benefit of those who may have been uncertain about the ideological origins of Tarrant's feverish Islamophobic *ressentiment*, the cover page of his digital manifesto featured a telling clue: the SS symbol of the "Schwarze Sonne," or "Black Sun."[4]

A few months later, in August 2019, an anti-immigrant zealot murdered twenty-two Hispanics at a Walmart store in El Paso, Texas. Prior to carrying out this gruesome deed, the killer, following the Christchurch murderer's lead, posted a hate-filled manifesto on the dark web claiming that the "attack [was] a response to the *Hispanic invasion of Texas*." It soon became clear that Camus's "Great Replacement" ideologeme played a key role in the killer's thinking. As he explained, "I'm only defending my country from *cultural and ethnic replacement brought on by an invasion*."[5]

Two years earlier, at the subsequently infamous "Unite the Right" rally in Charlottesville, Virginia, orchestrated by leaders of the Alt-Right, white nationalists organized a torchlight parade reminiscent of Sturmabteilung (SA) processions during the Nazi era. Within minutes, the marchers' "You will not replace us!" chant metamorphosed into "Jews will not replace us!" thus confirming the ideological connection between National Socialism and the U.S. white-supremacist movement.

Should any further proof concerning those ideological affinities be necessary, one might cite the notorious "Hailgate" episode that took place at a National Policy Institute (NPI) summit that was held in Washington, DC, in November 2016, following Donald Trump's stunning triumph in the U.S. presidential election. At the event, the Alt-Right charlatan and NPI president Richard Spencer's rallying cry, "Hail Trump! Hail our people!" was greeted by a flurry of outstretched arms that simulated the "Hitler *Gruß*" and enthusiastic shouts of "Sieg Heil!"[6]

Earlier that year, Spencer—then at the height of his notoriety—was queried about the intellectual origins of the Alt-Right worldview. His response offers an important clue with respect to Heidegger's ideological serviceability for the twenty-first-century New Right:

When I was thinking about the new standpoint, it was one that had a different philosophical basis than the kind of quaint Anglo-American conservatism outlined in,
say, Russell Kirk's *The Conservative Mind*. I was thinking about something like
the French New Right, something like the Traditionalism of [Julius] Evola, something like Nietzsche, German idealism, and Heidegger. I just wanted to go to all
these places that conservatives resisted. It was kind of a joke between Paul Gottfried and I [*sic*] that conservatives considered all these people to be liberal. They
were liberal fascists because they didn't believe in free markets and family values
or something.[7]

"The May 26 Demonstrators and Heidegger"

Since the 1950s, Dominique Venner had been an animating and shady presence among neofascist groups that flourished on the margins of French political
life. Like other "revolutionary nationalists," Venner opposed decolonization in
the name of white European supremacy. During the 1950s, Venner had served as
a "para" in the Algerian War (1954–62). Following Charles de Gaulle's 12 May
1958 coup, Venner oversaw *Jeune Nation*, a journal that doubled as the political
wing of the OAS (Organisation de l'armée secrete), the paramilitary organization whose acts of domestic terrorism brought metropolitan France to the brink
of civil war.

In 1961, as the OAS bomb attacks reached fever pitch following a failed
summons to insurrection, Venner and five other *Jeune Nation* militants were ar-
rested for sedition and convicted following a yearlong trial. Venner spent sixteen months in prison prior to being released.

Insight into the political motivations behind Venner's theatrical suicide can
be gleaned from the curiously titled online manifesto that he published in the
hours that preceded his death: "The 26 May Demonstrators and Heidegger."
Venner's title alluded to a peculiar coincidence: the next installment of the
Manif pour Tous protest movement was scheduled to occur on Sunday, 26 May.
Coincidentally, 26 May was also the anniversary of Heidegger's death, thirty-
seven years earlier, in 1976. Venner, it seems, interpreted this fortuitous con-
juncture as a positive political omen: a case of "preestablished harmony."

In Venner's suicide note, he detailed the links between his own neofascist
convictions and Heidegger's fundamental ontology. One important commonal-
ity concerned Heidegger's disavowal of "transcendence" in favor of a neopagan
affirmation of *Diesseitigkeit* qua "Being-in-the-world." "We must remember,"

Venner asserted, "that, as Heidegger phrased it appositely in *Being and Time*, the essence of man lies in his existence and not in a world 'beyond.' It is in the here and now that our destiny plays itself out, up until the very last moment."[8]

By acknowledging Heidegger's self-understanding as a philosopher of "facticity" and "Being-in-the-world," Venner sought to highlight the ideological continuities between historical fascism and neofascism. Since the early 1960s, one of the ideological hallmarks of the Nouvelle Droite—a political movement whose creation Venner had overseen and nurtured—was its rejection of Christianity in favor of neopaganism.

The embrace of neopaganism offered numerous political and strategic advantages. Above all, it paved the way for a return to the standpoint of "Indo-Europeanism" as a euphemism for "Aryanism." Thereby, it served as a means of reintroducing, via terminological subterfuge, the ideology of Aryan racial supremacy. Over time, the recourse to neopaganism proved to be an effective mechanism of regaining acceptance for the idea of race thinking, despite the legacy of annihilation and carnage it had wrought. The link between neopaganism and neofascism was at the heart of Venner protégé Alain de Benoist's influential 1981 study *How Can One Become Pagan?*[9]

At this point, the ideological disconnect between Venner's neofascist standpoint and the pro-Catholic Manif pour Tous demonstrations emerged. After all, Venner's suicide had taken place in the most hallowed bastion of French Catholicism. His deed had been, fundamentally and undeniably, an act of defilement. It demonstrably reaffirmed the Nouvelle Droite's neopagan self-understanding: its opposition, following Nietzsche, to the Judeo-Christian "slave revolt" in morals. The religious divide between Venner and the Manif pour Tous movement—whose proponents sought to challenge the French Republic's commitment to *laïcisation*, or "secularism"—helps to explain Venner's underlying motivation: to redirect this groundswell of popular discontent toward the racist ends of "population replacement."

"A Samurai of the Occident"

Another aim of the numerous Heidegger allusions that suffused Venner's suicide note was to convince the public that his iconoclastic deed was modeled on Heideggerian "authenticity": specifically, Heidegger's conception of

"Being-toward-death." In ancient Stoicism—another serviceable example of neopaganism—suicide, in contrast to Christianity, was esteemed as an affirmation of freedom vis-à-vis the vagaries of "fate." As Venner explained in a passage that was littered with references to Heidegger, "This final moment is as important as the rest of one's life. That is why it is essential to remain true to oneself until the very end. One triumphs over 'nothingness' by deciding for oneself and by remaining true to one's 'destiny.' There is no chance of escaping this exigency, since only in this life are we offered the possibility either 'to be ourselves' or to be 'nothing.' "[10]

Venner stressed that his provocative gesture was intended, first and foremost, as a political deed. To prove his point, he invoked the names of three prominent fascist sympathizers who had also taken their own lives: fellow literati whom Venner regarded as fraternal spirits and comrades in arms. The first two, Henry de Montherlant (1895–1972) and Pierre Drieu la Rochelle (1893–1945), had been *collaborateurs* and vigorous supporters of fascism *à la française* during the "dark years" of the Nazi occupation (1940–44). The third literary suicide cited by Venner was the Japanese ultranationalist Yukio Mishima (1925–70). Mishima had committed *seppuku*, in 1970, following an attempt to incite a coup among officers at Japanese army headquarters. Here, it is perhaps of more than passing interest to note that Venner's autobiography, which was published in 2012, was titled *Un Samouraï de l'occident: Le Bréviaire des insoumis* (A Samurai of the Occident: A Handbook for the Indomitable).[11]

I have dwelled on the historical and political context of Venner's suicide at some length, since, when he emerged from prison in 1962, Venner played a key role in reformulating the ideology of neofascism, redirecting its focus away from past struggles that had already been lost—the Third Reich, *l'État Français* (Vichy), and the Algerian War—and toward a future in which the goals of Aryan supremacy could be realized on a pan-European scale.

"Europe for the Europeans"

The Dominique Venner episode merits scrutiny, insofar as it exemplifies the various ways that the New Right, on both sides of the Atlantic, has made copious use of Heidegger's thought to advance its retrograde ethnonationalist political agenda. As Venner remarked in "Qu'est-ce que le nationalisme?" (1963), "Militants of a white race need to find ideological support beyond their borders:

support that elucidates their struggle, praises their courage, denounces the
repression by which they are victimized, and that catalyzes the struggle for
survival among white peoples everywhere against those who seek to destroy
them."[12]

Venner realized that postwar fascism, in order to be successful, would have
to undergo an *aggiornamento*: it would have to recalibrate its strategy to accommodate the realignments and transformations of international politics. In
order to rise to the geopolitical challenges of the Cold War and decolonization,
neofascism would need to abandon the nation-state framework. Venner and his
collaborateurs, such as the cofounder of GRECE (Groupement de recherche et
d'étude pour la civilisation européene) and Nouvelle Droite mastermind Alain
de Benoist, concluded that, henceforth, only a reconstituted *pan-European fascism* could offset the influence of the Soviet Union and the United States, the
non-European superpowers whose aspirations to continental mastery jeopardized the neofascist desideratum of "Europe for the Europeans." The proponents
of neofascism viewed the idea of "Fortress Europe" as a geostrategic prerequisite for translating their dystopian vision of an ethnically homogeneous, Indo-
European "empire" into reality. Hence, it soon became apparent that the New
Right's summons to European "autonomy" was merely a façade: a smokescreen that concealed the movement's Aryan-supremacist aspirations, its desire
to implement "Old Dreams of a New Reich."

Venner, de Benoist, and their fellow Grècistes realized that only a suprana-
tional, pan-European fascism could adequately safeguard the goal of European
racial supremacy. In their view, achieving this goal had become an urgent matter in light of the anticolonial revolts that, under the banner of "tier mondisme,"
were surging throughout the developing world.

Fundamentally, Venner, de Benoist, et al. sought to restore the anticommunist alliance that Nazi Germany, following its defeat at Stalingrad, had mobilized during the concluding years of World War II: a coalition whose stated
mission was to defend Western civilization against the "racial threat" posed by
"Judeo-Bolshevism." Nazi propagandists likened the Red Army's battlefield
advances during the war's final stages to the return of Genghis Khan and his
"Mongol-Asiatic" hordes.[13] The Nouvelle Droite pined for the halcyon days of
the Légion des Volontaires Françaises (LVF) and the Brigade Charlemagne,
whose fighters, under the watchful eye of the Waffen SS, had served on the
eastern front during the closing stages of the war.

The Politics of Fear

In the aftermath of the deadly white-supremacist attacks in Christchurch, New Zealand, and El Paso, Texas, many political commentators suggested that the "Great Replacement" was a comparatively recent political trope, whose topicality could be traced to the publication of Renaud Camus's *Le Grand Remplacement*, in 2012.[14] Yet this conclusion represents merely a partial truth.

The myth that "indigenous Europeans" are facing an "immigration stampede"—"inundation" by migrants from the developing world seeking revenge against their former colonial overlords—has a much older pedigree. It originated with Dominique Venner's realization, during the early 1960s, that postwar fascism urgently needed an ideological overhaul. The bogey of "population replacement" reflected the recalibration of neofascist doctrine following the "setbacks" of decolonization. Although the battles for Indochina and French Algeria had been lost, the struggle for an ethnically homogeneous "Fortress Europe" was just beginning. The Nouvelle Droite understood itself as the intellectual masterminds behind this new strategy.

Since the Nouvelle Droite's inception, one of its defining rhetorical themes has been to portray white Europeans as "victims" and colonial peoples as "aggressors," thereby reversing the opposition between perpetrators and victims. The Nouvelle Droite characterized European immigration policy as a "conspiracy" or "plot" orchestrated by political elites whose aim is "population exchange": "le grand remplacement" or "Bevölkerungsaustausch." Stoking the politics of fear, the Nouvelle Droite warned that liberal immigration policies are destined to culminate in the racial decimation of *européens de souche*, or "indigenous Europeans."[15] The ultimate goal of these political elites is to engineer a "reverse Holocaust," allowing the unwashed masses from the developing world to rise up and target "autochthonous Europeans" for annihilation. Alleging that the dystopian vision of Jean Raspail's *Camp of the Saints* is well on its way to becoming a reality, the Nouvelle Droite succeeded in catalyzing the racial anxieties of average Europeans.

The ideological currency that "population replacement" enjoys today among right-wing intellectuals on both sides of the Atlantic reflects the Nouvelle Droite's proficiency in relegitimating fascist discourse by whitewashing the movement's legacy of political criminality. By discursively airbrushing the excesses of historical fascism and by seeking to mask neofascism's racist and

authoritarian aims, the Nouvelle Droite has rendered the tenets of European
race thinking acceptable to the political mainstream.

In *Attack of the Antidemocrats*, Samuel Salzborn has confirmed the New
Right's pivotal role in effectuating a sea change in postwar political culture:
"The increasing sophistication of fascist and extreme right-wing discourses in
Europe, particularly notable in such parties as the National Front, the Alleanza
Nazionale, and the Freiheitliche Partei Österreichs [FPÖ], has resulted from a
conscious strategy adopted by . . . New Right thinkers to adapt their ideology
and style of self-presentation to a postwar political habitat inhospitable to
overtly racist, anti-liberal, and revolutionary demands for the overthrow of liberal democracy and the creation of a new order."[16]

The Actuality of the Conservative Revolution

The Nouvelle Droite's efforts to conjure the specter of an imminent "racial
apocalypse"—a revolt by inferior, nonwhite peoples against their former colonial
masters—was prefigured by Oswald Spengler's dystopian vision, in *The Hour of
Decision* (1933), of impending "Colored Revolutions": Spengler's racialist shorthand for contemporary anticolonial movements. Spengler argued that decoloni-
alization portended a heretical turn in the course of world history: an unprecedented
role reversal of "masters" and "slaves" that jeopardized European racial survival.
The new risk meant that, following centuries of brutal European colonialism, Europeans themselves might become the new victims. Thereby, Spengler amplified
his account of the West's spiritual collapse in *Decline of the West* (1918, 1922) by
dramatizing the emerging external threat posed by anticolonialism:

> Ever since the Boxer Revolution in China, the Indian Mutiny, and the revolt of the
> Mexicans against the Emperor Maximilian, there will be found . . . everywhere
> one and the same thing: *hatred of the white race and an unconditional determina-
> tion to destroy it.* . . . Danger is knocking at the door! The colored races are not
> pacifists. They do *not* cling to a life whose length is its sole value. They take up
> the sword when we lay it down. Once they feared the white man; now they despise
> him. Once they were filled with terror at our power. . . . Today, they . . . rise up and
> look down upon the whites as on a thing of yesterday.[17]

Spengler, along with Heidegger and Carl Schmitt, was one of a select coterie of
conservative revolutionary thinkers whose ideas the European New Right, in its

multifarious national guises—Nouvelle Droite, Neue Rechte, Nuovo Destra, Nuevo Derecho—sought to mobilize for contemporary political ends.

Historically, one of the conservative revolutionary movement's significant achievements was having usurped the idea of revolution from the political left and refashioned it for the ends of the Right. The conservative revolution's emergence during the 1920s represented a watershed in the history of German conservatism. Its representatives displayed little nostalgia for the demise of the hidebound traditionalism of the *Kaiserreich*. Conversely, they hailed Mussolini's March on Rome, in October 1922, as an invaluable precedent: confirmation that "direct action"—"propaganda of the deed"—could be appropriated for the ends of the radical Right. (Hitler's failed Munich Beer Hall Putsch of 1923 was modeled on Il Duce's coup d'état.) The conservative revolutionary program was epitomized by the title of Hans Freyer's 1930 call to arms, *Revolution von Rechts* (Revolution from the Right). When, in *Logic as a Question Concerning the Essence of Language* (1934), Heidegger extolled a recent meeting between Hitler and Mussolini as a prototype of existential *Geschichtlichkeit*— "When an airplane transports the Führer from Munich to Venice in order to meet with Mussolini, *then history occurs*. The flight becomes *a historical event [ein geschichtliches Geschehen]*"—his remarks epitomized the conservative revolutionary ethos of "total mobilization."[18]

In "La Révolution conservatrice" (1979), Alain de Benoist, writing under the cover of a pseudonym, identified conservative revolutionary thought as the ideational template that had inspired the Nouvelle Droite's efforts to supplant left-wing ideological hegemony via a systematic infusion of far-right ideas. The Nouvelle Droite's political project, de Benoist affirmed, represented a "continuation of the conservative revolution."[19]

Upon meeting Alain de Benoist for the first time in 1964, Armin Mohler (1920–2003)—the Waffen SS volunteer and former secretary of Ernst Jünger, whose monograph *Die konservative Revolution in Deutschland* (1950) rehabilitated conservative revolutionary thought for an entire generation of far-right intellectuals—was gratified to discover the key role that Heidegger and Schmitt's ideas played in the development of Nouvelle Droite worldview.[20] The Nouvelle Droite has been especially receptive toward Heidegger's affirmation of "rootedness," "native soil," ethnic belonging, and resolute "decision." All of these precepts have been instrumental in defining the content and parameters of the New Right standpoint.

Another reason that the Nouvelle Droite venerated conservative revolutionary thought derived from the fig leaf of intellectual respectability that the alliance with "spiritual fascists" like Heidegger, Schmitt, and Jünger provided. By cultivating this lineage, the Nouvelle Droite seized an opportunity to propagate a highbrow, intellectually sophisticated version of fascism: hence an approach better suited to reestablishing the movement's ideological legitimacy in the eyes of mainstream conservatives and a middle class whose democratic loyalties were beginning to waver. As Pierre-André Taguieff has confirmed in "La Stratégie intellectuelle de la Nouvelle Droite en France," the turn to the "conservative revolution enabled the Nouvelle Droite to eliminate positive and direct references to National Socialism, hence to avoid relying on authors who were associated with 'racist,' 'anti-Semitic,' and 'fascist' discourse"—notwithstanding the Nouvelle Droite's advocacy of "a racism that was no less radical."[21]

The sleight of hand involved in the New Right's strategy of ideological "camouflage" merits careful scrutiny. After all, numerous conservative revolutionary intellectuals—notably, Heidegger and Schmitt—enthusiastically joined the Nazi Party and dedicated themselves to realizing its aims. Even those who, like Jünger and Spengler, refused to join contributed to Nazism's success by paving the way for the broad acceptance of fascist ideology.

In 1963, Venner and de Benoist cofounded a "metapolitical" organization, Europe Action, whose message was amplified by a like-named journal. A year later, de Benoist became *Europe Action*'s editor in chief.

In keeping with the Nouvelle Droite's "metapolitical" turn, Europe Action undertook a tactical retreat from day-to-day politics. Instead, the New Rightists embraced a strategy of "total ideological saturation." Above all, they concentrated on "winning the battle of ideas": not as an end in itself but in an effort to lay the groundwork for an eventual seizure of political power.

The collaboration between Venner and de Benoist culminated in the formation of GRECE in 1968. (The allusion to "European civilization" played on the idea of the West's pre-Christian, "Indo-European" heritage.) Under de Benoist's stewardship, GRECE flourished as a far-right think tank tasked with establishing right-wing ideological hegemony, also known as a "Gramscism of the Right."

In keeping with the goal of achieving "total ideological saturation" for New Right ideas, GRECE spawned an extensive network of think tanks and journals: *Nouvelle École*, *Éléments*, *Krisis,* and the *Cercle Proudhon* in France;

Kriticon, Mut!, wir selbst, and the Thule Seminar in Germany; *Orientations* and
Vouloir in Belgium; and the Cercle Avalon in Switzerland—to name only the
most prominent. One indication of GRECE's impressive, pan-European reach
was that *Éléments*, which was edited by de Benoist, engendered a chain of like-
named sister publications or clones in Germany (*Elemente*), Italy (*Elementi*),
Russia, (*Elementy*), and Spain (*Elementos*). By overseeing the formation of ideologically kindred groups in Germany, Italy, Spain, Belgium, and Russia,
GRECE engendered a hall-of-mirrors effect. Hence, by the mid-1980s, the
Nouvelle Droite's objective of restoring intellectual respectability to key "elements" of fascist ideology seemed well within reach. Over the course of the
next decade, de Benoist became, by consensus, the éminence grise of the European New Right.

The Nouvelle Droite's "ideological saturation" strategy would come to fruition during the 1980s, with the electoral breakthrough of the National Front,
under the stewardship of Jean-Marie Le Pen. In the words of one commentator,
the National Front's emergence "signified a successful implementation of
[Nouvelle Droite] political goals through step-by-step achievements in the
struggle for a right-wing cultural hegemony: an attempt to achieve influence in
the pre-political sphere."[22] In this respect, the "metapolitical" strategy that was
jointly pursued by Dominque Venner and Alain de Benoist, which required taking leave of practical politics in favor of laying the ideological groundwork for
the broader acceptance of far-right ideas, paid off handsomely.

At the same time, a closer examination shows that the alliance between the
Nouvelle Droite and the National Front went far beyond the level of ideational
influence. During the mid-1980s, in keeping with the strategy of "entrisme,"
numerous New Rightists—publicists, opinion leaders, and *énarques* (graduates
of l'École Nationale d'Administration), such as Yvan Blot, Bruno Gollnisch,
Jean-Yves Le Gallou, and Bruno Mégret (to mention only the better-known
names)—migrated from GRECE and its sister organization, the Club d'Horloge,
to leadership positions within the National Front.[23]

Having learned the lessons of "metapolitical" struggle, upon joining the National Front, these former Nouvelle Droitistes focused on transforming the New
Right's ethnopopulist credo into a concrete political force. Given the two organizations' pronounced ideological affinities and common political agenda, the political
merger between the Nouvelle Droite and the National Front was a natural fit. As
Timothy McCulloch observes in an article on the political symbiosis between the

Nouvelle Droite and the National Front, whereas, circa 1980, "there were no *nouvelle droitistes* in the politburo of the National Front, by 1994, there were *six*. . . . Without this evolution in Nouvelle Droite influence, it is highly unlikely the National Front would have incorporated concepts such as 'National preference' into party policy."[24] Soon, the National Front, with its nativist agenda, its horror of *métissage*, and its openly racist sloganeering—"la France aux français" and "la priorité nationale"—reminiscent of the protofascist "leagues" of the 1930s, implanted itself on the French political landscape as a permanent antidemocratic menace.

Following the precedent set by the National Front, in recent years a wide array of European far-right parties—the Austrian Freedom Party (FPÖ), Italy's La Lega, and the Alternative for Germany (AfD), to name only the most prominent—whose ties to the Nouvelle Droite and GRECE are well documented, have made significant political inroads. The Austrian Freedom Party, notwithstanding its neo-Nazi roots, was part of the governing coalition in Austria in 2000–2005 and 2017–19. La Lega played a major role in Italy's coalition government from 2018 to 2019. In 2017, the Alternative for Germany—which was founded in 2013 as an anti-euro party—became the official opposition party in the Bundestag, having received 12.8 percent of the vote in the federal elections that year. The upshot of these developments has been a fundamental realignment of European politics: a shift that has significantly benefited the forces of authoritarian ethnic nationalism, which, henceforth, seem destined to play a significant role in determining Europe's political future.

Legitimizing Neoracism: "Ethnopluralism" and the "Right to Difference"

An important strategy that the Nouvelle Droite has deployed in order to rehabilitate the legacy of European race thinking was to present itself as a champion of "racial difference": hence as an advocate of cultural and political "pluralism." In advancing this argument, the Nouvelle Droite cautiously concealed its earlier commitments to neocolonialism and white supremacism.[25] Instead, it flaunted its allegiance to the values of "ethnopluralism."

However, closer scrutiny reveals that the movement's embrace of "ethnopluralism" and "cultural difference" functioned as a rhetorical smokescreen that sanitized the precepts of traditional race thinking, retrofitting them for contemporary political use. Thereby, the Nouvelle Droite sought to mislead the public into believing that it had abandoned historical fascism's commitment to racial hierarchy.

In "The New Cultural Racism in France," Pierre-André Taguieff deftly exposed the rhetorical subterfuge of the Nouvelle Droite's "differentialist racism" strategy. Taguieff showed that, by relying on an essentialized conception of "cultural difference," the Nouvelle Droite merely contrived a new argument to justify ethnic separatism: "The New Right's 'anti-racism' uses ideas of collective identities hypostatized as inalienable categories. . . . A communitarian type [of racism] establishes difference or group identity as an absolute. In this case, it is less a question of inequality than of incommunicability, incommensurability, and incomparability. The human species is broken down into self-contained, closed totalities. The differentialist imperative is the need to preserve the community as is, or to purify it."[26]

Like old-school European racists, New Right "ethnopluralists" firmly opposed the heresies of "miscegenation" and "racial mixing." They acknowledged the legitimacy of racial equality only insofar as the various races remained permanently "separate." In sum, they favored a neosegregationist agenda of "separate but equal."

Another important clue with respect to the Nouvelle Droite's attitude toward race is provided by the movement's relentless polemic against the legacy of *droits de l'homme*, or human rights. By seeking to base citizenship on "ethnicity" rather than "legal equality," the Nouvelle Droite, while celebrating the "right to difference"—a code word for "hierarchy"—essentially offered a new writ for ethnic cleansing.

In essence, the Nouvelle Droite sought to provide a warrant for a new form of apartheid: a version deceptively couched in the pseudoegalitarian jargon of the "right to difference." Fundamentally, however, the Nouvelle Droite's ethnopluralist defense of "racial difference" was little more than a rhetorically modified version of traditional race thinking.

The Nouvelle Droite's strategy of ideological camouflage notwithstanding, its basic political and cultural aspirations paralleled those of interwar fascism. This continuity helps to explain why the Nouvelle Droite has expended so much energy trying to erode the precepts of democratic legitimacy. By undermining the tenets of Western humanism, the New Right has sought to destroy the normative core of the reigning democratic political consensus. In order to advance these goals, it has subjected the discourse of human rights to a battery of relentless and prolonged attacks.

Unsurprisingly, New Right ideologues have found Heidegger's "antihumanism" extremely congenial to their antiegalitarian agenda. In addition, Heidegger's understanding of "authentic historicity" in terms of the primacy of the *Volksbegriff* has often served as a template for the New Right's ethnopopulist assault on the legacy of moral universalism.

Heidegger, GRECE, and the "Identitarian Movement"

Assessing the ideological affinities between the conservative revolutionaries and the New Right, Michael O'Meara, in *New Culture, New Right*, has explored the impact of Heidegger's thought on one of the Nouvelle Droite's most important political progeny, the "Identitarian Movement." As O'Meara explains, "The most important components of GRECE's historical philosophy come from Martin Heidegger. Heidegger's anti-modernist thought began to influence [GRECE's] metapolitical project . . . in the early 1980s. Like [Nietzsche], Heidegger rejected Christian/modernist metaphysics, viewing Man and History, Being and Becoming, as inseparable. . . . When [the past] is experienced as *authentic historicity* . . . 'it is something to which I can return again and again.' . . . Heidegger believed that [the past] continues to exist in the form of a Heritage Group or an Identity that is able to 'determine a future in the present.' "[27]

Echoing O'Meara's assessment, in *Rising from the Ruins*, Joakim Andersen has highlighted the importance of Heidegger's contribution to the Nouvelle Droite ideology of "cultural difference": in truth, a placeholder and euphemism for "racial difference." As Andersen observes, "The New Right, influenced by Heidegger, argues that we are *authentic*, true to ourselves, *when we are living our culture*. Our culture provides us with models for a good life, and it is when we incarnate these age-old role models in our own time, with our kin, . . . that our lives become truly meaningful. Culture gives us meaning and explains to us who we are and why we're here; *our culture provides us with an Identity*."[28]

In *Attack of the Antidemocrats*, Samuel Salzborn has underlined the importance of conservative revolutionary thought for the New Right worldview. However, in contrast to O'Meara and Andersen, Salzborn perceives significant ideological affinities between the Nouvelle Droite and National Socialism: a kinship that the New Right—in keeping with its project of ideological camouflage—has long been at pains to deny. Salzborn refuses to be taken in by this gambit. As he remarks, "The predominant intellectual-historical points of reference for the New Right are those intellectuals of the Weimar period who furnished National Socialism with its 'ideological infrastructure': thinkers such as Arthur Moeller van den Bruck, Oswald Spengler, Othmar Spann, and Martin Heidegger."[29]

In *Black Wind, White Snow*, Charles Clover, seconding Salzborn's assessment, views the Nouvelle Droite's reliance on the conservative revolutionary worldview as revelatory with respect to the movement's unspoken political aspirations. Clover observes that, in light of the fact that the conservative revolution was composed predominantly of "ex-Nazis"—"the philosopher Martin Heidegger, the legal theorist Carl Schmitt, [and] esoteric author Julius Evola"— the conservative revolutionary connection was tantamount to a "smoking gun." As Clover remarks, "The [Nouvelle Droite] has kept the flame alive for a German movement known during interwar politics as the 'conservative revolution' theorists: influential intellectuals radically opposed to liberalism and parliamentary democracy . . . and dedicated to the creation of a new post-liberal, nationalistic order."[30]

In *Sur la Nouvelle Droite*, Taguieff emphasizes the impact that Heidegger's "critique of modernity" had on Alain de Benoist and other New Right ideologues. Taguieff remarks that, although it would be tempting to situate de Benoist among the French "left Heideggerians" (Derrida, Foucault, etc.), to do so would be misleading, insofar as "before and after his encounter with Nazism, Heidegger took his bearings from the German 'conservative revolution.' Consequently, for de Benoist, unlike the 'left Heideggerians,' it was never a question of advancing under the camouflage of borrowed Heideggerian language. Instead, by relying on Heideggerian *Denkwege*, de Benoist was merely remaining self-consistent. Heidegger's 'critique of modernity' allowed de Benoist to embrace 'biologism' and to radically call into question the reign of 'techno-science.' "[31]

In de Benoist's autobiography, *Mémoire vive* (2012), he confirmed Taguieff's insight concerning the pivotal role that Heidegger played in the development of the Nouvelle Droite paradigm: above all, Heidegger's *völkisch* and "rooted" critique of cosmopolitan citizenship. Inspired by Heidegger's "critique of reason," de Benoist denounced "liberalism," "universalism," and "tolerance" qua domination incarnate. In a classic case of ideological reversal, de Benoist pilloried liberal democracy as "totalitarian," insofar as it purportedly abetted the annihilation of "cultural difference." In a paroxysm of hyperbole, de Benoist accused "liberal tolerance" of fomenting "cultural extinction." On another occasion, he exalted the Nouvelle Droite project as a form of "résistance" to "egalitarian *Gleichschaltung.*" As one leading Nouvelle Droite ideologue, Guillaume Faye, explained, by repatriating immigrants to their "countries of origin," the New Right would effectively be "liberating" them from the "slavery" of "[democratic] universalism." Conversely, when it came to the well-documented political misdeeds of conservative revolutionary thinkers such as Heidegger and Schmitt, de Benoist's lips remained sealed.[32]

In political manifestos such as *Beyond Human Rights* and *Toward a European Renaissance*, de Benoist argued that the current "state of emergency" demonstrated that the West's survival depended on the suppression of political liberalism.[33] The Nouvelle Droite has frequently appealed to Social Darwinist imperatives of "self-preservation" in order to reaffirm the validity of race thinking, claiming that peoples whose "biological existence" has been threatened are within their rights to employ all means at their disposal, including the repatriation nonwhite immigrants.

In *Mémoire vive*, de Benoist explains the derivation of the Nouvelle Droite's rejection of democratic humanism from Heidegger's critique of modernity as an age of unremitting *Gottes-* and *Seinsverlassenheit*: "Nihilism is the historical process whereby supersensible reality eviscerates itself, ceases to believe in its own sovereignty, to the point where *Being itself loses all meaning and significance.* 'Nihilism,' writes Heidegger, 'is the history of Being that inexorably and by degrees reveals the death of the Christian God.' . . . With modernity, the rise of nihilism is *accelerated.* . . .The contemporary situation represents the logical end point and denouement of this trajectory."[34]

The preceding remarks confirm the extremely selective nature of de Benoist's historical vision. When it comes to highlighting the shortcomings of Western liberalism, de Benoist does not hesitate to pull out all of the stops. Conversely, when the genocidal practices of National Socialism are at issue— by historical consensus, the apex of twentieth-century political criminality— his voice suddenly becomes inaudible.

Although it would be misleading to exaggerate Heidegger's contribution to the development of the Nouvelle Droite's "metapolitical" strategy by portraying him as the movement's philosophical preceptor, determining the nature and extent of his influence on the New Right remains an important task: especially in light of the pivotal role that the New Right has played in rehabilitating counterrevolutionary doctrine. Although the intellectual sources of Nouvelle Droite ideology are eclectic and diverse, Heidegger's name has repeatedly surfaced as a key inspiration and influence. As Chetan Bhatt has noted in "White Extinction: Metaphysical Elements in Contemporary Western Fascism," "If we consider the influences on the European New Right . . . we find the philosophy of pessimism (Julius Evola, Oswald Spengler) and authentic Being (Martin Heidegger, Ludwig Klages, Ernst Jünger), the rejection of liberalism (Carl Schmitt, Dominique Venner), natural order, hierarchy and race (Hans Günther, Vilfredo Pareto), racial science and philosophical anthropology (Hans Blüher, Cesare Lombroso, Arnold Gehlen), the racial soul (Ludwig Ferdinand Clauß, René Guénon, Gustave Le Bon), and occultism (Guénon, Julius Evola, Savitri Devi)."[35]

Understandably, much of the critical literature on the Nouvelle Droite has zeroed in on its political and ideological ties to interwar fascism. Despite the movement's prodigious efforts to distance itself from historical fascism, most commentators who have closely tracked its evolution refuse to be taken.

In "Plus ça change: The Fascist Pedigree of the Nouvelle Droite," Roger Griffin has implored scholars to penetrate beyond the pseudoegalitarian, rhetorical veneer of the Nouvelle Droite worldview: to recognize that, despite the semantic smokescreen the movement has constructed in order to conceal its ideological lineage, as far as matters of substance go, *very little has changed.* As Griffin correctly observes, the Nouvelle Droite "originated as a response to the need recognized by French neofascists in the early 1960s to change their ideology and tactics without abandoning their fundamental values or goals." Ultimately, the Nouvelle Droite's "hagiographic respect for the major figures of the conservative revolution, taken together with its stress on 'cultural hegemony,' can be seen as part of a highly refined revisionist strategy for dehistoricising fascism, and thus expurgating it of its indigestible connotations, while staying true to its fundamental historical mission: to replace the decadence of liberal democracy with a 'new order' in which national/ethnic identities are intensified rather than diluted, and the differences between peoples enhanced rather than eroded."[36]

Although the Nouvelle Droite has undergone numerous ideological transformations since its inception during the 1960s, as Griffin's remarks suggest, it is important to recognize the continuities with historical fascism. Among the more important elements of continuity are an endorsement of the Aryan myth, a vindication of neopaganism that rejects Judeo-Christian monotheism, a glorification of Nordic culture, and the propagation of Holocaust denial—one of the defining ideologemes of postwar neofascism. The fact that *Nouvelle École*—coedited by Alain de Benoist and the public face of GRECE—included a moving tribute to the recently deceased Nazi "Race Pope" Hans Günther in its winter 1968–69 issue confirms that Griffin's concerns merit serious consideration.[37]

In "From Fascism to the Nouvelle Droite: The Dream of Pan-European Empire," Tamir Bar-On has exposed the hypocrisy of de Benoist's appeal to "ethnopopulism" as a political model intended to combat the "cultural genocide" perpetrated by "Western universalism." Although de Benoist has repeatedly insisted that his "differentialist racism" is "pluralist" and "egalitarian," Bar-On convincingly shows that he has in effect resurrected the rallying cry "Europe for the Europeans," while giving it another name: "the 'people' that de Benoist is largely concerned with are the 'silent majority' of white Europeans who face supposed 'cultural extinction' as a result of uncontrolled immigration and the multicultural, egalitarian politics of a Europe dominated by the ethos of the liberal left."[38]

Le Pen "Family Values"

In contemporary Europe, the wager on ethnopopulism has portended a recodification of citizenship law in accordance with the precepts of jus sanguinis, or "right of blood." Hence, champions of ethnic nationalism have consistently sought to supplant the republican-democratic "civic" understanding of citizenship with a morally regressive definition that accords primacy to the "existential" prerogatives of "rootedness" and "ethnicity."

Viewed from the standpoint of social contract theory, the criterion of jus sanguinis seeks to exchange a moral or deontological understanding of citizenship predicated on the "volonté générale" for a conception that is "rooted" in "being." According to the consanguinity model, legislation is no longer the result of deliberative decisions made by the demos. Instead, the ethnopopulist paradigm redefines norms ontologically as obedience to a set of inherited, preexisting "existents," or *Seiende*: "blood," "soil," "heritage," and "Heimat." Once norms have been reconceived in this manner, however, they become, to all intents and purposes, synonymous with "submission."

Ethnopopulism's ascendancy has become one of the defining features of the contemporary global political landscape. In Europe and North America, a rising tide of xenophobia cum ethnic chauvinism has upended inherited normative assumptions about the desirability of rule of law, procedural democracy, and human rights. Consequently, today, nearly all polities in the Northern Hemisphere and beyond have been beset by challenges from authoritarian populist parties whose endorsement of ethnic citizenship has eroded the inherited understanding of democratic legitimacy. As Arjun Appadurai has observed in *The Great Regression*, "The central question of our times is whether we are witnessing the worldwide rejection of liberal democracy and its replacement by some sort of populist authoritarianism. Strong signs of this trend are to be found in Trump's America, Putin's Russia, Modi's India and Erdoğan's Turkey. In addition, we have numerous examples of already existing authoritarian governments [Viktor] Orbán in Hungary, [Andrzej] Duda in Poland), and major aspirants to authoritarian right-wing rule in France, Austria and other European countries."[39]

One of the primary aims of these antidemocratic political movements has been to supplant the civic-egalitarian norms that emerged with the "age of democratic revolutions" with the values of ethnic particularism. This sea change in the political self-understanding of modern societies heralds a shift from the inclusionary precepts of equal citizenship to the exclusionary logic of blood and ethnicity. It portends an definitive breach with the "third wave of democratization."[40] Thereby, a new breed of soulless autocracies and uncharismatic despotisms risks supplanting the virtues of public reason and political self-rule. "Having annulled intermediary organizations and institutions, [the new autocracies] supplant the constitutional-democratic norms of political 'distance' via direct communication with the *Volk*, and the illusory *Gemeinschaft* of 'leaders' and 'followers.' "[41]

In Hungarian Prime Minister Viktor Orbán's notorious "illiberal democracy" speech (2014), he tersely summarized these developments as follows: "There is a race underway to find the method of community organization, the state, which is most capable of making a nation and a community internationally competitive. . . . The most popular topic in thinking today is trying to understand how systems that are *not Western, not liberal, not liberal democracies, and perhaps not even democracies*, can nevertheless make their nations successful."[42]

Unsurprisingly, the resurgence of ethnic nationalism, in its various guises and manifestations, has served as a pretext for the resurrection of race thinking.

Stuart Hall, in his W. E. B. Dubois lectures, upon referencing the "horrendous human and historical consequences that have followed from the application of racialized classifying systems to social life," highlighted, in timely fashion, the disturbing revival of the "fateful triangle" of "race, nation, and ethnicity" in contemporary political life.[43]

In France, the National Front leadership has consistently demonstrated that Hall's anxieties concerning the renewed political currency of race thinking in an era of neoliberal destabilization were well founded. Informed accounts of the National Front's transformation from a motley clique of ex-Vichyites, "paras," and OAS conspirators to one of France's leading political parties have singled out Jean-Marie Le Pen's willingness to stoke racial fears for political gain as a crucial turning point. In the national elections of 1981, the National Front accrued a paltry 0.18 percent of the vote—Le Pen, for his part, failed to garner the five hundred signatures necessary to appear on the presidential ballot. Conversely, during the 1986 legislative elections, the National Front, brandishing the slogan, "Three million unemployed equals three million immigrants too many," was handsomely rewarded at the polls, gaining some thirty-five deputies.[44]

By misleadingly linking France's ongoing economic crisis with the issue of Muslim immigration, by playing on fears of "insecurity" and "identity loss" in a time of social and economic turmoil, Le Pen established the political formula that the National Front would successfully exploit for years to come. By deploying an ideological framework that was "profoundly reactionary, racist, anti-communist, and authoritarian," the National Front offered a political outlet for the frustrations and anxieties of social strata who feared that their identities were slipping away.[45]

Nouvelle Droite ideologues—Grècistes and Club d'Horlogistes—who reinvented themselves as National Front cadres pushed Le Pen, following the setback of 1981, to play the "ethnopopulist" card. Thereby, they appropriated the political Left's defense of "multiculturalism," transforming it into a justification of ethnic separatism.

Henceforth, the Nouvelle Droite's "differentialist racism" became a staple of National Front rhetoric: a convenient way of resisting the dangers of "race-mixing," or *métissage*, while denying that one is a "racist"—thus Le Pen's infamous declaration, "I love North Africans, but their place is in the Maghreb, not in Metropolitan France."[46] A similar logic pervaded Le Pen's "concentric circle" theory of politics: "I like my daughters better than my cousins, my cousins better than my neighbors, my neighbors better than strangers, and strangers better than foes." In 2012, when Le Pen's granddaughter Marion Maréchal-Le Pen was elected as the youngest deputy ever to the French National Assembly, Le Pen senior gloated, "Notre famille est de bonne race!"[47]

Upon inheriting the party presidency from Le Pen *père* in 2011, Marine Le Pen did her best to uphold Le Pen "family values." Addressing the topic of Muslim immigration, she proclaimed, "Their [Muslim immigrants'] attitudes and ways of being in society . . . are in total contradiction with the makeup of the French soul." In 2017, sounding the alarm with respect to the Middle East refugee crisis, she declared—in stark defiance of existing EU asylum law—"I am not a monster. If [immigrant] vessels are in danger, one must rescue the passengers, returning them to their countries of origin. If one allows them to enter the borders of the European Union, they might never leave."[48]

Upon learning of Dominique Venner's suicide in May 2013, Marine Le Pen broadcast the following words of condolence: "We wish to convey our whole-hearted respect for Dominique Venner, whose final gesture, an eminently political act, sought to bestir the people of France from their slumber."[49] What is astonishing about Le Pen's statement is that, despite her awareness of Venner's checkered past as a neofascist activist and convicted political conspirator, she had no compunction about lavishing praise on his suicide—notwithstanding its status as a blasphemous act that was committed in France's most venerated religious sanctuary.

"Ontological Rootedness" and "Ethnopluralism"

Venner's suicide note illustrates the multifarious ways that the New Right has found ideational support in Heidegger's thought in its metapolitical efforts to discredit Europe's reigning democratic political consensus. Heidegger's antipathy to universal norms and his correlative endorsement of "ontological rootedness" and *völkisch* particularism have emerged as key points of reference in the far right's efforts to redefine European citizenship in ethnopopulist terms. As Julian Göpffarth notes in "Heidegger's Philosophy in Contemporary German New Right Nationalism," the language of Heidegger's fundamental ontology has proved highly serviceable for the New Right's project of "discursive camouflage":

The German New Right puts forward an alternative, Heidegger-inspired nationalism grounded in *history* and *spirit* [that] . . . draws on narratives of German nationhood present in Heidegger's philosophy and early German anti-enlightenment
nationalism. . . . Heidegger's *Dasein* is used to reformulate an exclusive idea of
nationhood in the context of a liberal democratic political language in which . . .
racist nationalism and anti-Semitism are socially questionable and legally banned.
. . . Heidegger's anti-liberalism and [his] conviction that cultural decline and nihilistic modernity could be overcome by a fundamental rethinking of Being under
the guidance of German hyper-nationalism provided a useful intellectual resource
for the German New Right.[50]

Hence, it should not come as a surprise that Heidegger's decisionistic insistence
that we must "choose ourselves" has led to his canonization as a prophet of the
European Identity Movement: the activist, internet-savvy, anti-immigrant youth
wing of the European Far Right, which has repeatedly sounded the alarm about
the perils of "cultural mixing" and "population replacement."[51]

A good illustration of Göpffarth's thesis concerning Heidegger's outsized influence among Neue Rechte militants derives from the Austrian Identitarians
Martin Sellner and Walter Spatz, who celebrate "Heidegger's true, 'ethnopluralist' message." According to Sellner and Spatz, Heideggerian *Seinspolitik* justifies "the freedom and self-realization of every *Volk* and of every culture within
the framework and context of its own character."[52] Similarly, in *Eurasian Mission*, Russia's leading Heideggerian, Alexander Dugin, has summarized
Heidegger's commitment to "ethnocentrism" as follows: "We are deeply convinced that our common goal aims at the protection of the *specific nature of nations, cultures, confessions, languages, values, and philosophical systems*, for
therein lies the 'ebullient richness' of our continent."[53]

However, as we have already noted in the case of the Nouvelle Droite, Sellner's, Spatz's, and Dugin's glorification of *völkisch* self-assertion merely in-
strumentalizes the language of democratic self-determination for the ends of
ethnic chauvinism. Once the pseudoegalitarian veneer is stripped away, their
arguments provide a template for the exclusion of groups that fail to conform to
the fiction of an ethnically homogeneous citizenship. As Spatz asserts, condemning the refugee "invasion," "The link between a *Volk* and a specific territory [*Raum*] is undeniable. *Belonging* is something that a *Volk* does on its own
land. . . .The migrant *belongs to no one*. It is a nomadic form of existence, the
Daseinsform of a chameleon."[54] Once the *Völk* is defined primarily in ethnic

terms, the citizenship rights of immigrants and minority groups are immediately jeopardized; the threat of demoting these groups to the rank of second-class citizens is never far off.

In *Sezession*—since 2003, the quasi-official organ of the Neue Rechte—one finds numerous encomia to Heidegger's *Denken* as the metapolitical ground or basis for the rising tide of pan-German chauvinism. As Sellner asserts in "My Path to Heidegger," "There is no such thing as a 'free thinking' or a 'free-floating subject' that lies encrusted beneath the layers of tradition. Instead, the quest for Dasein's essence and Being shows that *it is always rooted in a concrete, ethnocultural soil* [*in einem ethnokulturellen Boden verwurzelt*]. . . . Heidegger realized that an understanding of Being [*Seinsverständnis*] *always derives from a* 'Volk.' . . . It grows *out of the soil* [*Boden*]."[55]

In the Federal Republic of Germany (FRG), the "Identitarian" standpoint has been cultivated by a coterie of far-right intellectual provocateurs who are closely allied with the Alternative for Germany and PEGIDA, a clunky acronym for "Europeans United against the Islamicization of the Occident."[56] (In 2015, PEGIDA's founder, Lutz Bachmann, was forced to step down temporarily when a photo of him imitating Hitler surfaced. In 2016, Bachmann was convicted of inciting hatred for demeaning asylum seekers as "cattle," "scum," and "trash.")[57]

From the Neue Rechte's perspective, the advantages of Heidegger's "rooted" approach to *Denken* and *Wohnen* (thinking and dwelling) seemed compelling, since it offered an "existential" rationale for replacing the prevailing, *civic* understanding of citizenship with an *ethnic* definition predicated on the "right of blood." Embracing Heidegger's "antihumanism," the Neue Rechte has portrayed the "ideas of 1789" as the political equivalent of original sin: a fateful misstep that opened the door to the evils of democracy, egalitarianism, and popular sovereignty. Hence, among proponents of the Neue Rechte, Heidegger's conception of "rootedness-in-soil" as the *fons et origo* of political authenticity has enjoyed a notable resurgence.

The Neue Rechte has consistently championed Heidegger's thought as an ethnopolitical alternative to the dislocations of neoliberalism and the global cosmopolis. At the height of the Middle East refugee crisis, Martin Lichtmesz—a regular *Sezession* contributor and the doyen of the Austrian Neue Rechte—lauded Heidegger's fundamental ontology as extraordinarily *timely*, since "[Heidegger's] *Denken . . . praises borders*: the borders between natural science and philosophy, between the ontological and the ontic, Being and Dasein, and, last but not least, between *Volk* and *Volk*."[58] (Lichtmesz's claim is little more than a fabrication: in *Being and Time*, the term "borders"—*Grenzen*—is nowhere to be found.) Unsurprisingly, one of the Neue Rechte's preferred slogans is, "Secure borders for a secure future" (*Sichere Grenzen, Sichere Zukunft*).[59]

In response to the controversy over Heidegger's anti-Semitism that followed the *Black Notebooks'* publication, proponents of the Neue Rechte rushed to the Master's defense. Erik Lehnert, the director of the Institut für Staatspolitik (IfS)—a Neue Rechte think tank modeled after GRECE—accused Heidegger's critics of demonstrating "a total incapacity for empathy with respect to the spiritual situation of the 1930s and 1940s," since, at the time, "the nexus between world Jewry, Americanism, and Bolshevism" had been "scientifically established" (*sic*!) to such a degree that "no one seriously called it into question." Lehnert alleged that Zionist efforts to relocate European Jews to Palestine confirmed that Heidegger's anxieties about "Jews as agents of dislocation [*Entortung*]" were well founded. (That German Jews' decision to emigrate, far from being voluntary, was a result of Nazi persecution seems to have escaped Lehnert's attention.) According to Lehnert, the fact that Heidegger's anti-Semitic utterances provoked such an outpouring of criticism retrospectively validated his suspicions concerning the existence of a world Jewish conspiracy.[60]

The Return of the Repressed: A *Völkisch* "Alternative for Germany"

Until recently, Nouvelle Droite/Neue Rechte perspectives remained a relatively marginal phenomenon in Germany. In part, this failure resulted from the immunizing effect of the Nazi past, which had relegated discussions of *völkisch* nationalism to the periphery. However, in 2015, as the Middle East refugee crisis peaked, the situation changed dramatically. As a result of the party's surprisingly strong showing in the September 2017 federal elections, the AfD emerged as the official opposition party in the Bundestag. Despite the AfD's modest electoral falloff in September 2021, when it slumped to 10.3 percent of the vote, in all likelihood, it will remain a political force to be reckoned with for the foreseeable future.

In *Mut zur Identität* (The Courage for Identity; 1988), the Neue Rechte author Pierre Krebs lauded Heidegger's *Denken* as a watershed in the history of political thought, since it taught that (1) all existential questions are ultimately political questions and (2) all political questions are ultimately racial questions. Following Heidegger's lead, Krebs postulated that the "ultimate questions" of contemporary political life are twofold: they concern the "loss of spirituality" owing to the domination of modern technology and the threat to the white race posed by an increasingly militant Third Worldism. To support his case, Krebs cited Spengler's warning in *Man and Technics* (1931) concerning the imminent threat of "white extinction." "Is there today any member of the white race," inquired Spengler, "who can sense what is going on on this earth? Anyone who can sense the magnitude of the danger that hangs over and threatens the mass of races?" Echoing Spengler, Krebs claimed that the preservation of European identity hinges on the existential challenge confronting the white race: whether or not, in the future, indigenous Europeans would be able to maintain their racial superiority.[61]

Following German reunification in 1990, numerous obstacles that had previously hindered the Neue Rechte from advancing its ethnonationalist agenda dissipated. Led by a new generation, the movement's champions made a concerted effort to break free from the margins of German political life. Proponents of the Neue Rechte wagered that, by freeing the FRG from the constraints of the Western Alliance, a reunified Germany could resume its historical role qua "master of Mitteleuropa." They also realized that an essential precondition for Germany's reemergence as a "self-confident" nation was to remove the stigma of the Nazi past.

An unprecedented opportunity to achieve this end emerged in 1995 with the commemorations surrounding the fiftieth anniversary of the end of World War II. The Neue Rechte historian Karlheinz Weißmann waged a vigorous campaign—"Gegen das Vergessen" (Against Forgetting)—that disputed the postwar commonplace that 8 May 1945, the date of Nazi Germany's "collapse," signified a day of "liberation." Instead, Weißmann and other Neue Rechte publicists argued that National Socialism's defeat had precipitated a new series of national humiliations at the hands of the Red Army and the victorious Allies. Thereby, Weißmann and his fellow revisionists shrewdly transformed the post-Holocaust mantra "Never Forget!" into its opposite: a plea to commemorate *German victimhood*, while disregarding the suffering and misery that Nazi aggression had inflicted on others. That Germany's newspaper of record, the *Frankfurter Allgemeine Zeitung* (*FAZ*), had agreed to publish Weißmann's controversial appeal provided his gambit with a semblance of mainstream respectability.[62]

Weißmann's efforts to downplay Nazi criminality and to elicit sympathy for the Germans as "victims" transgressed long-standing taboos about German culpability. Henceforth, revisionist arguments about the Nazi past that, at the time of the *Historikerstreit* (1986–87), had incited a furor, increasingly gained a public hearing.

The Neue Rechte's obsession with "identity loss" reflected the racialist myth that the German "gene pool" was being imperiled by successive immigration "waves"—often described via recourse to the prejudicial metaphor of "Überflutung," or "inundation"—and the cosmopolitan—hence *anti-völkisch*—aspirations of the European Union. As Erik Lehnert, alluding to the "existential" correspondence between "soul" (*Seele*) and "native soil" (*Boden*), observed, "It is important to remember that such a thing as the German soul exists. Hence, there must exist a corresponding place [*Ort*]." Weißmann, for his part, stressed the importance of "remedying [Germany's] spiritual void" as one of the Neue Rechte's central tasks. Thereby, both Lehnert and Weißmann recurred to the trope of a *Rassenseele*, which was a standard component of Aryan "race mysticism."[63]

Neue Rechte publicists venerate the conservative revolution as a sacrosanct German "Identitätsort": a locus of German identity. Hence, they accord the conservative revolutionary *Denkhabitus* a pivotal role in the restoration of German identity.[64] Proponents of the Neue Rechte recognized that only by permanently divorcing conservative revolutionary thought from the Nazi past might one refashion it in a manner palatable for consumption by the political mainstream.

It was at this juncture that Heidegger's ideas began to gain currency among Neue Rechte ideologues. For example, in the introduction to the controversial anthology *Die selbstbewusste Nation* (The Self-Confident Nation; 1994), editors Heimo Schwilk and Ulrich Schacht, reprising the idiom of conservative revolutionary *Kulturkritik*, mobilized the authority of Heidegger's "Letter on Humanism" in order to arraign the Bundesrepublik's cultural and political failings: a "hyper-moralist," media-driven culture, soulless consumerism, and an incapacity for national self-assertion.[65]

Gerd Bergfleth's contribution to *Die selbstbewusste Nation*, "Erde und Heimat," represents another good example of the way that Neue Rechte intellectuals found Heidegger's philosophy serviceable for their critique of postwar Germany's rapprochement with democratic values. Bergfleth extolled Heidegger's understanding of *Boden* and *Erde* as a "metaphysical breakthrough": a hermeneutic tour de force that recaptured the chthonic depths of German "spiritual traditions." Bergfleth lauded the metapolitical potential of Heidegger's deployment of *Boden* and *Erde*: concepts that, according to Bergfleth, were well suited to disrupting the "identity-destroying" consequences of *Verwestlichung*, or the Federal Republic of Germany's "turn toward the West," a process, claimed Bergfleth, that was incompatible with indigenous German cultural and political traditions. According to Bergfleth, by grounding fundamental ontology in *Boden*, *Erde*, and *Heimat*, Heidegger paved the way for rehabilitating the ideology of German exceptionalism, the unjustly maligned *Sonderweg*: "The Germans have a special responsibility for *the fate of the Earth*, insofar as they have *a metaphysical link to it*. They must follow their *special path* [*Sonderweg*], which leads away from the superficial Enlightenment and toward an understanding of *Myth*. The antimodern German tradition, represented by Martin Heidegger and Ernst Jünger, will do battle with modernity and the ecological, economic, and technological disaster it has wrought. A *religion of the Earth* must reassert itself and, thereby, reconnect humankind with the Earth."[66]

Heidegger as Preceptor of a "Self-Confident Nation"

In keeping with the Nouvelle Droite's metapolitical orientation, the Neue Rechte sought to incite an acute rightward shift of German political culture. As Weißmann commented in a 1999 interview, "[We are concerned] with *spiritual influence*: we are not interested in stratospheric intellectual pursuits, but instead, with influence on lecture halls and seminar rooms, as well as influence on minds; if those minds happen to be situated on the shoulders of *Machtpolitiker* and political influencers, so much the better."[67]

Loyal to the Nouvelle Droite playbook, Weißmann and Dieter Stein agreed that reviving the conservative revolutionary standpoint was the optimal way to achieve these ends. As Roger Woods has confirmed in *Germany's New Right*, "[The Neue Rechte's] interest in the conservative revolution meant that intellectuals such as Carl Schmitt, Martin Heidegger, Ernst Jünger, Oswald Spengler [began] experiencing a comeback as the innovative thinkers behind the movement."[68] Echoing Wood's claim, in 2016, the editors of *Sezession* declared that their "goal . . . [was] to surmount the limitations of 'modern' ideologies by critically and honestly acknowledging the [value of] the conservative revolutionary tradition: of 'secret Europe.' "[69]

The strategic and ideological confluence of these two influential currents of the European New Right, the Nouvelle Droite and the Neue Rechte, was the fruit of a historic meeting, in 1966, between Alain de Benoist and the German Neue Rechtler Henning Eichberg that was brokered by the former Waffen SS officer Arthur Ehrhardt (1896–1971).[70]

In the wake of the electoral setback that the neo-Nazi NPD (Nationaldemok-ratische Partei Deutschlands) endured in 1969, the fortunes of the Neue Rechte grew apace, a shift that prefigured the transition from "electoral politics" to "metapolitics." In 1970, the Neue Rechte stalwart Caspar von Schrenk-Notzing inaugurated the review *Criticón*, the movement's founding organ. (At *Criticón*, one of Schrenk-Notzing's collaborators was the AfD cofounder and deputy chairman Alexander Gauland. During the 1990s, Gauland also contributed to the national revolutionary weekly *Junge Freiheit*.) In 1980, the New Rightist Pierre Krebs established the Thule Seminar, a far-right think tank that was en-visioned as the German equivalent of GRECE. Shortly thereafter, the historic 1966 meeting between Alain de Benoist and Henning Eichberg began to pay additional dividends, as Eichberg founded *wir selbst: Zeitschrift für Nationale Identität*. In 1986, Schrenk-Notzing reemerged to establish *Elemente*, the Ger-man namesake and corollary of the Nouvelle Droite's *Éléments*.[71]

The Neue Rechte has supplemented these journalistic ventures with a book se-ries, Edition Antaios, which specializes in monographs by prominent New Right and "IBD" (Identitäre Bewegung Deutschland) authors, such as Weißmann, Re-naud Camus, Harold Seubert, Martin Lichtmesz, Martin Sellner, Walter Spatz, and Götz Kubitschek. (The publishing house derived its name from a *Jahrbuch*, or "an-nual," that was cofounded during the late 1950s by Ernst Jünger and Mircea Eliade.)

In 2020, the Federal Office for the Protection of the Constitution (Bundesamt für Verfassungsschutz, or BfV), in keeping with the prerogatives of "militant de-mocracy," charged Edition Antaios with popularizing political views that under-mined Germany's "free basic democratic order" (*freiheitlich-demokratische Grundordnung*). As a result, the publishing house was placed on a national watch-list of right-wing extremist organizations. In 2019, a similar fate befell the IBD owing to its fraternization with various far-right hate groups. Among the groups that were named in the complaint against the IBD were the "Ein Prozent"—a ref-erence to the percentage of the German population that the movement would need to "win over" in order to topple the "Merkel-Dictatorship"—and an affili-ated publication, *Compact-Magazin*.[72]

The Neue Rechte augmented the aforementioned cultural-political undertak-ings by establishing an extensive network of institutes and think tanks: the

Christian Social Union (CSU)–affiliated Studienzentrum Weikersheim, the Bibliothek des Konservatismus in Berlin (the brainchild of the irrepressible Schrenk-Notzing), the Desiderius-Erasmus-Stiftung, which is currently the AFD's official think tank, and the Institut für Staatspolitik, which was founded in 2000 by Kubitschek and Weißmann.[73] (In German, "Weißmann"—nomen est omen—means "white man.")

Kubitschek, a former editor of *Junge Freiheit*, has also gained notoriety as a far-right provocateur. In 2000, Kubitschek was expelled from the *Bundeswehr* owing to his ties to neo-Nazi groups. In 2008, he made headlines when, along with other members of the so-called Konservative Subversive Aktion (KSA) group, he disrupted a reading by Nobel Prize–winning author Günter Grass in Hamburg.[74] (The point of this "action," if there was one, was to protest the admixture of "morality" and "politics" that was characteristic of Grass's interventions as a public intellectual—a recurrent Neue Rechte complaint.) Kubitschek has also been a frequent speaker at PEGIDA rallies in neighboring Dresden.

In recent years, the Institut für Staatspolitik, which is directed by Kubitschek, has increasingly gained visibility as a pilgrimage site for far-right intellectuals, IBD and IBÖ (Identitäre Bewegung Österreich) activists, AfD members associated with "Der Flügel" (a radical faction headed by the controversial Thuringian party leader, Björn Höcke), and journalists in search of a colorful political story. As the authors of a recent study of the *Identitären* explain, "A functional division of labor has developed on the right side of the German political spectrum. Members of right-wing parties who stand for election network with . . . and count on support from street-fighting right-wing activists. The AfD conducts political campaigns, while Neue Rechte publicists organize summer universities and launch public campaigns to 'mobilize patriots.' Meanwhile, the Identitarians reap the benefits from the discursive exposure of their pet themes."[75]

One would be hard-pressed to deny the significant political inroads that the Neue Rechte has made, the fruits of its openly declared "metapolitical" strategy of "total ideological saturation." "With the influence it wields on the AfD, the Neue Rechte currently possesses an instrument to impart its political ideas [more widely]."[76]

Worrisomely, in recent years, significant sectors of the German electorate have moved closer to Neue Rechte positions on citizenship, immigration, and the need for a strong German identity. These developments confirm, as one astute observer of the far-right political scene has remarked, that "a process of normalization [of Neue Rechte ideas] has begun."[77]

Against "Population Replacement"

In a 2003 interview, Dieter Stein, the editor of the Neue Rechte flagship organ *Junge Freiheit*, asserted that the Neue Rechte's central task was to reestablish the legitimacy of authoritarian nationalism, thereby facilitating Germany's rebirth as a "self-confident nation." One measure of the Neue Rechte's success is that, between 2008 and 2021, *Junge Freiheit*'s circulation spiked from fifteen thousand to twenty-nine thousand.[78]

Neue Rechte intellectuals view the revival of German nationalism as an urgent political task. They contend that, since the "collapse" of 1945, Germany has been unjustly and excessively penalized: subjected to a vindictive "Carthaginian peace" by the victorious Allies. They characterize the Allies' "political reeducation" campaign of the 1950s as tantamount to "brainwashing." Hence, according to the Neue Rechte, for decades, German identity has been unfairly suppressed and maligned. However, the flaw in the Neue Rechte's case for a return to "normal" German nationalism is that its advocates abstract from the potential links between the course of German historical development and the excesses of the Nazi period.

The proponents of the Neue Rechte display a persecution complex and an obsession with conspiracy theories that is widely shared among extremists on both sides of the political spectrum. Thus, in solidarity with fellow IB activists, Kubitschek and Weißmann have alleged that the European immigration crisis of 2015 was a "plot" to destroy the genetic integrity of the *Volk*, thereby tapping into a groundswell of xenophobia whose historical roots run deep. They have maligned former chancellor Angela Merkel's asylum policies as a case of *Bevölkerungsaustausch* (population replacement), thereby implying that native Germans are being "replaced" by racially inferior peoples from the developing world.[79] The Neue Rechte has condemned the German constitution's equal protection clause. And, in a German version of the National Front's "préférence nationale," it seeks to replace these constitutional safeguards with a definition of citizenship predicated on ethnicity or jus sanguinis.

In keeping with Carl Schmitt's *Concept of the Political*, Kubitschek and his allies claim that, in politics, everything depends on the capacity to distinguish friends from enemies: a distinction that, in the last analysis, hinges on whether or not one belongs to the *Volk*. As Kubitschek explains,

> I am convinced that, in a state of exception [*Ausnahmezustand*], or in times of need, as the threats to . . . one's own group along ethnic, cultural, and civic lines become clear, so does the question of who "We are" and who "We are not." . . In other words, when people in this land, in one or another respect, have had enough, the question of [political] loyalty is bound to arise, as it does already when it is a question of customs, values, and the legal statutes that Islam—as a religion that places unreasonable demands on the conduct of everyday life—views as fundamental and unquestionable.[80]

In posing the question of "who 'We are' and who 'We are not,' " Kubitschek recurred to a theme that was central to Heidegger's understanding of National Socialism as a movement that demanded an existential "decision" or commitment by virtue of which the *Volk* "chooses itself."[81] However, to reconceive politics primarily through the lens of the "friend/enemy" dichotomy—in terms of the Identitarian logic of "who 'We are' and who 'We are not' "—means transforming it into a permanent *Ausnahmezustand*. By suspending *Rechtsstaatlichkeit*, the "state of exception" licenses all manner of discrimination and persecution in the name of *völkisch* self-preservation.

"Releasement and Resistance"

In order to further gauge the impact that Heidegger's thought has had on the Neue Rechte, a good place to start is a volume published by Edition Antaios in 2014: *Gelassen in den Widerstand: Ein Dialog über Heidegger*, a colloquy between the Austrian *Identitären* Martin Sellner and Walter Spatz that seeks to reevaluate Heidegger's philosophical legacy in light of the ends of national revolutionary politics. (*Gelassenheit*, a keyword in the later Heidegger, is conventionally translated as "releasement." The *ethos* of *Gelassenheit* recommends the passive subordination of human will and action to the "sendings of Being." A plausible rendering of the title, therefore, might be the oxymoronic "Tranquility in Resistance.")

Sellner and Spatz's title plays on the idea of Heidegger as a *Widerstandskämpfer*, although nothing could be further from the truth. Such lexical duplicity is characteristic of the Neue Rechte's efforts to insulate conservative revolutionary thought from the inhumanity that was endemic to Nazism. The "Widerstand" trope assumes additional significance, since Neue Rechte ideologues have repeatedly implored its followers to undertake acts of "resistance" against Germany's legally constituted government, whose political legitimacy they contest, just as, during the 1920s, the conservative revolutionaries refused to acknowledge the legitimacy of the Weimar Republic.

In the Neue Rechte's efforts to undermine the *Rechtsstaat*, it has frequently invoked the integral nationalist distinction between *le pays réel* and *le pays légal*—hence its familiar political mantra, "Germany will survive the Bundesrepublik" (in truth, a poorly disguised summons to insurrection). Neue Rechte activists are accomplished demagogues and social media adepts who excel at inciting popular discontent, a mood they hope to channel toward the end of overturning Germany's "basic democratic order."

Gelassen in den Widerstand illustrates how, among supporters of the Neue Rechte, Heidegger's thought has become a constant point of reference as well as a valuable source of intellectual legitimacy. Parroting the idiolect of Heideggerian *Zivilisationkritik*, Sellner and Spatz portray modernity as a condition of total "uprootedness" (*Entwurzelung*). They have also endorsed Heidegger's apologetic claim that, although both the Third Reich and the Western democracies ultimately succumbed to the domination of modern "technics," National Socialism alone harbored the potential to surmount these afflictions and, thereby, to realize the bliss of "another Beginning." According to this revisionist perspective, Nazism's depredations were primarily attributable to excessive *Western influence*: above all, a surfeit of "technics." Thereby, the political deformations of the German *Sonderweg* remain uninterrogated—hence fundamentally intact.

Sellner and Spatz endorse Heidegger's "metapolitical" standpoint, since it contains invaluable directives that point toward a "third way" beyond the limitations of capitalism and socialism. They argue that only by reprising the values of ethnocultural "rootedness" and grounding politics in the *Volksbegriff* might German identity withstand the destructive effects of neoliberalism and multiculturalism.

Sellner and Spatz seek to substantiate these claims by invoking a litany of Heideggerian ideological platitudes, whose self-evidence they take for granted. "Modernity," they assert, "robs us of the ability to feel at home as a *Volk*. It also robs us of decisiveness [*Entschlossenheit*] and of the Event [*Ereignis*]. As a countermeasure, we need to emphatically reconnect with the *Volk* and its *Volk*-Being [*Volk-Sein*]. Only thereby may we escape the existential hollowness of modernity. By emphasizing *Heimat* and *Tradition*, we bid adieu to multiculturalism."[82]

Sellner and Spatz adhere to the Neue Rechte insistence that scholarly attempts to "work through" the pathologies of German history have outlived their usefulness. They fault "critical history" for hindering reunited Germany's capacity for national "self-assertion," which they define, following Heidegger, in terms of the *Volk*'s ability to "choose itself." They insist that acts of *völkisch* "self-preservation" have become more necessary than ever in light of the "identity-destroying" consequences of "multiculturalism" and so-called *Gender-wahnsinn* (gender madness)—the Identitarians' term of derision for sexual equality and gay marriage. Invoking Heidegger's notion of *Geschichtlichkeit*, Sellner and Spatz claim that only peoples who wholeheartedly embrace "*Volk* and heritage [*Herkunft*] retain the capacity to make history."[83]

As Sellner and Spatz make their argument for the identity-enhancing benefits of "ethnic separatism," they sound the alarm about the dangers of excessive Jewish influence. They claim that, should Germany ignore the imperatives of *völkisch* unity, it risks succumbing to the "boundless, 'Ahasverian,' cold and rootless spirit" of Western modernity.[84] The expression "Ahasverian" conjures the demeaning racial stereotype of the "wandering Jew," a trope with a long and ugly history.[85] The clear implication is that, should Germany fail to meet the challenges of "*völkisch* self-assertion," it will surrender to "Jewification" (*Ver-judung*), as it did during the Weimar Republic. Thereby, Sellner and Spatz echo Heidegger's complaint in the *Black Notebooks* that the "ruination" of Western modernity stems primarily from excessive Jewish influence.[86]

Analogous professions of racial intolerance and cultural prejudice occur throughout the essay. Sellner and Spatz characterize "the Anglo-American way of life" as a form of "cultural cancer": an affliction that conservative revolutionary thinkers correctly attributed to "racial mixing" or "mongrelization." They describe the ancient Greeks as a "Nordic *Volk*": a misapprehension that, during the heyday of European racism, was widespread among Aryan supremacists.[87]

Despite Sellner and Spatz's assimilation of Heideggerian *Kulturpessimismus*, they discern a modicum of hope on the horizon. Their optimism derives from what they disdainfully characterize as the "invasion of illegals" (*Invasion Illegaler*), which they view as a potential turning point in the political culture of the Bundesrepublik. In their view, the refugee crisis presages the end of

German passivity and—invoking yet another Heidegger trope—the emergence of "völkischer Entschlossenheit": a "resolve" or "decisiveness" that foreshadows the reemergence of a "combative" (*kämpferisch*) spirit.

In conclusion, Sellner and Spatz contend that "only by relying on the *Volk* can we ensure *rootedness* and *resistance* [*Boden und Widerstand*]." Recourse to *Bodenständigkeit* is the only way to prevent what the authors hyperbolically describe—in what is, presumably, an allusion to modern technics—as "the drama of annihilation that is transpiring before our eyes today, in which man is being uprooted [*entwurzelt*] and made 'poor-in-world' [*weltarm*]." With this claim, we are offered a consummate example of the way that Heidegger's exaggerated "critique of modernity" can be transformed into a catalyst for political extremism.[88] To resurrect the conservative revolutionary program that Heidegger championed would annul the advances in political freedom that the Federal Republic of Germany has achieved since its inception in 1949.

Marc Jongen: The Conservative Revolutionary "Leap"

In light of the preceding account, it should not come as much of a surprise that Heideggerian influences have shaped the AfD's political program. Often, this impact has resulted from the interventions of the AfD deputy speaker Marc Jongen (1968–).

Jongen received a PhD in philosophy from the University of Karlsruhe, where his supervisor was Germany's leading Heideggerian, Peter Sloterdijk (1947–). Jongen's dissertation, *Nichtvergessenheit: Aus der Einleitung in das Theorieprojekt* (Against Forgetting: From the Introduction to the Theory Project; 2009), builds on Heidegger's understanding of modernity as the ne plus ultra of *Seinsvergessenheit*. Jongen interprets Heidegger's summons to "overcome metaphysics," as well as his reconceptualization of truth as *alētheia*, as postmetaphysical keys to surmounting modernity qua *Seinsvergessenheit* and hence as a prescription for returning to ontological "origins." In 2016, Jongen was elevated to the post of the AfD's chief policy planner. The German press commonly refers to Jongen as the AfD's "Partei-Philosoph."[89]

In Jongen's evaluation of post-1945 German political culture, what alarms him most is the destruction of national identity by unpatriotic "leftists" and "liberals." This accusation coalesces with one of the Neue Rechte's central ideological objectives: to supplant the cultural hegemony of the 1968 generation with the political ideas of conservative revolutionary thinkers. In Jongen's reflections on Germany's political future, he repeatedly turns to the question of immigration. Immigration, claims Jongen, inevitably leads to *Überfremdung*: inundation by foreigners. He labels the idea that immigrants can be successfully integrated into German society the great "Lebenslüge" (self-deception) of the Bundesrepublik.

In another example of hyperbole, Jongen contends that the influx of non-German-speaking foreigners has placed the future of the German language itself at risk. Relying on arguments popularized by Thilo Sarrazin in *Deutschland schafft sich ab* (Germany Is Committing Suicide; 2010), Jongen alleges that, in the near future, the ethnic specificity of German culture will be unrecognizable, ignoring the fact that immunizing oneself from outside influences is, in all likelihood, a recipe for cultural decline.

According to Jongen, threats to German identity are omnipresent: "Every day, thousands of culturally alien, mostly male, mostly Muslim migrants illegally cross the German border; with each passing day, Germany is becoming a Syrian village, an Iraqi suburb, without a preexisting infrastructure. Whoever believes that the danger is past is merely providing encouragement to the hundreds of thousands of migrants in North Africa and the Near and Middle East who have been successfully rebuffed, yet who merely await the next major migration wave."[90]

Nevertheless, like Sellner and Spatz, Jongen regards the refugee crisis as a blessing in disguise: as an opportunity for the Germans to awaken from the blandishments of the U.S.-induced "culture industry." "The real affliction," observes Jongen, reprising an argument from Heidegger's 1929–30 lecture course *Die Grundbegriffe der Metaphysik*, "is our incapacity to sense our [current] state of affliction."[91] Hence, in a best-case scenario, the crisis might provoke Germans to rediscover their "destiny" as a "self-confident nation" and rally around the claims of *völkisch* togetherness.

According to Jongen, one of the prerequisites for national rebirth is to wrest German "culture" from the clutches of "self-hating" sixty-eighters, whose cosmopolitan, pro-European views have prevailed at the expense of German ethnic identity. Jongen maintains that committed German nationalists must restore culture's anthropological, "meaning-establishing" (*Sinn-stiftende*) function. Thereby, Jongen has reprised Heidegger's claims that *Bodenständigkeit* is a precondition for cultural "flourishing."

Echoing Carl Schmitt, Jongen maintains that the Federal Republic of Germany has entered into a permanent *Notzustand*, or state of emergency. Consequently, to reinforce the "We" in narrowly ethnic terms has become a matter of
national survival, hence the imperative of reforming Germany's citizenship
laws, rejecting jus soli, or equal citizenship, and restoring the *Volksbegriff*: a
concept of national belonging predicated on "ethnicity" or "blood."

In "Migration and *Thymos*-Training," a paper that Jongen presented at Kubitschek's Institut für Staatspolitik in February 2017, he urged reanimating the "national will" via an infusion of Platonic *Thymos*—"Mut," or "courage"—a term that
Jongen misleadingly translated as "Zorn" (wrath). This "wrath," continued Jongen—in what seemed to be an oblique reference to PEGIDA—must be directed
against asylum seekers and irresponsible politicians who, in thrall to a post-'68, an-
tinational *Schuld-Komplex*, seek to promote a self-destructive "Wilkommenskult"
(welcome cult) at the expense of a "self-confident" national identity. In conclusion,
Jongen, drawing on his philosophical training, urged his fellow Germans to make
a Kierkegaardian "Sprung," or "leap": from Kantian "Mündigkeit" (maturity) to
conservative revolutionary "Männlichkeit" (manliness).[92]

In 1934, Heidegger, referring to National Socialism, recommended a similar
"leap": "There can be no gradual and steady transition from the nonessential to
the essential. In order to join a community [*Gemeinschaft*], *each individual
must dare to take the leap*."[93]

Björn Höcke: " 'Yes' to the 'We'!"

Among Neue Rechte ideologues, Jongen is hardly alone in seeking to consign the Freudian trope of "working through the past" to the historical dustbin,
thereby "emancipating" Germany from its "national guilt complex." Among
Neue Rechte thinkers, the complaint that Holocaust commemoration has been
elevated to the status of a new "secular theology" and pillar of "political correctness" has become a recurrent leitmotif. Rejecting the neofascist obsession
with Holocaust denial, the Neue Rechte's strategy has been to belittle or trivialize its historical import. AfD cofounder and party chief Alexander Gauland
echoed the Neue Rechte's "Holocaust trivialization" strategy when, in a now-
infamous speech, he alleged that, when viewed against the backdrop of "1,000
years of successful German history," Hitler and the Nazis amounted to a "speck
of bird shit."[94]

In January 2017, the Thüringen AfD party leader and Neue Rechte activist Björn Höcke made headlines when he derided the Berlin Holocaust Memorial as a "monument of shame" (*ein Denkmal der Schande*): a blemish that detracted from Germany's capacity for national self-assertion. On an earlier occasion, Höcke, reprising terminology that had been popular under National Socialism, raised hackles when he lauded the prospect of Germany's "thousand-year future." Thereby, Höcke echoed the view of another controversial AfD politician, who claimed that excessive focus on the Holocaust adversely affected Germany's capacity for "Führertum": its ability to produce decisive and resolute political leaders.[95]

In a recently published dialogue, *Nie Zweimals in denselben Fluss* (Never Twice in the Same Stream), Höcke praised Heidegger's "metapolitical" contributions to the Neue Rechte worldview as a "Heimatsphilosoph." According to Höcke, "Heidegger's critique of technology and his interest in preserving nature and landscape—not as subjectively defined 'environments,' but as forests, valleys, fields, animals and plants of our *Heimat* that are in need of real protection—reflect the conservative bent of my political thinking."[96]

Höcke has frequently invoked Heidegger's authority in support of the Neue Rechte topos of the *Selbstbewusste Nation*. "As Germans," observes Höcke, "we must ask '*who we are*.' *We need to say 'Yes' to this We*. The German *Volk* must detach itself from the matrix of the contemporary Zeitgeist. It must surmount its 'Seinsvergessenheit' and instead come closer to its 'Seinsordnung.'" "Of course," avows Höcke, "*that is Heidegger*."[97]

A featured speaker at PEGIDA rallies and Institut für Staatsforschung seminars, Höcke has consistently been one of the most visible public presences on the far-right "scene." Moreover, since the AfD's *völkisch* turn in 2016, he has acted as a liaison between the various currents of the German far right: the IfS, the AfD, the IBD, and PEGIDA. Höcke also heads the AfD's *völkisch* wing, "Der Flügel," which holds annual meetings at the Kyffhäuser Monument, a sacred pilgrimage site among German nationalists.

From "Protest" to "Resistance"

By urging a return to an ethnic definition of citizenship, the Neue Rechte has sought to undermine the Federal Republic's reigning democratic political consensus. Thereby, it has sought to incite a "revolution from the right."

In recent years, leading Neue Rechte ideologues have urged their followers to transition from peaceful protest to "active resistance." On these grounds, one must take seriously the Neue Rechte's discursive commitment to overturning Germany's "basic democratic order" by any means necessary, including force, should circumstances prove ripe. As one journalist has recently noted, "Under the pressure of circumstances, a party of civil war has emerged in proximity to the AfD and PEGIDA. Its enthusiasm for violence is palpable and insatiable. AfD deputy speaker Alexander Gauland has misleadingly sought to conceal the party's *völkisch* political tendencies beneath a middle-class veneer. Among followers, his 'excuses' for the excesses double as a justification for the attacks. He and his *compagnons de route* present themselves as moderates. However, such rhetorical deception belies their actions: in truth, they are arsonists [*Brandstifter*]."[98]

The Neue Rechte's self-understanding as "revolutionists" helps to explain their intemperate "antiparliamentarism": their insistence that, in order to effectuate genuine change, one must act outside the existing political "system." In this respect, they have fully internalized Carl Schmitt's disparagement of parliament as a *Schwatzbude*, or "gossip chamber": a bourgeois debating society that lacks the capacity for Heideggerian *Entschlossenheit*, for undertaking decisive political action.

In the Neue Rechte's rhetorical assault against the "Merkel-Diktatur," it insinuates that German citizens have been deprived of a meaningful "alternative" (hence, *Alternative* for Germany) to the reigning liberal-democratic consensus. In order to combat "political tyranny," the Neue Rechte claims that the *Volk* must take matters into its own hands. If not, *Deutschtum*'s racial integrity will be submerged in a sea of cultural difference. In this way, the Neue Rechte has highlighted one of the European Union's genuine weaknesses—its "democratic deficit"—a failing that it exaggerates in order to argue for the EU's dissolution and a return to the parochialism of ethnic nationalism.

As Claus Leggewie warns in *The Anti-Europeans*, in light of the Neue Rechte's insurrectionary turn, "it is no longer a question of 'mere words.' " Instead,

> In the most recent events sponsored by the Institut für Staatspolitik, the summons to *Widerstand* has been issued, a summons made familiar by the PEGIDA demonstrations in neighboring Dresden. Is the Neue Rechte now pressing toward "the Deed" [*die Tat*], since it is convinced that, in light of the *Bundesregierung*'s failure to manage the "refugee crisis," the situation has reached a breaking point? . . . In other words, does *Widerstand* mean merely a *verbal radicalism*, . . . or will the

Radical Right succumb to the temptation to enter into the fray, either on the side of right-wing political parties, or in extraparliamentary movements, street demonstrations, or actions against refugee shelters or mosques?[99]

By mischaracterizing the Bundesrepublik as a "dictatorship," the Neue Rechte has propagated a "lexical inversion" worthy of Hegel's "verkehrte Welt." It denigrates champions of the *Rechtsstaat*, such as former chancellor Angela Merkel, as "tyrants." Conversely, Neue Rechte activists, who openly favor a return to dictatorship, misleadingly portray themselves as defenders of *Volkssouveränität* (popular sovereignty). In truth, however, they have merely reprised Carl Schmitt's tendentious definition of democracy as the "identity between leaders and led": a classic recipe for the abuses of authoritarian populism.

One of the Neue Rechte's glaring inconsistencies is that it encourages a grassroots "revolt" for the sake of establishing new forms of political authoritarianism. However, once the rhetorical smokescreen dissipates, its proximity to the mind-set of interwar fascism becomes increasingly apparent. In Neue Rechte discourse, the idea of a "worthy opponent" has ceased to exist. Instead, as the just-quoted remarks by Kubitschek demonstrate, politics has been reduced to distinguishing *Freund* from *Feind*.

Writing in *Die Zeit*, Thomas Assheuer has shed important light on the political stakes involved in the Neue Rechte's ideological ascendancy:

> Far-right is *far-right, not conservative*. Its goal is not to *preserve*, but to *destroy*. It is not interested in expanding the boundaries of the liberal public sphere; instead, it wants to *eliminate* it. The Neue Rechte dreams of an ethnically homogeneous *Volk*, of an organic state, and of a renewed German sovereignty predicated on *Machtpolitik*: that is, stripped of equality before the law, an independent judiciary, without migrants, without any obligation to "work through the past," and without the restrictions of the European Union. Its heroes are Vladimir Putin, Victor Orban, and Jaroslav Kaczyński. Whatever one says about the Neue Rechte, one cannot accuse it of duplicity: *its proponents say what they mean*. And should they come to the power, one may rest assured that their *deeds* will measure up to their words.[100]

By instrumentalizing Heidegger's philosophy for the sake of making inroads among the *Bildungsbürgertum*, the Neue Rechte has exulted in portraying itself as an "alliance of the righteous": a sincere and well-intentioned grouping that has been unjustly "persecuted" by the political establishment because of its willingness to "speak truth to power." In the words of the Austrian Identitarian Martin Sellner, "Today, [Heidegger] speaks to us [i.e., the Neue Rechte] since we are the last remaining oppositional force: a force that, along with its inconvenient truths, has been constrained by those who are in power to seek refuge underground. Although we dwell in 'darkness,' we inhabit a space beyond 'political correctness' and coercive political intrigue. Thereby, we represent the last bastion of intellectual freedom [*Denkfreiheit*]."[101]

Here, we encounter yet another meretricious "lexical inversion." Heidegger, a philosopher who zealously supported the Nazis, has been rebranded by the Neue Rechte as an *oppositional thinker*: an intellectual dissident and *Widerstandskämpfer* and a fearless detractor of "political correctness."

It seems that, recently, the Neue Rechte's strategy of transgression and gratuitous provocation, as honed by the likes of Kubitschek, Sellner, and Lichtmesz, has finally backfired. In 2019, the Austrian government opened an investigation into Sellner's ties to the Christchurch, New Zealand, mosque murderer, Brenton Tarrant, who, following an email exchange with Sellner, donated €1,500 to the IB's Austrian wing. In July 2021, the Austrian parliament passed the so-called Symbolgesetz, banning the public display of the identifying symbols of five politically extremist groups. Among the banned emblems was the black and gold representation of the Greek letter lambda, which, since 2012, has been the highly visible public symbol of the Austrian and German Identitäre.[102]

In March 2020, the Office for the Protection of the Constitution in Berlin announced that it was placing Höcke's "Der Flügel" under surveillance as a threat to Germany's "free basic democratic order." One of the reasons for the BfV's decision was the escalating ties between "Der Flügel" and members of the neo-Nazi NPD.[103] Then, in April, BfV director Thomas Haldenwang revealed that he had also decided to place Kubitschek's Institut für Staatspolitik under investigation because of its increasing links to various far-right organizations.

In March 2021—approximately six months before the federal elections that were scheduled to take place in September—Haldenwang announced that he was placing the AfD as a whole under investigation, thereby authorizing surveillance by Germany's domestic intelligence service.[104] With its luster tarnished by the ignominy of further federal scrutiny, the AfD's electoral fortunes sank. Whereas in 2017 it had garnered 12.9 percent of the vote, placing third overall, in 2021 its totals diminished to 10.3 percent, resulting in a disappointing fifth-place finish. For the time being at least, the AfD's rise to prominence seems much less inevitable than many pundits had originally assumed.

Alexander Dugin: Heidegger's Dubious Russian Disciple

Unlike other New Right thinkers, Alexander Dugin (1962–) has made little effort to mask his fascist political allegiances. Coming of age during Soviet communism's twilight years, Dugin revered Nazism as the ideology that provided maximal political leverage to oppose an increasingly senescent and moribund "state socialism," *from the right*. In keeping with these convictions, as a youth, Dugin joined the Black Order of the SS, a secret organization that was affiliated with the esoteric Yuzhinskii Circle. Led by the shaman and polymath Yevgeny Golowin, the Black Order of the SS was dedicated to exploring the link between Russian nationalism and Aryanism. According to reliable reports, members were obligated to address Golowin as "Reichsführer SS."[105]

As Dugin avowed in "Fascism: Borderless and Red" (1997), what the motherland needed, following communism's ignominious collapse during the early 1990s, was a "Russian national socialism": "*an authentic, real, radically revolutionary and consistent fascism, a fascist fascism.*" Fusing Nietzsche with the Waffen-SS, Dugin characterized Russian fascism as a "revolutionary, rebellious, romantic, idealistic [form of nationalism] appealing to a great Myth and transcendental Idea . . . [that] gives birth to a society of heroes and supermen. . . . The nature of fascism [is] a new hierarchy, a new aristocracy, [that] is based on natural, organic, and clear principles: dignity, honor, courage, and heroism."[106]

When the *Black Notebooks* appeared in 2014–15, Dugin must have felt wholly confirmed in his Heidegger loyalties upon encountering Heidegger's conjectures—uttered in the aftermath of the Hitler-Stalin pact—concerning the geopolitical affinities between *"Deutschtum und Russentum."*[107] It would be difficult to formulate a more felicitous distillation of Dugin's political credo.

Among Heidegger's New Right acolytes, Dugin occupies a niche that is sui generis. For one, Dugin is a self-professed Heideggerian who has published numerous monographs and commentaries on Heidegger's work. Among his better-known contributions are *Heidegger and the Possibility of Russian Philosophy* (2011), *Heidegger: The Philosophy of Another Beginning* (2012), and *Martin Heidegger: The Last God* (2012).

Dugin's notion of the "Fourth Political Theory"—which Dugin has promoted as the successor ideology to the politically bankrupt precedents of liberalism, fascism, and communism—is predicated on the "völkisch" and "rooted" inflections of Heidegger's fundamental ontology. As Joakim Andersen has observed in *Rising from the Ruins: The Right of the 21st Century*, "The Fourth Political Theory's . . . central category is Heidegger's *Dasein*. Instead of abstractions, it concerns our *real identities*."[108] In a recently published monograph, *Political Platonism: The Philosophy of Politics* (2019), Dugin has reaffirmed the Heideggerian fundament of his political thinking, asserting, "The construction of the Fourth Political Theory is based . . . on Heidegger's philosophy and represents the development of its implicit content."[109]

"Putin's Brain"

Dugin's exceptional status among New Right Heidegger acolytes is also reflected in his privileged access to an influential coterie of foreign-policy advisers surrounding Vladimir Putin. The jacket copy of *Political Platonism* boasts, "For more than a decade, Dugin has been an advisor to Vladimir Putin and the Kremlin on geopolitical matters."[110]

Although the nature and extent of Dugin's influence on Putin has been a matter of dispute, following Russia's annexation of Crimea in 2014, a spate of commentaries appeared that referred to Dugin as "Putin's Brain" or "Putin's Rasputin."[111] The articles reflected the fact that, following Russia's military intervention in Crimea and eastern Ukraine, Putin, on several occasions, cited Dugin's doctrine of "Neo-Eurasianism" as an ideological justification for Russian aggression. (In 2003, with the Kremlin's blessing, Dugin established a Eurasian Party. In 2004, he founded a Eurasian Youth Organization, whose goal was to indoctrinate Russian youth in the ideology of Russian nationalism.)

In the decade that followed Putin's unexpected rise to the presidency of the Russian Federation (1999–), he searched for an ideology to replace communism. Putin's growing attraction to Dugin's Neo-Eurasianism reflected his political evolution from reluctant democrat to avowed autocrat. As outlined and promoted by Dugin, Neo-Eurasianism sought to provide postcommunist Russia with a geopolitical *raison d'être*: with an orientation that reaffirmed the Russian Empire's expansionist ambitions under tsardom, hence a "mission" that would reverse the Soviet Union's extensive territorial losses under Mikhail Gorbachev and Boris Yeltsin.

One sign of Dugin's growing influence among Kremlin foreign-policy elites emerged in 2011–12, when Putin, in an effort to offset his plummeting standing in national opinion polls, proposed the creation, under Russian leadership, of a "Eurasian Union": thereby tacitly endorsing the expansionist program that Dugin had advocated since his days as a lecturer at the Academy of the Russian General Staff.[112]

As the Ukraine crisis escalated in 2014, Putin repeatedly invoked "Neo-Eurasianism" as a mandate for Russia's geopolitical "push to the south." In May 2014, Russian separatists in the Donbass region of eastern Ukraine brandished the term in order to justify their declaration of a "Union of Novorossiya" or "Greater Russia." In August 2014, Putin once again used the term in a presidential directive that he addressed to the "Insurgents of Novorossiya." Neo-Eurasianism has, undoubtedly, been Dugin's greatest contribution to "Putinism." Claus Leggewie has denounced Dugin as a "desk murder" for his role in furnishing the ideological rationale behind Russia's southern imperial expansion—its geostrategic "push to the Caspian Sea."[113]

Dugin has also managed to influence Putin's views on a variety of controversial cultural themes: "Limits on personal freedom, a traditional understanding of the family, intolerance of homosexuality, and the centrality of Orthodox Christianity to Russia's rebirth as a great power."[114] As Dugin gloated in November 2016 following Trump's electoral victory, "In contrast with Hillary Clinton, Trump does not view LGBT supporters, feminists, and postmodernists as the be-all and end-all of 'progress.' From now on, the only thing that they can hope for will be to get medical treatment for their perversions."[115]

Following Moscow's annexation of Crimea, Putin's approval ratings skyrocketed. Most Russians agreed with Putin's misleading claim that Crimea and eastern Ukraine were, historically, part of Russia. Hence, they enthusiastically supported Moscow's reliance on military might to enforce its dubious claim to sovereignty.

Following Russia's military intervention in Crimea, Dugin's cachet among New Right intellectual circles also escalated dramatically. In May 2014, he was one of the featured speakers at a coven of far-right political leaders and ideologues that was held at the Liechtenstein Palace in Vienna. Although the gathering was supposed to be secret, its existence was unmasked by the Austrian journalist Bern-hard Odehnal.

The organizers had billed the conference as a twenty-first-century "Congress of Vienna," thereby alluding to the "Holy Alliance," orchestrated by Prince Metternich in 1815, to suppress the rising tide of European democracy. Other high-profile attendees included the Austrian Freedom Party (FPÖ) chairman, Heinz-Christian Strache; Marine Le Pen's leading political adviser, Aymeric Chauprade; and Marion Maréchal-Le Pen, at the time the National Front's "ris-ing star." Among the themes discussed at the meeting was "how to save Europe from liberalism and the 'satanic' gay lobby."[116]

Dugin, ever a stranger to moderation, became intoxicated with his own ce-lebrity. In support of the eastern Ukrainian independence movement, he de-clared, "I believe that one must kill, kill, and kill. I make this claim in my capacity as professor."[117] Among the students at Moscow State University, Dugin, by making this pronouncement, had clearly overreached. To protest Dugin's bloodthirsty, exterminationist rhetoric, they organized a petition that was signed by some ten thousand students. Shortly thereafter, Dugin was stripped of his position.

"Dasein's Existence Is *Völkisch*"

In *The Fourth Political Theory* (2013), Dugin took his bearings from Heidegger's reformulation of the *Seinsfrage* during the 1930s in accordance with the "metapolitics of the historical *Volk*."[118] Relying on this Heideggerian demarche for conceptual leverage, Dugin asserted, "Dasein's existence is *völkisch*. To exist in concrete, human terms means . . . to exist as a German, Frenchman, Russian, American, African. . . . *Völkisch existence is the reality that most closely approximates the essence of man*."[119] During the early 1990s, Dugin's numerous encounters with the Nouvelle Droite proved crucial in his transformation from an avowed neofascist to Russia's leading proponent of "ethno-differentialism," or racism with a "human face."[120]

Dugin's fulminations against Western liberalism as the zenith of *Machen-schaft* demonstrate the degree to which he had internalized Heidegger's "affect against logocentrism and rationalism, universalism and humanism."[121] It was in this spirit that, in *Heidegger: The Philosophy of Another Beginning*, Dugin en-thusiastically reprised Heidegger's denigration of "Anglo-Saxon liberalism" in

Die Geschichte des Seyns (1939) as the zenith of "planetary idiocy."[122] Dugin's characterization of "liberalism" as a "pandemic"—as a form of political contagion that must be urgently *eradicated*—openly echoed the Nazi lexicon of "virology":

> Calculating reason at the basis of liberalism and its values are the last stage of *degeneration of Western European ontology. It is impossible to go any lower.* We must look for the roots of liberalism *as a fatal and deadly pandemic in Europe.* But it is in the U.S. that this political phenomenon has acquired its ultimate form. . . . Man of the global world, a "liberal," accepting and recognizing the normativity of the "American way of life," is the kind of person who is a *patented idiot* from the philosophical . . . point of view, a *documented idiot, an idiot parading his foolishness above his head like a banner.*[123]

In "Donald Trump: The Swamp and the Fire"—an article that Dugin published in 2016, following Donald Trump's victory in the U.S. presidential elections—Dugin, faithful to the New Right's "negative branding" strategy, proclaimed, "*We need a Nuremberg Trial for liberalism.*" Dugin classified liberalism hyperbolically as "the last totalitarian political ideology of modernity." "Let us close this page of history," he urged.[124]

As the foregoing quotations attest, rhetorical excess and emotional revulsion are trademarks of Dugin's discursive idiolect. These traits bespeak a neofascist mind-set that denies its opponents' existential legitimacy.

Dugin has also lowered himself to justifying Heidegger's Nazism on ideological grounds, claiming that, since Heidegger was justifiably opposed to Bolshevism and Americanism—both of which were dominated by the same "technological frenzy"[125]—he had no choice but to embrace the Third Reich as a political bulwark against these complementary political evils. (That Heidegger's commitment to Nazism meant supporting a regime for which the commission of mass atrocities was a state-sanctioned credo leaves Dugin seemingly unfazed.)

In almost the same breath, Dugin managed, cagily, to vindicate Heidegger's anti-Semitism. As Dugin explains, Heidegger, following Nietzsche, viewed the Old Testament—a text that, Dugin reminds us, was canonized by a "Semitic people"—as incompatible with "Indo-European" traditions. Hence, when viewed from an "ethnopopulist" perspective, Heidegger's efforts to combat "culturally alien" Jewish influences represented a case of *défense légitime.*[126]

According to Dugin, one of Heidegger's salutary achievements as the philosopher of "another Beginning" concerned his efforts to keep corrosive Jewish intellectual influences at bay. One of the ways that Heidegger achieved this desideratum was through his critique of "logocentrism." Dugin reminds us that, although the primacy of "logos" may be traced back to the deformations and missteps of the Socratic School, "the same is true for Judaism, in the case of Philo the Jew and, above all, in Medieval Judaism and the Kabbalah." Echoing Heidegger, Dugin explained that, today, we are experiencing the endgame of a process of cultural decomposition that has been abetted by the "unfettered explosion of modern technics."[127]

The Geopolitical Mission of "Mother Russia"

As Volker Weiß has noted in *The Authoritarian Revolt*, Dugin's understanding of geopolitics has from its inception been Heideggerian through and through. At nearly every turn, it was informed by the existential imperatives and messianic structure of Heideggerian *Raumpolitik*. As Weiß observes, "The central ideas of Dugin's 'cultural theory of space,' the correlation between *Sein und Raum*, or Being and Space, derive from Heidegger's writings."[128]

However, in adapting the secular eschatology of Heideggerian *Seinsgeschichte* to Russian circumstances, Dugin appended an all-important twist: in light of National Socialism's "collapse," "Mother Russia" inherited Germany's "mission" as world-historical "redeemer." In monographs such as *The Last War of the World Island: The Geopolitics of Contemporary Russia*, Dugin insisted that Russia's "Eurasian mission" was not merely *regional* but *planetary*. As Dugin avowed with alarming frankness, "*All the powers and states in the world that possess tellurocratic properties depend on whether Russia will cope with this historic challenge and preserve and strengthen its sovereignty.*"[129]

Dugin's allusion to "tellurocratic properties" expressed his understanding of history as a geopolitical struggle between the "tellurocratic" (or land-based) powers of the Neo-Eurasian "heartland" versus the "thalassocratic" (or maritime) powers of England and the United States. In Dugin's view, the struggle for "world mastery" between Russia and the United States represented a "struggle unto death," or *Vernichtungskampf*.

Dugin portrayed this battle—the "Last War of the World Island"—as an *eschatological struggle*: an apocalyptical conflict between "good" and "evil."

Since the Western "thalassocracies"—Great Britain and the United States—were exclusively focused on *material gain*, they were the main carriers of "European nihilism" and "planetary *Machenschaften*." Conversely, Russia embodied what Dugin called a "heroic civilization" of the "land-based type." According to Dugin, Russia championed a *"vertical, hierarchical, Messianic structure of government."* Hence, Russia was the only "planetary" power capable of reanimating the "traditionalist" values of *"faithfulness, asceticism, honor, and loyalty."*[130]

In *The Last War of the World Island*, Dugin consistently portrayed the struggle between the Neo-Eurasian "heartland" and the seafaring "thalassocracies" as *Armageddon*. As Dugin observes,

> The Eurasian civilization, established around the Heartland with its core in the Russian *narod* [people], *is much broader than contemporary Russia*. . . . To guarantee its territorial security, Russia must take military control over the zones attached in the south and the west, and in the sphere of the northern Arctic Ocean. Moreover, if we consider Russia a *planetary-tellurocratic pole*, then it becomes apparent that its direct interests extend *throughout the Earth and touch all the continents, seas, and oceans*. Hence, it becomes necessary to elaborate *a global geopolitical strategy for Russia*, describing in detail the specific interests relating to each country and each region.[131]

Muscovite Metapolitics: Dugin and the Nouvelle Droite

Dugin, in solidarity with his Nouvelle Droite *compagnons de route*, defined success in "metapolitical" terms: as winning the battle for "ideological hegemony." In 2008, when he was appointed director of the Center for Conservative Research at Moscow State University, Dugin announced that his top priority was to acquaint Russian youth with conservative revolutionary thinkers such as Heidegger, Carl Schmitt, and Ernst Jünger. Consequently, under Dugin's tutelage, "a large portion of the Center's activities involved the clarification, reinterpretation, and adaptation of the ideas of the Counter-Enlightenment and the conservative revolution as they apply to Russian politics, global affairs, and international relations. Especially important in the agenda of Dugin's Center was the legacy and ideas of René Guénon, Julius Evola, Carl Schmitt, Martin Heidegger, and Oswald Spengler."[132]

As Stephen Shenfield has observed in *Russian Fascism: Traditions, Tendencies, and Movements*, Dugin's eschatological enthusiasm for the "conservative revolution" offers a telltale ideological clue: the "smoking gun" that "identifies Dugin unequivocally as a fascist." "For Dugin," continues Shenfield, the "conservative revolution is 'the Last Revolution,' 'the Greatest Revolution in history,' . . . the Return of the Angels, the Resurrection of the Heroes, and the uprising of the heart against the dictatorship of reason."[133]

Since Dugin's youthful dalliances in Yevgeny Golowin's Yuzhinskii Circle, he had been attracted to mysticism as an intellectual counterweight to the epistemological rigidity of dialectical materialist orthodoxy. Dugin's aversion to the methodological constraints of "scientific socialism" inspired his veneration of fascism as an effective means of combating the ideology of "state socialism."

Dugin's youthful attraction to Julius Evola's "spiritual fascism"—during the 1980s, he translated Evola's *Pagan Imperialism* into Russian—helps to explain his fascination with the esoteric dimensions of Heidegger's thought: Heidegger's veneration of "secret Germany" (*geheimes Deutschland*) and, at a later point, the "Fourfold" (*Geviert*): gods and mortals, heaven and earth. Dugin's propagation of "spiritual racism"—an epithet that is often used in conjunction with Evola's "Traditionalism"—emerged unambiguously in his early monograph *Hyperborean Theory* (1993): "The Aryan," Dugin insisted, "according to his essence, is not defined by *biology*, but instead by his *metaphysical mission*. . . . Aryans are a race . . . of *Nordic Warrior-Priests*."[134]

Dugin's background as a Heidegger initiate played an important role in his efforts to endow Russian geostrategic thinking with a higher sense of purpose: with a "calling" that, in the words of Anton Barbashin and Hannah Thoburn, was simultaneously "mystical, spiritual, emotional, and messianic"—hence with an orientation toward "transcendence" that fused politics and the mystical longings of a revivified Russian Orthodoxy.[135]

Dugin found additional "spiritual" inspiration for his steadily evolving Neo-Eurasian worldview in Heidegger's *Philosophy of Another Beginning*—the subtitle of Dugin's most important Heidegger commentary, which was published in 2011.[136]

The Heideggerian theme that Dugin found most congenial for his "Hyperborean," neo-Aryan designs was the "Fourfold" (*das Geviert*): Heidegger's speculative appellation for the presencing or interplay between "heaven and earth, mortals and divinities." In later essays such as "Building, Dwelling, Thinking," the Fourfold provided the foundation or ground for Heidegger's postmodern pagan cosmology. It proffered a vision or world-picture that offered "mortals" a respite from "modernity" as an age of total and unremitting "Gottesverlassen-heit" (abandonment by gods). The Fourfold harbored an esoteric redemptive promise: "hints" concerning the advent of the "god to come."[137]

Heidegger's treatment of "dwelling" (*Wohnen*) reprised his endorsement, during the Nazi era, of "rootedness-in-soil" as a normative touchstone. On these grounds, Julian Young, in one of the few scholarly articles on the Four-fold, interpreted Heidegger's understanding of "Earth" as providing a warrant for the New Right's "ethnopluralism." According to Young, "Heidegger always thought within the unspoken presupposition of a one-to-one correspondence between *ethnic communities* and *natural places*. . . . He viewed modernity's mingling of populations as simply *the destruction of dwelling*. . . . The idea of different communities of dwellers sharing the same 'earth' and 'sky' simply does not cross his mind." Young concluded with a dig at Heidegger's gratuitous obscurantism: "Among the many 'mysteries' surrounding 'the Fourfold' is the almost total absence of any attempt by Heidegger scholars to explain what it is.[138]

What mesmerized Dugin about the Fourfold was Heidegger's "geo-meta-physics" or "earth-mysticism": its antipositivist, *mystical* conception of "Earth," an approach that reinforced Dugin's efforts to endow geopolitics with a *higher, spiritual mission*. As Dugin observes in *The Rise of the Fourth Political Theory* (2017), "I agree with Heidegger that the Earth (*Erde*) in *das Geviert* (Fourfold) is a philosophical Idea, as is world (*Welt*) (or heaven [*Himmel*]). Germany is an Idea, as is Russia. Earth is dialectically linked with the sky. Their *battle* forms the Dasein of a concrete *Volk*. Heidegger founded an existential understanding of the *Volk*. . . . This point is the basis of the Fourth Political Theory."[139]

The Fourfold provided support for Dugin's view of the mystical, salvific role that "Mother Russia" was destined to play in the drama of world history. Thus, according to Dugin, it was the *Russian narod*, or *Volk*, rather than Germany, that embodied the ontological-historical key to realizing "another Beginning." For Dugin, the formal structure of Heideggerian *Seinsgeschichte* remained in-tact. Heidegger had merely wagered on the wrong *Volk*, or *narod*.

Dugin sought to rectify Heidegger's "error" by envisioning Russia as a "Third Rome": as the rightful heir to the Roman Empire. According to Dugin, twenty-first-century Russia was the land-based "Behemoth," whose "Eurasian Mission" was to annihilate the Anglo-American "Leviathan" as the "New Carthage."[140]

"Words That Kill": Oslo, 22 July 2011

Words are never merely "words." As philosophers of ordinary language have noted, they are also "speech acts." In addition to their semantic properties, words also entail perlocutionary effects, pragmatic consequences for human action.

The Nouvelle Droite formulated the concept of "idées-forces" to indicate the causal relationship between political ideas and their effects.[141] In contrast with poetry or a conversation among friends at a café, "idées-forces" delimits a class of ideas whose raison d'être is to have a determinate political impact.

The sophists were among the first to appreciate the manipulative capacities of rhetoric: its power to persuade people to act against their own interests. If we turn to the effects of language qua *ideology*, its abilities to influence human behavior escalate exponentially. As linguistic paradigms, ideologies discourage criticism and reinforce credulity. Because of their aversion to ambiguity and their penchant for reducing complex issues to prefabricated responses, ideologies function in a manner that is similar to "myth."

As is the case with myth, ideology is less concerned with *truth* than it is with *narrative consistency*—hence its effectiveness in keeping dissonant views at bay. This explains ideology's efficacy in furnishing the "worldviews" on which the twentieth century's totalitarian political systems were based. As the political philosopher Michael Freeden has observed, "Ideologies ... map the political and social world for us. Every ... ideology is one such instance of imposing a pattern—some form of structure or organization—on how we read—and misread—political facts, events, occurrences, and actions." Ideologies are indispensable to making sense of the social and political world. Yet, as Freeden hastens to add, " 'making sense' does not always mean making *good* or *right* sense."[142]

Whereas the twentieth century's major political ideologies—communism, fascism, and Nazism—ultimately discredited themselves, conservative revolutionary thought, which hovered between Nazism and fascism, has managed to survive. As we have seen, today, among the global New Right, it is undergoing a significant revival.[143]

Insight into the nature of political ideologies allows us to distinguish between gradations and types of violence. Whereas criminal violence is often circumstantial and devoid of broader social or cultural aims, political violence, as a product of ideology, is motivated by a preexisting ideational template. Consequently, one of the defining traits of political violence is that it justifies violent actions in the name of an *idea*.

On 22 July 2011, Anders Behring Breivik, a thirty-two-year-old Oslo resident, perpetrated an act of terrorism that was unprecedented by Norwegian standards. Although Breivik's killing spree lasted only seventy-five minutes, in that short amount of time, he murdered seventy-seven defenseless innocents—a "kill rate" of approximately one per minute. Although the deed itself was brief, it had been years in the planning stages.

The massacres that Breivik committed in Oslo and Utøya were no random undertaking. They had been underwritten and licensed by an ideological template: a discursive regime that, in the words of the British scholar of neofascism Paul Jackson, owed much to "the New Right thinking of figures such as Alain de Benoist and his attempt to invert racism through the discourse of 'differentialism.' "[144]

In the online manifesto that Breivik posted the morning of the attack, he expressed the fear that Europe was in the throes of a "tidal wave" of "Islamization." As the drama of "population replacement" reached its peak, Europe would become *Eurabia*: Sharia would become the law of the land, and Nordic-looking, "indigenous Europeans," like Breivik, would soon become a minority. Breivik's Islamophobia was, to be sure, delusional and overwrought. At the same time, his paranoia had been stoked and shaped by a preexisting political script.

Breivik's massacre was, unequivocally, a political crime: a misdeed that, as subsequent analyses have shown, had been ideologically framed and motivated. Breivik "christened" his online manifesto—a rambling, fifteen-hundred-page, "cut-and-paste" document—*2083: A European Declaration of Independence*. The date 2083 alluded to the four hundredth anniversary of the Battle of Vienna, when European troops halted the advance of Ottoman armies, thereby sparing western Europe from the threat of Muslim domination.

Breivik's manifesto expressly referenced the Nouvelle Droite's "ethno-differentialism."[145] Faithful to the New Right's "ethnopluralist" line, Breivik stressed that he was neither a neo-Nazi nor a white supremacist. Hence, he "would not hesitate to sacrifice [his] own life for the English, Slavic, Jewish, Indian, Latin or French tribes in their fight against the EUSSR/US hegemony."[146] As a "Nordic European," Breivik was merely defending his "tribe."

Significantly, Breivik's manifesto was also suffused with references to the conservative revolution: a movement that he repeatedly invoked as a touchstone of political authenticity. Characterizing his motivations, Breivik described himself as a "martyr for the conservative revolution."[147] He portrayed his "ideological journey" as a course that led from "indoctrinated multiculturalist zealot to conservative revolutionary." "They may physically kill a Justiciar Knight," Breivik observed. Though the path may be arduous, those who join "will be remembered as conservative revolutionary pioneers."[148]

Frustrated by the unwillingness of mainstream conservatives to support the idea of deporting Muslims, en masse, to their homelands, Breivik avowed, "if these writers are too scared to propagate a conservative revolution and armed resistance, then other writers will have to." At another point in his manifesto, Breivik stated, "I am a commander of the Knights Templar. Our organization was set up in London in 2002." Its ultimate goal was to effectuate a "conservative revolution," which Breivik characterized as "the only solution for free Europeans." "There is no greater glory," Breivik continued, "than dying selflessly while protecting your people from . . . demographical annihilation."[149]

The Breivik episode reminds us that not only do words have consequences, but violent words have violent consequences. Those who exalt the conservative revolutionary standpoint—a worldview that is predicated on a masculinist warrior ethos and an aesthetics of violence—glorify a discursive framework whose celebration of the "deed," as with the *Tatkreisler* (Hans Zehrer et al.), stands as an invitation to excess.

In retrospect, we know that Breivik's justification of his sanguinary deed in *A European Declaration of Independence* did not fall on deaf ears. A review of Brenton Tarrant's anti-Muslim screed "The Great Replacement" confirms that Breivik was one of the Christchurch, New Zealand, mosque murderer's role models and heroes.[150]

POSTSCRIPT

Heidegger and *Heimat*

Heidegger remained sufficiently a Nazi after the war that he was
convinced that world opinion was totally dominated by Jews.
—Hans-Georg Gadamer, "The German University and German Politics: The
Case of Heidegger" (1986)

HEIDEGGER'S EXISTENTIAL "DECISION" FOR HITLER WAS not—as Heidegger
loyalists have contended—a case of philosophical "self-misunderstanding."
Nor did it result from an anomalous "metaphysical *lapsus*" on Heidegger's
part: a "miscue" that was spurred by Heidegger's having temporarily lost sight
of the "critique of Western metaphysics." Nor was it an "error"—"die grösste
Dummheit meines Lebens," as Heidegger once put it—that Heidegger "rectified" by belatedly criticizing the empirical failings of "really existing" National
Socialism.[1] As Ernst Tugendhat—in a remark that I cited earlier—observed,
"Heidegger's Nazism was no accidental affair. . . . [Instead], a direct path led
from his philosophy—from its de-rationalized concept of truth and the concept
of self-determination defined by this—to Nazism."[2]

Ultimately, Heidegger's criticisms of empirical National Socialism never impelled him to seriously call into question his abiding metaphysical commitment
to the movement's "inner truth and greatness," which, as we have seen, he defined in terms of the "confrontation between planetary technology and modern
man." His misgivings never caused him to abandon the conviction that, despite
the movement's "phenomenal" imperfections, it represented an "authentic"
step toward realizing "another Beginning": an *Ereignis*, or Event, that would

rescue humanity from the tyranny of European nihilism. Hence, some twenty years after the *Stunde Null*, Heidegger continued to insist that "*National Social-ism . . . moved in the right direction.*" The problem was that the movement's ar-chitects and executors—that is, the NSDAP leadership—"were far too limited in their thinking to acquire an explicit relationship to what is really happening today and has been underway for three centuries."[3]

In those rare moments of self-examination in which Heidegger probed the failure of his political wager on Nazism, he insisted that there had been nothing *inherently* wrong with that commitment. Thus, he described the debacle of his rectorate as merely a case of *bad timing*. In essence, the *kairos* had been prema-ture. As Heidegger commented after the war, "*The error was that the 'time' was not yet ripe. . . .* [It] was due to my failure to recognize the immaturity of the [his-torical] 'forces.' "[4] Heidegger had merely been mistaken in his assumption that, as he put it, "world-historical *Denken* . . . could be established and cultivated at this particular moment."[5] Thereby, "Heidegger the fox" (Arendt) cagily held out the possibility that, at some future date, the *kairos* would be more propitious—at which point "authentic" National Socialism might stage a comeback.[6]

In "The Rectorate, 1933–34: Facts and Thoughts," Heidegger claimed that the rectorate episode, in and of itself, had been "meaningless" (*bedeutungslos*). It merely illustrated "the essential, metaphysical situation of 'science,' which has been consumed by 'technics,' and which, consequently, has proven to be re-fractory to all the attempts at renewal."[7] But seeking to attribute responsibility for the "German catastrophe" to "metaphysics" and "technics" was merely an-other strategy of avoidance on Heidegger's part. At another point, he sought, disingenuously, to explain away his political folly as a premature attempt to reconcile the *Seinsgedanke* with "the administrative requirements of an institu-tion of public instruction."[8]

The *Black Notebooks'* publication demonstrates that, even after the war, Heidegger's commitment to the idea of a Jewish world conspiracy remained undiminished. In *Anmerkungen I–V* (1942–48), for example, Heidegger excori-ated "world journalism" (*Weltjournalismus*) as a Jewish plot to subdue Ger-many and, thereby, to prevent its regeneration. " 'Spirit' that masquerades as world journalism," claimed Heidegger, is "*more devastating than the fallout generated by an atomic bomb.*" The Jews, worshipers of a "vengeful" God, had orchestrated a "revenge industry" (*Racheindustrie*), claimed Heidegger. "To-day," he railed, "an ancient *spirit of revenge* encircles the Earth. The intellectual

history of this revenge will never be written, for to do so would inhibit the revenge itself. . . . The public sphere itself [*Öffentlichkeit*] is already [a form of]
revenge."⁹

According to Heidegger, the Jews, by leveraging the *Schuldfrage*, had sought
to impose their "slave morality" (*Sklavenmoral*) on the Germans. He absolved
himself of the need to make amends for his commitment to Nazi rule on philosophical grounds, arrogantly claiming that "moral judgments [are] incompatible with the loneliness of *Denken*."¹⁰ Heidegger reprised this line of defense in
the Nietzsche lectures that he published in 1961, declaring, "Neither moral, nor
cultural, nor political standards suffice when it comes to the responsibility that
Denken, according to its essence, must confront," thereby reaffirming that "essential thinking," instead of clarifying matters, merely "explains away."¹¹

Despite compelling evidence to the contrary, Heidegger maintained that it
was the "Western powers" (*Westmächte*) that bore the ultimate responsibility
for the European catastrophe of 1939–45. Their "thoughtlessness [*Gedankenlosigkeit*]," Heidegger insisted, "surpasses *1000-fold* the irresponsible evils that
Hitler visited upon Europe." Heidegger claimed that the "reeducation of the
German *Volk*" under the Allied occupation was tantamount to its "degradation
to the status of helots." The *real* tragedy of the war was that "the German *Volk*
and land have become a singular KZ [concentration camp] *unlike anything the
world has ever seen and will ever see*." According to Heidegger, with the Allied
occupation of Germany, the "machinery of death" (*Tötungsmaschinerie*) that
was once employed by the Nazis was "inflicted on the Germans themselves."¹²

The irreparable flaw of Heidegger's repudiation of Western philosophy as
a "metaphysics of subjectivity"—as a process of "domination," whereby "beings" are systematically manipulated and debased qua "standing reserve"
(*Bestand*)—became glaringly apparent in *Anmerkungen I–V* (GA 97), as Heidegger contemplated the origins of the Nazi *Vernichtungslager*. Oblivious to the
deformations of the German *Sonderweg*, Heidegger attributed responsibility for
the extermination camps not to National Socialism but instead to Western metaphysics. In Heidegger's view, the camps were merely an extension of the West's
limitless capacity for instrumental reason and technological domination. Hence,
"National Socialism [failed] because it turned into 'rational socialism.' "¹³

By disingenuously attributing the Third Reich's failures to the disintegrative
effects of *Machenschaft*—which, according to Heidegger, was itself a product
of "world Jewry's" unbridled penchant for "calculation, huckstering, and

self-insinuation"—his explanatory scheme rashly devolved into "blaming the victims."[14] After the war, he doggedly insisted, "The modern system of total-itarian dictatorship derived from *Jewish-Christian monotheism* [*jüdisch-christlichen Monotheismus*]."[15] Time and again, when it came to fathoming the reasons for the German catastrophe, Heidegger refused to recognize the Nazis' murderous ideology of racial domination as a contributing variable or cause. In-stead, blinded by his commitment to the political theology of German exception-alism, Heidegger insisted that the fault lay with Germany's enemies.

Notwithstanding Heidegger's various prevarications and denials, in the sec-ondary literature, an exculpatory consensus has emerged that credits him with having definitively broken with the regime at the time of the Battle of Stalin-grad (1942–43): that is, once it had become clear that Nazism had been soundly defeated. However, these empathic interpretations of Heidegger's conduct overlook the fact that, at this point in time, there was little of the Third Reich, as a regenerative political project, left to support. Instead, what remained was the ideology of "total war." Moreover, it is well known that, during the last two years of the war, supporters of Nazism began abandoning the regime in droves.[16]

As Markus Gabriel has pointed out in "Heidegger's Anti-Semitic Stereo-types," Heidegger's "enlistment" for Nazism had always been primarily *idea-tional* and *philosophical*. It derived from his belief in the transformative capacities of National Socialism qua "movement" as opposed to a commitment to the NSDAP qua "institution" or "party."[17] As Heidegger admitted in retro-spect, "[With Nazism], I perceived the prospect of a gathering and renewal of the *Volk*, and a path leading to the attainment of its Western-historical essence [*geschichtlich-abendländischen Bestimmung*]."[18] Thus, in light of Gabriel's ob-servations concerning the philosophical grounds of Heidegger's political com-mitment, his belated disillusionment with "really existing" National Socialism would seem to count for very little, since his faith in Nazism's "inner truth and greatness" persevered well into the postwar era.

At base, there was never any *prise de conscience* on Heidegger's part con-cerning the inherent criminality of the regime he supported. The Freudian trope of "working through the past" never held any interest for him.[19] Consequently, following the war, Heidegger remained impervious to the prodigious ethical and political requirements of German reconstruction. Instead, in keeping with the Nietzschean ethos of "active nihilism," Heidegger rationalized Nazi brutal-ity as something that was ontologically required by the higher imperatives of

Seinsgeschichte. This conviction emerged with Heidegger's disturbing claim that "the path leading from Being to Thinking hews closely to the edge of annihilation [*Vernichtung*]."[20]

Seinsgeschichte as *Seinsdogmatik*

In the postwar period, Heidegger's thought was increasingly marked by a rigid and inflexible *Seinsdogmatik*: an ontological dogmatism that contrasted sharply with his earlier "existential" summonses to "decision" and "authenticity." In *Von der Existenzialontologie zur Seinsgeschichte*, Winfried Franzen has aptly characterized this ontological fundamentalism as the "hypertrophy of Heidegger's 'Seinsbegriff.' "[21] Consequently, in his later philosophy, "[Heidegger] elevated Being to the rank of *absolute subject of history*. 'Man,' conversely, was condemned to total subjection to Being and its fateful 'Sendings' [*Schickungen*]."[22]

It is not difficult to find ample textual support for Franzen's claim that, by hypostasizing the *Seinsgedanke* as a metaphysical Absolute—a primordial *Macht* or power, whose inscrutable "emanations" surpass the meager cognitive capacities of the lowly human understanding—Heidegger succeeded in rendering human action and will all but superfluous. For example, how should one interpret Heidegger's tautological declaration in "Recollection in Metaphysics" that "the history of Being is neither the history of man and humanity, nor the history of the human relation to beings and to Being. *The history of Being is Being itself, and only Being*";[23] or his complementary assertion in the "Letter on Humanism" that "man does not decide whether and how beings appear, whether and how god and the gods or history and nature come forward into the lighting of Being, come to presence and depart. The advent of beings lies in the *destiny of Being* [*Seinsgeschick*]. Hence, for man it is always a question a finding what in this essence corresponds to such destiny."[24] As Karl Löwith observed in *Heidegger: Thinker in a Destitute Age*, Heidegger's conception of the destiny of Being remained unconvincing, insofar as, instead of being based on "rational adjudication," it depended on a "suspension of disbelief": "Heidegger's claim concerning the necessity of his *Denken* will only convince those who already believe that his *Denken* has itself been 'sent' by Being: a 'destining of Being' [*Seinsgeschick*] that expresses the 'dictate of the truth of Being.' Such matters resist rational adjudication."[25]

If the "Sendings" of *Seinsgeschick* are as enigmatic and inscrutable as these asseverations imply, it becomes difficult to imagine how humanity, individually or collectively, might establish a meaningful relationship to the ontological problematic that Heidegger is describing, to say nothing of *Seinsgeschichte*, more generally. So extreme did Heidegger's aversion to inherited philosophical positions become that, ultimately, he deprived himself of the conceptual and discursive tools necessary to render his doctrines intelligible and coherent. Thus, as one sympathetic critic has observed, the dilemma that beset Heidegger's later work concerns "the extent to which one can counter philosophy with an approach that, . . . in the guise of 'authentic thinking' [*eigentliches Denken*], exempts itself from philosophy's requirements."[26] Especially telling in this respect was Heidegger's polemical dismissal of "Enlightenment" in *What Is Called Thinking?* (1954) as a standpoint that "darkens the essential heritage of thinking."[27]

The conceptual confusions and ambiguities of *Seinsgeschick* help to explain the later Heidegger's persistent recourse to questionable etymologies and ungrounded linguistic speculation in order to compensate for the escalating dearth of phenomenological "concreteness." This explains the increased prominence of obscure, quasi-mystical formulations such as "thinking is thanking" (*Denken ist Danken*), "Openness to the Mystery" (*Offenheit zum Mysterium*), and the "Fourfold" (*das Geviert*): "gods and mortals, heaven and earth"[28]—thus the legitimacy of Karl Löwith's insinuation that Heideggerian *Seinsgeschick* was essentially a form of "disguised theology" (*verkappte Theologie*).[29]

Insofar as Heidegger's reformulation of the "task of thinking" was increasingly tied to an escalating rhetorical and linguistic obscurantism, it frequently transgressed the limits of discursive intelligibility, the Kantian "bounds of sense." Since the *Seinsgedanke*, qua "transcendens," defied the epistemic capacities of ordinary language, Heidegger's *Denken* openly flirted with mysticism—hence his assertion in the "Letter on Humanism" that, "if man wishes to find himself once again in 'proximity' to Being [*in die Nähe des Seins*], he must, first and foremost, learn how to *exist in the Nameless* [*im Namenlosen zu existieren*]."[30] But what "existing in the Nameless" might entail is something that Heidegger declined to specify or define.

Adding to the confusion, Heidegger in his later work increasingly amalgamated "philosophy" and "poetic saying" (*dichterisches Sagen*). Whereas "the thinker says Being," declaimed Heidegger, "the poet names what is Holy."[31]

Blurring the lines between *Dichten und Denken* impelled Heidegger to embrace the cognitive value of myth. In light of the inadequacies of "Western metaphysics," the epistemological advantages of myth, as a type of privileged access to the mysteries of "Being" as "the Holy," presented themselves to Heidegger as increasingly promising.

Accordingly, in *What Is Called Thinking?*, Heidegger confirmed that the superiority of pre-Socratic philosophy derived from the fact that, in ancient Greece, *mythos* and *logos* subsisted in primordial unity. Heidegger regarded their subsequent estrangement as a primary symptom of philosophy's irreversible decline:

> *Mythos* stakes a primordial claim that concerns all human beings a priori. . . . *Logos* says the same thing as *mythos*. In contrast with the customary view of the history of philosophy, *mythos* and *logos* do not enter into philosophy as antitheses. Instead, the early Greek thinkers . . . employ *mythos* and *logos* to mean the same thing. *Mythos* and *logos* only enter into opposition when *mythos* and *logos* have forfeited their primordial essence, which already occurred with Plato. A prejudice . . . that derives from the Platonism of modern rationalism holds that *mythos* was destroyed by *logos*. But nothing *religious* can ever be destroyed by *logic*; it can only be destroyed by the god's withdrawal.[32]

Insofar as "Western metaphysics" bore responsibility for the *Seinsverlassenheit* (abandonment by Being) of modern man, Heidegger advocated the "end of philosophy" as a precondition for resurrecting the "task of thinking."[33] Hence, in *Zur Sache des Denkens*, Heidegger counseled "turning away from philosophy" and toward a more "essential" (*wesentlich*) or "originary" (*anfänglich*) thinking: a reorientation that required "overcoming metaphysics" and its replacement by a more "primordial" (*ursprünglich*) "thinking of Being."[34]

It is not hard to see that Heidegger's "ontological fatalism" conditioned his visceral antipathy to the values of democratic self-determination. As Alfons Söllner has commented, "[Heidegger's] evocative linguistic magic leads to a *mimesis of fate* rather than to an analysis of concrete social causes of the [contemporary] crisis. . . . The authoritarian sense or non-sense of Heidegger's thought lies in its jargon and its linguistic gestures."[35]

Heidegger's *Seinsdogmatik* consistently demanded that human thought and will capitulate before the "destinings" and "emanations" of Being. As he wrote to Erhard Kästner in 1963, "No human calculation and action can, in and of itself, bring about a turn in the present state of the world, if only because human dealings are molded by the state of the world and at its mercy."[36] Three years later, when pressed by *Der Spiegel* to comment on whether philosophy could shed light on the contemporary historical situation, Heidegger emphatically demurred: "The sole possibility that is left for us is to prepare a sort of *readiness*, through *Denken* and *Dichten*, for the appearance of the god or for the absence of the god in an age of decline [*Untergang*]; for, in the face of the god who is absent, we *perish* [*gehen unter*]."[37]

The later Heidegger increasingly sacrificed the *lumen naturale* of reason to a neopagan cosmology that focused on "naming the unnamable": the "Holy" in the form of the "absent god."

Another consequence of Heidegger's reformulation of the "task of thinking" as "Openness to the Mystery" and "existing in the Nameless" was his abandonment of meaningful human intentionality: a terminus that was consonant with Heidegger's ideologically conditioned rejection of the "metaphysics of subjectivity." Thus, following the "Turn," prospects for meaningful Being-in-the-world and authentic Being-with-others all but disappeared from Heidegger's *Denken*. They were effectively sidelined by the heteronomous and self-subsistent imperatives of *Seinsgeschick*.

Heidegger demoted "man" to the status of a lowly "shepherd of Being" (*Hirt des Seins*). Conversely, he ennobled language ontologically as the "House of Being." However, in doing so, Heidegger pointedly devalued the intersubjective, communicative dimension of language: the indispensable role that language plays in facilitating understanding. Instead, true to the paradigm of "antihumanism," Heidegger declared, "Language speaks, not man." "Man 'speaks,'" Heidegger continued, "only insofar as he *passively* [*geschicklich*] *corresponds to language*."[38] By ascribing a primordial, ontological function to language, Heidegger reconceived language as a form of heteronomy. Language no longer served immanent, human ends. Instead, Heidegger presented language as "the Master of man [*die Herrin des Menschen*]."[39]

Heidegger's ontological dogmatism also manifested itself in the totalizing character of his technology critique. As Heidegger observed in the *Der Spiegel* interview, "The essence of man is framed, claimed, and challenged by a power which manifests itself in the essence of technology, a power that man himself does not control."[40] "Everything," declared Heidegger, stands under the sign of the "disconsolate frenzy of unbounded technics and rootless organization of the average man. The spiritual decline of the Earth has progressed so far that peoples are in danger of losing their last spiritual strength, the strength that makes it possible even to *see* the decline and to appraise it as such. . . . The darkening of the world, the flight of the gods, the destruction of the Earth, the reduction of human beings to a mass, the hatred and mistrust of everything creative and free has already reached such proportions throughout the whole Earth."[41]

The intransigence and rigidity of *Seinsgeschick* resulted in Heidegger's inability to formulate meaningful inner-worldly distinctions: a debility that culminated in a type of acute judgmental paralysis. No matter where Heidegger trained his Medusa-like, ontological gaze, the end result was the same: the same "frenzy of unbounded technics and rootless organization of the average man," the same implacable reign of *Machenschaft* and *Gestell*. As he avowed in 1945, "What Ernst Jünger conceptualized as the 'Herrschaft' and 'Gestalt' of the 'Worker' betrays the universal domination of the 'Will to Power' [*Wille zur Macht*] with respect to planetary history. Today, everything stands within its grip, whether it is called communism, fascism, or world democracy."[42]

The impoverishment of Heidegger's *Zeitdiagnose*—his inability to distinguish between totalitarian forms of political rule and "world democracy," whatever its failings and limitations—reflected Heidegger's more general devaluation of intersubjectivity and "practical reason." Ultimately, the ebb and flow of phenomenal history paled in comparison with the majesty of *Seinsgeschichte* qua *Ereignis*. This ontologically conditioned impasse exemplified Heidegger's *inability to think*—no small irony in light of the fact that, in *Gelassenheit* (1955), Heidegger leveled the accusation of "thoughtlessness" (*Gedankenlosigkeit*) against all intellectual perspectives that failed to measure up to the sublimity of the *Seinsgedanke*. Ultimately, the onto-ontological difference—the distinction between "Being" and "beings"—which Heidegger regarded as his foremost philosophical strength, proved to be his greatest weakness.

In *What Is Called Thinking?*, Heidegger reprised this pessimistic diagnosis of the times, claiming that, from the standpoint of *Seinsgeschichte*, World War II had "decided nothing." So far removed from the "lifeworld" was the *Seinsgedanke* that even the toppling of the tyrannical and genocidal Hitler-*Diktatur* failed to register: "What has the Second World War actually decided—not to speak of its terrible consequences for our *Vaterland*, especially, the laceration down its middle? The world war has decided *nothing*, if here we take 'decision' in the strong sense, as it pertains uniquely to the essential destiny of man on this Earth. Only the indecisiveness of what remains comes a little more clearly into view."[43]

Heidegger's supporters have effusively praised the prescience and timeliness of his technology critique.[44] However, a more sober and measured assessment suggests a very different verdict. For, by disavowing action and contestation in the prosaic sphere of phenomenal history, Heidegger's ontological determinism ended up reinforcing the reign of technological *Machenschaft* that he purportedly sought to criticize. As Alexander Schwan observes appositely in "*Zeitkritik* and Politics in Heidegger's Later Philosophy,"

> Whether it is a question of Christianity, socialism, Marxism, nationalism, racism, biologism, psychologism, sociologism, positivism, materialism, Americanism, liberalism or democracy, *Heidegger perceives only the unity and uniformity of the contemporary world*. All of these phenomena contribute to the *calculation, planning, and breeding of the totality of beings*. . . . By leveling and amalgamating these variegated and divergent tendencies qua "machinations" of the "will to will," Heidegger fortified and reaffirmed these tendencies philosophically. Insofar as meaningful distinctions disappeared, Heidegger rendered questions of moral-political responsibility obsolete. . . . Ultimately, [Heidegger's] ontological-historical assessment of the totalitarian tendencies of the age . . . offered nothing that might contribute to the overcoming of National Socialism.[45]

The Search for an "Other Public"

According to a widespread misapprehension, following the war Heidegger retreated from politics, finding solace in "poetic revealing" and the serenity of *Gelassenheit*—a trope that Heidegger had assimilated from the mystical doctrines of Meister Eckhart (1260–1328)—"releasement toward things" or "letting beings be."

However, this understanding of Heidegger's *Denkweg* is only partially true. Following his *Lehrverbot*, Heidegger consciously sought out an "other public." He perceived this path as an important step on the road to rehabilitation. Thus, beginning in 1949, Heidegger undertook a series of well-publicized lectures—titled "Insight into That Which Is"—in order to warn his fellow Germans about the evils of technology and the "Atomic Age."

The lectures were presented at a variety of elite civic venues. At the Bremen Club, Heidegger addressed a monied aristocracy that was composed of captains of industry, shipping magnates, and merchants. According to eyewitness accounts, the attendees revered Heidegger as a "demigod" and embraced his portentous musings on *Seinsgeschick* as a source of religious consolation.[46] In March 1950, at the Bühlerhöhe sanatorium—a fashionable spa in the upper Schwarzwald—Heidegger spoke to a public that consisted of the local patriciate. In June, Heidegger delivered a revised version of the first lecture, "Concerning the Thing," at the Bavarian Academy of Fine Arts in Munich.

Heidegger's peculiar choice of venues raised numerous eyebrows. According to Rüdiger Safranski, the public increasingly began to wonder "whether Heidegger was not perhaps a 'vogue philosopher' or indeed a charlatan. Was he, they asked, still respectable as a scholar?"[47]

In light of Heidegger's ban on teaching, many of those who decided to attend viewed their presence as a form of protest against the Allied occupation authorities. Heidegger's efforts to attribute the Holocaust to the excesses of modern technology were well received by a public that had little appetite for addressing the *Schuldfrage*, to say nothing of the so-called pathologies of German historical development. Instead, in keeping with the mood of *Vergangenheitsverdrängung* (repression of the past) that predominated during the Adenauer era (1949–62), many Germans preferred to view the Nazi dictatorship as a *Betriebsunfall*, or "industrial accident." In the words of a foreign observer, "The Germans act as though the Nazis were a strange race of Eskimos who came down from the North Pole and somehow invaded Germany."[48]

Heidegger's neo-Spenglerian indictment of the excesses of modern technology proved to be an efficacious strategy of avoiding the sensitive topic of German culpability—in essence, by "changing the subject." By identifying *Technik* and *Gestell* as the "culprits," Heidegger intimated that national self-scrutiny was superfluous, since the veritable causes of the German catastrophe were *external*. Thereby, Heidegger succeeded in shifting attention to the forces that he viewed as real "perpetrators": "Russia and America," nations he denounced as the primary carriers of *Machenschaft*, or the "disconsolate frenzy of unchained technics and rootless organization of the average man."[49] No special leap of the imagination was required to appreciate the fact that the *Siegermächte* (victors) against whom Heidegger directed his polemical focus currently had hundreds of thousands of troops stationed on German soil.

Heidegger's lamentations about the evils of planetary technology also played exceptionally well in light of the emerging national consensus about the

Germans as victims of Nazism and as a "community of suffering." After all, in December 1949, as Heidegger stepped to the podium in Bremen, many German cities remained landscapes of devastation: *Trümmerhaufen* (heaps of rubble) to which they had been reduced by the Allies' punitive and indiscriminate bombing campaign during the final two years of war.

Heidegger began his Bremen Club discourse by stating, "Nineteen years ago, I gave a lecture here in which I uttered things which are only now being slowly understood. . . . I took a *risk* then, and I will take a *risk* again today!"[50] However, as a man and as a thinker, Heidegger remained inherently *risk averse*. Hence, Hannah Arendt's description of Heidegger, in a letter to Jaspers, as "charakterlos" (lacking in character), "in the sense that *he literally has none. . . .* This living in Todtnauberg, grumbling about *Zivilisation*, and writing *Sein* with a 'Y' is really a kind of mouse hole he has crawled back into. . . . He rightly assumes that nobody is likely to climb 1200 meters to make a scene; and if somebody did, he would lie a blue streak, . . . fast-talking himself out of everything unpleasant."[51]

In light of Arendt's critique, it seems pertinent to inquire, exactly how much of a "risk" did Heidegger take that evening in Bremen, when, in lecturing on "das Gestell," he relativized the Nazi "extermination camps" by equating them with "mechanized agriculture [*motorisierte Ackerbau*]" and—alluding to the Soviet blockade of Berlin in 1948—"the blockading and starvation of nations." "Agriculture," claimed Heidegger, "is a mechanized food industry, no different from the manufacture of corpses in gas chambers and extermination camps, or the blockade and starvation of nations, or the manufacture of hydrogen bombs."[52] Instead of *risking* anything, Heidegger merely restated a widely held "immoral equivalence": that the criminality of the Allies was on a par with that of the Germans. Thereby, Heidegger contributed to the repression of the *Schuldfrage*. Instead of providing "insight into that which is," Heidegger proffered rationalizations and pseudoexplanations that obscured the historical specificity of the events in question. By doing so, Heidegger confirmed that, in truth, he was the archetypal "conformist."

The Primacy of German Suffering

Following the war, Heidegger reinvented himself as a "public intellectual." In this capacity, his central concern was German suffering and the injustices of the Allied occupation.

The topic of German suffering is legitimate and important. Heidegger's failing or *lapsus* concerned his insensitivity to the massive suffering that Nazi Germany had inflicted on others. Once again, Heidegger's *Deutschtümelei* interfered with his *Urteilskraft*, his "faculty of judgment."[53]

Heidegger's narrow focus on German misery, in tandem with his refusal to explore the missteps of the German *Sonderweg*, conveniently allowed him to circumvent the "reality principle": that is, that German suffering had resulted from the brutal "war of aggression" it had launched against its hapless neighbors. The publication of the *Black Notebooks* demonstrates that Heidegger continued to support Nazi policies even after his involvement with the regime in an official capacity had ceased.

One of the foremost symptoms of "German misery" stemmed from the massive influx of German nationals—in toto, approximately, twelve million—who had either fled the advancing Red Army or had been forcibly expelled from the East. Seven million of these "expellees"—so-called *Reichsdeutsche*—hailed from the four provinces that Germany had forfeited after the war in accordance with the Yalta and Potsdam accords: East Prussia, Silesia, Pomerania, and Brandenburg. The remaining five million expellees were so-called *Volksdeutsche*: ethnic Germans who had resided in lands outside the Reich. Among the *Volksdeutsche* were three and a half million *Sudetendeutsche*: German residents of Bohemia and Moravia, the Czech provinces that, in 1939, had been forcibly incorporated into the Reich—in violation of the 1938 Munich Pact—as "protectorates." Many Sudeten Germans had resettled in neighboring Bavaria in the hope of an early return to their lost *Heimat*.

The expellees, or *Vertriebene*, comprised 16.5 percent of West Germany's population. They formed a powerful, revanchist-minded political lobby, the Bund der Heimatsvertriebenen und Entrechteten (League of Expellees and Disenfranchised, or BHE). Since many of the expellees had been expulsed from their homelands by Soviet troops—which, after the war, had remained as "occupiers"—they were virulently anticommunist. Many expellees advocated a bellicose, irredentist foreign policy, adamantly insisting on their "Heimatrecht." Consequently, in many significant respects, the expellees' ideological agenda coincided with that of the Nazis. As one chronicler of the expellees' plight explains, "The refugees' hostility to communism had its roots in long-standing anti-Soviet prejudices, intensified by Nazi propaganda. These preconceptions were reinforced by the traumatic experiences they had suffered during their flight or expulsion from their homelands as the Red Army moved westwards during 1944–45. They blamed the Soviet Union and its communist satellite states in Eastern Europe for the loss of their homes, tending to forget that the actions of Soviet troops and indigenous populations were in response to the atrocities committed by the National Socialists during the Second World War."[54]

In light of the Bund der Heimatvertriebenen's revanchist political designs, the Allies denied the expellees the right to form a political party. But as the Cold War escalated, constraints on the expellees' organizational aspirations began to weaken, despite the fact that many of the *Vertriebenen* were former Nazi Party members. (Eight out of the thirteen founding members of the BHE were ex-Nazis.) In 1964, BHE activists played a pivotal role in the creation of the Nation-aldemokratische Partei Deutschlands, or NPD, Germany's first neo-Nazi party.[55]

The term *Entrechteten*—literally "those who have been divested of their rights"—in the BHE appellation referred to former Nazis who had been banned from positions of authority because of their involvement with the Third Reich. Heidegger, because of his *Lehrverbot*, qualified as *Entrechteter*: a designation that highlighted the unfairness of the proscriptions that ex-Nazis had been forced to endure. Thereby, the BHE leadership sought to portray its members as the *real victims*.

Heidegger's self-understanding as a public intellectual—his efforts to preserve the memory of German suffering—coalesced fully with the agenda of the Bund der Heimatvertriebenen und Entrechteten. However, what was glaringly absent from his campaign to highlight the legacy of *German misery* was a concomitant acknowledgment of the misfortunes that Germany had visited on others.

Heidegger addressed the injustices of German suffering in his capacity as a *Festredner*, or keynote speaker, at numerous commemorative events and public occasions. A good example was the memorial address that he presented in 1955 in honor of the 175th birthday of the Swabian composer Conrad Kreutzer (1780–1849). Heidegger's speech—which was published in 1959 as *Gelassenheit*—has assumed a quasi-legendary status in the Heidegger canon. In it, Heidegger developed numerous key ideas of his later *Denken*. Hence, *Gelassenheit* has been regarded as emblematic of Heidegger's shift from an ethos of authentic "decision" to "releasement," in keeping with the ontological fatalism of *Seinsgeschick*.

In truth, however, there was much more at stake in the address. It broached themes that are of pivotal importance for comprehending Heidegger's self-understanding in the postwar period as a "metapolitical" thinker: as a thinker who actively sought to influence and shape the identity of the nascent Federal Republic of Germany. An attentive reading of Heidegger's text suggests that he strove to assume the role of *praeceptor Germaniae*, in a manner that paralleled his political self-assertion during the 1930s. Hence, under the changed political circumstances of the 1940s and 1950s, Heidegger reinvented himself as the spokesperson for Germany as a "community of suffering."

Heimatlosigkeit and Irredentism

To highlight the exigencies of German suffering, Heidegger accorded the problem of *Heimatlosigkeit* (homelessness) pride of place in his later thought. In light of the cataclysmic displacement of some twelve million *Reichs*- and *Volksdeutsche*, in postwar Germany, these dilemmas presented themselves as especially acute. Nevertheless, what stood out in Heidegger's discussions of these themes was *his exclusive preoccupation with German suffering*, to the exclusion of the suffering that other peoples had endured at the hands of the recently defeated *Grossdeutsche Reich*.

The selective character of Heidegger's treatment of these issues reflected the persistence of his Germanocentrism. In *An Introduction to Metaphysics*, Heidegger had elevated the Germans to the status of the "most metaphysical Volk" as well as the "most endangered Volk."[56] As we have seen, according to Heidegger, the "destiny of the West" was endemically tied to *German destiny*. After the war, Heidegger's commitment to the ideology of German exception-alism was no less hypertrophic than it had been during the 1930s. Here, it is worth recalling Heidegger's observation in *What Is Called Thinking?* that the most significant consequence of the Second World War had been the "terrible consequences for our *Vaterland*—especially, the laceration down its middle."

Heidegger perceived the problem of German *Heimatlosigkeit* as especially dire. In addition to the forlorn situation of the *Heimatvertriebenen*, the Allies had partitioned Germany into four "occupation zones." As Heidegger pointed out, thereby they had effectively *dismembered the Vaterland*. Although the U.S., British, and French occupation zones were formally relinquished in 1955, Russians troops continued to occupy East Germany until 1994.

Not only had Germany forfeited its political sovereignty. When viewed from the standpoint of *Seinsgeschichte*, the dilemmas of German *Heimatlosigkeit* threatened to undermine the "destiny" and "mission" of Western humanity. To make matters worse, the *Siegermächte* now in control of Europe's "fate" were the United States and Russia: the two powers that, during the 1930s, Heidegger had already identified as the primary carriers of *Machenschaft*: the "frenzy of unbounded technics" that was responsible for the postwar epidemic of *Heimatlosigkeit*.

Hence, in Heidegger's eyes, the fundamental problem of postwar Europe centered on how the German *Volk* might reestablish *an authentic relationship to Heimat* and *Boden*. Only in this way might it reconnect with the "salvific" ontological mission that Heidegger continued to ascribe to *Deutschtum*. Conversely, the Allies, by perpetuating Germany's *Heimatlosigkeit*, had effectively *severed the Volk from its "essence."* Thereby, they had jeopardized *Seinsgeschichte* as an eschatological project or *Ereignis*. As Heidegger observed in *Holzwege*, "As 'destining' [*geschicklich*], Being is inherently *eschatological*."[57]

Consequently, by embracing the plight of the *Heimatsvertriebenen* in *Gelassenheit*, Heidegger was not merely pursuing a political agenda in the narrow sense. In his eyes, the ultimate stakes were *ontological-historical*. "Many Germans have lost their *Heimat*," observed Heidegger. "They have been forced to leave their villages and towns; they have been expelled from the native soil of their *Heimat* [*vom heimatlichen Boden Vertriebene*]." It would be difficult, he continued, to exaggerate the metaphysical stakes of such uprooting and displacement, insofar as "the flourishing of any genuine, native work depends on its rootedness in the native soil of the *Heimat* [*aus der Tiefe des heimatlichen Bodens*]."[58] As Robert Metcalf has correctly pointed out in "Rethinking 'Bodenständigkeit' in the Technological Age," "A careful examination of the famous 'Gelassenheit' speech of 1955 demonstrates that, in fact, *Bodenständigkeit* is the core concept around which everything else turns."[59]

By insisting, as he had during the National Socialist period, that "the flourishing of any genuine, native work depends on its rootedness in the native soil of the *Heimat*," Heidegger insinuated that "bodenlos," or "unrooted" peoples— Jews, Sinti and Roma, and non-German immigrants—were spiritual cripples. From an "existential" perspective, they lacked fecundity; hence, they were incapable of cultural excellence. In Heidegger eyes, this spiritual defect meant that "unrooted peoples" were ontologically less worthy. Thereby, the disturbing correlation between *Bodenständigkeit* and the *Rassengedanke* persisted in Heidegger's postwar thinking.

In a *Festrede* that Heidegger held in Provence in 1958, he reiterated his view concerning the necessary correlation between "rootedness in the native soil of the *Heimat*" and cultural flourishing. "There can be no essential work of spirit," affirmed Heidegger, "without *primordial rootedness-in-soil* [*ursprüngliche Bodenständigkeit*]."[60]

Heidegger's "aesthetics of rootedness" coalesced with the Nazi understanding of *Heimat* as the ground or basis of a unified *Volksgemeinschaft*. In the realm of *Kulturpolitik*, the Third Reich sought to "coordinate" local and regional cultural institutions in order to generate a "national working group that promoted an '*authentic*, great art of the homeland, a *German Heimat culture*.' " In order to achieve this aim, the Nazis simultaneously tried to eliminate all traces of foreign cultural influence. The NSDAP leadership promoted so-called *Heimatkultur* as a "truly indigenous art [*eigentlich bodenständige Kunst*]."[61]

In Heidegger's eyes, the perils of *Heimatlosigkeit* signified a *civilizational crisis* as well as an *ontological-historical crisis*. Both crises manifested themselves through *Bodenlosigkeit*: a planetary "loss of rootedness." As Heidegger lamented in *Gelassenheit*, "The *rootedness-in-soil* [*Bodenständigkeit*] of contemporary humanity *is threatened at its core*. The loss of rootedness [*Verlust der Bodenständigkeit*] is not something that is caused merely by external circumstances or fortune. Nor is it due solely to the indolence of and superficial lifestyle of human beings. The 'loss of rootedness' stems from the spirit of the [Atomic] Age into which we all were born."[62]

Heidegger's allusion to the "Atomic Age" was unquestionably timely. However, in Heidegger's view, the nuclear arms race was symptomatic of a more fundamental, ontological-historical impasse: it was merely another expression of "Gestell," or "Enframing." As Heidegger explained in *Gelassenheit*, "Modern, technological instruments of news reporting *seduce, overwhelm, and control human beings hourly*." Their "predominance" or "sway" (*Walten*) demonstrated that *Heimatlosigkeit* had disrupted not only the lives of the *Heimatvertriebenen* but, more insidiously, the lives "of those who have remained at home" (*der in der Heimat Gebliebenen*).[63]

What was striking about Heidegger's *Zeitdiagnose*—his "critique of modernity"—was its inordinate *one-sidedness*. When it came to detailing the destructive effects of technology and postwar "media culture," Heidegger became positively loquacious. Conversely, when it came to the unprecedented criminality of the Hitler state, he remained strangely silent.

At one point in *Gelassenheit*, Heidegger, in solidarity with the *Heimatsver-triebenen*, proceeded to enumerate the various *Länder* (provinces) that Germany had forfeited following the "collapse" of 1945: "Mitteldeutschland [a stand-in for Prussia], East Prussia, Silesia, and Bohemia."[64] Readers expecting a critique of Nazi *Bevölkerungspolitik* in the "Ostgebiete"—that is, the Third Reich's genocidal policies of conquest, population transfer, and extermination that had precipitated Germany's postwar territorial forfeitures—would, yet again, find themselves disappointed.

Moreover, by placing Bohemia on a list of Germany's "lost" provinces—a list that included "Mitteldeutschland," East Prussia, and Silesia—Heidegger insinuated that it was rightfully German. However, prior to its annexation by the Third Reich in March 1939, Bohemia had never been part of Germany. In fact, prior to the Nazi takeover, only 20 percent of the region's inhabitants were ethnic Germans.[65]

In light of the Third Reich's draconian plans for the "Germanization" of the region (along with neighboring Moravia), Heidegger's inclusion of Bohemia on this list is especially disturbing. Following the fall of France, Nazi leaders estimated that it would be necessary to exterminate or expel half of the protectorate's indigenous Czech population. Of the region's 92,000 Jews, only 14,000 survived the war. Roma inhabitants experienced a similar fate: merely 583 out of 6,500 survived. The "deputy protector" of Bohemia and Moravia was Reinhard Heydrich. (It was Heydrich—head of the SD, or *Sicherheitsdienst*, and nicknamed "The Hangman"—who, in January 1942, had presided over the Wannsee Conference). Following Heydrich's assassination by Czech partisans in June 1942, the Nazis, acting on orders from Hitler and Himmler, executed the entire male adult population of Lidice, twenty kilometers west of Prague. The town's women and children were consigned to concentration camps.

Heidegger and *Heimatsdiskurs*

As the case of the *Heimatvertriebenen* suggests, Heidegger's adoption of *Heimatsdiskurs* reflected a widespread fear during the postwar period that Germany's "essence" was in danger of being despoiled by a variety of sinister foreign influences. Thereby, the ethnocentrism and xenophobia that were so pervasive during the Nazi era persisted—albeit in a different guise.

Here, one of the ironies of the postwar period was that, whereas the Nazis had sought to establish a racially pure *Herrenstaat*, the "collapse" of May 1945 had produced a chaotic, multiethnic jumble, as a tidal wave of displaced persons (DPs) and refugees streamed in from the East. Whereas the DPs, presumably, had a *Heimat* from which they had been expelled, the refugees were truly *hei-matlos*. When combined with the 6 million slave laborers already on German soil, the number of DPs rapidly swelled to 8 million, although the Allies' repatriation program reduced their number to 1.2 million by the end of the year.[66]

In postwar Germany, the resurgence of an indigenous *Heimatsdiskurs*—a central leitmotif of Heidegger's *Denken* during the 1950s—was part of a conscious effort to offset the perceived risks of foreign contamination. As Heidegger lamented in the *Black Notebooks*, "*Foreign Being [Fremdes Wesen] distorts and disrupts our specific essence. Why is it that the Germans are so susceptible to being seduced by that which is foreign [zu fremdem Wesen]?*"[67] As Florian Grosser observes in "Heidegger, the Politics of Space, and the Space of Politics," Heidegger's "emphasis on 'Nearness' [*Nähe*] and on 'regional belonging' [entail] a concept of communal homogeneity that . . . facilitated *othering* and *exclusion*."[68]

The *Heimatsdiskurs* vogue also reflected a central pillar of the expellees' political agenda: that is, their insistence on a "Recht auf Heimat," a "right to return" to their "native homeland," notwithstanding the fact that, in the case of many *Reichsdeutsche*, the *Heimat* in question had been acquired by conquest, displacing the original habitants (as in the case of the Warthegau) or turning them into second-class citizens (as in the case of the Sudetenland). Moreover, the expellees' assertion of a "Recht auf Heimat" stood in flagrant violation of the Yalta and Potsdam accords.

It would be tempting to perceive *Heimatsdiskurs*, because of its regional focus, as being at odds with the traditional discourse of German nationalism. However, a closer examination shows that this was not really the case. Instead, as a rule, *Heimatsdiskurs complemented* German nationalism's ethnochauvinist aspirations. As such, it was its constant companion. Their complementary relationship was consolidated with the rise of the *Heimatsschutz* (homeland protection) movement during the *Kaiserreich*. As one commentator has noted, "A multicentered vision of Germany reappeared not as a *reaction* to the modern German state but as the fundament of a new and more intense emotional bond to the nation. . . . Protecting landmarks within this hierarchy of places

translated local diversities from the past into national similarities in the present."
An important consequence of this symbiosis of the local with the national was
the "emergence of a radical nationalism that was more organized than anything
seen until then among the audiences who supported preservation and its related
activities."[69]

Historically speaking, *Heimatsdiskurs* overlapped with the more distasteful
aspects of the "German ideology," including the dissemination and populariza-
tion of the *Rassengedanke*. As Rudy Koshar notes in "The Antinomies of
Heimat: Homeland, History, and Nazism," "The [*Heimatsschutz*] movement's
goal of creating an undamaged and untainted German race . . . had serious
implications. It contained a *mythic element* [as well as] a call for a return to 'origins.' . . . *Myth* entered the world of *racial politics*, which took on more organized shape in the late Kaiserreich. Conserving the visual integrity of the nation
intersected broadly with attempts to conserve racial characteristics and to give
politics a 'biologistic' basis."[70] Koshar's observations confirm that Heidegger's
enthusiasm for the idiolect of *Heimat* and *Boden* during the 1950s was *ideologically freighted*: that his recourse to this lexicon betrayed his enduring allegiance to key elements of the *Volksbegriff*.

Heidegger's profligate reliance on *Heimatsdiskurs* suggests that, as far as the
worldview of German nativism was concerned, Heidegger, after the war, *doubled down*. This was especially true for his writings on the poetry of the Ale-
mann native Johann Peter Hebel (1760–1826). In essays such as "Hebel, der
Hausfreund" (1957) and "Sprache und Heimat" (1960), Heidegger's celebration of Hebel's attachments to *Heimat* and *Boden* often transcended his concern
with Hebel's poetic achievements. In "Hebel, der Hausfreund," for example,
seeking to allay the suspicion that Hebel's decision to write poetry in the Alemannic dialect might be construed as "provincial," Heidegger emphatically
rose to Hebel's defense. "Dialect [*Mundart*]," declared Heidegger, "is the mysterious source of every mature language. From it, there flows all that the spirit
of language conceals within itself."[71]

On first view, Heidegger's vindication of dialect might seem innocuous and
inconsequential. However, when viewed in light of Heidegger's accompanying
celebration of the *redemptive mission of poetry*—the poet, claimed Heidegger,
"*names what is Holy*"—his exaltation of *Mundart* betrayed a more parochial
and "rooted" agenda. Time and again, Heidegger insisted that "what is Holy"
and "primordial" derive exclusively from what is *heimatgebunden*. Hence,

forms of *Dichten* and *Denken* that *bypassed* or *neglected* what is "rooted" and *bodenständig* represented forms of linguistic "degeneracy." As Heidegger asserted forcefully in "Sprache und Heimat," language that is *authentic "is always a particular language that is innately derived from what is Volk-related* and *tribal [in die Völkerschaften und Stämme geschickhaft hineingeboren]. . . . It is always the language of a Heimat. . . . Language is language as mother tongue [Muttersprache].*" "Dialect," added Heidegger, "is not only *language of the mother [die Sprache der Mutter]*, it is also the *mother of language" [die Mutter der Sprache].*"[72]

In keeping with Heidegger's glorification of *Mundart* and *Muttersprache* as repositories of "authenticity," he expressly devalued the temptations of "Weltsprache," or "cosmopolitan language": "In the 'world-hour' of our 'world-age' [*Weltstunde unseres Weltalters*]," lamented Heidegger, "the inherited and traditional relationship between *language, mother tongue, dialect and Heimat [Sprache, Muttersprache, Mundart und Heimat] is out of joint.*" In Heidegger's eyes, the advent of a "Weltsprache" threated to substitute a "language that is universally comprehensible and uniquely binding" for the assurances and comforts of *Heimat* and "rootedness." Although this "Weltsprache" was, perhaps, not yet a reality, Heidegger warned that many signs pointed to its imminent "triumph" (*Herrschaft*).[73]

"Rootedness" and Fundamental Ontology: *Schollenromantik* Redux

In texts such as "Hebel, der Hausfreund" and "Sprache und Heimat," Heidegger's recourse to the semantics of "rootedness," *Heimat*, and *Boden* reprised the *Schollenromantik* idiom of Nazi-era addresses such as "Schlageter" (1933) and "Why Do We Stay in the Provinces?" (1934). In the 1934–35 edition of the *Deutsches Führerlexikon*, Heidegger, vaunting his own provincial roots, boasted, "I stem from Alemannic-Swabian peasant stock [*Bauerngeschlecht*] that, on my maternal side (Kempf), has inhabited the same plot of land since 1510."[74]

Before and after the war, Heidegger exalted "rootedness-in-soil" as a touchstone of philosophical authenticity. For example, in "Why Do We Stay in the Provinces?," he credited the rugged Schwarzwald topography with being the inspiration for his *Denken*. "My philosophical work," declaimed Heidegger, "is intimately rooted in and related to the peasants' work [*Arbeit der Bauern*]." To

illustrate this point, Heidegger provided examples that were drenched in ba-
thos: "When the young farm boy drags his heavy sled, piled high with beech
logs, up the slope and then down the dangerous slopes to his house, when the
herdsman, lost in thought and slow of step, drives his cattle up the slope, when
the peasant in his shed prepares the numerous shingles for his roof, . . . *my Arbeit is of the same sort.* The inner relationship between my own *Arbeit* and the
Schwarzwald and its people stems from a centuries-long and irreplaceable *rootedness [Bodenständigkeit] in the Alemannian-Swabian soil.*"[75]

It would be shortsighted to underestimate the epistemological significance of
these assertions with respect to Heidegger's *Denken*, his repeated insistence
that "rootedness-in-soil" was a sine qua non of philosophical authenticity.

Heidegger's treatment of agrarian life as an exemplary instance of "primordial *Existenz*" devolved from his construction of *Seinsgeschick*. His denigration
of "conceptualization" impelled him to seek out the "ground" of truth in what
was "original" and "primordial": sources that were untainted by "mediation."
This explains his apotheosis of "anfängliches Denken."[76] Just as the rustic simplicity of "bäuerliches Leben" (peasant life) predated the decadence of modern
Zivilisation, the "primordiality" of *Seinsgeschick* preceded the corruptions of
"Western metaphysics." Reprising the idiom of *Zivilisationskritik*, Heidegger
regarded both "civilization" and "metaphysics" as *Verfallsphänomene*, or manifestations of "decline."

In *On the Way to Language* (1959), Heidegger once again recurred to agrarian metaphors to characterize his *Denkart*. "*Denken* is not a means of knowledge [*Mittel fürs Erkennen*]," claimed Heidegger. "*Denken plows furrows in
the soil of Dasein.*" "*Denken*," he added, "must possess a *pungent odor*."
Heidegger discovered an important precedent for his views on the interrelationship of "Denken" and "plowing" in Nietzsche's claim that "thinking should
smell like a cornfield on a summer evening.'"[77]

Heidegger's metaphorics tell us something essential about his epistemic priorities: his predilection for *Vernunftkritik* was merely the flip side of his provincial attachments and longings.

In *Philosophical Terminology*, Adorno observed, "The more pronounced
such rural-agrarian resonances become [in Heidegger's work], the more socially conditioned value judgments accrue—judgments that proclaim the superiority of peasant Dasein, insofar as it subsists in closer proximity to 'Origins.' "[78]
Adorno regarded Heidegger's recourse to rustic metaphorics as a cautionary

tale about the errors and delusions of *Ursprungsphilosophie*. By invoking a *fundamentum inconcussum* or "Grund" that preceded the separation between subject and object, *Ursprungsphilosophie* rejected "conceptualization" as *epistemologically flawed*.

It was but a short step from Heidegger's embrace of a *Schollenromantik* idiom to his enthusiasm for *Blut und Boden* ideology. His celebration of the epistemological benefits of *mythos*—"*Mythos*," Heidegger once enthused, "names Being in its primordial looking-into and shining-forth"—heralded his ideological "Turn" during the early 1930s.[79] In "Why Do We Stay in the Provinces?," Heidegger avowed, "My whole work is sustained and guided by the world of these mountains and their people."[80] We would be doing his philosophy a disservice if we to refused take seriously the ontological implications of such claims and others like it.

Mundart and *Muttersprache*

Heidegger's defense of "Mundart," as language that is "fatefully" (*geschickhaft*) tied to *Heimat* and *Boden*, went hand in hand with his rejection of "cosmopolitanism" as an emissary of what is "foreign" (*das Fremde*). Heidegger feared that the penetration of "foreign" elements threatened to corrupt and defile the integrity of *Muttersprache* and *Heimat*. Thus, in "Sprache und Heimat," Heidegger lamented the "foreign" derivation of the word "Dialekt." On these grounds, Heidegger preferred "Mundart," whose Germanic roots he viewed as a sign of linguistic authenticity.[81]

Heidegger's veneration of *Mundart* and *Muttersprache* reflected the obsession with *Sprachreinigung* (linguistic purification) that emerged during the *Kaiserreich* and crested with the Nazi era. As Eduard Engel—one of the leading representatives of *völkisch*-militant *Sprachpurismus*—declared at the height of World War I, "The world-historical hour has struck! From now on, all waffling and hesitation . . . must end, and the battle cry must resonate, far and wide: 'Speak German!' *Language is Volk, and Volk is language! . . .* Only a German-speaking, German *Volk* will become and remain a *Herrenvolk*." Alluding to the plague of foreign words and idioms that had despoiled the German *Sprachbereich*, Engel implored his *Volksgenossen* to "eradicate this cancerous growth on the body of the German language, the German *Volkstum*, and German honor."[82] Thereby, he set the stage for the *Jagd auf Fremdwörter*: an effort to ferret out and extirpate non-German linguistic influences. As the Romanist Leo Spitzer remarked in a prescient study of the *Sprachreinigung* movement, "Fremdwörterhatz"—the "hunt" for foreign words—rapidly metamorphosed into a "Fremdvölkerhatz" (a "hunt" for foreign peoples).[83] Adorno echoed Spitzer's concerns in *Minima Moralia*, observing that "foreign words are the *Jews of language*."[84]

Heidegger's paeans to the regenerative attributes of *Muttersprache* reprised a discourse of ethnolinguistic chauvinism that, by the early 1930s, had essentially fused with Nazi race doctrine. His defense of *Muttersprache* intersected with the "mother-tongue fascism" vogue that reached its zenith under Nazism. As Christopher Hutton has shown in *Language and the Third Reich*, "mother-tongue fascism's" ideological signature was the *racialization of language*:

> In National Socialist Germany, the German language was the optic of increasingly intense penetration by professional linguists committed to the notion of *mother tongue*. These linguists believed it was their sacred duty to protect and preserve the mother tongue, to contribute to the salvation of the German people itself and its liberation from history, hybridity, and social divisions, and the horrors of assimilation, thereby reconnecting it with the foundation of national being. Reverence for the mother tongue reached at points a mystical level. It was expressed in the language of the cult and had complex links with the German pagan ideal of a pre-patriarchal, matriarchal order.[85]

As Hutton's remarks suggest, the "mother tongue" was divinized as a *mystical fundament* from which there emanated unique, life-sustaining qualities. Whereas the language of sacred texts, as the language of patriarchy, connoted the authority of *dead* over *living* language, the *Muttersprache*, insofar as it was "rooted" in the "life rhythms" of Mother Earth, was regarded as an inexhaustible source of *energy and vitality*.

"Mother-tongue fascism" highlighted the *chthonic* and *rooted* components of the National Socialist worldview. These valences emerged clearly in ideological cognates such as *Muttererde* (Mother Earth) and *Mutterboden* (maternal soil).

Nazi ideology was a syncretic phenomenon: an admixture or mélange. The vindication of "mother-tongue rights" was a core component of this admixture. With its "pan-German" roots, Nazism had always been a language-rights movement. Its emergence was inseparable from "Indo-European linguistics," which provided a pseudoscholarly basis for the idea of Aryan racial supremacy. It should come as no surprise that the vindication of "mother-tongue rights" (*Recht auf*

Muttersprache) became a key element of the Third Reich's plans to enfranchise the politically *heimatlose Volksdeutche* by establishing a "Greater Germany."

"Linguistic purification," or *Sprachreinigung*, was deemed essential to creating a unified *Volksgemeinschaft*. National Socialist ideologues viewed "language as the collective and unconscious template of a worldview that was race- and *Volk*-specific: a template whose consummate expression was *Dichtung*."[87] Heidegger's *Muttersprache* obsession reprised one of the central pillars of German linguistic nationalism: an abiding fear of *linguistic degeneracy* that paralleled the *völkisch* movement's preoccupation with the threat of *racial degeneration*.

Writing in 1965, the Germanist Klaus Ziegler cautioned that, in order to "work through" the depredations and excesses of National Socialism, "one must also take into account the continuities with the historical present. . . . Although National Socialism is no longer concretely present," Ziegler continued, "do we not still find specific patterns of thought and ideological models out of which it once developed? I'm afraid that this is indeed the case in ways that are extensive, deeply rooted, dangerous, and disturbing, insofar as, today, many adherents of this ideology remain inadequately aware of their indebtedness to National Socialism. In certain cases, *there is no awareness at all*." Such continuities were evident, added Ziegler, in the fashionable "polemics against the Enlightenment and its legacy of individualistic, rational, and critical, thinking." These exaggerated polemics culminated in a "mystical absolutization of *Volk* and '*Muttersprache*'" and in "dubious" efforts to seek consolation in a salvific understanding of "Dichtung," now charged with restoring a "perfect world" (*heilen Welt*).[88] Although Heidegger was nowhere directly named in Ziegler's essay, Ziegler's reflections deftly exposed the delusory aspirations of Heidegger's inflated conception of "poetic saying" (*dichterisches Sagen*).

In "Words from Abroad," Adorno acknowledged the ideological intolerance that suffused Heidegger's glorification of "Muttersprache" and "Heimat-Diskurs." Echoing Ziegler's concerns, he praised "foreign words" as expressions of *otherness* and *nonidentity*. Therein, he concluded, lay their commitment to "truth": "With the foreign word [the writer] can effect a beneficial interruption of the *conformist moment of language*. . . . [Hence], the discrepancy between the foreign word and the language can be made to serve *the expression of truth*. Language participates in *reification*: . . . it creates the illusion that what is said is immediately equivalent to what is meant. By acknowledging itself as a token, the foreign word . . . makes itself . . . *the bearer of dissonance*."[89]

Provincialism versus "Public Reason"

The prominence and persistence of the themes of *Heimat*, *Verwurzelung*, and *Bodenständigkeit* in Heidegger's later work, his exaltation of these topoi as emblems of ontological *authenticity*, attest to profound continuities in Heidegger's pre- and postwar *Denken*. They confirm that the later Heidegger doubled down on his earlier rejection of "cosmopolitanism" and "public reason," perspectives that Kant associated with the "enlarged thinking" that rescues individuals from the pitfalls of intellectual isolation and experiential impoverishment.[90] Instead, Heidegger continued to embrace a self-avowed *philosophical provincialism*: a standpoint that narrowly associated truth and meaning with "the native soil of the Heimat."

Kant realized that, by relying on the community of reasoning individuals, or *sensus communis*, we immunize ourselves against the debilities of intellectual insularity. When perceived in this light, philosophical judgment is an intrinsically associative-communal process: it is *dialogical* rather than *monological*, *communicative* rather than *didactic*. As such, it is the antithesis of philosophical solipsism. Kant's "enlarged mentality" was an act of *intellectual self-overcoming*. It demanded that we abstract from the contingencies and limitations of our particularity in order to incorporate other perspectives and standpoints. As Hannah Arendt remarked appositely, "The greater the reach—the larger the realm in which the individual is able to move from standpoint to standpoint—the more *general* will be her thinking."[91]

One of the later Heidegger's major failings was that he repeatedly linked the idea of "meditative thinking" (*besinnendes Denken*) to the concepts of *Boden*, *Erde*, *Ort*, and *Raum*. In *Gelassenheit*, for example, Heidegger enthusiastically endorsed a remark by Hebel that likened human beings to "plants that emerge from their rootedness in the Earth [*den Wurzeln aus der Erde*]" in support of his conviction that "there can be no essential work of spirit without *primordial rootedness-in-soil* [*ursprünglichen Bodenständigkeit*]."[92] Before and after 1945, Heidegger approached "authenticity" from the perspective of "rootedness-in-soil." *Bodenständigkeit* remained the indispensable touchstone for Heidegger's conception of ontological flourishing. As Robert Minder commented appositely, "Not only does *Bodenständigkeit*, as the criterion of artistic capacity, continue to haunt Heidegger's writings. He shared this delusion with an entire generation of Hitler loyalists."[93]

Heidegger's claims about the ontological superiority of "primordially rooted" forms of life call to mind the reactionary politics of Integral Nationalism: Maurice Barrès's celebration of "la terre et les morts"—"the soil and the dead"—as touchstones of identity and authenticity. Barrès's infamous catchword was, essentially, a translation of *Blut und Boden* into French. By stripping nationalism of its original "civic" significance, Barrès—the first French writer to employ the term "nationalism"—helped redefine nationalism along "ethnic" lines. Barrès claimed that " 'real' Truth and Justice were relative and literally rooted in the earth." In *Scènes et Doctrines du nationalisme*, he added, "A creature is viable only in the measure where he is transformed according to his character and hereditary ways. The historic sense, this high naturalist sentiment, this acceptance of *determinism*, is what we mean by nationalism."[94] In this respect, he was a seminal precursor of fascist ideology.[95]

During the Dreyfus Affair, Barrès maintained that the trappings of due process were superfluous; Dreyfus's *race*, in and of itself, was sufficient proof of his guilt. Barrès held that all Jews were potential traitors, since, as "déracinés" (the title of his 1897 novel), they lacked substantial ties to "la nation," which Barrès had reconceived as unthinking devotion to "la terre et les morts."

André Gide, in his *Journaux*, formulated the consummate response to Barrès's—and Heidegger's—glorification of "enracinement" as the supreme criterion of political belonging. "*Men are not plants!*" exclaimed Gide. "For them, *mobility is essential*."[96]

Following the German "collapse" of 1945, Heidegger's "retreat" to the insularity of "meditative thinking" did not mean that he had transformed himself into a resolutely antipolitical thinker. To be sure, he abandoned the discourse of *völkisch* self-assertion that characterized his thought during the 1930s. By the same token, to have persisted with this idiolect would have been senseless in light of the changed geopolitical situation.

Instead, Heidegger revived his earlier discourse of *earth, soil, space, Vaterland*, and *Heimat*. He recalibrated it in accordance with the requirements and demands of an occupied and divided Germany. Nevertheless, the ideological prejudices and structural characteristics that animated his earlier exaltation of "ontological rootedness" remained firmly in place. Although the historical and political context had shifted, the basic tropes of Heidegger's prewar attachment to the idiom of *Heimat, Boden*, and *Erde* persisted, essentially, unaltered.

ACKNOWLEDGMENTS

IT IS SOMETIMES SAID THAT A BOOK PRACTICALLY "writes itself." As far as *Heidegger in Ruins* is concerned, this was hardly the case. Given the ever-expanding accumulation of Heidegger commentaries, monographs, and edited compilations, it is important that the benchmark for future contributions remain high. Throughout the writing of the present study, I have done my best to honor this maxim.

Draft versions of many of the chapters originated as lectures that were held at several European universities in 2014 and 2015. In Germany, I would like to thank my various hosts: Professors Michael Forster and Markus Gabriel of the Faculty of Philosophy at the University of Bonn; Professor Christian Wiese, Faculty of Theology, the University of Frankfurt; Professors Marion Heinz and Sidonie Kellerer, Faculty of Philosophy, the University of Siegen; Professor Dan Diner, director of the Leibniz Institute for History and Culture–Simon Dubnow in Leipzig; and Professor Jürgen Zarusky of the Institut für Zeitgeschichte in Munich. Professor Matthias Bormuth, president of the Karl Jaspers Society and director of the Karl Jaspers Haus at the University of Oldenburg, was kind enough to offer me a platform to present an early version of chapter 4.

I would like to profusely thank Professor Marlène Laruelle, the director of the Institute for European, Russian, and Eurasian Studies at George Washington University, for her generosity in inviting me to participate in an eye-opening international symposium on Heidegger's *Black Notebooks* at Moscow State University in October 2015. Also in October 2015, I was privileged to participate in a lively colloquium on Heidegger and the Jews in Stockholm, Sweden, that was convened by Lizzie Scheja and the Swedish Association for Jewish Culture. I would also like to acknowledge the support of my colleagues at the Center for Modern European Studies (CEMES) at the University of Copenhagen, where I served as honorary professor from 2011 to 2015. During my sojourns in Copenhagen, the friendship of Professors Peter Madsen and Gert Sørenson, who cosponsored my public lectures on the *Black Notebooks*, proved especially valuable.

I am pleased to acknowledge the hospitality and superlative working conditions that were provided by Dr. Ulrich von Bülow, director of the German Literature Archive at Marbach.

Throughout the writing process, my labors were greatly assisted by the interlibrary loan staff at the CUNY Graduate Center, who tirelessly fulfilled my unending (or so it must have seemed) requests for journal articles and books, in German, French, and various other languages.

My research on *Heidegger in Ruins* benefited immensely from the receipt of two grants from the Alexander von Humboldt Stiftung and from a generous stipend from the CUNY Research Foundation. I profited enormously from two anonymous readers' reports that were commissioned by Yale University Press. I would also like to acknowledge the invaluable assistance and expertise I received from my copyeditor, Andrew Katz.

I would like to express my gratitude to my editor at Yale University Press, Bill Frucht, for his goodwill, his generosity, and, above all, his patience, as what began as a relatively circumscribed monograph on the *Black Notebooks* metamorphosed into something considerably more ambitious: an effort to reconstruct the key stages of Heidegger's *Denkweg* on the basis of the new insights and directives that the *Notebooks* provided. As the original conception for *Heidegger in Ruins* expanded and the length of the manuscript grew apace, Bill never lost confidence that his initial wager on the project was well placed.

Finally, I would like to thank—in more ways than words can express—my lovely wife, Caroline Rupprecht. Throughout the writing of *Heidegger in Ruins*, Caroline—an accomplished comparativist and a native German speaker—was my constant interlocutor. Caroline acted as my muse, my confidante, and my *daimonion*, all rolled into one. At various points, she selflessly put her own work aside in order to read—and reread—countless chapter drafts. Her insights and criticisms were unfailingly on the mark. Whatever failings the book possesses are entirely my doing. Whatever merits it may possess have been enhanced immeasurably by her superior powers of judgment and discernment.

NOTES

A Note on Sources

1. For additional information, see Alfred Denker, foreword to *Briefwechsel, 1932–1975*, by Martin Heidegger and Kurt Bauch, ed. Almuth Heidegger (Freiburg: Karl Alber, 2010), 9–12. See also the illuminating account in Reinhard Mehring, *Heideggers "Grosse Politik": Die semantische Revolution der Gesamtausgabe* (Tübingen: Mohr Siebeck, 2016), 239–40.
2. Karl Löwith, *Martin Heidegger and European Nihilism*, ed. Richard Wolin, trans. Gary Steiner (New York: Columbia University Press, 1995), 236. The correspondence between Heidegger and Löwith was published as the second volume of the projected thirty-five-volume *Briefausgabe*. See Martin Heidegger and Karl Löwith, *Briefwechsel, 1919–1973*, ed. Alfred Denker (Freiburg: Karl Alber, 2017).
3. Martin Heidegger, *Beiträge zur Philosophie*, GA 65 (Frankfurt: Klostermann, 1989), 414.
4. Martin Heidegger, *Anmerkungen I–V*, GA 97 (Frankfurt: Klostermann, 2015), 325.

Introduction

1. Judith Werner, *Poesie der Vernichtung: Literatur und Dichtung in Martin Heideggers "Schwarzen Heften"* (Wiesbaden: J. B. Metzler, 2018), 3, 8. For an assessment of the first wave of debates, see Jan Eike Dunkhase, "Beiträge zur neuen Heidegger-Debatte," *H-Soz-Kult*, 13 March 2017, https://www.hsozkult.de/publicationreview/id/reb-25610. Among the other relevant contributions, see Ingo Farin and Jeff Malpas, eds., *Reading Heidegger's "Black Notebooks," 1931–1941* (Cambridge, MA: MIT Press, 2015); Andrew J. Mitchell and Peter Trawny, eds., *Heidegger's "Black Notebooks": Responses to Anti-Semitism* (New York: Columbia University Press, 2016); Peter Trawny and Andrew Mitchell, eds., *Heidegger, die Juden—noch einmal* (Frankfurt: Klostermann, 2015); Jean-Luc Nancy, *La Banalité de Heidegger* (Paris: Editions Galilée, 2015); Eggert Blum, "Die Heidegger-Debatte nach den 'Schwarzen Heften,'" *Stimmen der Zeit* 12

(2015); Marion Heinz and Sidonie Kellerer, eds., *Heideggers "Schwarze Hefte": Eine philosophisch-politische Debatte* (Berlin: Suhrkamp, 2016); Hans-Helmuth Gander and Magnus Striet, eds., *Heideggers Weg in die Moderne. Eine Verortung der "Schwarzen Hefte"* (Frankfurt: Klostermann, 2017); Günter Figal et al., eds., *Heideggers "Schwarze Hefte" in Kontext: Geschichte, Politik, und Ideologie* (Tübingen: Mohr Siebeck, 2018); Marion Heinz and Tobias Bender, eds., *"Sein und Zeit" neu verhandelt: Untersuchungen Heideggers Hauptwerk* (Hamburg: Felix Meiner, 2019); Thomas Rohkrämer, *Martin Heidegger: Eine politische Biographie* (Paderborn: Ferdinand Schöningh, 2020); "Jenseits von Polemik und Apologie: Die 'Schwarzen Hefte' in der Diskussion," in *Heidegger-Jahrbuch*, vol. 12 (Freiburg: Karl Alber, 2020); and Lorenz Jäger, *Martin Heidegger: Ein deutsches Leben* (Berlin: Rowohlt, 2021).

2. Peter Trawny, "Nachwort des Herausgebers," in *Überlegungen II–VI*, GA 94, by Martin Heidegger (Frankfurt: Klostermann, 2014), 533.

3. Andrew J. Mitchell and Peter Trawny, "Editors' Introduction," in *Martin Heidegger's "Black Notebooks,"* xx.

4. Martin Heidegger, *Überlegungen XII–XV*, GA 96 (Frankfurt: Klostermann, 2014), 196.

5. Martin Heidegger, *Überlegungen VII–XI*, GA 95 (Frankfurt: Klostermann, 2014), 266.

6. Martin Heidegger, *Anmerkungen I–V*, GA 97 (Frankfurt: Klostermann, 2015), 148.

7. Heidegger, *Überlegungen XII–XV*, GA 96, 225.

8. Heidegger, *Überlegungen II–VI*, GA 94, 27. In *Politische Philosophie in Deutschland: Studien zu ihrer Geschichte* (Munich: Deutscher Taschenbuch Verlag, 1974), Hermann Lübbe describes the emergence of a dogmatic "Deutschland Metaphysik" as an integral component of the "Ideas of 1914." As the epitome of this mentality, Lübbe cites the Marburg neo-Kantian Paul Natorp's (1854–1924) dictum: "The German aims to conquer the world, not for his own sake, but instead for that of humanity; not in order, thereby, *to gain something*, but instead *as an act of generosity*" (194). Lübbe traces the development of this "Deutschland Metaphysik" back to Johann Gottlieb Fichte's *Addresses to the German Nation* (1807–8). He explains that, by elevating "German thinking, German philosophy, and German science" to the status of a metaphysical *summun bonum*, Fichte endowed "what was merely factual with the character of necessity." Hence, Fichte's demarche is only "comprehensible as the metaphysical doubling of what is merely factual, thereby transforming it into an inner essence" (196–97).

9. Martin Heidegger, *Hölderlins Hymnen "Germanien" und "Der Rhein,"* GA 39 (Frankfurt: Klostermann, 1980), 133–34

10. Martin Heidegger, *Einführung in die Metaphysik*, GA 40 (Frankfurt: Klostermann, 1983), 41; Heidegger, *Introduction to Metaphysics*, trans. Ralph Manheim (New Haven, CT: Yale University Press, 1959), 38.

11. Carl Schmitt, *Der Begriff des Politischen* (Berlin: Duncker und Humblot, 1963), 49.

12. Carl Schmitt, *Glossarium: Aufzeichnungen aus den Jahren 1947–1951* (Berlin: Duncker und Humblot, 1993), entry of September 25, 1947. See Martin Heidegger, "Seminar über Hegels *Rechtsphilosophie*," in *Seminare: Hegel-Schelling*, GA 86 (Frankfurt: Klostermann, 1998),171–78; Heidegger's engagement with Schmitt's *Freund-Feind* opposition occurs on pages 173–75. Ultimately, Heidegger faulted Schmitt's approach for being excessively "liberal," insofar as Schmitt treated "state," "movement," and "Volk" as separate spheres, instead of recognizing their common ontological derivation in the *Seinsfrage*.

13. Martin Heidegger, *Sein und Wahrheit*, GA 36/37 (Frankfurt: Klostermann, 2001), 91.

14. Heidegger, *Anmerkungen I–V*, GA 97, 20.

15. On the metamorphoses of the construction of the Jew as *Feindbild*, or "enemy," see Steven Aschheim, " 'The Jew Within': The Myth of the 'Judaization' of German Culture," in *Jewish Responses to German Culture: From the Enlightenment to the Second World War*, ed. Jehuda Reinhard and Walter Schatzberg (Hanover, NH: University of New England Press, 1985), 212–41. For Heidegger's remark to Jaspers, see Karl Jaspers, *Philosophische Autobiographie* (Munich: Piper, 1977), 101.

16. Raphael Gross, *Carl Schmitt and the Jews*, trans. Joel Golb (Madison: University of Wisconsin Press, 2007). For Schmitt's critique of Jewish *Bodenlosigkeit*, see Carl Schmitt, "Völkerrechtliche Großraumordnung mit Interventionsverbot für raumfremde Mächte," in *Staat, Grossraum, Nomos* (Berlin: Duncker und Humblot, 1994), 294, 317–18. Schmitt's essay was published in 1941; thus, his passing reference to the glories of "colonization" may be safely interpreted as an endorsement of Nazi *Drang nach Osten*.

17. Heidegger, *Überlegungen VII–XI*, GA 95, 50.

18. Martin Heidegger, *Beiträge zur Philosophie: Vom Ereignis*, GA 65 (Frankfurt: Klostermann, 1989), 282.

19. Heidegger, *Überlegungen VII–XI*, GA 95, 274.

20. Heidegger, *Überlegungen VII–XI*, GA 95, 124.

21. Trawny, "Nachwort des Herausgebers," 533; see Heidegger, *Überlegungen II–VI*, GA 94, 115, 124.

22. I treat these expurgations and omissions in detail in chapter 1, "The Heidegger Hoax."

23. Concerning Günter Figal's resignation as president of the International Heidegger Society, see Radio 102.3, "So denkt man nicht, wenn man Philosophie treibt," *Dreyeckland*, 9 January 2015. See also "Das Ende des Heideggerianertums," interview with Günter Figal, *Badische Zeitung*, 23 January 2015; and Antonio Carioti, "Donatella di Cesare si dimette: È ancora polemica sulla Società Heidegger: 'Siete provinciali,' " *Corriere della Sera*, 30 March 2015. See my contribution to this debate, "Addio Heidegger!," *Corriere della Sera*, 17 April 2015.

24. Günter Figal, foreword to *Heideggers "Schwarze Hefte" in Kontext*, v–vi.

25. Figal, "Das Ende des Heideggerianertums."

26. Otto Pöggeler, *Der Denkweg Martin Heideggers* (Pfullingen: Neske, 1994), 316.

27. Giorgio Agamben, "La Peur prépare à tout accepter," *L'Obs*, 17–23 September 2015.

28. Agamben's allegation that the *Black Notebooks* were never intended for publication is false.

29. Martin Heidegger, *Being and Time*, trans. John Macquarrie and Edward Robinson (New York: Harper and Row, 1962), 165.

30. Trawny and Mitchell, "Editors' Introduction," xxiv–xxv. Although the volume in question promises a critical engagement with Heidegger's anti-Semitism, the editors, relying on the inherently polysemous and indeterminate nature of "textuality" as an excuse, renounce the undertaking before they even begin: "Perhaps there is no text that can resist an anti-Semitic appropriation (or interpretation) and this is just a fact about texts. But what follows from this is that a response to anti-Semitism that seeks to identify whether a certain text is or is not anti-Semitic is doomed from the start" (xxiii).

31. Sabine Prokhoris, "Désigner l'immonde," *Libération*, 16 November 2017.

32. Jean-Luc Nancy, "Heidegger Incorrect," *Libération*, 12 October 2017.

33. Jean-Luc Nancy, *La Banalité de Heidegger* (Paris: Galilée, 2015).

34. See Donatella di Cesare, *Heidegger, die Juden, und die Shoah* (Frankfurt: Klostermann, 2015); di Cesare, "Das·Sein und der Jude," in *Heidegger und die Juden—noch einmal*, ed. Peter Trawny (Frankfurt: Klostermann, 2015), 74.

35. Pierre Bourdieu, "Back to History," in *The Heidegger Controversy: A Critical Reader*, ed. Richard Wolin (Cambridge, MA: MIT Press, 1993), 266.

36. Heidegger, *Überlegungen II–VI*, GA 94, 142.

37. Ibid., 135. At the same time, Heidegger affirmed that, in keeping with the requirements of political realism, he was willing to tolerate "vulgar National Socialism." Although he lamented the "platitudes of *völk*-bound thinking" and the proliferation of "cultural philistinism" that accompanied Nazism's rise, he acknowledged that "such circumstances are impossible to escape" and, hence, that "mediocrity is unavoidable."

38. Martin Heidegger to Elfride Heidegger, 8 September 1920, in *"Mein liebes Seelchen!" Briefe Martin Heideggers an seiner Frau Elfride, 1915–1970*, ed. Gertrud Heidegger (Munich: Deutsche Verlagsanstalt, 2005), 116.

39. Heidegger, *Einführung in die Metaphysik*, GA 40, 208; Heidegger, *Introduction to Metaphysics*, 199.

40. Heidegger, *Einführung in die Metaphysik*, GA 40, 208; Heidegger, *Introduction to Metaphysics*, 199.

41. Martin Heidegger to Fritz Heidegger, 2 March 1932, in *Heidegger und der Antisemitismus: Positionen im Widerstreit. Mit Briefen von Martin und Fritz Heidegger*, ed. Walter Homolka and Arnulf Heidegger (Freiburg: Herder, 2016), 26.

42. Heidegger, *Überlegungen II–VI*, GA 94, 111.

43. Ibid., 189. Heidegger repeats this claim in "Vom Wesen der Wahrheit," in *Sein und Wahrheit*, GA 36/37: "*Blut* and *Boden* are a, to be sure, powerful and necessary, yet insufficient condition for the Dasein of a *Volk*" (263).

44. Karl Löwith, "My Last Meeting with Heidegger in Rome, 1936," in Wolin, *Heidegger Controversy*, 184. For a detailed account of the "spiritual racism" of Günther and Clauss, see Hans-Jürgen Lutzthöft, *Der Nordische Gedanke in Deutschland: 1920–1940* (Leipzig: Ernst Klett, 1971); for a good treatment in English, see Christopher Hutton, *Race and the Third Reich* (Cambridge, UK: Polity, 2005).

45. For important exceptions to this oversight, see Dieter Thomä, "Heidegger und der Nationalsozialismus: In der Dunkelkammer der Seinsgeschichte," in *Heidegger Handbuch: Leben, Werk, Wirkung*, ed. Thomä (Stuttgart: Metzler, 2013), 108–32; and Florian Grosser, *Revolution Denken: Heidegger und das Politische, 1919–1969* (Munich: Beck, 2009), 116–20.

46. Martin Heidegger, "The Self-Assertion of the German University," in Wolin, *Heidegger Controversy*, 35.

47. Heidegger, *Being and Time*, 153–63, 235–41, 352–58.

48. Martin Heidegger, "Liebeserklärung an die Provence," in *Reden und andere Zeugnisse eines Lebensweges*, GA 16 (Frankfurt: Klostermann, 1995), 551.

49. Heidegger, *Überlegungen XII–XV*, GA 96, 56.

50. Martin Heidegger, *Sein und Zeit*, GA 2 (Frankfurt: Klostermann, 1977): "Der moderne Mensch, das heißt, der Mensch seit der Renaissance, ist fertig zum Begrabenwerden" (401); Heidegger, *Being and Time*, 452.

51. Heidegger, *Überlegungen II–VI*, GA 94, 124.

52. The phrase "from Dublin to Vladivostok" derives from the work of the Belgian neofascist Jean-François Thiriart, the author of *Un Empire de 400 millions: l'Europe* (Brussels: Sineco, 1964). For a clarification of its employment by the New Right, see Anton Shekhovtsov, *Russia and the Western Far Right: Tango Noir* (New York: Routledge, 2018), 192.

53. For an excellent treatment of this theme, see the recent study by Paul Hanebrink, *A Specter Haunting Europe: The Myth of Jewish Bolshevism* (Cambridge, MA: Harvard University Press, 2018).

54. Heidegger, "Gelassenheit," in *Reden und andere Zeugnisse eines Lebensweges*, GA 16, 521. Inexplicably missing from this list was Pomerania.

55. Heidegger, *Einführung in die Metaphysik*, GA 40, 41.

56. Emil Angehrn, "Ursprungsdenken und Modernitätskritik," in Gander and Striet, *Heideggers Weg in die Moderne*, 98–99.

57. Martin Heidegger, *Logik: Die Frage nach der Wahrheit*, GA 21 (Frankfurt: Klostermann, 1995), 79.

58. Heidegger, *Überlegungen II–VI*, GA 94, 124. For a recent critique of the deleterious consequences of Heidegger's neglect of traditional criteria of "validity" and "coherence," see Sidonie Kellerer, "Philosophy or Messianism?," in *Confronting Heidegger: A Critical Dialogue on Politics and Philosophy*, ed. Gregory Fried (Lanham, MD: Rowman and Littlefield, 2019), 179–208.

59. Emmanuel Levinas, *Ethics and Infinity*, ed. Philip Nemo, trans. Richard A. Cohen (Pittsburgh: Duquesne University Press, 1985), 39–41.

60. Theodor Adorno, *Negative Dialectics*, trans. E. B. Ashton (New York: Seabury, 1972), 61–96.

61. Günther Anders, "On the Pseudo-Concreteness of Heidegger's Philosophy," *Philosophy and Phenomenological Research* 8 (1948): 341. For an informative discussion of Anders's relationship to Heidegger, see Jason Dawsey, "Ontology and Ideology: Günther Anders's Philosophical and Political Confrontation with Heidegger," *Critical Historical Studies* 4, no. 1 (2017): 1–27. In *The Fundamental Concepts of Metaphysics*, trans. William McNeill (Bloomington: Indiana University Press, 1982), Heidegger spoke of "terror" as providing an incentive to serious philosophy: "Only where there is the perilousness of being seized by terror do we find the bliss of astonishment—being torn away in that wakeful manner that is the breath of all philosophizing and which the greats among the philosophers called 'enthusiasm'—as witnessed by the last of the greats, Friedrich Nietzsche" (366).

62. Anders, "On the Pseudo-Concreteness of Heidegger's Philosophy," 355. See also Herbert Marcuse's comments in "Heidegger's Politics: An Interview," in *Heideggerian Marxism*, ed. Richard Wolin and John Abromeit (Lincoln: University of Nebraska Press, 2005): "If you look at [Heidegger's] view of human existence, being-in-the-world, you will find a highly repressive, highly oppressive interpretation . . .: 'Idle talk, curiosity, ambiguity, falling and being-thrown-into, concern, being-toward-death, anxiety, dread, boredom,' and so on. Now this gives a picture which plays well on the fears and frustrations of men and women in a repressive society—a joyous existence: overshadowed by death and anxiety; human cereal material for the authoritarian personality" (169–70).

63. Christian von Krockow, *Die Entscheidung: Eine Untersuchung über Ernst Jünger, Carl Schmitt, und Martin Heidegger* (Stuttgart: Enke, 1958); Johannes Fritsche, *Historical Destiny and National Socialism in Heidegger's "Being and Time"* (Berkeley: University of California Press, 1999); Charles Bambach, *Heidegger's Roots: Nietzsche, National Socialism, and the Greeks* (Ithaca, NY: Cornell University Press, 2003); Daniel Morat, *Von der Tat zur Gelassenheit: Konservatives Denken bei Martin Heidegger, Ernst Jünger, und Friedrich Georg Jünger, 1920–1960* (Göttingen: Wallstein, 2007); Grosser, *Revolution Denken*.

64. Otto Pöggeler, "Heidegger, Nietzsche, and National Socialism," in *The Heidegger Case: A Casebook* (Philadelphia: Temple University Press, 1993), 12. In *Historical Destiny and National Socialism in Heidegger's "Being and Time,"* Fritsche explores in detail the implications of Pöggeler's claim concerning the politically fraught nature of Heideggerian *Geschichtlichkeit*.

65. Hans Freyer, *Revolution von Rechts* (Jena: Diedrichs, 1931). The reference to Freyer seems especially germane, insofar as he and Heidegger served together on the Ausschuss für Rechtsphilosophie, an elite subcommittee of Hans Frank's Academy of German Law.

Chapter 1. The Heidegger Hoax

1. See Theodore Kisiel, "Heidegger's *Gesamtausgabe*: An International Scandal of Scholarship," *Philosophy Today* 39, no. 1 (1995): 4; Rainer Marten, "Grabhalter mit letzter Treuebereitschaft," *Die Zeit* 11 (18 March 2015): "Seit Jahren nehmen die Herausgeber Martin Heideggers Werk in Beschlag. Das ist ein Skandal, der endlich ein Ende haben muss"; Lorenz Jäger, "Allesamt Spielarten der Seinsvergessenheit," *Frankfurter Allgemeine Zeitung*, 3 March 2015; Reinhard Mehring, *Heideggers Überlieferungsgeschick: Eine dionysische Selbstinszenierung* (Würzburg: Königshausen und Neumann, 1992).

2. For example, see Heidegger's preface to the Nietzsche lectures, in which he states, "In the text of the lectures, unnecessary words and phrases have been deleted, involuted sentences simplified, obscure passages clarified, and oversights corrected." Martin Heidegger, *The Will to Power as Art*, trans. David Krell (New York: HarperCollins, 1990), xl.

3. Friedrich Nietzsche, *The Will to Power*, trans. Walter Kaufmann (New York: Vintage, 1968), 22. For an informative discussion of Darwin's influence on Nietzsche, see John Richardson, *Nietzsche's New Darwinism* (New York: Oxford University Press, 2004).

4. Martin Heidegger, *Schellings Abhandlung über das Wesen der menschlichen Freiheit*, GA 42 (Frankfurt: Klostermann, 1995), 40–41. The passage was omitted in the original publication of *Schellings Abhandlung über das Wesen der menschlichen Freiheit* (Max Niemeyer Verlag: Tübingen, 1971).

5. Martin Heidegger, *Einführung in die Metaphysik* (Tübingen: Max Niemeyer, 1953).

6. Jürgen Habermas, "Work and Weltanschauung: The Heidegger Controversy from a German Perspective," in *The New Conservatism: Cultural Criticism and the Historians' Debate*, trans. Shierry W. Nicholsen (Cambridge, MA: MIT Press, 1989), 161.

7. Jürgen Habermas, "Martin Heidegger: On the Publication of the Lectures of 1935," in *The Heidegger Controversy: A Critical Reader*, ed. Richard Wolin (Cambridge, MA: MIT Press, 1993), 191, 196.

8. Hannah Arendt, *The Origins of Totalitarianism* (New York: Harcourt Brace, 1958): "To-talitarianism in power invariably replaces all first-rate talents . . . with those crackpots and fools whose lack of intelligence and creativity is still the best guarantee of their loy-alty" (339).

9. Habermas, "Martin Heidegger," 197.

10. Otto Pöggeler, *Heidegger's Path of Thinking*, trans. Daniel Magurshak and Sigmund Barber (Atlantic Heights, NJ: Humanities Press, 1990), 276–77 (translation slightly al-tered). The philosophically rich correspondence between Heidegger and Pöggeler has recently been published as volume 3 of the Heidegger *Briefausgabe*. See Martin Heidegger and Otto Pöggeler, *Briefwechsel, 1959–1976*, ed. Kathrin Busch and Chris-toph Jamme (Freiburg: Karl Alber, 2021). The correspondence reveals that Heidegger enthusiastically endorsed the interpretation of his "path of thought" that Pöggeler devel-oped in *Das Denkweg Martin Heideggers*, which was first published in 1963. (Heidegger esteemed Pöggeler's sensitivity to the nuances of his philosophical trajectory, above all, with respect to the "Turn" of the early 1930s.) However, differences began to emerge with the publication of Pöggeler's ensuing Heidegger study, *Philosophie und Politik bei Heidegger* (Freiburg: Karl Alber, 1972), which was more critical of Heidegger's thought.

11. Martin Heidegger, *Einführung in die Metaphysik*, GA 40 (Frankfurt: Klostermann, 1983), 208; hence, the wording in the 1953 and 1983 editions remained unchanged: "Was heute vollends als Philosophie des Nationalsozialismus herumgeboten wird, aber mit der inneren Wahrheit und Größe dieser Bewegung (nämlich mit der Begegnung der planetarisch bestimmten Technik und des neuzeitlichen Menschen) nicht das Geringste zu tun hat, das macht seine Fischzüge in diesen trüben Gewässern der 'Werte' und der 'Ganzheiten.' " For the English translation, see Heidegger, *Introduction to Metaphysics*, trans. Ralph Manheim (New Haven, CT: Yale University Press, 1959), 199.

12. Petra Jaeger, "Nachwort der Herausgeberin," in *Einführung in die Metaphysik*, GA 40, 233–34.

13. Martin Heidegger, " 'Only a God Can Save Us': *Der Spiegel*'s Interview with Martin Heidegger (1966)," in Wolin, *Heidegger Controversy*, 102.

14. Heidegger, *Einführung in die Metaphysik*, GA 40, 234.

15. Pöggeler, *Heidegger's Path of Thought*, 277.

16. Karl Jaspers, "Letter to the Freiburg University de-Nazification Commission," in Wolin, *Heidegger Controversy*, 150.

17. Martin Heidegger, "Das Rektorat, 1933–34: Tatsachen und Gedanken," in *Reden und andere Zeugnisse eines Lebensweges*, GA 16 (Frankfurt: Klostermann, 2000), 391–92.

18. See the illuminating discussion in Lutz Hachmeister, *Heideggers Testament: Der Phi-losoph, Der Spiegel, und die SS* (Berlin: Ullstein: 2014), 198.

19. Habermas, "Work and Weltanschauung," 162.

20. Christian Lewalter, letter to the editor, *Die Zeit*, 13 August 1953. Heidegger's letter ap-peared one month later in *Die Zeit*, 24 September 1953.

21. Martin Heidegger, *Überlegungen VII–XI*, GA 95 (Frankfurt: Klostermann, 2014), 209.

22. Otto Pöggeler, *Heidegger in seiner Zeit* (Munich: Wilhelm Fink, 1999), 268.

23. Quoted in Elzbieta Ettinger, *Hannah Arendt/Martin Heidegger* (New Haven, CT: Yale University Press, 1995), 28.

24. This is the interpretation that appeared in the purportedly "corrected," *Gesamtausgabe* edition of *Einführung in die Metaphysik* (GA 40); Heidegger, "Only a God Can Save Us," 104.

25. Rainer Marten, "Ein rassistisches Konzept von Humanität," *Badische Zeitung*, 28 December 1987.

26. Ibid. See also Hartmut Buchner, "Fragmentarisches," in *Erinnerung an Martin Heidegger*, ed. Günther Neske (Pfullingen: Neske, 1977), 47–51.

27. Both remarks are cited in Heinrich W. Petzet, *Auf einen Stern zugehen: Begegnungen und Gespräche mit Martin Heidegger* (Frankfurt: Societät Verlag, 1983), 232, 82. For a good treatment of philosophical anthropology that discusses Heidegger's proximity to the movement, see Joachim Fischer, *Philosophische Anthropologie: Eine Denkrichtung im 20. Jahrhundert* (Munich: Karl Alber, 2020).

28. Martin Heidegger, *What Is Called Thinking?*, trans. Albert Hofstadter (New York: Harper and Row, 1968), 67.

29. Heidegger, "Das Rektorat, 1933–34," 375.

30. Heidegger, *Einführung in die Metaphysik*, GA 40, 142; Heidegger, *Introduction to Metaphysics*, 133.

31. Martin Heidegger, *Der Wille zur Macht als Kunst*, GA 43 (Frankfurt: Klostermann, 1985), 193 (emphasis added). For a partial list of the editorial omissions and manipulations that pervade Heidegger's Nietzsche lectures, see Gregory Fried, *Heidegger's Polemos: From Being to Politics* (New Haven, CT: Yale University Press, 2001), 251–57.

32. Martin Heidegger, *Die Geschichte des Seyns*, ed. Peter Trawny (Frankfurt: Klostermann, 1998); for the relevant background, see Eggert Blum, "Die Marke Heidegger," *Die Zeit* 47 (27 November 2014). See Peter Trawny, *Heidegger und der Mythos einer jüdischen Weltverschwörung* (Frankfurt: Klostermann, 2014), 51.

33. That the determination of who qualified as a Jew under National Socialism was arbitrary—hence devoid of an "objective" basis—is suggested by Hermann Göring's notorious declaration, "It is I who will decide who is a Jew!" Quoted in Diemut Majer, *"Non-Germans" under the Third Reich: The Nazi Judicial and Administrative System in Germany* (Baltimore: Johns Hopkins University Press, 2003), 60.

34. For the context and background of Hitler's speech, see Hans Mommsen, "Hitler's Reichstag Speech of 30 January 1939," *History and Memory* 9 (1997): 147–61.

35. Martin Heidegger, *Hölderlins Hymnen "Germanien" und "Der Rhein,"* GA 39 (Frankfurt: Klostermann, 1980), 214.

36. Ibid. See Adam Soboczynski, "Was heist 'N. soz.'? Hätte der massive Antisemitismus des Philosophen Martin Heidegger früher belegt werden können?," *Die Zeit* 13 (26 March 2015).

37. Ibid.

38. Heidegger, "Das Rektorat, 1933–34," 404.

39. Martin Heidegger, "The Age of the World Picture," in *The Question Concerning Technology and Other Essays*, trans. William Lovitt (New York: Harper and Row, 1977), 84.

40. I have addressed some of these problems and things in my book *The Seduction of Unreason: The Intellectual Romance with Fascism from Nietzsche to Postmodernism*, 2nd ed. (Princeton, NJ: Princeton University Press, 2019).

41. Martin Heidegger, "Das Gestell," in *Bremer und Freiburger Vorträge*, GA 79 (Frankfurt: Klostermann, 1994), 27. See also Berel Lang, *Heidegger's Silence* (Ithaca, NY: Cornell University Press, 1996).

42. Martin Heidegger, "Die Frage nach der Technik," in *Vorträge und Aufsätze* (Pfullingen: Neske Verlag, 1954), 5–36. Needless to say, the deception was perpetuated in the English-language publication of Heidegger's text, "The Question Concerning Technology," in *Question Concerning Technology*. Despite the fact that the editorial sleight-of-hand first came to light during the 1980s, it has never been corrected in subsequent editions of the anthology.

43. Habermas, "Work and Weltanschauung," 159–60.

44. Martin Heidegger, "Die Grundfrage der Philosophie," in *Sein und Wahrheit*, GA 36/37 (Frankfurt: Klostermann, 2001), 39.

45. Theodor Adorno, *Minima Moralia*, trans. E. F. N. Jephcott (London: New Left Books, 1974), 110.

46. See Hachmeister, *Heideggers Testament*, 195.

47. Heidegger's deception was first revealed by the University of Siegen philosopher Sidonie Kellerer in "Rewording the Past: The Postwar Publication of a 1938 Lecture by Martin Heidegger," *Modern Intellectual History* 11 (2014): 575–602. Martin Heidegger, *Holzwege* (Frankfurt: Klostermann, 1950), 111.

48. Kellerer, "Rewording the Past," 579.

49. See the account in Hugo Ott, *Martin Heidegger: A Political Life*, trans. Allan Blunden (New York: Basic Books, 1990), 359–68.

50. Martin Heidegger, *Off the Beaten Path*, trans. Julian Young and Kenneth Baynes (New York: Cambridge University Press, 2002), 245.

51. See Soboczynski, "Was heist 'N. soz.' "?

52. This fact was confirmed to me in a personal conversation with the University of Siegen philosopher Marion Heinz, who edited *Gesamtausgabe* 44, *Nietzsches metaphysische Grundstellung im abendländischen Denken: Die ewige Wiederkehr des Gleichen* (Frankfurt: Klostermann Verlag, 1986).

53. See Thomas Assheuer, "Er verstand sich als Revolutionär: Ein Interview mit Marion Heinz," *Die Zeit* 11 (18 March 2015).

54. Alexander Cammann and Adam Soboczynski, "Martin Heidegger: Es ist wieder da! Silvio Vietta macht das unbekannte 'Schwarze Heft' öffentlich!," *Die Zeit* 5 (23 January 2014).

55. Peter Trawny, "Nachwort des Herausgebers," in *Anmerkungen I–V*, GA 97 (Frankfurt: Klostermann, 2015), 521.

56. Reinhard Mehring, *Heideggers "Grosse Politik": Die semantische Revolution der Gesamtausgabe* (Tübingen: Mohr Siebeck, 2018), 282.

57. Heidegger confirmed this fact in a letter to Hannah Arendt of June 1974, after the contract had been signed with Klostermann. See Heidegger to Arendt, 20 June 1974, in *Briefwechsel: 1925–1975* (Frankfurt: Klostermann, 2001), 251.

58. See Friedrich-Wilhelm von Herrmann, "Die Edition der Vorlesungen Heideggers in seiner Gesatmausgabe letzter Hand," *Freibürger Universitätsblätter* 21 (1986): 153–72.

59. Ibid.

60. See Mehring's comments on von Herrmann's statement in *Heideggers "Grosse Politik,"* 270–72.

61. See Kisiel, "Heidegger's *Gesamtausgabe*." See also Rainer Marten, "Grabhalter mit letzter Treuebereitschaft": "Seit Jahren nehmen die Herausgeber Martin Heideggers Werk in Beschlag. Das ist ein Skandal, der endlich ein Ende haben muss." In addition, see Lorenz Jäger, "Allesamt Spielarten der Seinsvergessenheit," *Frankfurter Allgemeine Zeitung*, 3 March 2015; and Mehring, *Heideggers Überlieferungsgeschick*.

62. See Richard Wolin, "Heidegger hielt 'Endlösung' für notwendig,' " *Hohe Luft-Magazin*, 28 March 2015; Vittorio E. Klostermann, "Eine verlässliche Ausgabe und ein unredlicher Angriff," *Hohe Luft*, 31 August 2015; and my response to Klostermann, "J'accuse! Eine Antwort auf Vittorio Klostermann," *Hohe Luft*, 2 November 2015. See also Wolin, " 'Eine Art Schadensabwicklung': Antwort auf Vittorio E. Klostermann," *Vierteljahrshefte für Zeitgeschichte* 64 (2016): 169–71.

63. See Robert Michael and Karin Doer, eds., *Nazi-Deutsch/Nazi German: An English Lexicon of the Language of the Third Reich* (Westport, CT: Greenwood, 2002).

64. Quoted in *Ausgewählte Dokumente zur Geschichte des Nationalsozialismus, 1933–1945*, vol. 4, ed. Hans-Adolf Jacobsen and Werner Jochmann (Bielefeld: Neue Gesellschaft, 1961), 4–5.

65. Gregory Fried and Richard Polt, "Editors' Introduction," in *Nature, History, State*, by Martin Heidegger (London: Bloomsbury Academic, 2013), 12.

66. Ibid.

67. Heidegger, *Hölderlins Hymnen "Germanien" und "Der Rhein,"* GA 39, 210.

68. See the entry "Führer, der 'Führer,' " in *Vokabular des Nationalsozialismus*, ed. Cornelia Schmitz-Berning (Berlin: de Gruyter, 2007), 240–45.

69. *Knaurs Koversations-Lexikon A–Z* (Berlin: T. H. Knaior, 1934), 450.

70. Der Reichsorganisationsleiter der NSDAP, *Organisationsbuch der NSDAP* (Munich: Eher, 1943), 86.

71. Martin Heidegger, *Über Wesen und Begriff von Natur, Geschichte, und Staat*, in *Heidegger-Jahrbuch*, vol. 4 (Freiburg: Karl Alber, 2009), 77.

72. Martin Heidegger, "Seminar über Hegels *Rechtsphilosophie*," in *Seminare: Hegel-Schelling*, GA 86 (Frankfurt: Klostermann, 1998), 170–71. For an overview of Heidegger's involvement with the Academy of German Law, see Werner Schubert, ed., *Weitere Nachträge (1934–1939): Ausschüsse für Rechtsphilosophie, für die Überprüfung der rechtswissenschaftlichen Studienordnung und für Seeversicherungsrecht* (Frankfurt: Peter Lang, 2019).

73. Martin Heidegger, "Die deutsche Universität," in *Reden und andere Zeugnisse eines Lebensweges*, GA 16, 298–99.

74. Heidegger, *Sein und Zeit*, GA 2, 385 (emphasis added); Martin Heidegger, *Being and Time*, trans. John Macquarrie and Edward Robinson (New York: Harper and Row, 1962), 452.

75. Ibid.

76. Daniel Morat, *Von der Tat zur Gelassenheit: Konservatives Denken bei Martin Heidegger, Ernst Jünger und Friedrich Georg Jünger* (Göttingen: Wallstein Verlag, 2007), 114.

77. Daniel Morat, "No Remigration: Martin Heidegger and Ernst Jünger in the Early Federal Republic of German," *Modern Intellectual History* 9 (2012): 668.

78. Arno Münster, *Heidegger: La Science allemande et le National-Socialisme* (Paris: Editions Kimé, 2002), 68, 72. I have formulated a set of similar arguments in the *Politics of Being: The Political Thought of Martin Heidegger* (New York: Columbia University Press, 2016); see especially chapter 2, "*Being and Time* as Political Philosophy," 16–66.

79. For a representative treatment of "Heidegger and pragmatism," see Mark Okrent, *Heidegger's Pragmatism: Understanding, Being, and the Critique of Metaphysics* (Ithaca, NY: Cornell University Press, 1991). The virtues of Okrent's study are many. However, its inattention to the "historicity" of *Being and Time*—that is, the book's contextual situatedness—explains its inability to fathom *Being and Time*'s influence qua *Zeit- and Zivilisationskritik*: that is, as a "critique of the historical present."

80. Hubert Drefyus, *Being-in-the-World: A Commentary on Heidegger's "Being and Time"* (Cambridge, MA: MIT Press, 1991), vii.

81. Karl-Heinz Bohrer, *Ästhetik des Schreckens: Die pessimistische Romantik und Ernst Jüngers Frühwerk* (Munich: Ullstein, 1978), 334–35, 341.

82. Pierre Bourdieu, *The Political Ontology of Martin Heidegger*, trans. Peter Collier (Stanford, CA: Stanford University Press, 1991).

83. Martin Heidegger, *Grundbegriffe der aristotelischen Philosophie*, GA 17 (Frankfurt: Klostermann, 2002), 15.

84. See Charles Bambach's lucid reflections on *Bodenständigkeit* in *Heidegger's Roots: Nietzsche, National Socialism, and the Greeks* (Ithaca, NY: Cornell University Press, 2003): "Heidegger was convinced that 'originary philosophy' could only be done in dialogue with politics . . . as the historical-ontological site within which Dasein struggled to find its own sense of *being rooted*: in a community, a *Volk*, a tradition, and a history. On this reading, politics is a *politics of the earth*, a geopolitics, whose ultimate meaning is *ontological* in the sense that it becomes the site for the unfolding of basic human possibilities. . . . [The] earth becomes what the ancient Greeks called 'chton,' the place where humans go and form a homeland" (14).

85. Heidegger, *Anmerkungen I–V*, GA 97, 20.

86. Anna Bramwell, *Blood and Soil: Richard Walther Darré and Hitler's "Green Party"* (Bourne End, UK: Kensal, 1985): "[Darré] had become acquainted during the late 1920s with National Socialist activists and sympathizers, most of them living in Thuringia, and interested in two things: peasant-agrarian problems and the decline of German culture. . . . He knew Hanns Johst, playwright and the author of a popular work on Schlageter; met Jünger and, later, Heidegger" (75). In "Blut und Boden: The Ideological Basis of the Nazi Agricultural Program," *Journal of the History of Ideas* 28 (1967), Charles Lovin outlines Darré's understanding of the racial correspondence between "Blut" and "Boden" as follows: "*Blut und Boden* is the phrase that lies at the very heart of all Darré's thinking. *Blut* . . . is used as the heading for his racial theories. Under *Boden*, or soil, all his notions on agriculture appear. . . . If one sentence can be found to express Darré's basic conception of the meaning of agriculture, it will be his declaration that 'the German soul with its warmth is rooted in its agriculture and in a real sense always grew out of it.' Darré believed . . . that the farmer [*Bauer*] was the basis of German society and the backbone of the Nordic race. His principal means of emphasizing the importance of the farmer was the equation of the terms 'farmer' and 'noble'" (282). Uwe Mai discusses Darré's status as the 'real ideologue behind Himmler' in *"Rasse und Raum": Agrarpolitik, Sozial-und Raumplanung im NS-Staat* (Paderborn: Schöningh, 2002), 15.

87. See Adam Epstein, " 'Blood and Soil': The Meaning of the Nazi Slogan Chanted by White Nationalists in Charlottesville," *Quartz*, 13 August 2017. In Heidegger's Hölderlin lectures (1934–35), he lauded this "fateful" rapport of the *Volk* to its *Heimat* as "*politics in the highest and most authentic sense*." Heidegger, *Hölderlins Hymnen "Germanien" und "Der Rhein,"* GA 39, 214.

88. Martin Heidegger, *Basic Concepts of Aristotelian Philosophy*, trans. Robert Metcalf (Bloomington: Indiana University Press, 2009), 13.

89. Kurt Sontheimer, *Antidemokratisches Denken in der Weimarer Republik* (Munich: Nymphenerger Verlagshandlung, 1962).

90. For an important addition to this literature, see Victor Klemperer, *Language of the Third Reich: LTI: Lingui Tertii Imperii*, trans. Martin Brady (London: Athlon, 2006).

91. Ernst Cassirer, *The Myth of the State* (New Haven, CT: Yale University Press, 1946), 282–83.

92. Ibid., 284.

93. Michel Foucault, *Dits et Écrits*, vol. 3 (Paris: Gallimard, 1977), 390–98. Foucault's remarks originally appeared in an interview with Knut Boesers in *Literaturmagazin* 8 (1977): 60–68.

94. Martin Heidegger, *Logik: Die Frage nach der Wahrheit*, GA 21 (Frankfurt: Klostermann, 1995), 79.

95. See my article "The Swan Song of French Nietzscheanism," *Los Angeles Review of Books*, 9 July 2018.

96. G. W. F. Hegel, preface to the *Phenomenology of Spirit*, trans. A. W. Miller (New York: Oxford University Press, 1977), 47.

97. Herbert Schnädelbach, *Zur Rehabilitierung des animal rationale* (Frankfurt: Suhrkamp Verlag, 1992), 13.

98. See Friedrich Nietzsche, *Ecce Homo*, trans. R. J. Hollingdale (New York: Penguin, 2004), 131, 112; Nietzsche, *Twilight of the Idols, or How to Philosophize with a Hammer*, trans. Richard Polt (Indianapolis: Hackett, 1997). Needless to say, these criticisms of Nietzsche are intended to help in contextualizing his thought; they are not meant to dismiss it.

99. Martin Heidegger, *Vorträge: 1915–1932*, GA 80, vol. 1 (Frankfurt: Klostermann, 2016); Heidegger, *Vorträge: 1934–1967*, GA 80, vol. 2 (Frankfurt: Klostermann, 2020); Uwe Justus Wenzel, "Eine Ausgabe letzter Hände," *Neue Zürcher Zeitung*, 3 April 2015; also see Reinhard Mehring, review of *Vorträge: 1915–1932*, GA 80, vol. 1, by Martin Heidegger, *Philosophischer Literaturanzeiger* 69 (2016): 233–38.

100. Wenzel, "Eine Ausgabe letzter Hände"; Arnulf Heidegger, "Heideggers 'Schwarze Hefte': 'Der Vorwurf geht ins Leere,' " *Die Zeit* 12 (19 March 2015); Thomas Meyer, "Im Editionsbunker: Neues von Martin Heidegger," *Süddeutsche Zeitung*, 8 December 2020.

Chapter 2. Heidegger in Ruins

1. See Martin Heidegger to Elfride Heidegger, 19 March 1933, in *"Mein liebes Seelchen": Briefe Martin Heideggers an seine Frau Elfride, 1915–1970*, ed. Gertrud Heidegger (Munich: Deutsche Verlag-Anstalt, 2005), 186.

2. Martin Heidegger, *Überlegungen II–VI*, GA 94 (Frankfurt: Klostermann, 2014), 124.
   For a perceptive commentary on these passages, see Emmanuel Faye, "Kategorien oder
   Existenzialien: Von der Metaphysik zur Metapolitik," in *Heideggers "Schwarze Hefte":
   Eine philosophisch-politische Debatte*, ed. Marion Heinz and Sidonie Kellerer (Berlin:
   Suhrkamp, 2016), 100–121.
3. Heidegger, *Überlegungen II–VI*, GA 94, 27.
4. Martin Heidegger, *Überlegungen XII–XV*, GA 96 (Frankfurt: Klostermann, 2014), 46.
5. *Über Wesen und Begriff von Natur, Geschichte, und Staat*, in *Heidegger-Jahrbuch*, vol. 4
   (Freiburg: Karl Alber, 2009), 82.
6. Martin Heidegger, *Einführung in die Metaphysik*, GA 40 (Frankfurt: Klostermann,
   1983), 41; Heidegger, *Introduction to Metaphysics*, trans. Ralph Manheim (New Haven,
   CT: Yale University Press, 1959), 38.
7. Martin Heidegger, *Der Anfang des abendländischen Denkens. Heraklit*, GA 55 (Frankfurt: Klostermann, 1987), 108, 123 (emphasis added).
8. Heidegger, *Überlegungen II–VI*, GA 94, 194 (emphasis added).
9. Heidegger, *Überlegungen XII–XV*, GA 96, 195: "Alles muss durch die völlige Verwüstung hindurch. Nur so ist das zweitausendjährige Gefüge der Metaphysik zu erschüt-
   tern." In this respect, Jünger's influence on Heidegger, as the literary inheritor of
   Nietzschean "active nihilism," proved to be pivotal. As Ernst Jünger proposed in " 'Nationalismus' und Nationalismus" (1929), "The true will to struggle [*Kampf*] and genuine
   hatred are attracted by everything capable of *destroying the opponent. Destruction
   [Zerstörung]* is the optimal means of defining contemporary Nationalism. The first part
   of our task is 'anarchistic,' and whoever acknowledges this point, during this initial
   stage, will welcome *everything that can destroy*. We will take up our position only where
   raging fire has paved the way, only where the flamethrower has achieved the Great
   Purification through Nothingness." Jünger, " 'Nationalismus' und Nationalismus," in
   Politische Publizistik, 1919–1933, ed. Sven Berggötz (Stuttgart: Klett-Cotta, 2001), 506.
10. Martin Heidegger, *Überlegungen VII–XI*, GA 95 (Frankfurt: Klostermann, 2014), 274.
11. Heidegger, *Überlegungen II–VI*, GA 94, 124.
12. Martin Heidegger, "Wehrdienst der Freiburger Studentenschaft," in *Reden und andere
    Zeugnisse eines Lebensweges*, GA 16 (Frankfurt: Klostermann, 2000), 103.
13. See G. W. F. Hegel, *Lectures on the Philosophy of History*, trans. H. B. Nesbitt (New
    York: Cambridge University Press, 1975): "The History of the world is none other than
    the progress of the consciousness of Freedom; a progress whose development according
    to the necessity of its nature, it is our business to investigate" (54).
14. See Steven Aschheim, "Nietzsche and the German Radical Right," in *The Intellectual
    Revolt against Liberal Democracy: 1875–1945*, ed. Zeev Sternhell (Jerusalem: Israel
    Academy of the Humanities, 1996): "For the German radical right of 1918–1933 . . . Ni-
    etzsche was the most authoritative and inspirational source. . . . As its sympathetic
    chronicler, Armin Mohler, put it, the 'conservative revolution' would have been 'un-
    thinkable' without Nietzsche" (159).
15. Charles Bambach, *Heidegger's Roots: Nietzsche, National Socialism, and the Greeks*
    (Ithaca, NY: Cornell University Press, 2003), 281. See also Christian von Krockow, *Die
    Entscheidung: Eine Untersuchung über Ernst Jünger, Carl Schmitt, und Martin
    Heidegger* (Stuttgart: Enke, 1958); and Daniel Morat, *Von der Tat zur Gelassenheit:*

Konservatives Denken bei Martin Heidegger, Ernst Jünger, und Friedrich Georg Jünger (Göttingen: Wallstein Verlag, 2007).

16. In *Metaphysics: Concepts and Problems*, trans. Edmund Jephcott (Stanford, CA: Stanford University Press, 2001), Theodor Adorno astutely warned against naively viewing the history of philosophy as "an 'eternal conversation of philosophical minds' carried on down the millennia, which has nothing to do with history" (65).

17. See Martin Heidegger, *Sein und Zeit*, GA 2 (Frankfurt: Klostermann, 1977), 30; Heidegger, *Being and Time*, trans. John Macquarrie and Edward Robinson (New York: Harper Row, 1962): "We understand [our] task as one in which *by taking the question of Being as our clue*, we are to *destroy* the traditional content of ancient ontology until we arrive at those primordial experiences in which we achieved our first ways of determining the nature of Being" (44).

18. Martin Heidegger, *Kant und das Problem der Metaphysik*, GA 3 (Frankfurt: Klostermann, 1999), 273.

19. Martin Heidegger, *Vom Wesen der Menschlichen Freiheit: Einleitung in der Philosophie*, GA 31 (Frankfurt: Klostermann, 1983), 292.

20. On this question, see the important study by Ulrich Sieg, *Geist und Gewalt: Deutsche Philosophen zwischen Kaiserreich und Nationalsozialismus* (Munich: Hanser, 2013). For an account of Nietzsche's influence on Heidegger, see Otto Pöggeler, *Friedrich Nietzsche und Martin Heidegger* (Bonn: Bouvier, 2002). See also Klaus Vondung, *The Apocalypse in Germany*, trans. Stephen Ricks (Columbus: University of Missouri Press, 2000), especially part 4, "The Existential Apocalypse."

21. See Luc Ferry and Alain Renaut, eds., *Why We Are Not Nietzscheans*, trans. Robert de Loaiza (Chicago: University of Chicago Press, 1997), 178. I discuss the meaning of Heidegger's "spiritual fascism" at length in chapter 3, "Heidegger and Race." In "Zur Immatrikulation" (5 May 1933), for example, Heidegger stressed the centrality of "*geistig-politischen Führerschaft*" (spiritual-political leadership). Heidegger, *Reden und andere Zeugnisse eines Lebesweges*, GA 16, 95.

22. Martin Heidegger to Fritz Heidegger, 28 October 1932, in *Heidegger und der Antisemitismus: Positionen im Widerstreit*, ed. Walter Homolka and Arnulf Heidegger (Freiburg: Herder, 2016), 31.

23. Hans Zehrer, "Die Revolution von Rechts," *Die Tat*, April 1933, 1.

24. Karl Prümm, *Die Literatur des soldatischen Nationalismus der 20er Jahre: Gruppenideologie und Epochenproblematik*, 3 vols. (Kronberg: Scriptor Verlag, 1974).

25. Klaus Theweleit, *Männerphantasien: Die Angst vor der Körperauflösung*, 2 vols. (Berlin: Matthes und Seitz, 1977).

26. Florian Brückner, *In der Literatur unbesiegt: Werner Beumelburg als Kriegsdichter in der Weimarer Republik und Nationalsozialismus* (Berlin: LIT Verlag, 2017), 11.

27. Quoted in Kurt Sontheimer, *Antidemokratisches Denken in der Weimarer Republik* (Munich: Nymphenbürger Verlag, 1960), 125.

28. Martin Heidegger, "Die deutsche Universität," in *Reden und andere Zeugnisse eines Lebesweges*, GA 16, 299–300.

29. Martin Heidegger to Fritz Heidegger, 2 March 1932, in *Heidegger und der Antisemitismus*, 26; Werner Beumelburg, *Deutschland in Ketten: Von Versailles bis zum Youngplan* (Oldenburg: Gerhard Stalling, 1931).

30. Beumelburg, *Deutschland in Ketten*, 62–63.

31. Martin Heidegger to Fritz Heidegger, 2 March 1932, *Heidegger und der Antisemitismus*, 27.

32. Hans Grimm, "Überbevölkerung und Kolonialproblem" (1922), in *Der Schriftsteller und die Zeit: Eine Bekenntnis* (Munich: Albert Langen, 1931), 92.

33. Ernst Keller, *Nationalismus und Literatur: Langemarck, Weimar, Stalingrad* (Bern and Munich: Franke, 1970), 129.

34. Friedrich Nietzsche, *Beyond Good and Evil: Prelude to a Philosophy of the Future*, trans. Walter Kaufman (New York: Vintage, 1989), 176–77.

35. Vondung, *Apocalypse in Germany*.

36. Friedrich Nietzsche, "Why I Am a Destiny," in *"On the Genealogy of Morals" and "Ecce Homo,"* trans. Walter Kaufmann (New York: Vintage, 1968), 327.

37. Fritz Stern, *The Politics of Cultural Despair: A Study in the Rise of German Ideology* (Berkeley: University of California Press, 1961).

38. Heidegger, *Überlegungen, XII–XV*, GA 96, 29.

39. Bambach, *Heidegger's Roots*, 251.

40. See Charles Bambach, *Heidegger, Dilthey, and the Crisis of Historicism* (Ithaca, NY: Cornell University Press, 1995): "Spengler's sermonizing about the decline of Western culture . . . appeared to [Heidegger] as the contemporary sign of a profoundly Nietzschean nihilism" (215).

41. Heidegger, *Überlegungen II–VI*, GA 94, 484, 502.

42. Heidegger, *Überlegungen XII–XV*, GA 96, 238, 281 (emphasis added).

43. Peter Trawny, *Heidegger und der Mythos einer jüdischen Weltverschwörung* (Frankfurt: Klostermann, 2014), 133.

44. Heidegger, *Überlegungen XII–XV*, GA 96, 274. For Heidegger's early engagement with Spengler, see the text of his 1923 Freiburg University lecture course *Ontology: The Hermeneutics Facticity* (Bloomington: Indiana University Press, 1999), 28–32. On 10–12 May 1932, Heidegger informed Fritz that he had mailed a copy of Spengler's monograph *Der Mensch und die Technik: Beitrag zu einer Philosophie des Lebens* (Munich: CH Beck, 1931). Heidegger also passed along a recent press dossier, "Der deutsche Sozialismus nach Adolf Hitler: Oswald Spengler und der Aufstieg des Nationalsozialismus," analyzing the relationship between Spengler and National Socialism that had recently been published in *Das Neue Deutschland* (Leipzig, 1932). See Martin Heidegger to Fritz Heidegger, 10–12 May 1932, in *Heidegger und der Antisemitismus*, 29, 146.

45. Martin Heidegger, "Das Rektorat, 1933–34: Tatsachen und Gedanken," in *Reden und andere Zeugnisse eines Lebensweges*, GA 16, 375.

46. Michel Winock, "L'Éternel refrain de la décadence," *L'Histoire* 76 (1985): 97.

47. See Bambach, *Heidegger's Roots*, 280.

48. Jürgen Habermas, "The Great Influence," in *Philosophical-Political Profiles*, trans. Frederick Lawrence (Cambridge, MA: MIT Press, 1983), 57.

49. See Jeffrey Herf, *Reactionary Modernism* (New York: Cambridge University Press, 1984). As Martin Travers has observed in *Critics of Modernity: The Literature of the Conservative Revolution, 1890–1933* (New York: Peter Lang, 2001), the reactionary modernists produced "a literature of *Ungleichzeitigkeit* ('Non-Contemporaneity'), whose recognition of the crisis of modernity drew it forward into the modern period, as

the solutions, totalizing, sectarian and sometimes populist, that it offered to that crisis, drew it back into the Romantic utopias of the nineteenth century and, in certain instances, back further still, into idealized notions of medieval guilds or chivalric oligarchies" (9).

50. Hannah Arendt, "Heidegger at Eighty," in *Heidegger and Modern Philosophy*, ed. Michael Murray (New Haven, CT: Yale University Press, 1979), 293–303.
51. See Marion Heinz's account in Thomas Assheuer, "Er verstand sich als Revolutionär," *Die Zeit* 11 (12 March 2015).
52. Martin Heidegger to Fritz Heidegger, 28 October 1932, in *Heidegger und der Antisemitismus*, 30. Heidegger's allusion to the Jews' "state of panic" referred to the consequences of the economic "Crash" of 1929.
53. Assheuer, "Er verstand sich als Revolutionär."
54. Martin Heidegger to Fritz Heidegger, 21 December 1931, in *Heidegger und der Antisemitismus*, 21–22.
55. See Ulrich Sieg, *Geist und Gewalt: Deutsche Philosophen zwischen Kaiserreich und Nationalsozialismus* (Munich: Hanser, 2013).
56. Fritz Heidegger to Martin Heidegger, 3 April 1933, in *Heidegger und der Antisemitismus*, 33.
57. Ian Kershaw, *Hitler: A Biography* (New York: Norton, 2010), 276.
58. Martin Heidegger to Fritz Heidegger, 13 April 1933, in *Heidegger und der Antisemitismus*, 35 (emphasis added).
59. Heidegger, *Überlegungen XII–XV*, GA 96, 235 (emphasis added).
60. Stern, *Politics of Cultural Despair*, 268.
61. Julian Göpffarth, "Rethinking the German Nation as German Dasein: Intellectuals and Heidegger's Philosophy in Contemporary German New Right Nationalism," *Journal of Political Ideologies* 25 (2020): 261.
62. George Mosse, *The Crisis of German Ideology: The Intellectual Origins of the Third Reich* (New York: Grossett and Dunlap, 1964), 306–7.
63. Susanne Lettow, "Heideggers Politik des Rassenbegriffs," in Heinz and Kellerer, *Heideggers "Schwarze Hefte,"* 237.
64. Sontheimer, *Antidemokratisches Denken*, 249.
65. *Großes Brockhaus Lexikon*, 15th ed., vol. 19 (Leipzig, 1928), 650.
66. For background, see Hans Kellersohn, "Volk, völkisch, völkische Bewegung," in *DISS-Journal* 33 (2017): 9–12; see also Reinhart Koselleck et al., "Volk, Nation, Nationalismus, Masse," in *Geschichtliche Grundbegriffe*, vol. 7, ed. Werner Conze and Otto Brunner (Stuttgart: Klett-Cotta, 1992), 141–431.
67. Heidegger, *Einführung in die Metaphysik*, GA 40, 42; Heidegger, *Introduction to Metaphysics*, 38 (emphasis added).
68. Heidegger, *Einführung in die Metaphysik*, GA 40, 42; Heidegger, *Introduction to Metaphysics*, 38 (emphasis added).
69. For the classic account of the ideology of German exceptionalism, see Gerd Faulenbach, *Die Ideologie des deutschen Weges: Die deutsche Geschichte in der Historiographie zwischen Kaiserreich und Nationalsozialismus* (Munich: Beck, 1980). As Faulenbach explains,

With the founding of the Second Empire in 1871 . . . it became de rigueur to reread German history as a process culminating in unification. Thereafter, the Wilhelmine era was defined by a markedly ideological image of the German Empire. . . . The new monarchical system was promoted as a peculiarly and specifically *German* form of political rule that was distinctly superior to Western parliamentary models, . . . [a] view that was elevated to the status of unchallengeable dogma. German thinkers celebrated the specific characteristics of *German spiritual life* and *German culture*—German idealism, German romanticism, historicism, and so forth—as a specifically *German* form of cultural-political achievement. As the First World War erupted—a conflict that was also fought under the banner of a *Kulturkrieg* [clash of cultures]—the unique, salvific mission of *Germanentum* rigidified into a dogma. Among historians, philosophers, and theologians, such views hardened into what may be denominated "the German ideology." (7)

70. Martin Heidegger, *Hölderlins Hymnen "Germanien" und "Der Rhein,"* GA 39 (Frankfurt: Klostermann Verlag, 1980), 210.

71. Heidegger, *Überlegungen II–VI*, GA 94, 111.

72. See Otto Pöggeler, "Den Führer führen: Heidegger und kein Ende," *Philosophische Rundschau* 32 (1985): 26–67.

73. Martin Heidegger, "Ansprache an Leipzig," in *Reden und andere Zeugnisse eines Lebensweges*, GA 16, 192.

74. Martin Heidegger to Fritz Heidegger, 13 April 1933, 35.

75. Martin Heidegger, "The Self-Assertion of the German University," in *The Heidegger Controversy: A Critical Reader*, ed. Richard Wolin (Cambridge, MA: MIT Press, 1993), 31.

76. Heidegger, *Hölderlins Hymnen "Germanien" und "Der Rhein,"* GA 39, 133–34.

77. Heidegger, *Introduction to Metaphysics*, 43.

78. Herbert Marcuse and Martin Heidegger, "An Exchange of Letters," in Wolin, *Heidegger Controversy*, 162.

79. Heidegger, *Hölderlins Hymnen "Germanien" und "Der Rhein,"* GA 39, 133–34 (emphasis added). See also Rainer Marten, "Heidegger and the Greeks," in *The Heidegger Case: On Philosophy and Politics*, ed. Tom Rockmore and Joseph Margolis (Philadelphia: Temple University Press, 1992): "The ancient Greeks *are*; they have not passed away. . . . They are just now coming into their own *in the Germans*. . . . Western man—historical, philosophical, and originally Greek—*ultimately reappears as German*" (169).

80. In *Mein Kampf*, trans. Ralph Manheim (New York: Houghton Mifflin, 1998), for example, Hitler vilified Kurt Eisner, the Jewish leader of the Munich *Räterepublik*, as an "Oriental," who, under the pretense of representing Bavarian interests, ultimately betrayed them (556–57). Similarly, in *The Myth of the Twentieth Century*, Alfred Rosenberg denigrated "the Roman-Syrian-Jewish Myth that rejects the supreme value of race" in favor of a nebulous, extraterritorial "universalism." Rosenberg, *The Myth of the Twentieth Century: An Evaluation of the Spiritual-Intellectual Confrontations of Our Age*, trans. James B. Whisker (Torrance, CA: Noontide, 1982), 383. With the advent of the Middle East refugee crisis in 2015, the trope of "inundation" (*Überflutung*) by uncivilized "Asiatic hordes" made a comeback among proponents of right-wing German nationalism.

81. Martin Heidegger to Fritz Heidegger, 2 March 1932, in *Heidegger und der Antisemitismus*, 26.

82. Hannah Arendt, *The Origins of Totalitarianism* (New York: Harcourt Brace, 1958), viii–ix. See also Dan Diner and Seyla Benhabib, eds., *Zivilisationsbruch: Denken nach Auschwitz* (Frankfurt: Fisher Verlag, 1988); and Dan Diner, *Beyond the Conceivable: Studies on Germany, Nazism, and the Holocaust* (Berkeley: University of California Press, 2000).

83. See Markus Gabriel, "Heideggers widerwärtige Thesen über den Holocaust," *Die Welt*, 15 March 2015. As Gabriel observes, *Anmerkungen I–V* (GA 97) "presents us with a distorted image of German history from 1942 to 1948; behind that image, the mask of unregenerate Nazi thinking grins at us. . . . The question that arises in light of the publication of the [*Black Notebooks*] becomes: to what extent was Heidegger's abandonment of philosophy in favor of '*Denken*' entwined with his 'spiritual National Socialism.' "

84. Heidegger, *Anmerkungen I–V*, GA 97 (Frankfurt: Klostermann Verlag, 2015), 20; and see my commentary on these claims in "Heidegger's Philosophy of Violence," *Chronicle Review*, 2 March 2015.

85. For a discussion of "Holocaust inversion," see Robert Wistrich, "Holocaust Inversion and Anti-Semitism," in *Anti-Semitism before and since the Holocaust*, ed. Anthony McEligott and Jeffrey Herf (Basingstoke, UK: Palgrave Macmillan, 2017), 37–49.

86. Monika Schwarz-Friesel, "Der Tatort Sprache in Deutschland. Antisemitismus im öffentlichen Kommunikationsraum," *Tribune* 189 (2009): 48. For Adorno's discussion of secondary anti-Semitism, see Adorno, "Schuld und Abwehr. Eine qualitative Analyse zum Gruppenexperiment" (1955), in *Gesammelte Schriften*, vol. 9, part 2 (Frankfurt: Suhrkamp, 1997), 121–324.

87. Martin Heidegger, *Die Geschichte des Seyns*, ed. Peter Trawny (Frankfurt: Klostermann, 1998). For the relevant background, see Eggert Blum, "Die Marke Heidegger," *Die Zeit* 47 (27 November 2014). See Trawny, *Heidegger und der Mythos einer jüdischen Weltverschwörung*, 51.

88. Heidegger, *Überlegungen XII–XV*, GA 96, 46.

89. Heidegger, Der Anfang des abendländischen Denkens. Heraklit, GA 55, 108.

90. Heidegger, *Überlegungen XII–XV*, GA 96, 262.

91. Danielle Cohen-Levinas, "Un exister païen: Heidegger, Rosenzweig, Levinas," *Le Genre Humain* 56–57 (2016): 657–72.

92. Christian Tilitzki, *Die Deutsche Universitätsphilosophie in der Weimarer Republik und im Dritten Reich*, vol. 1 (Berlin: Akademie Verlag, 2002), 551.

93. Heidegger, *Überlegungen II–VI*, GA 94, 27.

94. Quoted in Max Domarus, *Hitler: Speeches and Proclamations, 1932–45*, vol. 2 (London: I. B. Taurus, 1990–2004), 1055–58.

95. Günther Anders, "The Pseudo-Concreteness of Heidegger's Existentialism," *Philosophy and Phenomenological Research* 8 (1947): 337–71.

96. Theodor Adorno, *Against Epistemology*, trans. Willis Domingo (Cambridge, MA: MIT Press, 1986), 187–88.

97. Jürgen Habermas, "Work and Weltanschauung: The Heidegger Controversy from a German Perspective," in *The New Conservatism: Cultural Criticism and the Historians' Debate*, trans. Shierry Weber Nicholsen (Cambridge, MA: MIT Press, 1989), 159–60.

98. Jürgen Habermas, *Nachmetaphysiches Denken: Philosophische Aufsätze* (Frankfurt: Suhrkamp, 1988), 167; Habermas, "Themes in Postmetaphysical Thinking," in *Postmetaphysical Thinking: Philosophical Essays*, trans. William Mark Hohengarten (Cambridge, MA: MIT Press, 1988), 12.

99. Emmanuel Levinas, "La Philosophie et l'idée de l'infini," in *En Découvrant l'existence avec Husserl et Heidegger* (Paris: J. Vrin, 1974), 170.

100. Claude Lefort, *Democracy and Modern Political Theory*, trans. David Macey (Minneapolis: University of Minnesota Press, 1989).

101. Hannah Arendt, *On Revolution* (New York: Penguin, 1962), 255.

102. Jürgen Habermas, "America and the World," *Logos* 3 (2004): 4. On the normative significance of the Axial Age, see Karl Jaspers, *The Origin and Goal of History*, trans. Michael Bullock (New York: Routledge, 2014), 18–22.

103. Heidegger, *Überlegungen VII–XI*, GA 95, 97.

104. Heidegger, *Überlegungen XII–XV*, GA 96, 56.

105. Ibid., 243 (emphasis added).

106. Thomas Assheuer, "Heideggers *Schwarze Hefte*: Die vergiftete Erbe," *Die Zeit*, 21 March 2014.

107. Heidegger, *Überlegungen VII–XI*, GA 95, 209.

108. Ingo Farin, "The *Black Notebooks* in Their Historical and Political Context," in *Reading Heidegger's "Black Notebooks," 1931–1941*, ed. Ingo Farin and Jeff Malpas (Cambridge, MA: MIT Press, 2015), 300. As Markus Gabriel rightly observes in "Heideggers Antisemitische Stereotypen," the recent controversies over Heidegger and anti-Semitism have, regrettably, led to a proliferation of "apologetic interpretations." In *Heidegger und der Antisemitismus*, 221.

109. Heidegger, *Überlegungen XII–XV*, GA 96, 218.

110. Heidegger, "Liebeserklärung an die Provence," in *Reden und andere Zeugnisse eines Lebensweges*, GA 16, 551.

111. For the Kassel lectures, see Martin Heidegger, *Der Begriff von Zeit*, GA 64 (Frankfurt: Klostermann Verlag, 2004). See also Heidegger, "Der Zusammenhang der vorstehenden Exposition des Problems der Geschichtlichkeit mit den Forschungen Wilhelm Diltheys und den Ideen des Grafen von Yorck," in *Sein und Zeit*, GA 2, 397–404, #77. For a discussion of the role that *Bodenständigkeit* played in the development of Heidegger's early existential ontology, see the illuminating study by Jaehoon Lee, "Heidegger en 1924: L'influence de Yorck von Wartenburg dans son interprétation de Descartes," in *Heidegger: Le sol, la communauté, la race*, ed. Emmanuel Faye (Paris: Éditions Beauchesne, 2014), 25–47.

112. See Richard Zneimer, "The Nazis and the Professors: Social Origin, Professional Mobility, and Political Involvement of the Frankfurt University Faculty, 1933–1939," *Journal of Social History* 12 (1978): 148.

113. Toni Cassirer, *Mein Leben mit Ernst Cassirer* (Hildesheim: Gerstenberg, 1981), 138.

114. Rosenberg, *Myth of the Twentieth Century*, 387; Alfred Rosenberg, *Der Mythus des zwanzigsten Jahrhunderts: Eine Bewertung des psychischen und seelischen Gestaltenkampf unserer Zeit* (Munich: F. Eder Verlag, 1930).

115. Shulamit Volkov, "Anti-Semitism as a Cultural Code: Reflections on the History and Historiography of Imperial Germany," in *Leo Baeck Yearbook* 23 (1978): 31. See also

Volkov, *Germans, Jews, and Anti-Semites: Trials in the Emancipation* (New York: Cambridge University Press, 2006), 67–118.

116. Raphael Gross, *Carl Schmitt and the Jews*, trans. Joel Golb (Madison: University of Wisconsin Press, 2007), 11.

117. See Herf, *Reactionary Modernism*; and Sontheimer, *Antidemokratisches Denken*.

118. Heidegger, *Überlegungen VII–XI*, GA 95, 326. The editors of *Martin Heidegger's "Black Notebooks": Responses to Anti-Semitism* feign surprise that the *Notebooks* "reveal . . . anti-Semitic content within [Heidegger's] very thinking of the history of being," a discourse that they had "never before seen in Heidegger's published writings." However, in light of Heidegger's proximity to the reactionary idiom of *Zivilisationskritik*, should one really be surprised? See Andrew J. Mitchell and Peter Trawny, "Editors' Introduction," in *Martin Heidegger's "Black Notebooks,"* xvii.

119. Johannes Fritsche, *Historical Destiny and National Socialism in Heidegger's "Being and Time"* (Berkeley: University of California Press, 1999), xii.

120. See the discussion of Sombart's work in Jerry Muller, *Capitalism and the Jews* (Princeton, NJ: Princeton University Press, 2012), 57–59.

121. Jean-Paul Sartre, *Anti-Semite and Jew: The Etiology of Hatred*, trans. George Becker (New York: Schocken, 1995), 8; David Nirenberg, *Anti-Judaism: The Western Tradition* (New York: Norton, 2013), 5.

122. The provenance of this proverb is difficult to trace. It has often been attributed— erroneously—to the writer Kurt Tucholsky. It surfaced in Erich Maria Remarque's novel *Der schwarze Obelisk* (Cologne: Kiepenheuer und Witsch, 1956). Hannah Arendt recounted it in *The Origins of Totalitarianism*, 5.

123. Jennifer Gosetti-Ferencei, *Heidegger, Hölderlin and the Subject of Poetic Language: Toward a New Poetics of Dasein* (New York: Fordham University Press, 2004), 6–7.

124. Heidegger, *Überlegungen II–VI*, GA 94, 66.

125. Martin Heidegger, *Beiträge zur Philosophie: Vom Ereignis*, GA 65 (Frankfurt: Klostermann, 1989), 435.

126. Heidegger, *Anmerkungen I–V*, GA 97, 91.

127. Heidegger, *Einführung in die Metaphysik*, GA 40, 142; Heidegger, *Introduction to Metaphysics*, 133.

128. Heidegger, *Überlegungen XII–XV*, GA 96, 29.

129. Hans-Georg Gadamer, *Gesammelte Werke*, vol. 3 (Tübingen: Mohr, 1987), viii. Also see Gadamer's remarks about the later Heidegger and language in Alfons Greider, "A Conversation with Hans-Georg Gadamer," *Journal of the British Society for Phenomenology* 26 (1995): "Heidegger's language and style [were] . . . boorish, barbarian— like an elephant going through the primeval forest. . . . *This is not language any more.* . . . The later Heidegger too became monological" (120, 123, 118).

130. Habermas, "Great Influence," 59.

131. G. W. F. Hegel, *Phenomenology of Spirit*, trans. Terry Pinkard (New York: Cambridge University Press, 2014), 44.

132. Theodor Adorno, "Why Still Philosophy?," in *Critical Models: Interventions and Catchwords*, trans. Henry W. Pickford (New York: Columbia University Press, 1998), 15.

133. Theodor Adorno, *Lectures on Negative Dialectics: Fragments of a Lecture Course*, trans. Rodney Livingston (Cambridge, MA: Polity, 2008), 67.

134. Immanuel Kant, "An Answer to the Question: 'What Is Enlightenment?,'" in *Kant: Political Writings*, ed. Hans Reiss (New York: Cambridge University Press, 1991), 54.

135. See, for example, John Wild, "Being, Meaning, and the World," *Review of Metaphysics* 18 (1965): 411–29. Wild suggests that Heidegger "has never carefully examined the relation between Being and world, nor stated his reasons for choosing the former over the latter." He concludes, "I don't think that many of us will be converted from our 'un-Sein-like' ways by this *Seinsmystik*" (429).

136. Ernst Tugendhat, *Self-Consciousness and Self-Determination*, trans. Paul Stern (Cambridge, MA: MIT Press, 1984), 187.

137. Winfried Franzen, *Von Existentzialontologie zur Seinsgeschichte: Eine Untersuchung über die Entwicklung der Philosophie Martin Heideggers* (Meisenheim am Glan: Anton Hein, 1976), 150.

138. Karl Löwith, *Heidegger: Denker in dürftiger Zeit* (Frankfurt: Fischer, 1953), 59.

139. Iain Thomson, "Understanding Technology Ontotheologically, or: the Danger and the Promise of Heidegger, an American Perspective," in *New Waves in the Philosophy of Technology*, ed. Jan Karre Berg Olsen, Evan Selinger, and Søren Riis (Basingstoke, UK: Macmillan, 2008), 148.

140. Martin Heidegger, *Logik: Die Frage nach der Wahrheit*, GA 21 (Frankfurt: Klostermann, 1995), 54, 64, 79.

141. Heidegger, *Hölderlins Hymnen "Germanien" und "Der Rhein,"* GA 39, 247.

142. Martin Heidegger, *Anmerkungen VI–XI*, GA 98 (Frankfurt: Klostermann, 2016), 43.

143. Martin Heidegger, "Nietzsche's Word: 'God Is Dead,'" in *The Question Concerning Technology and Other Essays*, trans. William Lovitt (New York: Harper and Row, 1977), 112.

144. Immanuel Kant, *Critique of Pure Reason*, trans. Paul Guyer and Allen Wood (New York: Cambridge University Press, 1998), A315/B372.

145. Herbert Marcuse, *Negations: Essays in Critical Theory*, trans. Jeremy J. Shapiro (Boston: Beacon, 1968), 136.

146. Martin Heidegger, "The Origin of the Work of Art," in *Poetry, Language, Thought*, trans. Albert Hofstadter (New York: Harper and Row, 1977). See my discussion in *The Politics of Being: The Political Thought of Martin Heidegger* (New York: Columbia University Press, 2016), 118–23.

147. For a discussion that, in the face of much countervailing evidence, embraces the purportedly "progressive" implications of the "post-truth" standpoint, see Steve Fuller, *Post-Truth: Knowledge as a Power-Game* (London: Anthem, 2018). Fuller holds that "post-truth" corresponds to a world that has become "post-fact"—that is, in which agreement concerning the factual-evidentiary basis of truth has disappeared. Hence, he concludes, "Truth turns out to be whatever is decided by the empowered judge in the case at hand" (28).

148. See Martin Sellner, "Mein Denkweg zu Heidegger," *Sezession* 64 (February 2015): 11.

149. For a survey of the Identitarian movement written by a sympathizer, see José Pedro Zúquete, *The Identitarians: The Movement against Globalism and Islam* (South Bend, IN: Notre Dame University Press, 2018).

150. Thomas J. Main, *The Rise of the Alt-Right* (Washington, DC: Brookings Institution Press, 2017), 216.

151. Greg Johnson, "Between Two Lampshades: Michael Enoch Interviews Greg Johnson, Part 1," *Counter-Currents*, June 2015, www.counter-currents.com/2015/06/between-two-lampshades-1/.
152. Graham Macklin, "Greg Johnson and Counter-Currents," in *Key Thinkers of the Radical Right*, ed. Mark Sedgwick (New York: Oxford University Press, 2019), 204.
153. Arendt, "What Is *Existenz* Philosophy?," in *Essays in Understanding* (New York: Harcourt Brace, 1994), 187. For a discussion of Heidegger's embrace of *Vernunftkritik*, see my essay "Vernunftkritik nach den *Schwarzen Heften*," in *Heideggers "Schwarze Hefte": Eine philosophisch-politische Debatte*, ed. Marion Heinz and Sidonie Kellerer (Frankfurt: Suhrkamp, 2016), 397–415.
154. Martin Heidegger, "Letter on Humanism," in *Basic Writings*, ed. David Krell (New York: Harper and Row, 1977), 234.
155. Martin Heidegger, "'Only a God Can Save Us': *Der Spiegel*'s Interview with Martin Heidegger (1966)," in Wolin, *Heidegger Controversy*, 107.
156. David Krell, "Heidegger's *Black Notebooks*," *Research in Phenomenology* 45 (2015): 131.
157. Adorno, "Why Still Philosophy?," 9.
158. Heidegger, "Only a God Can Save Us," 111.
159. Lutz Hachmeister, *Heideggers Testament: Der Philosoph, Der Spiegel, und die SS* (Munich: Propylaen, 2013), 198 (emphasis added).
160. Heidegger, *Überlegungen VII–XI*, GA 95, 408.
161. Martin Heidegger, *Nietzsches Metaphysik*, GA 50 (Frankfurt: Klostermann, 2007), 70.
162. See, for example, Agnes Heller, "Parmenides and the Battle of Stalingrad," *Graduate Faculty Philosophy Journal* 19 (1997): 247–62. For a critical overview of this questionable scholarly consensus, see Bambach, *Heidegger's Roots*: "In 1942 and after, Heidegger does not embrace an anti-political style; rather his politics go underground. . . . Henceforth, Heidegger will advocate a new politics of the anti-political: an originary politics of the *arche* that dispenses with, extinguishes, and deracinates the aggressively nationalist dimension from the old politics of the earth, the homeland, the soil, and the fatherland. . . . What will emerge in the next two and one-half years is a language of German autochthony stripped of all geopolitical references. And yet, the same structural principles will remain in place" (187).
163. Gabriel, "Heideggers Antisemitische Stereotypen," 224.
164. Tugendhat, *Self-Consciousness and Self-Determination*, 218.
165. Ibid.

Chapter 3. Heidegger and Race

1. Ernst Nolte, *Politik und Geschichte im Leben Heidegger* (Munich: Propylaen, 1991), 130.
2. Jeff Malpas, introduction to *Reading Heidegger's "Black Notebooks,"* ed. Ingo Farin and Jeff Malpas (Cambridge, MA: MIT Press, 2016), 6.
3. Adolf Hitler, *Mein Kampf*, trans. Ralph Manheim (Boston: Houghton Mifflin, 1988), 283.
4. The date of Heidegger's entry into the Party is itself significant. May 1 was the official day of National Socialist Party Unity. In addition, in an attempt to wean German workers from socialism, Hitler declared it the "National Day of Labor."

5. Martin Heidegger, "Das Rektorat, 1933–34: Tatsachen und Gedanken," in *Reden und andere Zeugnisse eines Lebensweges*, GA 16 (Frankfurt: Klostermann, 2000), 401, 414.

6. Thomas Rohkrämer, "Heidegger, Kulturkritik, und völkische Ideologie," in *Heideggers "Schwarze Hefte": Ein philosophisch-politische Debatte*, ed. Marion Heinz and Sidonie Kellner (Frankfurt: Suhrkamp, 2016), 261.

7. Martin Heidegger, *Einführung in die Metaphysik*, GA 40 (Frankfurt: Klostermann, 1983), 165.

8. Martin Heidegger, "Aus der Tischrede bei der Feier des Fünfzigjährigen Bestehens des Institutes für Pathologische Anatomie," in *Reden und andere Zeugnisse eines Lebensweges*, GA 16, 151.

9. Martin Heidegger, *Überlegungen II–VI*, GA 94 (Frankfurt: Klostermann Verlag, 2014), 135.

10. Martin Heidegger to Elfride Heidegger, 8 September 1920, in *"Mein liebes Seelchen!": Briefe Martin Heideggers an seine Frau Elfride, 1915–1970*, ed. Gertrud Heidegger (Munich: Deutsche Verlagsanstalt, 2005), 116.

11. Heidegger, *Einführung in die Metaphysik*, GA 40, 152.

12. See, for example, Dieter Thomä, "Wie antisemitisch ist Heidegger?," in Heinz and Kellerer, *Heideggers "Schwarze Hefte,"* 215.

13. Heidegger, *Überlegungen II–VI*, GA 94, 115 (emphasis added).

14. See, for example, Franz Neumann, *Behemoth: The Structure and Practice of National Socialism* (New York: Oxford University Press, 1942). On these grounds, Neumann referred to Nazi rule as a "polycracy."

15. See Karl Löwith, "My Last Meeting with Heidegger in Rome, 1936," in *The Heidegger Controversy: A Critical Reader*, ed. Richard Wolin (Cambridge, MA: MIT Press, 1993),142.

16. Martin Heidegger to Otto Wacker, 26 April 1933, in *Reden und andere Zeugnisse eines Lebensweges*, GA 16, 84. See also the discussion in Anton M. Fischer, *Martin Heidegger: Der gottlose Priester—Psychogramm eines Denkers* (Zurich: Rüffer and Rub, 2008): "Heidegger declined to justify the milder 'Reich' law; instead, he approvingly forwarded Wacker's memo to his deans" (287).

17. Walter Eucken to Willy Andreas, 22 August 1933, quoted in Bernard Grün, *Der Rektor als Führer? Die Universität Freiburg i. Br. von 1933 bis 1945* (Freiburg/Munich: Karl Alber, 2010), 194.

18. See Martin Heidegger, "Telegramm an den Reichskanzler," in *Reden und andere Zeugnisse eines Lebensweges*, GA 16, 105.

19. Martin Heidegger, "National Socialist Education," in Wolin, *Heidegger Controversy*, 55–60.

20. Martin Heidegger, "Die Universität im Neuen Reich," in *Reden und andere Zeugnisse eines Lebensweges*, GA 16, 763.

21. See "Politische Schulung an der Universität Freiburg," in the *Freiburger Studentenzeitung*, 16 May 1933; cited by Guido Schneeberger, *Nachlese zu Heidegger: Dokumente zu seinem Leben und Denken* (Bern: Buchdruckerei A. G. Suhr, 1962), 40.

22. Cited in Grün, *Der Rektor als Führer?*, 220.

23. Quoted ibid., 218.

24. Quoted ibid.

25. See Eugen Fischer, *Die Rehobother Bastarde und das Bastardierungsproblem* [*sic*] *beim Menschen* (Jena: Gustav Fischer, 1913), 1.

26. Quoted in Peter Weingart, Jürgen Kroll, and Kurt Bayertz, *Rasse, Blut, und Gene: Geschichte der Eugenik und Rassenhygiene in Deutschland* (Frankfurt: Suhrkamp, 1988), 385.

27. Quoted in Grün, *Der Rektor als Führer?*, 218.

28. Heidegger exulted about the "call" to the University of Berlin in letters of 4 and 5 September 1933; see, Heidegger to Eugen Fehrle, 4 September 1933, and Heidegger to Elisabeth Blochmann, 5 September 1933, in *Reden und andere Zeugnisse eines Lebensweges*, GA 16, 163–65. Unfortunately, the records of the University of Berlin deliberations were destroyed. However, we do know that Heidegger's University of Berlin *Ruf* bypassed the normal faculty channels and was orchestrated directly by the minister of education, Bernhard Rust.

29. Quoted in Helmut Heiber, *Die Universität unter dem Hakenkreuz: Der Professor im dritten Reich*, part 1 (Munich: K. G. Saur, 1991), 28.

30. Martin Heidegger, "Declaration of Support for Adolf Hider and the National Socialist State," in Wolin, *Heidegger Controversy*, 50.

31. Gerd Tellenbach, "Verlautbarungen," in *Martin Heidegger und das "Dritte Reich": Ein Kompendium*, ed. Bernd Martin (Darmstadt: Wissenschaftliche Buchgesellschaft, 1989), 160.

32. Heidegger, "Ansprache am 11 November 1933 in Leipzig," in *Reden und andere Zeugnisse eines Lebensweges*, GA 16, 192.

33. Heidegger, *Überlegungen II–VI*, GA 94, 111.

34. Martin Heidegger, *Überlegungen XII–XV*, GA 96 (Frankfurt: Klostermann, 2014), 56.

35. Raphael Gross, *Carl Schmitt and the Jews*, trans. Joel Golb (Madison: University of Wisconsin Press, 2007), 268.

36. Martin Heidegger, "Der Spruch des Anaximander," in *Holzwege*, GA 5 (Frankfurt: Klostermann, 1977), 327.

37. Quoted in Ulrich Sieg, "Die Verjudung des deutschen Geistes: Ein unbekannter Brief Heideggers," *Die Zeit* 52 (29 December 1989): 19.

38. Richard Wagner, "Das Judenthum in der Musik," in *Gesammelte Schriften u. Dichtungen*, 4th ed., vol. 5 (Berlin: Deutches Verlaghaus Bong, 1913), 68.

39. Wilhelm Marr, *Der Sieg des Judenthums über das Germanenthum* (Bern: Costenoble, 1879), 8.

40. Hitler, *Mein Kampf*, 270.

41. Martin Heidegger to Elfride Petri, 18 October 1916, in *"Mein liebes Seelchen!,"* 51.

42. Martin Heidegger, "Bitte von Ausdehnung des Lehrvertrages Abzusehen" (letter to Dr. Otto Wacker, 13 April 1934), in *Reden und andere Zeugnisse eines Lebensweges*, GA 16, 269.

43. Martin Heidegger, "Das Rektorat, 1933–34: Tatsachen und Gedanken," in *Reden und andere Zeugnisse eines Lebensweges*, GA 16, 414.

44. See Hubert Fehr, "Ur- und Frühgeschichte," in *Die Freiburger Philosophische Fakultät, 1920–1960*, ed. Eckhard Wirbelauer and Frank-Rutger Hausmann (Freiburg: Freiburger Beiträge zu Wissenschafts- und Universitätsgeschichte, 2006), 544.

45. Ibid., 545.

46. Volker Losemann, *Nationalsozialismus und Antike* (Hamburg: Hoffmann and Campe, 1977), 11.

47. See Klaus von See, *Deutsche Germanen-Ideologie* (Frankfurt: Athenäum, 1971), 10. See also Volker Losemann, "Nationalistische Interpretationen der römisch-germanischen Auseinandersetzung," in *Arminius und die Varusschlacht*, ed. Rainer Wiegels (Paderborn: Ferdinand Schönigh, 1995), 419–32.

48. Martin Heidegger, *Sein und Wahrheit*, GA 36/37 (Frankfurt: Klostermann, 2003), 89.

49. Martin Heidegger to Elisabeth Blochmann, 20 September 1930, in *Briefwechsel*, ed. Joachim Storch (Marbach: Deutsche Schillergesellschaft, 1989): "ich stimme damit nicht für die goldene Mitte, sondern dafür dass die Wirklichkeit des Volkes und der Stämme und ihren eigenen Quellen in Kräften zurück findet" (38).

50. Martin Heidegger to Werner Jaeger, 12 December 1932, quoted in Frank Edler, "Heidegger and Werner Jaeger on the Eve of 1933: A Possible Rapprochement," *Research in Phenomenology* 27 (1997): 122.

51. Ibid.

52. Katie Fleming, "Heidegger, Jaeger, Plato: The Politics of Humanism," *International Journal of the Classical Tradition* 19 (2012): 99.

53. Hitler, *Mein Kampf*, 183.

54. Jonathan Chapoutot, *Greeks, Romans and Germans* (Berkeley: University of California Press, 2015), 12.

55. William M. Calder, "Werner Jaeger and Richard Harder: An *Erklärung*," *Quaderni torici* 17 (1983): 106.

56. See Herbert Cancik, "Der Einfluß Friedrich Nietzsches auf klassische Philologie in Deutschland bis 1945: Philologen am Nietzsche-Archiv (I)," in *Philolog und Kultfigur: Friedrich Nietzsche und seine Antike in Deutschland*, Herbert Cancik and Hildegard Cancik-Lindermaier, eds. (Stuttgart: Metzler Verlag, 1999), 231–51.

57. Werner Jaeger, *Humanistische Reden und Vorträge* (Boston: De Gruyter, 1960), 19.

58. Werner Jaeger, "Die Erziehung des politischen Menschen und die Antike," *Volk im Werden* 1, no. 3 (1933): 47. See also Jaeger's earlier study *Das Problem des Klassischen und die Antike: Acht Vorträge* (Leipzig: B. G. Teubner, 1930).

59. Martin Heidegger, "The Self-Assertion of the German University," in Wolin, *Heidegger Controversy*, 31.

60. Martin Heidegger to Kurt Bauch, 14 March 1933, in *Briefwechsel, 1932–1975* (Freiburg: Karl Alber Verlag, 2011), 14.

61. See Heinrich W. Petzet, *Auf einen Stern zu gehen: Begegnungen und Gespräche mit Martin Heidegger* (Frankfurt: Societäts-Verlag), 34.

62. Richard Harder, review of *Die Selbstbehauptung der deutschen Universität*, by Martin Heidegger, *Gnomon* 9 (1933): 440–42.

63. One should also recall that Heidegger chose a maxim from Plato's *Sophist* (244a) as the epigraph of *Being and Time*: "For manifestly you have long been aware of what you mean when you use the expression 'Being.' We, however, who used to think we understood it, have now become perplexed." Martin Heidegger, *Sein und Zeit*, GA 2 (Frankfurt: Klostermann, 1977), 1; Heidegger, *Being and Time*, trans. John Macquarrie and Edward Robinson (New York: Harper and Row, 1962), 1.

64. Martin Heidegger, *Vom Wesen der Wahrheit: Zu Platons Höhlengleichnis und Theatät*, GA 34 (Frankfurt: Klostermann, 1988), 100.

65. Plato, *The Republic*, trans. G. M. A. Grube (Indianapolis: Hackett, 1992), 375e 1–2–376c 1–2 (51).

66. See C. D. C. Reeve, *Philosopher Kings: The Argument of Plato's "Republic"* (Indianapolis: Hackett, 2006): "First, the complete guardians receive only primary education, and this gives no access to forms. Second, they have true opinion, and a settled disposition to cling to it, but they are never said to have knowledge. Third, it is 'political courage' that enables them to cling to their true beliefs in the face of 'pleasure or a fear.' . . . But political courage is the virtue characteristic of guardians, not a philosopher king" (182).

67. Heidegger, *Vom Wesen der Wahrheit*, 100 (emphasis added).

68. For a discussion of this episode, see Christos Evangeliou, "Plato and Sicilian Power Politics: Between Dion and Dionysus II," in *Politics and Performance in Western Greece: Essays on the Hellenic Heritage of Sicily and Southern Italy*, ed. Heather Reid, Davide Tanasi, and Susi Kimbell (Sioux City, IA: Parnassos, 2017), 289–301.

69. Max Kommerell, *Der Dichter als Führer in der deutschen Klassik: Klopstock, Herder, Goethe, Schiller, Jean Paul, and Hölderlin* (Berlin: Bondi, 1928).

70. Martin Heidegger, *Hölderlins Hymnen "Germanien" und "Der Rhein,"* GA 39 (Frankfurt: Klostermann Verlag, 1980), 51–52 (emphasis added).

71. Kommerell, *Der Dichter als Führer in der deutschen Klassik*, 478.

72. Their correspondence is contained in Max Kommerell, *Briefe und Aufzeichnungen: 1919–1944*, ed. Inge Jens (Olten: Walter, 1967). For Heidegger's tribute, see "Max Kommerell: Zum Gedächtnis," in *Reden und andere Zeugnisse eines Lebensweges*, GA 16, 364.

73. Kommerell, *Dichter als Führer in der deutschen Klassik*, 455, 478.

74. Kurt Hildebrandt, quoted in Robert Norton, *Secret Germany: Stefan George and His Circle* (Ithaca, NY: Cornell University Press, 2001), 412.

75. Kurt Hildebrandt, *Platon: Der Kampf des Geistes um die Macht* (Berlin: Bondi, 1932). Hildebrandt, *Einleitung zu Platons, "Der Staat"* (Leipzig: Kroner Verlag, 1933), 364. It is significant that, in a letter that Heidegger wrote to Carl Schmitt on 22 August 1933 proposing a political alliance, Heidegger praised Schmitt's allusion in the *Concept of the Political* to the figure of *Basileus*, or "philosopher king." As Heidegger commented, "With respect to the citation from Heraclitus [Fragment 53 on "war," or *polemos*], I was especially pleased to see that you did not neglect to mention *Basileus*, which provides the maxim with its content and meaning." In Heidegger, *Reden und andere Zeugnisse eines Lebensweges*, GA 16, 156.

76. Friedrich Wolters, "Herrschaft und Dienst," *Jahrbuch für die geistige Bewegung* 1 (1910): 11. See Ute Oelmann, "The George Circle: From *Künstlergesellschaft* to *Lebensgemeinschaft*," in *A Poet's Reich: Politics and Culture in the George Circle*, ed. Melissa Lane and Martin A. Ruehl (Rochester, NY: Camden House, 2011): "The final object for Wolters was the 'geistige Tat,' which would redeem the German nation and guarantee its future as cultural and intellectual hegemon of the West" (32).

77. Robert E. Norton, *Secret Germany: Stefan George and His Circle* (Ithaca, NY: Cornell University Press, 2002), 416.

78. Ibid., 585.

79. For more on Hölderlin's "vaterländische Umkehr," see Friedrich Beissner, *Hölderlins Übersetzungen aus dem Griechischen* (Stuttgart: Metzler, 1931), 147–86. Heidegger cited Beissner's book in *Hölderlins Hymne "Der Ister,"* GA 53 (Frankfurt: Klostermann, 1983), 156–57; and in *Hölderlins Hymnen "Germanien" und "Der Rhein,"* GA 39, 126.

80. See Norbert von Hellingrath, *Hölderlin: Zwei Vorträge* (Munich: Hugo Bruckmann, 1922), 31–32. See the helpful discussion in Charles Bambach, *Heidegger's Roots: Nietzsche, National Socialism, and the Greeks* (Ithaca, NY: Cornell University Press, 2003), 241–46.

81. Heidegger, *Hölderlins Hymnen "Germanien" und "Der Rhein,"* GA 39, 101.

82. Heidegger, "Die deutsche Universitatät," in *Reden und andere Zeugnisse eines Lebensweges*, GA 16, 290.

83. Norbert Rath, "Kriegskamerad Hölderlin: Zitate zur Sinngebungsgeschichte," in *Neue Wege zu Hölderlin*, ed. Uwe Beyer (Würzburg: Königshausen and Neumann, 1994), 219–20.

84. Heidegger, *Hölderlins Hymnen "Germanien" und "Der Rhein,"* GA 39, 215.

85. Kommerell, *Der Dichter als Führer in der deutschen Klassik*, 474. In a fascinating autobiographical account of the George-*Kreis*'s immense influence on German academics during the 1920s, Hans-Georg Gadamer confirmed the pivotal role that Heidegger's encounter with Kommerell's work played in the philosopher's turn toward Hölderlin as the "poet of the Germans." See Gadamer, "Die Wirkung Stefan Georges auf die Wissenschaft" (1983), in *Gesammelte Werke*, vol. 9 (Tübingen: Mohr Siebeck, 1993), 262.

86. Heidegger, *Hölderlins Hymnen "Germanien" und "Der Rhein,"* GA 39, 73.

87. Ibid., 163.

88. Claudia Albrecht, "Dient Kulturarbeit den Sieg? Hölderlin-Rezeption von 1933–1945," in *Hölderlin und die Moderne: Eine Bestandsaufnahme*, ed. Gerhard Kurz, Valérie Lawitschka, and Jürgen Wertheimer (Tübingen: Attempo, 1995), 153–73.

89. See Martin Heidegger, *Erläuterungen zu Hölderlins Dichtung*, GA 4 (Frankfurt: Klostermann, 1981). The dedication to von Hellingrath, which had been elided from the previous editions of *Erläuterungen zu Hölderlins Dichtung*, was restored in the *Gesamtausgabe* edition. However, Heidegger's claim in the 1936 edition that the only point of publishing the essay was to honor von Hellingrath's memory was suppressed without mention.

90. Quoted in Günther Penzoldt, "Das innere Reich im dritten Reich," *Die Zeit* 14 (2 April 1965).

91. Horst Denkler, "Janusköpfig: Zur ideologischen Physiognomie der Zeitschrift, 'Das innere Reich,' " in *Die deutsche Literatur im Dritten Reich: Themen, Traditionen, Wirkungen*, ed. Horst Denkler and Karl Prümm (Stuttgart: Reclam, 1976), 384.

92. Walter Benjamin, "Wider ein Meisterwerk: Zu Max Kommerell, *Der Dichter als Führer in der deutschen Klassik*," in *Gesammelte Werke*, vol. 3, *Kritiken und Rezensionen* (Frankfurt: Suhrkamp, 1980), 252–59.

93. Quoted in Peter Hoffmann, "The George Circle and National Socialism," in Lane and Ruehl, *Poet's Reich*, 309. On the affinities between the *Männerbund*, as a legacy of the "community of the trenches," and National Socialism, see Alfred Baeumler, *Männerbund und Wissenschaft* (Berlin: Junker und Dünnhaupt, 1934).

94. See David Fernbach's review of *Secret Germany: Stefan George and His Circle*, by Robert Norton, *New Left Review* 18 (2002): 149–53.

95. Peter Hoffmann, "George Circle and National Socialism," 289.

96. Melissa S. Lane and Martin A. Ruehl, introduction to *Poet's Reich*, 6.

97. Ibid.

98. Woldemar Uxkull-Gyllenband, *Das revolutionäre Ethos bei Stefan George* (Tübingen: J. C. B. Mohr, 1933), 8.

99. Kurt Hildebrandt to Arvid Brodersen, 7 January 1935, quoted in Peter Hoffmann, *Stauffenberg und seine Brüder* (Munich: Deutsche-Verlag Anstalt, 1992), 502.

100. Jussi Backman, "The Traditional Breakdown of the Word: Heidegger's Encounter with Language," *Gatherings: The Heidegger Circle Annual* (2011): 54.

101. Martin Heidegger, *Zu Herders Abhandlung "Über den Ursprung der Sprache,"* GA 85 (Frankfurt: Klostermann, 1999), 61, 69–72.

102. Quoted in Hoffmann, "George Circle and National Socialism," 296.

103. Max Kommerell, *Briefe und Aufzeichnungen 1919–1944*, ed. Inge Jens (Freiburg: Olten, 1967), 27.

104. Benjamin to Scholem, 16 June 1933, in *The Correspondence of Walter Benjamin and Gershom Scholem* (Cambridge, MA: Harvard University Press, 1992), 59. See Elke Siegel, "Contested Legacies of German Friendship: Max Kommerell's 'The Poet as Leader in German Classicism,'" *Telos* 176 (2016): 77–101. Siegel observes that "Benjamin respected Kommerell's brilliant critical sensibilities, which were in some respects akin to his own," while adding the important qualifier that, nevertheless, "Kommerell was part of a 'Germany,' secret or not, that was responsible for Benjamin's ultimate demise" (78).

105. Hannah Arendt, *Origins of Totalitarianism* (New York: Harcourt Brace, 1958), 339.

106. Quoted in Volker Losemann, "Die Dorier im Deutschland der 30er und 40er Jahre," in *Zwischen Rationalismus und Romantik: Karl Otfired Mülller und die antike Kultur*, ed. William M. Calder (Hildesheim: Weidmannsche Verlagsbuschhandlung, 1998), 421.

107. Heidegger to Jaeger, 12 December 1932, quoted in Edler, "Heidegger and Werner Jaeger on the Eve of 1933," 125.

108. Volker Losemann, "Classics in the Second World War," in *Nazi Germany and the Humanities: How German Academics Embraced Nazism*, ed. Wolfgang Bialis and Anson Rabinbach (London: Oneworld, 2007), 421.

109. Werner Jaeger, *Paideia*, vol. 1 (Berlin: De Gruyter, 1934), 149 (emphasis added).

110. Heidegger, *Sein und Zeit*, GA 2, 509; Heidegger, *Being and Time*, 327.

111. Herbert Marcuse, "Heidegger's Politics: An Interview," in *Heideggerian Marxism*, ed. Richard Wolin and John Abromeit (Lincoln: University of Nebraska Press, 2005), 172.

112. Johannes Fritsche, *Historical Destiny and National Socialism in Heidegger's "Being and Time"* (Berkeley: University of California Press, 1999): " '*Entschlossen-in-den-Tod vorlaufen*'—to resolutely run ahead into death—was how the acts of those who were later called the 'Helden von Langemarck' (heroes of Langemarck) were characterized" (2, 3).

113. Theodor Adorno, *Jargon der Eigentlichkeit*, vol. 5 of *Gesammelte Schriften* (Frankfurt: Suhrkamp Verlag, 1970), 505.

114. Heidegger, *Sein und Zeit*, GA 2, 508; Heidegger, *Being and Time*, 436.

115. Domenico Losurdo, *Heidegger and the Ideology of War: Community, Death, and the West,* trans. Marella Morris and Jon Morris (Amherst, NY: Humanity Books, 2001), 46–47.

116. See Andreas Kaas, *Lehrerlager, 1932–1945: Politische Funktion und Pädogogische Gestaltung* (Bad Heilbrunn: Klinkhardt, 2004).

117. See Losurdo, *Heidegger and the Ideology of War,* 47; see also Hugo Ott, *Heidegger: Unterwegs zu seiner Biographie* (Frankfurt: Campus, 1988), 151.

118. Martin Heidegger, "An die am Ferienlager Todtnauberg (Schwarzwald) teilnehmenden Herren Dozenten und Assistenten," in *Reden und andere Zeugnisse eines Lebensweges,* GA 16, 171–72.

119. See Jaeger, *Paideia,* vol. 1, 129. Jaeger's "Tyrtaios düber die wahre *Aretē*" essay first appeared in *Sitzungsberichte der Preussischen Akademie der Wissenschaften zu Berlin* (1932): 537–68. An English translation, "Tyrtaeus on True *Aretē*," was published in Jaeger, *Five Essays,* trans. Adele Fiske (Montreal: Mario Cassalini, 1966), 103–42.

120. Heidegger, *Hölderlins Hymnen "Germanien" und "Der Rhein,"* GA 39, 214, 220.

121. Jaeger, *Paideia,* vol. 1, 129.

122. Heidegger, *Hölderlins Hymnen "Germanien" und "Der Rhein,"* GA 39, 51–52.

123. Pierre Bourdieu, *L'Ontologie politique de Martin Heidegger* (Paris: Editions de Minuit, 1988); first printed in *Actes de la Recherches en Sciences Sociales* (1975): 109–56.

124. Martin Heidegger, "Der Ursprung des Kunstwerkes," in *Holzwege,* 35.

125. See the discussion in Losemann, "Classics in the Second World War," 311.

126. Martin Heidegger, *Der europäische Nihilismus,* GA 46 (Frankfurt: Klostermann, 1986), 264.

127. See Werner Schubert, introduction to *Weitere Nachträge (1934–39): Ausschüsse für Rechtsphilosophie, für die Überprüfung der rechtswissenschaftlichen Studienordnung und für Seesversicherungsrecht* (New York and Berlin: Peter Lang, 2019), 9–44.

128. *Karlsruher Zeitung,* 29 June 1933, 2.

129. Kurt Bauch, "Konzept eines Gutachtens über Martin Heidegger" (1938), epilogue to Heidegger and Bauch, *Briefwechsel, 1932–1975,* 164. According to Bauch's testimony, Heidegger subscribed to the *Völkischer Beobachter* well before 1933. Bauch's assertion is confirmed by Fritz Heidegger in a letter to Martin of 13 January 1932, in which he expresses his "heartfelt thanks" for the copy of the "V.B." that his brother had recently sent him. In *Heidegger und der Antisemitismus: Positionen in Widerstreit. Mit Briefen von Martin und Fritz Heidegger,* ed. Walter Homolka and Arnulf Heidegger (Freiburg: Herder, 2016), 25.

130. Bernd Rüthers, *Unbegrenzte Auslegung: Zum Wandel der Privatrechtsordnung im Nationalsozialismus* (Tübingen: Mohr and Siebeck, 2012), 101.

131. See Gottfried Feder, *Hitler's Official Program and Its Fundamental Ideas* (New York: Routledge, 2010), 32.

132. Ott, *Martin Heidegger,* 180.

133. Heidegger, *Überlegungen II–VI,* GA 94, 27.

134. *Großes Brockhaus Lexikon,* 15th ed., vol. 19 (Leipzig, 1928), 650.

135. Martin Heidegger, *Logik als die Frage nach dem Wesen der Sprache,* GA 38 (Frankfurt: Klostermann, 1998), 65.

136. For an example, see Gregory Fried and Richard Polt, 'Translators' Foreword," in *Being and Truth,* by Martin Heidegger (Bloomington: Indiana University Press, 2010): "For

orthodox National Socialists, *Volk* was primarily defined in racial terms, but Heidegger attacks this biological interpretation" (xvii). Cf. Heidegger's observation in "Letter to the Rector of Freiburg University" (4 November 1945), in Wolin, *Heidegger Controversy*: "I demonstrated publicly my attitude toward the Party by . . . [practicing] spiritual resistance during the last 11 years. . . . Between 1934 and 1944, thousands of students were trained to reflect on the metaphysical basis of our age; I opened their eyes to the world of spirit and to its great traditions in the history of the West" (66).

137. Lutz Hachmeister, *Heideggers Testament: Der Philosoph, Der Spiegel, und die SS* (Munich: Propyläen, 2013), 211–12.

138. This scenario was featured in Steven Spielberg's film *Raiders of the Lost Ark*. Upon viewing images of Macchu Pichu, Himmler was convinced that only full-blooded Aryans could have constructed the ancient Incan city. On the *Ahnenerbe*, see Michael Kater's pioneering study *Die "Ahnenerbe" des SS, 1935–1945: Ein Beitrag zur Kulturgeschichte des dritten Reiches* (Stuttgart: Deutsche Anstalt-Verlag, 1974).

139. Peter Longerich, *Heinrich Himmler*, trans. Jeremy Noakes and Lesley Sharpe (New York: Oxford University Press, 2012), 279. See Eric Kurlander, "Hitler's Supernatural Sciences: Astrology, Anthroposophy, and World Ice Theory in The Third Reich," in *Revisiting the Nazi Occult: Histories, Realities, Legacies*, ed. Monica Black and Eric Kurlander (Rochester, NY: Camden House, 2015): "As an antidote to 'Jewish' physics, Nazi leaders sponsored Hans Hörbiger's world ice theory, which postulated that events in the Bible and the putative destruction of Atlantis were caused by moons of ice hitting the Earth" (132).

140. Alfred Rosenberg, *Der Mythus des 20. Jahrhunderts: Eine Wertung der Seelisch-geistigen Gestaltenkämpfe unserer Zeit* (Munich: Hohenreichen, 1935), 4.

141. Ibid., 5.

142. These affinities were especially palpable when it came to Heidegger's anti-Semitism. As François Rastier has observed in *Naufrage d'un prophète: Heidegger aujourd'hui* (Paris: Presses Universitaire de France, 2015), "The *Black Notebooks* reveal that, as far as anti-Semitism is concerned, Heidegger's thinking differs not in the least from that of Hitler and Rosenberg" (21).

143. Waldemar Gurian, *Um des Reiches Zukunft: Nationale Wiedergeburt oder politische Reaktion?* (Freiburg: Herder, 1932), 76–77.

144. For a good summary of this research, see Dan Stone, "Nazi Race Ideologues," *Patterns of Prejudice* 50 (2016): 445–57.

145. Ibid., 456.

146. As Peter Staudenmaier observes in *Between Occultism and Nazism: Anthroposophy and the Politics of Race in the Fascist Era* (Leiden: Brill, 2014): "Esoteric beliefs . . . contributed to the eclectic ideology of high-level Nazi figures such as Alfred Rosenberg, Rudolf Hess, and Heinrich Himmler. Neo-pagan predilections and a preoccupation with prehistory and mythology fit well with occult lore about Atlantis and Aryans" (14). For background and context, see Brigitte Hamann, *Hitler's Vienna: A Dictator's Apprenticeship*, trans. James Thornton (New York: Oxford University Press, 1999); see also Fritz Stern's venerable account, *The Politics of Cultural Despair: A Study in the Rise of the Germanic Ideology* (New York: Doubleday, 1965).

147. Goodrick-Clarke, *The Occult Roots of Nazism: Secret Aryan Cults and Their Influence on Nazi Ideology* (London: I. B. Tauris, 2004), vi–vii.

148. Ibid.
149. George Mosse, "The Mystical Origins of National Socialism," *Journal of the History of Ideas* 22 (1961): 81.
150. Ibid., 96.
151. For the locus classicus, see Martin Broszat, "Die völkische Ideologie und der National-sozialismus," *Deutsche Rundschau* 84 (1958): 53–68.
152. Neumann, *Behemoth*, 38–39.
153. See Hans Lutzhöft, *Der nordische Gedanke in Deutschland, 1920–1940* (Stuttgart: E. Klett, 1971).
154. Martin Heidegger, *Überlegungen VII–XI*, GA 95 (Frankfurt: Klostermann, 2014), 325–26.
155. Karl Larenz, "Volksgeist und Recht," *Zeitschrift für deutsche Kulturphilosophie* (1935): 40, 42.
156. Helmut Nicolai, *Die Rassengesetzliche Rechtslehre* (Munich: F. Eher, 1932), 26.
157. Heidegger, *Einführung in die Metaphysik*, GA 40, 165.
158. In the introduction to *The Bloomsbury Companion to Heidegger* (London: Bloomsbury, 2013), the editors, Francois Raffoul and Eric Nelson, insist that "Heidegger's orientation toward the question of the people includes a radical critique of biologism. What matters is how our own being is put into question, . . . [which] implies that the question of 'who we are' remains as a question, the question of human uncanniness" (6). These observations purportedly demonstrate that, in opting for Nazism, Heidegger contradicted his own philosophical strictures and stipulations, which pertain to the mystery and indeterminacy of "human uncanniness." What the authors fail to understand is that, in ways that are almost too numerous to mention, Heidegger associated National Socialism with the qualities of "human uncanniness" he was seeking. In other words, the movement satisfied the criteria he had established, instead of contradicting them. In an essay on "Heidegger, Nietzsche, and National Socialism," Robert Bernasconi recognizes the problems characteristic of this defense of Heidegger. Bernasconi observes that, although Heidegger's critique of Nietzsche's biologism could be construed as "a way of being political"—i.e., of criticizing Nazi race doctrine—nevertheless, this critique would have been "limited to an attack on only one group within the Nazi Party." As such, it was an attack "only in the sense that he was marking his own distance from biologism. It did not have a critical edge beyond that." Bernasconi, "Heidegger, Nietzsche, and National Socialism," in Raffoul and Nelson, *Bloomsbury Companion to Heidegger*, 51.
159. Hannah Arendt, "What Is Existential Philosophy?," in *Essays in Understanding, 1930–1954: Formation, Exile, Totalitarianism* (New York: Harcourt Brace, 1994), 187.
160. Heidegger, "Self-Assertion of the German University," 33–34.
161. Heidegger, *Logik als die Frage nach dem Wesen der Sprache*, GA 38, 153.
162. Zeev Sternhell, *Neither Right, nor Left: Fascist Ideology in France*, trans. David Maisel (Princeton, NJ: Princeton University Press, 1986), 248.
163. Ibid., 257.
164. See Nicolas Kessler, *Histoire politique de la jeune droite: Une révolution conservatrice française* (Paris: L'Harmattan, 2001). Despite the merits of Kessler's study, it displays a surfeit of empathy toward his protagonists. As a result, he fails to probe the role that

these conservative revolutionaries *à la française* played in discrediting the Third Republic. See also John Hellman, *The Knight Monks of Vichy: Uriage, 1940–1945* (Montreal: Queens University Press, 1993).

165. Sternhell, *Neither Right, nor Left*, 263. For more on Bergéry, see Philippe Burrin, *La Dérive fasciste: Jacques Doriot, Marcel Déat, Gaston Bergéry* (Paris: Seuil, 1986).

166. Heidegger, *Logik als Frage nach dem Wesen der Sprache*, GA 38, 66.

167. Martin Heidegger, "Zum 30. Januar 1933. Kolbenheyer," in *Sein und Wahrheit*, GA 36 (Frankfurt: Klostermann, 2000), 209–13.

168. Heidegger, *Logik als Frage nach dem Wesen der Sprache*, GA 38, 61.

169. Ibid., 66.

170. Ibid., 65.

171. Martin Heidegger, *Sein und Zeit* (Frankfurt: Klostermann, 1977), 134.

172. Heidegger, *Logik als eine Frage nach dem Wesen der Sprache*, GA 38, 153.

173. Heidegger, *Überlegungen II–VI*, GA 94, 189.

174. Martin Heidegger to Elfride Heidegger, 19 March 1933, in *"Mein liebes Seelchen!,"* 141.

175. Heidegger, *Überlegungen II–VI*, GA 94, 66.

176. Ibid., 124 (emphasis added).

177. Heidegger, *Überlegungen XII–XV*, GA 96, 235 (emphasis added).

178. Heidegger, *Sein und Wahrheit*, GA 36/37, 263.

179. Martin Heidegger, "Hönigswald aus der Schule des Neukantianismus," in *Reden und andere Zeugnisse eines Lebensweges*, GA 16, 132.

180. Martin Heidegger, "Aus der Tischrede bei der Feier des fünfzigjährigen Bestehens des Instituts für Pathologischie Anatomie," in *Reden und andere Zeugnisse eines Lebensweges*, GA 16, 151 (emphasis added).

181. Heidegger, "Self-Assertion of the German University," 30, 33.

182. Martin Heidegger to Elfride Heidegger, 19 March 1933, in *"Mein Liebes Seelchen!,"* 141.

183. Quoted in Eva-Maria Ziege, *Mythisches Kohärenz: Diskursanalyse des völkischen Antisemitismus* (Konstanz: UVK Verlag-Gesellschaft, 2002), 37, 39. Also see Jean-Pierre Faye, *Langages totalitaires* (Paris: Hermann, 1972).

184. See Reinhart Koselleck, "Volk, Nation, Masse," in *Geschichtliche Grundbegriffe*, vol. 7, ed. Otto Brunner and Werner Conze (Stuttgart: Klett-Cotta, 2004), 411–12.

185. In *The Nationalization of the Masses: Political Symbolism and Mass Movements in Germany from the Napoleonic Wars through the Third Reich* (New York: Howard Fertig, 1975), George Mosse remarks, "We can detect a basic continuity that extends from the struggle for national liberation against Napoleon to the political liturgy of the Third Reich" (19). In *Prelude to Nation States: The French and German Experiences, 1789–1815* (Princeton, NJ: Van Nostrum, 1967), Hans Kohn notes that, in *Von deutscher Art und Kunst*, Herder was one of the first "to regard the terms German and 'creative' or 'original' as almost synonymous, while French represented the opposite." At a later point, with the German Romantics,

> The national community gained a new central importance for all cultural life. The concept of individuality, unique and all-containing, was transferred from the

individual to the national community, which appeared as a higher individual of infinite relevance and endowed with creative force. The nation was no longer a legal society of individuals entering into union according to general rational principles; instead, it was an incomparable and unique organic growth, an original phenomenon of nature and history, leading its own life according to the laws of growth. . . . This national individuality, alive, growing, and striving, often stirred by desires for power and expansion, appeared as a manifestation of the Divine with a special mission to fulfill. . . . The national community or the state—the Romantics did not establish any clear distinction—became the source of all aesthetic and soon also political and ethical creativity (152, 171).

186. Heidegger, *Hölderlins Hymnen "Germanien" und "Der Rhein,"* 220.
187. Heidegger, *Sein und Zeit*, GA 2, 508: "Denn aber das schicksalhafte Dasein als In-der-Welt-sein wesenhaft als Mitsein mit Anderen existiert, ist sein Geschehen ein Mitgeschehen und bestimmt als Geschick. Damit bezeichnen wir das Geschehen der Gemeinschaft, des Volkes . . . Miteinandersein in derselben Welt und in der Entschlossenheit für bestimmte Möglichkeiten sind die Schicksale im vorhinein schon geleitet in der Mitteilung und im Kampf wird die Macht des Geschickes erst frei. Das schicksalhafte Geschick des Daseins in und mit seiner ‚Generation' macht das volle, eigentliche Geschehen des Daseins aus . . . Die eigentliche Wiederholung einer gewesenen Existenzmöglichkeit—dass das Dasein seinen Helden wählt—gründet existenzial in der vorlaufenden Entschlossenheit; den in ihr wird allererst die Wahl gewählt, die kämpfende Nachfolge und Treue zum Wiederholbaren frei macht"; Heidegger, *Being and Time*, 436. For a commentary on this passage, see Fritsche, *Historical Destiny and National Socialism*, 1–28.
188. See, for example, Kurt Sontheimer's pathbreaking study *Antidemokratisches Denken in der Weimarer Republik* (Munich: Nymphenbürger Verlagsanstalt, 1962). One of the merits of Sontheimer's book is that he painstakingly documents the elements of ideological continuity between the "conservative revolutionary" thinkers and National Socialism. Unfortunately, Sontheimer's work has never been translated into English.
189. Kurt Sontheimer, "Antidemocratic Thought in the Weimar Republic," in *The Road to Dictatorship*, trans. Lawrence Wilson (London: Oswald Wolfe, 1964), 42–43.
190. Daniel Morat, *Von der Tat zur Gelassenheit: Konservatives Denken bei Martin Heidegger, Ernst Jünger, und Friedrich Georg Jünger* (Göttingen: Wallstein, 2007), 113–14.
191. Heidegger, *Sein und Wahrheit*, GA 36/37, 89.
192. Heidegger, *Überlegungen II–VI*, GA 94, 27.
193. Heidegger, *Sein und Wahrheit*, GA 36/37, 89.
194. See, for example, his condemnation of "[world] Jewry's endemic propensity to *planetary criminality.*" Quoted in Peter Trawny, *Heidegger und der Mythos der jüdischen Weltverschwörung* (Frankfurt: Klostermann, 2014), 51. See my article "On Heidegger's Anti-Semitism: The Peter Trawny Affair," *Antisemitism Studies* 1 (2017): 245–79. Martin Heidegger, *Nietzsches Metaphysik*, GA 50 (Frankfurt: Klostermann, 2007), 70.
195. Heidegger, *Logik als Frage nach dem Wesen der Sprache*, GA 38, 81.
196. Ibid. On Heidegger's "exclusionary," Eurocentric ontological-historical biases, see Rainer Marten's important essay "Heidegger and the Greeks," in *The Heidegger Case:*

On Philosophy and Politics, ed. Tom Rockmore and Joseph Margolis (Philadelphia: Temple University Press, 1992), 167–87. According to Marten, Heidegger held that "Western man represents the human race, because western man is the only one with a history. And what about the Egyptians and the Indians, the Sumerians, the Chinese, and the Aztecs? Without question, they have no history at the point where history is defined narrowly and 'rigorously'—that is, qua *historicity*" (169).

197. Heidegger advanced these Social Darwinist, geopolitical arguments consistently in *Über Wesen und Begriff von Natur, Geschichte, und Staat*, in *Heidegger-Jahrbuch*, vol. 4 (Freiburg: Karl Alber, 2009), 53–88.

198. Heidegger, *Überlegungen XII–XV*, GA 96, 243.

199. Heidegger, *Sein und Wahrheit*, GA 36/37, 91.

200. Adolf Hitler, Hamburg speech, 17 August 1934, reprinted in *Führerworte*, vol. 1, ed. Arnold Schley (Berlin: Freiheit Verlag, 1935), 174.

201. Heidegger, "Self-Assertion of the German University," 35; Martin Heidegger, "Political Texts, 1933–1934," in Wolin, *Heidegger Controversy*, 42, 44.

202. Martin Heidegger, *Heraklit* (Frankfurt: Klostermann, 1983), 180–81, 108.

203. I discuss this theme at length in chapter 4.

204. Heidegger, *Überlegungen II–VI*, GA 94, 121, 113.

205. Martin Heidegger to Elisabeth Blochmann, 7 November 1918, in *Briefwechsel*, 12.

206. Heidegger *Überlegungen II–VI*, GA 94, 115 (emphasis added).

207. Heidegger, "Self-Assertion of the German University," 34.

208. Cornelia Schmitz-Berning, *Vokabular des Nationalsozialismus* (Berlin: De Gruyter, 2007), 77.

209. Quoted in Rainer Zitelmann, *Hitler: Selbstverständnis eines Revolutionärs* (Stuttgart: F. A. Herbig, 1989), 44.

210. Heidegger, "Self-Assertion of the German University," 33.

211. On this point, see Francesco Cassata, *A Destra del fascismo: Profilo politico di Julius Evola* (Turin: Bollati Bolingheri, 2003). See Julius Evola, "Sul problema della 'razza dello spirito,' " *Vita Italiana*, Feburary 1942, 153–59. In 1938, Evola wrote a preface to the Italian edition of *The Protocols of the Elders of Zion*, published by the Italian race thinker Giovanni Preziosi's house, La Vita Italiana: *L'Internazionale ebraica: I 'Protocolli' dei 'savi anziani' di Sion* (Rome: La Vita Italiana, 1938), 9–31. For a helpful clarification of the meaning of "spiritual fascism," see Peter Staudenmaier, "Anti-Semitic Intellectuals in Fascist Italy: Promoting 'Spiritual Racism,' " in *Intellectual Anti-Semitism*, ed. Sarah Danielsson and Frank Jacob (Würzburg: Könighausen and Neumann, 2018), 95–116. Staudenmaier's article confirms that the customary separation between "biological" and "spiritual" racism is historically untenable. Hence, he concludes, "By linking biological and spiritual aspects of anti-Semitic animus, spiritual racism formed an unusually potent worldview during the ascendency of Fascism" (95).

212. Julius Evola, *Rivolta contro il mondo moderno* (Milan: Ulrico Hoepli, 1934); German translation: Evola, *Erhebung wider die moderne Welt* (Stuttgart: Deutsche Verlags Anstalt, 1935). On Heidegger and Evola, see the illuminating article by Thomas Vasek, "Ein spirituelles Umsturzprogramm," *Frankfurter Allgemeine Zeitung*, 30 December 2015.

213. See Richard Drake, "Julius Evola, Radical Fascism, and the Lateran Accords," *Catholic Historical Review* 74 (1988): 403–19.

214. Gottfried Benn, "Sein und Werden," *Die Literatur* 37 (1935): 283.

215. Quoted in Jason Horowitz, "Taboo Italian Thinker Is an Enigma to Many, but Not to Bannon," *New York Times*, 10 February 2017.

216. I explore Dugin's role as Russia's leading Heidegger disciple in chapter 6. In this respect, it is also significant that, following Mikhail Gorbachev's introduction of Glasnost, Dugin, during his initial forays to western Europe, cultivated an intellectual friendship with one of Italy's leading neofascist "Evoliani": the self-described "Nazi Maoist" Claudio Mutti. Mutti's Parma-based publishing house, All'insegna del Veltro, published Dugin's book *Continente Russia*. It is through Mutti that Dugin was introduced to the éminence grise of the French Nouvelle Droite Alain de Benoist. See the account in Anton Shekhovtsov, *Russia and the Western Far Right: Tango Noir* (New York: Routledge, 2018), 44.

217. Julius Evola, "Le SS: Guardia e ordine della revolutizione crociuncinata," *Vita Italiana*, August 1938, 164–73.

218. Aaron Gillette, *Racial Theories in Fascist Italy* (New York: Routledge, 2002), 156. On the *Ordensburgen*, see Harald Scholtz, "Die NS 'Ordensburgen,' " *Vierteljahrshefte für Zeitgeschichte* 4 (1967): 269–99. The German Federal Archive contains a thick dossier detailing Evola's interactions with the SS. For a good summary of these dealings, see Horst Junginger, "From Buddha to Adolf Hitler: Walter Wüst and the Aryan Tradition," in *The Study of Religion under the Impact of Fascism*, ed. Junginger (Leiden: Brill, 2008), 105–77.

219. For an excellent discussion of Evola's hypertrophic anti-Semitism, see Peter Staudenmaier, "Racial Ideology between Fascist Italy and Nazi Germany: Julius Evola and the Aryan Myth, 1933–43," *Journal of Contemporary History* 55 (2020): 473–91.

220. See Evola's account of their meeting in *The Path of the Cinnabar*, trans. Sergio Knipe (London: Integral Tradition, 2009), 173–74. See also Renzo de Felice, *The Jews in Fascist Italy*, trans. Robert L. Miller (New York: Enigma Books, 2001), 229–39.

221. Gillette, *Racial Theories in Fascist Italy*, 157.

222. Quoted in Andrea Mammone, *Transnational Neofascism in France and Italy* (New York: Cambridge University Press, 2015), 169. The MSI was the postwar successor to Mussolini's National Fascist Party.

223. See, for example, Hans Jonas, "Gnosticism and Modern Nihilism," *Social Research* 19 (1952): 430–52.

224. Heidegger, *Sein und Zeit*, GA 2, 237; Heidegger, *Being and Time*, 223.

225. Julius Evola, "Die Waffen des geheimen Krieges," 7. "Die Waffen des geheimen Krieges" was one of three lectures that Evola presented at the Deutsch-Italienische Gesellschaft in Berlin in June 1938. The other two lectures were "Arische Lehre des heiligen Kampfes" and "Gral als nordisches Mysterium." Evola, "Julius Evola Ahnenerbe Germanien SS Archiv 3 Vorträge über Gralsmysterium und Reichsgedanke (1938, 68 S., Text)," Internet Archive, accessed 6 June 2012, https://archive.org/details/juliusevolaahnenerbegermanienssarchiv3vortraegeuebergralsmysteriumundreichsgedanke193868s.text.

226. Julius Evola, *Grundrisse der faschistischen Rassenlehre* (Berlin: Eduard Runge Verlag, 1942), 46.

227. See René Guénon, *La Crise du monde moderne* (Paris: Editions Bossard, 1927). Evola translated Guénon's work into Italian in 1937.

424 NOTES TO PAGES 162-169

228. See Leon Poliakov, *The Aryan Myth: A History of Racist and Nationalist Ideas in Europe* (New York: Basic Books, 1965); see also Stefan Arvidsson, *Aryan Idols: Indo-European Mythology as Ideology and Science*, trans. Sonia Wichmann (Chicago: University of Chicago Press, 2003).

229. Umberto Eco, "Ur-Fascism," *New York Review of Books*, 22 June 1995.

230. Vasek, "Ein spirituelles Umsturzprogramm."

231. Christoph Scheuermann, "The Steve Bannon Project: Searching in Europe for Glory Days Gone By," *Der Spiegel*, 29 October 2018, http://www.spiegel.de/international/world/stephen-bannon-tries-rightwing-revolution-in-europe-a-1235297.html. For Bannon's claim that he wanted to turn Breitbart into the "platform of the alt-right," see Sarah Posner, "How Donald Trump's New Campaign Chief Created an Online Haven for White Nationalists," *Mother Jones,* 22 August 2016.

232. See Ernst Bloch, *Thomas Münzer: Theologe der Revolution* (Frankfurt: Suhrkamp, 1962).

233. Johann Gottlieb Fichte, *Nachgelassene Werke*, vol. 3 (Berlin: De Gruyter, 1962), 265.

234. Johann Gottlieb Fichte, *Addresses to the German Nation*, ed. Gregory Moore (New York: Cambridge University Press, 2009), 48, 195.

235. Ibid., 87. See the discussion of this theme in Hans Sluga, *Heidegger's Crisis* (Cambridge, MA: Harvard University Press, 1993), 31–39.

236. Mosse, *Nationalization of the Masses*, 6.

237. Friedrich Schlegel, "Vom Wiener Kongress zum Frankfurter Bundestag, 10. September 1814–31. Oktober 1818," in *Kritische Friedrich-Schlegel-Ausgabe*, vol. 29 (Paderborn: Ferdinand Schönigh, 1980), 67–68.

238. Klaus Vondung, *The Apocalypse in Germany*, trans. Stephen Ricks (Columbia: University of Missouri Press, 2001), 178, 180.

239. Heidegger, *Einführung in die Metaphysik*, GA 40, 49–50 (emphasis added).

240. Herbert Marcuse and Martin Heidegger, "An Exchange of Letters," in Wolin, *Heidegger Controversy*, 161.

241. Heidegger, *Überlegungen II–VI*, GA 94, 481.

242. Heidegger, *Überlegungen XII–XV*, 243.

243. Heidegger, *Überlegungen VII–XI*, GA 95, 96–97 (emphasis added).

244. Heidegger, *Überlegungen XII–XV*, GA 96, 281 (emphasis added).

245. Trawny, *Heidegger und der Mythos einer jüdischen Weltverschwörung*, 133.

246. Heidegger, *Überlegungen II–VI*, GA 94, 484, 502.

247. Richard Wagner, "The Jews in Music," in *Wagner on Music and Drama*, trans. H. Ashton Ellis (New York: Da Capo, 1964), 59.

248. Raul Hilberg, quoted in Claude Lanzmann, *Shoah: The Complete Text of the Acclaimed Holocaust Film* (New York: Da Capo, 1995), 60.

249. Heidegger, *Überlegungen XII–XV*, GA 96, 56.

250. Heidegger, *Natur, Geschichte, und Staat,* 82: "Volk und Raum [gehören] wechselseitig zusammen. Aus dem spezifischen Wissen eines Volkes um die Natur seines Raumes erfahren wir erst, wie die Natur in ihm offenbar wird. Einem slawischen Volke würde die Natur unseres deutschen Raumes bestimmt anders offenbar werden als uns, den semitischen Nomaden wird sie vielleicht überhaupt nie offenbar."

Chapter 4. *Arbeit macht frei*

1. Martin Heidegger, "Labor Service and the University" and "The Call to Labor Service," in *The Heidegger Controversy: A Critical Reader*, ed. Richard Wolin (Cambridge, MA: MIT Press, 1991), 42–43, 53–55; Heidegger, "Der deutsche Student als Arbeiter," in *Reden und andere Zeugnisse eines Lebensweges*, GA 16 (Frankfurt: Klostermann, 2000), 198–208.

2. Martin Heidegger, *Logik als Frage nach dem Wesen der Sprache*, GA 38 (Frankfurt: Klostermann, 1998), 153.

3. For two representative examples, see Otto Pöggeler and Anne-Marie Gethmann-Siefert, eds., *Heidegger und die praktische Philosophie* (Frankfurt: Suhrkamp, 1988); and François Raffoul and David Pettigrew, *Heidegger and Practical Philosophy* (Albany: SUNY Press, 2002).

4. Martin Heidegger, *Being and Time*, trans. John Macquarrie and Edward Robinson (New York: Harper and Row, 1962), 99.

5. Martin Heidegger, *Einführung in die Metaphysik*, GA 40 (Frankfurt: Klostermann, 1983), 152.

6. See, for example, the extended discussion of *Arbeit* in Heidegger's 1934 lecture course *Logik als Frage nach dem Wesen der Sprache*, GA 38, 153–55.

7. Martin Heidegger, *Nietzsches metaphysische Grundstellung im abendländischen Denken: Die ewige Wiederkehr des Gleichen*, GA 44, ed. Marion Heinz (Frankfurt: Klostermann Verlag, 1986). In the course of the discussion that spans pages 254, 283, 286, and 289, Heidegger praised Jünger and Spengler as the "authentic heirs of Nietzsche."

8. Martin Heidegger, *Zu Ernst Jünger*, GA 90 (Frankfurt: Klostermann, 2001), 226–27.

9. Martin Heidegger, "Das Rektorat 1933/34: Tatsachen und Gedanken," in *Reden und andere Zeugnisse eines Lebensweges*, GA 16, 375. For a translation of Jünger's essay "Total Mobilization," see Wolin, *Heidegger Controversy*, 119–39.

10. Jünger, "Total Mobilization," 127, 128.

11. Ibid., 146.

12. Carl Schmitt, "Die Wendung zum totalen Staat," in *Positionen und Begriffe im Kampf mit Weimar-Genf-Versailles* (Berlin: Duncker und Humblot, 1940), 172–73.

13. Walter Benjamin, "Theorien des deutschen Faschismus," in *Gesammelte Werke*, vol. 3 (Frankfurt: Suhrkamp, 1972), 240.

14. Oswald Spengler, *Preussentum und Sozialismus* (Munich: C. H. Beck, 1920), 32, 99.

15. Ibid., 3.

16. Christoph Werth, *Sozialismus und Nation: Die deutsche Ideologiediskussion zwischen 1918 und 1945* (Darmstadt: Westdeutscher Verlag, 1996), 182.

17. The so-called "archeofuturist" current of the French Nouvelle Droite, headed by Guillaume Faye, a cofounder of the far-right think tank GRECE, takes its ideological bearings from Jünger's work. In recent years, the Budapest-based, neofascist publishing house Arktos, which was founded by the Swedish ex-Nazi Daniel Friberg, has translated many of Faye's books into English, including *Archeofuturism* (2003). Following the model established by Jünger in *Der Arbeiter*, archeofuturism glorifies the power and might of modern technology, which it seeks to "tame" by integrating with the "organic"

framework of a racially pure *Volksgemeinschaft*, or "national community." As far back as the 1970s, the "archeofuturists" have been rabidly anti-Semitic. They have also viciously opposed Islam and Arab immigration. For an analysis, see Stéphane François's chapter "Guillaume Faye and Archeofuturism," in *Key Thinkers of the Radical Right: Behind the New Threat to Liberal Democracy*, ed. Mark Sedgwick (New York: Oxford University Press, 2018), 91–102.

18. Ernst Jünger, *Der Arbeiter: Herrschaft und Gestalt* (Stuttgart: Klett-Cotta, 1980), 73. See also Martin Meyer, *Ernst Jünger: Die Biographie* (Munich: Hanser Verlag, 1990), 171.

19. Werth, *Sozialismus und Nation*, 181.

20. Martin Heidegger to Kurt Bauch, 1 May 1942, in *Briefwechsel* (Freiburg: Karl Albers Verlag, 2010), 78. See also Martin Heidegger, *Überlegungen XII–XV*, GA 96 (Frankfurt: Klostermann, 2014), 274.

21. Martin Heidegger, "Die deutsche Universität," in *Reden und andere Zeugnisse eines Lebensweges*, GA 16, 302–3.

22. Martin Heidegger, "25 Jahre nach unserem Abiturium," in *Reden und andere Zeugnisse eines Lebensweges*, GA 16, 281–82.

23. See Ernst Jünger, *Politische Publizistik, 1919–1933*, ed. Sven Berggötz (Stuttgart: Klett-Cotta, 2001). Between 1927 and 1933, Jünger published seventeen articles in *Widerstand*.

24. Heidegger, "Das Rektorat 1933/34," 371.

25. Koppel Pinson, *Modern Germany* (London: Macmillan, 1966), 486.

26. Friedrich Nietzsche, *The Will to Power*, trans. Walter Kaufmann (New York: Vintage, 1968), 465.

27. Heidegger, *Zu Ernst Jünger*, GA 90, 239–40; Friedrich Nietzsche, "On Old and New Tablets," in *Thus Spake Zarathustra*, trans. Walter Kaufmann (New York: Penguin, 1966), 196–214. See also Otto Pöggeler, "Heidegger, Nietzsche, and Politics," in *The Heidegger Case: On Philosophy and Politics*, ed. Tom Rockmore and Joseph Margolis (Philadelphia: Temple University Press, 1992), 114–40.

28. Martin Heidegger to Kurt Bauch, 7 June 1936, in *Briefwechsel*, 29–30.

29. Hans Jonas, "Heideggers Entschlossenheit und Entschluss," in *Erinnerungen an Martin Heidegger*, ed. Günther Neske (Tübingen: Neske Verlag, 1977), 227.

30. Martin Heidegger to Kurt Bauch, 9 August 1935, in *Briefwechsel*, 22.

31. Jeffrey Herf, *Reactionary Modernism: Technology, Politics, and Culture in the Weimar Republic and the Third Reich* (New York: Cambridge University Press, 1984), 3, 29.

32. Quoted in David Landes, "The Jewish Merchant: Typology and Stereotypology in Germany," *Leo Baeck Institute Yearbook* 19 (1974): 21; see also Paul Mendes-Flohr, "Werner Sombart, 'The Jews and Modern Capitalism,'" *Leo Baeck Institute Yearbook* 21 (1976): 87–108.

33. See Barbara Besslich, *Wege in die "Kulturkrieg": Zivilisationskritik in Deutschland, 1890–1914* (Darmstadt: Wissenschaftliche Buchgesellschaft, 2003).

34. Richard von Schaukal, "Wir und die Juden," *Das Gewissen* 1 (1919): 27.

35. Dan Diner, *Weltordnungen: Über Geschichte und Wirkung von Recht und Macht* (Frankfurt: Fischer, 1993), 131–32.

36. Oswald Spengler, *Decline of the West: Form and Actuality*, vol. 1, trans. Charles Francis Atkinson (New York: Knopf, 1947), 317–18, 318–19, 320–21.

37. Martin Heidegger to Elfride Petry, 8 September 1916, in *"Mein liebes Seelchen!"*: *Briefe Martin Heideggers an seine Frau Elfride, 1915–1970*, ed. Gertrud Heidegger (Munich: Deutsche-Verlagsanstalt 2005), 112, 116. For Heidegger's complaint about "Verjudung," see Ulrich Sieg, "Die Verjudung des deutschen Geistes: Ein unbekannter Brief Heideggers," *Die Zeit* 52 (29 December 1989): 19.

38. Heidegger, *Überlegungen XII–XV*, GA 96, 243. Heidegger's recourse to "Menschentümlichkeit"—a neologism that is not found in colloquial German—is noteworthy. Standard usage would suggest the use of *Menschentum* (mankind) or *Menschheit* (humanity). *Menschentümlichkeit* conveys mockery or scorn. Hence, it is a lexical device that further denies the Jews' "humanity."

39. Karl Jaspers, *Philosophische Autobiographie* (Munich: Piper, 1977), 101.

40. Ernst Jünger, *Kampf als inneres Erlebnis* (Berlin: Mittler, 1922), 57.

41. Quoted in Daniel Morat, *Von der Tat zur Gelassenheit: Konservatives Denken bei Martin Heidegger, Ernst Jünger und Friedrich Georg Jünger* (Göttingen: Wallstein Verlag, 2007), 79.

42. Heidegger, *Zu Ernst Jünger*, GA 90, 237–38.

43. Jünger, *Der Arbeiter*, 99, 107.

44. Ibid., 68.

45. Meyer, *Ernst Jünger*, 88.

46. Martin Heidegger, "Brief über den Humanismus," *Wegmarken*, GA 9 (Frankfurt: Klostermann, 1976), 314; Morat, *Von der Tat zur Gelassenheit*, 84.

47. Friedrich Nietzsche, *Genealogy of Morals/Ecce Homo*, trans. Walter Kaufmann and R. J. Hollingdale (New York: Vintage, 1967), 258.

48. Thomas Mann, "Deutschland und die Deutschen," in *Essays*, vol. 2, *Politik*, ed. Hermann Kunske (Frankfurt: Suhrkamp Verlag, 1977), 294. Also see Herf, *Reactionary Modernism*: "After the war, the conservative revolutionaries associated irrationalism, protest against the Enlightenment, and a romantic cult of violence with a cult of 'technics'" (25); and Karl Dietrich Bracher, *The German Dictatorship: The Origins, Structure, and Effects of National Socialism*, trans. Jean Steinberg (New York: Holt, Rinehart, and Winston, 1970): "As a political organization, and certainly as totalitarian rule, National Socialism made singularly effective use of modern industrial and technological methods. This was a presupposition both for propagandistic and organizational *Gleichschaltung* and for the plans of expansion" (331).

49. On this point, see Jost Hermand, *Old Dreams of a New Reich: Völkisch Ideas and National Socialism* (Bloomington: Indiana University Press, 1992).

50. Joseph Goebbels, editorial, *Deutsche Technik*, March 1939, 105–6.

51. Peter Schwerber, *Nationalsozialismus und Technik: Die Geistigkeit der nationalsozialistischen Bewegung* (Munich: Eher Verlag, 1930). See also the illuminating discussion of these questions in Herf, *Reactionary Modernism*, 193.

52. Martin Heidegger, *Introduction to Metaphysics*, trans. Ralph Manheim (New Haven, CT: Yale University Press, 1959), 199.

53. Heidegger, *Überlegungen XII–XV*, GA 96, 67.

54. Ibid., 82. For Heidegger's justification of the Final Solution, see *Anmerkungen I–V*, GA 97 (Frankfurt: Klostermann, 2015), 20.

55. Martin Heidegger, *Holderlins Hymnen "Germanien" und "Der Rhein,"* GA 39 (Frankfurt: Klostermann, 1980), 134. As Oliver Precht remarks in *Heidegger: Zur Selbst- und Fremdbestimmung seiner Philosophie* (Hamburg: Felix Meiner, 2020), Heidegger envisioned philosophy's task as "providing National Socialism with the requisite spiritual superstructure" (147).

56. Martin Heidegger, "Der Student als Arbeiter," in *Reden und andere Zeugnisse eines Lebensweges*, GA 16, 205 (emphasis in original). During the 1920s, *Gestalt* became a popular term of art among German intellectuals. Not only did it figure in the subtitle of Jünger's *Der Arbeiter: Gestalt und Herrschaft* (Gestalt and Domination); Spengler also employed it in the subtitle of volume 1 of *Untergang des Abendlandes: Gestalt und Wirklichkeit* (Gestalt and Actuality). In both cases, *Gestalt* connoted an unalterable, structural feature of the modern world. Methodologically, it suggested a *holistic* as opposed to an *atomistic* approach to understanding human existence. Lastly, in a nod to Nietzsche's *amor fati*, it also reflected a cosmological "destiny," whose *Schlag*, or "imprint," transcended humanity's paltry, subjective preferences.

57. For Spengler's widespread impact, see Manfred Schroeter, *Der Streit um Spengler: Eine Kritik seiner Kritiker* (Munich: Beck, 1922). See also Werth, *Sozialismus und Nation*, 43–54; and Volker Weiss, *Deutschlands Neue Rechte: Angriff der Elite von Spengler zu Sarrazin* (Paderborn: Verlag Ferdinand Schönigh, 2011).

58. Friedrich Nietzsche, *Writings from the Late Notebooks*, ed. Rüdiger Bittner (Cambridge: Cambridge University Press, 2003), 146 (Notebook 9, Autumn 1887).

59. Nietzsche, *Will to Power*, 463.

60. Nietzsche to Joseph Paneth, May 1884, quoted in Karl Löwith, *From Hegel to Nietzsche: The Revolution in Nineteenth-Century Thought*, trans. David E. Green (New York: Columbia University Press, 1991), 189.

61. David Ohana, "The Case of Ernst Jünger," in *Nietzsche, Godfather of Fascism? On the Uses and Abuses of a Philosophy*, ed. Jacob Golomb and Robert S. Wistrich (Princeton, NJ: Princeton University Press, 2002), 284.

62. Morat, *Von der Tat zur Gelassenheit*, 153.

63. Heidegger, *Einführung in die Metaphysik*, GA 40, 208.

64. Martin Heidegger, *Nietzsches Metaphysische Grundstellung im abendländischen Denken: Die ewige Wiederkehr des Gleichen*, GA 44 (Frankfurt: Klostermann, 1986), 257.

65. Heidegger, "Das Rektorat 1933/34," 375.

66. Martin Heidegger, *Besinnung*, GA 66 (Frankfurt: Klostermann, 1997), 27–28.

67. Heidegger, *Zu Ernst Jünger*, GA 90, 265, 239–40.

68. Martin Heidegger, *Nietzsche: Europäischer Nihilismus*, GA 48 (Frankfurt: Klostermann, 1986), 73.

69. Ibid., 138.

70. Domenico Losurdo, *Heidegger and the Ideology of War: Community, Death, and the West*, trans. Marcella Morris and Jan Morris (Amherst, NY: Humanity Books, 2001), 171–72.

71. Heidegger, *Nietzsche: Europäischer Nihilismus*, GA 48, 205.

72. Ibid.

73. Ibid.

74. Marc Bloch, *L'Étrange Défaite* (Paris: Société des Éditions Franc-Tireur, 1946).

75. Herf, *Reactionary Modernism*, 30.

76. Ernst Jünger, "Die Maschine," *Der Standarte* 15 (1925), reprinted in Jünger, *Politische Publizistik*, 161.

77. Martin Heidegger, *Schellings "Über das Wesen der menschlichen Freiheit,"* GA 42 (Frankfurt: Klostermann, 1988), 40–41.

78. Elliot Neaman, "Ernst Jünger," in Sedgwick, *Key Thinkers of the Radical Right*, 24.

79. Ernst Jünger, "Abgrenzung und Verbindung," *Die Standarte* 2 (13 September 1925): 2; Jünger, " 'Nationalismus' und Nationalsozialismus," *Arminius*, 27 March 1927, 8–9.

80. Hans-Peter Schwarz, *Der konservative Anarchist: Politik und Zeitkritik Ernst Jüngers* (Freiburg: Rombach, 1962).

81. See Ernst Jünger, *Strahlungen* (Tübingen: Heliopolis, 1949): "After the earthquake one lashes out at the seismograph. Yet one cannot blame the barometer for the typhoon, unless one wants to be classed a savage" (9).

82. Ernst Jünger, *Werke* (Stuttgart: Klett-Cotta, 1969); Jünger, *Sämtliche Werke* (Stuttgart: Klett-Cotta, 1978).

83. See Jünger, *Politische Publizistik*.

84. See "André Müller spricht mit dem Dichter Ernst Jünger," *Die Zeit* 50 (8 December 1989).

85. Ernst Jünger, "Revolution und Idee," *Völkischer Beobachter*, 24–25 September 1923.

86. Ernst Jünger, "Über Nationalismus und die Judenfrage," *Die Kommenden* 38 (1930): 445–46.

87. Jünger, "Total Mobilization," 136.

88. Nicolaus Wachsmann, "Marching under the Swastika: Ernst Jünger and National Socialism under the Weimar Republic," *Journal of Contemporary History* 33–34 (1998): 587–88.

89. Thomas Mann to Agnes Meyer, 14 Dezember 1945, in *Briefe, 1937–1947* (Frankfurt: Fischer, 1963), 464.

90. Martin Heidegger, *Sein und Zeit*, GA 2 (Frankfurt: Klostermann, 1977), 220–21. Heidegger observes, "This term [Care] has been chosen not because Dasein happens to be proximally and to a large extent 'practical' and economic, but because the Being of Dasein itself is to be made visible as Care. . . . Dasein, when understood ontologically, is Care" (71); Heidegger, *Being and Time*, 83–84.

91. See Heidegger's extensive treatment of this question in his 1929–30 lecture course *The Fundamental Concepts of Metaphysics: World, Finitude, Solitude*, trans. William McNeill and Nicholas Walker (Bloomington: Indiana University Press, 1995); see, above all, part 2, 167–365.

92. Charles Guignon, *Heidegger and the Problem of Knowledge* (Indianapolis: Hackett, 1983), 200. See also the instructive explication of *Sorge* in Günther Anders, "The Pseudo-Concreteness of Heidegger's Existentialism," *Philosophy and Phenomenological Research* 8 (1948): " 'Sorge' designates both 'Dasein's' relation to itself: it is a 'Sein,' 'dem es um es Selbst geht' (a 'modus existendi characterized by its concern for itself'); as well as its relation to its world of 'Umgang' ('dealing' and 'communications'). Thus it is 'interest' in the broadest sense of the word that is made the fundamental feature of 'Dasein' " (345).

93. Heidegger, "Der deutsche Student als Arbeiter," 234.

94. Martin Heidegger, "Zur Eröffnung der Schulungskurse für die Notstandsarbeiter der Stadt an der Universität," in *Reden und andere Zeugnisse eines Lebensweges*, GA 16, 232.

95. Heidegger, "Der deutsche Student als Arbeiter," 234.

96. Martin Heidegger, "Die Selbstbehauptung der deutschen Universität," in *Reden und andere Zeugnisse eines Lebensweges*, GA 16, 113; Heidegger, "The Self-Assertion of the German University," in Wolin, *Heidegger Controversy*, 34.

97. Martin Heidegger, "Zur Immatrikuation," in *Reden und andere Zeugnisse eines Lebensweges*, GA 16, 96.

98. Ibid.

99. Heidegger, *Being and Time*, 89, 90.

100. Ibid. 97–98.

101. Ibid., 97.

102. Martin Heidegger, *Ontologie: Hermeneutik der Faktizität*, GA 63 (Frankfurt: Klostermann Verlag, 2018).

103. Heidegger, *Logik als Frage nach dem Wesen der Sprache*, GA 38, 133.

104. Heidegger, *Überlegungen VII–XI*, GA 95, 97. In the passage in question, Heidegger speaks of world Jewry's "Weltlosigkeit."

105. Martin Heidegger, *Bremer und Freiburger Vorträge*, GA 79 (Frankfurt: Klostermann Verlag, 1994), 56.

106. On this point, see Frank Dikötter, *The Tragedy of Liberation: A History of the Chinese Revolution* (London: Bloomsbury, 2013).

107. Byron Williston, "The Question Concerning Geo-Engineering," *Technē: Research in Philosophy and Technology* 21 (2017): 212.

108. Theodor Adorno, "Why Still Philosophy?," in *Critical Models: Interventions and Catchwords*, trans. Henry W. Pickford (New York: Columbia University Press, 1998), 16. For Nietzsche's discussion of "backworldsmen," see "Von den Hinterweltern," in *Also Sprach Zarathustra*, in *Sämtliche Werke: Kritische Studienausgabe* vol. 4, eds. Giorgio Colli and Mazzino Montinari (Berlin: De Gruyter, 1967–77), 35–38.

109. Theodor Adorno, *The Jargon of Authenticity*, trans. Knut Tarnowski and Frederic Will (Evanston, IL: Northwestern University Press, 1973), 108–9.

110. See Joan Campbell, *Joy in Work, German Work: The National Debate, 1800–1945* (Princeton, NJ: Princeton University Press, 1989), 327–28.

111. For a good account, see Wolfgang Abendroth, *A Short History of the European Working Class* (New York: Monthly Review Press, 1973).

112. Martin Heidegger, "National Socialist Education," in Wolin, *Heidegger Controversy*, 59 (emphasis in original).

113. Martin Heidegger, "Arbeitsdienst und Universität," in *Reden und andere Zeugnisse eines Lebensweges*, GA 16, 125–26; see also Heidegger, "Labor Service and the University," in Wolin, *Heidegger Controversy*, 42–43.

114. Campbell, *Joy in Work, German Work*, 328.

115. Martin Heidegger, *Beiträge zur Philosophie: Vom Ereignis*, GA 65 (Frankfurt: Klostermann, 1989), 36ff.

116. Martin Heidegger, "Zur Immatrikulation," in *Reden und andere Zeugnisse eines Lebensweges*, GA 16, 95, 96.

117. Jünger, *Der Arbeiter*, 119, 151. See also Leonard Krieger, *The German Idea of Freedom* (Chicago: University of Chicago Press, 1957).

118. See Campbell, *Joy in Work, German Work*, 146.

119. Paul Horneffer, "Die Religion der Arbeit," *Deutsche Pfeiler* 2 (1922–23): 5–13.

120. Campbell, *Joy in Work, German Work*, 248.

121. Paul Horneffer, *Der Weg zur Arbeitsfreude* (Berlin: Hobbing, 1928).

122. Campbell, *Joy in Work, German Work*, 249–50.

123. Martin Heidegger, "The Call to Labor Service," in Wolin, *Heidegger Controversy*, 54.

124. Martin Heidegger, *Sein und Wahrheit*, GA 36/37 (Frankfurt: Klostermann Verlag, 2001), 86. In these passages, Heidegger's characterization of the ontological meaning of "work" reflects Aristotle's understanding of *technē* as a purposive or goal-directed transformation of nature, a transformation in accordance with human "ends" (*telei*).

125. Heidegger, *Logik als Frage nach dem Wesen der Sprache*, GA 38, 100.

126. Kiran Klaus Patel, *"Soldaten der Arbeit": Arbeitsdienste in Deutschland und den USA, 1933–1945* (Göttingen: Vandenhoeck and Ruprecht, 2003), 117; Michel Foucault, "Means of Correct Training," in *Discipline and Punish*, trans. Alan Sheridan (New York: Vintage, 1977), 170–94.

127. See Wolfgang Schlicker, "Arbeitsdienstbestrebungen des deutschen Monopolkapitals in der Weimarer Republik unter besonderer Berücksichtigung des Deutschen Institutes für Technische Arbeitschulung," *Jahrbuch für Wirtschaftsgeschichte*, 1971–73, 95–122.

128. David Schoenbaum, *Hitler's Social Revolution: Class and Status in Nazi Germany, 1933–1939* (New York: Norton, 1997), 115.

129. The interview with Hanns Johst first appeared in the *Frankfurter Volksblatt*, 27 January 1934. See Adolf Hitler, *Reden und Proklamationen, 1922–45*, vol. 1, ed. Max Domarus (Leonburg: Pamminger und Partner Verlagsgesellschaft, 1973), 349. Cf. Frank Trommler, "Die Nationalisierung der Arbeit," in *Arbeit als Thema in der deutschen Literatur vom Mittelalter bis zur Gegenwart*, ed. Reinhold Grimm and Jost Hermand (Königstein: Athenäum, 1979): "The brutal concomitant to the nationalization of *Arbeit* came to light shortly after Hitler's accession to power with the elimination of the workers' movement and the murder of thousands of Communists and Socialists" (121).

130. Quoted in Trommler, "Die Nationalisierung der Arbeit," 102; Adolf Hitler, in *Reden und Proklamationen*, 10 April 1933 (First Congress of the German Arbeitsfront) and 24 October 1933 (Berliner Sportpalast).

131. Adolf Hitler, "Rede vor dem Reichstag," 20 February 1938, in *Reden und Proklamationen*, 792.

132. Martin Heidegger to Karl Jaspers, 22 November 1922, in *Briefwechsel* (Frankfurt: Klostermann; Munich: Piper, 1990), 33.

133. Adolf Hitler, quoted in Schoenbaum, *Hitler's Social Revolution*, 62.

134. Karl Arnhold, *Das Ringen um die Arbeitsidee* (Berlin: DAF, 1938), 77.

135. Quoted in Wolfgang Brückner, *"Arbeit Macht Frei": Herkunft und Hintergrund der KZ-Devise* (Opladen: Leske and Budrich Verlag, 1998), 122–24.

136. Konstantin Hierl, "Rede," in *Der Parteitag der Arbeit, 6–13 September 1937* (Munich: Franz Eher, 1938), 90.

137. Quoted in Werner Conze, "Arbeit," in *Geschichtliche Grundbegriffe* (Stuttgart: E. Klett Verlag, 1972), 214–15.

138. Quoted in Eberhard Jäckel, *Hitler's Weltanschauung: A Blueprint for Power*, trans. Herbert Arnold (Cambridge, MA: Harvard University Press, 1981), 51. See also Reginald H. Phelps, "Hitlers 'grundlegende' Rede über den Antisemitismus," *Vierteljahrshefte für Zeitgeschichte* 16 (1968): 390–420.

139. Peter Dudek, *Erziehung durch Arbeit: Arbeitslagerbewegung und freiwilliger Arbeitsdienst, 1920–1935* (Opladen: Westdeutscher Verlag, 1986), 14 (emphasis added).

140. Heidegger, "Labor Service and the University," 42–43.

141. Bracher, *German Dictatorship*, 214, 216.

142. Ibid., 216.

143. Anson Rabinbach, "Aesthetics of Production in the Third Reich," *Journal of Contemporary History* 11 (1976): 66, 67, 68.

144. Schoenbaum, *Hitler's Social Revolution*, 117–18.

145. Ibid., 45.

146. Adolf Hitler, in *Deutsches Lesebuch für Volksschulen*, vol. 4 (Berlin: Deutscher Schulverlag, 1944), 261.

147. Trommler, "Die Nationalisierung der Arbeit," 120.

148. Max Horkheimer and Theodor W. Adorno, *Dialectic of Enlightenment: Philosophical Fragments*, trans. Edmund Jephcott (Stanford, CA: Stanford University Press, 2002), xviii.

149. Martin Heidegger, "Schöpferische Landschaft: Warum bleiben wir in Provinz," in *Aus der Erfahrung des Denkens*, GA 13 (Frankfurt: Klostermann Verlag, 1983), 9, 10, 11.

150. Heidegger, "Self-Assertion of the German University," 33–34.

151. Heidegger, "Schöpferische Landschaft," 9–11.

152. Ibid., 11.

153. Martin Heidegger, "Zum Hochzeitstag von Fritz und Liesel Heidegger," in *Reden und andere Zeugnisse eines Lebensweges*, GA 16, 53.

154. Heidegger, *Fundamental Concepts of Metaphysics*, 5.

155. Heinrich W. Petzet, *Auf einen Stern zugehen: Begegnungen und Unterhaltungen mit Martin Heidegger, 1929–1976* (Frankfurt: Societät Verlag, 1983), 87.

156. See Sieg, "Die Verjudung des deutschen Geistes."

157. Martin Heidegger, *Der Feldweg,* GA 77 (Frankfurt: Klostermann Verlag, 1995), 17; Walther Darré, *Das Bauerntum als Lebensquell der Nordischen Rasse* (Munich: T. S. Lehmanns Verlag, 1929), 277. For more on Darré, see Anna Bramwell, *Blood and Soil: Richard Walther Darré and Hitler's "Green Party"* (Bourne End, UK: Kensal, 1985). Reviews of this book have exposed its excessive sympathies for Darré's Nazism.

158. Bramwell, *Blood and Soil*, 76.

159. See Michael Kater, "Die Artamanen: Völkische Jugend in der Weimarer Republik," *Historische Zeitschrift* 213 (1971): 577–638.

160. Walther Darré, "Farmers and the State," in *Nazi Ideology before 1933: A Documentation*, ed. Barbara Land and Leila Rupp (Manchester: Manchester University Press, 1978), 133.

161. Darré, *Das Bauerntum als Lebensquell der Nordischen Rasse*, 46.

162. Ibid., 40.

163. Ibid., 311.

164. Adolf Hitler, *Mein Kampf*, trans. Ralph Manheim (New York: Houghton Mifflin, 1943), 304–5.

165. Clifford A. Lovin, "*Blut und Boden*: The Ideological Basis of the Nazi Agricultural Program," *Journal of the History of Ideas* 28 (1967): 286.

166. Walther Darré, *Erkenntnisse und Werden* (Goslar: Blut und Boden Verlag, 1940), 24–26.

167. Heidegger, "Zum Hochzeitstag von Fritz und Liesel Heidegger," in *Reden und andere Zeugnisse eines Lebensweges*, GA 16, 55.

168. Martin Heidegger, *Über Wesen und Begriff von Natur, Geschichte, und Staat*, in *Heidegger-Jahrbuch*, vol. 4 (Freiburg: Karl Alber, 2009), 82.

169. Ibid., 81–82 (emphasis added).

170. Quoted in Bramwell, *Blood and Soil*, 63.

171. Peter Fritzsche, *Germans into Nazis* (Cambridge, MA: Harvard University Press, 1999).

172. Dudek, *Erziehung durch Arbeit*, 151.

173. See Klaus Kirin Patel, " 'Auslese' und 'Ausmerze': Das Janusgesicht der nationalsozialistischen Lager," *Zeitschrift für Geisteswissenschaften* 54 (2006): *"Arbeitsdienst* became the binding model that was subsequently copied by other organizations" (344).

174. Quoted in Patel, *"Soldaten der Arbeit,"* 107.

175. Erving Goffman, *Asylums: Essays on the Social Situation of Mental Patients and Other Inmates* (New York: Anchor, 1961).

176. The seminal importance of the *Männerbund* idea in the political self-understanding of National Socialism was acknowledged by Alfred Baeumler in *Männerbund und Wissenschaft* (Berlin: Junker und Dünnhaupt, 1934).

177. Andreas Kraas, *Erziehungslager, 1932–1945: Politische Funktion und pädagogische Gestaltung* (Bad Heilbrunn: Klinckhardt Verlag, 2004), 12.

178. Albrecht Günther, "Das Lager," *Deutsches Volkstum*, 1934, 809.

179. Michael Wildt, "Der Begriff der Arbeit bei Hitler," in *Arbeit im Nationalsozialismus*, ed. Marc Buggeln and Michael Wildt (Oldenbourg: De Gruyter, 2004), 18.

180. Georges-Arthur Goldschmidt, "Travail et National Socialisme," *Allemagne d'aujourd'hui* 40 (1973): 12.

181. The KZ's evolution is painstakingly traced in Nicolaus Wachsmann, *KL: A History of the Nazi Concentration Camps* (New York: Farrar, Straus and Giroux, 2014).

182. Dolf Sternberger, "Vorbemerkung," in *Aus dem Wörterbuch des Unmenschen*, ed. Dolf Sternberger, Gerhard Storz, and Wilhelm Emanuel Süskind (Munich: Beck, 1962), 72.

183. Martin Heidegger, *Überlegungen II–VI*, GA 94 (Frankfurt: Klostermann Verlag, 2014), 115 (emphasis added).

184. Otto Pöggeler, *Philosophie und Nationalsozialismus am Beispiel Heideggers* (Opladen: Westdeutscher Taschenbuchverlag, 1989), 29.

185. Quoted in Hugo Ott, *Martin Heidegger: Unterwegs zu seiner Biographie* (Frankfurt: Campus, 1988), 215. Heidegger's text, "The University in the New Reich," was published two months later in a National Socialist organ, *Der deutsche Student*. See Wolin, *Heidegger Controversy*, 43–45.

186. Heidegger, "Wehrdienst der Freiburger Studentenschaft," in *Reden und andere Zeugnisse eines Lebensweges*, GA 16, 103.

187. Heidegger, "Call to Labor Service," 42–43.

188. Schoenbaum, *Hitler's Social Revolution*, 145.

189. Quoted in Klaus Kirin Patel, "Education, Schooling, and Camps," in *A Companion to Nazi Germany*, ed. Shelley Baranowski, Armin Nolzen, and Claus-Christian W. Szejnmann (New York: Wiley, 2015), 186.

190. Martin Heidegger, "Die Universität im neuen Reich," in *Reden und andere Zeugnisse eines Lebensweges*, GA 16, 762.

191. Martin Heidegger, "Seminar über Hegels *Rechtsphilosophie*," in *Seminare: Hegel-Schelling*, GA 86 (Frankfurt: Klostermann, 1998), 177.

192. Heidegger, "Die Universität im neuen Reich," 761–62.

193. For a good account, see Ott, *Martin Heidegger*, 214–23.

194. Ibid., 214.

195. Heidegger, *Sein und Wahrheit*, GA 36/37, 91.

196. Heidegger, "National Socialist Education," 56.

197. See Peter Fritzsche, *Germans into Nazis* (Cambridge, MA: Harvard University Press, 1998).

198. Heidegger, "National Socialist Education," 58. See also Guido Schneeberger, *Nachlese zu Heidegger: Dokumente zu seinem Leben und Denken* (Bern: Buchdruckerei A. G. Suhr, 1962), 201.

199. Martin Heidegger, "An die am Ferienlager Todtnauberg (Schwarzwald) teilnehmenden Herren Dozenten und Assistenten," in *Reden und andere Zeugnisse eines Lebens*, GA 16, 170.

200. See Victor Klemperer, *Language of the Third Reich: A Philologist's Notebook* (London: Athlone, 2000), 185.

201. "Festakte der Tagung der badischen Schreinmeister," *Freiburger Zeitung* 240 (4 September 1933); reprinted in Schneeberger, *Nachlese zu Heidegger*, 122.

202. Martin Heidegger, "Zur Eröffnung der Schulungskurse für die Notstandsarbeiter der Stadt an der Universität," 234.

203. Heidegger, "Call to Labor Service," 53–54.

204. Ibid.

205. Ibid.

206. Heidegger, *Logik als Frage nach dem Wesen der Sprache*, GA 38, 128.

207. Heidegger, "Nationalsozialistische Wissensschulung," *Der Alemanne: Kampfblatt der Nationalsozialisten Oberbadens*, 1 February 1934, 9; quoted in Schneeberger, *Nachlese zu Heidegger*, 199 (emphasis in original).

208. Heidegger, *Logik als Frage nach dem Wesen der Sprache*, GA 38, 154.

209. Ibid., 100. See also Aristotle, *Metaphysics*, trans. W. D. Ross (New York: Oxford University Press, 1991), book 1, 983a: "From wonder, men, both now and at the first, began to philosophize, having felt astonishment originally at the things which were more obvious, indeed, amongst those that were doubtful; then, by degrees in this way having advanced on words, and, in process of time, having started difficulties about more important subjects."

210. Heidegger, *Logik als Frage nach dem Wesen der Sprache*, GA 38, 162.

211. See Winfried Franzen, "Die Sehnsucht nach Härte und Schwere: Über ein zum NS-Engagement disponierendes Motiv in Heideggers Vorlesung 'Die Grundbegriffe der Metaphysik' von 1929/1930," in Pöggeler and Gethmann-Siefert, *Heidegger und die praktische Philosophie*, 78–92.

212. See Ott, *Martin Heidegger*, 244.

213. Anders, "Pseudo-Concreteness of Heidegger's Existentialism."
214. Graham Harmon, "The McCluhans and Metaphysics," in *New Waves in Philosophy of Technology*, ed. Jan Kyrre Berg Olsen, Evan Selinger, and Søren Riis (Basingstoke, UK: Palgrave Macmillan, 2009), 112.
215. Adorno, *Jargon of Authenticity*, 5.

Chapter 5. Earth and Soil

1. Martin Heidegger, *Sein und Zeit*, GA 2 (Frankfurt: Klostermann, 1977), 66; Martin Heidegger, *Being and Time*, trans. John Macquarrie and Edward Robinson (New York: Harper and Row, 1962), 93.
2. Heidegger, *Sein und Zeit*, GA 2, 150; Heidegger, *Being and Time*, 112.
3. See, for example, Jeff Malpas, *Heidegger and the Thinking of Place: Explorations in the Topology of Being* (Cambridge, MA: MIT Press, 2012).
4. Martin Heidegger, *Aus der Erfahrung des Denkens*, GA 13 (Frankfurt: Klostermann, 1983), 23.
5. Martin Heidegger, *Wegmarken*, GA 9 (Frankfurt: Klostermann, 1976), 421.
6. For a good example, see Don Ihde, *Heidegger's Technologies: Post-Phenomenological Perspectives* (New York: Fordham University Press, 2010).
7. Jeff Malpas, *Heidegger's Topology: Being, Place, and World* (Cambridge, MA: MIT Press, 2006), 302–3.
8. Martin Heidegger, "Zum Hochzeitstag von Fritz und Liesel Heidegger," in *Reden und Andere Zeugnisse eines Lebensweges*, GA 16 (Frankfurt: Klostermann, 2000), 53.
9. Hans Jonas, "Heideggers Entschlossenheit und Entschluss," in *Antwort: Martin Heidegger im Gespräch*, ed. Günther Neske and Emil Kettering (Pfullingen: Neske Verlag, 1988), 223.
10. Martin Heidegger, *Einführung in die Metaphysik*, GA 40 (Frankfurt: Klostermann, 1998), 43; Heidegger, *Introduction to Metaphysics*, trans. Ralph Manheim (New Haven, CT: Yale University Press, 1959), 39.
11. Martin Heidegger, *Logik als die Frage nach dem Wesen der Sprache*, GA 38 (Frankfurt: Klostermann, 1998), 40 (emphasis in original).
12. Walther Darré, *Neuadel aus Blut und Boden* (Munich: Lehmann Verlag, 1930). See also, Anna Bramwell, *Blood and Soil: Richard Walter Darré and Hitler's "Green Party"* (Bourne End, UK: Kensal, 1985). Bramwell's study is a disconcertingly positive evaluation of Darré's legacy. Abstracting from her protagonist's commitment to "race thinking," she portrays Darré as a "dissident" National Socialist who anticipated the environmentalism of the German Green Party. Neither of these claims is genuinely sustainable.
13. Victor Klemperer, *Language of the Third Reich*, trans. Martin Brady (New York: Continuum, 2006), 22.
14. Martin Heidegger, *Anmerkungen I–V*, GA 97 (Frankfurt: Klostermann, 2015), 60.
15. Martin Heidegger, " 'Only a God Can Save Us': *Der Spiegel*'s Interview with Martin Heidegger (1966)," in *The Heidegger Controversy: A Critical Reader*, ed. Richard Wolin (Cambridge, MA: MIT Press, 1991), 106.

16. Shulamit Volkov, "Anti-Semitism as a Cultural Code," in *Germans, Jews, and Anti-Semites: Trials in Emancipation* (New York: Cambridge University Press, 2002), 67–157.

17. Martin Heidegger to Elfride Heidegger, 19 March 1933, in *"Mein Liebes Seelchen!":* *Briefe Martin Heideggers an seine Frau Elfride, 1915–1970*, ed. Gertrud Heidegger (Munich: Deutsche Verlag-Anstalt, 2005), 186.

18. Martin Heidegger, *Überlegungen II–VI*, GA 94 (Frankfurt: Klostermann Verlag, 2014), 164.

19. Martin Heidegger, *Parmenides*, trans. André Schuwer and Richard Rojewicz (Bloomington: Indiana University Press, 1992), 112.

20. Johann Jakob Bachofen, *Der Mythos von Orient und Occident: Eine Metaphysik der Alten Welt*, ed. Manfred Schröter (Munich: C. H. Beck'sche Verlagsbuchhandlung, 1926).

21. Walter Burkert, "Griechische Mythologie und die Geistesgeschichte der Moderne," in *Les Études classiques aux XIXe et XXe siècles: Leur place dans l'histoire des idées*, ed. Willem den Boer (Geneva: Fondation Hardt, 1980), 187.

22. Martin Heidegger, *Zur Bestimmung der Philosophie*, GA 56/57 (Frankfurt: Klostermann Verlag, 1985), 15–17.

23. Martin Heidegger, *Phänomenologische Interpretationen zu Aristotles*, GA 61 (Frankfurt: Klostermann Verlag, 1985), 170.

24. Martin Heidegger, *Überlegungen XII–XV*, GA 96 (Frankfurt: Klostermann Verlag, 2014), 46.

25. Martin Heidegger, "The Self-Assertion of the German University," in Wolin, *Heidegger Controversy*, 38, 36.

26. Charles Bambach, *Heidegger's Roots: Nietzsche, National Socialism, and the Greeks* (Ithaca, NY: Cornell University Press, 2003), 14 (emphasis added).

27. Quoted in Hans-Jürgen Sandkühler, *Philosophie im Nationalsozialismus* (Hamburg: Meiner Verlag, 2009), 174

28. Martin Heidegger, *Introduction to Metaphysics*, trans. Ralph Manheim (New Haven, CT: Yale University Press, 1959), 38.

29. Martin Heidegger, "Der Ursprung des Kunstwerkes," in *Holzwege*, GA 5 (Frankfurt: Klostermann, 1977), 35.

30. Martin Heidegger, *Hölderlins Hymne "Germanien" und "Der Rhein,"* GA 39 (Frankfurt: Klostermann, 1983), 106.

31. Martin Heidegger, *Vom Wesen der Wahrheit. Zu Platons Höhlengleichnis und Theätet*, GA 34 (Frankfurt: Klostermann, 1988), 145 (emphasis added).

32. Heidegger, "Der Ursprung des Kunstwerkes," 28.

33. Martin Heidegger, "National Socialist Education," in Wolin, *Heidegger Controversy*, 56.

34. Heidegger, *Hölderlins Hymne "Germanien" und "Der Rhein,"* GA 39, 217.

35. Heidegger, "Der Ursprung des Kunstwerkes," 29.

36. Dieter Thomä, *Die Zeit des Selbst und die Zeit danach* (Frankfurt: Suhrkamp Verlag, 1994), 586.

37. Hannah Arendt, "What Is Existential Philosophy?," in *Essays in Understanding, 1930–1954: Formation, Exile, Totalitarianism* (New York: Harcourt Brace, 1994), 181.

38. Heidegger, *Anmerkungen I–V*, GA 97, 47.

39. George Mosse, *The Crisis of German Ideology: The Intellectual Origins of the Third Reich* (New York: Grosset and Dunlap, 1964), 16.

40. Quoted in Karl Dietrich Bracher, *The German Dictatorship*, trans. Jean Steinman (New York: Holt, Rinehardt, and Winston, 1970), 10.

41. Bambach, *Heidegger's Roots*, xx.

42. Martin Heidegger, *Sein und Wahrheit*, GA 36/37 (Frankfurt: Klostermann, 2001), 14.

43. Martin Heidegger, *Prolegomena zur Geschichte des Zeitbegriffs*, GA 20 (Frankfurt: Klostermann, 1988), 104.

44. Ibid., 423.

45. Martin Heidegger, *Einführung in die Philosophische Forschung*, GA 17 (Frankfurt: Klostermann, 2006), 214.

46. Heidegger, *Sein und Zeit*, GA 2, 49; Heidegger, *Being and Time*, 61.

47. Heidegger, "Zum Hochzeitstag von Fritz und Liesel Heidegger," 53.

48. See the illuminating discussion of these themes in Sidonie Kellerer, *Zerissenner Moderne: Descartes bei den Neukantianern, Husserl, und Heidegger* (Konstanz: Konstanz University Press, 2013), 202.

49. Heidegger, *Sein und Zeit*, GA 2, 30; *Being and Time*, 44. See Stefan Günzel, "Heideggers und Deleuzes Geopolitische Leseart von Nietzsche," in *Geophilosophie: Nietzsches philosophische Geographie* (Berlin: Akademie Verlag, 2001), 146–54. As Heidegger observes in *Being and Time*, paragraph 74, "*Repetition is an explicit handing-down [Überlieferung]*: the retrogression to the possibility of historically prior Dasein." Heidegger, *Sein und Zeit*, GA 2, 509; Heidegger, *Being and Time*, 437.

50. Martin Heidegger, *Grundbegriffe der aristotelischen Philosophie*, GA 18 (Frankfurt: Klostermann, 2002), 15.

51. Heidegger, "Self-Assertion of the German University," 32.

52. Bambach, *Heidegger's Roots*, 20.

53. Paul Yorck von Wartenburg, *Die Philosophie des Grafen Paul Yorck von Wartenburg*, ed. Karlfried Gründer (Göttingen: Vandenhoeck and Ruprecht, 1970), 174–75.

54. Martin Heidegger, *Nietzsche: Europäischer Nihilismus*, GA 48 (Frankfurt: Klostermann, 1986), 205.

55. Robert Minder, *Der Dichter in der Gesellschaft: Erfahrungen mit deutscher und französischer Literatur* (Frankfurt: Suhrkamp Verlag, 1968), 247–48 (emphasis added).

56. Louis Dean Valencia-Garcia, "The Rise and Fall of the Alt-Right in the Digital Age," in *Far-Right Revisionism and the End of History*, ed. Valencia-Garcia (New York: Routledge, 2020), 314.

57. Heidegger, *Anmerkungen I–V*, GA 97, 20.

58. Martin Heidegger, *Die Bremer und Freiburger Vorträge*, GA 79 (Frankfurt: Klostermann, 1994), 27.

59. Heidegger, *Sein und Zeit*, GA 2, 526, 531, 529; Heidegger, *Being and Time*, 450, 454, 452.

60. Paul Yorck von Wartenburg, *Bewusstseinsstellung und Geschichte* (Hamburg: Meiner Verlag, 1991), 46.

61. Ibid. For the controversy surrounding the ideological valences of *Bodenständigkeit* in Heidegger's early work, see Emmanuel Faye, "La 'vision du monde' antisémite de Heidegger à l'ombre de ses *Cahiers noirs*," in *Heidegger: Le sol, la communauté, la race*, ed. E. Faye (Paris: 2014), 307–27; and Dieter Thomä, "Weltlosigkeit und Bodenlosigkeit:

Der frühe Heidegger und das jüdische Denken," in *"Sein und Zeit" neu verhandelt*, ed. Marion Heinz and Tobias Bender (Hamburg: Meiner Verlag, 2019), 379–413. Thomä's essay proceeds according to the mistaken assumption that, by successfully contesting Faye's arguments, he can exonerate Heidegger.

62. Rogers Brubaker, *Citizenship and Nationhood in France and Germany* (Cambridge, MA: Harvard University Press, 2008), 1, 9.

63. Martin Heidegger, *Die Grundbegriffe der Metaphysik: Welt, Endlichkeit, Einsamkeit*, GA 29–30 (Frankfurt: Klostermann, 1983), 244; Heidegger, *Fundamental Concepts of Metaphysics: World, Finitude, Solitude*, trans. William McNeill and Nicholas Walker (Bloomington: Indiana University Press, 1982), 163.

64. For an account of Heidegger's Karlsruhe address, see Guido Schneeberger, *Nachlese zu Heidegger: Dokumente zu seinem Leben und Denken* (Bern: Buchdrückerei A. G. Suhr, 1962), 10–12.

65. Heidegger, "Self-Assertion of the German University," 32.

66. Heidegger, *Sein und Zeit*, GA 2, 395; Heidegger, *Being and Time*, 447.

67. Martin Heidegger, "Schlageter," in Wolin, *Heidegger Controversy*, 41.

68. Heidegger, *Logik als Frage nach dem Wesen der Sprache*, GA 38, 80–81.

69. Martin Heidegger, *Über Wesen und Begriff von Natur, Geschichte, und Staat*, in *Heidegger-Jahrbuch*, vol. 4 (Freiburg: Karl Alber, 2009), 81, 80.

70. Wilhelm Volz, "Lebensraum und Lebensrecht des deutschen Volkes," *Deutsche Arbeit* 24 (1925): 174.

71. Heidegger, *Natur, Geschichte, und Staat*, 79, 81.

72. Anne Harrington, *Reenchanted Science: Holism in German Culture from Wilhelm II to Hitler* (Princeton, NJ: Princeton University Press, 1995), 181.

73. Ibid.

74. Heidegger, *Natur, Geschichte, und Staat*, 81–82.

75. Heidegger, *Überlegungen II–VI*, GA 94, 124.

76. Karl Haushofer, *Grenzen in ihren Geographischen und politischen Bedeutung* (Berlin: Kurt Vowinckel, 1927), 98. For a discussion of Haushofer's book, see David Murphy, *Heroic Earth: Geopolitical Thought in Weimar Germany* (Kent, OH: Kent State University Press, 1997), 31–32.

77. Quoted in Richard Hennig and Leo Korholz, *Einführung in die Geopolitik* (Leipzig: Teubner, 1934), 48. For a treatment of the "law of expanding spaces," see Horace B. Davis, "Conservative Writers on Imperialism," *Science & Society* 18 (1954): 310–25.

78. Quoted in Murphy, *Heroic Earth*, 1.

79. Heidegger, *Natur, Geschichte, und Staat*, 79, 80.

80. Immanuel Kant, "Physical Geography," in *Natural Science*, ed. Eric Watkins (New York: Cambridge University Press, 2012), 434–679; Herder's thoughts on geography are contained in Books I and II of *Ideen zur Philosophie der Geschichte der Menschheit*, vol. 1 (Berlin: Aufbau, 1965), 13–46.

81. Geoffrey Parker, *Western Geopolitical Thought in the Twentieth Century* (New York: Routledge, 2015), 12.

82. Martin Heidegger to Fritz Heidegger, 2 March 1932, in *Heidegger und der Antisemitismus: Positionen im Widerstreit*, ed. Walter Homolka and Arnulf Heidegger (Freiburg: Herder, 2016), 27.

83. Woodruff Smith, *The Ideological Origins of Nazi Imperialism* (New York: Oxford University Press, 1986), 230.

84. Franz Neumann, *Behemoth: The Structure and Practice of National Socialism* (New York: Oxford University Press, 1942), 147.

85. Heidegger, *Überlegungen II–VI*, GA 94, 18.

86. Otto Pöggeler, "Heidegger, Nietzsche, and Politics," in *The Heidegger Case: On Philosophy and Politics*, ed. Tom Rockmore and Joseph Margolis (Philadelphia: Temple University Press, 1991), 133.

87. Carl Schmitt, *Der Begriff des Politischen* (Berlin: Duncker und Humblot, 1963), 67.

88. Heidegger, *Sein und Wahrheit*, GA 36/37, 90.

89. Schmitt, *Der Begriff des Politschen*, 46–47 (emphasis added).

90. See Ulrich Sieg, "Die Verjudung des deutschen Geistes," *Die Zeit* 52 (22 December 1989).

91. Heidegger, *Sein und Wahrheit*, GA 36/37, 90–91.

92. Adolf Hitler, "Wesen und Ziel des Nationalsozialismus," 3 July 1927, in *Reden, Schriften, Anordnungen*, ed. Bärbel Dusik (Munich: K. G. Saur, 1992), 2/1, 406.

93. As Holger Herwig shows in his biography of Haushofer, *Demon of Geopolitics: How Karl Haushofer "Educated" Hitler* (Lanham, MD: Rowman and Littlefield, 2016), under the Third Reich, Haushofer's upward career mobility was hampered by the fact that he had a Jewish wife, whom he refused to divorce.

94. Adolf Hitler, *Mein Kampf*, trans. Ralph Manheim (New York: Houghton Mifflin, 1943), 643.

95. Ibid., 653–54.

96. Heidegger, *Einführung in die Metaphysik*, GA 40, 41–42; Heidegger, *Introduction to Metaphysics*, 38.

97. Heidegger, *Einführung in die Metaphysik*, GA 40, 49; Heidegger, *Introduction to Metaphysics*, 46.

98. Martin Heidegger, "Hölderlin und das Wesen der Dichtung," in *Erläuterungen zu Hölderlins Dichtung*, GA 4 (Frankfurt: Klostermann, 1944), 44.

99. Heidegger, *Einführung in die Metaphysik*, GA 40, 180; Heidegger, *Introduction to Metaphysics*, 171.

100. Heidegger, *Einführung in die Metaphysik*, GA 40, 174; Heidegger, *Introduction to Metaphysics*, 157.

101. Heidegger, *Einführung in die Metaphysik*, GA 40, 66; Heidegger, *Introduction to Metaphysics*, 62 (emphasis added).

102. For a discussion of the distinctive combination of aesthetics, fundamental ontology, and "state-founding" in Heidegger's work, see Joseph Chytry, *The Aesthetic State: A Quest in Modern German Thought* (Berkeley: University of California Press, 1989), chap. 7, "Heidegger: Ontology and Anarchy," 371–408. For a critique of the romantic approach to state formation, see Carl Schmitt, *Political Romanticism*, trans. Guy Oakes (Cambridge, MA: MIT Press, 1988).

103. Heidegger, *Hölderlins Hymnen "Germanien" und "Der Rhein,"* GA 39, 120.

104. Minder, *Der Dichter in der Gesellschaft*, 250–51.

105. Alfred Baeumler, "Hellas und Germanien," in *Studien zur deutschen Geistesgeschichte* (Berlin: Junker und Dünnhaupt, 1937), 305.

106. Heidegger, *Hölderlins Hymnen "Germanien" und "Der Rhein,"* GA 39, 144.

107. Ibid., 74. See also Domenico Losurdo, *Heidegger and the Ideology of War: Community, Death, and the West,* trans. Marella Morris and John Morris (Amherst, NY: Humanity Books, 2001). That, in the apologetic literature on Heidegger, Losurdo's indispensable study is rarely cited I regard as further evidence of *Verdrängung* (repression) of Heidegger's "military nationalism."

108. Heidegger, *Hölderlins Hymnen "Germanien" und "Der Rhein,"* GA 39, 216, 214.

109. Ibid., 120.

110. Ibid., 163.

111. Manfred Frank, *Gott im Exil: Vorlesungen über einer neuen Mythologie* (Frankfurt: Suhrkamp, 1988), 105–7.

112. On this theme, see Robert Williamson, *The Longing for Myth in Germany: Religion and Aestheticism from Romanticism to Nietzsche* (Chicago: University of Chicago Press, 2004).

113. Heinrich Block, "Eurasien," *Zeitschrift für Geopolitik* 3 (1926): 15–16.

114. Hermann Lautensach, "Geopolitik und Schule," *Geographischer Anzeiger* 28 (1927): 342.

115. Martin Heidegger, *Vom Wesen der Wahrheit. Zu Platons Höhlengleichnis und Thäetet,* GA 34 (Frankfurt: Klostermann Verlag, 1988), 145 (emphasis added). Heidegger invokes the figure of a nation of "Dichter und Denker" in his *Parmenides* lectures of 1942–43, GA 54 (Frankfurt: Klostermann, 1982): "The more primordial Beginning," observes Heidegger, "like the First Beginning, can only be achieved by a Western-historical *Volk* of *Dichter und Denker*" (114).

116. Heidegger, *Überlegungen XII–XV,* GA 96, 235. For Heidegger's denigration of "Negroes" as "geschichtlos" (without history), see *Logik als Frage nach dem Wesen der Sprache,* GA 38, 81.

117. Friedrich Nietzsche, *Zur Genealogie der Moral,* KSA IV (Berlin: De Gruyter, 1980), 324–25 (emphasis added).

118. Heidegger, *Natur, Geschichte, und Staat,* 82.

119. Ibid.

120. Ibid.

121. Ibid. (emphasis added).

122. Ibid.

123. For a masterful account of German *Ostforschung,* see Michael Burleigh, *Germany Turns Eastwards: A Study of "Ostforschung" in the Third Reich* (Cambridge: Cambridge University Press, 1988).

124. Hitler, *Mein Kampf,* 642.

125. Ibid., 598.

126. Quoted in Jeffrey Herf, *Reactionary Modernism: Technology, Politics, and Culture in the Weimar Republic and the Third Reich* (New York: Cambridge University Press, 1984), 139.

127. Werner Sombart, *The Jews and Modern Economic Life,* trans. Mortimer Epstein (Kitchener, ON: Batoche Books, 2001), 240.

128. Quoted in Reginald Phelps, "Hitlers Grundlegende Rede über den Antisemitismus," *Vierteljahrshefte für Zeitgeschichte* 16 (1968): 14.

129. Heidegger, *Natur, Geschichte, und Staat*, 81.

130. Ibid., 82.

131. Sander L. Gilman, "Cosmopolitan Jews vs. Jewish Nomads," in *Heidegger's "Black Notebooks": Responses to Anti-Semitism*, ed. Andrew J. Mitchell and Peter Trawny (New York: Columbia University Press, 2015), 31.

132. Mosse, *Crisis of German Ideology*, 9.

133. Heidegger, *Überlegungen XII–XV*, GA 96, 67.

134. Harrington, *Reenchanted Science*, 181.

135. Heidegger, *Sein und Wahrheit*, GA 36/37, 91.

136. Heidegger, *Überlegungen VII–XI*, GA 95, 97.

137. Heidegger, *Die Grundbegriffe der Metaphysik*, GA 29–30, 262.

138. Martin Heidegger, "Die Weltlichkeit der Welt," in *Sein und Zeit*, GA 2, 85–151; Heidegger, "The Worldhood of the World," in *Being and Time*, 91–147.

139. Ibid.

140. Hitler, *Mein Kampf*, 649, 626, 140.

141. Heidegger, "Der Ursprung des Kunstwerkes," 8.

142. Heidegger, *Hölderlins Hymne "Germanien" und "Der Rhein,"* GA 39, 205.

143. Heidegger, *Logik als Frage nach dem Wesen der Sprache*, GA 38, 153.

144. On this point, see the invaluable study by Hubert Brunträger, *Der Ironiker und der Ideologe: Die Beziehungen zwischen Thomas Mann und Alfred Baeumler* (Würzburg: Königshausen und Neumann, 1993), 80. For Heidegger's engagement with Klages, Spengler, and Scheler, see "Four Interpretations of Our Contemporary Situation: The Opposition of Life (Soul) and Spirit in Oswald Spengler, Ludwig Klages, Max Scheler, and Leopold Ziegler," in *Die Grundbegriffe der Metaphysik*, GA 29–30, 103–7. For Scheler's role as a prominent advocate of *Zivilisationskritik*, see John Raphael Staude, *Max Scheler: An Intellectual Biography* (New York: Free Press, 1968). On Heidegger's relationship to the Stefan George-*Kreis*, see Francois Rastier, *Naufrage d'un prophète: Heidegger aujourd'hui* (Paris: Presses Universitaires de France, 2015).

145. Hans Vaihinger, "Der Mythos und das Al Ob: Ein Fragment" (1927), quoted in Philipp Teichfischer, *Die Masken des Philosophen: Alfred Baeumler in der Weimarer Republik* (Marburg: Techtum, 2009), 176.

146. For an excellent overview of these tendencies—an account that includes an insightful presentation of Heidegger's work—see Nitzan Lebovic, *The Philosophy of Life and Death: Ludwig Klages and the Rise of Nazi Biopolitics* (New York: Palgrave Macmillan, 2013).

147. Friedrich Nietzsche, *Das Geburt der Tragödie aus dem Geist der Musik*, in *Sämtliche Werke*, vol. 1 (Berlin: De Gruyter, 1988), 143.

148. See the discussion in Tobias Bevc, *Kulturgenese als Dialektik von Mythos und Vernunft: Ernst Cassirer und die Kritische Theorie* (Würzburg: Königshausen und Neumann, 2005), 159–61.

149. Mircea Eliade, *The Myth of the Eternal Return* (Princeton, NJ: Princeton University Press, 1954), ix. For a treatment of the political-ontological affinities between Eliade and Heidegger, see David Dubuisson, *Twentieth-Century Mythologies: Dumézil, Lévi-Strauss, and Eliade*, trans. Martha Cunningham (New York: Routledge, 2014), chap. 16, "Metaphysics and Politics: Heidegger and Eliade," 221–33. For a lucid discussion

of Eliade and political myth, see Robert Ellwood, *The Politics of Myth: C. G. Jung, Mircea Eliade, and Joseph Campbell* (Albany: SUNY Press, 1999), chap. 3, "Mircea Eliade and Nostalgia for the Sacred," 79–126. For Eliade's filiations with Corneliu Codreanu and the Legionnaire movement, see Florian Turcanu, *Mircea Eliade: Le Prisonnier de l'histoire* (Paris: La Découverte, 2003).

150. Ludwig Klages, *Vom kosmogonischen Eros* (Bonn: Bouvier, 1988), 179–80; for Heidegger's treatment of Klages, see *Die Grundbegriffe der Metaphysik*, 105–7.

151. Ernst Bloch, *The Heritage of Our Time*, trans. Neville Plaice and Stephen Plaice (Cambridge, MA: Polity, 1991). Bloch cites the following observation from Klages's three-volume opus *Geist als Widersacher der Seele*: "The earth is steaming with the blood of the slain as never before, and the ape-like element is flaunting the spoils from the smashed temple of life." According to Bloch, "while the first part of the sentence depicts capitalism plus murder, its conclusion illustrates . . . the telepathic theft where 'primeval souls' anticipate genuine ones, and Tarzan prototypes copy mystery" (316).

152. Günzel, *Geophilosophie*, 150–54.

153. Frank Edler, "Alfred Baeumler on Hölderlin and the Greeks: Reflections on the Heidegger-Baeumler Relationship," *Janus Head* 1 (1999), https://oajournals.blogspot.com/search?q=edler.

154. Immanuel Kant, *The Critique of Pure Reason*, trans. Paul Guyer and Allen Wood (New York: Cambridge University Press, 1998), 704.

155. Jeffrey Barash, "Ernst Cassirer, Martin Heidegger, and the Legacy of Davos," *History and Theory* 51 (2012): 444.

156. Martin Heidegger, "Review of Ernst Cassirer, *Mythical Thought*," in *Kant and the Problem of Metaphysics*, trans. Richard Taft (Bloomington: Indiana University Press, 1997), 180.

157. Martin Heidegger, *Kant und das Problem der Metaphysik*, GA 3 (Frankfurt: Klostermann, 1991), 245. Heidegger's Cassirer review originally appeared in the *Deutsche Literaturzeitung* 21 (1928): 1000–1012.

158. Heidegger, "Review of Ernst Cassirer, *Mythical Thought*," 188.

159. Ibid.

160. Ibid., 190.

161. Ibid.

162. Heidegger, *Sein und Wahrheit*, GA 36/37, 12 (emphasis added).

163. Heidegger, *Einführung in die Metaphysik*, GA 40, 164–65; Heidegger, *Introduction to Metaphysics*, 155.

164. Heidegger, *Überlegungen II–VI*, GA 94, 115.

165. Ibid., 124.

166. "Davos Disputation between Ernst Cassirer and Martin Heidegger," in Heidegger, *Kant and the Problem of Metaphysics*, 204.

167. Jeffrey Barash, "Ernst Cassirer's Theory of Myth," in *The Symbolic Construction of Reality: The Legacy of Ernst Cassirer*, ed. Barash (Chicago: University of Chicago Press, 2007), 115.

168. Ernst Cassirer, *Nachgelassene Manuskripte und Texte*, vol. 9 (Hamburg: Meiner, 2008), 167.

169. See Lebovic, *Philosophy of Life and Death*, 196.

170. Ernst Cassirer, *The Myth of the State* (New Haven, CT: Yale University Press, 1946), 284–85.

171. Emilio Gentile, *The Sacralization of Politics in Fascist Italy*, trans. Keith Botsford (Cambridge, MA: Harvard University Press, 1996). See also Stanley Payne, *The History of Fascism* (Madison: University of Wisconsin Press, 1967), 215.

172. Paul Simon, *Mythos oder Religion* (Paderborn: Druck und Verlag der Bonifacius-Druckerei, 1935), 111.

173. Quoted in Uriel Tal, "Political Faith of Nazism Prior to the Holocaust," in *Religion, Politics and Ideology in the Third Reich* (New York: Routledge, 2004), 21. For more on Simon, see Ulrich Lehner, "Das Menschliche an der Kirche Christi," *Theologie und Glaube* 106 (2016): 63–69.

174. Martin Heidegger, *Metaphysical Foundations of Logic*, trans. Michael Heim (Bloomington: Indiana University Press, 1984), 209 (emphasis added).

175. Otto Pöggeler, *Heidegger in seiner Zeit* (Munich: Wilhelm Fink, 1999), 127.

176. See Heidegger's comments on modernity as an age of "devitalization" (*Entlebung*), in *Zur Bestimmung der Philosophie*, GA 56/57, 88–89.

177. On the search for "holism" as a distinguishing feature of German "reactionary modernism," see Harrington, *Reenchanted Science*. Heidegger was keenly interested in the work of one of Germany's leading "holistic" biologists, Baron Jakob von Uexküll. In Heidegger's 1929–30 lecture course *Die Grundbegriffe der Metaphysik: Welt, Endlichkeit, Einsamkeit*, GA 29–30, Heidegger discussed Uexküll's work enthusiastically, lauding his vitalistic approach for having rescued biology from the discipline's prevailing mechanistic prejudices. Heidegger also praised Uexküll's exemplary, holistic understanding of "Umwelt," or of the integration of the animal within its environment: an understanding of nature in which the organism's "wholeness is not exhausted through the bodily wholeness of the animal, but rather the bodily wholeness is first itself understood on the basis of an original wholeness [with the environment]" (379–80). In *Reenchanted Science*, Harrington speculates that Heidegger's concept of "Being-in-the-world" may have derived from Uexküll's "Umwelt-Begriff." However, there is an additional connection between Uexküll and Heidegger: they served together on the *Ausschuss für Rechtsphilosophie*, a prestigious and ambitious subcommittee of Hans Frank's Academy of German Law.

178. Georg Lukács, *The Destruction of Reason*, trans. Peter Palmer (London: Merlin, 1980), 533.

179. Wilhelm Reich, *The Mass Psychology of Fascism*, trans. Vincent Carfagno (New York: Farrar, Strauss and Giroux, 1970), 76, 382.

180. On Mann's development, see Brunträger, *Der Ironiker und der Ideolog*.

181. Thomas Mann, *Reden und Aufsätze*, vol. 1 (Frankfurt: Suhrkamp Verlag, 1965), 470. Görres, known for his veneration of myth, was a leading figure of the Heidelberg school of Romanticism.

182. Alfred Bachofen, *Versuch über die Gräbersymbolik der Alten*, ed. Karl Albrecht Bernoulli and Ludwig Klages (Basel: Helbing und Lichterhahn, 1925).

183. Alfred Bachofen, *Mutterrecht*, quoted in Georg Dörr, *Muttermythos und Herrschaftsmythos* (Würzburg: Könighausen und Neumann, 2007), 55.

184. Robert Norton, *Secret Germany: Stefan George and His Circle* (Ithaca, NY: Cornell University Press, 2002), 296.

185. Bambach, *Heidegger's Roots*, 275–76.
186. The story is told in *Thomas Mann und Alfred Baeumler: Eine Dokumentation*, ed. Marianne Baeumler, Hubert Brunträger, and Hermann Kurzke (Würzburg: Königshausen und Neumann, 1989), 463. For a detailed account of the fate of the Marburg philosophy chair vacated by Heidegger, see Christian Tilitzki, *Deutsche Universitätsphilosophie in der Weimarer Republik und im dritten Reich*, vol. 1 (Berlin: Akademie Verlag, 2002), 185–94, 216–18, 545–91. For more on the relationship between Heidegger and Baeumler, see Rüdiger Safranski, *Martin Heidegger: Between Good and Evil*, trans. Ewald Osers (Cambridge, MA: Harvard University Press, 1999), 236–37.
187. See Martin Heidegger to Karl Jaspers, 3 November 1928, in *Briefwechsel, 1919–1963*, ed. Hans Saner (Munich: Piper Verlag, 1990), 95.
188. See Tilitzki, *Deutsche Universitätsphilosophie in der Weimarer Republik und im dritten Reich*, 589.
189. Alfred Baeumler to Manfred Schroeter, 4 May 1925, in *Thomas Mann und Alfred Baeumler*, 117.
190. Alfred Baeumler, "Nietzsche und Bachofen," *Neue Schweizer Rundschau* 28 (1928): 323–43; see Max Whyte, "The Uses and Abuses of History in the Third Reich: Alfred Baeumler's 'Heroic Realism,' " *Journal of Contemporary History* 43 (2008): 178.
191. Alfred Baeumler, "Nietzsche und der Nationalsozialismus," in *Nationalsozialistische Monatshefte* 5 (1934): 291, 294–95; reprinted in Baeumler, *Studien zur deutschen Geistesgeschichte* (Berlin: Junker und Dünnhaupt, 1943), 283–94.
192. Quoted in Tilitzki, *Deutsche Universitätsphilosophie in der Weimarer Republik und im dritten Reich*, 573.
193. Ibid., 574–75.
194. Friedrich Nietzsche, "The Use and Abuse of History," in *Untimely Meditations*, trans. R. J. Hollingdale (New York: Cambridge University Press, 1997), 75.
195. Edler, "Alfred Baeumler on Hölderlin and the Greeks." Heidegger's attraction to the "cult of dead heroes" was spurred by his reading of Werner Jaeger's essay *Tyrtaios über die wahre Aretē* (Berlin: De Gruyter, 1932); see my discussion of the Heidegger-Jaeger encounter in chapter 3.
196. Heidegger, "Self-Assertion of the German University," 32–33.
197. Martin Heidegger to Elisabeth Blochmann, 25 May 1932, in *Briefwechsel*, ed. Joachim Storch (Marbach: Deutsche Schillergesellschaft, 1990), 50.
198. Martin Heidegger to Werner Jaeger, 12 December 1932, quoted in Frank Edler, "Martin Heidegger and Werner Jaeger on the Eve of 1933," *Research in Phenomenology* 27 (1997): 123–25.
199. Heidegger, *Hölderlins Hymnen "Germanien" und "Der Rhein,"* GA 39, 164.
200. Bambach, *Heidegger's Roots*, 46.
201. Daniel Meyer, "Die Entdeckung des griechischen Mythos: Heideggers geschichtsphilosophische Wende," *Germanica* 45 (2010): 11.
202. Martin Heidegger to Elfride Heidegger, 19 March 1933, in *"Mein Liebes Seelchen,"* 186; Heidegger, *Überlegungen II–VI*, GA 94, 124.
203. Heidegger, *Hölderlins Hymnen "Germanien" und "Der Rhein,"* GA 39, 214, 220.
204. Heidegger, *Überlegungen XII–XV*, GA 96, 29. See my discussion of this theme in chapter 3.

205. Bambach, *Heidegger's Roots*, 230 (emphasis added).

206. Cassirer, *Myth of the State*, 279, 280.

207. Ibid., 280.

208. Ibid., 282.

209. Claude Lefort, *L'Invention démocratique* (Paris: Fayard, 1981), especially chap. 1, "Droits de l'homme et politique," 45–83.

210. Cassirer, *Myth of the State*, 283–84.

211. Hans Blumenberg, *The Legitimacy of the Modern Age*, trans. Robert M. Wallace (Cambridge, MA: MIT Press, 1986).

212. Jürgen Habermas, *Postmetaphysical Thinking*, trans. William Mark Hohengarten (Cambridge, MA: MIT Press, 1993), 42.

213. Heidegger, "Only a God Can Save Us," 96.

214. Hannah Arendt, "What Is Existential Philosophy?," in *Essays in Understanding, 1930–1954: Formation, Exile, Totalitarianism* (New York: Harcourt Brace, 1994), 178.

215. Ibid. A disagreement concerning the nature of "spontaneity" in Kant's *Critique of Pure Reason* was one of the key elements of dissensus in the Cassirer-Heidegger debate at Davos.

216. Martin Heidegger, "Letter on Humanism," in *Basic Writings*, trans. David Krell (New York: Harper and Row, 1979), 234.

217. Karl Jaspers, "Letter to the Freiburg University Denazification Committee, December 22, 1945," in Wolin, *Heidegger Controversy*, 149.

Chapter 6. From Beyond the Grave

1. Dominique Venner, "Les Manifestants du 26 mai et Heidegger," Dominique Venner's website, accessed 25 June 2020, http://www.dominiquevenner.fr/.

2. Alain Ruscio, "Dominique Venner, une 'tête pensante' du fascisme français," *Histoire Coloniale et Postcoloniale*, 22 May 2013, https://histoirecoloniale.net/Dominique-Venner-une-tete-pensante.html. According to a news report that surfaced in 2017, *Camp of the Saints* was also one of Steve Bannon's favorite books. See Sarah Jones, "The Notorious Book That Ties the Right to the Far-Right," *New Republic Daily*, 2 February 2018.

3. Jean-Marie Le Pen, *Les Français d'abord* (Paris: M. Lafont, 1984), 181.

4. See Nicholas Goodrick-Clarke, *Black Sun: Aryan Cults, Esoteric Nazism, and the Politics of Identity* (New York: NYU Press, 2002). The symbol of the *Schwarze Sonne* adorned the SS Ordensburg at Schloss Wewelsburg. Goodrick-Clarke remarks on its currency among neo-Nazi cults (149–50). For example, in 1992, it became the logo for the Thule-Seminar website, Thule-Netz. (The Thule-Seminar—founded by Pierre Krebs in 1980 and a namesake of Rudolf von Sebottendorf's Munich-based Thule-Gesellschaft—was a leading organ of the German Neue Rechte.)

5. Tim Arago, "Minutes before El Paso Killing, Hate-Filled Manifesto Appears Online," *New York Times*, 3 August 2019.

6. Adam Bhala Lough's documentary *Alt-Right: Age of Rage* (Gravitas Ventures, 2018) reproduces Spencer's infamous reenactment of the Nazi "Hitler *Gruß*."

7. George Hawley, *Making Sense of the Alt-Right* (New York: Columbia University Press, 2018), 61.

8. Venner, "Les Manifestants du 26 mai et Heidegger."

9. Alain de Benoist, *Comment peut-on être païen?* (Paris: Albin Michel, 1981). On de Benoist, see Tamir Bar-On, *Where Have All the Fascists Gone?* (New York: Routledge, 2008).

10. Venner, "Les Manifestants du 26 mai et Heidegger."

11. Dominique Venner, *Un Samourai de l'occident: Le Bréviaire des insoumis* (Paris: Éditions Pierre Guillaume de Roux, 2013). See Heinrich Himmler, foreword to *Die Samurai: Ritter des Reiches in Ehre und Treue*, by Heinz Corazza (Berlin: Franz Eher Verlag, 1936). See also Gerhard Krebs, "German Perspectives on Japanese Heroism during the Nazi Era," in *Mutual Perceptions and Images in Japanese-German Relations, 1860–2010*, ed. Sven Saaler, Kudō Akira, and Tajima Nobuo (Leiden: Brill, 2017), 327–48.

12. Dominique Venner, "Qu'est-ce que le nationalisme?," *Europe-Action* (May 1963), 5. See also Joseph Algazy, *La Tentation néo-fasciste en France: 1944–1965* (Paris: Fayard, 1984), 269.

13. See Aristotle Kallis, "The Construction of a Negative Mega-Narrative: The 'Jewish-Bolshevik-Plutocratic Alliance,' " in *Nazi Propaganda and the Second World War* (Basingstoke, UK: Palgrave Macmillan, 2005), 83–92.

14. For a statistically based, edifying refutation of "population replacement" hysteria, see Frédéric Lemaître, "Un Pamphlet suscite un débat sur l'islam," *Le Monde*, 3 September 2010; see also Christian Geyer, "Thilo Sarrazin rend l'Allemagne plus bête," *Frankfurter Allgemeine Zeitung*, 9 Septembre 2010.

15. See Ruth Wodak, *The Politics of Fear: The Shameless Normalization of Far-Right Discourse* (Los Angeles: Sage, 2020).

16. Roger Griffin, "Plus ça change: The Fascist Pedigree of the Nouvelle Droite," in *The Development of the Radical Right in France: From Boulanger to Le Pen*, ed. Edward Arnold (Basingstoke, UK: Palgrave Macmillan, 2000), 241.

17. Oswald Spengler, *Jahre der Entscheidung* (Munich: Beck Verlag, 1933), 104.

18. Martin Heidegger, *Logik als Frage nach dem Wesen der Sprache*, GA 38 (Frankfurt: Klostermann, 1998), 84. On the fraternal ties between Mussolini and Hitler, see Volker Weiß, "Mussolini und Hitler: Brüder im Geist," *Die Zeit*, 17 August 2013. See also Christian Goeschel, *Mussolini and Hitler: The Forging of the Fascist Alliance* (New Haven, CT: Yale University Press, 2018).

19. Alain de Benoist, "La Révolution conservatrice," *Éléments* 20 (1977): 3.

20. Armin Mohler, "Wir feine Konservativen," in *Vergangenheitsbewältigung, oder wie man den Krieg nochmals verliert* (Krefeld: Sinus Verlag, 1980), 91–103. See also Karlheinz Weißmann, *Armin Mohler: Eine politische Biographie* (Schellroda: Edition Antaios, 2011), 181. During the 1950s, Mohler, who wrote a *Habilitationsschrift* under Karl Jaspers's supervision at the University of Basel in 1950, served as Ernst Jünger's personal secretary. After meeting Alain de Benoist, Mohler served on the editorial board of the Nouvelle Droite journal, *Nouvelle École*.

21. Pierre-André Taguieff, "La Stratégie culturelle de la Nouvelle Droite en France," in *Vous avez dit fascismes?*, ed. Antoine Spire (Paris: Editions Montalba, 1984), 20.

22. Samuel Salzborn, "Renaissance of the New Right in Germany? A Discussion of New Right Elements in German Right-Wing Extremism Today," *German Politics and Society* 34 (2016): 37.

23. Other Grècistes who joined the National Front ranks are Jean-Claude Bardet, Jean-Jacques Moureau, and Pierre Vial. See the discussion in Pierre-André Taguieff, *Sur la Nouvelle Droite* (Paris: Descartes and Cie, 1994), 284. In *Visages de la Nouvelle Droite: Le GRECE et son histoire* (Paris: Presses de la Fondation Nationale des Sciences Politiques, 1988), Anne-Marie Duranton-Crabol shows that, during the 1970s, the Grècistes practiced another form of "entrisme," advising several influential members of French President Valéry Giscard d'Estaing's entourage (125–27).

24. See Timothy McCulloch, "The Nouvelle Droite in the 1980s and 1990s: Ideology and Entryism, the Relationship with the Front National," *French Politics* 4 (2006): 158–59. According to McCulloch, "Bruno Mégret was delegate general in charge of party studies, propaganda, training, and communication, while Yvan Blot was the personal adviser of Jean-Marie Le Pen." See also Ariane Chebel d'Appollonia, *L'Extrème Droite en France: De Maurras à Le Pen* (Brussels: Editions Complexe, 1994), 335–39.

25. Fabrice Laroche (pseudonym for Alain de Benoist) and Gilles Fournier, *Verité pour l'Afrique de Sud* (Paris: Editions Saint Just, 1965).

26. Pierre-André Taguieff, "The New Cultural Racism in France," *Telos* 98–99 (1993–94), 111, 116–17.

27. Michael O'Meara, *New Culture, New Right: Anti-Liberalism in Postmodern Europe* (Budapest: Arktos, 2014), 144.

28. Joakim Andersen, *Rising from the Ruins: The Right of the 21st Century*, trans. Gustav Hörngren (London: Arktos, 2018), 93.

29. Samuel Salzborn, *Angriff der Antidemokraten: Die völkische Rebellion der Neuen Rechten* (Weinheim and Munich: Juventa Verlag, 2017), 39.

30. Charles Clover, *Black Wind, White Snow: The Rise of Russia's New Nationalism* (New Haven, CT: Yale University Press, 2016), 262.

31. Taguieff, *Sur la nouvelle droite*, 23–24.

32. Quoted in Tamir Bar-On, "Fascism to the Nouvelle Droite: The Dream of Pan-European Empire," *Journal of Contemporary European Studies* 16 (2008): 340; see Alain de Benoist (writing under the pseudonym Robert de Herte), "La stratégie de l'attention," *Eléments* 33 (1980): 2; and Guillaume Faye, "La Société multiraciale en question," *Eléments* 48–49 (1983–84): 76. In a similar vein, one of de Benoist's ideological allies, Michael O'Meara, claims that "the culture fostered by liberal market societies [is] 'ethnocidal' " (*New Culture, New Right*, 51).

33. See de Benoist, *Beyond Human Rights: Defending Freedoms* (London: Arktos, 2011).

34. Alain de Benoist, *Mémoire vive: Entretiens avec François Bousquet* (Paris: Éditions du Fallois, 2012), 311.

35. Chetan Bhatt, " 'White Extinction': Metaphysical Influences in Contemporary Western Fascism," *Theory, Culture, and Society* 38 (2021): 7.

36. Griffin, "Plus ça change," 240, 248.

37. See Pierre-André Taguieff, "L'Héritage nazi: Des nouvelles droites européennes à la littérature niant le génocide," *Les Nouveaux cahiers* 64 (1981): 9. On the Nouvelle Droite's

support for Holocaust denial, see Valérie Igounet, *L'Histoire du négationnisme* (Paris: Seuil, 2000), 161–80.

38. Bar-On, "Fascism to the Nouvelle Droite," 340.

39. Arjun Appadurai, "Democracy Fatigue," in *The Great Regression*, ed. Heinrich Geiselberger (Cambridge, UK: Polity, 2017), 1.

40. Samuel Huntington, *The Third Wave: Democratization in the Late Twentieth Century* (Norman: University of Oklahoma Press, 1991). According to Huntington's periodization, the "first wave" of democratization coincided with the democratic revolutions of the eighteenth century, the "second wave" took place with the collapse of the central European monarchies following World War I, and the "third wave" emerged during the mid-1970s with the democratic transitions in Portugal and Spain.

41. Günter Frankenburg, *Autoritärismus: Verfassungstheoretische Perspektiven* (Frankfurt: Suhrkamp, 2020), 18.

42. Csaba Tóth, "Full Text of Viktor Orbán's Speech at Băile Tuşnad (Tusnádfürdő) of 26 July 2014," *Budapest Beacon*, 29 July 2014, https://budapestbeacon.com/full-text-of-viktor-orbans-speech-at-baile-tusnad-tusnadfurdo-of-26-july-2014/.

43. Stuart Hall, *The Fateful Triangle: Race, Nation, Ethnicity*, ed. Kobena Mercer (Cambridge, MA: Harvard University Press, 2017), 33.

44. D'Appollonia, *L'Extrème Droite en France*, 334.

45. Jean-Marie Vincent, "Pourquoi l'extrême droite?," *Les Temps Modernes* 465 (1985): 1777.

46. Quoted in Dan Stone, *Goodbye to All That: A History of Europe Since 1945* (New York: Oxford University Press, 2014), 191.

47. Jean-Marie Le Pen, "Notre famille est de bonne race!," *Le Point* 2534 (3 June 2012).

48. Marine Le Pen, interview with David Pujadas on *L'Émission Politique*, France 2, 9 February 2017, http://www.non-stop-zapping.com/actu/tv/marine-le-pen-agacee-par-david-pujadas-dans-lemission-politique-elle-replique-sechement.

49. Quoted in *Le Monde*, 22 May 2013: "Tout notre respect à Dominique Venner dont le dernier geste, éminemment politique, aura été de tenter de réveiller le peuple de France. MLP."

50. Julian Göpffarth, "Rethinking the German Nation as German Dasein: Intellectuals and Heidegger's Philosophy in Contemporary German New Right Nationalism," *Journal of Political Ideologies* 25 (2020): 248–73. See also Ronald Beiner, *Dangerous Minds: Nietzsche and Heidegger and the Return of the Far Right* (Philadelphia: University of Pennsylvania Press, 2018), 67–69.

51. See Mathilde Forestier, "Die identitäre Bewegung in Frankreich: Ein Porträt," *Journal EXIT Deutschland* 3 (2014): 117–47. See also Jakob Bruns, Kathrin Glösel, and Natascha Strobl, eds., *Die Identitären: Handbuch zur Jugendbewegung der Neuen Rechten in Europa* (Munich: Unrast Verlag, 2016). Heidegger discusses the "Wir-Frage" (the We-Question) in section 12 of *Logik als Frage nach dem Wesen der Sprache*, GA 38, "Das Selbst und die Selbstverlorenheit," 48–56. After posing the "Wir-Frage" in terms of the problem of "self-loss" (*Selbstverlorenheit*), he adumbrates a "solution" in the following section, "Wir sind das Volk kraft der Entscheidung" (We are *das Volk* by virtue of the power of decision). Heidegger claimed that "self-loss" is overcome and the "We-Question" resolved once the *Volk* succeeds in "choosing itself."

52. Martin Sellner and Walter Spatz, *Gelassen in den Widerstand: Ein Gespräch über Heidegger* (Schnellroda: Antaios Verlag, 2015), 49.

53. Alexander Dugin, *Eurasian Mission: An Introduction to Neo-Eurasianism* (London: Arktos, 2014), 21.

54. Sellner and Spatz, *Gelassen in den Widerstand*, 32.

55. Martin Sellner, "Mein Denkweg zu Heidegger," *Sezession* 64 (February 2015): 11.

56. See Micha Brumlik, "Das alte Denken der Neuen Rechte," *Blätter für deutsche und internationale Politik* 3 (2016): 82.

57. "Lutz Bachmann muss wegen Volksverhetzung zahlen," *Handelsblatt*, 3 May 2016. See Ralf Havertz, *Radical-Right Populism in Germany: AfD, Pegida, and the Identitarian Movement* (New York: Routledge, 2021).

58. Martin Lichtmesz, *Kann nur ein Gott uns retten? Glauben, Hoffen, Standhalten* (Schnellroda: Antaios Verlag, 2014).

59. Andreas Speit, "Reaktionärer Klan: Die Entwicklung der Identitären Bewegung in Deutschland," in *Das Netzwerk der Identitären: Ideologie und Aktions der Neuen Rechten*, ed. Speit (Berlin: Ch. Links Verlag, 2019), 19.

60. Erik Lehnert, "Martin Heideggers 'Schwarze Hefte,' " *Sezession* 25 (June 2014), 50–51. For fifteen years, Lehnert has been a ubiquitous presence in Neue Rechte circles. In 2008, he became the chief financial officer of the Institut für Staatspolitik (IfS). He serves on the editorial board of *Sezession* and is a member of the editorial committee of Antaios Verlag, the Neue Rechte publishing house that is formally allied with the IfS and *Sezession*. Since 2018, Lehnert also worked in the Bundestag, or German Federal Parliament, as an adviser to Harald Weyel, an AfD delegate from North Rhine-Westphalia.

61. Pierre Krebs, "Unser inneres Reich," in *Mut zur Identität*, ed. Krebs (Struckum: Verlag für Ganzheitliche Forschung und Kultur, 1988), 25.

62. Since German reunification, the *Frankfurter Allgemeine Zeitung* had engaged in a controversial campaign to rehabilitate conservative revolutionary eminences such as Heidegger, Carl Schmitt, and Ernst Jünger, a development that suggested troubling parallels between the *FAZ* and the Neue Rechte agenda. See John Ely, "The 'Frankfurter Allgemeine Zeitung' and Contemporary National Conservatism," *German Politics and Society* 13 (1995): 81–121; Elliot Neaman, "A New Conservative Revolution? Neonationalism, Collective Memory, and the New Right in Germany Since Unification," in *Antisemitism and Xenophobia in Germany after Unification*, ed. Hermann Kurthen, Werner Bergmann, and Rainer Erb (New York: Oxford University Press, 1997), 190–209; and Jay Julian Rossellini, *Literary Skinheads: Writing from the Right in Reunified Germany* (West Lafayette, IN: Purdue University Press, 2000).

63. Lehnert quoted in Ellen Kositza and Götz Kubitschek, introduction to *Tristesse Droite: Die Abende von Schnellroda*, ed. Kositza and Kubitschek (Schnellroda: IfS, 2015), 26; "Kriminelle Akte," interview with Karlheinz Weißmann, *Junge Freiheit* 36 (31 August 2001): 3.

64. For a helpful account, see Tobias Adler-Bartels, "Der radikale Konservatismus und die offene Gesellschaft: Der Kulturkampf um die Identität der *Berliner Republik*," in *Offene oder geschlossene Kollektividentität*, ed. Yves Bizeul, Ludmila Lutz-Auras, and Jan Rohgalf (Berlin: Springer Verlag, 2019), 61–86. Also see Volker Weiß, "Die konservative Revolution; Geistiger Erinnerungsort der 'Neuen Rechte,' " in *Erinnerungsorte der*

extremen Rechten, ed. Martin Langebach and Michael Sturm (Wiesbaden: Springer Verlag, 2015), 101–20.

65. Heimo Schwilk and Ulrich Schacht, introduction to *Die Selbstbewusste Nation: "Anschwellender Bocksgesang" und weitere Beiträge zu einer deutschen Debatte*, ed. Schwilk and Schacht (Berlin: Ullstein, 1994), 14–15.

66. Gerd Bergfleth, "Erde und Heimat," in Schwilk and Schacht, *Die Selbstbewusste Nation*, 101–23. Bergfleth saddled the Frankfurt School and Jewish intellectuals with responsibility for postwar Germany's *Heimatsverlust*, insofar as the "remigrants" purportedly favored a culture that was *"heimatsfremd*, devoid of origins and roots, enlightened, intellectualized, and cynical" (106).

67. Karlheinz Weißmann, "Der Nationalsozialismus war eine genuin linke Idee: Karlheinz Weißmann im Gespräch mit Peter Krause und Dieter Stein," *Junge Freiheit* 36 (28 August 1998): 4.

68. Roger Woods, *Germany's New Right as Culture and as Politics* (Basingstoke, UK: Palgrave Macmillan 2007), 83. This sentiment is echoed by Salzborn in *Angriff der Antidemokraten*: "The New Right's ideational-historical points of reference are those Weimar-era intellectuals who furnished the ideological basis for National Socialism: Arthur Moeller van den Bruck, Oswald Spengler, Othmar Spann [and] Martin Heidegger" (39).

69. "Gelassen in Widerstand: Martin Sellner und Heidegger," *Sezession im Netz*, 1 January 2016. The allusion to "secret Europe" plays on the doctrine of "secret Germany" that was integral to the credo of the Stefan George-*Kreis*. Although George himself died in December 1933—ten months after the Nazi *Machtergreifung*—his glorification of "geistige Führertum" in poetry collections such as *Der siebente Ring* and *Das innere Reich* bore ideological affinities with the National Socialist worldview. Following George's death, several of his closest disciples—e.g., the classics scholar Kurt Hildebrandt—boarded the Nazi bandwagon.

70. Eichberg discusses his initial encounter with de Benoist in Matthias Brodkorb, "Über Habitus, Ideologie, und Praxis: Im Gespräch mit Henning Eichberg," *Endstation Rechts*, 5 June 2010, http://www.endstation-rechts.de/news/ueber-habitus-ideologie-und-praxis-im-gespraech-mit-henning-eichberg-teil-1.html. See also the informative account of their meeting in Darius Harwardt, *Verehrter Feind: Amerikabilder deutscher Rechsintellecktueller in der Bundesrepublik* (Frankfurt: Campus, 2019), 197–99.

71. Volkmar Wölk, "Der gescheiterte Aufstieg," *Der Rechte Rand* 157 (2015): 10; Volker Weiß, *Die autoritäre Revolte: Die Neue Rechte und der Untergang des Abendlandes* (Stuttgart: Klett Cotta, 2017), 30–31. See Alain de Benoist, "Sur la Nouvelle Droite Allemande," *Éléments* 86 (October 1996); and Thomas Assheuer's observations on the important role that Nouvelle Droite figures such as de Benoist played in the genesis of the Neue Rechte worldview, in "Neue Rechte: Germanische Thing-Zirkel," *Die Zeit* 14 (1 April 2018): "The Neue Rechte . . . established the Thule-*Kreis* and journals like *Criticón*; and later, during the late 1980s, they created their own weekly. . . . They begin describing the Germans as an 'oppressed' *Volk*, which before long would disappear into the European Union. Armin Mohler's disciples study the books of the French philosopher Alain de Benoist in order to effectuate a 'right-wing counterrevolution.' They attack liberalism at its weakest point: social atomization and 'lonely' individuals."

72. See Stefan Goeritz, *Rechtsextremismus und Rechtsterrorismus in Deutschland: Eine analytische Einführung für Polizei und das Sicherheitsbehörde* (Hilden: Verlag Deutsche Polizeiliteratur, 2021), 72–73. See also "Verbindungen der extrem rechten 'Identitären' in Deutschland und Österreich," Drucksache 19/32632, 1 October 2021, https://dserver. bundestag.de; "Verfassungsschutz stuft Compact-Magazin als rechtsextremistisch ein," *Der Tagesspiegel*, 12 October 2021.

73. Studienzentrum Weikersheim was founded in 1979 by the CDU politician Hans Filbinger. Filbinger was forced to resign his position as minister-president of Baden-Württemberg in 1978 when it came to light that, during the final months of World War II, he handed down summary death sentences to opponents of National Socialism. See Volker Weiß, *Deutschlands Neue Rechte: Angriff der Eliten* (Paderborn: Ferdinand Schöningh, 2012), 41–42.

74. See Eckhard Fuhr, "Konservative Spontis attackieren Günter Grass," *Die Welt*, 9 September 2008.

75. Julian Bruns, Kathrin Glösel, and Natascha Strobl, introduction to *Die Identitären*, 11.

76. Helmut Kellershohn, "Volk, Staat und Nation: Konturen des völkischen Nationalismus in der 'Jungen Freiheit,'" in *Die Wochenzeitung "Junge Freiheit": Kritische Analysen zu Programmatik, Inhalten, Autoren, und Kunden,* ed. Stephan Braun and Ute Vogt (Wiesbaden: VS Verlag für Sozialwissenschaften, 2007), 106.

77. Weiß, *Die autoritäre Revolte*, 26. As an example of the shift to the right on the part of Germany's so-called C parties, the CSU party chief and interior minister Horst Seehofer proposed reintroducing the notion of *Heimat*, despite its checkered legacy, as a national rallying cry to replace *Leitkultur* and *Nation*. See his commentary in the *Frankfurter Allgemeine Zeitung*, "Warum Heimatverlust die Menschen so umtreibt," 29 April 2018. Seehofer's detractors have complained, understandably, that the concept is laden with racist and xenophobic connotations. See, for example, the article that appeared in the *Stuttgarter Zeitung*, "Heimat ist eindeutig weiß, christlich und männlich," 28 March 2018. In the article "Horst Seehofer: Heimat, wie er sie sieht" (3 May 2018), the *Die Zeit* author Ferdinand Ott commented that the aim of Seehofer's *Heimat* mania was to restore a type of "blond and blue-eyed cultural hegemony." That Seehofer has been an outspoken critic of the refugees from the Middle East, who, according to the *Grundgesetz*, or German constitution, are legal asylum seekers, provides legitimate grounds for such concerns.

78. Dieter Stein and Moritz Schwarz, "Interview mit Jörg Schönbohm," *Junge Freiheit* 47 (7 February 2003). For the *Junge Freiheit*'s circulation increase, see Statista, "Verkaufte Auflage der Wochenzeitung Junge Freihet vom 3. Quartal 2013 bis zum 3. Quartal 2021," accessed 25 March 2021, https://de.statista.com/statistik/daten/studie/1248368/ umfrage/verkaufte-auflage-der-jungen-freiheit/.

79. Many of these themes had already surfaced, to great controversy and fanfare, in Thilo Sarrazin's *succès de scandale Deutschland schafft sich ab: Wie Wir unser Land aufs Spiel setzen* (Munich: Deutsche Verlags-Anstalt, 2010), which sold over one million copies. See Götz Kubitschek and Karlheinz Weißmann, *Sarrazin lesen: Was steckt in "Deutschland schafft sich ab"* (Schnellroda: Sezession, 2010).

80. See the exchange of letters between Kubitschek and Armin Nassehi in the appendix to Armin Nassehi, *Die letzte Stunde der Wahrheit* (Hamburg: Murman Verlag, 2015), 329.

81. Heidegger, *Logik als die Frage nach dem Wesen der Sprache*, GA 38, 55. Posing the question, "Who are we *really*? [*Wer sind wir selbst?*]," Heidegger responded that we realize ourselves through "the will of a state . . .: the *will-to-domination* [*Herrschaftswille*] and *form-of-domination* [*Herrschaftsform*] of a *Volk* over itself. In the form of *Dasein*, we insert ourselves . . . into belonging-to-the-*Volk* [*Zugehörigkeit zum Volk*], we stand in the *Being of the Volk*, we are this *Volk* itself" (77).

82. Sellner and Spatz, *Gelassen in den Widerstand*, 20.

83. Ibid.

84. Ibid., 28, 25. The endorsement of ethnic identity and national chauvinism that one finds in *Gelassen in den Widerstand* was already a central theme of Neue Rechte discourse following the *Wende* (Turn) of 1989–90. See, for example, Schwilk and Schacht, *Die Selbstbewusste Nation*.

85. For an excellent overview, see Richard I. Cohen, "The 'Wandering Jew' from Medieval Legend to Modern Metaphor," in *The Art of Being Jewish in Modern Times*, ed. Barbara Kirschenblatt-Gimblett and Jonathan Karp (Philadelphia: University of Pennsylvania Press, 2008), 147–77.

86. Martin Heidegger, *Überlegungen XII–XV*, GA 96 (Frankfurt: Klostermann Verlag): "Eine der verstecktesten Gestalten des Riesigen und vielleicht die älteste [ist] die Zähe Geschicklichkeit des Rechnens und Schiebens und Durcheinandermischens, wodurch die Weltlosigkeit des Judentums gegründet wird" (67).

87. Sellner and Spatz, *Gelassen in den Widerstand*, 39. On German anti-Americanism, see Dan Diner, *America in the Eyes of the Germans: An Essay on Anti-Americanism*, trans. Allison Brown (Princeton, NJ: Markus Wiener, 2002).

88. Sellner and Spatz, *Gelassen in den Widerstand*, 38, 51, 37, 47. In *Deutschlands Neue Rechte*, Volker Weiß provides a lucid discussion of the integral relationship between *Kulturpessimismus* and conservative revolutionary *Denken*.

89. See Klaus Weber, "Salonfaschisten: Über die reaktionäre Ideologie des Philosophen Peter Sloterdijk und seines AfD-Schülers Marc Jongen," *Junge Welt*, 27 October 2020; Göpffarth, "Rethinking the German Nation as German Dasein," 253.

90. Marc Jongen, *Die Weltwoche* 19 (12 May 2016): 60.

91. Ibid.

92. Marc Jongen, "Migration und Thymos-Training," presentation at the IfS, 17 February 2017, available on YouTube: https://www.youtube.com/watch?v=cg_KuESI7rY (accessed 6 July 2020).

93. Heidegger, *Logik als Frage nach dem Wesen der Sprache*, GA 38, 19.

94. See Ijoma Mangold, "Alexander Gauland: Spiel mit der Schuld," *Die Zeit* 24 (7 June 2018), https://www.zeit.de/2018/24/alexander-gauland-afd-vergangenheitsrevision-rechtspopulismus.

95. "Acht Zitate zeigen, wie gefährlich der AfD-Rechtsaußen wirklich ist," *Focus On-Line*, 24 January 2017.

96. Björn Höcke, *Nie zweimal in denselben Fluss* (Ludwighausen and Berlin: Manuskriptum Verlagsbuchhandlung, 2018), 47.

97. Quoted in Justus Binder and Reinhard Bingener, "Das wird man wohl noch aushalten dürfen," *Frankfurter Allgemeine Zeitung*, 11 November 2015: " 'Wir müssen als Deutsche fragen, wer wir sind,' sagt er. 'Wir brauchen ein Ja zum Wir.' Das deutsche Volk müsse sich von der 'Zeitgeistmatrix' lösen, es müsse aus seiner 'Seinsvergessenheit' heraustreten und stattdessen wieder seiner 'Seinsordnung' näherkommen. 'Ja, das ist Heidegger.' " Also see Pascal Zorn, "Höcke und Heidegger," *Hohe Luft*, 3 December 2015, https://www.hoheluftmagazin.de/2015/12/hoecke-und-heidegger/.

98. Volker Zastrow, "AfD: Die neue völkische Bewegung," faz.net, 11 November 2015; https://www.faz.net/aktuell/politik/inland/afd-die-neue-voelkische-bewegung-13937439.html.

99. Claus Leggewie, *Anti-Europäer: Breivik, Dugin, al-Suri & Co.* (Frankfurt: Suhrkamp Verlag, 2017), 45. Leggewie's fears would seem to be confirmed by the recent controversy over the "manhunts" against immigrants and foreigners in the course of the far-right demonstrations in Chemnitz and elsewhere. See "Chemnitz und die Folgen: Die Deutungsschlacht," *Die Zeit* 38, 13 September 2018.

100. Thomas Assheuer, "Neue Rechte: Germanische Thing-Zirkel," *Die Zeit* 14 (1 April 2018), https://www.zeit.de/2018/14/neue-rechte-nationalismus-konservatismus-zirkel.

101. Martin Sellner, "Gelassen in den Widerstand," interview, *Sezession*, 1 January 2016.

102. See Jason Wilson, "Christchurch Shooter's Links to Austrian Far Right 'More Extensive than Thought,' " *Guardian*, 15 May 2019. On the Austrian "Symbolgesetz," see Jüdisches Forum für Demokratie und gegen Antisemitismus, "Die Identitäre Bewegung und ihre 'Demonstration gegen das Symbolgesetz' am 31 Juli 2021 in Wien," 3 August 2021, https://www.jfda.de/post/die-identit%C3%A4re-bewegung-und-ihre-demonstration-gegen-das-symbolgesetz-am-31-juli-2021-in-wien.

103. See Sabine am Orde, "Entscheidung des Verfassungsschutzes: Der 'Flügel' ist rechtsextrem," *Taz*, 12 March 2020, https://taz.de/Entscheidung-des-Verfassungsschutzes/!5671396/.

104. "Institut Kubitschek unter Verdacht: Im Verfassungsschutz-Visier," *Taz*, 23 April 2020; Wolfgang Wiedemann-Schmidt, "Der AfD und der Verfassungsschutz in den Abgrund," *Der Spiegel*, 4 March 2021.

105. Andreas Umland, "Aleksandr Dugin's Transformation from a Lunatic Fringe Figure to a Mainstream Political Publicist, 1890–1998: A Case Study in the Rise of Late and Post-Soviet Russian Fascism," *Journal of Eurasian Studies* 1 (2010): 146.

106. A translation of Dugin's article, "Fascism: Borderless and Red," may be found in Andreas Umland, "Fascist Tendencies in Russia's Political Establishment: The Rise of the International Eurasian Movement," History Network, 29 May 2009, https://historynewsnetwork.org/article/88134; the article was originally available on Dugin's website, http://arcto.ru/, but has been taken down along with other English translations of key texts from the 1990s—"Conservative Revolution: The Third Way" (1991) and "The Metaphysics of National Bolshevism" (1997)—that attest to Dugin's fascist affinities and predilections. As Umland points out in "Fascist Tendencies in Russia's Political Establishment," "Throughout the 1990s, Dugin repeatedly eulogized, in disguised or open form, inter-war European and contemporary Russian fascism." However, since his rise to political prominence, he has, "for obvious reasons, been eager to disassociate himself

from German Nazism, at times strongly condemning Hitler's crimes, and now often introduces himself as an 'anti-fascist.'"

107. Heidegger, *Überlegungen XII–XV*, GA 96, 57.

108. Andersen, *Rising from the Ruins*, 93.

109. Alexander Dugin, *Political Platonism: The Philosophy of Politics*, trans. Michael Millerman and Ciarán Ó Conaill (London: Arktos, 2019), 87–88.

110. Ibid. *Political Platonism* is littered with Heidegger references, including extended discussions of "the *Volk* as Dasein," "the existential structure of the *Volk*," and "the project of authentic society: the existential empire."

111. See, for example, Anton Shekhovtsov, "Putin's Brain," *Eurozine*, September 2014; see also Robert Zubrin, "Putin's Rasputin: Meet Aleksandr Dugin, the Mystical High Priest of Russian Fascism Who Wants to Bring about the End of the World," *Skeptic* 20 (2015): 21; Julia Smirnova, "Putins Vordenker: Ein rechtsradialer Guru," *Die Welt*, 11 July 2014; As Veronika Dorman pointed out in *Libération*, "Alexandre Douguine: chantre de l'eurasisme anti-américain en Russie" (27 April 2014), during the Ukraine crisis, Dugin's influence was especially noticeable in the case of two key Putin advisers: the economist Sergei Glazyov and the president of the Russian Duma Sergei Narychkin.

112. See John Dunlop, "Aleksandr Dugin's *Foundations of Geopolitics*," *Demokratizatsiya* 12 (2004): 43–44.

113. Leggewie, *Anti-Europäer*, 62. For Putin's support for the idea of "Greater Russia," see Marlene Laruelle, "The Three Colors of Novorossiya, or the Russian Nationalist Mythmaking of the Ukrainian Crisis," *Post-Soviet Affairs* 32 (2016): 55–74.

114. Ibid.

115. Alexandre Douguine, "La Victoire de Donald Trump," *Katechon*, 10 November 2016.

116. Bernhard Odehnal, "Gipfel treffen mit Putins fünfter Kolonne," *Der Tagesanzeiger*, 3 June 2014. See the useful discussion in Anton Shekhovtsov, *Russia and the Western Far Right: Tango Noir* (New York: Routledge, 2018), 199.

117. Quoted in Marlene Laruelle, introduction to *Eurasianism and the European Far Right: Reshaping the Europe-Russia Relationship*, ed. Laruelle (Lanham, MD: Lexington Books, 2015), vii.

118. Heidegger, *Überlegungen II–VI*, GA 94, 124.

119. Alexander Dugin, *Heidegger: Die Möglichkeit der russischen Philosophie* (Moscow, 2011), 115, quoted in Brumlik, "Das alte Denken der neuen Rechten," 85. For a complete list of Dugin's books on Heidegger, see http://evrasia-books.ru.

120. See Alexander Shekhovtsov, "Alexander Dugin and the West European New Right, 1989–1994," in Laruelle, *Eurasianism and the European Far Right*, 35–54.

121. Leggewie, *Die Anti-Europäer*, 73–74.

122. Martin Heidegger, *Die Geschichte des Seyns*, GA 69 (Frankfurt: Klostermann, 1998), 74.

123. Alexander Dugin, *Heidegger: The Philosophy of Another Beginning* (Washington, DC: Raddix/Washington Summit, 2014), 162–64 (emphasis added).

124. Alexander Dugin, "Donald Trump: The Swamp and the Fire," The Fourth Political Theory, accessed 9 November 2018, http://www.4pt.su/en/content/donald-trump-swamp-and-fire.

125. Martin Heidegger, *Einführung in die Metaphysik*, GA 40 (Frankfurt: Klostermann, 1983), 40–41; Heidegger, *Introduction to Metaphysics*, trans. Ralph Manheim (New Haven, CT: Yale University Press, 1959), 37.

126. Dugin, *Heidegger: Die Möglichkeit der russischen Philosophie*, 115, quoted in Brumlik, "Das alte Denken der neuen Rechten," .

127. Alexander Dugin, *The Fourth Political Theory*, trans. Mark Selboda and Michael Millerman (London: Arktos, 2012), 234.

128. Weiß, *Die autoritäre Revolte*, 200.

129. Alexander Dugin, *The Last War of the World Island: The Geopolitics of Contemporary Russia*, trans. John Bryant (London: Arktos, 2015), 10.

130. Ibid., 8.

131. Ibid., 13.

132. Vadim Rossman, "Moscow State University's Department of Sociology and the Climate of Opinion in Post-Soviet Russia," in Laruelle, *Eurasianism and the European Far Right*, 66.

133. Stephen Shenfield, *Russian Fascism: Traditions, Tendencies and Movements* (New York: Routledge, 2000), 194.

134. Quoted in Andreas Umland, "Faschismus à la Dugin," *Blätter für Deutsche und Internationale Politik* 12 (2007): 1432.

135. Anton Barbashin and Hannah Thoburn, "Alexander Dugin and the Philosophy Behind Putin's Invasion of Crimea," *Foreign Affairs*, 31 March 2014.

136. An English translation by Nina Kouprianova appeared in 2014, under the imprint of the Alt-Right impresario Richard Spencer's Washington Summit Publishers. At the time, Kouprianova and Spencer were husband and wife. The preface to the English translation was written by Paul Gottfried, the doyen of American paleoconservativism, who, in 2007, along with Spencer, coined the term "Alternative Right." See Jacob Siegel, "The Alt-Right's Jewish Godfather: How Paul Gottfried—Willing or Reluctant—Became the Mentor of Richard Spencer and a Philosophical Lodestone for White Nationalists," *Tablet*, 29 November 2016.

137. Martin Heidegger, "Building, Dwelling, Thinking," in *Poetry, Language, Thought*, trans. Albert Hofstadter (New York: Harper and Row, 1977), 143–61.

138. Julian Young, "The Fourfold," in *The Cambridge Companion to Heidegger*, ed. Charles B. Guignon (New York: Cambridge University Press, 2006), 273; Frederick Olafson, "The Unity of Heidegger's Thought," in Guignon, *Cambridge Companion to Heidegger*, 117. See also Matthew Sharpe, "In the Crosshairs of the Fourfold: Critical Thoughts on Alexander Dugin's Heidegger Interpretation," *Critical Horizons* 21 (2020): 167–87.

139. Alexander Dugin, *The Rise of the Fourth Political Theory*, trans. Michael Millerman (London: Arktos, 2017), 212.

140. Carl Schmitt reprised the biblical figures of Behemoth and Leviathan in *Der Leviathan in der Staatslehre des Thomas Hobbes: Sinn und Fehlschlag eines politischen Symbols* (Hamburg: Hanseatische Verlagsanstalt, 1938).

141. See Joan Anton Mellon, "The Idées-Forces of the European New Right," in *Varieties of Right-Wing European Extremism*, ed. Andrea Mammone, Emmanuel Godin, and Brian Jenkins (London: Taylor and Francis, 2013), 67–82. Citing earlier literature, Mellon characterizes "idées-forces" as the fundamental and operative nuclei of a given ideology.

142. Michael Freeden, *Ideology: A Very Short Introduction* (New York: Oxford University Press, 2003), 4–5.

143. For a standard comparison, which includes an extensive discussion of Integral Nationalism, see Ernst Nolte, *Three Faces of Fascism: Action Française, Italian Fascism, and National Socialism* (New York: Henry Holt, 1966).

144. Paul Jackson, "The License to Hate: Fascist Rhetoric in Anders Breivik's Manifesto *2083: A European Declaration of Independence*," *Democracy and Security* 9 (2013): 252. For more on the discursive-ideological "licensing" of political violence, see Aristotle Kallis, *Genocide and Fascism: The Eliminationist Drive in Fascist Europe* (London: Routledge, 2008). The source for Breivik's ideas about "population replacement" was the Norwegian blogger Peter Jensen ("Fjordman"). It is worth noting that, shortly after Breivik's attacks, the Neue Rechte published an anthology of Jensen's texts: Fjordman, *Europa verteidigen: Zehn Texte*, ed. Martin Lichtmesz and Manfred Kleine-Hartlage (Schnellroda: Edition Antaios, 2011).

145. See Leggewie, *Anti-Europäer*, 27.

146. Quoted in Aage Borchgrevink, *A Norwegian Tragedy: Anders Behring Breivik and the Massacre at Utøya*, trans. Guy Puzey (Cambridge, UK: Polity, 2015), 356.

147. Quoted in Asne Seierstad, *One of Us: The Story of Anders Breivik and the Massacre in Norway* (New York: Farrar, Straus and Giroux, 2015), 285.

148. Quoted in Roger Griffin, *Terrorist's Creed: Fanatical Violence and the Human Need for Meaning* (Basingstoke, UK: Palgrave Macmillan, 2012), 210.

149. Anders Breivik, *2083: A European Declaration of Independence*, 123, 1068, 107, 585, available at translated.by, accessed 2 September 2019, https://translatedby.com/you/2083-a-european-declaration-of-independence-otkrytyi-perevod/original/?page=123.

150. See the analysis in Andreas Önnerfors, " 'The Great Replacement': Decoding the Christchurch Terrorist Manifesto," Center for the Analysis of the Radical Right (CARR), 18 March 2019, https://www.radicalrightanalysis.com/2019/03/18/the-great-replacement-decoding-the-christchurch-terrorist-manifesto/: "The analysis demonstrated compelling parallels to Norwegian terrorist Breivik in terms of the intentions to kill and the use of a language of power. . . . Tarrant says he was in contact with the 'reborn Knights Templar' around 'Knight Justiciar' Breivik, whom he admires deeply."

Postscript

1. Heidegger quoted in Heinrich W. Petzet, *Auf einen Stern zugehen: Begegnungen und Gespräche mit Heidegger, 1929–1976* (Frankfurt: Societätsverlag, 1983), 43.

2. Ernst Tugendhat, *Selbstbewusstsein und Selbsterhaltung* (Frankfurt: Suhrkamp, 1979), 143.

3. Martin Heidegger, " 'Only a God Can Save Us': *Der Spiegel*'s Interview with Martin Heidegger (1966)," in *The Heidegger Controversy: A Critical Reader*, ed. Richard Wolin (Cambridge, MA: MIT Press, 1993), 111.

4. Martin Heidegger, *Anmerkungen I–V*, GA 97 (Frankfurt: Klostermann, 2015), 98.

5. Ibid.

6. Hannah Arendt, "Heidegger the Fox," in *Essays in Understanding: 1930–1954: Formation, Exile, Totalitarianism* (New York: Harcourt Brace, 1994), 362–63.

7. Martin Heidegger, "Das Rektorat, 1933–34: Tatsachen und Gedanken," in *Reden und andere Zeugnisse eines Lebensweges*, GA 16 (Frankfurt: Klostermann, 2000), 374.

8. Heidegger, *Anmerkungen I–V*, GA 97, 127.

9. Ibid., 444, 461. See Judith Werner, "Heidegger e la *Lügenpresse*," in *Quaderni neri di Heidegger*, ed. Donatella di Cesare (Milan: Udine, 2016), 145–54.

10. Heidegger, *Anmerkungen I–V*, GA 97, 174.

11. Martin Heidegger, *Nietzsche*, vol. 1 (Pfullingen: Neske, 1961), 603.

12. Heidegger, *Anmerkungen I–V*, GA 97, 250, 82, 100, 151.

13. Martin Heidegger, *Überlegungen XII–XV*, GA 96 (Frankfurt: Klostermann, 2014), 195 (emphasis added).

14. See Martin Heidegger, *Überlegungen VII–XI*, GA 95 (Frankfurt: Klostermann, 2014), 97.

15. Heidegger, *Anmerkungen I–V*, GA 97, 438.

16. See, for example, Agnes Heller, "Parmenides and the Battle of Stalingrad," *Graduate Faculty Philosophy Journal* 19 (1997): 247–62.

17. Markus Gabriel, "Heideggers Antisemitische Stereotypen," in *Heidegger und der Antisemitismus: Positionen im Widerstreit*, ed. Walter Homolka and Arnulf Heidegger (Freiburg: Herder, 2016), 224. See also Jan Süsselbeck's superb discussion of Heidegger and anti-Semitism, "Chiffre der planetarischen Technik," *Literaturkrititk.de* 6 (2015), https://literaturkritik.de/id/20648.

18. Heidegger, "Das Rektorat, 1933–34," 374.

19. See Theodor Adorno, "The Meaning of Working through the Past," in *Critical Models: Interventions and Catchwords*, trans. Henry Pickford (New York: Columbia University Press, 1998), 89–104.

20. Heidegger, *Überlegungen VII–XI*, GA 95, 50.

21. Winfried Franzen, *Von der Existenzialontologie zur Seinsgeschichte* (Meisenheim am Glan: Anton Hain, 1975), 141.

22. Ibid., 125.

23. Martin Heidegger, *Nietzsche*, vol. 2 (Pfullingen: Neske Verlag, 1961), 489.

24. Martin Heidegger, "Brief über den Humanismus," in *Wegmarken*, GA 9 (Frankfurt: Klostermann, 1976), 330–31.

25. Karl Löwith, *Heidegger: Denker in dürftiger Zeit* (Frankfurt: Fischer, 1953), 59.

26. Gethmann-Siefert, "Heidegger und Hölderlin: Die Überforderung des 'Dichters in dürftiger Zeit,'" in *Heidegger und die praktische Philosophie*, ed. Otto Pöggeler and Annemarie Gethmann-Siefert (Frankfurt: Suhrkamp, 1988), 131–32.

27. Martin Heidegger, *Was heißt Denken?*, GA 8 (Frankfurt: Klostermann, 2002), 214.

28. See Martin Heidegger, "Gelassenheit," in *Reden und andere Zeugnisse eines Lebensweges*, GA 16, 528.

29. See the discussion of this point in Wiebrecht Ries, *Karl Löwith* (Stuttgart: Metzler, 1992), 34–48.

30. Martin Heidegger, "Brief über den Humanismus," in *Wegmarken*, GA 9, 319.

31. Martin Heidegger, "Nachwort zu: Was ist Metaphysik?," in *Wegmarken*, GA 9, 312.

32. Heidegger, *Was Heißt Denken?*, GA 8, 12.

33. "Das Ende der Philosophie und die Aufgabe des Denkens" (1964) represents an important waystation in Heidegger's abandonment of philosophy in favor of—as Gadamer once put it—"poeticizing gnosis." See Heidegger, *Zur Sache des Denkens*, GA 14 (Frankfurt: Klostermann, 2007), 67–80. For Gadamer's remark, see Hans-Georg Gadamer, *Gesammelte Werke*, vol. 3 (Tübingen: Mohr, 1987), viii.

34. Heidegger, *Zur Sache des Denkens*, GA 14, 15.

35. Alfons Söllner, "Left Students of the Conservative Revolution: Neumann, Kirchheimer, and Marcuse," *Telos* 61 (1984): 59.

36. Martin Heidegger to Erhart Kästner, 24 December 1963, in *Briefwechsel, 1953–1974* (Frankfurt: Insel Verlag, 1986), 59.

37. Heidegger, "Only a God Can Save Us," 107.

38. Martin Heidegger, *Der Satz vom Grund*, GA 10 (Frankfurt: Klostermann, 1997), 151.

39. Martin Heidegger, *Vorträge und Aufsätze*, GA 7 (Frankfurt: Klostermann, 2000), 148.

40. Heidegger, "Only a God Can Save Us," 107.

41. Martin Heidegger, *Einführung in die Metaphysik*, GA 40 (Frankfurt: Klostermann Verlag, 1983), 35.

42. Heidegger, "Das Rektorat, 1933–34," 375.

43. Heidegger, *Was heißt Denken?*, 71.

44. Justifications of Heidegger's *Technik-Kritik* undoubtedly reached a "credo quia absurdum" moment with Jean-Luc Nancy's comments on the Islamic fundamentalist massacre in Nice, on Bastille Day (14 July) 2016, in which 84 innocent passersby were murdered and 450 wounded in a vicious truck attack. Neglecting to mention that the perpetrator justified his murderous assault in the name of the Islamic State, Nancy interpreted the episode from the standpoint of Heidegger's technology critique. Hence, Nancy blamed the attack on "fundamentalist modernity," which "keeps trucks, machines, and businesses in constant movement." For Nancy, it was as though *the truck itself*, as an instance of *Machenschaft*, had committed the massacre independently of the fundamentalist ideology that motivated the deed: an ideology, moreover, whose goal was a restoration of the medieval Caliphate. See Nancy, "Un Camion lancé," *Libération*, 19 July 2016. See also the rejoinder by François Rastier, "Terrorisme de Nice à Edmonton, la faute au camion?," *Sens Public*, 31 January 2017.

45. Alexander Schwan, "Zeitkritik und Politik in Heideggers Spätphilosophie," in *Heidegger und Praktische Philosophie*, ed. Otto Pöggeler and Annemarie Gethmann-Siefert (Frankfurt: Suhrkamp, 1988), 96–97.

46. See Gottfried Benn and F. W. Oelze, *Briefe* (Wiesbaden: Limes, 1980). See also the account in Petzet, *Auf einen Stern zu gehen*.

47. Rüdiger Safranski, *Martin Heidegger: Between Good and Evil*, trans. Ewald Osers (Cambridge, MA: Harvard University Press, 1999), 390.

48. Quoted in Margaret Bourke-White, *Dear Fatherland, Rest Quietly: A Report on the Collapse of Hitler's "Thousand Years"* (New York: Simon and Schuster, 1946), 5.

49. Heidegger, *Einführung in die Metaphysik*, GA 40, 40–41.

50. Quoted in Petzet, *Auf einen Stern zugehen*, 62. The earlier lecture that Heidegger referred to was "Das Wesen der Wahrheit."

51. Hannah Arendt to Karl Jaspers, 29 September 1949, in *Correspondence: 1926–1969* (New York: Harcourt Brace, 1992), 42.

52. Martin Heidegger, "Das Gestell," in *Vorträge und Aufsätze*, GA 7 (Frankfurt: Klostermann Verlag, 1994), 27.

53. In *Martin Heidegger: Eine politische Biographie* (Paderborn: Schöningh, 2020), Thomas Rohkrämer concludes that the later Heidegger's ethereal focus on *Seinsgeschichte* and *Seinsvergessnheit* resulted in his unconscionable insensitivity to "human suffering" (241). The weakness of Rohkrämer's approach lies in his tendency to isolate Heidegger's ideological zealotry from his philosophy by arguing that it derived from the *Zeitgeist*, thereby insinuating that Heidegger should not be held accountable for the aspects of the *Zeitgeist* that he chose to imbibe.

54. Ian Connor, *Refugees and Expellees in Postwar Germany* (Manchester: Manchester University Press, 2014), 190–91.

55. For background, see Anil Menon, "Postwar Forced Resettlement of Germans Echoes through the Decades," *The Conversation*, accessed 9 November 2020, https://theconversation.com/postwar-forced-resettlement-of-germans-echoes-through-the-decades-137219. See also John David Nagel, *The National Democratic Party: Right Radicalism in the Federal Republic of Germany* (Berkeley: University of California Press, 1971), 21–23, 140–43.

56. Heidegger, *Einführung in die Metaphysik*, GA 40, 41.

57. Martin Heidegger, "Der Spruch des Anaximander," in *Holzwege*, GA 5, 327.

58. Heidegger, "Gelassenheit," 521.

59. Robert Metcalf, "Rethinking 'Bodenständigkeit' in the Technological Age," *Research in Phenomenology* 42 (2012): 49.

60. Martin Heidegger, "Liebeserklärung an die Provence" (20 March 1958), in *Reden und andere Zeugnisse eines Lebensweges*, GA 16, 551.

61. Rudy Koshar, *Germany's Transient Pasts: Preservation and National Memory in the Twentieth Century* (Chapel Hill: University of North Carolina Press, 1998), 100.

62. Heidegger, "Gelassenheit," 522.

63. Ibid.

64. Ibid., 521: "Mitteldeutschland . . . Ostpreußen, das schlesische Land und das Böhmerland."

65. See Chad Bryant, *Prague in Black: Nazi Rule and Czech Nationalism* (Cambridge, MA: Harvard University Press, 2005), 3.

66. See Anna Holian, *Displaced Persons in Postwar Germany* (Ann Arbor: University of Michigan Press, 2011), 3.

67. Heidegger, *Anmerkungen I–V*, GA 97, 47.

68. Florian Grosser, "Heidegger, the Politics of Space, and the Space of Politics," *Geographica Helvetica* 72 (2017): 93.

69. Koshar, *Germany's Transient Pasts*, 47–48, 99.

70. Rudy Koshar, "The Antinomies of *Heimat:* Homeland, History, and Nazism," in *Heimat, History and Fatherland: The German Sense of Belonging*, ed. Jost Hermand and James Steakley (New York: Peter Lang, 1996), 118.

71. Martin Heidegger, "Hebel, der Hausfreund," in *Aus der Erfahrung des Denkens*, GA 13 (Frankfurt: Klostermann, 1983), 134.

72. Heidegger, "Nachwort zu: Was ist Metaphysik?," 312; Martin Heidegger, "Sprache und Heimat," in *Aus der Erfahrung des Denkens*, GA 13, 156.

73. Ibid., 156, 155.

74. Martin Heidegger, *Das deutsche Führerlexikon, 1934–35* (Berlin: Otto Stollberg, 1934), 180.

75. Martin Heidegger, "Schöpferische Landschaft: Warum bleiben wir in Provinz," in *Aus der Erfahrung des Denkens*, GA 13, 9–11.

76. See Martin Heidegger, *Die Geschichte des Seyns*, GA 69 (Frankfurt: Klostermann, 1998): "Ontological-historical thinking [*seynsgeschichtliche Denken*] is always thinking in terms of *origins* [*anfängliches Denken*]; it refuses to squander itself by focusing on the historical course of opinions and doctrines" (87).

77. Martin Heidegger, "Das Wesen der Sprache," in *Unterwegs zur Sprache* (Pfullingen: Neske, 1959), 173, 21.

78. Theodor Adorno, *Philosophische Terminologie: Zur Einleitung*, vol. 1 (Frankfurt: Suhrkamp, 1973), 152.

79. Martin Heidegger, *Parmenides*, trans. André Schuwer and Richard Rojewicz (Bloomington: Indiana University Press, 1992), 112.

80. Heidegger, "Schöpferische Landschaft," 10.

81. Heidegger, "Sprache und Heimat," 155.

82. Eduard Engel, *Sprich Deutsch! Ein Buch zur Entwelschung* (Leipzig: Hesse und Becker, 1918), 6.

83. Leo Spitzer, *Fremdwörterhatz und Fremdvölkerhass: Eine Streitschrift gegen die Sprachreinigung* (Vienna: Manz Verlag, 1918).

84. Theodor Adorno, *Minima Moralia*, trans. E. F. N. Jephcott (London: New Left Books, 1974), 110.

85. Christopher Hutton, *Language and the Third Reich: Mother Tongue Fascism, Race, and the Science of Language* (New York: Routledge, 2003), 6.

87. Klaus Ziegler, "Deutsche Sprache-und Literaturwissenschaft im Dritten Reich," in *Deutsches Geistesleben und Nationalsozialismus. Eine Vortragsreihe der Universität Tübingen*, ed. Andreas Fitner (Tübingen: Wunderlich, 1965), 150.

88. Ibid., 159.

89. Theodor Adorno, "Words from Abroad," in *Notes to Literature*, vol. 2, trans. S. W. Nicholsen (New York: Columbia University Press, 1995), 189.

90. Immanuel Kant, *Critique of Judgement*, trans. James Meredith (New York: Oxford University Press, 1952), 152–53.

91. Hannah Arendt, *Lectures on Kant's Political Philosophy* (Chicago: University of Chicago Press, 1983), 43.

92. Heidegger, "Gelassenheit," 521.

93. Robert Minder, "Heidegger, Hebel, und die Sprache von Messkirch," in *Der Dichter in der Gesellschaft: Erfahrungen mit deutscher und französischer Literatur* (Frankfurt: Suhrkamp Verlag, 1968), 228.

94. Quoted in Charles Stewart Doty, *From Cultural Rebellion to Counterrevolution: The Politics of Maurice Barrès* (Athens: Ohio University Press, 1976), 154. See also Raoul Girardet, *Le Nationalisme Française: 1871–1914* (Paris: Armand Colin, 1966), 185–89.

95. See Maurice Barrés, *Scènes et doctrines du nationalisme* (Paris: Plon, 1925), 80, 81. See also Judith Sirkus, *Sexing the Citizen: Morality and Masculinity in France, 1870–1920* (Ithaca, NY: Cornell University Press, 2011), 94.

96. Quoted in Minder, "Heidegger, Hebel, und die Sprache von Messkirch," 258.

INDEX

Academy of German Law, 135
active nihilism, 134, 180, 192–93. *See
also under* Nietzsche, Friedrich
Adorno, Theodor: on *Arbeitsideologie* of
Heidegger, 221; on contradictions
in Heidegger's thought, 81; on death
in Heideggerian ontology, 129–30;
on Heidegger's jargon, 205, 243,
365; on Heidegger's Nazism, 97;
on philosophy's nature, 91, 402n16;
on popularity of Heidegger's
philosophy, 23; and purity of
German language, 381, 383; on
rural-agrarian ideas of Heidegger,
204, 380
AfD. *See* Alternative for Germany
Agamben, Giorgio, 9–11, 391n28
Ahasverian, 339
Almirante, Giorgio, 161
Alternative for Germany, 18, 318, 329,
330, 334, 335, 340–47
Alt-Right, the: Breitbart News and, 163;
Charlottesville rally of, 308; Hei-
degger and origins of, 308; websites
of, 95
Anabaptist Messianism, 164
Anders, Günther, 23, 241–42
Andreas, Willy, 105

"another beginning": active nihilism and,
192; in *Black Notebooks*, 58; catastrophic vision of, 66–67, 168; Germany's role in, 132, 144, 150, 154,
275; and Greece, 67, 286; Nazi Germany and, 97–99, 191, 194, 359,
338; opposition to, 154, 271; Russia
as key to, in thought of Alexander
Dugin, 355; and Stefan George,
126; and Werner Jaeger's "Third
Humanism," 113
Antaios (Edition), 334, 337
anti-modernism, 86, 320
anti-Semitism: and "antirace" idea in
Nazism, 59, 168, 203, 281–82; capi-
talistic stereotypes of, 69–70, 87,
181; internal logic of, 88; Jews as
desert people (nomads) in, 59, 87–
88, 169, 225–27, 263, 279–83; medieval nature of, 5; Nazi ideology
of, 136; polyvalence of, 86; pork
consumption and, 226; spiritual
form of, 12, 85, 102, 126, 182,
422n211. *See also under* Heidegger,
Martin
Arbeit: anti-Semitic conception of, 216;
and authenticity in Heidegger's
thought, 16, 170–72; as a calling

461

Gadamer, Hans-Georg, 90, 415n85
Gauland, Alexander, 334, 342
Gehlen, Arnold, 34, 323
Gelassenheit, 337, 372
geophilosophy, 261, 273–74
geopolitics, 227, 250, 264–71, 274, 285
George, Stefan: call for messianic leader by, 124; Nazi support of, 126; on poetry and myth, 274, 293; as political leader, 120; racism of, 125; violence and, 125–26
Gesellschaft and *Gemeinschaft*, 87, 141, 251, 260
Gide, André, 385
Gnosticism, 161–62
Gobineau, Comte Arthur de, 292
Goebbels, Joseph: and dictum about year *1789*, 253; Ernst Jünger and, 197; Germanist background of, 274; on technology, 102, 186–87, 195
Goffman, Erving, 228
Gollnisch, Bruno, 317
Golowin, Yevgeny, 347, 354
Görres, Joseph, 295, 298, 299
Gottfried, Paul, 309, 455n136
Grabowsky, Adolf, 265
Great Replacement, The, 307–8, 313, 358
GRECE, 18, 312, 316–18, 320, 324, 326, 425n17, 447n23
Greece: and Dorian connection, 127–28; and German connection, 153, 157, 203, 286; and the Greek beginning, 7, 34, 51, 60, 67, 75–76, 113–18, in Heidegger's thought, 254, 297–300; and Jaeger's Plato interpretation, 127; in Nietzsche's thought, 300; rootedness of, 256–57; science in, 257; in thought of Johann Gottlieb Fichte, 165
Green Party, 435n12
Grimm, Hans, 65, 265–67, 299
Gross, Walter, 140
Grossraum, 6, 18, 267
Guénon, René, 162, 323, 353

Gundolf, Friedrich, 274
Günther, Erich, 274
Günther, Hans, 15, 52, 86, 140, 142–43, 259, 324

Habermas, Jürgen, 13, 28, 39, 68, 81
Haldenwang, Thomas, 346
Hall, Stuart, 326
Harder, Richard, 114–16
Haubold, Helmut, 106
Haushofer, Karl, 17, 247, 264, 269, 439n93
Hebel, Johann Peter, 19, 378–79
Hegel, Georg Wilhelm Friedrich: Heidegger seminar on 5, 48–49, 232; "labor of the concept" of, 91; progress of freedom and, 61, 67, 305; reason and, 54, 91
Heidegger, Almuth, 56
Heidegger, Fritz, 14, 62, 69–73, 75, 76–77, 403n44, 417n129
Heidegger, Hermann, 36, 42, 55, 57
Heidegger, Martin: Adolf Hitler and, 14–15, 27, 70–72, 75, 101, 105, 233; alienation in philosophy of, 204–5; anti-authoritarianism of, 246; antihumanism of, 163, 320, 329, 366; and anti-Semitic claim of Jewish planetary criminality, 35–36, 79, 83; and anti-Semitic claim that Jews were black marketers, 182; and anti-Semitic conception of Jews as enemy, 5; anti-Semitic treatment of Freud by, 84; and anti-Semitic treatment of Jews as having empty rationality, 282; anti-Semitic usage of *Verjudung* by, 223, 268; anti-Semitism after World War II, 360–62; art in philosophy of, 274–75; being-toward-death as "warrior ethos" in thought of, 129, 273; break with Nazi regime of, 98; Catholicism of, 5, 143; "concepts" in thought of, 91; conservative nature of philosophy of, 24–25, 61, 77,